Speculum Sermonis

DISPUTATIO

VOLUME 1

Speculum Sermonis

Interdisciplinary Reflections on the Medieval Sermon

Edited by

Georgiana Donavin, Cary J. Nederman, and Richard Utz

BREPOLS

British Library Cataloguing in Publication Data

Speculum sermonis : interdisciplinary reflections on the medieval sermon. – (Disputatio ; 1)
1.Sermons, Medieval – History and criticism 2.Preaching – History – Middle Ages, 600-1500
I.Donavin, Georgiana II.Nederman, Cary J. III.Utz, Richard J., 1961-
252'.00902

ISBN 2503513395

D/2004/0095/59
ISBN 2-503-51339-5

Contents

Abbreviations ix

Acknowledgements xi

Introduction xiii
GEORGIANA DONAVIN

I. How Sermons Reflect Their World(s)

The Word Made Flesh: Preaching and Community from the Apostolic to the Late Middle Ages 3
LEO CARRUTHERS

'Going to the Gate of Life': The Carthage Amphitheatre and Augustine's Sermons on Saints Perpetua and Felicitas 29
JOHN KITCHEN

Susanna Victrix, Christus Victor: Lenten Sermons, Typology, and the Lectionary 55
CATHERINE BROWN TKACZ

Time and Again: A Response to Leo Carruthers, John Kitchen, and Catherine Brown Tkacz 81
JEFFREY BURTON RUSSELL

II. How Sermons Reflect *Upon* Their World(s)

'Let Us Love One Another': Liturgy, Morality, and Political Theory in Chrysostom's Sermons on Rom. 12–13 and II Thess. 2 89
STEPHEN MORRIS

Preaching the Dead from Their Graves: Bernard of Clairvaux's Lament on His Brother Gerard 113
WIM VERBAAL

'Spare the Rod and Spoil the Child': Proverbial Speech Acts, Boy Bishop Sermons, and Pedagogical Violence 139
EVE SALISBURY

Bernardino of Siena Visualizes the Name of God 155
EMILY MICHELSON

Sermons Reflecting Upon Their World(s): A Response to Stephen Morris, Wim Verbaal, Eve Salisbury, and Emily Michelson 179
PETER HOWARD

III. How Sermons are Reflected in Other Literatures

Illumination of the Intellect: Franciscan Sermons and *Piers Plowma* 195
DAVID STRONG

Unauthorized Preaching: The Sermon in Jean Bodel's *Jeu de Saint Nicolas* 219
LYNN T. RAMEY

The Conversion of Mary Magdalene and the Musical Legacy of Franciscan Piety in the Early German Passion Plays 233
PETER V. LOEWEN

Interdisciplinary Craft: A Response to Peter Loewen, Lynn T. Ramey, and David Strong 257
ELIZABETH SCHIRMER

IV. Reflections *Upon* Sermons

Speech-Reporting Strategies in 'Dramatic Preaching': With Examples from East Slavic Festal Sermons 271
INGUNN LUNDE

Relic or Strategy: The Middle Dutch Sermon as a Literary Phenomenon 293
THOM MERTENS

Fashioning Devotion: The Art of Good Friday Preaching in Chaucerian England 315
HOLLY JOHNSON

A Statistical Treatment of Sin and Holiness in Sermons from the Early Middle Ages (500–1100) 335
MARTINE DE REU

Multilingualism in Medieval Sermons: A Response to Thom Mertens, Martine De Reu, Ingunn Lunde, and Holly Johnson 363
SIMON FORDE

Bibliography 371
GEORGIANA DONAVIN

Contributors 405

Index of Names 411

Abbreviations

CCSL	Corpus Christianorum Series Latina (Turnhout: Brepols, 1954–)
CCCM	Corpus Christianorum Continuatio Mediaeualis (Turnhout: Brepols, 1966–)
CPG	Clavis Patrum Graecorum, ed. by M. Geerard and F. Glorie, 5 vols (Turnhout: Brepols, 1974–87)
CSEL	Corpus Scriptorum Ecclesiasticorum Latinorum (Vienna, 1866–)
IMSSS	International Medieval Sermon Studies -Society
NPNCF	Nicene and Post-Nicene Christian Fathers (New York, 1887–92; Oxford, 1890–1900)
PG	*Patrologiae Cursus Completus*, Series Graeca, ed. by Jacques-Paul Migne, 162 vols (Paris: Garnier, 1857–66)
PL	*Patrologiae Cursus Completus*, Series Latina, ed. by Jacques-Paul Migne, 221 vols (Paris: Garnier, 1844–64)

Acknowledgements

The editors of this volume are grateful to the members of the International Medieval Sermon Studies Society, whose research inspired the idea for this publication and whose encouragement was unflagging. Many members of the society have contributed essays here. We are particularly indebted to Simon Forde for suggesting ways to make this first issue of Disputatio disputatious and for his many efforts as liaison to Brepols to see this book in print and to establish a successful series. During the research that led to the conceptualization of this volume, the Gore Endowment at Westminster College provided a generous Summer Grant that allowed Georgiana Donavin to collaborate with contributors. In the processes of selecting essays and editing them, many students from both Westminster College and Texas A&M diligently participated—and, we hope, gained some valuable experience for their continued life of scholarship. We thank Alexander Lemons for early communications with contributors and research on the bibliography. Phillip Gray, Sara Jordan, Jeff Lee and Megan Savageau dedicated many hours to researching stray details, proofreading and formatting. In the final corrections and compilation of the manuscript, Timothy Asay was indispensable. Nathan Gale, a graduate student in English at the University of Northern Iowa, helped to compile the index. Beyond student aid, the staff for Instructional Technology at Westminster College, especially Meggan Levitt, Carol Poelman and Stephan Ross, ensured the manuscript's electronic transmission to other computers. And finally, we are so thankful for the kind but exacting attention of our copyeditor, Maryna Mews.

Acknowledgements

Introduction

GEORGIANA DONAVIN

Disputatio is a new book series providing multi-disciplinary perspectives on medieval intellectual cultures. Its inaugural volume, *Speculum Sermonis: Interdisciplinary Reflections on the Medieval Sermon*, is concerned with the medieval sermon, a discourse often arising from and speaking to the intellectual forums of the church, university and court. In the case of popular preaching in the Middle Ages, the sermon often translated the academic to the unlettered through the mutually accepted medium of oral delivery.

This anthology of essays about the medieval sermon investigates not only medieval, but also contemporary academic traditions and practices. Its purpose is to illustrate how different disciplines study medieval sermons and reciprocally, how the sermon informs the discipline's conclusions about the Middle Ages. It is therefore a collection with an epistemological slant, inquiring into the methodologies through which medievalists 'know' the sermon and how the sermon allows for 'knowledge' of the medieval period. To this end, the authors of the essays in this volume hail from diverse fields of study, including social history, archaeology, liturgiology, history of theatre, linguistics, literature, and others. The title of the volume invokes the image of the *speculum*, or mirror, and its 'reflections' in order to suggest a multiplicity of academic perspectives and representations of the past. Not only the title of the volume, but also of the book series hint at the variety of disciplinary perspectives within. Following the medieval educational practice of the debate, or *disputatio*, *Speculum Sermonis* accords with the title of the book series by providing response papers that add significantly to, and sometimes challenge, the grouping of essays upon which they comment. In total, this volume presents fourteen essays, divided into four sections, each concluding in its own response paper. Through the diversity of academic approaches and sometimes through scholarly disagreement, this volume conveys a rich conversation about medieval sermons and provides an extensive bibliography at the end for those who are inspired to enter it. The bibliography offers a listing of primary sermon collections and scholarship about them after 1980, an arbitrary marker, admittedly, but in general a date after which many medievalists became more conscious of the theories and preconceptions informing their disciplinary paradigms. Comprehensive bibliographies of older sermon scholarship are plentiful, the best and most recent presented in *The Sermon*, edited by Beverly Mayne Kienzle for Brepols's Typologie series.[1] Since the theme of *Speculum Sermonis* is the divergence and confluence of various disciplinary perspectives, the bibliography also includes a short section on sources about interdisciplinarity in academe.

The idea of interdisciplinarity deserves some attention before a discussion of how the essays included in this volume conform to it. In *Blackberry Winter*, Margaret Mead comments on the value of interdisciplinarity and attributes the following quotation to a remark by her husband, Luther. Providing an architectural metaphor for research across the fields, Luther says:

> I would like to see us build a new room [. . . that] would have no door [. . .] a Commons Room to which [researchers] would drift in from those [other] rooms marked geology, anthropology [. . .] logic, mathematics, psychology, linguistics, and many others [. . .]. All these would drop in and linger. The room would have great windows [. . . and the] landscape that we gaze on and try to understand is an epic portion of human experience.[2]

Long before interdisciplinarity came into fashion with the challenges posed to the compartmentalization of universities by such new programs as women's studies, medievalists were regulars in the parlour to which our colleagues from literature, history, theology and other fields come. Sometimes the object of our discussions has been truly interdisciplinary, as J. T. Klein defines the term in *Interdisciplinarity: history, theory and practice*. Klein states that research across the fields produces 'a new, single, intellectually coherent entity', synthesis of a wide variety of information, and conclusions that outstrip any one school of thought. [3] For their essays in *Speculum Sermonis*, several of the authors combine modes of research from different disciplines to form new conceptions about medieval sermons and what they represent. For instance, through the interweaving of church history, liturgiology and art history, Catherine Brown Tkacz demonstrates a rich tradition of the use of Susanna, heroine of the Book of Daniel, as a type of Christ—a tradition that might be surprising to many scholars in any one of the fields whose evidence and methodologies Tkacz employs. Yet through the integration of patristic sermons,

[1] *The Sermon*, ed. by Beverly Mayne Kienzle, Typologie des sources du Moyen Age occidental, fascicules 81–83 (Turnhout: Brepols, 1999).

[2] Margaret Mead, *Blackberry Winter: My Earlier Years* (New York: Simon and Schuster, 1972), pp. 289–90.

[3] J. T. Klein, *Interdisciplinarity: history, theory and practice* (Detroit: Wayne State University Press, 1990), p. 57.

multiple lectionaries and artistic depictions, the tradition of this Christological woman appears strong and vibrant. Similarly, Peter Loewen brings together scholarship from the histories of church, theatre, literature and music to show how Franciscan thought on penitence and the rhetoric of music affects the composition of the songs assigned to Mary Magdalene in thirteenth-century German Passion plays.

Interdisciplinary scholarship such as Tkacz's and Loewen's paints a broad, new picture of the Middle Ages and its sermons through agility with the brushstrokes of single disciplinary methods and an eye for the academic mixing that intensifies colour. Not all of the authors for *Speculum Sermonis*, however, combine disciplinary methods; some rely on the paradigms of a single field of study in order to reveal how particular approaches bear particular fruits. For instance, Emily Michelson discovers in the sermons of Bernardino of Siena explanations which art historians might use to interpret the popular IHS monogram. By compiling essays that both cross disciplinary lines and rest in a single field of study, *Speculum Sermonis* illuminates both the potential and restrictions of traditional academic approaches to research. The effect of gathering both sorts of essays delivers, overall, what Lewis E. Gilbert, Director for Interdisciplinary Programs at the Earth Institute, Columbia University would call a multidisciplinary outlook. He distinguishes interdisciplinarity from multidisciplinarity in the following way: while interdisciplinary study arrives at 'more than the linear sum of its [disciplinary] parts', multidisciplinary endeavour 'assembles, in an additive fashion, knowledge from more than one discipline', but 'disciplinary identity' is retained.[4] In this excavation of disciplinary methods, however, may be unearthed the common foundations upon which may be built a new edifice of interdisciplinary knowledge, congruous, proportionate and balanced. One brace that might be installed there is the principle of performance, an idea to return to after a summary of the contents of the volume.

The first section of essays is entitled 'How Sermons Reflect Their World(s)'; it illustrates how scholars from different fields employ sermons to reconstruct medieval communities, architectures, rhetorical devices, beliefs about women and artistic representations.

Leo Carruthers's essay begins this section and the entire collection because it is not only a fine example of scholarship, but also a helpful introduction to the many different contexts for medieval sermons. Approaching the sermon from the point of view of religious history, Carruthers details the sorts of communities that made and were made by sermons. With 'The Word Made Flesh' from John 1. 14 as his title, Carruthers alludes to 'the Christ of John's Gospel, the Logos as a declaration of faith, and the proclamation of that faith by preachers and teachers through the ages, which led to the founding of a wide variety of communities'. Carruthers begins with the first kerygmatic Christian communities and traces the use of sermons through the

---

[4] Lewis E. Gilbert, 'Disciplinary Breadth and Interdisciplinary Knowledge Production', *Knowledge, Technology, and Policy*, 11. 1–2 (Spring/Summer, 1998), p. 6.

patristic age, monasticism, court life, universities, the mendicant movement and other aspects of medieval society. His broad historical treatment focuses on the idea that many religious groups throughout history can be identified by common types, themes or scenes for preaching. Thus, in the apostolic age, sermons offered an 'element of proclamation in Christian apologetic' as inspired preachers conveyed the 'good news' that would draw others to the new religion. In the patristic age, 'generations of theologians spent their lives developing doctrine, defending the gospel against heresies and misunderstandings, composing extensive commentaries on the Bible, and publishing numerous sermons on these subjects [. . .]'. Patristic sermons, in other words, offered a much expanded body of believers consistent doctrines for a coherent community. Later, among the mendicants, preaching tours to important cities, and especially those where universities were burgeoning, characterized the friars' spiritual journey. Overall, Carruthers demonstates that the history of religion can be organized according to the communities' distinct approaches to, and uses for, sermons.

In the second essay in this section, John Kitchen shows the value of archaeological research to sermon studies in 'Going to the Gate of Life: The Carthage Amphitheatre and Augustine's Sermons on Saints Perpetua and Felicitas'. Kitchen demonstrates that an important and previously unnoticed source for Augustine's rhetoric of opposition in these sermons is the oppositional architecture of the Carthage Amphitheatre, where Perpetua and Felicitas were martyred. Since many early Christians perceived the attainment of salvation in agonistic terms—as, for instance, a fight against evil—Augustine employed the vocabulary of conflict when describing the martyrdom and significance of these two saints. He adapted this vocabulary in part from Perpetua's *Passio sanctarum Perpetuae et Felicitatis,* which includes a dream of the author's martyrdom, depicting her enemy as a 'foul Egyptian' and herself a victorious wrestler against this devilish nemesis. However, after having participated on an excavation team, Kitchen notes that the layout of the Carthage Amphitheatre, with the Gate of Life and Gate of Death at either end, supports or stages the sermon's vocabulary of oppositions. In Perpetua's *Passio* and Augustine's sermons, the Gate of Life, the exit for surviving gladiators, and the Gate of Death, the repository for the bodies of those killed in the amphitheatre, take on a different meaning. In these Christian discourses, the martyrdom of these women allows them to enter the Gate of Life, or eternal salvation. While the architecture of the amphitheatre governs the symbolism of Augustine's sermons on the saints, Augustine develops a series of contrasting events and themes proceeding from the overarching symbolism. Alluding to Augustine's theory of signs in the *De doctrina Christiana,* Kitchen remarks that '[a]s a place associated with killing and madness, the physical structure of the amphitheatre itself operates as a *signum* [. . .]', itself in binary opposition to the edifice of the Church. In sum, Kitchen's analysis of Augustine's sermons and their structural counterpart in the amphitheatre increases our awareness of the sources for antithesis in medieval discourse.

The final essay in this section, Catherine Brown Tkacz's '*Susanna Victrix, Christus Victor*: Lenten Sermons, Typology and the Lectionary' reveals what medieval Lenten sermons have to say about the lectionary, church art and views of women. Because in medieval sermons, lectionaries and forms of art, Susanna, the heroine of the Book of Daniel, is so often depicted as a type of Christ, her story supports the Church's teachings concerning the spiritual equality of women and men. Tkacz's argument focuses on the pairing in the Lenten lectionary of the story of Susanna from Chapter 13 of the Book of Daniel with Chapter 8 of the Gospel of John. Daniel 13 conveys the events surrounding the false accusation of adultery and final justification of Susanna; John 8. 1–11 tells of Jesus's mercy toward a woman rightfully charged with adultery. While many have assumed that the pairing of the two narratives underscores the parallel lives of the two women, Tkacz demonstrates that verses 1–11 were added rather late to the gospel of John and that the original pairing in the lectionary reflected Susanna's status as a type of Christ. Because of her false accusal, her dignity before a corrupt tribunal and even her words of prayer before her ostensible death, Susanna offers a comparison to and a prefiguration of Christ at his trial and crucifixion. Tkacz offers a plethora of persuasive evidence for Susanna's status as a type of Christ, including patristic sermons, a variety of lectionaries and also visual evidence. Of the latter, she notes, for instance, an embroidered vestment made for Philip Hosden, abbot of St Gertrude's Church in Louvain. The front of this garment shows Christ's arrest in Gethsemane and Susanna's arrest in the garden side by side. Tkacz concludes her essay with an analysis of a fifteenth-century Lenten sermon from Bavaria that represents Susanna as a Christological figure. She asserts that her 'research on Susanna indicates what valuable information about women in Christianity may be retrieved through the full recovery of the traditions of women as types of Christ'.

In his response to the essays of Carruthers, Kitchen, and Brown, Jeffrey Burton Russell points out the similarity in their employment of the concept of time. In 'Time and Again' Russell demonstrates how the Christian belief in the eternal nature of God's time informs each essay and becomes a foundation for interpreting discrete events in medieval history through the sermon.

The next section of essays is entitled 'How Sermons Reflect *Upon* Their World(s)'. The sermons analyzed in this section by scholars of political, literary and art history comment upon the significance, social value and morality of medieval practices. In 'Let Us Love One Another: Liturgy, Morality, and Political Theory in Chrysostom's Sermons on Rom. 12–13 and II Thess. 2', Stephen Morris elucidates John Chrysostom's comments on a Christian's public obligations. According to Chrysostom, the appropriate response to the Eucharist is the surrendering of one's life to God in a perpetual effort to love the community of Christian believers. Through devotion to what is best for the whole body of Christ, a Christian learns to curb sinful self-destruction, live in obedience to the God-ordained government of superiors and rule subordinates in righteousness and charity. While the sermons on the Romans attend to private behavior with public consequences, the sermons on II

Thessalonians, preached in Constantinople for an audience including the emperor and others in high places of government, focus more on the public body. Speculating about how the emperor might have digested Chrysostom's sermons, Morris declares that the emperor would have learned 'his personal duty to maintain the imperial unity as a prerequisite for participating in the Eucharist'. Also, he might have considered 'it his responsibility to assist his subjects in living ethical, Christian lives.'

Making a transition from political to literary analysis, Wim Verbaal provides a close reading of Bernard of Clairvaux's funeral sermon for his brother Gerard. In 'Preaching the Dead from Their Graves: Bernard of Clairvaux's Lament on His Brother Gerard', Verbaal illustrates the value of treating sermons as literature—and how the narrator of a sermon can function as a representative of the sermon's' audience. As Verbaal points out, the sermons on the Canticle, of which the funeral sermon is a part, 'do not testify so much to Bernard's oratorical skills as to his talents as an author. They are not meant to be heard but to be read, to be studied with attention'. Employing literary analysis allows for a sophisticated evaluation of the narrator, Bernard's first person singular ('ego'). Verbaal contends that Bernard's use of 'ego' is less for biographical reference than for his audience's improvement. That is, by authoring an 'ego' that mimics the audience's response to the content of the sermon text, the narrative voice speaks as a bridge between the readers and the message. To illustrate how this process works, Verbaal chooses to assess a sermon that seems intimately autobiographical, Sermon 26 from the collection on the Canticle, a sermon on the death of Bernard's brother Gerard. While Bernard's grief for his brother permeates this sermon, the main point, according to Verbaal, is the way that Sermon 26 operates in the context of other sermons on the Canticle. The sermons preceding 26 highlight several themes enacted by Bernard's narrator when he grieves over Gerard. Besides the motif of inside/outside, other binary oppositions such as straight/crooked and black/beautiful in the sermons leading up to 26 foreshadow conclusions there. By the end, the reader is brought inside the mysteries of the text and in harmony with Bernard's narrator through the understanding of the death of death and the life of all in the spirit. Bernard's Sermon 26 reflects *upon* its world as it mirrors the reader's journey to Christian comprehension.

In '"Spare the Rod and Spoil the Child": Proverbial Speech Acts, Boy Bishop Sermons, and Pedagogical Violence', Eve Salisbury expands the scope of literary analysis to demonstrate how sermons comment not only upon their immediate audience, but also upon larger social systems. Specifically, she shows how boy bishop sermons 'reveal the intensity of the pre-modern debate on how best to raise and educate children [. . .]'. Sermons by boy bishops, school boys elected to replace their adult superiors at Christmastime, internalize, lament or repudiate the practices of corporal punishment so common in homes and classrooms. Because the boy bishop represented all children beaten for misbehaviour, the Holy Innocents and St Nicholas, who reversed the mortal effects of violent crime, the boy bishop was in a position to speak for victims. Yet, because a master wrote the boy bishop's sermon, the victim's own voice was silenced and replaced by one who often meted out blows. Through this discursive ventriloquism, the message of the boy bishop sermons could be unstable, in the same discourse offering jokes about the harshness of the master and defending the efficacy and morality of the proverb 'Spare the rod and spoil the child'. In her study of three boy bishop sermons—one delivered at St Paul's in 1495, another at Gloucester in 1558 and Erasmus's *Homily to the Child Jesus* from 1512—Salisbury discovers that only Erasmus's sermon clearly replaces the defence of corporal punishment with a plea to the audience for *imitatio Christi*, while the other two defend the practice of corporal punishment.

The last essay in this section, Emily Michelson's 'Bernardino of Siena Visualizes the Name of God' demonstrates the interdependency between Bernardino's fifteenth-century sermons and his monogram of Jesus's Holy Name. She explains how the sermons provide a multi-layered exegesis of the monogram and how the monogram functions as a prop for preaching. Since Bernardino was a celebrated Observant preacher and since the monogram with the letters 'IHS' inside a sun was famous—even the cause of a heresy trial—Michelson's essay illustrates how collaboration between art and church history can inform and offer new conclusions for even the most studied event of our medieval past. Although Bernardino is often remembered for and painted with the monogram, especially by Sano di Pietro, Michelson argues that Bernardino himself was more concerned with the sermonic words inspiring the audience to worship Jesus's name and the program of a faithful life that the monogram inspired. In fact, the heresy trial, in which Bernardino was accused of inspiring worship of the colors in the monogram itself and thus rendering it an idol, demonstrates Michelson's point: Bernardino was exonerated because he successfully defended the traditional worship of the name of God and made a distinction between such worship and inappropriate adoration of the symbol promoting the name. Throughout her essay, Michelson expertly describes the meanings that Bernard developed for the monogram through his sermons and the methods he employed to encourage meditation of Jesus's name through the monogram during the sermons. As Michelson remarks, 'Bernardino's fundamental intention, the one which overshadows all the others, is that the monogram should transform or bolster the faith of the person who beholds and contemplates it'. Michelson's investigation of the history and artistic context for the monogram, as well as her close reading of Bernardino's sermons about it, help us to understand more clearly one of the most famous images in Western Christianity.

Responding to the essays in Section II, Peter Howard offers further evidence for how the sermons invoked here reflect upon their worlds. Because of their hortatory nature, he contends, sermons cast their reflection through persuasion. He argues for a rigorous contextualizing in sermons scholarship, especially for the need to analyze a sermon's meaning from the rhetorical situation for which it was composed or delivered. Howard's essay is a good example of the principle of disputation in this volume: he initiates the sort of debate that can happen between scholars who regard sermons as rhetorical and those who view them as representational.

The third section of essays is entitled, 'How Sermons are Reflected in Other Literatures'. Here, the authors explain what *Piers Plowman* and several medieval plays have to say about certain medieval sermons. Beginning this section, David Strong illustrates how Franciscan theology and sermon practice influenced the composition of William Langland's *Piers Plowman*. In 'Illumination of the Intellect: Franciscan Sermons and *Piers Plowman*', he demonstrates the similarity between Bonaventure's university sermons and Langland's fourteenth-century Middle English poem. The 'substantive import' of both Bonaventure's sermons and *Piers Plowman* 'awakens their audience to a divine presence within this world'. 'In effect', Strong argues, '*Piers* functions as a literary sermon indebted to Franciscan thought, specifically that strain emphasizing the spiritual value of creation and its innate link to the Creator'. Bonaventure's emphasis on the individual's spiritual quest is depicted in the wanderings of Long Will in *Piers*. Through an allegory personifying important aspects of the world and humanity, such as Hunger and Imaginatyf, *Piers Plowman* makes tangible the concept of God's immanence. Strong connects the poem's allegoresis to the Franciscan tradition of preaching to the uneducated people, of having to render difficult theological concepts understandable. Even though Bonaventure's *Collationes in Hexaemeron* were written to rebut Averroism and antifraternalism at the University of Paris, they nevertheless defend faith and an awareness of God in creation as paths to knowledge in unpretentious language. Bonaventure's contemporaries remark upon the simplicity and clarity of his treatment of metaphysics, and similarly, Langland's use of dreams makes comprehensible the meeting of human and divine. While both Bonaventure and Langland are concerned with the accessibility of ideas, their approach is not so much to simplify, but to engage the audience's understanding through analogies to common experience. In sum, as 'Franciscan ideology inspires connections between the erudite and the common, the aesthetic and the natural, Langland embraces this idea, using it to justify his emphasis upon individual capabilities in the search for higher truth'.

In the first of two essays about medieval drama, Lynn T. Ramey's 'Unauthorized Preaching: The Sermon in Jean Bodel's *Jeu de Saint Nicolas*' provides an example of how medieval theatre comments upon medieval preaching. The *Jeu de Saint Nicolas*, performed in Arras on 5 December 1200, is remarkable as a very early example of vernacular religious theatre and as a timely commentary upon crusade preaching. Including many references to sermons, the play is introduced by *li preechieres* and punctuated by the town criers' mock preaching. The action includes a battle between Christians and Muslims, a tavern scene where thieves are encouraged to steal the open treasure of the Muslim ruler, a miracle whereby St Nicholas preserves the treasure, and a conversion of the Muslims in the face of the saint's power. Since *li preechieres* incorrectly summarizes this plot in the beginning and Connart, the town crier, parodies Crusade sermons by summoning the Muslims to battle, the play calls the truthfulness of preaching into question. Ramey situates the play's radical critique in the context of the miserably failed Third Crusade, whose glories were promised in sermons, but never attained. Ramey concludes that while the *Jeu de Saint Nicolas* 'intentionally capitalized on the horizon of expectations of the sermon', it highlights the interchanges between theatre and pulpit, illustrating the performative nature of preaching and the potential for sermonizing in performance. By rendering his own play a sermon, Jean Bodel 'casts doubt on the play's own message', and gives 'his medieval audience a coded warning—one needs to listen to preachers and playwrights with caution, for, as any public voice, their messages can be deceiving'.

Like David Strong, Peter V. Loewen is concerned with connections among Franciscans, sermons and literature in 'The Conversion of Mary Magdalene and the Musical Legacy of Franciscan Piety in the Early German Passion Plays'. Like Ramey's essay, Loewen's treats medieval drama. By examining two of the earliest examples of German passion plays, the *Großes Benediktbeurer Passionsspiel* (*c.* 1250) and the *Wiener Passionsspielfragment* (*c.* 1300), Loewen demonstrates how Franciscan thought on penitence and the rhetoric of music, flowering in the same century as the plays considered, affects the composition of the songs assigned to Mary Magdalene. In both plays, the Magdalene sings goliardic songs celebrating beauty, vanity and lechery; she also confesses her spiritual correction through songs of penitence. In her sinful songs, the Magadalene's materialism, focusing on clothes and cosmetics, and her physical abandon to dancing and lechery enact the typical German Franciscan depiction of the sinner. For instance, the sermons of Berthold of Regensburg (*c.* 1210–72) focus on pride and licentiousness and employ *exempla* of immodest women to illustrate these sins. The proper penitence for one so proud as to use the church service as a stage for the display of fine clothing would be the imitation of the humble, pure and unadorned Virgin Mary. In her penitential lyrics in the Passion plays, the Magdalene repudiates her former ornaments and promiscuity while committing her life to Christ. Significantly, the Magdalene's Goliardic songs are melodically simple and her penitence lyrics tonally complex, illustrating the spiritual gorgeousness she has achieved by throwing off baubles. Loewen concludes that '[m]usic and words function together in the German Passion plays as scriptural exegesis'.

Elizabeth Schirmer responds to the essays in Section III. Noting that each of the authors makes a comparison between the generic properties of sermons and other vernacular literatures, Schirmer illustrates the subversive and complicated nature of such literary exchanges. She makes a case for historicizing the local contexts for the sermon's uses of vernacular literature and for the literature's employment of sermons.

The final section of essays, 'Reflections *Upon* Sermons', especially emphasizes how different disciplinary methodologies cast their light upon the medieval sermon. As the essays highlight various angles of the sermon—linguistic properties, generic conventions, modes of representation or frequency of stock phrasing—they provide diverse pictures of the medieval sermon and illustrate how the sermon signifies in distinct fields.

Ingunn Lunde provides our first essay in this section, 'Speech-Reporting Strategies in "Dramatic Preaching": With Examples from East Slavic Festal Sermons'. Here, she employs the methods of linguistic pragmatics in order to explain the dramatic effects of the sermons of Kirill, bishop of Turov. The reference to 'speech-reporting' in the title signifies the reported speeches in Kirill's sermons, the words of a biblical figure spoken by the preacher as narrator. The analytical categories for linguistic pragmatics include *deixis*, framing, voice and perspective. Exploring *deictic* markers in Kirill's sermons, in other words, those characteristics which highlight time, space and person, Lunde finds that '[m]arkers may point in several directions, creating multiple perspectives or even ambiguities with regard to speaker and addressee [. . .]'. This multiplicity and ambiguity serves the preacher's goal of moving the audience through the dramatic representation of a biblical text. Along with *deictic* markers, Lunde demonstrates how framing devices add meaning and relevance to the sermon material. In the same sermon for the Third Sunday after Easter, Kirill juxtaposes the various accounts of the scene at Christ's empty grave by the four evangelists in order to corroborate the resurrection narrative. Although Kirill's sermons often create unified meaning from multiplicity, Lunde notes as she uses 'voice' as a category of analysis, that sometimes Kirill highlights conflict. For example, the *Sermons for the Fourth and Sixth Sundays after Easter* offer dialogues between the conflicting voices of Doubting Thomas or the Jews and Christ. Lunde argues overall that speech-reporting lends immediacy to Kirill's sermons and that the techniques of linguistic pragmatics explain the workings of dramaturgy in the pulpit. The multiple perspectives that Kirill invokes through dramatic speeches cause the congregation to think about divine authority and and 'maximise the participation of the audience by stimulating their perceptual, emotional and cognitive involvement'.

Considering the difference between vocal preaching and the composition of sermons, Thom Mertens establishes the importance of analyzing the medieval sermon as a written text in 'Relic or Strategy: The Middle Dutch Sermon as a Literary Phenomenon'. While essays previously described for this volume have focused similarly on literary analysis, Mertens especially emphasizes how an examination of the material, historical and rhetorical features of manuscripts differs from a consideration of the sermon as delivered speech. As Mertens points out, 'The silent identification of the spoken and written sermon blurs on the one side the question of what we actually know about preaching itself, and on the other side the question of proper characteristics, conventions, and functions of the written sermon'. By distinguishing between the spoken and written, Mertens aims to clarify the circumstances surrounding Middle Dutch preaching and sermon composition. He discovers that in many cases when preachers write down their own sermons or when listeners take notes, predicatory features, such as direct addresses to the audience, are eliminated in favor of recording the gist of the message. One interesting exception to this general rule, he remarks, occurs when nuns write out the sermons of their confessors, either by copying a manuscript or composing from a dictation. The sermons of Claus of Euskirchen and Jan Storm have been preserved in this way.

Perhaps, the inclusion of features needed to involve the audience in a speech and keep their attention allowed the nuns to preach these sermons in the refectory as spiritual entertainment. Mertens cites the example of one prioress, Alijt Bake, who was not content to speak others' sermons in her own voice, but composed her own for delivery when she found others insufficient for Palm Sunday. Through references to Alijt and the other anonymous copyists, Mertens demonstrates how widely divergent might be the original invention of a medieval sermon and its circumstances for dissemination and delivery. When investigating sermons not meant for delivery, Mertens finds that the few extant from Middle Dutch evince the same purpose as Sunday sermons, the catechization of the laity in their own vernacular. Preaching conventions might be maintained in sermon collections meant for individual reading in order to mimic the Sunday experience. Mertens concludes that while it may not be practical or wise to treat the medieval sermon as a literary phenomenon only, being aware of the differences between speaking and writing, or hearing and reading sermons leads to clearer analysis.

While Mertens focuses on the written nature of sermons, Holly Johnson returns to ways in which literary analysis reveals the oral and representational. In her estimation, macaronic sermons on the Passion preached in late medieval England give a particularly dramatic rendering of Christ's sufferings. In 'Fashioning Devotion: The Art of Good Friday Preaching in Chaucerian England', Johnson illustrates that Passion sermons, like the liturgy for Good Friday, evoke the presence of the crucifixion as they represent Jesus's death vividly and invite the congregation to witness and participate. In contrast to the dryly didactic Latin sermons of those such as Bishop Thomas Brinton, the macaronic sermons, Johnson argues, were often preached in English and reflect popular devotion, tempered and confined by the structure and systems of development of the scholastic form. The three examples of macaronic sermons that Johnson invokes are an unedited sermon showing the influence of the *Vita Christi* from the Lambeth Palace manuscript, a sermon invoking the pietà by William Melton and an interactive sermon by Henry Chambron, who invites the audience to take part. With each of these examples, Johnson highlights the visual effects that encourage the congregation to imagine Christ's Passion and commit the lesson to memory. According to Johnson, '[t]he interplay between images and narrative in these sermons creates a tension between stasis and action, a tension connected to that which is created by the interplay between doctrine and drama, or theology and pathos'. As these sermons invoke images that bear cultural, historical and religious weight, they imprint the Passion and its meaning upon the memories of the audience.

For the volume's final essay, Martine De Reu argues the efficacy of computerized textual analysis in 'A Statistical Treatment of Sin and Holiness in Sermons from the Early Middle Ages (500–1100)'. Admitting that automatic analysis of machine readable texts is often distrusted by scholars in the history of ideas, she reminds her readers that concordances and methods for style analysis have long been accepted, and contends that a statistical analysis can be a helpful addition to more traditional methods of research. For instance, computerized searches for the number of instances in which a word or its synonyms are used in a certain text can help to confirm a reader's impressions. In this essay, De Reu applies a statistical analysis to the discussion of the vices and virtues in early medieval sermons and related works. She searches for uses of the seven deadly sins, the theological virtues and the monastic virtues in Merovingian, Carolingian and tenth- and eleventh-century sermons and other treatises, such as penitentials. In order to ensure a representative and relevant sample of texts, she consults a number of secondary resources on the medieval sermon, including histories and bibliographies, which she lists in Appendix I. Appendix II outlines the numerous sermons composed between 500 and 1100 that make up the subject matter for this study. With the subject matter for her statistical analysis clarified, she demonstrates how sermons treat the vices and virtues differently in different ages and rhetorical contexts. Helpful charts illustrate the generalizations drawn from statistical analysis. For instance, Chart 3 makes clear that the discourses of the Carolingian period emphasize faith, much beyond the discourses of the Merovingian era or texts from the tenth- and eleventh-centuries. Because of this emphasis on faith, De Reu notes that the 'Carolingian preachers succeeded in giving their sermon collections an identity, all the while borrowing so extensively from their predecessors'. De Reu argues that, without statistical analysis, it may be difficult for modern readers to recognize the particularly Carolingian innovation in sermons because of such heavy use of earlier models for preaching. Finding an explanation for the Carolingian focus on faith in Charlegmagne's reforms for preaching, she notes that the *Admonitio generalis* outlines the authorized subject matter for sermons and underscores the need for the ruler and the preachers to instruct the people in right belief.

Simon Forde responds to the essays in this final section by considering how multilingualism is a condition of both medieval preachers and contemporary medievalists.

While the essays in *Speculum Sermonis* take both single-disciplinary and interdisciplinary approaches, an interdisciplinary objective for the whole anthology is the presentation of shared foundations for more cross-collaboration about sermons. For the four sections of this volume, the respondents focus and expand on conclusions common to the authors. Even beyond the syntheses of the respondents, one overriding commonality, an idea providing a bridge across all of the authors and their fields here, is that of performance. All of the essays in *Speculum Sermonis* concur in demonstrating a performative element in sermons, whether these essays discuss the theatrical or the theoretical, the pulpit as a stage, or its language as productive of events, ideas, social codes and personal behaviors. Essays depicting the pulpit as a scene or a counterpart to theatre and spectacle include, in the order that they are presented in this volume, Salisbury's, Michelson's, Ramey's Loewen's, Lunde's and Johnson's. Salisbury examines the boy bishop's impersonation of authority, Michelson characterizes the IHS monogram as a preaching prop, Ramey compares the action of the *Jeu de Saint Nicolas* to Crusade preaching, Loewen finds the music of German Passion plays imbued with Franciscan sermons, Lunde examines the linguistic properties of dramatic dialogue in Slavic sermons, and Johnson illustrates how macaronic sermons re-enact the Passion. These essays demonstrate that religious drama and the sermon's connection to it are fertile areas of study for not only historians of theatre, but also for art historians, musicologists, linguists, literary critics and others. Not all sermon texts, however, benefit from an analysis of their histrionics or from suppositions about the impact of their oral delivery, as both Mertens's and Verbaal's essays make clear. Many sermons were written for private reading and devotion, and therefore their performativity rests not in the actual creation of a scene, but in the power of their language imprinted upon the reader. As De Reu's analysis of the use of virtues and vices illustrates, the terminology of righteousness and sinfulness employed in sermons has complicated connections to both private and social religious thought and practice. Whether or not a sermon is delivered, its invocations can manifest themselves graphically on both social and human body, as Salisbury explains in her reading of corporal punishment in boy bishop sermons. With the language of sermons performing various religious concepts and actions, it can even, according to Leo Carruthers, create and identify communities. The essays of this volume cooperate in defining how the sermon produces for its medieval audience the reality–or the vision of reality–it would perpetuate. These definitions are sometimes the result of discrete disciplinary methods of inquiry. It is now up to the readers to combine fields of vision in their own work.

Not only for past audiences, but also for contemporary scholars, the medieval sermon often re-enacts the past and becomes a substitute for medieval space, as in Kitchen's treatment of the Carthage Amphitheatre; for medieval practice, as in Morris's politicization of Chrysostom's sermons; and for medieval thought, as in Strong's discovery of Franciscan ideals in both Bonaventure's preaching and *Piers Plowman*. That a body of evidence such as the sermon provides a trace of the past may be a scholarly truism, and as such, it should yield to inspection about how divergent fields draw out the traces. The following pages provide a new look at disciplinary hermeneutics, as well as possibilities for combining different modes of interpretation. *Speculum Sermonis: Interdisciplinary Reflections on the Medieval Sermon* refracts the different angles and lights from which scholars in various disciplines view the sermon and the multiplicitous images of the medieval past that the sermons project in scholarly discourse.

I

How Sermons Reflect Their World(s)

The Word Made Flesh: Preaching and Community from the Apostolic to the Late Middle Ages

LEO CARRUTHERS

I. The New Testament as 'Sermon': Mirror of a Preaching Community

The short title used above, 'The Word Made Flesh', may be taken as a paradigm for how sermons and related religious texts ('word') allow us an insight into human history ('flesh'). It comes, of course, from the famous opening chapter of John's Gospel (1. 14) where Christ, the Logos, the eternal, uncreated Word of God, becomes flesh in the person of Jesus, a man born of woman at a given place in time.[1] This is seen as the fulfilment of the Old Testament tradition of the word of God being proclaimed to the chosen people through the prophets. In the Christian conception of cosmology, God the Creator is the first community, composed before time began of Father, Son and Holy Spirit. The second community, from a monotheistic viewpoint, is that existing between Creator and creation, especially the human race, material beings with a free will capable of knowing and loving Yahweh, 'the One who is', i.e. being itself, the spiritual essence of life. And the third community is the nuclear human family, man, woman and child, God's chosen instrument for the creation of new life. The man Jesus Christ, again in the Christian conception, is a focus and a realization of these three types of community: the Holy Trinity, the created and the uncreated, the human family—in a word, the Word made flesh. John's pithy phrase claims that the incarnation of Christ is the fullest expression of communication between God and his creatures in terms that the limited human mind can grasp.

---

[1] Scripture quotations in English are based on *The Holy Bible*, Revised Standard Version (London: Catholic Truth Society, 1966).

How this idea generated Christian communities in various times and places, from biblical times to late medieval Europe—with the evidence of texts—is the focus of the present paper. The 'Word' is taken to mean both the Christ of John's Gospel, the Logos as a declaration of faith, and the proclamation of that faith by preachers and teachers through the ages, which led to the founding of a wide variety of communities. To develop this thoroughly would require a whole history of the Church side by side with the history of preaching, but this has been done by other and better-qualified scholars, most recently by the contributors to the *Typologie* volume on *The Sermon*.[2] No attempt will here be made to define the terms 'preaching' or 'sermon', except to say that they can and do have a very wide sense: 'sermon' is an 'overlapping genre' which, as others have pointed out, includes many types of text and discourse.[3] This is one reason why the field of sermon studies must, of its nature, be interdisciplinary, since it touches on so many areas of specialization whose encounter can only be mutually beneficial. Bearing this in mind, my focus here will be on the notion of community in the Christian context and the exploration of the intimate connection between, on the one hand, word and text (speech/writing), and, on the other hand, word and community (theory/practice).

For the earliest period, we are obviously hampered by a relative shortage of texts other than the Bible, and must rely to some extent on oral tradition. One of the great changes in medieval European society was the gradual transition from oral to written transmission as a means of general communication, a subject which has attracted many recent historians.[4] In this respect, the Bible itself is a forerunner and an example, an inspiration which generated a desire to preserve knowledge in a written form; for all three of the world's principal monotheistic faiths, Judaism, Christianity and Islam, are traditionally held to be religions of the Book, of the written word—a word believed by their followers to have been divinely revealed to humans in various stages. My own limited competence, as well as the problem of space, will make it necessary to keep my remarks to the Christian tradition. But the fact that preaching also existed among non-Christian groups, of whom Jews undoubtedly formed the most important element in medieval Europe, should not be overlooked. A recent summary of medieval Jewish sermons points to the homogeneous nature of the Jewish

[2] *The Sermon*, ed. by Beverly Mayne Kienzle, Typologie des sources du Moyen Age occidental, fascicules 81–83 (Turnhout: Brepols, 2000). There is of course a very extensive body of historical and literary criticism in all areas related to the subject, as this volume's bibliography testifies.

[3] See Beverly Kienzle's introduction to *The Sermon*, especially the definitions discussed in 'Essential Characteristics of the Sermon', pp. 150–59; also 'Overlapping of the sermon and other genres', pp. 964–65.

[4] For example: Laura Kendrick, *Animating the Letter: The Figurative Embodiment of Writing from Late Antiquity to the Renaissance* (Columbus: Ohio State University Press, 1999); Michael T. Clanchy, *From Memory to Written Record: England 1066–1307* (Oxford: Blackwell, 1979, 2nd edn 1993).

community and the absence among them of the typical Christian distinction between preaching to the people and preaching to a more learned clergy.[5]

But to go back to the beginning, at least from a Christian viewpoint, let us recall the first kerygmatic community, that of the Jewish Christians in Jerusalem as described in the Acts of the Apostles. Christians were not meant to form an exclusive esoteric group, like Roman soldiers meeting in the temples of Mithra, but rapidly became, after the first Pentecost, both kerygmatic and didactic. The Greek word *kerygma* meant both 'proclamation' in the secular sense and, later, 'preaching' in the religious sense; it is used more narrowly, however, to characterize the element of proclamation in Christian apologetic, as contrasted with *didache* or its instructional element.[6] In biblical criticism, it is a term for what is believed to be recoverable as a single original core of the 'good news' within the varied New Testament writings (Gospels, Acts, Epistles), giving them internal unity.[7] In its purest form, this can be reduced to the person of Christ himself: 'I am the way, the truth and the life' (John 14. 6). But it must include the teachings of his followers which make up a large part of the New Testament: the pattern of preaching in Acts 2–13, and Paul's preaching of the cross and resurrection. This is in fact a peculiarly Christian use of the term *kerygma*, specific to the New Testament, since there is no tradition either in the Hebrew Scriptures, or in the Greek translation known as the Septuagint, of the word being associated with this type of religious proclamation.[8] The *kerygma* appears in its simplest form in the 'discourses' attributed to St Peter, reported in several parts of the Acts of the Apostles: firstly, those in Jerusalem following the day of Pentecost (2. 14–40 and 3. 12–26), and secondly, his preaching in Caesarea (10. 28–43) which is part of the early mission to the Gentiles. Whatever one's view of the nature of inspiration, these texts are believed to preserve the first-century preaching tradition which was accepted by the medieval Church as the authentic proclamation of the Apostles. From the earliest times, therefore, the connection between preaching and community is evident: whether directed inwards to Christians, or outwards to non-Christians, preaching aims to create and strengthen communities of believers by teaching them the faith and inspiring enthusiasm for it.

---

[5] Marc Saperstein, 'The Medieval Jewish Sermon', in *The Sermon*, ed. by B.M. Kienzle, pp. 175–201.

[6] *The Oxford Dictionary of the Christian Church* (afterwards *ODCC*), ed. by F. L. Cross and E. A. Livingstone (Oxford: Oxford University Press, 1957, 3rd edn 1997), p. 478 *Didache*, 924 *Kerygma*. All of the entries in this excellent reference work are accompanied by useful bibliographies of primary and secondary sources.

[7] Lower-case 'gospel' is used as a common noun equivalent to 'proclamation' or *kerygma*, while Gospel (with a capital letter) refers to the four New Testament books traditionally so named.

[8] See John L. McKenzie, *Dictionary of the Bible* (London & Dublin: Chapman, 1976), p. 689, 'Preaching'.

Many anecdotes from the Acts of the Apostles vividly illustrate the power of preaching. One evening, for example, in Troas (a city of Asia Minor), when the brethren were gathered together to break bread, St Paul spoke at length, his sermon going on until midnight.

> And a young man named Eutychus was sitting in the window. He sank into a deep sleep as Paul talked still longer; and being overcome by sleep, he fell down from the third storey and was taken up dead. But Paul went down and bent over him, and embracing him said, 'Do not be alarmed, for his life is in him' (Acts 20. 9–10).

One cannot help wondering if the name Eutychus, which in Greek means 'fortunate', was not in fact a nickname given to this drowsy young man precisely because of his lucky escape from death.[9] Following his revival, Paul went back upstairs to have a meal and then, untroubled by the accident, continued talking to the community all night long, until daybreak.

II. A Window on the Patristic Age

The end of the first century marks the Church's entry into the post-apostolic and post-biblical age. Without attempting to discuss the complex arguments surrounding the dates of death of the twelve Apostles, or the dating and authorship of the various books of the New Testament, suffice it to say that in the medieval West, the canon was held to be complete with the Apocalypse, or Book of Revelation. Its author, John, was probably writing during the persecution of the Emperor Domitian (81–96), most likely towards the end of that period (94–95), indicated by the spread and establishment of the Church in Asia as mentioned in the book.[10] Also from the first century there is at least one other text, known as the *Didache*, which, without being canonical, is accepted as both apostolic and orthodox; indeed it was quoted as Scripture by one of the early Church Fathers, St Clement of Alexandria (*c.* 150–215).[11] The statement of faith known as the Apostles' Creed is not a formula of apostolic origin, though in the West it was believed, certainly by the fourth century, to have been jointly composed by the twelve Apostles themselves.[12] Proof of this lies in the *Explanatio symboli*, a sermon written by St Niceta(s), Bishop of Remesiana (*c.*

---

[9] This suggestion is my own. For the etymology see McKenzie, *Dictionary of the Bible*, p. 254, 'Eutychus'.

[10] From an early period controversy has surrounded the author of the last book of the New Testament; it is unlikely to have been John the Evangelist, contrary to what was commonly believed in the Middle Ages. See McKenzie, *Dictionary of the Bible*, pp. 38–41, 'Apocalypse'.

[11] *ODCC*, p. 478, 'Didache'.

[12] *ODCC*, p. 89, 'Apostles' Creed'.

370–414), a primary witness for the history of the Apostles' Creed and the oldest attestation for the expression 'the communion of saints' (*communio sanctorum*) which is contained therein.[13] A thousand years later the attribution to the twelve Apostles was being repeated in didactic vernacular treatises such as the fourteenth-century English *Book of Vices and Virtues*: 'And þer beþ twelue [articules of þe feiþ], after þe noumbre of þe twelue apostles, þat setten hem and ordeyned hem to kepen and to holden to alle hem þat willeþ be saued.'[14]

The Apostolic Age is followed by the patristic, beginning with St Clement of Rome (d. *c.* 102), second or third bishop after St Peter and author of an Epistle to the Corinthians, and St Ignatius, third Bishop of Antioch (d. *c.* 107), author of a series of letters to early Christian communities. Another early Epistle to the Corinthians, once attributed to Clement of Rome, is described as 'the earliest surviving Christian sermon'.[15] From the first words of his authentic Epistle to the Corinthians, Clement shows his concern to promote peace and harmony within the community:

> Because of our recent series of unexpected misfortunes and set-backs, my dear friends, we feel there has been some delay in turning our attention to the causes of dispute in your community. We refer particularly to the odious and unholy breach of unity among you, which is quite incompatible with God's chosen people.[16]

Sadly, this would become a familiar theme echoed throughout history by caring bishops anxious to restore unity in the midst of human dissension.

The patristic age is considered to have lasted for about five or six hundred years, coming to a close in the West with St Isidore of Seville (*c.* 560–636) and in the East with St John of Damascus (*c.* 657–749). This is a very long time, longer than we tend to realize as we look back and see it as a single block. Many generations of theologians spent their lives developing doctrine, defending the gospel against heresies and misunderstandings, composing extensive commentaries on the Bible, and publishing numerous sermons on these subjects; they also kept records of Church history and related the faith to the philosophy of their age.[17] Those who were entitled

---

[13] *ODCC*, p. 1147, 'St Niceta' (Remesiana is now Bela Palanka, in modern Serbia). On the Communion of Saints see also *A New Dictionary of Christian Theology*, ed. by Alan Richardson and John Bowden (London: SCM, 1983), pp. 114–15.

[14] 'And there are twelve articles of the faith, according to the number of the twelve Apostles, who fixed them and who commanded all who desire to be saved to observe them' (my translation). *The Book of Vices and Virtues*, ed. by W. Nelson Francis, Early English Text Society, o.s. 217 (London: Oxford University Press, 1940), 6/20–26. This is a Middle English version of the French *Somme le Roi* (1279).

[15] *ODCC*, p. 360, 'St Clement of Rome'.

[16] *Early Christian Writings. The Apostolic Fathers*, trans. by Maxwell Staniforth (Harmondsworth, Middlesex: Penguin Classics, 1968), p. 23.

[17] *ODCC*, p. 1233, 'Patristics'.

to be known as Fathers of the Church were, to begin with, bishops as witnesses of the Christian tradition; but the title was applied more particularly, from the fourth century onwards (by St Basil), to writers whose authority on doctrinal matters carried special weight. They were considered to be infallible only when they taught a doctrine unanimously, since the teaching of individuals was admittedly liable to error. Some of those whose orthodoxy on certain matters might be questioned, such as Tertullian (*c.* 160–225) and Origen (*c.* 186–254), are nevertheless numbered among the Fathers because of the contribution made by their writings to the expression of doctrine and a deepening of theological awareness.[18] The influence of these early writers is incalculable; nor should it be supposed to die out with the end of the patristic age, as their sermons and other tracts continued to be read for hundreds of years. To mention but one example among many, St Caesarius of Arles (*c.* 470–542), himself one of the Church Fathers and a preacher of distinction, made a collection of ninety-five sermons, mainly by Augustine and other African bishops, which was still being copied in the ninth century, in a Carolingian manuscript known as *The Homiliary of Wolfenbuttel*.[19]

III. Rules and Sermons: Glimpses of Monastic Life

For most of the writers mentioned so far, the idea of the Christian community is identical with that of the universal Church, seen as the mystical body of Christ, expressed on an everyday, practical level by the association of believers united around their bishop. The latter is both a teacher and administrator, a function always associated with the important cities of the Roman Empire in which Christian assemblies were first founded—hence Clement of Rome's concern with unity (quoted above), a paradigm for bishops' preaching. Later in the patristic period, however, we note the beginning of new kinds of religious movements, new forms of social organization, which bring us closer to the notion of 'community' as a distinct way of life within the larger body of the Church: this is the ascetic and monastic tradition. But it should be recalled that for most of Christian history, and for most people, the typical community has remained the diocese and its subdivision, the parish, the first focused on the bishop, the second on his vicar, the parish priest. In the modern period, too, many of the larger reformed denominations have retained an episcopal organization; and even where this is not the case, the parish or weekly assembly, led by a minister (appointed or elected), still represents the basic community. The use of the word 'community' in connection with the consecrated or monastic way of life is, therefore,

---

[18] *ODCC*, p. 600, 'Fathers of the Church'.

[19] Thomas N. Hall, 'The Early Medieval Sermon', in *The Sermon*, ed. by B. M. Kienzle, p. 227 (pp. 203–69).

a narrowing of the meaning, though it may be the first one to spring to mind for many specialists of religious orders and their sermons which figure so largely in later medieval preaching.

The New Testament model is clearly not monastic, but it is communitarian. The monastic way of life is an attempt to return to a certain communitarian ideal, while at the same time integrating the ascetic precepts of poverty, chastity, and obedience. According to the Acts of the Apostles, the first community in Jerusalem held all things in common—though it is rather unfortunate that from the very start, an element of fear and hypocrisy was present. The sudden deaths of Ananias and his wife struck fear among the believers, who began to look on St Peter with a kind of awe that, biblical though it may be, must have horrified the Protestant reformers of a later age as an unworthy attitude, a forerunner of 'medieval superstition'. The unhappy couple dropped dead—apparently struck down by God, but in accordance with Peter's severe judgement—because of their hypocrisy and dishonesty (Acts 5. 1–11). In a community which laid emphasis on sharing material wealth for the good of all, they bowed to social pressure; but rather than being open and above board in their actions, they tried to conceal part of their possessions.

The beginning of the consecrated religious life is attributed to the Desert Fathers, St Antony (*c.* 251–356) and St Pachomius (*c.* 290–346), both of whom founded communities in Egypt. Of the two, Antony was by nature more eremitical (solitary), but in spite of himself, he attracted a number of disciples through his holiness and asceticism, so that in *c.* 305, after twenty years of solitude in the desert, he found it necessary to organize his followers into a community under his rule; they did not, however, have much common life comparable to the later religious orders. Pachomius, who was more coenobitic (communitarian), founded a monastery *c.* 320, which soon attracted large numbers of monks; at his death he was ruling as abbot-general over nine monasteries for men and two for women. In both cases, we see a connection between the written word and the community, of their own day and later. The seven epistles attributed to Antony, which survive in a Latin version printed by Migne, were known to St Jerome (*c.* 345–420), who also translated the letters of Pachomius and, perhaps even more important, the latter's monastic Rule.[20] The Rule of Pachomius influenced St Basil (*c.* 330–79), Bishop of Caesarea, whose Rule remains dominant in Eastern monasticism down to the present day. Monasticism grew rapidly in Syria, Palestine and Asia Minor, and flourished in the Byzantine Empire, where it enjoyed great influence within society. The tradition has of course endured in the eastern Church, where monasteries tend to be independent of each other, not belonging to a religious order as would become the norm in the West.

Monasticism first spread to the Latin Church during the fifth century as the literature of the East, beginning with the Desert Fathers and St Basil, became known.[21]

---

[20] *ODCC*, p. 80, 'St Antony of Egypt', p. 120, 'St Pachomius'.

[21] *ODCC*, p. 1102, 'Monasticism'.

The Rule of Pachomius influenced the similar rules of many other founders: St John Cassian (*c.* 360–433), responsible for bringing the Egyptian tradition to Gaul (at Marseille); St Caesarius (*c.* 470–542), who was a monk at Lérins before becoming Archbishop of Arles; and St Benedict (*c.* 480–550), Abbot of Subiaco and Monte Cassino, called the 'patriarch of Western monasticism' because of the major role played by his Rule.[22] Various new types of religious community thus evolved, differing in the extent of their common life, the taking of religious vows, and the nature and purpose of their common activities. In Europe the coenobitic tradition, as opposed to the eremitical, would rapidly dominate, for women as well as for men. Coenobites live in common, whereas hermits, by definition, live alone; but coenobites may also be anchorites in separate dwellings observing a rule of silence, though living as a community of monks in a common enclosure. This way of life is now followed in the West chiefly by the Carthusian Order, not founded until 1084 by St Bruno at the Grande Chartreuse, combining Benedictine monachism and eremitical asceticism.

The eastern tradition was also influential in the development of Irish monasticism, with its vigorous ascetical practices. It is interesting to note how quickly such communities took root in Ireland, a country which proved an exception to the rule of the city-based bishoprics. But then, the island had never been part of the Roman Empire, and the 'barbarian' Celts (i.e. those outside the Roman sphere of influence) had not developed an urban culture. The conversion of Ireland took place during the fifth century, precisely when monasticism first developed in the West; and down to the eleventh century when the internal diocesan system was finally organized, the basic unit of the Irish Church was the monastery rather than the town. Indeed, it was the monasteries which contributed to the development of towns, not the other way round; and as for coastal ports, there were none of any importance until the Viking Age, from the ninth century onwards. Early Irish monasticism was in turn brought to the Continent by men such as St Columbanus (*c.* 543–615), founder of monasteries in Luxeuil and Bobbio. Some of the sermons of Columbanus have been preserved, or at least sermons attributed to him.[23] If they were not composed by Columbanus himself, they do issue from his tradition; and the fact that his monastic Rule was widely used in the seventh century is sufficient explanation for the attribution.

By the ninth century, however, the Benedictine Rule had become pre-eminent in western Europe. The later Middle Ages saw the creation of new monastic orders following the Rule, notably the Cistercians, founded at Cîteaux in 1098 by a group of seven monks including St Robert of Molesme (1027–1110) and St Stephen Harding (d. 1134); their intention was to return to a stricter and more primitive form of

[22] David Hugh Farmer, *The Oxford Dictionary of Saints* (Oxford: Oxford University Press, 1978, 4th edn 1997), *s.v.* Benedict. Farmer (afterwards *ODS*) also gives full references to primary and secondary sources, including, whenever possible, editions of sermons and other writings by the saints themselves.

[23] Thomas N. Hall, 'The Early Medieval Sermon', p. 241.

monasticism than was current among the Benedictines of the day.[24] Perhaps the most famous Cistercian of all was the great preacher, St Bernard (1090–1153), who entered Cîteaux as a young man and later founded the order's fourth house at Clairvaux. A large number of Bernard's sermons have been preserved, including many which contain internal references showing they were preached to his own community, or were at least based on sermons which had earlier been delivered orally. Even though analysis of the differences between oral and written forms of sermons demonstrates that the texts as they have been preserved were not necessarily preached directly in their present form, they still show a close connection between sermons and community life, offering a window into how Bernard addressed the brethren and aroused their feelings.[25]

The Cistercian order spread very rapidly all over Europe and the Latin East: at the time of St Bernard's death it already had three hundred and forty-five houses, and it went on to a grand total of seven hundred and forty by the end of the following century, most of which survived up to the Reformation.[26] But the Cistercian success does not necessarily mean that the older Benedictine houses were all in decay, for their schools and churches were often closely involved with the life of the towns. Nor were they without their share of famous preachers, who inspired the common people and not just the brethren. In Bury St Edmunds, Suffolk, a contemporary account of the rule of Abbot Samson (elected in 1182) tells how he liked to preach to the people in English, in his local Norfolk dialect; and furthermore, so important was preaching to him that he gave orders for the erection of a pulpit 'to allow the congregation to hear the sermons clearly'.[27] This is one of the earliest known references to the use of a pulpit in any English church.

Benedictine preachers sometimes included women, at least when speaking to their own monastic communities, since women were technically forbidden to preach or teach in public.[28] One famous example is St Hildegard, Abbess of Bingen (b. 1098–d. 1179), many of whose writings have been preserved—even homilies, though this is rather exceptional for a woman.[29] Speaking both to her own community and to the

---

[24] The classic account is that by Dom David Knowles, *The Monastic Order in England, 943–1216* (Cambridge: Cambridge University Press, 1940, corr. 1949). See also *ODCC*, p. 354, 'Cistercian Order'.

[25] B. M. Kienzle, 'The Twelfth-Century Monastic Sermon', in *The Sermon*, ed. by Kienzle, esp. p. 294.

[26] For a general survey of preaching by monks and their influence see Carolyn Muessig, *Medieval Monastic Preaching*, Studies in Intellectual History, 90 (Leiden: Brill, 1998).

[27] Jocelin of Brakelond. *Chronicle of the Abbey of Bury St Edmunds*, trans. by Diana Greenway and Jane Sayers (Oxford: Oxford University Press, 1998), p. 37.

[28] See Alcuin Blamires, 'Women and Preaching in Medieval Orthodoxy, Heresy and Saints' Lives', *Viator*, 26 (1995), 135–53.

[29] See Beverly Kienzle, *The Sermon*, p. 153.

wider Church, Hildegard demonstrates anxiety about the accurate transmission of her text, the natural concern of a literate person: 'let no man be so audacious as to add anything to this writing, or to take anything away from it [...]. But let the faithful receive these words with a devout affection of the heart'.[30] Another unusual example of a woman preacher, some of whose sermons have been preserved, is St Umiltà (or Humility) of Faenza (1226–1310). Her religious life started out with her husband when they both agreed to enter the Benedictine double house of Faenza, though Umiltà later became a solitary. She eventually went on to found new houses of the Vallambrosan order (a reformed branch of the Benedictines) in Faenza and Florence, where she died. In an apparent contradiction—for hermits, like the Desert Fathers, tend to become the unwilling centre of new communities—it was during her life as a recluse that she began to write and deliver her sermons.[31]

IV. Sermons and Society: Scholars, Kings and Commoners

But there are other types of communities in addition to those already mentioned, the diocese and parish on the one hand, the monastery on the other. Nor should the Church's insistence on its universality (the meaning of the word 'catholic'), its vision of itself as transcending the bounds of human limitations, be forgotten. Not only in the cloister, therefore, but in court, city and university, kerygmatic and didactic communities were involved in spreading the word.[32] The universality of this movement is illustrated in a striking Spanish illumination of 1109 showing the Angel of God preaching to the faithful united, the latter symbolized by a flock of birds of different species.[33] Medieval preaching, it has been said, 'was closely linked to the widespread growth and development of cities in the High Middle Ages. As an important aspect of Christian communal life, the preaching of sermons often provided a mirror in which the life of the medieval city was reflected'.[34] A certain number of

---

[30] From *Liber Divinorum Operum Simplicis Hominis*, quoted in *Medieval Women's Visionary Literature*, ed. by Elizabeth Alvilda Petroff (New York and Oxford: Oxford University Press, 1986), p. 157.

[31] See Petroff, *Medieval Women's Visionary Literature*, pp. 235–6. Many of Umiltà's 'sermons' are of mixed genre, often tending towards prose meditations reflecting her inner mystical life, as Petroff's examples illustrate.

[32] Note the full title of *Medieval Sermons and Society: Cloister, City, University*, ed. by Jacqueline Hamesse, Beverly M. Kienzle, Debra Stoudt, and Anne Thayer (Louvain-la-Neuve: FIIEM, 1998).

[33] Used as the cover illustration, in colour, of *Medieval Sermons and Society.* For further details of the manuscript and its illuminations see, in the same volume, James R. Blaettler, SJ, 'Preaching the Power of Penitence in the *Silos Beatus*', pp. 35–61 (at p. 40 for the date 1109).

[34] Phyllis B. Roberts, 'Preaching in/and the Medieval City', in *Medieval Sermons and Society*, p. 151 (pp. 151–64).

secular European courts—imperial and royal—may thus be mentioned as offering a new perspective on preaching and community, especially in the case of those which went beyond their most obvious role as centres of administration by becoming the focus of intellectual life and cultural renewal. Such cases seem always to owe their existence to charismatic rulers who went out of their way to found schools and to promote learning. The court of the Emperor Constantine (reigned 306–37) must surely take pride of place in this respect, since his own conversion was to prove a major event in the history of the Roman Empire and of the Church. An emperor who provided bibles and built great basilicas in Rome, Jerusalem and Constantinople was an obvious source of inspiration to later rulers who, in various ways, contributed to the development of Christian communities. At least one later Byzantine emperor, Leo VI (reigned 886–912), went a step further by becoming a preacher himself, many of whose homilies (as well as other writings such as religious poetry) have survived.[35]

In the West, two Germanic monarchs stand out, not because they preached but because their courts were notable for the encouragement of learning, which led to a revival of preaching. While many other kings could no doubt be mentioned, there are very few who were called 'Great' by their successors: they are Charles, king of the Franks (reigned 768–814) and, from 800, Holy Roman Emperor (*Carolus Magnus* becoming 'Charlemagne' in the later French tradition), and Alfred, king of the West Saxons (reigned 871–99). Both of these enlightened men sought the help of learned monks in order to found schools which would renew the tradition of scholarship and sanctity in their kingdoms; and curiously enough, both turned to teachers who were not of their own nationality or language, simply because they wanted the best. Thus it was that Charles invited an Anglo-Saxon, Alcuin of York, to found the royal school at Aachen (Aix-la-Chapelle), while Alfred turned to the Welsh monk, Asser, Abbot of St David's, to develop learning in Winchester, capital of Wessex. To Asser is attributed a famous *Life of Alfred*, a panegyric designed almost to sanctify its hero, in which there is clearly an unstated wish to compare the Anglo-Saxon king to the great Frankish emperor.[36] The influence of the schools founded by these men was immense, and their transnational character was a sign of greater things to come in the field of learning. It led to what has been called 'a virtual explosion of sermon-writing and collecting activity in response to the demand for new preaching materials', thus producing the Carolingian homiliaries and sermonaries.[37] In England, an impetus was given not only to Latin scholarship but also to the composition of vernacular texts, giving us further insight into the social and political conditions of their day. Of particular note are the

[35] See Theodora Antonopoulou, *The Homilies of the Emperor Leo VI* (Leiden: Brill, 1997).

[36] See Nora K. Chadwick, 'The Celtic Background of Early Anglo-Saxon England', in *Celt and Saxon: Studies in the Early British Border*, ed. by N. K. Chadwick and K. H. Jackson (Cambridge: Cambridge University Press, 1963), pp. 323–52: 352 n1. The attribution of the Life is uncertain, but its intention is clear.

[37] Thomas N. Hall, 'The Early Medieval Sermon', p. 221.

English homilies of Ælfric, Abbot of Eynsham (d. 1020?), and Wulfstan, Archbishop of York (d. 1023): masterpieces of thought and style, these sermons can scarcely be equalled in any language other than Latin. Both writers give a vivid impression of millenarian fears which were current before and after the year 1000, though both, it must also be said, thoroughly disapproved of attempts to pin down Gospel predictions to a particular date.[38]

Out of the schools was to develop a new kind of international institution, the university, though not in either Aachen or Winchester. The earliest examples in Europe are those of Paris, Oxford and Salerno, all in the late twelfth century, and all arising out of the increasing numbers of students flocking to hear the teachers in the schools. An early feature of university life in Paris was the division of students into so-called 'nations', such as the 'English nation', which did not correspond to a clearcut ethnic or linguistic category but was merely a way of grouping together all north European students. It is interesting to recall that many authors of sermons, well-known in their own countries, were also—perhaps primarily—schoolmen of international standing. An English theologian like Stephen Langton (*c.* 1150–1228) was a leading preacher and teacher in the Paris schools before being made a cardinal in 1206 and Archbishop of Canterbury the following year.[39] One may easily picture the intellectual Stephen—the first English archbishop appointed since the Norman Conquest who was neither a monk nor a minister of the crown—staying in contact with his friends and colleagues at the university, and keeping up to date with those exciting developments taking place in the academic community during his lifetime. For it was only in 1207 that the Paris schools were first known as *Universitas magistrorum*; in 1209 Cambridge University was founded by scholars fleeing Oxford in a 'town and gown' dispute; Oxford itself received its first chancellor and papal constitution in 1214; and Paris likewise received its first official statutes from Pope Innocent III in 1215.

Another feature of university life, of interest to the present purpose, was the founding of halls of residence, in which students were obliged to lead a form of community life based on monastic practice, with shared rooms, meals, prayer and study. This was the origin of the college system still found in some ancient universities like Oxford and Cambridge. In Paris, colleges were abandoned during the upheavals of the French Revolution; nevertheless, the popular title of the university, the Sorbonne, still recalls the older system. The name is taken from a hall of residence founded in 1253–57 by a professor of theology, Robert of Sorbon (1201–74), canon of Cambrai and chaplain to the saintly king, Louis IX (reigned 1226–70); it was later applied to the faculty of theology, and eventually to the whole university. There is

---

[38] See Leo Carruthers, 'Ending the Millennium: Eschatology and Orthodoxy in the Late Anglo-Saxon Church', *Medioevo*, 26 (2001), 1–23.

[39] See Phyllis B. Roberts, *Stephanus de Lingua-tonante: Studies in the Sermons of Stephen Langton* (Toronto: Pontifical Institute of Mediaeval Studies, 1968).

plenty of evidence from later centuries of sermons composed by university professors for their students and colleagues, sometimes affording glimpses of particular events or disputes within the scholarly community; some of the sermons of John Wyclif (*c.* 1330–84), who taught at Oxford in the period 1361–81, were written for strictly academic occasions.[40] It has even been argued that macaronic sermons, exhibiting varying degrees of language mixing (Latin and the vernacular), must have been delivered as they stand, because only an educated, bilingual audience, such as those found in the monasteries and universities, would have been able to understand the Latin elements; and it is a fact that all known macaronic sermons are of the scholastic type often associated with the universities.[41] If this argument is accepted, then the existence of macaronic sermons is itself a window into the social and linguistic context in which such texts were produced.

Returning for a moment to royal courts, one cannot ignore unusual cases where kings themselves became preachers, thus turning court into congregation. The Emperor Leo VI has already been mentioned. But the best-known example is Robert of Anjou (*c.* 1275–1343), king of Naples from 1309, who 'probably wrote and certainly delivered sermons on various occasions', as 'an integral part of his royal strategy' and in order to 'display the sacral state of his office'.[42] His sermons can be classified according to the occasions when they were preached, all reflecting different degrees of community interaction: state affairs, religious ceremonies and royal visitations, relations with the papal court at Avignon, and with the university of Naples. But their content tends to be commonplace, even when delivered on clearly identifiable occasions such as the inception of a new university master.[43] While these sermons throw a fascinating light on how a king could cast himself in a sacred role, apparently without having sought ecclesiastical approval to do so, their deliberately non-specific, non-topical, and non-controversial nature may be disappointing to those seeking realistic glimpses of court and university life.

But many sermons, it must be admitted, tend to be like that. It may be that the absence of 'the small-change of daily life' is an inherent characteristic of the genre, which by its nature often aims at the abstract and general; while some sermons 'do offer fragmentary insights into social attitudes', not all scholars are satisfied to see

---

[40] Edith Dolnikowski, 'Preaching at Oxford: Academic and Pastoral Themes in Wyclif's Latin Sermon Cycle', in *Medieval Sermons and Society*, pp. 374 and 382 (pp. 371–86).

[41] Siegfried Wenzel, *Macaronic Sermons: Bilingualism and Preaching in Late-Medieval England* (Ann Arbor: University of Michigan Press, 1994), pp. 74 and 124. Reviewed by Leo Carruthers in *Medieval Sermon Studies*, 39 (Spring 1997), 17–21.

[42] Darleen Pryds, '*Rex praedicans*: Robert d'Anjou and the Politics of Preaching', in *De l'homélie au sermon: histoire de la prédication médiévale*, ed. by Jacqueline Hamesse and Xavier Hermand (Louvain-la-Neuve: IEM, 1993), pp. 241 and 244 (pp. 239–62).

[43] Darleen Pryds, 'Court as *Studium*: Royal Venues for Academic Preaching', in *Medieval Sermons and Society*, p. 353 (pp. 343–56).

them being 'merely plundered for their incidental comments, or read as transcripts of life'.[44] On the other hand, there are clear examples of sermons and sermon-series, like the early fifteenth-century English *Jacob's Well*, which devote a great deal of time to addressing social issues, often in a very concrete way, making readers feel as if they were really present right here 'in this church' alongside a very lifelike medieval congregation.[45] It is hard to say if this is purely the result of the writer's art—literary 'realism' in the novelistic sense—or a series of 'photographs' of the parish community as its various members come in for attack.[46] The preacher, conscious of producing an effect which might range from terror to boredom, reminds the audience of their duty to sit still and not to run out of church (22/18), while he often berates them for chatting together (115/19), or for falling asleep while he is talking (290/22)! With all due deference to the prudent requirements of literary and historical criticism, it seems to me that a major homiletic work of this type offers genuine insights into many aspects of the daily life of its place and time, i.e. an urban parish in late medieval England.

A further type of non-monastic community which may be mentioned is the pilgrim group, whose peripatetic, transitory nature makes it rather different from the permanent establishments hitherto evoked. No doubt some people travelled alone, but from an early date we have accounts of pilgrims banding together to make the long and arduous journey to the Holy Land. Indeed, the whole point of the Crusades was, officially, to regain European control of Palestine so that the pilgrim routes would stay open to Christians. The Crusades also have a significant connection with sermons, since they were launched by the open-air preaching of Pope Urban II on 27 November 1095 at the Council of Clermont; his example was followed in later generations by other inspiring leaders, such as St Bernard of Clairvaux, who preached the second Crusade in 1147.[47] In Europe itself, many sites, of which Rome, Compostella and Canterbury are only the most famous, were likewise the object of pilgrimage, which necessitated a certain amount of organization to accommodate the crowds. This led to the building of ever-larger churches and basilicas, the main focus of piety, but also, as in Jerusalem, to the need for hospices or halls of residence where pilgrims could find shelter.

---

[44] Helen Leith Spencer, *English Preaching in the Late Middle Ages* (Oxford: Clarendon Press, 1993), p. vii.

[45] *Jacob's Well*, ed. by Arthur Brandeis, Early English Text Society, o.s., 115 (London: Kegan Paul, 1900); see page 232/16 for the reference to 'in þis cherch'.

[46] For a detailed treatment of its social criticism see Leo Carruthers, 'Know Thyself: Criticism, Reform and the Audience of *Jacob's Well*', in *Medieval Sermons and Society*, pp. 219–40.

[47] For a thorough discussion see Penny J. Cole, *The Preaching of the Crusades to the Holy Land, 1095–1270* (Cambridge, MA: Medieval Academy of America, 1991).

These events are reflected in the composition of travel books, both realistic and fictional, describing the sacred places in the Holy Land as well as important ecclesiastical sites on the way there and back, from Rome to Constantinople.[48] One of the earliest true accounts is that of an Egyptian woman, Egeria, whose journey was apparently made in the years 381–84.[49] More than a millennium later, another woman, Margery Kempe, author of the first autobiography in the English language (composed 1436–38), describes a whole series of pilgrimages she made to Jerusalem, Rome and Compostella, in which she makes it clear how important it was to get in with the right pilgrim group in order to travel in comfort and safety.[50] These were temporary, *ad hoc* communities in which preaching and teaching took place, though not always to everyone's liking, as Margery soon discovered: people were highly irritated by her preachy talk, which sounded like Lollardy, though Margery vigorously refuted the charge of heresy and denied that she was doing anything unauthorized. She also gives a most interesting picture of the English church and hospice in Rome, the Hospital of St Thomas of Canterbury, where pilgrims could stay and where the religious community who ran the place preached to the residents.[51]

Among the most famous fictional texts relating to pilgrimages must be mentioned two nearly contemporary works from the fourteenth century, Chaucer's *Canterbury Tales*[52] and the anonymous *Mandeville's Travels*.[53] In the former, the pilgrimage framework makes a heterogeneous group into a community of *raconteurs* and listeners, which Chaucer himself describes as a 'fellowship' and a 'company'.[54] Some of their tales involve or include sermons and, in fact, the collection finishes with a homiletic text—the so-called Parson's Tale, not a story at all but a long sermon on the sacrament of Penance. As for the fictitious 'Sir John Mandeville', though his pilgrimage ends up in the realm of fantasy, it is based on a number of earlier travel writers who really did make the journey to Jerusalem. The fictional works are mentioned here because of the light they throw on real-life communities of various kinds, including those of a temporary nature (the pilgrim group) and those of a more permanent status (the guardians of the holy sites and the wardens of the pilgrim hospices).

---

[48] See Scott Westrem, 'Departures and Returns in Medieval Travel Narratives', in *Prologues et Epilogues*, ed. by Leo Carruthers and Adrian Papahagi (Paris: AMAES 24, 2001), pp. 93–112.

[49] *ODCC*, p. 534, 'Egeria'.

[50] *The Book of Margery Kempe*, ed. by Sanford Meech Brown and Hope Emily Allen, Early English Text Society, o.s., 212 (Oxford: Oxford University Press, 1940).

[51] *The Book of Margery Kempe*, especially pp. 80–81, 94–95.

[52] *The Riverside Chaucer*, ed. by Larry D. Benson (New York: Houghton Mifflin, 1987).

[53] *Mandeville's Travels*, ed. by M. C. Seymour (Oxford: Clarendon Press, 1967).

[54] See Derek Brewer, 'From the Many to the One: Prologue and Epilogue in the *Canterbury Tales*', in *Prologues et Epilogues*, p. 65 (pp. 55–72).

V. Preaching Revival: Canons and Mendicants

During the twelfth and thirteenth centuries newer forms of religious life came into being, less monastic in their origins, aims and practice, though still much influenced by the monastic tradition. The canons regular and the mendicant friars are the best-known of these, and all are related, directly or indirectly, to the history of preaching. Whatever their specificity, we do not need to imagine solid walls standing between them and other types of preachers or other forms of community, since many famous canons and mendicants also became university professors, bishops and even popes.

Canons were originally the clergy (excluding monks) who formed the official staff of a diocese, but the word was gradually limited to the secular clergy belonging to a cathedral or collegiate church and sharing in its revenues.[55] At first subject to no particular rule, the development of their common life, including the practice of poverty, chastity and obedience, was part of the Gregorian reform, a movement to revive the faith and morals of the Church led by the pope himself, Gregory VII (reigned 1073–85). The fact that Gregory was a monk before becoming pope no doubt influenced his austere and ascetic view of the duties of the clergy. Despite internal divisions and much opposition, it is now accepted that Gregory's example and the activities of his successors, especially Urban II (1088–99), did much to regenerate the Church. One of the results of this was the development among canons of a more organized community under a rule, from which they are known as canons regular, with a way of life much resembling monks except that they remained attached to a parish church or cathedral. In the twelfth century, they largely adopted the so-called Rule of St Augustine, an ancient but previously little-known rule for clerks living in common, from which they are known as Augustinian (or Austin) Canons. At the same time, many of them were influenced by St Bernard and Cistercian customs. Some, such as the Victorines in Paris (1113), became influential in their turn.[56] The Premonstratensians (1120) even founded daughter houses and began to spread like a religious order.[57] But the canons, as a whole, never had a central organization of this type; their houses were independent, while following roughly the same Augustinian Rule. For this reason they remained subject to the local bishop and were often involved in pastoral activities of a kind typified by the later English sermon-series, *Jacob's Well*.[58] A good example of a canon regular who became both a bishop and a

[55] *ODCC*, p. 131, 'Augustinian Canons'; p. 131, 'Augustinian Hermits or Friars'; p. 277, 'Canon'; p. 281 'Canons Regular'.

[56] Founded in 1113 by William of Champeaux (1070–1121), the most famous scholar of his day and a teacher of Abelard, they were canons regular who took their name from the dedication of their house to St Victor.

[57] Also called Norbertines, and in England, White Canons, they were founded in 1120 by St Norbert (1080–1134), a friend of St Bernard's, at Prémontré near Laon.

[58] Its anonymous author appears to have been an Austin canon like John Mirk, as may be gleaned from an analysis of the target audience. See Leo Carruthers, 'Know Thyself: Criticism,

prolific preacher is Jacques de Vitry (*c.* 1165–1240), who was for a time Bishop of Acre (1216–28); the author of a multitude of sermons, he kept in mind the practical needs of his colleagues for whom he produced a shorter series of *Sermones feriales*, designed for preachers who just wanted to have a few sermons at hand.[59] Through this sermon-collection, we therefore gain an insight into a certain conception of a professional fellowship, just one aspect of a bishop's fatherly role.

The other major new element in religious life was the foundation of the mendicant orders, in particular the Dominicans and Franciscans which both came into existence at the beginning of the thirteenth century, with specific aims going beyond the bounds of monasticism.[60] St Dominic (1170–1221) and St Francis (1181–1226) were alike in their insistence on corporate poverty and begging, from which the orders they founded took the name mendicant. Francis, though younger, was the first to create a new community: men, often older than himself, attracted to his poverty and inspired by his charismatic sermons, who joined him on preaching tours. From these humble beginnings grew an official order. In 1209, when the number of his followers had reached twelve, he drew up a short and simple rule and went to Rome to secure the pope's (oral) approval; he was probably present at the Fourth Lateran Council in 1215 and somehow escaped the command to adopt an existing religious rule. The rapid growth of the movement, with new communities already being founded outside Italy, led to the adoption of a more complex rule which finally obtained the papal seal in 1223, by which time Francis himself had given up any official position within the order. If Francis ever wrote any sermons, none has survived; stories of his preaching come later. The *Fioretti*, or 'Little Flowers of St Francis' (composed after his death), explains how the order's growth, and the preaching which accompanied it to the four corners of the earth, was prefigured and symbolized by the birds to whom the saint himself once preached; and however unlikely the feathered congregation, this must surely be the most famous of all accounts of a medieval sermon![61] It may also be noted that Francis was putting into effect (for the reality of his action is not called into question) what to others had been only a symbol, as in the Silos manuscript illumination referred to above, where the birds represent humanity.

As for Dominic, his religious life followed a more conventional route, and his order, both more ecclesiastical in origin and less 'romantic' in the popular mind, was quicker to receive official approval. Dominic himself was an Augustinian canon, and

---

Reform and the Audience of *Jacob's Well*'.

[59] See Carolyn Muessig, 'Jacques de Vitry's Sermones feriales et communes: text and context', in *De l'homélie au sermon: histoire de la prédication médiévale*, p. 65 (pp. 51–82).

[60] The classic history is again by Dom David Knowles, *The Religious Orders in England*, I, *1216–1340*; II, *The End of the Middle Ages* (Cambridge: Cambridge University Press, 1948–1957).

[61] *I Fioretti di San Francesco* (ch. 16), many times edited and translated. The text consulted is *The Little Flowers of St Francis*, trans. by W. Heywood (Assisi: Edizioni Porziuncula, 1982).

the order grew out of a preaching mission against the Albigensians led by his bishop, Diego, in 1205; on Diego's advice they adopted a new style of itinerant, mendicant preaching in imitation of the Apostles, and by 1215, Dominic was in charge of the mission's base in Toulouse. At first they naturally followed the Rule of St Augustine, like other canons; but this was modified by insisting on the need for study and preaching, and by granting dispensations from conventual observances so that the brothers could go on preaching missions. Thus fairly quickly, between 1216 and 1218, a new preaching order came into existence, whose constitutions gained papal approval in 1220. Unfortunately, none of Dominic's sermons, any more than those of Francis, has survived; he died soon after the order had become established, and perhaps there had never been any time, in a hectic life filled with preaching, to do any writing. But this absence of texts from the early years was soon to give way to a flood of mendicant compositions. Unlike the older monastic foundations which had often been built in isolated rural areas, both the Dominicans and the Franciscans were essentially urban, aiming at the needs of town-dwellers. Furthermore, they rapidly became associated with the universities which, as we saw, were developing at precisely the same time, and in which exegesis and theology went hand in hand with preaching. In this way Paris, for example, became an important centre for the copying and dissemination of Latin sermon collections which were widely used as models, an early case of what has been called 'mass communication'.[62]

Two other mendicant orders should be mentioned, as their way of life, though slightly older in origin, became assimilated to that of the Dominicans and Franciscans. The Carmelites traced their beginnings to hermits living on Mount Carmel in the Holy Land in the late twelfth century; but by 1247 they had received permission to found houses in European cities and had taken on the same type of activities, preaching and teaching, as the followers of Dominic and Francis.[63] The fourth mendicant order is that of the Augustinian hermits or friars, not to be confused with the Augustinian Canons previously dealt with. The friars did not come into existence as a mendicant order until 1256, when three congregations of Italian hermits, all following the Augustinian rule, were united by Pope Alexander IV. From that time onwards, they came more and more to resemble the existing mendicant orders and to engage in similar activities, study, teaching and preaching. While there were many kinds of Christian homilists and sermon writers in the Middle Ages—popes and monks, bishops and nuns, canons and kings (not to mention others who were condemned as 'heretics' by Church authorities)—it is perhaps the mendicant friar who comes across as the typical late medieval preacher. This is surely because of the intense intellectual

---

[62] David d'Avray, *The Preaching of the Friars. Sermons Diffused From Paris Before 1300* (Oxford: Oxford University Press, 1985), pp. 3–4.

[63] *ODCC*, p. 289, 'Carmelites'; p. 497, 'Dominican Order'; p. 634, 'Franciscan Order'.

activity of all four mendicant orders, and the sheer volume of their sermon production, which outweighs all other groups in terms of surviving manuscripts.[64]

VI. Saints' Lives: Heavenly Visions and Lady Abbesses

It is typical of the history of religious orders that a period of enthusiasm and expansion is often followed by one of stagnation and decay, with a corresponding loss of reputation and respect among the general population. This is not necessarily a permanent state and frequently leads to revival and reform, with a return to a more austere way of life in accordance with the founder's ideals. It may be said that moments of awakening and revival, together with the communities that spring up at such times, are characterized by their kerygmatic rather than their didactic nature, even though the distinction may be theoretical; for the community and its preaching are kerygmatic precisely because they *proclaim* the faith with a renewed sense of discovery.[65] Even where such reforms are successful, new times and circumstances give rise to fresh needs within the Church, and new charismatic leaders rise to meet the challenge. One interesting example is that of the Swedish saint, Bridget or Birgitta (1303–73), who in 1346 founded a convent in Vadstena. Her visions and *Revelations*, recorded by her spiritual directors, had a wide influence in her own time and in the following generations.[66] Although she was not a preacher in the conventional sense, and has not left any written sermons, Birgitta was very clear in her perception of herself as a prophetess in the Old Testament tradition: a woman chosen by God to convey his word in a special way to her own generation, who, in pursuit of her vision, did not hesitate to take popes and kings to task.[67] One naturally recalls other women visionaries of the same type, like Hildegard of Bingen (1098–1179) and Catherine of Siena (1347–80), whose dramatic lives are well documented in texts of various kinds, such as letters and biographies, in addition to sermons.

Birgitta is normally known in English as St Bridget of Sweden.[68] The reference to the country is necessary in order to distinguish her from the fifth/sixth-century Irish

---

[64] See Carolyn Muessig, 'Sermon, Preacher and Society in the Middle Ages', *Journal of Medieval History*, 28 (2002), p. 84 (pp. 73–91).

[65] Beverly Kienzle comments on the didactic, hortatory and at times kerygmatic nature of preaching in her introduction to *The Sermon*, p. 155.

[66] The original Latin text was soon translated into other languages and several copies have been preserved in Middle English. The most recent English edition is *The Liber Celestis of Bridget of Sweden*, ed. by Roger Ellis, Early English Text Society, o.s., 291 (Oxford: Oxford University Press, 1987).

[67] For a perceptive study of Birgitta and her text, see Rosalynn Voaden, *God's Words, Women's Voices: The Discernment of Spirits in the Writing of Late-Medieval Women Visionaries* (York: York Medieval Press; Woodbridge: Boydell & Brewer, 1999), ch. 3.

[68] Farmer, *ODS*, classifies the Swedish saint under the English form Bridget, with Birgitta in

saint, Brigid (Bridget) of Kildare (d. 525), about whom it is worth saying a little more before returning to Bridget of Sweden. Patroness of Ireland and second in this title only to St Patrick, who is said to have baptized her, she is the object of several early Lives in Latin and Old Irish, which include fantastic accounts of her miracle-working.[69] Confused by the legends that clung to her in the Middle Ages, some critics have questioned Brigid's authenticity and sought to identify her with a shadowy Celtic goddess of the same name, Brig or Brigit, the Brigantia of Roman sources. It is certainly no coincidence that the Irish saint's feast-day is 1 February, the first day of spring in the ancient Celtic calendar and associated with the fire-cult of the goddess Brig. But current scholarship has now re-established St Brigid's historicity.[70] The fact that she was a real person does not, however, authenticate all aspects of her popular cult, some of which probably derived from the pagan goddess whose name she bore; such confusion is quite common in medieval literature, where legendary deeds are often ascribed to real heroes and saints. A popular form of devotion still found today in many Irish homes is the use of a cross woven from rushes, known as St Brigid's Cross, believed to have first been made by the saint herself in an effort to explain the faith to a dying man. During the golden age of Irish monasticism, Brigid's cult extended to churches of Irish origin in Britain and Europe, and there are copies of her life in Old French, Middle English and German. It is, therefore, less surprising than one might otherwise think to find the name being used in Sweden for the fourteenth-century Bridget/Birgitta. She must have been familiar with the story of Sweden's conversion to Christianity, which had taken place about three hundred years before: for despite some earlier attempts, it really got under way only in the year 1000 with the baptism of King Olaf by St Sigfrid, an English monk from Glastonbury—thus linking Sweden and Norway with the insular missionary tradition.[71]

The order founded in Vadstena met with great success, at one time having as many as seventy houses. Their most original feature was that they were composed, according to St Bridget's instructions, of double communities of women and men, sixty nuns and twenty-five monks (priests, deacons and lay brothers), each group having separate quarters but praying together in church. Different sections of the church building were allotted to each, while a further area was open to lay people,

---

parenthesis. Writers in English normally use the spelling Bridget.

[69] See *ODS*, *s.v.* 'Brigid', with bibliography of editions of the Lives. Note that the Irish saint is classified under the Irish spelling Brigid, with the English forms Brigit, Bridget and Bride given as alternatives.

[70] See Catherine McKenna, 'Apotheosis and Evanescence: The Fortunes of Saint Brigit in the Nineteenth and Twentieth Centuries', in *The Individual in Celtic Literatures: CSANA Yearbook* 1, ed. by Joseph F. Nagy (Dublin: Four Courts Press, 2001), pp. 74–108.

[71] See *ODS*, *s.v.* 'Sigfrid'. Although an English Benedictine monastery in Sigfrid's time, Glastonbury was originally a Celtic foundation which tradition linked to St Patrick. The Apostle of Ireland was indeed a British Celt, born, he tells us, on the west coast of Britain.

whose presence at conventual prayer and preaching was central to Bridget's plan.[72] Remarkably enough, while the confessor-general was responsible for spiritual direction, it was the lady abbess who ruled the whole convent, both men and women, in temporal affairs. There was only one such house in England, Syon Abbey, founded in 1415 by King Henry V. It is not often recalled that the impulse behind this unusual step—importing a Swedish order—most likely came from Henry's sister Philippa, who was Queen of Sweden at the time, a benefactress of the Bridgettines whose tomb may still be seen in the church at Vadstena.[73] The English foundation was originally at Twickenham, moving to Isleworth in 1431, where it remained up to the Reformation.[74] Nearby was the Carthusian monastery of Sheen (just across the river at Richmond), another royal foundation of the same date; and the two communities, Carthusian and Bridgettine, together formed a major religious nucleus in pre-Reformation England. In spite of its eremitical origin, the Carthusian order had by this time developed a strong ministry in the promotion of lay piety by composing and copying religious texts in the vernacular, an activity with which Syon Abbey also became associated. An example is Symon Wynter, monk of Syon, who wrote (in the 1420s) a 'Life of St Jerome' for a member of the royal family, Lady Margaret Holland, Duchess of Clarence.[75] Margery Kempe, the pilgrim, records making a visit to Syon Abbey in 1434.[76] Born probably in the year of St Bridget's death (1373), Margery had great devotion to the Swedish mystic and liked to think of herself as following in her footsteps; in her autobiography she refers more than once to Bridget's famous book, the *Liber Celestis* or *Revelations*, which she knew well.

The Bridgettine Order was not the first experiment in double communities headed by an abbess, for Vadstena was probably modelled on the famous abbey of Fontevraud, near Tours. Founded in 1099 by Robert d'Arbrissel, the French monastery had been a double community from the beginning, ruled by the lady

[72] The laity did not, however, come into contact with the nuns, who prayed on a raised platform with direct access to the convent at an upper level. This triple division of the church, to allow for the simultaneous presence of what might almost be called a triple community, is no longer visible in Vadstena, due to structural alterations following the Reformation.

[73] Philippa was the wife of Eric of Pomerania, King of Norway (1396), later King of Denmark and Sweden (1412), all three countries having formed the Union of Kalmar in 1397. Eric succeeded his aunt, Margaret I, Queen of Denmark (d. 1412), who had actively encouraged the spread of the Bridgettine Order.

[74] At the Reformation the double community went abroad and after 1695 was restricted to nuns; the order did not return permanently to England (at a new location) until 1861. See J. R. Fletcher, *The Story of the English Bridgettines of Syon Abbey* (South Brent, Devon: Syon Abbey, 1933).

[75] See *Cultures of Piety: Medieval English Devotional Literature in English*, ed. by Anne Clark Bartlett and Thomas H. Bestul (Ithaca & London: Cornell University Press, 1999), ch. 7 (this chapter is by Claire Waters).

[76] *The Book of Margery Kempe*: see the editors' note to 245/31–32.

abbess. Double communities of men and women existed elsewhere too, such as the Benedictine monastery of Admont in Austria; but here the ruler was the abbot, though the nuns played a role in both transcribing and preaching (they could deliver sermons to their sisters when the abbot was prevented).[77] Even Fontevraud was not the first of its kind, since double communities ruled by an abbess had been known before, in the early days of Frankish monasticism, as well as in Anglo-Saxon England and Celtic Ireland. The English example is that of Whitby in Northumbria, founded in 657 by St Hilda (614–80), a high-born lady related to the Northumbrian king with whom she had been baptized.[78] Northumbria was very much within the Celtic sphere of influence, having been evangelized by the Irish monk from Iona, St Aidan (d. 651), who personally encouraged Hilda to enter religion. As abbess of Hartlepool, she organized community life according to the rule she had learnt from mainly Irish sources, therefore based on the Rule of St Columbanus (d. 615). Hilda would certainly have known of many Irish monasteries by reputation, and she may well have taken inspiration from Kildare, where there was a double monastery with the abbess as head. This custom was supposed to go back to Brigid herself, who had died there more than a hundred years before (*c.* 525), although there is no documentary proof that Kildare had been a double monastery as far back as Brigid's day. Nevertheless, on the basis of Brigid's Lives, Irish missionaries of Hilda's time would have believed it to be the case. Indeed, the same is true for the Irish monks who spread St Brigid's cult on the Continent; the early Irish saints were renowned as missionaries, their influence long remaining preponderant in foundations such as Luxeuil, Bobbio, St. Gallen, and Salzburg. So it is not altogether improbable to suggest that St Bridget (Birgitta) of Sweden, when composing her order's rule, could have looked back beyond Fontevraud and taken inspiration from a more ancient role-model—that she is to be placed, in fact, in a line of foundresses going back to her own namesake, Brigid (Bridget) of Kildare.

VII. Conclusion: Sermon as Logos in Place and Time

What has been attempted in the present paper is to follow two strands of thought, one concerning the history of preaching, the other, the growth of various types of community, and to establish connections between them. This is one aspect of the interdisciplinary nature of sermon studies, illustrating how sermons throw light on

[77] See Stephan Borgehammar, 'Who Wrote the Admont Sermon Corpus–Gottfried the Abbot, His Brother Irimbert, or the Nuns?', in *De l'homélie au sermon: histoire de la prédication médiévale*, pp. 47–51 (he concludes that it was Gottfried). Also Beverly Kienzle, *The Sermon*, p. 166.

[78] See *ODS*, *s.v.* 'Hilda'.

many different sides of medieval history and literature—which the sermons themselves grew out of and in turn fertilized. The discipline now known as 'sermon studies', while dating back in some respects to the nineteenth century, has only fairly recently, since the 1970s, gathered sufficient momentum to enable it to place itself upon a firm methodological basis which has generated a large body of international research.[79] The diversity of approaches is often reflected in current work, as here, since 'the sermon provided a fluid genre, to and from which other types of literature could be created'.[80]

We began by looking at the *kerygma*, or core element, of preaching in the first Christian communities, to which St Paul made such a valuable contribution. It may be said that all Christian preaching tends, to a greater or lesser degree, to fulfill four functions: to proclaim (*kerussein*), to witness (*marturien*), to evangelize (*evangelizein*), and to teach (*didaskein*). All are represented in New Testament discourses, and all recur constantly throughout the history of preaching. Clearly the emphasis laid on each of these four aspects will vary from minimal to maximal in a given sermon or didactic text, depending on author, audience and purpose; but they are rarely entirely absent, nor can they always be easily distinguished. In just the same way, the many types of human community reflect similar distinctions, depending on their founding charism; and while one of these four aspects may be of greater importance in a particular case, it does not necessarily exclude the others. The New Testament emphasizes that the communion of saints is based on their communion with the Father, through the Son, in the Spirit.[81] The Logos, the Word of God, speaks in each place and time in a language which is proper to each community.

From the Apostolic Age onwards, the creation of communities of various kinds, orthodox and unorthodox, ecclesial and heretical, has been connected with the inspired preaching of charismatic leaders. As a rule, both religious orders and heretical groups grew out of a single community of followers gathered around a radical founder, frequently misunderstood, often rejected, sometimes canonized by a later generation. This is often linked with preaching, traces of which may be preserved in texts of variable genres. Such documents may include the sermons of founders or their early followers, or the monastic rules attributed to the founder, traditionally said to reflect his/her teaching, or even more pneumatic works such as St Bridget's *Liber celestis*. Many texts have survived, even from the earliest period, the New Testament

---

79 For a good overview of pioneering work since the nineteenth century, and especially of recent trends in the field, see Carolyn Muessig, 'Sermon, Preacher and Society in the Middle Ages'.

80 Beverly Kienzle, Preface to *Medieval Sermons and Society*, p. viii.

81 See passages such as Colossians 1. 12, 1 John 1. 3, 2 Corinthians 13. 13, 1 Corinthians 15. 29, emphasizing the union of all believers, living and dead, in Christ. This is the source of the doctrine of the 'mystical Body' of Christ, though the expression as such is not used in the New Testament.

itself being part of a didactic and kerygmatic tradition given expression in a written form. This is how the phrase 'the word made flesh' has been applied in this article—exploring how the word, both preached orally and preserved in writing, tends to generate and strengthen community.[82] All preaching is, therefore, related to community, a universal remark that may be seen as applying to all religions at all times. Christian sermons allow us to glimpse 'many aspects of the religious life of the period', and they 'provide abundant commentary on beliefs and practices of various medieval communities': while this remark was made about the early Middle Ages, it is no doubt applicable to all periods.[83] A large number of references have been made to famous saints and founders, all of whom preached, many of whom wrote down their sermons, or whose oral discourses were noted and copied by others. This is not the place to list their writings; bibliographies are available in the standard reference works to which the *Typologie* volume on *The Sermon* is a most honourable addition. Also very enlightening are histories of preaching such as Jean Longère's pioneering *La Prédication médiévale*, whose chronological framework, beginning with the *kerygma*, has here been followed.[84]

The key word in sermon studies, as the present writer has elsewhere written, has long been interdisciplinarity. 'Specialists in Latin, the vernacular languages, history, philosophy, theology, politics and law, all found that sermons had something to give, and all found that much was to be learned from others working in different but related areas'.[85] By way of conclusion, it may be added that for many of us in academic life, the university continues to be, as it was in the early days of its foundation, in some sense a community, albeit rather distended in comparison with the time when preaching was a common feature of daily life in Paris and Oxford. Those teachers who are members of a religious order will enjoy an additional and specific dimension of fraternity. But other forms of common life, be it in the parish or synagogue, a trade guild or a workers' union, a society or an association, overlap in this role for many people. A scholarly group like the International Medieval Sermon Studies Society (IMSSS) may justifiably be seen as a type of community, based on common interests and research, enjoying a particular identity within the Academy.[86] It is natural that the

---

[82] This theme is explored in detail for a more limited period by Brian Stock, *The Implications of Literacy: Written Language and Models of Interpretation in the Eleventh and Twelfth Centuries* (Princeton: Princeton University Press, 1983).

[83] Thomas N. Hall, 'The Early Medieval Sermon', p. 245.

[84] Jean Longère, *La Prédication médiévale* (Paris: Etudes augustiniennes, 1983). This work includes an important bibliography of medieval sermons (primary and secondary sources), now brought up to date by the *Typologie* volume on *The Sermon*. Supplementary information on individuals and themes is often provided by the two other major reference works quoted above, *ODCC* and *ODS*.

[85] Leo Carruthers, in the Dedication to *The Sermon*, ed. by Kienzle, p. 16.

[86] The IMSSS was formally constituted in 1988 at the Dijon Sermon Studies Symposium. The impulse to create the Society grew out of a series of symposia organized in Oxford by

sermon, described by the second president of the IMSSS as the 'central literary genre' of the religious life of medieval Europe,[87] should continue to nourish and regenerate the academic community—one which, if no longer homiletic, is certainly didactic.

Gloria Cigman between 1979 and 1986. The Society holds its biannual meeting at various locations in Europe, sponsors sessions at the annual Medieval Congress in Kalamazoo, and publishes the journal *Medieval Sermon Studies*.

[87] Beverly Kienzle, in her conclusion to *The Sermon*, p. 983.

Going to the Gate of Life: The Archaeology of the Carthage Amphitheatre and Augustine's Sermons on Saints Perpetua and Felicitas

JOHN KITCHEN

> By the term gate any preacher can be meant because whoever opens the door of the heavenly kingdom is a gate.
>
> –Garnerus of Saint Victor

As we know from 'the shrines that failed', even medieval communities could consign their saints to quick oblivion.[1] In light of such a possibility, the extensive and persistent reminders of Perpetua and Felicitas appear all the more extraordinary. Early inscriptions mention their martyrdom; medieval mosaics bear their faces in the archiepiscopal palace of Ravenna; a nineteenth-century chapel commemorates them among the ruins of an amphitheatre in Islamic Tunisia; modern poetry evokes their dramatic confrontation; and contemporary horticulturalists call a white and reddish rose by their name.[2] Even if we narrow our consideration of their

---

[1] See Benedicta Ward, *Miracles and the Medieval Mind: Theory, Record and Event 1000–1215* (London: Scolar Press, 1982), p. 127.

[2] Inscriptions: Jacqueline Amat, *Passion de Perpérpetue et de Félicité suivi des actes: introduction, texte critique, traduction, commentaire et index* (Paris: Les Éditions du Cerf, 1996), pp. 25–27. On the debates regarding the exact dating of the inscriptions, Amat tends to concur with the more recent archaeological studies attributing the earliest epigraphical evidence to the Byzantine period rather than to the era of the martyrs' original cult as previous scholars had argued. Mosaics: *New Catholic Encyclopedia*, XI (New York: McGraw-Hill, 1967), p. 143; for other artistic depictions of Perpetua and Felicitas consult the studies listed by Cornelius Ioannes Maria Ioseph Van Beek, *Passio sanctarum Perpetuae et Felicitatis, vol. I: textum Graecum et Latinum ad fidem modicum MSS* (Nijmegen: Dekker & Van de Vegt, 1936), pp. 13–14; modern chapel: J. Cabrol and H. Leclercq, *Dictionnaire*

veneration to the geographic distribution of the early evidence alone, the martyrologies, we still find that the cult of Perpetua and Felicitas reached the major centres of the late antique and medieval Christian world. The churches of Italy, Syria, Gaul, and England remembered these women who died in a Carthaginian amphitheatre, along with their Christian companions, during Septimius Severus's persecution in 203.[3]

The sources relating the incident constitute a substantial hagiographic dossier that includes both Greek and Latin texts.[4] Among the various documents is testimony coming from the leading ecclesiastical figure who encountered the cult in its heyday. Similar to the other writings comprising the dossier, this testimony reveals the popularity of the two martyrs, but unlike the other evidence, it also intimates the (perplexing) outcome of so much devotion. Apparently, the veneration of these saints had reached such intensity by the fourth century, the account of their martyrdom had become so well-known, so much a part of Christian consciousness, particularly in the martyrs' North African homeland, that Augustine of Hippo, at an opportune moment, had to state what was—officially—obvious: '*nec scriptura ipsa canonica est*'. No matter what African Christians may have thought, and regardless of the story's 'revelations' and inspiration from 'the Spirit', the *Passio sanctarum Perpetuae et Felicitatis* did not have the status of Holy Scripture.[5]

---

d'archéologie chrétienne et de liturgie, XIV (Paris: Librairie Letouzey et Ané, 1939), p. 429, fig. 10121; modern poetry: Sarah Flower Adams, *Vivia Perpetua: A Dramatic Poem in Five Acts* (London: C. Fox, 1841); rose, known as 'Félicité et Perpetué': Peter Beales, *Botanica's Roses: The Encyclopedia of Roses* (Vancouver, BC: Raincoat Books, 1998), p. 238.

[3] For the martyrological testimony and the related scholarship on the widespread liturgical commemoration of Perpetua and Felicitas, see Van Beek, pp. 162, 165–66, 14–15. For an overview of the circumstances surrounding the martyrs' life and death, see Joyce E. Salisbury, *Perpetua's Passion: The Death and Memory of a Young Roman Woman* (New York; London, Routledge, 1997). Regarding the date of their execution, see Timothy David Barnes, *Tertullian: A Historical and Literary Study* (Oxford: Clarendon Press, 1971; repr. 1985), pp. 263–65; Herbert Musurillo, *The Acts of the Christian Martyrs* (Oxford: Clarendon Press, 1972), pp. xxvi–xxvii. Note that, in general, the reader is advised to consult the works of Van Beek and Amat, which are indispensable guides to all matters concerning the historical circumstances, sources, and scholarly literature pertaining to Perpetua and Felicitas.

[4] The extant documents constituting the early dossier of Saints Perpetua and Felicitas, including Augustine's sermons, are conveniently included in Van Beek's work (all citations and quotations of the *Passio* in this essay are from Van Beek's edition). Amat's edition also contains the Greek and Latin versions of the *Passio*, together with the *Acta*.

[5] Augustine, *De anima et ejus origine* 1.10.12, PL 44, 481. On the question of the *Passio* assuming the status of Holy Scripture, see the perceptive observations of Marc Van Uytfanaghe, 'L'empreinte biblique sur la plus ancienne hagiographie occidentale', in *Le Monde latin antique et la Bible*, ed. by Jacques Fontaine and Charles Pietri (Paris: Beauchesne, 1985), p. 572; see also Barnes, p. 79. For some time, scholars have claimed or implied that Augustine objected to African Christians regarding the account of Perpetua and

Augustine's response is intriguing. After all, his achievement as a Christian *rhetor* helped sustain the very condition he finds so perplexing.[6] As the region's indefatigable preacher, he represented the saints' most authoritative panegyrist, with his sermons in honour of Perpetua and Felicitas evoking in pithy, vivid rhetoric the feats of African Christianity's most celebrated local heroes.[7] Thus the hint of pastoral anxiety over the *Passio's* revered status suggests that Augustine's sermons on these saints function within a network of hagiographic, homiletic, theological, and communal expressions of the Christian belief system. In short, his sermons on these saints link and mediate the original documents to a community that his preaching conditions and reflects. Simply in terms of the 'meaning-effects' generated within this network of relations, the sermons on Perpetua and Felicitas deserve our attention.[8] However, while the earliest sources recording their martyrdom have received sustained treatment by hagiographic researchers and scholars of primitive Christianity, the issues concerning how the veneration of these saints developed in late antique and early medieval Europe have not been sufficiently addressed. In particular, Augustine's sermons dedicated to these martyrs have been largely neglected by researchers treating instead the pressing questions

---

Felicitas as 'canonical'. *Butler's Lives of the Saints: Complete Edition, Edited Revised and Supplemented by Herbert Thurston and Donald Attwater*, I (Westminster, MD: Christian Classics, 1926, repr. 1990), p. 493: '[. . .] these acts were [. . .] so highly esteemed that St Augustine found it necessary to issue a protest against their being placed on a level with the Holy Scriptures'; similarly, Brent Shaw, 'The Passion of Perpetua', *Past and Present*, 139 (1993), p. 37, with Salisbury, p. 170. But Augustine's comments cited to support this view explicitly concern Perpetua's vision of her brother Dinocrates (as recorded in the *Passio*), who after dying young from cancer languishes in a tormented afterlife from which Perpetua's prayer delivers him. Hence Augustine did **not** 'issue a protest against' the *Passio* being placed on the level of Scripture but rather objected to his opponent's appeal to it as an authoritative text in settling a theological debate over the efficacy of baptism. While I concur with the long-standing consensus regarding the *Passio*'s revered status, the position needs to be qualified, as recognized by Cecil M. Robeck, *Prophecy in Carthage: Perpetua, Tertullian, and Cyprian* (Cleveland: Pilgrim Press, 1992), p. 238, n. 68. For the specific listing of biblical books that Augustine regarded as 'canonical' see *De doctrina Christiana* 8.13, PL 34, 40–41.

[6] Compare Amat, p. 81.

[7] Including the fragments, there are over five hundred *sermones ad populum* attributed to Augustine, according to Pierre-Patrick Verbraken, *Études critiques sur les sermons authentiques de Saint Augustin* (Steenbrugge, 1976), pp. 17–18. For observations on Augustine's remarkable preaching activity, treated in light of the recently discovered sermons, see Peter Brown, *Augustine of Hippo: A Biography, A New Edition with an Epilogue* (Berkeley: University of California Press, 2000), pp. 441–62.

[8] Daniel Patte, *The Religious Dimensions of Biblical Texts: Greimas's Structural Semiotics and Biblical Exegesis* (Atlanta, GA: Scholars Press, 1990), p. 14.

concerning the authorship of the *Passio*, along with the linguistic, philological, and historical problems raised by the original sources.[9]

At its most basic level, then, the following discussion attempts to expand the scope of research treating the cult of Christian martyrs simply by offering an analysis of Augustine's sermons on Perpetua and Felicitas. At another (experimental) level, however, my analysis of Augustine's sermons attempts to bring to light aspects of his preaching that, to the best of my knowledge, have not been rigorously explored. As I shall elaborate, these aspects came to light in a rather unexpected fashion, specifically through a consideration of how archaeological remains might relate to Augustinian homiletics. To put the matter more precisely, I propose to situate Augustine's sermons on Perpetua and Felicitas within the context of my on-site study at the Carthage amphitheatre and the recent archaeological literature treating its architectural design.[10]

While a proposal to consider these sermons in light of the archaeological evidence may at first appear methodologically unconventional, the turn to the physical remains actually represents an attempt to realize the full implications of the insights offered by leading scholars treating Augustine's literary and religious imagination. Consider, for example, how Karl Morrison has called our attention to the 'malevolent sympathy' characterizing the ways in which patristic writers relied on the most repugnant classical models to express fundamental features of the Christian life. The struggle in the amphitheatre and the agonistic feats of gladiatorial combat become the images that Christian authors apply to themselves. As Morrison succinctly observes when considering the mimetic richness of such discourse:

> For Christians, hardly any place of worldly amusement was more abhorrent than the amphitheatre, the scene of martyrdom. And yet, Tertullian [. . .] was able to glory in the mutilation and slaughter of his co-religionists in the arena. [. . .] Augustine thought of the rhetorician's subdued style, of which he was a master, as a naked fighter, 'crushing the sinews and muscles of his foe with his most powerful limbs overcoming and destroying falsehood,' and Jerome portrayed himself in his theological conflicts as a warrior fighting to the death.[1]

---

[9] For brief discussions of Augustine's sermons on Perpetua and Felicitas, see Salisbury, pp. 170–76; Amat, pp. 80–81; W. H. Shewring, *The Passion of SS Perpetua and Felicity MM, A New Edition and Translation of the Latin Text, together with the Sermons of St Augustine upon the Saints* (London: Sheed and Ward, 1931), pp. xxix–xxx. On the issues and scholarship regarding the *Passio*'s anonymous authorship and redactions, see Amat, pp. 67–78; and, especially, the informative and compelling analysis of Thomas Heffernan, 'Philology and Authorship in the *Passio Sanctarum Perpetuae et Felicitatis*', *Traditio*, 50 (1995), 315–25.

[10] My examination of the material remains of the Carthage amphitheatre relies extensively on the archaeological research of David L. Bomgardner, 'The Carthage Amphitheater: A Reappraisal', *American Journal of Archaeology*, 93 (1989), 85–103; see now, by the same author, *The Story of the Roman Amphitheatre* (London; New York: Routledge, 2000).

In pursuing Morrison's insight, we find that Augustine himself shows a deep awareness of the amphitheatre's prominent place in the urban Mediterranean culture of his day, an awareness that reveals how promising may be the turn to archaeology and the amphitheatrical environment as a means of explicating textual material of late antique Christianity. For instance, the well-known story of Augustine's friend Alypius, who first became addicted to watching spectacles in Carthage, shows the popularity of viewing amphitheatrical sports as well as the 'malevolent sympathy' involved in appropriating such a sensual encounter to depict a spiritual condition. Coaxed by friends into watching a contest while he is in Rome, Alypius vows to keep his eyes covered during the event. But the moment a combatant is fatally struck, the '*clamor*' of the spectators 'hits' (*pulsasset*) him. Unable to resist the roar of the crowd, peering at the gory sight of a fallen gladiator, Alypius experiences an intoxicating exuberance as the vanquished fighter expires. It is an experience Augustine describes in terms of a moral defeat, a succumbing to sin, the fall of Alypius's soul:

> [...]aperuit oculos et percussus est grauiore uulnere in anima quam ille in corpore, quem cernere concupiuit, ceciditque miserabilius quam ille, quo cadente factus est clamor[...]. Ut enim uidit illum sanguinem, inmanitatem simul ebibit et non se auertit, sed fixit aspectum et hauriebat furias et nesciebat et delectabatur scelere certaminis et cruenta uoluptate inebriabatur. [12]

In light of such a description, we may say that the great extent to which agonistic play informs the way patristic authors viewed their rhetorical and religious activity, including the production of sermons, is a fact compelling us to consider another kind of network of relations altogether, namely that of the amphitheatrical environment and Augustine's preaching. In what follows, then, I shall explore how the archaeological research associated with the Carthaginian amphitheatre can bring to light the ways in which the design and function of such an edifice resonate in the

[11] Karl F. Morrison, *'I Am You': The Hermeneutics of Empathy in Western Literature, Theology, and Art* (Princeton: Princeton University Press, 1988), pp. 74–75.

[12] Augustine, *Libri tredecim confessionvm* 6.8, ed. by Pius Knöll, CSEL 33, pp. 127–28. The translation (with modifications) is that of R. S. Pine-Coffin, *Saint Augustine: Confessions* (Harmondsworth, Middlesex: Penguin Books, 1961; repr. 1983), p. 122 (unless otherwise stated the translations are my own); for comments on the passage see K. M. Coleman, 'Fatal Charades: Roman Executions Staged as Mythological Enactments', *Journal of Roman Studies*, 80 (1990), p. 58. 'So he opened his eyes and his soul was stabbed with a wound more deadly than any which the gladiator, whom he wanted to see, had received in his body, and he fell more miserably than he whose falling had given rise to the roar. [. . .] For as soon as he saw the blood he drank up the savageness, and he did not turn himself away but fixed his gaze and drank in the Furies without realizing what he was doing, and he was delighted by the wickedness of the contest and was drunk on the bloody pleasure.'

rhetorical strategies and religious thought underlying Augustine's sermons on Perpetua and Felicitas; how, in other words, the material remains and physical layout of an agonistic setting well known to Augustine are represented in the sermons' discourse and mythical structure.

First, let us consider the basic information and features pertaining to the edifice (though, of course, the brief overview offered here must be limited to the aspects that will eventually bear on my treatment of Augustine's sermons). According to a recent archaeological assessment of the site, 'the Carthage amphitheatre was probably originally built toward the end of the first century AD [. . .] and subsequently reconstructed soon after AD 165. It was one of the largest and most ornate amphitheatres in North Africa'.[13] Although the building has been repeatedly subjected to theft and to various attempts at reconstruction involving alterations that date from the modern period, the contemporary viewer is still able to distinguish the original elliptical shape of the structure and to sense its ancient proportions, along with other features that archaeological research has identified as part of the 'original masonry'.[14] Also detectable is the original arrangement of certain portals. When coming to the site in Carthage, the visitor to the amphitheatre approaches through the main entrance on the north side. Another large entrance appears at the southern sector, where the small, partially sunken, modern chapel dedicated to the saints stands. In addition to the main northern and southern gateways, there are two other portals worth noting–one located at roughly the centre of the eastern wall and another across from it at the western wall. Also readily noticeable are two long subterranean vaulted galleries, along the major and minor axes of the arena, which intersect at the centre.

The portals located at the east and west are of the greatest importance, for the position of these doorways, as we shall see, bears symbolic significance in Perpetua's *Passio* (as they undoubtedly did in Roman religion as well). The one located on the east side is called the '*porta Sanavivaria*', or 'The Gate of Life'. It is through this passage that victorious gladiators exited. The other passageway on the west side is known as the '*porta Libitinensis*', or 'The Gate of Death'. It is through this passage that the vanquished were taken.[15] The subterranean corridor leading to

[13] Bomgardner, 'Carthage Amphitheater', p. 102; *Roman Amphitheatre*, pp. 128–36.

[14] Bomgardner, 'Carthage Amphitheater', p. 91.

[15] Bomgardner, *Roman Amphitheatre*, p 137, explains: 'The layout and architecture of the arena itself reflected this duality between the alternative outcomes of life and death. Two portals known respectively as the *porta Sanavivaria* and the *porta Libitinensis* opened on to the arena from beneath the podium and its galleries and chambers. [. . .] The *porta Sanavivaria* was the 'Gate of Life' through which the victorious or spared gladiator strode in triumph and glory out of the arena, having defeated death itself, if only for a time. The *porta Libitinensis*, so named from the Roman goddess of funerals, Libitina, was the 'Gate of Death'. Through this gateway a figure dressed as Charun, the Etruscan demon of death and a traditional attendant of the gladiatorial combats, dragged the lifeless corpse of the luckless

The Gate of Death may still be entered today. After walking to the end of the tunnel leading to this gate, one will reach 'a cross-vaulted chamber', with a ledge large enough for a body to be placed. This is the section of the portal known as the '*spoliarium*', the place 'where the dead and dying were dragged to be dispatched, then stripped for burial'.[16] In considering the features of the amphitheatre, we should keep in mind the importance that the archaeologist Bomgardner gives to these east and west portals: 'From the logical opposition of the concepts of "The Gates of Life and Death", a physical opposition in the arena itself should be expected. These two gateways should form the vital axis for everything that occurred in the arena. I postulate, therefore, that these doorways should lie at the opposite ends of the minor axis of the arena'.[17]

Bomgardner refers to the 'logical opposition' of the two gates, but for our purposes, it is also worth considering how the portals function as symbolic opposites. For example, the *Passio* refers to the Gate of Life when Perpetua describes a dream the night before her martyrdom.[18] The dream involves a fight with a 'foul Egyptian' (*Aegyptius foedus*), skillfully manhandled by Perpetua in a wrestling match.[19] The description is especially revealing as it shows how an early

---

opponent. Charun had the job to test whether a gladiator was feigning death and to dispatch him with the large mallet that he carried, if necessary'.

[16] Bomgardner, 'Carthage Amphitheater', p. 89.

[17] Bomgardner, 'Carthage Amphitheater', p. 89.

[18] It is mentioned again in the *Passio* (20.8), when Perpetua and Felicitas are temporarily spared at the crowd's insistence. It is possible that the gates mentioned in the *Passio* are those of the civilian amphitheatre, which we have been treating and which has been thought to be the location of the martyrs' death. Indeed, the fact that a modern chapel was placed in that amphitheatre may be evidence of a tradition of popular piety associating the well-known and prominent civilian amphitheatre with the *Passio*. However, references in *Passio* 7.9 have led some scholars to argue that the military, rather than the civilian, amphitheatre was the place of the martyrs' execution. For the scholarly literature see Bomgardner, 'Carthage Amphitheater', p. 89. Regardless of whether the civilian amphitheatre currently under our discussion was the one in which the martyrs died, a consideration of its features in light of the *Passio* is still a legitimate undertaking, as Bomgardner himself states: 'Whether this martyrdom took place in the military or in the civilian amphitheater at Carthage, this account provides valuable information about the terminology, apparatus, and personnel of the arena, the procedure of public executions *ad bestias*, and the role of the crowd in effecting events in the arena of Carthage'. Note that the location of the military amphitheatre is still not known despite archaeological investigations considering the matter since the nineteenth century; see Bomgardner, *Roman Amphitheatre*, p. 249, n. 53.

[19] Note that the dream entails Perpetua's 'becoming male'; see, in general, Peter Habermehl, *Perpetua und der Ägypter order Bilder des Bösen im frühen afrikanischen Christentum: Ein Versuch zur Passio Sanctarum et Felicitatis* (Berlin: Akademischer, 1992); see also Robeck, pp. 57–69, who throughout his study discusses the various 'dream-visions' in the *Passio*, a subject that has been extensively treated: Peter Dronke, *Woman Writers of the*

Christian experience of martyrdom is expressed not only through agonistic imagery–such as Perpetua's rub down by assistants, the crowd's applause and her winning the victory branch–but also through the symbolic appropriation of the amphitheatre's layout.[20] After her defeat of the Egyptian, Perpetua claims that she 'began to go in glory toward The Gate of Life'[*et coepi ire cum gloria ad portam Sanavivariam*]. The brief interpretation of the dream, offered in the account's next line emphasizes Perpetua's confidence that her martyrdom will end in triumph: 'and I understood that I would not fight against beasts but against the devil; but I knew that the victory would be mine'[*et intellexi me non ad bestias, sed contra diabolum esse pugnaturam; sed sciebam mihi esse victoriam.*] (10.14–15).

Significantly, when considering Perpetua's glorious exit through The Gate of Life, Judith Perkins notes that 'what Perpetua calls her victory will, of course, be her death; she reveals a Christian logic as reversed as the imagery surrounding it'.[21] The nature of this reversed logic deserves further consideration as it is, I think, rooted in the amphitheatre's layout; it is also, as I shall argue, at work in Augustine's sermons on these saints. For the purposes of this discussion I shall resist interpreting the dream's victorious outcome as a wish-fulfillment, a kind of psychological compensation for the humiliating, public death awaiting the condemned.[22] Instead, let us concentrate on the way in which the narrative's presentation of the martyr's situation and of the Christian belief system mirrors the actual design of the amphitheatre. To that end, we must recognize how the Christian understanding of life and death interacts with the placement of the portals.

Middle Ages: A Critical Study of Texts from Perpetua (d. 203) to Marguerite Porete (d. 1310) (Cambridge: Cambridge University Press, 1984), pp. 1–17; Thomas Heffernan, *Sacred Biography: Saints and Their Biographers in the Middle Ages* (New York: Oxford University Press, 1988), pp. 185–230; Elizabeth Petroff, *Medieval Women's Visionary Literature* (New York: Oxford University Press, 1986), pp. 3–69; Kerstin Aspegren, *The Male Woman: A Feminine Ideal in the Early Church* (Stockholm: Almquist & Wiksell, 1990), pp. 133–43; Giselle de Nie, '"Consciousness Fecund through God": From Male Fighter to Spiritual Bride-Mother in Late Antique Female Sanctity', in *Sanctity and Motherhood: Essays on Holy Mothers in the Middle Ages*, ed. by Anneke B. Mulder-Bakker (New York: Garland, 1995), pp. 116–23.

[20] See *Passio*, 10.7, 12–13.

[21] Judith Perkins, *The Suffering Self: Pain and Narrative Representation in the Early Christian Era* (London; New York: Routledge, 1995), p. 110.

[22] For psychological approaches to the *Passio* see Mary Lefkowitz, 'The Motivations for St Perpetua's Martydom', *Journal of the American Academy of Religion*, 44 (1976), 417–21; Aline Rousselle, 'The Dreams of Vibia Perpetua: Analysis of a Female Christian Martyr', *Journal of Psychohistory*, 14 (1987), 193–206; Marie-Louise von Franz, *The Passio Perpetuae*, trans. by Elizabeth Welsh (Dallas, TX: Spring Publications, 1949); E. R. Dodds, *Pagan and Christian in an Age of Anxiety* (Cambridge: Cambridge University Press, 1985), pp. 47–53.

On the basis of the explicit reference to the *porta Sanavivaria*, we may begin to unravel how the *Passio* creates, with a logical rigour, a correspondence between the physical layout of the amphitheatre and the two opposing options facing the Christian under persecution. Perpetua may choose to witness to the Christian God through enduring punishment and, as a result, gain eternal life, or she may choose to renounce her Christianity by performing the pagan sacrifice, in which case eternal death ensues. As we have seen from the way the dream is recounted, the first choice leads to victory. Presumably, then, the second choice, had it been taken, would have led to defeat.[23] Likewise, if the first choice entails an exit through the Gate of Life, then the second choice would entail an exit through the Gate of Death. Thus, for the Christian who confronts persecution, dying is the victory symbolized by The Gate of Life; living is the defeat symbolized by the Gate of Death. Given, then, how the significance of the portals has been maintained in the *Passio*, there is no denying that the layout of the arena has become part of the way martyrdom's meaning is expressed. However, the reference points represented by the portals' physical opposition are symbolically reversed in the Christian appropriation of the amphitheatre's design. The major implication of such a reversal is apparent at the dream's close, in which the narrative depicts a triumphant Perpetua approaching the *porta Sanavivaria*. Of course, as someone who will surely die the next day from fatal wounds, Perpetua will be taken out through the *porta Libitinensis*, where her body will be placed on the *spoliarium*. Yet, in the eyes of the martyr, the *spoliarium* at the tunnel's end marks the threshold to paradise.[24] In other words, with the 'malevolent sympathy' at work here, the physical opposition has been reinvested, turned upside down by Christianity's symbolic logic—The Gate of Death has become The Gate of Life.

Our brief analysis of the portals' function offers a key insight that will be central to the treatment of Augustine's sermons. The archaeological research briefly discussed here has emphasized the importance of opposition in the arena, with the two physically opposed gates, as already stated, constituting 'the vital axis for everything that occurred'. Bomgardner's point is certainly worth repeating, for the environment in which the Christians die informs the meaning of their death. Clearly, the amphitheatre is the place where the arena's layout and the Christian belief system coalesce, where architecture and religion merge into a coherent expression of meaning conveyed through narrative. Thus, the salient feature of martyrdom's environment, the physical opposition of portals, has, in the important instance of Perpetua's dream, structured the symbolic world of the *Passio*. Indeed, though the

---

[23] As Tertullian, Perpetua's African contemporary, suggests: *De fuga in persecutione* 7.2, ed. by J. J. Thierry, CCSL 2.2 (Turnhout: Brepols, 1954), p. 1145. On the question of Tertullian as an author of the *Passio* see Amat, 67–78; and Heffernan, 'Philology', pp. 315–25.

[24] Compare, in general, Tertullian, *Ad martyras*, ed. by Eligius Dekkers, CCSL 1.1, pp. 3–8.

matter cannot be addressed in this brief discussion, the *Passio* itself is permeated with striking oppositions occurring on several levels (political, ecclesiastical, familial, corporeal, temporal and spatial). In short, while the point cannot be pursued here, I think there is sufficient evidence to say that the amphitheatre, like the role of Scripture in the *Passio*, functions as a key hermeneutical locus orienting and structuring the meaning of Christian martyrdom.[25] Keeping in mind, then, the importance of environment, of the physical and symbolic opposition of The Gates of Life and Death, let us turn to the sermons.

In total, Augustine wrote three sermons commemorating the two saints.[26] Although the sermons ostensibly honour the martyrs on their feast day (March 7), the various themes they address range widely, from a philosophical discussion on the human tendency to postpone death as long as possible to the significance of bodily resurrection.[27] In addition to offering a broad thematic scope, Augustine also attempts to interpret particular elements in the original *Passio*, especially material

---

[25] In connection to this point Bomgardner's hypothesis, *Roman Amphitheatre* p. 126, is especially intriguing: 'It is tempting to see the Christian burial in the apsed vaulted chamber beneath the seating of the amphitheatre at Thuburbo Maius as connected with a martyrdom in the arena, with the later establishment of a martyr's grave within the disused monument under a Christian emperor'.

[26] *Sermo* 280, 281, and 282, PL 38, 1280–1286; a fourth is included among the 'doubtful' sermons of Augustine (PL 39, 1715–1716); see Shewring, pp. xxix–xxx. Regarding the date of Augustine's sermons, in general, see Serge Lance, *Saint Augustin* (Paris: Fayard, 1999), p. 744. Lance, who provides a convenient list dating all of Augustine's main works, including the recently discovered material, attributes the sermons to the period spanning 392 to 430. With respect to the sermons on Perpetua and Felicitas, note that Verbraken, p. 127, who provides the known information pertaining to the dates of each sermon in Augustine's corpus, in this case lists no specific year for the sermons on the two martyrs but simply writes, under the category 'la datation': 'fête des saintes Perpétue et Félicité, martyres [7 mars]'. Although the March feast day of these saints was the occasion of preaching, it is important to consider the temporal observations of Brown, pp. 447–48, on Augustine's tremendous preaching activity in Carthage, brought to light by the recently discovered sermons: 'Augustine may have come to Carthage as early as May 397 and stayed until late September (that is, if he preached all in one season the sermons at the feasts of the saints, celebrated in Carthage between the months of May and September) [. . .] Even if this were not the case, Augustine certainly spent the summer months at Carthage in 397, and preached there continuously'.

[27] For a useful discussion treating the question of how the sermons were committed to writing, see Roy Deferrari, 'Saint Augustine's Method of Composing and Delivering Sermons', *American Journal of Philology*, 43 (1922), 97–123, who concludes: 'we know that his sermons were taken down by *notarii* [stenographers] as he delivered them'. Similarly, speaking of the sermons given in 404, Brown, pp. 457–58, remarks: 'For Augustine did not preach sermons, in the sense of delivering fierce denunciations of the gods. Rather, he gave his congregation what we would call a "teach-in"[. . .] They were preserved as they were spoken, by stenographers'.

related to gender. The previously mentioned dream in which Perpetua becomes male, the prayed for, pre-mature birth of Felicitas's child, and the obvious fact that the original document prominently portrays two women as Christian leaders are textual features that clearly engage Augustine. Significantly, then, his preaching attempts to offer explanations for the *Passio*'s most remarkable, and perhaps controversial, episodes. Naturally, I cannot address in detail all aspects of the sermons and the ways in which they treat the original text. In keeping with the goal of the paper, what I wish to consider now are the temporal and spatial references, for such features reveal most readily how the architecture and environment of the amphitheatre resonate in Augustine's sermons on Perpetua and Felicitas.

The most striking feature–and, I think, the key to understanding all the sermons dedicated to these saints–is the repetition of a prefix in the first sermon's initial line. The prefix reflects the 'present-centeredness' of Augustine's preaching, for the commemoration is not simply an encomium celebrating past deeds of Christian heroism; it is also a '*re*plication', a '*re*calling' and, most important, a '*re*-presentation' of the original event in Augustine's own time.[28] The preacher obviously assumes here that, in re-telling what happened, the event itself is re-created, as if the present words convey the reality of the past experience. As we notice from the sermon's opening, the temporal distance separating the past of the martyrs' death and the present of Augustine's preaching is dissolved in liturgical time, the cycle of ritual commemoration entailing the contemporary re-reading of a story that arouses both the physical senses and the minds of listeners:

> Hodiernus dies anniversaria replicatione nobis in memoriam revocat, et quodam modo repraesentat diem, quo sanctae famulae Dei Perpetuae et Felicitas, coronis martyrii decoratae, perpetua felicitate floruerunt, tenentes nomen Christi in praelio, et simul invenientes etiam suum nomen in praemio. Exhortationes earum in divinis revelationibus, triumphosque passionum, cum legerentur, audivimus; eaque omnia verborum digesta et illustrata luminibus, aure percepimus, mente spectavimus, religione honoravimus, charitate laudavimus.[29]

---

[28] While I think the phrase 'present-centeredness' captures the temporal significance of Augustine's preaching, note that it is taken out of a context quite different from that of the present discussion: T. G. Ashplant and Adrian Wilson, 'Present-Centered History and the Problem of Historical Knowledge', *The Historical Journal*, 31.2 (1988), 267.

[29] This day, with its annual replication, recalls to our memory, and in a way re-presents, the day on which the holy handmaids of God, Perpetua and Felicitas, adorned with the crowns of martyrdom, blossomed into perpetual felicity, clinging to Christ's name in war while earning their own name in reward. During the reading, we heard the exhortations of these women in their divine revelations, and we listened to their triumphant passion. All this, composed and brightened by the light of words, we heeded with the ear, beheld with the mind, honoured with ritual and praised with charity.

As a part of the liturgical re-presentation, then, the sermons attempt to evoke for Augustine's contemporaries the meaning of Christian martyrdom. The re-presentation occurs not only in liturgical time, as the above passage indicates, but also in liturgical space; and it is in the category of space that the archaeological remains associated with the Carthage amphitheatre bear the most obvious relevancy to Augustine's preaching. In the second part of the first sermon, Augustine refers explicitly to the amphitheatre, to a feature of its architecture (the *cavea*), and to the behaviour of crowds watching Christians die. As we are about to see, this portion of the sermon draws on the sensual experience of spectacles and on a salient feature of amphitheatrical design that the archaeological research has treated.

As expressions of that malevolent sympathy mentioned earlier, the appearance here (280.2) of comparative adjectives is arresting. There is nothing 'sweeter' (*suavius*), nothing 'braver' (*fortius*), nothing 'more glorious' (*gloriosius*) than the 'spectacle' of the martyrs' victorious 'contest' against their persecutors. After emphasizing the triumph of their martyrdom, Augustine refers explicitly to the amphitheatre as the place where the shouting crowd relishes the sight of 'holy bodies' put to death. The physical setting of the amphitheatre and the frenzied excitement of the onlookers thus play a prominent role in this portion of the sermon. Especially important is the fact that this setting, with its boisterous crowd, informs Augustine's portrayal of divine judgment. As the spectators enthusiastically watch the inane cruelties, looking down from their seats and ridiculing the Christians, 'the Lord' also watches from above, in his heavenly abode, derisively gazing at the unruly spectators. Such a description clearly depends on the amphitheatrical arrangement of seating, with its ascending rows of benches. However, in the Christian appropriation of the setting (entailing the insertion of Psalm 2. 1, 4), the crowd itself becomes the spectacle, looked down on and mocked by the divine judge seated on high:

> Tunc cum bestiis sancta objicerentur corpora, toto amphitheatro fremebant gentes, et populi meditabantur inania. Sed qui habitat in coelis, irridebat eos, et Dominus subsannabat eos.[30]

The emphasis on spatial re-presentation is maintained as the sermon continues, with an explicit reference to the *cavea*, the actual section of the amphitheatre containing the tiered rows of seats from which the spectators, arranged according to class, watched events.[31] Although there are now no remains of the *cavea's* seating

---

[30] Then, when the holy bodies were being thrown to beasts, throughout the amphitheatre 'the heathens were roaring, and the peoples were contemplating vanities. But He who dwells in heaven was laughing at them, the Lord was mocking them'.

[31] On the *cavea*, *gradus* and other features associated with amphitheatrical seating, see Bomgardner's discussion of the Colosseum, *Roman Amphitheatre*, pp. 9–20; see also Florence Dupont, *L'acteur-roi ou le théâtre dans la Rome antique* (Paris: Les Belles Lettres, 1985), pp.

blocks, the dimensions of other preserved *gradus* (stone seats) and the estimated size of the *cavea* allow for the application of a method by which the seating capacity of the Carthage amphitheatre may be calculated. By establishing a formula based on the *gradus* and surface area of the *cavea*, Bomgardner has been able to calculate the seating capacity of the Carthage amphitheatre, which he estimates held 'approximately 30,000 spectators'.[32] Undoubtedly, the edifice functioned as one of the largest popular meeting places in all of Carthage. However, similar to the way in which the spectators of martyrdom become the spectacle of God, the great *cavea* of the amphitheatre is dwarfed by another edifice, that of the church in which the account of the martyrs' death is read. Thus, shortly after referring to the divine mockery of the crowd, Augustine contrasts the seating capacity of the *cavea*, in which so many gathered to watch Christians die, with the large numbers who now fill the church on the martyrs' feast day:

> Nunc autem posteri illorum, quorum voces in carnem martyrum impie saeviebant, merita martyrum piis vocibus laudant. Neque tunc tanto concursu hominum ad eos, occidendos cavea crudelitatis impleta est, quanto nunc ad eos honorandos ecclesia pietatis impletur. Omni anno spectat cum religione charitas, quod uno die cum sacrilegio commisit impietas.[33]

The above passage contrasting *cavea* and *ecclesia* is important for the way in which the temporal and spacial re-presentations work in conjunction. The descendants of the people who once persecuted Perpetua and Felicitas are the ones who now praise them, with the temporal contrast emphasized not only by the adverbs *nunc* and *tunc*, but also by the past and present tenses of the main verbs ('*saeviebant [. . .] laudant*'; '*impleta est [...] impletur*'. Hence, in the annually re-presented sacrifice of the martyrs, the place and time of the past persecution are

---

51–57, with Augustine's views on spectacles discussed at pp. 19–24.

[32] Bomgardner, 'Carthage Amphitheater', p. 101.

[33] The descendants of those whose voices used to rage impiously against the martyrs' flesh now with pious voices praise the martyrs' merits. At that time, the cavea of cruelty was not filled with as many gathered for killing them [the martyrs] as the church of piety is now filled for honouring them. During every year charity watches religiously what on one day impiety committed sacrilegiously.

opposed and superceded by the place and time of the present commemoration. Indeed, the dual contrasts emerging in this short section of the sermon are too numerous to discuss in detail. A simple arranged listing of the various dichotomies should suffice to give an accurate impression of the rhetorical strategy at work in *Sermo* 280.2:

Space, Time and Spectators of Persecution	Space, Time and Spectators of Martyrs' feast
earthly amphitheatre	heavenly abode
crowd's gaze	God's gaze
crowd's mockery	God's mockery
impious	pious
ancestors raging	descendants praising
cavea of cruelty	*ecclesia* of piety
sacrilegious	religious
one day	every year
seeing with the eye of the flesh	seeing with the eye of the heart
rejoicing at dead bodies	lamenting persecutors' dead minds
dead martyrs	crowned martyrs
insult	exult
perfidious	faithful
temporal	eternal

The above arrangement of opposing elements could be greatly lengthened if the material from the other sermons was included. However, by this point in our discussion the significance of such juxtaposed contraries should start to become apparent. Clearly, the amphitheatrical environment is powerfully evoked in the sermon we have been considering, as indicated by the references to the martyrs' victorious combat, the roaring crowd, and the *cavea*. At the level of rhetoric, then, the sermon both appropriates and subverts the agonistic environment in which martyrdom occurs. On the one hand, it highlights the wickedness of the persecutors, who receive God's denunciatory judgment for their impious cruelty; on the other hand, it celebrates agonistic contest, the victorious outcome of the irreconcilable confrontation between persecutor and Christian. The latter aspect is especially significant, for the rhetorical emphasis highlighting the confrontation allows us to identify the sermon's defining feature. Similar to the original *Passio*, and as indicated by the textual dichotomies listed above, a rhetoric of opposition emerges as the sermon's chief characteristic. In other words, the rhetorical structure of the sermon mimics the physical design of the amphitheatre's 'vital axis'. The text of the sermon, with its sentences forming units of opposition, is itself a rhetorical representation of the portals' physical layout and symbolic meaning. At the level of rhetoric, it replicates what the archaeological research has identified as the most important feature in the layout of the Carthage amphitheatre–the opposition of the Gates of Life and Death.

To elaborate my argument, the list presented above is useful for the way it isolates the first sermon's specific components of opposition. As a re-presentation of martyrdom's meaning, the oppositional structure of the sermon corresponds to the 'symbolic logic' that arises in the *Passio* out of the physical opposition of the two portals. As indicated above, the persecutors inhabit a world of excess and cruelty. Rage, delight in mutilated bodies, the fleetingness of the occasion–these, I think, are the characteristics of a death experience. Indeed, Augustine refers to the crowd 'contemplating vanities'. Literally, they have 'focused their attention' (*meditabantur*) on 'empty things' (*inania*). Their world is one that cannot last, as Augustine emphasizes when contrasting the former *cavea* of cruelty with the current throng gathered in a church filled to capacity on the martyrs' feast day. Rooted in the reversed Christian logic discussed earlier, the sermon thus vindicates the martyrs as a vital source for the community's religious life. In short, similar to the shrines dedicated to the saints throughout North Africa, the church and the preaching itself or, as the essay's epigraph suggests, the preacher, function as 'gates of life', portals that give Augustine's contemporaries access to the martyrs' everlasting glory.[34]

The interpretation arguing that the sermon's spatial re-presentation highlights an opposition between the amphitheatre as a place of death and the church as a place of life is worth developing from another perspective. If we consider Augustine's *Enarrationes in Psalmos*, we find that the kind of explanation just offered for the contrast between *cavea* and *ecclesia* is supported by descriptions of Christian and amphitheatrical spaces connoting, respectively, the *loci* of life and death.[32] For instance, as 'crazed' spectators at the amphitheatre sit in the hot sun, a group stands in the shade watching 'the spectacle' of Augustine the preacher unraveling the meanings of a scriptural passage. The attending faithful, in turn, are seen by 'the Lord', the spectator *par excellence* 'plucking souls from death' (*eruat a morte animas eorum*). Likewise, the crowds that walk along the path 'to the amphitheatre' are going the way that 'leads to death' (*ducit ad mortem*). And 'the blessed who

---

[34] Brown, *The Cult of the Saints: Its Rise and Function in Latin Christianity* (Chicago, IL: University of Chicago Press, 1982), p. 86: '*Hic locus est*: "Here is the place", or simply *hic*, is a refrain that runs through the inscriptions on the early martyrs' shrines of North Africa. The holy was available in one place, and in each such place it was accessible to one group in a manner in which it could not be accessible to anyone else'.

[35] Regarding the designation of *Enarrationes* as sermons, Deferrari, pp. 97–98, notes: 'Among the church fathers, the terms *sermones, homiliae, tractatus, enarrationes*, etc., were used interchangeably for the most part [. . .].' In this regard, see Augustine, *Enarrationes in Psalmos* 118, proemium, ed. by Eligius Dekkers and Johannes Fraipont, CCSL 40, p. 1665; see also the comments reprinted by Migne, PL 36, 11.

dwell in the house' of the Lord 'will praise' and 'see' God 'for eternity' while those who delight at the sight of wild beast hunts (*venationes*) are destined to be saddened on the last day when they will 'see' that the 'Saviour' does not deliver them (*quibus Saluator saluti non erit*).[36]

These passages in the *Enarrationes* not only support the contention regarding the sermon's rhetorical and symbolic opposition conveyed through the juxtaposed spacial images of *cavea* and *ecclesia*; they also suggest how deeply Augustine's rhetoric of malevolent sympathy is rooted in a pervasive environment of spectacle. The sensual experience of the martyrs' feast, evoked in the sermons, goes hand in hand with watching amphitheatrical sports.[37] In other words, what is especially important about the *Enarrationes*, what the sermons on Perpetua and Felicitas omit when praising the great attendance at the saints' commemoration, is the fact that those spectators who gather in such numbers at the church are the very ones who also flock to the shows. In short, *Sermo* 280.2 is put in a different light–and, I think, enriched–when we realize that, during Augustine's time, some Christians find both events equally appealing:

> Nonne ipsi sunt qui theatra et amphitheatra implent per ludos et per alia spectacula, qui implent ecclesias per dies festos? [38]

When we turn from the way the sermons function rhetorically to consider the significance of their theological, or mythical, content, we notice again an emphasis on the opposition of life and death, an emphasis that emerges precisely when Augustine's consideration of the saints has led him to address key issues in the Christian belief system.

Consider, for instance, Augustine's interpretation of another dream recounted in the *Passio* (4.3–8). In the original story, Perpetua sees a ladder extending to heaven. The sides of the ladder are covered with sharp instruments, such as swords and

---

[36] *Enarrationes*, Ps. 32. 25, CSEL 38: 270; Ps. 39. 7, CSEL 38: 430; Ps. 147. 3, CSEL 40: 2141.

[37] Brown's description, *Augustine*, pp. 453, of the martyrs' feast as a sensual experience is worth quoting: 'For his [Augustine's] hearers the festival of a martyr was a time of torchlight vigils in the warm summer nights. It was a time of glory, marked by a suspension of the ordinary—by the chanting of songs, by the elevation of good wine, even by rhythmic dance. [. . .] To go to a feast of the martyrs was not necessarily to strive to imitate the endurance of martyrs. It was to draw sustenance through deep, almost non-verbal participation—through the excited throngs, through liquor, music and swaying movement—in the martyr's victory'. As the material from the new sermons suggests, it now appears that, while a student in Carthage, the young Augustine attended martyrs' feasts to meet women; see Brown, pp. 456–57.

[38] Are not those filling the theaters and amphitheatres during the games and other spectacles the ones who fill the churches during feast days? For similar remarks see, *Enarrationes*, Ps. 30. 2, CSEL 38, p. 203; Ps. 39. 10, CSEL 38, p. 433.

daggers, and at the bottom a large, menacing snake is ready to strike anyone who dares to climb. Perpetua dreams that she boldly steps on the snake's head and then proceeds to ascend. When treating the episode (*Sermo* 280.1), Augustine focuses on the significance of gender in the Christian myth of fall and redemption. Although he refers to the well-known Pauline verse emphasizing the equality of all in Christ, he nonetheless draws attention to feminine weakness. Even if Perpetua is not corporeally male, according to Augustine, her mental power and deeds compensate for her sex. More important, as a woman crushing the snake's head, Perpetua reverses the fall of humanity, which occurred because a woman did not resist the serpent:

> Quid enim gloriosius his feminis, quas viri mirantur facilius, quam imitantur? Sed hoc illius potissimim laus est, in quem credentes, et in cujus nomine fideli studio concurrentes, secundum interiorem hominem, nec masculus, nec femina inveniuntur; ut etiam in his quae feminae corpore, virtus mentis sexum carnis abscondat, et in membris pigeat cogitare, quod in factis non potuit apparere. Calcatus est ergo draco pede casto et victore vestigo, cum erectae demonstrarentur scalae, per quas beata Perpetua iret ad Deum. Ita caput serpentis antiqui, quod fuit praecipitium feminae cadenti, gradus factum est ascendenti.[39]

In light of the previous discussion, what is most striking in the quotation is not the fact that Augustine seems concerned with the martyr's absence of a phallus, but the way he situates the question of gender within the larger context of the Judeo-Christian account of humanity's fallen condition. In the above passage, Perpetua's dream is viewed as the redemptive counterpart of the first parent's sin: Eve loses paradise as a woman beguiled by the serpent; Perpetua regains paradise by crushing the snake's head as the first step toward her heavenly ascent. The whole understanding of fall and redemption is thus viewed in terms of female weakness and female strength. Hence Perpetua's dream offers Augustine the occasion to express the heart of the Christian myth in terms of an opposition between Eve and Perpetua. In losing paradise, Eve brings death into the world; in regaining paradise, through martyrdom, Perpetua attains eternal life. Significantly, when referring to the figures of the fall–Adam, Eve, and the serpent–Augustine repeatedly uses prepositions denoting agency (*per*) or cause (*propter*). It is *through* Eve that humanity's fall occurs. It is *through* Perpetua that humanity's redeemed condition is

[39] For what is more glorious than these women whom men more easily admire than imitate? Yet this is the praise especially of that one, in whom those believing and for whose name those fighting with faithful zeal are, according to the inner man, 'neither male nor female' [Galatians 3. 28]. So even among those who are women in body the power of the mind hides the flesh of the sex; and it would be loathsome to think that what was not able to appear in their corporeal parts was also not able to appear in their deeds. Hence the snake was crushed by the chaste foot and vanquishing heel when the raised ladder appeared by which Perpetua would go to God. In this way the head of the ancient serpent, which was the brink from which a woman fell, became the step on which a woman rose.

realized. Indeed, both martyred '*feminae* destroy the enemy who, *through* a woman, had destroyed man'. And their role as female soteriological agents reversing the fall is explicitly associated with the redemptive sacrifice of Christ. The incarnated God who took on human 'weakness' (*infirmus*) for humanity's sake 'appears unconquered' (*invictus*) in the victorious attainment of the martyrs' 'perpetual felicity' (*perpetuam felicitatem*).[40] Hence, another way to think about the theological significance associated with Eve, Perpetua and Felicitas is in terms of gates. According to the Augustinian view expressed in the sermons, sin enters the world through a woman, but the fallen condition is undone through the martyrs actualization of the redemptive sacrifice. The martyrs and Eve are thus gates of life and death (an image perhaps echoing, and challenging, Tertullian's claim that women, as daughters of Eve, are 'the devil's gateway'.)[41]

This same emphasis on the opposition of life and death emerges again when Augustine turns his attention to the actual condition of the martyrs' bodies on the day of resurrection.[42] At this point (280.5), the sermon becomes an exegesis on Luke 16. 19–26. Note that the exegesis heightens the opposition between 'the rich man' and poor Lazarus when explaining the corporeal state of the once mutilated bodies of the raised martyrs. The wealthy one who was clad in purple when alive begs for a drop of water in the afterlife, his parched body undergoing the eternal fire. In contrast, the flesh of ulcerated Lazarus is to be transformed on 'the day of retribution', shining among the angels. Augustine thus draws on and accentuates the opposition inherent in the biblical text to illustrate his understanding of the promise of resurrection awaiting the martyrs:

> Veniet autem retributionis dies, ubi corporibus redditis, totus homo recipiat quod meretur. Ubi et illius divitis membra quae qondam temporali purpura decorabantur, aeterno igne torreantur, et caro pauperis ulcerosi mutata inter Angelos fulgeat: quamvis etiam nunc ille guttam ex digito pauperis apud inferos sitiat, et ille in sinu justi deliciose requiescat. Sicut enim plurimum distat inter laetitias miseriasve somniantium et vigilantium; ita multum interest inter tormenta vel gaudia mortuorum et resurgentium; [. . .] gloriosissimi martyres pracipua sui honoris luce fulgebunt,

---

[40] *Sermo* 281.1 (PL 38, 1284), with the role of women in the redemption repeatedly emphasized; similarly, *Sermo* 282.2; also intriguing is Augustine's view of Felicitas's giving birth prematurely so that she may be executed with her fellow Christians (*Sermo* 281.3): 'Non aberat Evae poena, sed aderat Mariae gratia'.

[41] Tertullian, *De cultu feminarum* 1.2, ed. by Marie Turcan, Sources chrétiennes 173 (Paris: Les éditions du Cerf, 1971), p. 42: '[. . .] et Euam te esse nescis? [. . .] Tu es diaboli ianua.'

[42] On Augustine's understanding of bodily resurrection, see Caroline Walker Bynum, *The Resurrection of the Body in Western Christianity 200–1336* (New York: Columbia University Press, 1995), pp. 94–104.

ipsaque corpora in quibus indigna tormenta perpessi sunt, eis digna in ornamenta vertentur.[43]

As the above passage indicates, Augustine has structured this whole chapter of the sermon according to units of opposition, first between the rich man and poor Lazarus, then between the sleeping and the awake, and finally between the condition of the flesh during and after martyrdom. The last unit mentioned is especially important in light of the previous discussion concerning the Gates of Life and Death, for we notice again that a fundamental Christian belief is expressed in terms of opposition, an opposition intimately linked to the experience of martyrdom. According to the sermon, resurrection entails the reversal of opposing moral and corporeal conditions. With the resurrection, suffering is overturned by an eschatological judgment in which the body receives its due reward for unjustified ('*indigna*') punishments. The reconstituted and transformed flesh of the martyrs is meaningful only in light of its opposite, the cruel mutilations that initially deformed their bodies in the amphitheatre.

As we might expect on the basis of the material presented so far, the content of the sermons is permeated with oppositional pairs. Indeed, when Augustine's collection of homiletic texts on Perpetua and Felicitas is considered in its entirety, what emerges most prominently are carefully formulated modes of expression and thought structured according to 'relations of difference'.[44] Certainly, the original *Passio* displays such a tendency, and clearly that source left its mark on the sermons' rhetorical and mythical structure. But the sermons also develop oppositional relations that never appear or are only hinted at in the original document (e.g., *ecclesia/cavea* or Eve/Perpetua). In short, the sermons are hardly derivative. By way of conclusion, then, I think some general observations are needed to sense the overarching rationale underlying Augustine's homiletic commemoration and the broader implications of applying archaeological research to the study of this literature.

Perhaps most telling is how certain features of the sermons correspond with Augustine's own theory of signification outlined in his *De doctrina Christiana*.[45] As

---

[43] The day of retribution will come when, with bodies restored, the whole person receives what he deserves; when that rich man's limbs, which at one time were adorned in purple, burn with eternal fire, and the changed flesh of the poor man shines among the angels; although even now the former who is among the inhabitants of the dead thirsts for a drop from the poor man's finger and the latter rests delightfully in the bosom of the just one. For just as there is the greatest distance between the delights of the sleeping and the miseries of the awake, so too there is much difference between the torments of the dead and the joys of the resurrected; [. . .] the most glorious martyrs will shine in that special light of their honour, and those very bodies in which the undeserved torments were endured will be turned into ornaments worthy of them.

[44] Patte, p. 15.

[45] On the circumstances surrounding the composition of the work, see Conrad Leyser,

is well known, early on in that work he makes a distinction between 'things' and 'signs'(1.2). He defines *res* negatively as 'those things which are not used for signifying something, such as wood, stone, ram, and other such things of this kind' [*quae non ad significandum aliquid adhibentur, sicut est lignum, lapis, pecus, atque hujusmodi caetera*]. However, he immediately qualifies the definition by claiming that references to such objects in biblical texts also function as signs (or what we might call symbols):

> Sed non illud lignum quod in aquas amaras Moysen misse legimus, ut amaritudine carerent; neque ille lapis quem Jacob sibi ad caput posuerat; neque illud pecus quod pro filio immolavit Abraham. Haec namque ita res sunt, ut aliarum etiam signa sint rerum.[46]

Augustine's understanding of signs appears to be at work in the way the amphitheatre is presented in the sermons. Later in the discussion he states how a sign functions (2.1). A sign, 'besides the appearance that it conveys to the senses', causes of itself something else to come into thought [*praeter speciem quam ingerit sensibus, aliud aliquid ex se faciens in cogitationem venire*]. As a place associated with killing and madness, the physical structure of the amphitheatre itself operates as a *signum* in the texts we have examined. That is, it generates ideas that Augustine ties into the Christian belief system, so that the edifice comes to signify death, not simply because it formerly functioned as the place where martyrs died, but also because it continues to draw the attraction of Christians who flock there against their bishop's wishes. The amphitheatre is thus both a physical structure as well as a place of spiritual and moral decline in which persons such as Alypius are ruined. As we saw from the analysis of texts presented earlier, the amphitheatre is opposed by another architectural *signum*, the church. There the community gathers to hear and watch martyrdom's ritualized re-presentation, a sign of everlasting life. In a similar way, we may view the pairing of Eve and Perpetua or the martyrs' bodies before and after the day of resurrection, both theological themes that the sermons present in terms of opposed signs. Basically, the content of the homiletic texts that we have examined consists of such relations of signified difference. Since the main purpose of understanding and utilizing signs is, according to the *De doctrina*, the instruction of others in the faith, the juxtaposition of opposed *signa* appearing in the sermons is entirely consistent with the Augustinian method of preaching outlined in that work. Let us say, then, that the hermeneutical theory developed in the *De doctrina Christiana* also underlies the key oppositional elements detected in the sermons.

Authority and Asceticism from Augustine to Gregory the Great (Oxford: Clarendon Press, 2000), pp. 28–29.

[46] 'But not that wood which we read Moses put into the bitter waters [Exodus 15. 25]; nor that stone which Jacob placed on his head [Genesis 28. 2]; nor that ram which Abraham sacrificed instead of his son [Genesis 22. 13]. For these are things in such a way that they are also signs of other things'.

Of course, the amphitheatre as sign, as stone text signifying spiritual and moral ruin, again relates to the physical and symbolic world of the original *Passio*, in which the Gates of Life and Death function as symbolic opposites. In considering how the opposition of portals relates to the situation of early Christians in conflict, it is also worth recalling that literary critics, too, have highlighted 'binary opposition' as the defining feature of the narrative structure appearing in *passiones*, which constitute a literary genre distinct from hagiographic romance precisely because of the irreconcilable conflict between two contending forces.[47] Certainly, the fact that Augustine's sermons preserve such a structure suggests that the homiletic literature deserves to be investigated as part of the hagiographic dossier, as a source that reflects the mediating role played by the preacher's utilization of the original texts describing martyrdom.[48] Generally speaking, given the ways in which Augustine conforms to and departs from the original *Passio*, we may say that his utilization both draws on the narrative structure of the original document as well as re-works the material's content to serve more directly a pastoral and doctrinal (or ideological) agenda.[49]

However, when the archaeological research is brought into consideration, the limitation of the structural and historical-critical approach to such writings as Perpetua's *Passio* and Augustine's sermons becomes apparent. Something else, something more fundamental, emerges besides tropes, narratological architectonics and a kind of pastoral hermeneutics overseeing the reception of martyr-stories along lines suitable to the preacher. What does emerge is, I think, succinctly articulated by Thomas Reed, whose observations on medieval 'debate poetry' are readily applicable to the literature we have been discussing: '[. . .] the chances of a dialectical literary form having erupted so spontaneously are significantly enhanced in an age which habitually saw the world in terms of binary oppositions [. . .] the

---

[47] See Charles F. Altman, 'Two Types of Opposition and the Structure of Latin Saints' Lives', in *Medievalia et Humanistica*, n.s. 6 (1975), 1–11; Alison Eliott, *Roads to Paradise: Reading the Lives of the Early Saints* (Hanover, PA: Brown University Press, 1987), pp. 16–41. While the subject cannot be addressed in this brief discussion, the pervasiveness of the oppositional content in both the *Passio* and the sermons is a feature worth treating in light of the theoretical literature engaged with issues of opposition, contradiction, and difference (something I hope to explore in a future project). As already suggested by previous citations, especially useful in this regard would be Patte's work applying Greimas's structural semiotics to religious texts. Other theoretical possibilities might include Claude Lévi-Strauss, *Structural Anthropology* (Garden City: Basic Books, 1963) and Jacques Derrida, *Writing and Difference*, trans. by Alan Bass (Chicago, IL: University of Chicago Press, 1978).

[48] On the methodological importance of examining hagiographic dossiers, see Hippolyte Delehaye, *The Legends of the Saints: An Introduction to Hagiography*, trans. by V. M. Crawford (Notre Dame, IN: University of Notre Dame Press, 1961), pp. 125–47.

[49] See Mary-Ann Stouck, *Medieval Saints: A Reader* (Peterborough: Broadview Press, 1999), p. 39; Salisbury, pp. 172–76.

Middle Ages did consistently *speak* about the temporal world as an arena of contending opposites'.[50]

As Reed's comment suggests, it is a particular environment that emerges in the literature we have been examining, an environment that archaeology ostensibly treats. In this case, archaeology tells us that the physical setting actually is 'an arena of contending opposites', a setting that Augustine's preaching, as re-presentation, mediates to the community of believers. In advocating a move beyond tropes and narrative structure (a move facilitated here through archaeological findings), we may come to recover lost aspects of meaning that previously seemed so conventional as to be almost banal, not simply in Augustine's sermons but, as Reed's study indicates, in a wide range of medieval literature. To put the matter in another way, when Garnerus refers to the preacher as a 'gate' (*porta*) or, more to the point, when Matthew's Gospel (7.13–14) contrasts one 'gate [. . .] leading to destruction' with another 'gate [. . .] leading to life', or when John's Gospel (10. 9) calls Jesus a 'door', or even when medieval authors speak of 'the book of the heart', are we not compelled to consider the reasons why material objects figure so prominently in religious thought and rhetoric?[51] In the present case, the archaeological perspective generates new kinds of questions to ask the sources, the answers to which unexpectedly throw into relief an edifice of opposition inscribed on the discourse and theology of Augustine's preaching.

Finally, what the oppositions in the sermons and in the *Passio* unambiguously show is the great extent to which a specific environment conditions literary genres, rhetorical strategies, and conceptualizations of key Christian teachings, such as bodily resurrection and the redemption. It is because the vestiges of an agonistic environment mark the Christian belief system that the archaeological material discussed here proves so useful a tool in understanding the significance of the spatial references and theological content in Augustine's sermons on Perpetua and Felicitas. When the archaeological findings come into play, we can begin to understand some of the important ways in which amphitheatrical architecture and the Christian belief system interact. The physical emphasis on the opposition of portals, uncovered by the archaeological research, thus leads to a fuller understanding of the ways in which an agonistic edifice, homiletic rhetoric and Christianity's symbolic structure are interconnected. In a sense, it is by taking account of the function and meaning of

---

[50] Thomas L. Reed, *Middle English Debate Poetry and the Aesthetics of Irresolution* (Columbia, MO: University of Missouri Press, 1990), pp. 41–42, n. 3.

[51] Garnerus of Saint Victor, *Gregorianum*, 13.11, PL 193: 402; for the biblical references the text used is the Fourth Revised Edition of *The Greek New Testament*, ed. by Barbara Aland and others (Stuttgart: Deutsche Bibelgesellschaft and United Bible Societies, 2001); Eric Jager, 'The Book of the Heart: Reading and Writing the Medieval Subject', *Speculum* 17.1 (1996), 1–26; for illuminating comments on such 'metaphors', see Northrop Frye, *The Great Code: The Bible and Literature* (San Diego: Harvest/HJB, 1982), p. 59.

physical remains that we are able to perceive in Augustine's sermons how things become signs.[52]

[52] A partial version of this essay was read at the 2001 Northwestern Regional Meeting of the American Academy of Religion. The paper is the outgrowth of my experience in Carthage, Tunisia, where I had the opportunity to study first-hand some of the early material history associated with North African Christianity. I am most grateful to the archaeologists who kindly hosted and helped me in Carthage during the summer of 2000: Jeremy Rossiter, Tana Allen, and Sandy Bingham. For valuable suggestions I also thank my colleagues Rebecca Nagel and Selina Stewart. Especially appreciated is the patience of Michael May, reference librarian at the University of Alberta's Rutherford Library, who, for the preparation of this essay and on several other occasions, frequently offered the technical assistance I needed to conduct searches on the CD-ROM version of the Patrologia Latina (Chadwyck-Healey, 1994). Finally, I express my deepest gratitude to the Capuchin Friars of Saint Conrad's, Berkeley, who very kindly gave me a place to stay as I finished the essay.

Carthage Amphitheatre

Tunnel Leading to The Gate of Death

The Gate of Death and *Spoliarium*

Susanna Victrix, *Christus Victor*: Lenten Sermons, Typology, and the Lectionary

CATHERINE BROWN TKACZ

Lenten sermons on Susanna, the heroine of the Book of Daniel, prove to be dramatically valuable in reconstructing the tradition of innovative Christian regard for women, and for two reasons. First, liturgical preaching about specific women constitutes a substantive demonstration of how the Church promulgated the doctrine of the spiritual equality of the sexes, a doctrine only recently discussed in its own right.[1] Thus the study of Lenten sermons on Susanna complements the research already available on the doctrine itself. Second, Susanna proves to be particularly important within Christian tradition, for she is one of at least eight biblical women interpreted as a type of Christ and, in fact, she was included in the lectionary specifically as a type of Christ. Both of these reasons need clarification as a prolegomenon to the present study.

Prolegomenon

From the start, Christianity enabled women better to recognize themselves as being, equally with men, in the image of God.[2] For instance, holy women from at least the

---

[1] For this doctrine in the teachings of Christ, see Catherine Brown Tkacz, 'Jesus and the Spiritual Equality of Women', *Fellowship of Catholic Scholars Quarterly*, 24.4 (Fall 2001), 24–29. For this concept in patristic, medieval and Byzantine eras, see Catherine Brown Tkacz, 'Singing Women's Words as Sacramental Mimesis', *Recherches de théologie et philosophie médiévales*, 70 (2003), 43–96, esp. at nos 13–21, and Patricia Ranft, *Women and Spiritual Equality in Christian Tradition* (New York: St. Martin's Press, 1998).

[2] Patricia Ranft, *A Woman's Way: The Forgotten History of Women Spiritual Directors* (New York: Palgrave, 2000); review by Catherine Brown Tkacz, *Fellowship of Catholic Scholars Quarterly*, 25.2 (Spring 2002), 38–40. Tkacz, 'Singing Women's Words'; see also Laporte,

fourth century (St Olympias of Constantinople) have expressed their sense of spiritual equality by referring to themselves as the image of God, and the nun Baudovinia in her life of the abbess Radegund (*c.* 518–87) in detail describes her as 'good shepherdess', applying to her a famous metaphor for Christ himself.[3] German nuns in a Franciscan women's monastery daily beheld a visual reminder of their spiritual capacity to imitate Christ in holiness, for their refectory held a painting (1543) depicting three nuns following Christ, each of the four labouring to carry an inscribed cross.[4] A major means by which the faithful gained the recognition of women as the spiritual equals of men has been documented, namely, preaching of the doctrine per se. 'Women Are Equally Capable with Men of Obtaining Perfection' is the subject of a sermon by St Clement of Alexandria (d. 215)[5] and this doctrine was also preached by Sts Irenaeus, Theophilus of Antioch, Athenagoras of Athens (all three second century), John Chrysostom (340–407), Augustine (354–430), and others.[6] Another important means for inculcating this doctrine was by sermons on individual holy women, such as Susanna, who dynamically demonstrated their merits through their lives.

Susanna

Among such women, Susanna is notable as a type of Christ. Eight biblical women can now be identified as having been interpreted in mainstream Christianity from the early centuries on as prefigurations of Christ in his Passion: the widow of Zarephath, Ruth, Jephthah's daughter, Esther, Judith, Susanna, Jairus's daughter, and, from the parable,

---

Truax, and Rogers, in note 6 below. For additional sources, see Tkacz, 'Two Loves Built Two Cities. . .', *The University Bookman*, 39.2 (1999), 29–35. See also note 1 above.

[3] Ranft, *A Woman's Way*, p. 56 and index, *s.v.* 'Image'.

[4] Cologne: Wallraf-Richartz-Museum, Inv. 703; colour plate in *Glanz und Schmerz: Kölner Malerei aus dem Wallraf-Richartz-Museum*, ed. by Heiner Borggrefe and Vera Lüpkes (Cologne: Wienand, 1998), cat. no. 14, pp. 68–69. See also Tkacz, 'Singing Women's Words', at n. 47.

[5] Clement of Alexandria, *Stromateis* 4.19 (PG 8, 1330); Ranft, *Women and Spiritual Equality*, pp. 7–9; and William M. Daly, 'An Adverse Consensus Questioned: Does Sidonius' *Euchariston* (Carmen XVI) Show That He Was Scripturally Naïve?', *Traditio*, 55 (2000), 19–71, at 210–12.

[6] For instance, Clement of Alexandria, *The Instructor* 1.3–4, *Stromateis* 4.8, and *Exhortation to the Heathen* 6; Ranft, *Women and Spiritual Equality*, pp. 7–11. Also, John Chrystostom, 'In illud: vidi dominum', in *Jean Chrysostome, Homélies sur Ozias*, ed. by Jean Dumortier, Sources Chrétiennes, 277 (Paris: Cerf, 1981), p. 154. See also Jean Laporte, *The Role of Women in Early Christianity* (New York: Mellen, 1982); Jean A. Truax, 'Augustine of Hippo: Defender of Women's Equality?' *Journal of Medieval History*, 16 (1990), 279–99; Katherine A. Rogers, 'Equal Before God: Augustine on the Nature and Role of Women,' in *Nova Doctrina Vetusque: Essays on Early Christianity in Honor of Fredric W. Schlatter, S.J.* (New York: Lang, 1999), 169–85; and Barbara Finlay, 'Was Tertullian a Misogynist? A Reconsideration', *The Journal of the Historical Society*, 3.3–4 (2003), 503–25.

the woman who finds the lost drachma. Esteem for these women as types of Christ was eroded only in modernity, concommitant with the loss of awareness of typology.[7] Reconstruction has begun of their traditions, in the lectionary, in sermons in Greek, Latin, Syriac, Coptic, and in liturgical hymnody and art.[8] That Susanna was interpreted as a type of Christ and depicted as such was demonstrated in 1999.[9] But this interpretation proves to be more than simply compatible with Scripture: the synoptic Gospels themselves encode within their narratives the belief that Susanna prefigures Christ in his Passion.

The Gospel typology illumines the evidence of sermons and commentaries from the patristic era. Their study, coordinated with the evidence of the visual arts, allows a re-assessment and correction of the probable development of the lectionary in the West, which also can now be seen to present Susanna as a type of Christ.[10] In the ensuing centuries, this typological theme continues, with fresh elaborations, expressed in sermons, commentaries, mystery plays, and in the art found not only in manuscripts but also visible to the faithful at mass, in stained glass and fresco and bas relief in church buildings across northern Europe and in an eloquently embroidered vestment in Louvain. The integrated interdisciplinary methodology used here yields a rich understanding of why Maximus of Turin preached Susanna as *victrix* and Christ as *victor*, and sheds light on the perception of women in the early and medieval Church. For the fact that a woman can and did prefigure Christ in his Passion is a notable reminder that 'Women Are Equally Capable with Men of Obtaining Perfection'.

The account of Susanna, Chapter 13 of the Book of Daniel in the Vulgate, has from the earliest recorded times been in the calendar of readings for Lent. In the seventh century, when Roman usage became generally adopted in the West, this account was read in tandem with Chapter 8 of the Gospel of John. But why was the reading of Susanna's

---

[7] Caused by Protestant restrictions of typology (Tkacz, 'Susanna as a Type of Christ', p. 129) and Humanist and Enlightenment disparaging of women; Ranft, *Women and Spiritual Equality* pp. 213–15, 229–30; and Sister Prudence Allen, RSM, *The Concept of Woman, Volume II: The Early Humanist Reformation, 1250–1500* (Grand Rapids, MI: Eerdmans, 2002), esp. pp. 439–536, rev. by C. B. Tkacz, in *Review of Metaphysics*, 57 (2003), 863–64.

[8] See Catherine Brown Tkacz, 'Women as Types of Christ: Susanna and Jephthah's Daughter', *Gregorianum*, 85 (2004), 281–314; 'Recovering the Tradition of Women as Types of Christ', in submission; and 'The Doctrinal Context for Interpreting Women as Types of Christ', presentation at the XIV International Conference on Patristic Studies, Oxford University, 18–23 August 2002.

[9] Catherine Brown Tkacz, 'Susanna as a Type of Christ', *Studies in Iconography*, 20 (1999), 101–53; and Catherine Brown Tkacz, *The Key to the Brescia Casket: Typology and the Early Christian Imagination*, Collection des études Augustiniennes, série antiquité, 165; Christianity and Judaism in Antiquity Series, 15 (Turnhout: Brepols, for the Institut d'Études Augustiniennes and University of Notre Dame Press, 2001), esp. pp. 74–81.

[10] The evidence of sermons is regularly used to reconstruct probable lections for periods and places in the early Church without witness of an extant lectionary; see, for example, Gregory Dix, *The Shape of the Liturgy*, 2nd ed. (Westminster: Dacre Press, 1945).

history deemed suitable for Lent? And when and why did it become paired with John 8? The modern assumption is that Susanna, justly delivered from a false condemnation for adultery, balances the woman taken in adultery (John 8. 1–11), mercifully delivered by Jesus from a true charge of adultery, so that the reading of John 8. 1–11 drew to it the reading of Daniel 13.[11] Certainly this comparison of the two women came to be how the pairing of the two readings was understood (although Bede preaches a Lenten sermon on mercy and justice, based on John 8. 1–12, without citing any Old Testament lection.)[12] Rupert of Deutz (1075–1129) in his analysis of the lectionary finds Daniel 13 congruent (*congruit*) with John 8. 1–11, 'Nam haec per misericordiam, illa lapidationem evasit per justitiam' ('For this one through mercy, that one through justice evaded stoning').[13] Also, the commentaries found in two thirteenth-century copies of the *Bible Moralisée*[14] and in the *Concordantia caritatis* (written 1351) pair Susanna and the woman taken in adultery.[15] Yet this evidence is scant and late.

A comprehensive examination of the earliest evidence and of the dominant evidence of the succeeding centuries radically revises the picture. The complete opposite of the modern view may well be the case, namely, that the synoptic Gospels (especially Matthew) associate Susanna with the Passion of Christ, and this led to the reading of Susanna's history during Lent, even Holy Week. Moreover, the pairing of Daniel 13 with John 8 was perhaps intended to extend the typology of Susanna and Christ to all four Gospels. Only when these chapters were already paired liturgically did the verses about the woman taken in adultery, hitherto a floating element within Scripture, become fixed at the start of John 8. Because Susanna was already associated with that chapter, the woman taken in adultery was imported into it.

Biblical Studies

Chronologically, the first evidence to be considered are the Gospels themselves, John 8 and also the synoptic accounts of the Passion of Christ. Necessarily the present study

[11] For instance, Antoine Chavasse, 'Le Carême romain et les scrutins prebaptismaux avant le IXe siècle', *Recherches de science religieuse*, 15 (1948), 325–81 (pp. 359–60); Josef Pascher, *Das liturgische Jahr* (Munich: Hüber, 1963), p. 89.

[12] Bede, *Homelia 25 in Quadragesima* (CCSL 122, 178–83).

[13] Rupert of Deutz, *De divinis officiis per anni circulum*, 4.17 (CCCM 7, 130–31).

[14] The two pertinent manuscripts are Vienna, Österreichische Nationalbibliothek, Cod. 1179, fols 173[v]–74 (1220s); Paris, Bibliothèque nationale de France, lat. 11560, fols 212[v]–213, vol. 2 of 4 (*c.* 1235–45).

[15] *Concordantia caritatis*: the original, by Ulrich of Lilienfeld, 1351, is Lilienfeld, Cistercienserstift Bibliothek, Cod. 151, fol. 55[v]; also Eichstätt, University Library, Cod. st 212, fol. 54–55 (1/4 15th); Munich, Bayerische Staatsbibliothek, Clm 8832, fol. 54[v] (*c.* 1450).

uses the modern convention of citing Scriptures by numbers for chapter and verse, but the original practice was to cite a passage by incipit and explicit. Although now 'John 8. 12–59' sounds like part of a chapter, it was the whole chapter for the early Church.[16] Significantly, the original manuscripts of the Gospel of John lack the account of the woman taken in adultery (now John 7. 53–8. 11).[17] The pericope is also absent from the majority of lectionaries and synaxaria, from some manuscripts of the Diatesseron, from fifteen papyri (including eight from the third through fifth centuries), and from the Old Syriac, Coptic, Gothic, Armenian, and Georgian versions of the third through seventh centuries, as well as several early Fathers: Tertullian (220), Origen (254), Cyprian (258), Chrysostom (407), Nonnus (431), and Cyril of Alexandria (444).[18] Some biblical manuscripts include the passage later or earlier in the same Gospel, after John 21. 25[19] or after John 7. 36.[20] St Augustine in 413 treats the passage at the end of his discussion of John 7. 40–53, in one seamless sermon.[21] Even several manuscripts that include the passage at the start of John 8 mark it with asterisks or obeli to indicate that it is doubtful.[22] Other manuscripts include

---

[16] On numerical reference to Scripture see R. Loewe, 'The Medieval History of the Latin Vulgate', in *The Cambridge History of the Bible*, 2 (Cambridge: Cambridge University Press, 1969), pp. 102, 119; and Bruce M. Metzger, *The Early Versions of the New Testament: Their Origins, Transmission, and Limitations* (Oxford: Clarendon Press, 1977), pp. 347–48. On John 8, see also note 81 below.

[17] Kurt and Barbara Aland, *The Text of the New Testament: An Introduction to the Critical Editions and to the Theory and Practice of Modern Textual Criticism*, 2nd rev. and enl. ed., trans. by Erroll F. Rhodes (Grand Rapids, MI: Eerdmans, 1986), pp. 232, 307, 194. For the list of manuscripts, see also *The Greek New Testament*, ed. by Kurt Aland and others, 4th rev. edn. (Federal Republic of Germany: United Bible Societies, 1994), the end of the note signaled from John 8. 1. Albert Paretsky, OP, kindly called my attention to the early uncertainty over the authenticity and placement of this pericope.

[18] *Greek New Testament*, same note. See also Harry Merwyn Buck, Jr., 'The Saturday and Sunday Lessons from John in the Greek Gospel Lectionary' (unpublished doctoral dissertation: University of Chicago, 1954), Table One, showing that the numerous readings from John during *Pascha* (Easter) include only John 8. 31–42a on the Saturday before the Fourth Sunday of Easter. Regarding the tenth-century Georgian versions, Birdsall has examined numerous manuscripts beyond those used in the published editions and found that a few, at Tblisi, Sinai, and the Vatican, include the pericope, though after 7. 44; J. N. Birdsall, 'The Pericope Adulterae (John 7. 53–8. 11) in the Four Ancient Georgian Versions of the Gospels', Fourteenth International Conference on Patristic Studies, Oxford, 21 August 2003.

[19] *Greek New Testament*, same note, citing the manuscripts of 'Family 1' and a fifth-century Armenian manuscript (*f¹ arm*).

[20] Ibid., citing a manuscript from 1192 (225).

[21] Augustine, *In Iohannis evangelium tractatus*, 33.4-8 (CCSL 36, 306–11). For the date of 21 September 413, the Seventeenth Sunday after Pentecost, see headnote on p. 306.

[22] *Greek New Testament*, ibid., citing many manuscripts (E, S, 1077, 1443, 1445, etc.)

the passage in a different Gospel entirely, after Luke 21. 38[23] or after Luke 24. 53.[24] Considered without the migrant passage on the woman taken in adultery,[25] the eighth chapter of John narrates an exchange between the Pharisees and Jesus in which the issue of witnesses is focal (8. 13–18) as they try to tempt him to sacrilege and finally attempt to stone him (8. 59). And, as will be seen, it is these verses, 8. 12–59, which are found in the earliest lectionaries. Congruently, a number of early discussions of Susanna and Christ focus on just these parallels. In short, John 8 was initially known without the account of the woman taken in adultery, a passage that became fixed in that Gospel and in that chapter only relatively late.

The synoptic narratives of Christ's Passion, especially the Matthean account, provide compelling evidence regarding Susanna, for these narratives may well have been constructed to show that Susanna foreshadowed Christ. This hypothesis is revolutionary, the first demonstration that typology comparing a woman to Christ informs a Gospel narrative.[26] It suggests a profound respect for the spiritual equality and dignity of women. Significantly, the parallels here adduced between Daniel 13 (Theodotion's edition, here called Theodotion-Susanna) and the synoptic accounts are extensive. The number of false witnesses against Christ is specified as two (only in Matthew 26. 59–60), just as two false Elders perjure themselves in order to convict Susanna (Daniel 13. 34). The Matthean account records that Jesus was silent at his trial (Matthew 26. 63), just as Susanna was silent at her trial (Daniel 13. 26–40). A distinctive statement used just twice in the entire Bible links these accounts: Pilate's statement when he washes his hands, 'I am clean of the blood of this [just] one!' (Ἀθῷός εἰμι ἀπὸ τοῦ αἵματος τούτου', Matthew 27. 24) echoes Daniel's outcry, 'I am innocent of the blood of this [just] one!' (Καθαρὸς ἐγὼ ἀπὸ τοῦ αἵματος ταύτης, Theodotion-Susanna 46).[27] One of the oldest manuscripts of the Bible, the fourth-century Codex Vaticanus, brings the words of Daniel even closer to those of Pilate, replacing Καθαρὸς with Ἀθῷός 'innocent, free from'.[28]

Furthermore, it appears that the Matthean account of the Passion reflects a deliberate use of Susanna's great-voiced prayer as she faced death (Daniel 13. 42–43) to narrate Jesus's crying out in prayer in a 'great voice' before dying (Matthew 27. 46, 50).[29] The

---

[23] Ibid., citing the group of manuscripts known as 'Family 13' (*f*[13]).

[24] Ibid., citing 1333[c].

[25] Contemporary scholars also exclude those verses, without comment, when treating this chapter; see, e.g., J. Duncan M. Derrett, 'Exercitationes on John 8', *Estudios Biblicos*, 52.4 (1994), 433–51.

[26] For the fully documented argument, see Catherine Brown Tkacz, 'Aneboesen phone megale: Susanna and the Synoptic Passion Narratives,' forthcoming in *Gregorianum*.

[27] See also Tkacz, *Key to the Brescia Casket*, pp. 29, 35, 77–78, 81, 187.

[28] See apparatus of Alfred Rahlf's edition.

[29] The genesis of this research was my discussion of φωνῇ μεγαλῇ with Albert Paretsky, OP, at the Dominican House of Studies in Washington, DC, 14 August 2001.

accounts of Susanna's prayer and of Christ's exclamation before death each open with the predicate ἀνεβόησεν ('exclaimed') and the biblical phrase φωνῇ μεγαλῇ (Vulg. *voce magna*). While the phrase φωνῇ μεγαλῇ is common in the Bible, its conjunction with the predicate ἀνεβόησεν is rare, found only four times. Only twice is the full set of terms used of someone on the point of death, crying out in prayer. That is, this contextual coupling is unique to the two persons, Susanna and Christ. Both invoke God, and this is followed in Susanna's case with the statement, καὶ ἰδοὺ ἀποθνῄσκω (Vulgate: *Ecce morior*, 'Behold, I die') and in Jesus's case by his actual death:

> ἀνεβόησεν δὲ φωνῇ μεγαλῇ Σουσαννα καὶ εἶπεν, Ὁ θεὸς.. καὶ ἰδοὺ ἀποθνῄσκω[...]' (Theodotion-Susanna Verses 42–43)
>
> Exclamavit voce magna Susanna et dixit, 'Deus aeterne [...] Et ecce morior [...]' (Vulgate Daniel 13. 42–43).[30]
>
> ἀνεβόησεν ὁ Ἰησοῦς φωνῇ μεγαλῇ λέγων, Ἠλι ηλι [...] θεέ θεέ [...]'. κράξας φωνῇ μεγαλῇ ἀφῆκεν τὸ πνεῦμα. (Matthew 27. 46, 50)
>
> [...] clamavit Jesus voce magna dicens, 'Heli Heli.[...] Deus meus[...]'[...] clamans voce magna emisit spiritum. (Matthew 27. 46, 50)

The Matthean account has significant parallels with Daniel 13. the two false witnesses; the silence at the trial; the statement of Pilate and Daniel; the crying out with a great voice in prayer at the point of death. Christ's Passion is presented as fulfilling what Susanna's ordeal prefigured.

The other synoptic Gospels, especially Mark, also show the same typology. All three synoptic accounts share the pattern for the last words and death of Christ. Mark is quite close to Matthew here, with ἐβόησεν ὁ Ἰησοῦς φωνῇ μεγαλῇ (Vulg. 'Exclamavit Jesus voce magna'), the same final words for Christ, and a similar way of expressing his death (Mark 15. 34–37). Luke has a different predicate (φωνήσας) and records Jesus's final words as 'Father, into thy hands I commend my spirit' (Luke 23. 46). Mark describes false witnesses against Jesus (Mark 14. 55–59) and extends the parallel between Susanna and Christ by two additional details. First, he states that the false testimonies do not agree (Mark 14. 59), precisely the point by which Daniel exposed the perjury of the Elders (Daniel 13. 51–59). Second, Mark concludes that after their false testimony, all the chief priests condemned Jesus to death (Mark 14. 64). Susanna, too, was condemned to death right after the Elders' false testimony (Daniel 13. 41). These additional details in the Markan account evoke further similarities between the experiences of Susanna and Christ.

In the first century, then, Susanna may first be interpreted as a type of Christ, for the synoptic Gospels themselves may well present her experiences as prefiguring Christ's, both at his trial and at the very moment of sacrifice. And this need not surprise us, for

---

[30] See also Tkacz, 'Singing Women's Words', at n. 156.

Jesus's consistent teaching of the spiritual equality of the sexes[31] supports the idea that it was fitting to interpret Susanna as a type of Christ. The typological influence of Daniel 13 on the Matthean and other synoptic accounts of the Passion of Christ led naturally to the subsequent reading of Susanna's history during Lent. The priests and bishops whose preaching led to the compilation of the lectionary, it appears, were simply taking their cue from the Gospels themselves.

Further, a difference here between East and West is traceable to the Scriptures also. Because the edition of Theodotion is evidently the source for the synoptic parallels, it has Daniel's words, for instance, which are lacking from the Septuagint, and because Jerome used Theodotion for his translation of Daniel 13, Susanna as a type of Christ is better known in the West than in the East, which used the Septuagint. Even so, Susanna was known as a Christological type in the East: A Byzantine liturgical drama of Susanna, now lost, presented her as a prefiguration of Christ.[32] In the West, however, in art, sermons, and the lectionary, Susanna is prominent as a type of Christ.

Early Christian Evidence

The art, sermons, and commentaries of the ensuing three centuries predate the earliest lectionaries and therefore are critical in showing how Susanna was initially interpreted by Christians. Manifestly they understood her as a prefiguration of Christ. On a number of third- and fourth-century sarcophagi at Arles, the Vatican, Gerona, and Cahors, in frescoes in the catacombs, and on gold glass vessels at Oxford and the Louvre, Susanna is depicted as a type of Christ.[33] On three of these sarcophagi, namely, the 'sarcophagus of the Chaste Susanna' at Gerona, the famous 'Two Brothers' sarcophagus at the Vatican, and a sarcophagus lid at Cahors, Susanna being arrested in the garden is juxtaposed to Pilate washing his hands, a depiction that, on these three monuments, uncharacteristically omits Christ. In short, Susanna was so clearly a type of Christ that she could substitute for him visually. These images echo the typology apparently encoded in the Gospel narrative of the Passion. Moreover, the art demonstrates that typology was imagined creatively, and new expressions of it were invented in the visual arts. For instance, in the fresco in the Cemetery of Praetextatus (fourth century) Susanna appears as a lamb between two wolves, recalling the Lamb of God.[34]

Of unparalleled importance are the pair of Lenten sermons on Susanna preached by St Maximus of Turin in the fourth century and the related pair of typological depictions of

---

[31] See note 1 above.

[32] Kariophiles Mitsakis, Βυζαντινὴ Ὑμνογραφία (Thessalonike, 1971), 330–53 (p. 336). The play is ascribed to John or Nicolas of Damascus or Eustathios of Thessaloniki.

[33] Tkacz, 'Susanna as a Type of Christ', pp. 104–16, 136–43, with plates.

[34] Tkacz, 'Susanna as a Type of Christ', pp. 110, 141.

her on a late fourth-century ivorywork produced in northern Italy, the Brescia Casket.[35] The bishop's sermons, *On the Lord Accused before Pilate and on Susanna* (*De accusato Domino apud Pilatum et de Susanna*), comprise the earliest and fullest discussion of Susanna as a type of Christ. Although scholars have often mistakenly dated Maximus to the fifth century, revisionist research has corrected the dates for the delivery of his sermons to 395–415, or even decades earlier, if, for instance, Maximus lived from 336/46–*c.* 408.[36] His sermons on Susanna were quite popular.[37] Notably they rely on Matthew 27. 1–24. Moreover, he preached them during[38] or shortly before Holy Week.[39] Thus, Maximus paired Matthew 27 and Daniel 13 as Lenten lections in northern Italy in or shortly before Holy Week.

Maximus focuses on Susanna in her trial and also in her arrest as a type of Christ.[40] Each sermon draws on the Gospel narrative of Matthew 27, yet each also goes beyond the parallels within that text, elaborating such word play as *victor / victrix / vincere / victoria* and *salus / salvere / salvator*. Consistently the bishop presents both Christ and Susanna as overcoming, conquering, a point to which we shall return. Marvelling at Christ's silence before Pilate, the bishop explains:

> Non plane accusationem suam tacendo confirmat, sed despicit non refellendo. Bene enim tacet qui defensione non indiget, ambiat defendi qui metuit superari, festinet loqui, qui timet vinci. Christus autem cum condemnatur et superat, cum judicatur et vincet[...] Quod vincit Christus non orationis est sed virtutis; scit enim salvator[...] quomodo tacendo vinceret, quomodo non respondendo superaret[...] Suam enim salutem perdidit, ut salutem omnium lucraretur; in se vinci maluit ut victor esset in cunctis. Sed quid de Christo loquar? Susanna mulier inimicos suos tacuit et vicit. Non enim apud Danihelem iudicem verborum se oratione defendit, non patrocinii sermone tutata est; sed in sancta femina tacente lingua pro ea castitas loquebatur.[...] Castitas ergo Susannae et praesbyteros inpudicos convincit in paradiso, et in iudicio falsos accusatores obtinuit; bisque victrix reos facit testimonii, quos reos fecerat adulterii.[...] (CCSL 23, 228–29)[41]

---

[35] Tkacz, 'Susanna as a Type of Christ', pp. 103–9; idem, *Key to the Brescia Casket*, pp. 74–81.

[36] For the dates 395–415, see Almut Mutzenbecher, CCSL 23, pp. xxxi–xxxv. William Fahey suggests a life span of 336/46–*c.* 408; 'Maximus of Turin and His Late Antique Community' (unpublished doctoral dissertation, The Catholic University of America, 2002).

[37] Surveying the introductions to individual sermons in the CCSL edition of Maximus of Turin shows that those on Susanna and Christ (in 5 of 7 MSS) are better attested than most (in 1–4). See also remarks in PL 57, 351–52.

[38] For the first sermon being on 'post dominicam in Ramis prima', see PL 57, 190.

[39] The incipit of the sermon that follows the Susanna sermons refers to the second as preached *proxima dominica* 'last Sunday' (CCSL 23, 236).

[40] Maximus of Turin, *Sermo 57*: *De accusato Domino apud Pilatum et de Susanna* (CCSL 23, 228–30) and *Sermo 58*: *Item sequentia* (CCSL 23, 231–34).

[41] 'Clearly he does not confirm his accusation by not speaking; rather he despises it by not

Further, Maximus quotes Pilate and compares the statements of Daniel and Pilate (p. 229).

In the second sermon (CCSL 23.232–34), Maximus again compares Susanna to Christ, this time with closer parallelism highlighted by paired pronouns, names, or adverbs, *illa[...] hic* (lines 7–9, 14), *hunc[...] hanc* (17, 18–19), *Susannae[...] domini* (21, 23, 34–38), *Susannam[...] dominum* (24-25), *ibi[...] hic* (33–34), etc. Maximus presses the irony that the accusers themselves in each case were guilty of what they alleged against the innocent, so that the Elders were themselves guilty of adultery, and the Pharisees were themselves guilty of sacrilege. Further, the bishop presents the charges themselves as typologically related, 'for sacrilege can be called a serious adultery' (lines 9–10). (Similarly, Hippolytus of Rome [*c* 170–235/6] had construed the two Elders as types of Judaism and of heresy, tempting the Church to forsake her true spouse, Christ.[42]) Maximus recalls that in the first sermon he had compared the trials of Susanna and Christ; now he compares the place of the arrest of each: a garden: 'For Susanna was in a man's garden (*viri paradyso*) when she was surrounded by her accusers, and the Lord was in the garden of a vineyard (*hortuli paradyso*) when he was encircled by his betrayers; she suffered schemers there, he put up with betrayal here' (30–33). The outcomes of the two trials are also compared (34–41).

Precisely, the focal parallels of these two sermons are presented in two carved scenes on the front of the Brescia Casket: Susanna is shown arrested in the garden, and then she is shown at her trial, held by the Elders before Daniel. Uniquely, this fourth-century work pairs each typological depiction with a representation of the very event in the

---

refuting it. For one who needs no defence does well to keep silent, but let one who fears to be overcome defend himself and one who is afraid of being vanquished hasten to speak. When Christ is condemned, however, he also overcomes, and when he is judged, he also vanquishes[...] It is not by reason of speech but because of virtue that Christ vanquishes, for the Saviour[...] knows how to vanquish by keeping silent and how to overcome by not responding.[...] he lost His own life in order to gain life for all; he preferred to be conquered in himself in order to be the victor in everyone.

'But why should I speak of Christ? The woman Susanna was silent and vanquished her enemies. For she did not defend herself before Daniel the judge with much talk, she was not protected by a word of pleading, but chastity spoke on behalf of the holy woman while her tongue was silent.[...]Susanna's chastity, then, both refutes the lascivious Elders in the garden and prevails against the false accusers at her trial, and twice the victor, the woman proves guilty of perjury those whom she had also proven guilty of adultery.' Except for the last clause, the translation is that of Boniface Ramsey, OP, *The Sermons of St. Maximus of Turin*, Ancient Christian Writers, 50 (New York: Newman Press, 1989), pp. 137–38. All other translations in this essay are my own.

[42] Hippolytus of Rome, *Commentarium in Danielem*, Book 1; *On Susanna*, in *Hippolyte, Commentaire sur Daniel*, ed. by Maurice Lefèvre, Sources Chrétiennes, 14 (Paris: Cerf, 1947); *Hippolytus Werke* 1.1 (Leipzig: Akademie, 1897); English translation: *Ante-Nicene Christian Library*, 10 (1869), p. 477.

Passion of Christ that fulfills the prophetic type: on the lid of the ivorywork, in the top register, is carved Christ in the garden about to be arrested, and then, in the lid's second register, is depicted Christ held by soldiers at his trial before Pilate, who is shown washing his hands. Pilate's action, of course, recalls the words he spoke while washing them, one of the points of typological comparison between the two trials. The victory of Christ and of Susanna is also shown, for—even when threatened with death—they stand poised and serene.

The Christian understanding of the saints, including Susanna, and pre-eminently Christ, as victorious, merits specific attention with regard to striking diction Maximus uses of Susanna, for such diction is in fact standard and established as such through sermons. *Victrix*, a pithy term for 'victorious woman', was used of Susanna since at least the third century. Indeed, the diction for conquering is used consistently of saints from the patristic era onward, with, for instance, modern oratorios about Susanna by Stradella, Handel, and others culminating in chorally rich laud of her valour in the fight and praise of her as triumphant (*trionfante*).[43] Novatian (fl. 250) anticipates Maximus in finding her *bis victrix*, because even in danger she evaded both lust and death.[44] The medieval *Speculum virginum* praises her as *beata femina, victrix [...] sempiterni preconii laude cum triumpho* (blessed woman, victress [...] with the praise of the everlasting herald and with triumph).[45] Other writers personify her virtues and designate her chastity (*pudicitia*) or integrity (*integritas*) as *victrix*.[46] She is among the saints described by preachers and hagiographers as conquering (*superare*, *vincere*, νικάω)[47] their enemies, as triumphing (*triumphare*).[48] St Ambrose ascribes additional direct discourse to Susanna, having her assert, 'I could not be conquered, because I willed otherwise'.[49]

---

[43] Alessandro Stradella, *La Susanna*, libretto by G. B. Giardini (1681); G. F. Handel, *Susanna: Oratorium in drei Akten*, librettist unknown (1749).

[44] *De bono pudicitiae* 9.2 (CCSL 4, 122.17).

[45] CCCM 5, 148.

[46] Zeno of Verona, *Tractatus* 4.6 (CCSL 22, 13); Latin inscription on the engraving of Susanna by Willem van Swanenburg (1581/2–1612), from series *Thronus Iustitiae* (Amsterdam, 1606); Susan Dackerman, 'The Danger of Visual Seduction: Netherlandish Prints of Susanna and the Elders' (unpublised doctoral dissertation: Bryn Mawr College, 1995), cat. no. 92.

[47] For instance, *superare*: see Radulphus, Homily 11 (PL 155, 1532); *vincere*: see Augustine, *De Susanna* (PL 39, 1857), Hugh of St Victor, *De bestiis* (PL 177, 67), Hugo Lacerta (?) and others (before 1157), *Liber de doctrina* 119.9–13 (CCCM 8, 58); νικάω: see Asterius of Amasa, 'Sermon on Daniel the Prophet and Susanna' (PG 40, 244–45). For such language used of other saints, see for example Catherine Brown Tkacz, 'The Tormentor Tormented in Aelfric=s *Passio sancti Vincentii martyris*', *Ball State University Forum*, 24 (1984), 3–13 (pp. 9–12).

[48] For instance, *Triumphare*: see Jerome, Epistle 65.2.2 (CSEL 54, 618); *De virgine quadam antiochena*, in *Sanctuarium seu Vitae Sanctorum*, ed. Boninus Mombritius (Paris: Albert Fontemoing, 1910, repr. Hildesheim/New York: Georg Olms, 1978) 1. 108–10 at 108, lines 43–44. See also Zeno, *Speculum virginum*, and Swanenburg in notes 45–46 above.

[49] *De lapsu virginis* (PL 16, 370).

Antonius the Hermit, writing to a fellow religious, cites heroic examples including Thecla and Joseph; the first praised is

> Blessed Susanna, strongest in battle (*fortissima in bello*), who prevailed against the lust of those two Elders assailing her. Though they testified falsely against her and imposed many labors upon her, because of her patience and constancy God exalted (*exaltavit*) her in the end of her battle (*certaminis*) and humbled her enemies.[50]

Augustine in May 397 preaches that Daniel 13 is the account of her doing battle (*certentem*) and thereby demonstrating for us what it is to be an athlete of God (*athletam Dei*) in the arena (*theatrum*) of our heart. He prays that we may triumph with this victorious woman (*cum victrice triumphemus*).[51] Within the extensive tradition of presenting Susanna as victorious and a type of Christ, the fullest exposition of the theme comprises Maximus's two sermons during Holy Week.

St Ambrose in the 380s[52] summarily treats the silence of the Lord and of Susanna using the same material as Maximus; italics mark the closest verbal parallels. Again, the scriptural references are to the Gospel of Matthew:

> Accusatur dominus et tacet. Et *bene tacet qui defensione non indiget, ambiant defendi qui timent vinci. Non ergo accusationem tacendo confirmat, sed despicit non refellendo[...] Salus omnium* suam prodit, ut adquirat omnium. *Sed quid de* Deo *loquar*? *Susanna tacuit et vicit*; melior enim causa, quae non defenditur et probatur. (CCSL 143, 373–74)[53]

Elsewhere Ambrose reprises the comparison in treating fruitful silence: 'For there is an active silence (*negotiosum silentium*) as was that of Susanna, who did more (*plus egit*) by being silent than if she had spoken. The Lord himself by being silent was accomplishing the salvation of mankind' (*tacens operabatur salutem hominum*).[54] The same typology hovers nearby when, preaching on Psalm 38. 7, 'I have placed a guard over my mouth', the bishop of Milan recalls holy examples, pre-eminently 'Christus tacebat ante Pilati iudicium' as well as Moses (Exodus 14. 15), and 'Susanna, quae

---

[50] Epistle 20 (PG 40, 1058).

[51] *Tractatus de Susanna et Ioseph* 5.150–52; ed. by C. Lambot, *Revue Bénédictine*, 66 (1956), 28–38 (p. 33). For the date see G. G. Willis, *St Augustine's Lectionary* (London: SPCK, 1962), p. 28.

[52] Ambrose, *Expositio evangelii secundum Lucam*, 10.97 (CCSL 143, 373–74). See also Tkacz, 'Susanna as a Type of Christ', pp. 102–3, 117–19, 143–44.

[53] 'Accused, the Lord is silent. And certainly the one who has no need for defence can be silent: let those who fear to be conquered cast about to defend themselves. By being silent one does not confirm an accusation; rather one scorns it by not refuting it[...]. The safety/salvation (*salus*) of all mattered more to him than his own, as he aimed to obtain the salvation of all. But why should I speak of God? Susanna was silent and she conquered. Indeed her case is better, for she did not defend herself yet was proven [innocent].'

[54] Ambrose, *De officiis ministrorum* 1.3 (PL 16, 23–184, at 26). Some manuscripts record the last word as 'omnium', the word in the related passage by Maximus.

tacuit in periculis suis et dominus exaudivit eam'.[55] Elsewhere St Ambrose is prompted to recall Susanna and Christ: '"Nabuthe a duobus falsis testibus accusatus lapidatur"[...] Duobus testibus et Susanna est appetita: duos testes et Synagoga invenit, qui adversum Christum falsa jactarent' (Naboth having been accused by two false witnesses was stoned[...] By two witnesses Susanna also was desired; and two witnesses did the Synagogue find, who would hurl falsehoods against Christ).[56] Even this brief comment draws on the patterning after Daniel 13 found in Matthew, which alone records the number of witnesses against Christ.

St Augustine (354–430), in an influential set of sermons on the Gospel of John, provides additional early and valuable evidence pairing Susanna with Christ. He preached on John 8. 15–18 on 27 September 413, the Saturday before the eighteenth Sunday after Pentecost.[57] The pericope is from the lengthy dialogue between Jesus and the Pharisees who are trying to entrap him into heresy so that they can stone him. Significantly, Augustine treats Susanna as a Christological type when interpreting a text not from the synoptic Gospels: he is prompted by John 8. 17, Jesus's words about the Mosaic rule regarding witnesses, to consider Susanna. The bishop offers a mild instance of Susanna as a type of Christ: two false witnesses were against her; the whole people were false to Christ. Then the mystery of the Trinity engages his attention, with the thought that Susanna was supported by the trio of the Trinity:

> 'In lege', inquit, 'vestra scriptum est quia duorum hominum testimonium verum est. Ego sum qui de me testimonium perhibeo, et testimonium perhibet de me qui misit me Pater[...]'. Veritas quaeritur per duos testes? Ita plane, sic se habet humani generis consuetudo; sed tamen fieri potest ut et duo mentiantur. Susanna casta duobus falsis testibus urgebatur; numquid quia duo erant, ideo falsi testes non erant? De duobus dicimus aut de tribus? universus populus mentitus est contra Christum[...] Denique quando Susanna, casta femina fidelisque coniunx duobus falsis testibus urgebatur, Trinitas illi in conscientia atque in occulto suffragabatur; illa Trinitas de occulto unum testem Danielem excitavit, et duos convicit. (CCSL 36, 330–31)[58]

---

[55] Ambrose, *De explanatione psalmi 38*, 7 (CSEL 64, 189).

[56] Ambrose, *De Nabuthe Jezraelita* [3 Kings 21], 1.11 (PL 14, 731–56, at 745).

[57] Augustine, *In Iohannis evangelium tractatus* 36.10.15–18, 20 (CCSL 36, 330–31).

[58] '"In the law", he said, "your law, it is written that the testimony of two men is true. I am who gives testimony concerning myself, and testimony concerning me is also given by him who sent me, the Father[...]". The truth is sought through two witnesses? Yes, clearly, this is the custom of humankind. But nevertheless it can occur that two may lie. Susanna, chaste, was by two false witnesses oppressively urged; can we possibly conclude that because there are two, the witnesses are not false? Of two, do we speak, or of three? The entire population lied against Christ. [...]Therefore, when Susanna, chaste woman and faithful spouse, was by two false witnesses pressed, the Trinity was supporting her in her conscience and also in secret; the Trinity from secret raised up the one witness Daniel, and convicted the two.' Focal in the Torah (Genesis 17. 4, Exodus 3. 14), God's statement 'I am' is rendered literally here because Jesus is using it to reveal his divinity; see also M. J. Lagrange, OP, *Évangile selon Saint Jean* (Paris: Victor

In a neat rhetorical turn, Augustine balances the 'two false witnesses' by describing Susanna with two appositives, 'chaste woman and faithful spouse', and then has the three-fold Trinity raise up Daniel as one more witness for Susanna, so that the two-fold true character of Susanna added to Daniel makes a Trinitarian three to support her innocence. The bishop of Hippo again compared Susanna and the Lord in *Sermo 343*, 'On Susanna and Joseph'. To encourage his congregation, lest they fear that false witnesses might prevail against them, he reminded them that Christ and Susanna had endured that.[59] Quite briefly, Augustine in 401 implicitly likens the attitude of the Elders toward Susanna to the attitude of Judas in receiving the Eucharist at the Last Supper.[60]

In sum, the patristic evidence interprets Susanna as a type of Christ most often with reference to the Gospel of Matthew. Focal are the sermons of Maximus, preached during Holy Week or shortly before, in the latter half of the fourth century. The common elements treated relatively often in sermons on Susanna and Christ are the arrest in a garden, the false witnesses, silence at trial, and the trials themselves (including Pilate's name and words). St Ambrose, preaching on Luke's account of the Passion and in a sermon on Psalm 38, focuses on the typology. St Augustine adduces the typology twice, once in preaching on John 8.15–18 in the season of Pentecost of 412. This patristic evidence helps suggest modifications to the received history of the lectionary.

Lectionaries

The annual cycle of lections developed gradually.[61] By the fourth or fifth century, in both East[62] and West, pericopes were standardized.[63] In the late-fourth and early-fifth

---

Lecoffre, 1927), 250, 256–57; J. C. Coetzee, 'Jesus' Revelation in the *EGO EIMI* Sayings in Jn 8 and 9', in *South African Perspective on the New Testament*, ed. by J. H. Petzer and P. J. Hartin (Leiden: Brill, 1986), 170–77; and Jeffrey Burton Russell, *A History of Heaven: The Singing Silence* (Princeton: Princeton University Press, 1997), p. 9.

[59] *Tractatus de Susanna et Ioseph*, 28–38 (p. 30).

[60] Augustine, *Contra litteras Petiliani* 2.23.53.9–17 (CSEL 52, 52). For date, see Maureen A. Tilley, 'Anti-Donatist Works', in *Saint Augustine through the Ages: An Encyclopedia*, ed. by Allan Fitzgerald (Grand Rapids: Erdmanns, 1999), 34–39 (p. 36). The passage is discussed by Tkacz, 'Women as Types of Christ' (see note 8 above), at note 56.

[61] Jules Baudot, OSB, *The Lectionary: Its Sources and History*, trans. by Ambrose Cator (London: Herder, 1910), 119–21; Anton Baumstark, *Comparative Liturgy*, rev. by Bernard Botte,OSB, trans. by F. L. Cross (Westminster, MD: Newman Press, 1958), e.g., p. 132.

[62] The earliest complete lectionary for the whole liturgical year is from Jerusalem, it is known through fifth-century lectionaries in Early Syriac, Armenian, and Georgian, and became normative, modifying the earlier set of lections from Antioch; see Robert F. Taft, 'Lections' and 'Lectionary' in *The Oxford Dictionary of Byzantium* (hereafter *ODB*), 3 vols., ed. by Alexander P. Kazhdan (Oxford: Oxford University, 1991), s.v.

[63] See Gerhard Kunze, *Die Gottesdienstliche Schriftlesung*, I: *Stand und Aufgabe der*

centuries, 'some lections are already established by custom', the readings for Eastertide being the first to be fixed.[64] The annual pre-Easter fast was introduced in the late-second or early-third century and rapidly became important.[65] A reasonable inference is that the readings for Lent were defined relatively early. For the year as a whole, readings were defined for Sundays first and then for Saturday, the weekly pre-festive for Sunday.[66] By 340 the basic structure of the western Lent was established: Lent in Rome then consisted of a six-week fast, beginning on the sixth Sunday before Easter.[67] Within Lent, at first the emphasis was on its opening, middle and, of course, culmination. Weekday readings filled in somewhat later, with a complete coverage of days by about the seventh century.[68] Moreover, Gospel lections understandably had primacy: their pairing with Old Testament readings was an early custom, later revived, that was variable in the fourth century: Old Testament lections remained usual in Milan and in the Mozarabic and Gallican rites, but became rare in Rome, except during Lent, and in Africa.[69]

Susanna's history was among the lections defined relatively early, having been read in the early Church in the West during Lent from perhaps the fourth century.[70] Also, her history was and is among the numerous lections on Good Friday in the Coptic Church.[71] Precisely when during Lent Daniel 13 was read, however, varied for some centuries. Significantly, Daniel 13 was read in its entirety on such focal days as Thursday of Holy Week in Milan and the Third Sunday of Lent in Spain and, I suggest here for the first time, in Rome also.

Strikingly, in Milan the history of Susanna was read after Terce on Holy Thursday, 'consequently, on a feast day of the first order',[72] and in a context that emphasized her role as a type of Christ. The Milanese placing of Susanna is thus close to the Bishop of

---

Perikopenforschung (Göttingen, 1947); A. Allan McArthur, *The Christian Year and Lectionary Reform* (London: SCM, 1958); and William J. Diebold, 'Pericope', *Dictionary of the Middle Ages*.

[64] Willis, *St Augustine's Lectionary*, 10, see also 1–9.

[65] G. G. Willis, *A History of Early Roman Liturgy to the Death of Pope Gregory the Great*, Henry Bradshaw Society, Subsidia 1 (London: Henry Bradshaw Society, 1994), p. 87; Robert F. Taft, 'Lent', *ODB*, *s.v.*

[66] Taft, 'Lections'; Willis, *St Augustine's Lectionary*, pp. 4–5.

[67] See note 61 above.

[68] Taft, 'Lections'; Chavasse, 'Carême romain', 331–60.

[69] Willis, *St Augustine's Lectionary*, pp. 4–5. 'In Africa in St Augustine's day the Old Testament was in process of disappearance', Willis states, listing only twelve days with such readings, 'as well as some other days which cannot be identified'.

[70] Richard Delbrueck, *Probleme der Lipsanothek in Brescia* (Bonn: Hanstein, 1952), p. 129.

[71] Mother Lois Faraq, Coptic Orthodox nun, private communication, 9/15/99.

[72] Delbrueck, *Probleme der Lipsanothek*, p. 129, my translation. See also Fernand Cabrol, 'Épîtres', in *Dictionnaire des antiquités Chrétiennes*, ed. by J. M. Martigny, 3rd edn (Paris: Hachette, 1889), p. 293, n. 66.

Turin's placing of his set of sermons on her in the second half of the fourth century. In Milan, also, her lection was paired with a portion of Matthew 26–27, a Gospel always proclaimed during Holy Week.[73] Matthew is the Gospel with the strongest set of parallels with Daniel 13 (Matthew 27. 24, 46, 50, 59–60, 63).

In Milan on Holy Thursday, the readings within Terce present Susanna's experience as prefiguring Christ's, about to be betrayed by Judas, with the Psalm expressing the innocence of each in the face of false witnesses. The history of Susanna (Daniel 13) was the first lection. It was followed by the Psalm: 'Wicked witnesses whom I did not know rose up, questioning me. They returned to me evil for good. I, however, when they had molested me, clad myself in sackcloth and humbled my soul in fasting' (Ps. 34. 11–13). Next was a reading from Wisdom 2: 'The wicked said, thinking not rightly within themselves, "Let us surround the just man[...] If he is truly the Son of God, let God deliver him from our hands; let us condemn him to the foulest death"'. *In solo* was then sung 'He who ate my bread has enlarged treachery against me[...]'. The Gospel lection from Matthew culminated the readings: 'Then one of the twelve, who was called Judas Iscariot, went out to the chief priests and said to them, "What will you give me if I hand him over to you?"[74] Intriguingly, the liturgical pairing of Daniel 13 with Matthew 26. 14–16 extends Susanna's Christological typology, adding to the biblical parallels an implied comparison of the Elders with Judas, a pairing that St Augustine expressed in 401.[75] After Daniel 13 was read on Maundy Thursday, the continuing reading of Matthew during the ensuing hours included every narrative element recalling Susanna's experiences.[76] Surely several auditors, hearing Susanna's prayer at terce, would recall it at vespers when hearing Christ's prayer on the cross. Daniel's words, heard at terce on Thursday, would come to mind when Pilate's words were heard the next morning.

In Spain, Daniel 13 was read at matins on the Third Sunday of Lent, another emphasized occasion, being a Sunday in the middle of the fast. Not one of the synoptic Gospels, however, but John 8. 15–20 was the Gospel lection, 'Vos secundum carnem iudicatis[...]. In lege vesta scriptum est quia duorum hominum testimonium est

[73] For instance, in addition to the Milanese use discussed here, in Rome from the earliest known times the Gospel lections for the last Sunday of Lent and for Holy Thursday were Matthew 26–27 and Luke 22–23; Chavasse, 'Carême romain', 341 (cols A and B).

[74] *Manuale Ambrosianum ex codice saec. XI* [Cod. Ambr. I 55 Sup.], ed. by Marcus Magistretti, 3 vols. in 2 (Milan: Hoepli, 1897, 1905; repr., 1971), III, p. 181. For the span of the Gospel lection, see Stephan Beissel SJ, *Entstehung der Perikopen des römischen Meßbuchs: Zur Geschichte des Evangelienbücher in der ersten Hälfte des Mittelalters* (Freiburg im Breisgau: Herder, 1907; repr. 1967), p. 93.

[75] See note 60 above.

[76] On Thursday Matthew 26. 17–75 was read at vespers, on Friday first Matthew 27. 1–56 at matins and then Matthew 27. 57–61 at vespers, and on Saturday Matthew 27. 62—66 at matins; Beissel, *Entstehung der Perikopen*, 93. That is, Matthew 26–27 was read in full during the Triduum in Milan.

verum[...]'.[77] That is, Jesus speaks of judgement according to the flesh in contrast to divine judgment and adduces the Mosaic law's rule of two witnesses as a prelude to saying that both he and his Father give testimony concerning him. As noted earlier, in 413 St Augustine explicates John 8. 15–18 with reference to Susanna.[78] The lection in Spain runs longer, and includes a verse that makes a clear parallel with Susanna as a type of Christ, for just as Daniel 13 ends with her release, so the Spanish lection concludes that no one captured Christ then, because his hour had not yet come (John 8. 20).[79]

Rome's practice seems in part cognate with that in Spain, regarding the reading from John on the Third Sunday: Rome's 'évangile primitif' then was John 8. 12–59[80], in other words, the original chapter in full.[81] A quick development was the duplication of this entire lection on the next Sunday as well, so that on the Fourth Sunday John 8. 12–59 was read again.[82] Then John 8 was shifted to the Fourth Saturday.[83] Next this long, important reading was divided into three, with John 8. 12–20, 'Ego sum lux mundi', with reference to the law about witnesses, retained as the reading for the Fourth Saturday,[84] John 8. 46–59 read the day before (i.e., on Friday),[85] and John 8. 21–29 shifted earlier in Lent, to the Tuesday of the Second week of Lent.[86] Gregory the Great

---

[77] *Liber Comicus, sive lectionarius missae quo Toletana Ecclesia ante annos mille et ducentos utebatur* [Paris, BN, nouv. acq. lat. 2171 (11th c.)], ed. by Germanus Morin (Maredsous: Monasterium S. Benedicti, 1893), pp. 98–103. See also Cabrol, 'Épîtres', p. 264 n. 38, and Delbrueck, *Probleme der Lipsanothek*, p. 129.

[78] See at note 57 above.

[79] Nearly all of John 8, including the woman taken in adultery, was read in Spain in the second half of Lent: John 8. 15–20 on the Third Sunday of Lent, John 8.2–11 on the Friday after the Third Sunday, John 8. 51–53 and 58–59 on the Fourth Sunday (De Lazaro), John 8. 12–30 on the Wednesday after the Fourth Sunday, John 8. 31–39 on the Friday after the Fourth Sunday, John 7. 43–8.2 on the Monday of Holy Week, and John 8. 46–51 on the Tuesday of Holy Week; Beissel, *Entstehung der Perikopen*, pp. 80–83, 86.

[80] This was also the Gospel lection for that day in north Italy; Beissel, *Entstehung der Perikopen*, pp. 95–96, 98.

[81] See also at note 16 above.

[82] Chavasse, 'Carême romain', 341 (cols A and B), 345–46, 360. In the sixth or seventh century the reading on the Fourth Sunday was cut to just verses 12–20; p. 345.

[83] Chavasse, 'Carême romain', 341 (cols A and B), 345–46, 360.

[84] Chavasse, 'Carême romain', 352, 377. The reading is found in, e.g., the oldest extant Evangelary for this date; Germain Morin, 'Liturgie et basiliques de Rome au milieu du VIIe siècle d=après les listes d=Évangiles de Würzburg', *Revue Bénédictine*, 8 (1911) 296–330, at 303.

[85] Chavasse, 'Carême romain', 351, also 341 (col. C), 348–50, 352. Initially this was the practice in Rome, but not in Milan, where Lenten Fridays were aliturgical. Soon the practice spread North and is also found in, e.g., the Sacramentary of Bergamo (pp. 349–50).

[86] Chavasse, 'Carême romain', 341 (col. C), 356–57.

considered John 8. 46–59 important enough to use on Sunday, specifically, on the Fifth Sunday of Lent, as seen in his homiliary (593).[87] Other liturgical uses of this Gospel grew: by the eighth century John 8. 18–20 was read during the baptismal scrutinies on the Fourth Wednesday and the Fourth Saturday of Lent.[88]

Only in the late sixth century did the pericope of the woman taken in adultery, John 8. 1–11, appear as a lection. Then it is paired with Daniel 13 on the Saturday after the Third Sunday of Lent.[89] (This placing of the readings continued until after Vatican II, when the pair was shifted to the Monday after the Fifth Sunday of Lent.[90]) I suggest that the late arrival of John 8. 1–11 among the Lenten lections is due to the late assignment of that passage to the eighth chapter of John. It seems probable that Susanna, as a well-known type of Christ from the Gospels on, had already become associated with John 8. 12–59; Augustine is known to have preached on her with John 8. 15–18 in 413. Susanna's association with that Gospel chapter gave a reason for associating another woman, providentially freed from a charge of adultery, with that same chapter.[91]

On the level of the overt or manifest meaning[92] of the passages, Susanna and the woman taken in adultery constitute a contrasting pair of innocent and guilty, so that God's delivery of them shows his justice and his mercy, respectively. Typologically, the basis for associating these readings in the lectionary deepens: God, who had preserved the innocent Susanna from destruction from adultery, which is a figure for heresy,[93] had become incarnate as Jesus Christ. And Jesus, whose Passion would fulfill what Susanna's ordeal had prefigured, would by that same Passion grant release from destruction to the guilty, represented by the woman taken in adultery.

Arguably, the pairing of Daniel 13 and John 8 that survives even now in Lent was the original pairing in Rome on the Third Sunday of Lent, going back perhaps even to the fourth century. If so, Susanna's history was an ancient lection in Rome as well as in

---

[87] Chavasse, 'Carême romain', 360, also 341 (col. E).

[88] Chavasse, 'Carême romain', 375–77.

[89] This pair is in the oldest extant Roman lectionary, the *Comes* of Würzburg (Würzburg, Universitätsbibliothek, M.p.th.62 [*c.* 700]); edition in Morin, 'Évangiles de Würzburg', 303. Some lectionaries (e.g., the 8th-century Lindisfarne Gospels and the *Evangelarium of Burchard*, bishop of Würzburg) give only incipits and so do not define the span of the Gospel lection; D. Hurst, in CCSL 122, pp. ix, xii. See also Chavasse, 'Carême romain', 342 (col. D), 358, 359; Beissel, *Entstehung der Perikopen*, p. 175.

[90] *The Roman Missal [..].: Lectionary for Mass* (New York: Catholic Book Publishing, 1970), no. 252. Now, only in Year C is John 8. 12–20 read; otherwise just John 8. 1–11 is read.

[91] Interestingly, Robert E. Osborne, though unaware of the tradition of Susanna as a type of Christ, suggests that Susanna, being hemmed in on every side, was like Jesus, being set up by the Pharisees to be condemned whichever way he decided about the adulteress; R. E. Osborne, 'Pericope Adulterae', *Canadian Journal of Theology*, 12.4 (1966), 281–83.

[92] Russell, *History of Heaven* (at note 58 above), p. 8.

[93] See Maximus and Hippolytus on this point at note 42 above.

Milan and Spain. The only contrary argument is strained. Antoine Chavasse suggests that the original Old Testament lection for Rome on the Third Sunday of Lent in Rome was Isaiah.[94] After construing Isaiah 49. 8–15 as the epistle for the Gospel of the Fourth Sunday, John 9. 1–38 (the man born blind), Chavasse asserts that the Isaiah lection 'must then go back to the Third Sunday' when John 8. 12–59 was read, because 'the profound accord of these two texts argues in favour of this double function' for Isaiah 49. 8–15.[95] But the 'accord' seems slight. Specifically, he holds that Isaiah's prophecy of blessing for 'his qui in *tenebris*' (Isaiah 49. 9) corresponds with Jesus's proclamation, 'Ego sum lux mundi; qui sequitur me, non ambulat in *tenebris*' (John 8. 12, italics mine). In contrast to this supposition, documented evidence in the form of Augustine's sermon in 413 and also the lectionary in Spain demonstrates the perceived correspondence of John 8 with Daniel 13. Moreover, in each lection the law regarding two witnesses is obviously important. Given all this, and also the indisputable fact that the subsequent pairing in the Roman lectionary is John 8 with Daniel 13, it is reasonable to suppose that it was, simply, the original pairing.

Why, though, were the readings of John 8 and Daniel 13 shifted in the late sixth century from the Third Sunday in Lent to the following Saturday? The answer lies in the developing rituals in preparation for baptism on Holy Saturday. The liturgy for the Saturday after the Third Sunday in Lent incorporated one of the important pre-baptismal scrutinies, and the prayers for catechumens included petitions citing Old Testament exemplars, Abraham being in the petition for men and Susanna being in the petition for women.[96] Moreover, by 595 the church of Santa Susanna, dedicated to the Roman martyr, was defined as the stational church in Rome for that ferial day.[97] The two Susannas are religious heroines representing a range of possibilities. The Roman Susanna was a virgin who was martyred; the Old Testament Susanna was a wife and mother who was providentially rescued from death and who was also, importantly, a type of Christ. The unnamed woman of the Gospels offers a further, hopeful example of a sinner who was delivered from death by Jesus in person.[98] That Church and that pair of readings offer catechumens, especially women, a range of exemplary women to

---

[94] Chavasse, 'Carême romain', 342 (col. A), 346.

[95] Chavasse, 'Carême romain', 346, my translation.

[96] *Ordo ad catechumenum faciendum*; see, for instance, *Liber Sacramentorum Augustodunensis* (CCSL 159B), Rubric 443; *Liber Sacramentorum Engolismensis*, Rubric 695; *Liber Sacramentorum Excarpsus Bruxellensis* (CCCM 47, 100), Rubric 51.1; *Liber Sacramentorum Gellonensis* (CCSL 159, 51), Rubric 406; *The Sarum Missal*, ed. by. J. Wickham Legg (Oxford: Clarendon Press, 1916; repr. 1970), pp. 123–28, esp. p. 126.31–32.

[97] Valerie J. J. Flint, 'Susanna and the Lothar Crystal: A Liturgical Perspective', *Early Medieval Europe*, 4 (1995), 61–86 (p. 70 n. 23), citing Chavasse, 'Carême romain', 360, etc. Pascher, *Das liturgische Jahr* (see note 11 above), pp. 89–90, suggests *c.* 550 for assigning the scrutinies to this church.

[98] On women as models for all the faithful, as these women were for all the catechumens, see also Tkacz, 'Singing Women's Words', esp. at notes 72–83 and 192–94.

follow.[99] A further reason for correlating Susanna's history with preparation for baptism is the longstanding tradition of reading her experience of going to an enclosed garden to bathe and to anoint herself as a prefiguration of baptism, an analysis offered by Hippolytus of Rome and depicted occasionally in art, including the Doclea Cup, on which she is depicted as a type of Christ in his baptism,[100] and later tapestries, paintings, and manuscripts in which she stands beside or even within an enlarged baptismal font.[101]

In sum, the typological link between Susanna in Daniel 13 and Jesus in John 8 caused these passages to be paired in the lectionary, and once that had happened, then the possibility of correlating the justice of Susanna's delivery with the mercy of the adulteress's release caused the reading of the woman taken in adultery to become associated with John 8. This reconstruction corrects the history of the lectionary with regard to Susanna. Significantly, it also demonstrates a continuing Christian respect for the spiritual equality of women, such that it was completely natural to regard them as prefigurations of Christ.

Textual Evidence, 800–1200

Corroboration for this hypothesis is found in both the lack of sermons and commentaries that link Susanna and the woman taken in adultery and also the sustained interpretation in sermons, commentaries, and art of Susanna as a type of Christ. One sermon, perhaps by the Venerable Bede (d. 735),[102] circulated in Bavaria, for the Saturday after the Third Sunday in Lent. It treats Susanna without reference to any Gospel lection, as a model of all virtues and thus a 'figura Ecclesie' and, notably, as a type of the Blessed Virgin, who (because she was pregnant before marriage) was also falsely thought guilty of unchastity

[99] According to Flint the baptizands' mothers also had prominence in this liturgy during the Carolingian era; 'Susanna and the Lothar Crystal', 72–75.

[100] Hippolytus of Rome, *On Susanna* (see note 42 above), p. 16; Jean Danielou, 'Daniel', *Reallexikon für Antike und Christentum*, II (Stuttgart: Anton Hiersemann, 1957), cols 575–85 (580–81). For the Doclea Cup and other depictions of Susanna evoking baptism, see Tkacz, 'Susanna as a Type of Christ', pp. 116–17 with fig. 7

[101] Ibid. See also Pinturicchio's painting in the Vatican, 1492–94; N. Randolph Parks, 'On the Meaning of Pinturicchio's *Sala dei Santi*', *Art History*, 2.3 (1979), 290–317 (pp. 291–95). Also, the Hours of Charles the Bold and Margaret of York (before 1468), Duke and Duchess of Burgundy, formerly London, collection of Ronald A. Lee, now in a private collection, fol. 231; for plate, see James Douglas Farquhar, *Creation and Imitation: The Work of a Fifteenth-Century Illuminator* (Fort Lauderdale, FL: Nova University Press, 1976), fig. 73. Also the Hours of Louis de Laval (1469–89), Paris, Bibliothèque nationale de France, lat. 920, fols 315–316; Victor Leroquais, *Les Livres d'heures manuscrits de la Bibliothèque Nationale*, 2 vols. (Paris, [Maçon, Protat frères, impr.], 1927), no. 6 on 1.15–30, also p. lxxxi.

[102] For a survey of opinion on this, see Johannes Heil, *Kompilation oder Konstruktion? Die Juden in den Pauluskommentaren des 9. Jahrhundert* (Hannover: Hansche, 1998), p. 208.

and was also vindicated. That is, Bede likens the innocent vindicated Susanna, not to the guilty-but-forgiven adulteress, but to the innocent, vindicated Virgin. The sermon concludes by offering Susanna and the Virgin as exemplary victors in faith for monks to emulate, 'that each may battle (*certet*) well in this world, so that he may conquer (*vincat*) in the future'.[103]

Even writers who pair Susanna with John 8, and even those who do so in Lenten sermons, omit the woman taken in adultery and interpret Susanna as a type of Christ. Three Carolingian texts echo Augustine's discussion, beginning with the Commentary on John by the Venerable Bede. He strengthens the comparison of Susanna with Christ by citing Matthew 26. 61, a verse shown above to extend the typological parallels by specifying the number of false witnesses against Christ as two:

> Is it inevitable that two men speak true testimony? Did not two false witnesses deliver false testimony against Susanna? And when the Jews were seeking false testimony against Christ, the evangelist says, 'Finally there came two false witnesses'. *Can we possibly conclude that because there are two, the witnesses are not false? Of two, do we speak, or of three? The entire population lied against Christ.* (PL 92, 739–40; italics mark direct borrowing from Augustine)

Bede's version of this material is used again by Alcuin (735–804) in his commentary on the Gospel of John.[104] Notably, in a Lenten homily after Laetare Sunday Haimo of Auxerre (d. *c.* 855) uses the same material to explicate John 8. 12–19 ('Ego sum lux mundi...') in which Jesus recalls the Mosaic law regarding witnesses.[105]

An entire sermon on Susanna by Abelard (1079–1142) was preached to a woman's monastery, perhaps during Lent. Briefly and implicitly he compares her to Christ in it, by relating to Susanna and to Christ jointly Isaiah's famous messianic prophecy. When Susanna had been arraigned and had heard the false testimony against her, Abelard recalls, '[i]t is recounted that she did not speak, but wept, and looked up to heaven, so that first might be proved her patience, patience which the prophet had foretold in regard to Christ also, in these words, "Like a sheep is led to slaughter, and as a lamb before the shearer is silent, [he] will not open [his] mouth (*et non aperiet os suum*)"' (Isaiah 53.

---

[103] Inc.: *In praesenti lectione quam audistis, dilectissime, nobis lectum est de Susanna nobilissima foemina [..].* Text on pp. 75–78 in *Homéliare du Pseudo-Bède sur les Épîtres*, ed. by J. Gymnicus (Cologne, 1535). See also Michael Gorman, 'The Canon of Bede's Works and the World of Ps. Bede', *Revue Bénédictine*, 111.3–4 (2001), 399–445 (pp. 403, item 20, and 444, item 19). Michael M. Gorman graciously provided me with a copy of this text from his microfilm of its rare edition. Barré considers the homily anonymous; it circulated in Bavaria; Henri Barré, *Les homiliaires Carolingiens de l'École d'Auxerre*, Studi e Testi 225 (Città del Vaticano: Biblioteca Apostolica Vaticana, 1962), pp. 6–10, 212, Table III, and 279.

[104] PL 100, 858–59.

[105] Haimo of Auxerre, Benedictine monk of St Germain, *Homilia LV: Sabbato post Laetare* (PL 118, 322–27, at 324–25). Wrongly attributed in PL to Haymo, bishop of Halberstadt.

7).[106] In the prophecy, the subject of the predicate 'will not open' *non aperiet* is implied and the pronoun *suum* is generic, meaning potentially 'his' or 'hers'. As a result the prophecy fits Susanna also: '[s]he will not open [her] mouth'. Preaching may also have derived from the commentary on the Gospel of John by Rupert of Deutz (1075–1129), who likewise suggests Susanna as a type of Christ. Specifically, Rupert emphasizes that the Jews take Christ before Pilate because it is not lawful for them to kill someone (John 18. 29–32).[107] The circumstances of the Babylonian captivity, Rupert notes, were different in that it would have been possible to kill Susanna without consulting the Babylonian government.

Although the ensuing centuries have little record of new sermons on this typology, other texts express it freshly through 1562.[108] A variety of commentaries, German and Latin, on Susanna as a type of Christ are extant in manuscripts (1320–1475) of the enormously popular *Biblia pauperum*, and even elaborate the typology in new ways. Lenten plays in German and Corpus Christi processions at Ingolstadt (documented for 1498–1526) and Béthune (through 1562) suggest Susanna as a type of Christ. It is likely the typology was still being preached.

Visual Evidence, 1200–1558

Consistent with the content of the documented preaching are the artistic expressions of Susanna as a type of Christ, for instance, the illustrations of the *Biblia pauperum*.[109] For the present study, it is useful to consider especially those artworks actually visible within churches, because such art had the potential to be used by preachers as visual aids during sermons, and certainly it was available to the faithful for private meditation. Susanna as a type of Christ is found in churches depicted on wall and ceiling, in stained glass, on a sculpted lectern's bas reliefs, and on a brightly embroidered vestment. She is seen in the thirteenth-century dome fresco at Meldorf, in a fourteenth-century fresco in the church of Saint-Bauld in France (discussed below), and in the stained glass windows of the Frauenkirche in Munich (1480). Moreover, she was depicted prominently on the massive alabaster lectern at Tournai (1570–75), from which at mass the priest or deacon would have read her history and the Gospel of John during Lent, and, during Holy Week, the Matthean account of the Passion. The lectern depicts Christ before Pilate, and, directly below this, Susanna before the judge.

---

[106] Peter Abelard, *De sancta Susanna*, in *Opera*, 2 vols, ed. by Victor Cousin (Paris, 1849; repr. 1970), I, pp. 537-46, at 544. On the depiction of Susanna as a lamb, see above at note 34.

[107] Rupert of Deutz, *Commentaria in evangelium sancti Iohannis*, 13.613 (CCCM 9, 727).

[108] For specifics on the evidence cited in this paragraph, see Tkacz, 'Susanna as a Type of Christ', pp. 118–20, 122–26, 143–44.

[109] Tkacz, 'Susanna as a Type of Christ', ibid., also b/w figs 8–9. For the other artworks cited in this paragraph, see pp. 121–22, 126–27, 129—30, and figs 10–11.

Rarely does art pair Susanna with the woman taken in adultery. Although two manuscripts of the *Bible Moralisée* do so,[110] John Lowden has recently demonstrated that this work is idiosyncratic, made for members of the French royal family, and not known to be influential in thought or art generally.[111] Likewise, the *Concordantia Caritatis* juxtaposes the two women, but not one extant sermon is known to discuss Susanna with the woman taken in adultery.

In contrast, Susanna is dynamically visible as a type of Christ on the front of an embroidered vestment made for Philip Hosden, abbot of St Gertrude's church in Louvain (1558). The two focal events in which Susanna prefigured Christ appear adjacently to Christ: Christ being arrested in Gethsemane is above Susanna arrested in the garden, and Christ standing bound at his trial is above Susanna standing bound at her trial. The same explicit typology set forth in the sermons of Maximus of Turin and depicted on the Brescia Casket in the fourth century is still being depicted. Moreover, these embroidered typological medallions were placed where they could be clearly seen by communicants as they came forward to receive the eucharist.[112] Abbot Philip may well have preached on this typology while wearing the vestment itself.

In France in the church of Saint-Bauld, the chapel wall is covered with the remains of a fourteenth-century fresco of the history of Susanna. Only a French translation of the surviving inscription has been published: 'Elle endure mort et passion pour tout le monde' ('She endures death and passion for everyone').[113] This statement makes no sense if one considers merely the biblical account of Susanna, for she did not die, and in any case the death she had been condemned to would not have benefited anyone, let alone the whole world. The fresco and its inscription indicate that Susanna was familiar to the medieval French congregation as a type of Christ. It is likely that the original inscription was longer and compared Susanna to Christ '*who* endured death and Passion for the whole world'. That is, the decoration comprised a series of depictions from the history of Susanna, and the typology was made explicit through the inscription. Such public familiarity has been demonstrated for the Early Christian era, when it was necessary for the understanding of the depiction of Susanna as a lamb, recalling the Lamb of God, in the Catacomb of Praetextatus. That same popular familiarity with Susanna as a type of Christ is indicated by the frescoes in Saint-Bauld's as well.

---

[110] In 1999 I mistakenly construed these manuscripts as evidence that the lectionary was intended to link those two women; Tkacz, 'Susanna as a Type of Christ,' p. 133.

[111] John Lowden, *The Making of the Bibles Moralisées*, I, *The Manuscripts* (University Park, Pennsylvania State University Press, 2000).

[112] Louvain, Stedelijke Musea, inv. T/46. Dalmatic, with sixteen embroidered medallions. Made by Bartholomeus van de Kerckhoven; Tkacz, 'Susanna as a Type of Christ', pp. 129–30.

[113] Bernard Briais, *Loches et la Touraine du sud* (Chambray-lès-Tours, Association pour la promotion du tourisme en pays Lochois/CLD, 1984), 132–33.

Fifteenth-century Sermon

Finally, compelling evidence for the strength of the tradition of Susanna as a Christological type is found in a medieval Lenten sermon from Bavaria, extant in a fifteenth-century manuscript at Klosterneuberg.[114] The sermon, evidently preached in Holy Week, covers comprehensively the events from Christ's dining at Bethany through his Passion, citing copiously all four Gospels. The one Old Testament type of Christ presented is Susanna. And the point of comparison used is Susanna's words in her prayer, argued above to be parallel typologically in the synoptic Gospels with the moment of Christ's death on the Cross.[115] Indeed, her prayer opens the sermon:

> Lo, I die (*En morior*), although I have done none of the things that they falsely have testified against me'. It is clear that originally these words were spoken by Saint Susanna, when she, because of false testimony, had been condemned to death. On account of her innocence, she was finally delivered from this condemnation. I can, moreover, offer these words as a prelude of the Passion of Christ, whom the false and envious Jews condemned to death, who similarly, rising gloriously from conquered death, triumphed against them strenuously (*qui similiter de victa morte gloriose resurgens contra eos strennue triumphavit*). In these words is shown the benevolence and innocence of Christ in his death.[116]

Language associated with Susanna since the third century, when Novatian deemed her *bis victrix* (over both the lust and perjury of the Elders), and affirmed in the fourth century, when Maximus again termed her *bis victrix* and Christ *victor*, is in use yet, for the preacher describes Christ rising *de victa morte*, his rising and triumphing *similiter* to Susanna.

Conclusions

The original and abiding interpretation of Susanna was as a prefiguration of Christ. The very wording of the Bible's synoptic accounts of the Passion of Christ appear to be composed following the narrative template of Susanna's history. Early artworks and preaching consequently presented this typology, and it has now been shown that the calendar of readings was itself designed to promulgate it. The early preaching of

[114] *Sermo de passione Christi*. Klosterneuberg, Austria. Bibliotheca Canonicorum Regularum S. Augustini, CCl. 417, fols 133^{r}–44^{v}. Dr Floridus Röhrig, Can. reg., has kindly given me permission to edit and publish this text.

[115] See above after note 29.

[116] My transcription and translation, with capital letters, spacing, and punctuation normalized, abbreviations silently expanded, and breathing marks (for oral delivery) omitted. To preserve the word order of the second sentence I have made the active construction passive.

Novatian, Maximus, Ambrose, Augustine, and others is followed by new sermons (and artworks) treating the same typology, sermons by Bede, Haimo of Auxerre, Abelard, Rupert of Deutz, and the newly identified Bavarian sermon for Lent. Without reference to this traditional interpretation, the inscription on the fresco at Saint-Bauld would seem obscure or scandalous. With typological understanding, however, the meaning of the fresco is clarified. And, notably, the role of a woman as fit to foreshadow Christ himself is recovered. Just as bishop Maximus of Turin had preached in the fourth century, so a millennium later a church in France again presented Susanna as *victrix* and Christ as *victor* and in so doing, proclaimed the spiritual equality of men and women.

Clearly, it was through such experiences as hearing Lenten sermons presenting Susanna as a type of Christ, and seeing her so depicted in artworks in church, that Christian women were encouraged to respect their personal ability to be living images of Christ and to use their intellectual and spiritual capacities to achieve this. Such sermons on specific exemplary women complemented sermons that affirm 'Women Are Equally Capable with Men of Obtaining Perfection'. The Church, by proclaiming the lection of Daniel 13 in tandem with John 8 every Lent, sought to insure that the occasion for preaching Susanna as a type of Christ would be regular and emphasized. Only the modern loss of awareness of typology has vitiated this program. Significantly, at least three of the eight biblical women known as types of Christ were from the start featured in Lenten lections paired with Gospel readings selected to show the women to be types of Christ in his Passion: Susanna, the widow of Zarephath, and Esther. Each one, however, has been inadvertently displaced from this role in the post-Vatican II lectionary. The present research on Susanna indicates what valuable information about women in Christianity may be retrieved through the full recovery of the traditions of women as types of Christ. Hopefully each will prove *bis victrix*, first, in having been known from antiquity as a valiant type of Christ, until modernity lost awareness of her Christological valence, and soon again, in conquering the modern ignorance about women as types of Christ.

Time and Again: A Response to Leo Carruthers, John Kitchen, and Catherine Brown Tkacz

JEFFREY BURTON RUSSELL

These three clear and exciting articles examine a variety of important aspects of homilies, including community, typology, the unity between the heard and the visual, and the nature of time. The sermon has since earliest Christianity been intended to evangelize: to proclaim the truth of the Scriptures, to elucidate it, and to mediate it to an audience. It looks both backward and forward, back to the divine revelation of the Bible and forward to the present and future concerns of the audience. Many people currently think of a sermon as primarily intended to moralize, but moral suggestions and exhortations were subsidiary to the proclamation of the truth in its eternity.[1] Backward and forward; past, present, future: an underlying theme is the nature of time itself.

Current misunderstandings about time have sapped the basis for apprehending Christian sermons—and, I believe, Christianity itself. The deep meaning—the 'Deep Magic', in C. S. Lewis's famous phrase—of sermons is forgotten by historians, forgotten by many theologians, forgotten by most homilists, and forgotten by the Christian laity. For Augustine, by contrast, the meaning of time is that it is all informed by God's purpose.

The aim of the preacher, while declaring the Good News to the audience, is to create (in the case of non-Christians), or to strengthen (in the case of Christians), a community with Christ and in Christ. The concept of community is, as Leo Carruthers emphasizes, not merely important in, but absolutely fundamental to, Christianity. Without the community of believers in Christ, there would be no

[1] Rodney Stark's new books, *One True God* (Princeton: Princeton University Press, 2001) and, *For the Glory of God* (Princeton: Princeton University Press, 2003) demonstrate again (see also Mircea Eliade's corpus of writings) that religion and morality are not necessarily linked.

Christianity. As Carruthers argues, word and text were inseparable from word and community. People drew upon one another's assumptions. This is emphatically not to say that all ideas are 'socially' generated, nor to say that homilists said what their audiences wanted to hear (often quite the contrary!), but that there was a continuity between speaker and hearer. That continuity rested on the idea that the preacher considered himself a part of the congregation (a term applying to very diverse situations from people standing around in a forum or a marketplace to monks in a cloister to a university class), that the congregation considered itself part of the Communion of Saints through time and place, part of the Universal Church and the Mystical Body of Christ, along with the prophets, martyrs, and saints past, present, and future. Such a sense of community through time has seldom if ever been matched in human history.

Now, let us imagine a preacher and his audience—anywhere we like, in a forum or marketplace, a private home or a vaulted cathedral; the principle is the same. The preacher is mediating things that he knows about truth to an audience that wishes to understand. The preacher himself also learns as he teaches: he learns from what he is reviewing for himself, and he learns from the response of his hearers. Thus all present open deeper and broader. The group of individuals becomes a congregation becomes a community. That community does not exist only in that time and place: it is part of the larger Christian community in the whole world at that time: almost any Christian from any part of the world would have realized that mutual belonging. The individual congregations are part of the large congregation, the Church part of the large Church. Moreover, the congregation is part of the entire Christian community past, a living part of, and sign of, the Communion of Saints, the Universal Church, the City of God, the Body of Christ.

The 'Body of Christ' was not at all an abstraction *less real* than the people standing in the congregation, quite the contrary: the individuals were *less real* than the actual, eternal Body of Christ. 'Realism' in the ancient and medieval Christian tradition meant the opposite of what it does in modern 'materialist realism'. 'Realism' referred to the transcendent and ontological realities of which events, persons, and things in the world are signs. This is a strange concept for the modern mind, yet without understanding it, we cannot understand traditional sermons or the Christianity they represent and illustrate. It is not that reality is *either* spiritual *or* material, it is that it is *both* material and spiritual, both literal and figurative, and that spiritual reality is more real than material. *Praeter*, 'beyond', was a key world for Augustine and other preachers: we look beyond what we first see in order to see more and more and more.

All places are one in God; Christ is present everywhere in his community. All times are one in God: God knows every place and every moment eternally. No place and no time are privileged. Christ is no less real in London than in Jerusalem, no less real in 2004 than in AD 30 or even 500 BC. That is what we must get our minds around if we are to understand these sermons.

Take Kitchen's example of Augustine's sermons on the martyrdom of Perpetua and Felicity. What was going on in the minds of Augustine and his hearers? They understood that they, the congregation at Hippo at their time, were united with all Christians past, present, and future, in the Body of Christ; thus they understood that Perpetua and Felicity were not just dead people in the past, like Caesar and Cleopatra, but living members in Christ and thus immediately present. Not only Perpetua and Felicity, but also the amphitheatre in Carthage where they died, is eternally meaningful, as Kitchen shows in his explication of its archeology.

The Roman amphitheatre was a place of combat and death where gladiators fought for their lives with one another and wild beasts. It was a *cavea*, much like a modern football stadium, a large public open space for crowds and also a place of confinement for the combatants or victims. It had an arena opening into two opposite portals: the west portal, which was the 'gate of death' through which the dead and dying were dragged; and the east portal, the 'gate of life', through which the victorious combatants exited. Perpetua was condemned to the arena for refusing to sacrifice to Roman deities; and there she suffered, died, and was dragged out of the arena through the gate of death.

Sermons find the eternal meaning in this historical narrative by stressing its *types* and their *antitypes*, using those terms in their theological sense. The *cavea* is a type of hell and of death, its antitype a place of Christian worship. The crowd jamming the theatre lusting for blood is a type of sinners, of demons, of the City of Man or of Satan, of this evil eon; they replicate the crowd calling for Christ's death. They seek pleasure but find spiritual ruin; they watch the death of Perpetua as God observes their spiritual death; they condemn Perpetua and are themselves condemned by God. The antitype of the crowd is the Christian congregation, the City of God. The west gate, the gate of death, is the type of the mouth of hell; its antitype is the gate of life, the gate of heaven and salvation. In a powerful reversal of the antithesis, Augustine explains that whereas the ignorant think of the gate of death as leading to physical ruin and decay, the gate of death actually becomes the real gate of life, of eternal life in Christ. And whereas the ignorant think of the gate of life as leading to more years of enjoyment in this world, in the *real* world of Christianity it becomes the gate of death and ruin, of eternal annihilation. Perpetua, suffering defeat and death in the arena, *really* achieves victory and gains life. This manner of thinking may appear to be 'reversed logic', but it goes beyond logic and opens up to an eternal spiritual world where *res* (things and actions) are not just *res* but are *signs*—they *signify* the reality beyond the material and beyond logic. Perpetua is certainly a model of Christian behaviour, but more deeply she is a *type* of Christ, a sign of Christ, for she participates in Christ's sacrifice, a fundamental choice available to all Christians. Our own sacrifices are not only *like* Perpetua's and Christ's; they participate in the eternal sacrifice that God makes to redeem the world. This view is 'present-centred' only in the broader sense that all time is present: the words 'present' and 'now' represent moving points in God's eternity.

The liturgical meaning is also central. The Christian congregation gathers not only, or even mainly, to hear the sermon, but also to participate in the sacrifice of the Eucharist. The congregation enacts the eternal sacrifice liturgically as Perpetua performs it in the arena. How do the action of the Eucharist, the action of Perpetua, and the action of Christ tie together with regard to time? The action may be seen as a memorial of a past event; as a re-presentation of a past event; as a replication of the past event; or as a participation in an eternal event. For Augustine, the last two are most real: the *nunc* and *tunc* (present and past) that Kitchen observes are in one sense opposed, but they come together in now. *Nunc* and *tunc* dissolve into *semper et ubique* (always and everywhere). Christ's sacrifice is now. Perpetua's sacrifice is now. Our own sacrifice is now. Perpetua shares in Christ's eternal sacrifice. Individual actions are real events in the past; but on a *more real* level they are eternal. The acts and actors are types of the eternal.

The Old Testament Susanna is also a type of Christ, as Catherine Brown Tkacz demonstrates. How can this be, exclaims the modernist, for did not Susanna come before Christ? Before, after, here, there, now, then, always. In the eternal worldview of these sermons, all past and future are one in God. As much God's revelation as the New Testament, the Old Testament is full of types of all kinds—kings, liars, prophets, good people, cities, trees—but most importantly of types of Christ. Christian typology—certainly Augustine's—centred on Old Testament types of Christ such as Moses even more than it did on later types such as Perpetua.

Perpetua and Susanna are both innocents tormented by evildoers, and their courage leads them both to the kingdom of God. They also share an obvious characteristic: they are both women. The equality of women in Christ as types of Christ has been one of the salient points of Tkacz's work. She has shown that at least eight Old Testament female types of Christ exist, the most important of which may be Susanna, the heroine of the Book of Daniel.

Typology has a long and powerful tradition not only in Catholicism and Orthodoxy but also in Protestantism. The King James Version I read as a Protestant boy had innumerable notes on the parallels between the two Testaments (which I did not then understand), but most contemporary versions have only scattered typological notes or none at all. In the modern world, these concepts have become weakened, waved away as mere symbols or abstractions, but in Christian tradition they are more than symbols: they are *signs* of a reality deeper than any one place—or time. Typology has been almost lost in modern Christian thought. It does not even rate an entry in The Oxford Dictionary of the Christian Church.[2] Yet it is necessary to the understanding of most Christian literature and art, including, of course, sermons.

---

[2] Tkacz has a helpful article, 'Typology', in Allan D. Fitzgerald, OSA, *Augustine through the Ages: An Encyclopedia* (Grand Rapids, MI: Eerdmans, 1999), pp. 855–57.

Susanna was a devout Jew; she was falsely accused; she was accused in a garden; she was naked and exposed to the view of her enemies. She chose truth over falsehood at the risk of her life. Susanna, like Christ, was tempted to despair, tried for an alleged crime, faced with two false witnesses, and stood silent in the presence of her accusers. When, like Christ, she was condemned to death, she too 'exclaimed' to the Father 'in a great voice'. Where Daniel says, 'I am innocent of the blood of this just one', Pilate says, 'I am clean of the blood of this just one'.[3] The parallels are clear and were repeatedly explicated in sermons such as those of Maximus of Turin, in artworks such as the Brescia Casket and the Louvain vestment, and in the liturgy.

An eternal type pointing to ultimate divine reality may be projected from the New Testament 'backward' into the Old Testament or 'forward' into the Christian era. Susanna before the Christian era, and Perpetua in the Christian era, are both types of Christ. Why think this way? One answer Augustine and other homilists would give is that it is true. Another is that it helps tie the Old and New Testaments together as one divine revelation. A third is that the continuity continues now and into the future—a future that was not, as for moderns, indeterminate, but one that would end with the Second Coming and the Last Judgement,. A fourth is that each Christian, individually and communally can also be part of the Body of Christ. A fifth is that the community of the Christian saved is a continuation of the community of the pre-Christian saved. A sixth is that it points forward to the endtime and the kingdom of God. There are many more answers besides. Whether or not we believe in typology, it was a deep aspect of Christian thought even into the nineteenth century. Reviving an understanding of typology is of considerable importance both theologically and historically.

It remains to inquire why neither Christians nor religious scholars emphasize typology today. One reason is modernist dismissal of the harmony of Old and New Testaments. The decline of typology is linked to the decline of biblical study in religious studies departments and liberal theological schools and seminaries. There is much emphasis in both modern Protestantism and Catholicism on the 'horizontal' as opposed to the 'vertical', the emphasis upon the relationship of the community with itself rather than its relationship with God. To some extent, this may be a necessary corrective to past under-emphasis on the 'horizontal', but now the pendulum has swung so widely that the vertical is set aside and interactions among worshippers take precedence over *imitatio Christi*. However necessary and indispensable, the horizontal cannot lead into the deeper and deeper understanding that true sermons opening up the richness of the Bible can achieve.[4] On the other hand, simplistic 'literalism' or fundamentalism accepts only the Bible and thus loses the treasury of traditional interpretations, typology among them.

---

[3] Tkacz's revolutionary suggestion that the language of the Gospels may have actually drawn from that of Daniel 13 should provoke much scholarly investigation.

[4] Stark shows that the less a Church demands of its people, the less it offers the less it elicits response from the people—and the smaller the congregation becomes.

The decline of typology is also linked to the decline of authority. Few modern homilists dare to preach for four hours, as Fidel Castro did recently. As the churches have weakened during the past century, they have become less eager to instruct and more eager to please or even propitiate: 'apologetics' has taken on a whole new meaning. Becoming more inclusive, we lose the point. Without the Bible and the tradition of the Christian community, what is the point of Christianity at all?

Even if the Bible is not revealed and Christ is an illusion, the fact is that typology was a dominant mode of thought for 1800 years and well worth understanding. And if the Bible is revealed and Christ is not an illusion, then typology makes as much sense now as it did centuries ago. If typology is not understood, contemporaries will continue to find traditional sermons, literature, and artworks almost incomprehensible. The three essays in this section go a long way toward reviving this understanding.

II

How Sermons Reflect *Upon* Their World(s)

'Let Us Love One Another': Liturgy, Morality, and Political Theory in Chrysostom's Sermons on Rom. 12–13 and II Thess. 2

STEPHEN MORRIS

John Chrysostom (the 'Golden-Mouth') is perhaps the most famous, the most prolific, the most influential of the Greek-speaking fathers of the Church. The author of the standard Sunday eucharistic rite used each week by Orthodox Christians, Chrysostom delivered sermons considered the distillation of Eastern Christian theology, pastoral practice, and ethical behaviour. Liturgy books and manuscripts give the prayers and texts to be sung or read in the course of the services. Law codes describe what was or was not to be tolerated in public behaviour. It is the sermons we will examine here that show the interaction between the liturgy books and the law books, how the one reflects and shapes the others. In his vision, the Christian community expressing their mutual love through the ritual kiss at the Divine Liturgy was the embodiment of Christian virtue which, by its expression and maintenance of both love and order in both the personal and civic or political spheres, would forestall the coming of the Antichrist. Chrysostom's homiletic allusions to the sacramental practices of the Church in his day, as well as his direct discussion of these same matters, speak volumes that are consulted by liturgists attempting to reconstruct the historical development of Eastern Christian thought and practice. He wrote tracts and pamphlets in addition to his sermons, but it was the homilies that won him most attention. His popular sermons, sometimes interrupted by applause from the congregation, were taken down by stenographers, which he then edited prior to their 'publication'.

Born (probably in 349) in Antioch, the sophisticated and wealthy administrative centre of the Roman east, John was ordained deacon (in 381) and then priest (386) following his attempt at the ascetic life in the Syrian desert.[1] When the bishop of

[1] Biographical details for John are taken from J. N. D. Kelly, *Golden Mouth: The Story of*

Constantinople died in 397, John was taken (almost kidnapped) to be made the bishop of the capital city of the Roman Empire. He served in that post until his death in 404.

Those, however, were not years of peaceful ministry. As bishop of the capital, John was embroiled in doctrinal and political controversies from the beginning. His personal ascetic style and his deep concern for the poor, sick, and needy quickly won him powerful foes at the pampered court. Arcadius (the emperor)seems to have been particularly spineless and the empress Eudoxia was given to violent mood swings: easily angered but also possible to placate. He was exiled twice. Recalled once by the empress in response to the riots and demands of ordinary citizens, he died on the Black Sea coast during the second period of exile. His relics were escorted back to Constantinople in triumph in 438 by Theodosius II, son of Eudoxia and Arcadius, 'begging John to grant them pardon for all the injustices they had done him in ignorance'.[2]

John's sermons on the Romans seem to have been preached during his period of priestly ministry in Antioch in 392. Acclaimed from early on as 'one of his most finished productions' and lauded by the likes of Isidore of Pelusion,[3] the series of thirty-two extemporaneous homilies on Romans were taken down by stenographers and given by John a rather 'more thorough revision' than was usual before publishing them as a 'commentary' on the apostolic epistle.[4]

Chrysostom begins his Homily 20 on the Epistle to the Romans by turning to the beginning of Chapter 12: 'I appeal to you therefore, brethren, by the mercies of God, to present your bodies as a living sacrifice, holy and acceptable to God, which is your spiritual worship.'(Rom. 12. 1)[5]

After speaking in general about God's love for mankind (*philanthropia*) and pointing out his unspeakable concern and unutterable goodness for us, he moves on to persuading those who have received these benefits to exhibit a life worthy of the gift and be moved to compassion by the mercies of God.[6]

John Chrysostom–Ascetic, Preacher, Bishop (New York: Cornell University Press, 1995). For details of John's popularity in Antioch and his preaching/writing/editing style, see pp. 57 and 94; on applause during his preaching, see pp. 58, 60, 130–31

[2] Kelly, *Golden Mouth*, p. 290.

[3] Kelly, *Golden Mouth*, p. 90.

[4] Kelly, *Golden Mouth*, p. 94.

[5] Biblical quotes taken from *The New Oxford Annotated Bible, with the Apocrypha (Revised Standard Version)* (New York: Oxford University Press, 1973), unless otherwise noted.

[6] John Chrysostom, Homilies 20–24 on the Epistle to the Romans available in Migne, *PG* 60, 595–628. English translations based on those of by J. B. Morris and W. H. Simcox, revised by G. B. Stevens in NPNCF First Series, ed. by P. Schaff (n.p.: Christian Literature Publishing, 1889. Repr. Peabody, MA: Hendrickson, 1995) 11, pp. 496–521.

This act of response to God's mercies is to be an offering of 'your bodies', a 'living sacrifice, holy and acceptable to God, which is your spiritual worship.' The liturgical context and underpinning of this living sacrifice (which context Chrysostom took for granted) appears in the Greek terms which appear both in the epistle and the eucharistic liturgy with which Chrysostom presumed his congregation to be familiar. The appearance of *thusian* ('sacrifice') sets the stage and creates the context for everything that follows. It would have been impossible for Chrysostom's audience to hear the word 'sacrifice' and not immediately associate it with the Divine Liturgy itself, the 'mercy of peace, the sacrifice of praise' in which they were participating even as they heard Chrysostom preach.[7] Likewise, with the exhortation to live 'worthy of the gift', the eucharistic gifts of the Body and Blood of Christ cannot be far from the congregation's consciousness.[8] These 'intertextual resonances' are inescapable throughout the sermons dealing with Romans 12–13.

At its most basic level, intertextuality can simply refer to how authors quote or allude to earlier sources in writing their own texts. However, intertextuality critiques the claim that individual texts are 'discrete, closed-off entities', and instead argues that any particular text can be read only within the context of prior texts and larger cultural discourses that give it meaning. As one theorist put it: '[E]ach text becomes itself in relation to other texts, no text is self-contained.' Texts, by their very nature, play upon other texts.[9]

The resonances in the minds of the congregation as various words triggered other memories and associations were a significant factor in the popularity and effective nature of Chrysostom's preaching. The 'deep memory' of a psyche, where these 'bells would ring', is where the most fundamental work of a preacher takes place:

> This deep memory is the home of our dreams and of the symbols and myths that make up primitive religion. It is the world with which much in modern art and literature is

---

[7] On the common early Christian use of the term 'The Sacrifice' for what we now commonly call the Eucharist, see Gregory Dix, *The Shape of the Liturgy* (London: Dacre, 1945), pp. 111–15. For eastern Christian use of the term 'the Liturgy', much as the western Christians use the term 'the mass', see Timothy Ware, *The Orthodox Church* (London: Penguin ,1963; rev. edns 1993, 1997), p. 14. For an English translation of the *anaphora* ('eucharistic prayer, or 'consecration prayer', 'canon [of the mass]') of Chrysostom, see *The Divine Liturgy according to St. John Chrysostom, with appendices* (South Canaan, PA: St Tikhon's Seminary Press, 2nd edn, 1977) pp. 62–70.

[8] 'The gifts' is the common term among eastern Christians to describe the bread and wine intended for use at the altar, what western Christians would call 'the elements'. See the *anaphora* of St John Chrysostom for references to the bread and wine as 'gifts' offered by the people to God and offered—after the consecration—by God to the people.

[9] Stephen Davis, 'Crossed Texts, Crossed Sex: Intertextuality and Gender in Early Christian Legends of Holy Women Disguised as Men', *Journal of Early Christian Studies*, 10.1 (2002), 13.

> concerned. It is the level at which depth psychology attempts to effect therapy. The content of this metaphorical world is suggested to us by a number of clues: the person we fall in love with, the things we laugh or cry over, the fears that haunt us in the night. Since the things to be changed [by preaching] are the basic metaphors by which the psyche interprets reality, the tools to be employed are other, more adequate metaphors and stories.[10]

Chrysostom's great popularity sprang in part from his talent to tap into that 'deep memory' and offer other, more compelling metaphors by which his congregation could organize reality.

The 'spiritual worship' (RSV) or the older 'reasonable service' (KJV) is theological word-play in Greek: *logiken latreian*, or logical worship, revealed by the Logos or Word of God incarnate. The 'logical worship' is also distinct from, and superior to, the offering of animals by the Levitical priests in the Jerusalem temple under the Old Covenant, as Chrysostom points out.[11] This same phrase appears in the *anaphora* of Chrysostom himself to sanctify the eucharistic gifts at both Antioch and Constantinople.[12] The implication is that Christ himself, the Logos, revealed the act of worship to which John refers.

This oblation of the body was both a liturgical and an ethical act: ethical behaviour during the week could not be divorced from liturgical participation in the weekly eucharistic offering. Chrysostom repeatedly quotes the liturgical phrase 'sacrifice of praise' from the prophets to demonstrate both the superiority of the Christian oblation and the unified nature of the liturgical act and the moral life.[13]
But how, he asks, can the body be offered and yet remain alive? 'Let the eye look upon no evil thing, and it has become a sacrifice; let your tongue speak nothing filthy, and it has become an offering [*prosphora*, the bread given for use at the liturgy];[14] let your hand do no lawless deed, and it has become a whole burnt offering.'[15] But, he continues, it is not enough to simply refrain from doing evil. It is

---

[10] O. C. Edwards, *Elements of Homiletic* (New York: Pueblo Publishing, 1982), pp. 68–69. For an extended discussion of the role and function of the 'deep memory' and the work of preaching in relation to it, see Edwards, *Elements of Homiletic*, pp. 11, 66–70.

[11] Homily 20 (PG 60, 595; NPNCF 11, 496).

[12] *The Divine Liturgy of St. John Chrysostom*, p. 69. For the accuracy of the attribution of the *anaphora* to Chrysostom, see Robert Taft, 'The Authenticity of the Chrysostom *Anaphora* Revisted. Determining the Authorship of Liturgical Texts by Computer', *Orientalia Christiana Periodica*, 56 (1990), 5–51. Repr. in *Liturgy in Byzantium and Beyond* (Aldershot, Hampshire: Variorum, Ashgate, 1995).

[13] Homily 20 (PG 60, 595; NPNCF 11, 496)

[14] For an excellent study on the terminology, history, and uses of bread in the Christian liturgy (esp. eastern Christian use), see George Galavaris, *Bread and the Liturgy* (Madison, WI: University of Wisconsin Press, 1970.)

[15] Homily 20 (PG 60, 595–6; NPNCF 11, 496).

necessary to actively do good as well: 'Let the hand do alms, the mouth bless them that cross one, and the hearing find leisure evermore for lections of Scripture.'[16] Furthermore, these acts involve public behaviour, not simply private intentions or even isolated private actions: the eye must abstain from lechery, which necessarily involves at least one other person (i.e. a public context); the hand must abstain from greed (i.e. extend charity, which requires a recipient, a public); the feet must not carry one to the threatre or the brothel (both public spaces which cannot be entered—or avoided—without witnesses and subsequent notoriety and opprobrium or good repute). Even sexual intercourse with a prostitute, which presumably occurs in a private room, is a public act inasmuch as every sexual encounter creates a new entity ('one flesh,' as described in both the New Testament and in Chrysostom's other preaching) which affects—like ripples in a pond—those involved with the sexual partners.[17]

The eucharistic overtones of good behaviour are underlined when Chrysostom describes the descent of the heavenly fire to perfect and consume the offering of ethical personal behaviour:

> we shall not need the knife, altar, or fire any more, or rather we shall want the knife, altar, and fire which are not made-by-hands;[18] we shall need the spiritual fire and knife, which come to us from above, and our altar will be as spacious as the heavens. When Elijah offered his visible sacrifice, flame came down from above and consumed the whole: water, wood, and stones. How much more perfectly now will that same fire come down from above upon you? If you have anything in you that is malleable and worldly and yet still offer the sacrifice with a good intention, the fire of the Spirit will come down and burn away all that is worldly and perfect the whole sacrifice.[19]

This descent of the fire of the Spirit is too similar to the *epiclesis*, the invocation of the Father to send the Spirit down and make the eucharistic gifts of bread and wine into the body and blood of Christ to have escaped the notice of Chrysostom's audience.

Chrysostom also alludes to the spiritual and ritual preparation of the clergy to offer the Eucharist when he associates the personal behaviour of the lay Christian with the clerical preparatory acts: 'As he that ministers in the house of God, and officiates, of whatever sort he may be, collects himself [before the liturgy],and becomes more dignified; so we ought to be minded all our whole life as serving and

---

[16] Homily 20 (PG 60, 596; NPNCF 11, 496).

[17] I Corinthians 6. 15–17, Ephesians 5. 25–33; Chrysostom, Homily 18 on I Corinthians.

[18] A technical theological idiom, meaning 'made directly by God without human intervention'.

[19] Homily 20 (PG 60, 597; NPNCF 11, 497).

ministering.' [20] He goes on, likening the layfolk's moral behaviour to the sacrificial ministry of the clergy:

> And this will be so [consider our whole life as serving and ministering], if every day you bring him sacrifices, and become the priest of your own body, and of the virtue of your soul; as for example, when you offer soberness, or when you offer almsgiving or goodness or forbearance. For in doing this you offer 'a reasonable service', that is, one without anything that is bodily, gross, visible.'[21]

He also points out that his congregation must not conform to the fashion or vanity of fallen society if they are to walk or stand upright,[22] echoing the deacon's admonition to the congregation at the opening of the *anaphora* proper: 'Let us stand aright!'[23] Proper participation in the eucharistic offering depends on proper participation in civic affairs and public life.

The sermon goes on to exhort the faithful to embrace virtue, which is a person's true beauty, and to renew that beauty by repentance, tears, and good works.[24] He pauses to point out that one should praise virtue, especially if there is none in one's own life:

> For those who do not know so much even as what virtue may be, but reverence vice in its place, and take into their bed the harlot instead of the modest wife, how are they to be able to stand aloof from the present world? Wherefore we ought above all to have a correct estimate of things, and even if we do not follow after virtue, to praise virtue, and even if we do not avoid vice, to stigmatize vice, that so far we may have our judgements uncorrupted.[25]

While this might sound like hypocrisy to modern ears, to Chrysostom it is simply the acknowledgment of one's target behaviour: the goal or destination has to be agreed to before the task or journey is undertaken.

The homily concludes with the praise of humility, the mother of all good deeds and an admirable sacrifice in itself: 'Here [referring to Paul's words at Romans 12. 3] he is bringing before us the mother of good deeds, which is lowliness of mind, in imitation of his own Master.'

> So Paul too has taught us virtue in general terms, by requiring of us the admirable sacrifice; and being on the point of giving a more particular portrait of it, he begins

---

[20] For the fully developed rite of entrance, vesting, and preparation, see *The Divine Liturgy of St. John Chrysostom*, pp. 3–25.

[21] Homily 20 (PG 60, 597; NPNCF 11, 497), with a repetition of the 'logical worship' word-play.

[22] Homily 20 (PG 60, 597; NPNCF 11, 497).

[23] *The Divine Liturgy of St. John Chrysostom*, p. 62.

[24] Homily 20 (PG 60, 597; NPNCF 11, 497).

[25] Homily 20 (PG 60, 598; NPNCF 11, 498).

> from lowliness of mind as from the head and tells us, 'not to think more highly of one's self than one ought to think, but to think soberly.'[26]

Humility, humility, humility. Humility is the mother of virtue, which is both repercussion and continuation of the laity's participation in the sacrifice of the liturgy on Sunday.

Homily 21 (opening with Romans 12. 4) picks up where Homily 20 left off. Condemning haughtiness, Chrysostom points out to the congregation:

> Again he uses the same example as he does with the Corinthians[....] For great is the power of the medicine, and the force of this illustration for the correcting of this disease of haughtiness[....] When then we are in reality but one body, and members one of another, why do you separate yourself from the others by your haughtiness?[27]

He exhorts the congregation to do good deeds with a good attitude, not a bad temper; to give assistance to whomever in whatever form is required (financial, by words, or deeds); to love simplicity above all else and cleave to that which is good as Adam was told to cleave to his wife.[28] All Christians are family, having been 'born of the same pangs',[29] and the poor among the brethren will benefit the rich by praying for those who give them alms. Chrysostom connects this cheerful almsgiving and hospitality as expressions of love with the hospitality of Abraham toward the three angels (recounted in Genesis 18). A staple of patristic preaching, the encounter of Abraham with the angels was taken as an Old Testament revelation of the Trinity and an anticipation of the Eucharist.[30] Both of these allusions would have been familiar to the faithful in Antioch and the liturgical foundation for acts of charity towards the poor would have been underlined for them. Not only was the Eucharist the spiritual source of charity for the community but the source of its practical application as well. Liturgical practice in Chrysostom's day involved the bringing of gifts 'in kind' to the liturgy; from these the deacons would select the bread, wine, and other supplies required for the celebration of the liturgy that morning and the rest would be set aside for distribution to the poor later and throughout the rest of the week.[31] Chrysostom's descriptions of the bountiful banquet (meaning both

---

[26] Homily 20 (PG 60, 597; NPNCF 11, 499).

[27] Homily 21 (PG 60, 601; NPNCF 11, 501).

[28] Homily 21 (PG 60, 602–604; NPNCF 11, 502–503).

[29] Homily 21 (PG 60, 604; NPNCF 11, 503), referring to baptism.

[30] See Augustine of Hippo, *De civitate Dei* XVI.29; Paulinus of Nola, *Epistle* 13.21 and *Epistle* 23.40; also Hetty and Robert Roozemond, *Ikon: Inspired Art* (Echteld, Netherlands: Wijenburgh Foundation, n.d.), commentary on Plate 80 and Natalia and Vladimir Teteriatnikov, *Russian Icons of the Golden Age, 1400–1700* (Huntingdon, Pennsylvania: Juniata College, 1988), commentary on Plate 25.

[31] Dix, *The Shape of the Liturgy*, pp. 120–22, 250–51 and Robert Taft, *The Great*

Abraham's table and the altar laden with Communion and the offerings of the faithful) would have driven home that connection for his listeners.[32] Trinitarian divine communal life and mutual love of the brethren were both revealed in the Eucharist.

Chrysostom continues, pointing out that even Judas received alms from Christ as he was about to betray his master and that it is out-of-place for an almsgiver to judge if a recipient deserves the gift bestowed:

> Do not then busy yourself with men's lives and doings. For this is the very extreme of selfishness, for one loaf to be exact about a man's entire life. For if this person be a murderer, if a robber, or whatnot, does he therefore seem to you not to deserve a loaf and a few pennies? And yet your Master causes even the sun to rise upon him! And do you judge him unworthy of food even for a day?[33]

This insistence on giving-without-judging is tied to the social charity involved in both the celebration of the liturgy in Chrysostom's day and the celebration of the Last Supper itself, when the liturgy was first instituted. To give without judgement or condemnation is one of the primary prerequisites to receiving Communion, or even praying, oneself.

> And how can you say to God, 'Have mercy on me,' and ask of Him remission of sins, when you are insolent to one who is innocent, and hold him responsible for this hunger and great necessity, and then put all brute beasts in the shade when compared with your cruelty. The brute beasts seize the food they need by the compulsion of their bellies. But you, when nothing either pushes or compels you, devour and bite your brother, tearing at him, if not with your teeth, yet with words that bite more cuttingly. How then will you receive the holy oblation [the *prosphoran*, the bread given for use in the Liturgy and transformed into the Body of Christ], when you have empurpled your tongue in human gore? How give the kiss of peace, with mouth gorged with war? Nay, how enjoy every common nourishment, when you are gathering so much venom?[34]

It is impossible to exchange the kiss of peace with one so full of hate and arrogance. If the kiss of peace, one of the most important ritual expressions of charity and forgiveness and an indispensable pre-Communion act of preparation, was impossible to share with such a selfish one, how could Communion be shared?[35] How could

---

Entrance: A History of the Transfer of the Gifts and Other Pre-anaphoral Rites of the Liturgy of St. John Chrysostom (Rome: Pont. Institutum Studiorum Orientalium, 1975), pp. 12–26, 35–52; also ch. 5 passim, esp. pp. 178–86, 192–94.

[32] Homily 21 (PG 60, 606; NPNCF 11, 504).

[33] Homily 21 (PG 60, 607; NPNCF 11, 505).

[34] Homily 21 (PG 60, 608; NPNCF 11, 506).

[35] See Taft, *The Great Entrance*, pp. 50–51, 374–96; Dix, *The Shape of the Liturgy*, pp. 105–110; the *Vita* of St Mary of Egypt by Sophronius.

such a one even enjoy his own dinner in peace, knowing his poisonous attitude toward his neighbours? Chrysostom implies that such an attitude not only disqualifies one from receiving the Holy Communion but bars such a one from even attending or participating in any way in the offering and sanctification of the gifts, as it was standard practice to dismiss the catechumens and others not deemed competent to receive Communion before either the exchange of the kiss of peace or the transfer of gifts to the altar from the chapel where they had been prepared.[36] To refuse to share with those in need barred one from the public, sacramental life of the Church as well as denying any hope or expectation of mercy in one's personal life. This exclusion from Christian society and assembly would presumably end in damnation if there were no repentance; the damnation would be the result of those attitudes, of which the exclusion from sacramental society was a symptom–not a cause.[37]

It also seems apparent that Chrysostom could assume that most of his congregation that could exchange the kiss of peace and receive Communion would do so. There is no mention of the later widespread custom of those deemed 'worthy' of Communion (the baptized who were in no state of formal excommunication or penance) refusing to receive the *mysteria*.[38] Surely Chrysostom would have also castigated those who refused to receive so great a gift if this abstention from Communion were a respected alternative behaviour.[39] He could presume the social force of what was considered 'acceptable behaviour'; refusing Communion would have been considered so shameful that his congregation would have at least seriously considered reforming their actions and attitudes towards the needy rather than abstain from standing inline to receive the Communion with their peers.

Homily 22 continues the theme of compassion, but in this case, the compassion is for those who persecute the righteous. The proper rebuke to the evildoers is the charity of the righteous, by which they heap coals of fire upon the heads of the wicked; this compassion and heaping of coals is not to be done in the gleeful spirit of

---

[36] Juan Mateos, *La Celebration de la Parole dans la Liturgie Byzantine* (Rome: Pont. Institutum Studiorum Orientalium, 1971), pp. 156–58; also Taft, *The Great Entrance*, pp. 40–42, 194, and Dix, *The Shape of the Liturgy*, pp. 436–37.

[37] Homily 21 (PG 60, 608–609; NPNCF 11, 506). For a later, similar identification of vicious mistreatment of others as equivalent to cannibalism see the story concerning Blessed Basil, the Fool-for-Christ rebuking the Czar, Ivan the Terrible on the road outside Moscow during Lent and similar incidents in Dimitry Pospielovsky's *The Orthodox Church in the History of Russia* (Crestwood, NY: St. Vladimir's Seminary Press, 1998), p. 66.

[38] The common name in the Christian East was 'the mysteries' for what were commonly 'the sacraments' in the West; Chrysostom's Homily 85 on the Gospel of John.

[39] Just as he does castigate, on another occasion, those who take advantage of the kiss of peace for rowdy, unseemly behaviour in the church (obscene kisses) in his Homily 30 on II Corinthians. On the frequency of Communion during Chrysostom's time, see Taft, *The Great Entrance*, p. 13.

vengeance, but out of true concern for the welfare of the wicked.[40] The need for humility is stressed again, as in Homily 20. As an interesting aside, Chrysostom takes Romans 12. 16 ('Live in harmony with one another; do not be haughty, but associate with the lowly; never be conceited') and comments:

> Here again he [St Paul, the author of the epistle] insists much upon lowliness of mind. For there was a probability of their being full of high-mindedness, both on account of their city, and from various other causes; he therefore keeps drawing off the dead flesh around the wound, and lowers the inflammation.'[41]

Chrysostom alludes to St Paul's concern that the original Roman recipients of the epistle would be especially liable to temptations of pride because of the city in which they dwelt. Rome could provoke intense loyalty and pride among her inhabitants; is it possible that among 'the sundry other causes' might also be the very charity which was encouraged by the apostle and for which the Church in Rome was famous? Perhaps already when the epistle was written,[42] the organized charity of the Roman parish was taking shape, the charity for which she was said to 'preside in love' over the other churches and which supported beggars, widows, the imprisoned, and anyone who could be considered 'needy'.[43]

The organized charity of the Roman Church was famous throughout the Mediterranean world.[44] Even if not a source of arrogant pride in the time of St Paul, perhaps it was problematic in the days of Chrysostom. While praiseworthy in and of itself, the extent of this charity (the outgrowth of the Roman Christian participation in the eucharistic life of the Church) might have become a source of pride for the local Roman Christians; that the charity itself was something he would want to see maintained at Rome (if not expanded), is apparent in that this charity in action was exactly the sort of work that Chrysostom himself would undertake when he became bishop of Constantinople.[45]

---

[40] Homily 22 (PG 60, 612–13; NPNCF 11, 508–509).

[41] Homily 22 (PG 60, 610; NPNCF 11, 507).

[42] Probably written between AD 54–58, according to the Revised Standard Version's introduction to the epistle (p. 1361).

[43] For a fascinating discussion of the practical working out of this fame for Roman charity and almsgiving in terms of ecclesiastical primacy, see Nicolas Afanassieff's 'The Church Which Presides in Love' in *The Primacy of Peter*, no editor given (London: Faith Press, 1963), pp. 57–110.

[44] Eusebius, *Ecclesiastical History* 4.23, 9–11; see also Roman Garrison, *Redemptive Almsgiving in Early Christianity* (Sheffield, England: Sheffield Academic Press, 1993.) 93–94, also ch. 7 passim.

[45] Kelly, *Golden Mouth*, pp. 119–20, 141, 254.

Chrysostom begins Homily 24 with a reference to Romans 13. 11, '[knowing] what hour it is, how it is full time now for you to wake from sleep.' He thus reminds his flock that time is short until the Judgement Day comes and now is the chance to do good.[46] If they seize the opportunity, Chrysostom tells them, that day will be the day of salvation for them; they need only put on the armour of light and engage 'not in a war but a solemn dance and a feast day' in which all excessive use of food, wine, and sex are repudiated.[47] It is, John insists, not all drinking or sexual activity that he warns his flock to avoid; only the excessive, immoderate use of those good gifts God has given humanity. It is the two primary, 'deadly', passions that he is eager to save them from—lust and anger—by guiding them to avoid the most common circumstances—overfilled stomachs and drunkenness—that give rise to those sinful behaviours. (He even points out that Romans does not condemn making provisions for the flesh but the satisfaction of lusts or excessive desires of the flesh.)[48] It is by 'putting on Christ', a baptismal image and hymn based on Galatians 3. 27, that John encourages his listeners to take advantage of the time remaining until Judgement Day.[49]

He suggests that the faithful are spiritually asleep and invites them to prove they are awake by responding to the sermon. If they are awake, they should be able to tell him which prophet and which apostle had been read just moments ago (evidence that at that time it was standard practice to have readings from the Old Testament as well as the New Testament Epistles); but even if they are awake, he is afraid they are drunk and paying no attention to what they hear.[50] Invite the poor to your parties, he tells the people, and then your parties become a microcosm of the Church and a blessing for the host rather than a source of headaches, hangovers, and a host of other disorders. Sing psalms and hymns, pray, share the occasion with the poor and Christ himself will be present.[51]

Chrysostom then launches into a tirade against drunkenness, which leads to fornication or adultery which in turn leads to the shameful birth or abortion of illegitimate children. Abortion, John asserts, is even worse than murder because it prevents a birth from happening at all. Lest the men in the congregation think John was speaking primarily to the women, he turned to them and said: 'For you don't even let the harlot continue a mere harlot, but make her a murderess also. For even if the daring deed be hers, yet you are the cause of it.'[52]

---

[46] Homily 24 (PG 60, 621; NPNCF 11, 516.)

[47] Homily 24 (PG 60, 623; NPNCF 11, 518.)

[48] Homily 24 (PG 60, 624; NPNCF 11, 518.)

[49] Mateos, *La Celebration*, pp. 110–11, 118–19, 125–26.

[50] Homily 24 (PG 60, 625; NPNCF 11, 519.)

[51] Homily 24 (PG 60, 626; NPNCF 11, 520.)

[52] Homily 24 (PG 60, 627; NPNCF 11, 520.)

Not only was murder the result of sexual misbehaviour in the congregation, Chrysostom asserts, but idolatry also as the women engaged in profane magic to maintain their allure for their lovers or attract new ones. Furthermore, it was known that some of the men ignored their legitimate wives and children in favour of their mistresses and bastards; on the whole, the drunkenness that was the origin of the lustful desires could ruin untold lives and contribute to the downfall of society.

Was there an outburst of immoderate behaviour in Antioch, which demanded Chrysostom's response in 392? Most likely, he was preaching standard Christian ethics (although we cannot rule out a local scandal which caught the attention of his congregation) and moving freely from topic to topic by 'freely associating' images.

It was only by putting on Christ, reverting to the baptismal imagery employed earlier in the sermon, that society can be maintained and saved. By acting with moderation, sanctity could be embraced and salvation won. John continues in this vein by pointing out that there is safety in moderation, safety both now and in eternity. In moderation—if not outright poverty—we are kept free from harm:

> For it is not the having much, but the requiring little, that keeps us from being injured.[…] If we have little, even those that want to exploit us [either wicked humans now or devils on Judgement Day] are powerless to do so.[53]

John reminds the people that Christ lived moderately and cites the example of sitting on the grass rather than at an elaborate banqueting table to eat and having barley loaves rather than finer wheat loaves to eat. By referring to the sitting on the grass and eating barley loaves, Chrysostom is alluding to the miracle (feeding the 5000 with five loaves and two fish) recounted in the sixth chapter of the Gospel of John, a eucharistic type which again situates the moderation Chrysostom is enjoining his people to embrace in a liturgical/eucharistic context.

It is in Homily 23, however, that Chrysostom expands these ideas of Christian liturgical, sacramental life as the basis for ethical civic life to include political ramifications.[54] Preached as they were after the incident of 'the Statues', he underlines the role of the civil magistrates to maintain order and authority. It is this maintenance of order that seems to be the chief role of these secular authorities.

He begins by citing Romans 13. 1, 'Let every person be subject to the governing authorities', and insists that this applies to all members of society—even monks and priests![55] God has created authority in the universe, much as he has created marriage: not that he has chosen in advance and united every married couple or selected each government official but that he has made the universe in such a way that authority and marriage are inherent in its basic structure.[56] Every ruler is minister, a deacon

---

[53] Homily 24 (PG 60, 628; NPNCF 11, 521.)

[54] Homily 23 (PG 60, 613–21; NPNCF 11, 511–16).

[55] Homily 23 (PG 60, 613–5; NPNCF 11, 511).

[56] Homily 23 (PG 60, 615–6; NPNCF 11, 511–12).

(using the same term as the clerical office that assists the priest and bishop) who is doing God's work even if he is not aware that he is doing so. Without these divinely appointed rulers, all things would go to ruin as the world would be turned upside-down and the powerful devour the weaker.[57]

Chrysostom urges his listeners to see the good inherent in the institution of authority and to avoid citing one example of a bad ruler as an excuse to overthrow all government. Not only did St Paul need to encourage his originally intended audience to obey the magistrates and thereby disprove the common accusation that Christians were subversive revolutionaries, but Chrysostom evidently had a party of Christian anarchists in his flock whom he needed to discourage. It is no degrading thing to show deference to the government, Chrysostom continues; he furthermore points out that if it was honourable to obey the authorities while they were yet the officials of pagan Rome, how much more is it appropriate to obey them now that they have embraced Christianity and come into the family of the Church themselves![58]

Love, Chrysostom insists, fulfills all demands of authority and it is divine love, free from all passion (in contrast to human love which is tinged with envy, grudging, and jealousy), which is most able to fulfil those demands of authority. Therefore, 'let us love one another!' Chrysostom exclaims to his Antiochene flock–using the same phrase as they heard the deacon exclaim each week at the kiss of peace during the liturgy.[59] In loving one another with this divine love, the congregation will love God as well, give authority its due and keep the demands of the civil law.[60] It is this exclamation that ties all Chrysostom's themes together, linking morality, political theory, and liturgical practice.

He goes on to point out that because of this pure love, God never 'punishes' but only 'corrects' his wayward creatures and calls them with the voice of an injured or rejected lover. This intense divine love, contrasted with the unbending savagery of fallen humanity, makes it possible for those who finally love God as they ought to delight in the Lord (citing Psalm 37. 4) and experience his kingdom even now—'in as goodly a condition as they that dwell in heaven,' as Chrysostom says.[61] That this experience of love and delight cannot be divorced from the liturgical experience is implied in Chrysostom's use of Psalm 34. 8 as well: 'Taste and see that the Lord is

---

[57] Chrysostom uses again the metaphor of consumption to describe the wicked behaviour of the powerful towards the weak. For a roughly contemporary discussion of wicked folk consuming the body of the dragon [i.e. the Devil] and partaking of his wickedness in opposition to the faithful consuming the body of Christ in Communion and sharing his righteousness and life, see Augustine of Hippo's *On the Psalms* LXXIV.10,12–13.

[58] Homily 23 (PG 60, 615–17; NPNCF 11, 512–14).

[59] Taft, *The Great Entrance*, pp. 380–83.

[60] Homily 23 (PG 60, 619; NPNCF 11, 515).

[61] Homily 23 (PG 60, 621–12; NPNCF 11, 516.)

good,' a standard antiphon during the distribution of Communion.[62] To experience God, to taste what he offers is what the liturgy pledges in anticipation and is worked out in the 'real time' of the faithful's lives.

The sermons on the Epistle to the Romans were preached in Antioch, the 'wild, wild east' of the Roman Empire. Evidently facing a constant threat of chaos, John emphasized the maintenance of good order as the primary, even divine, duty of the civil government. Facing a faction of Christian anarchists who insisted that obedience to any secular authority undermined their dignity as Christians, Chrysostom extolled the virtue of obedience and cooperation with those charged by God to protect the safety of the people: the anarchists could not endanger the whole city by refusing to contribute their share of taxes and whatever else the government determined was required to keep the peace.[63] Although there were certainly government officials in the cathedral congregation when Chrysostom preached these homilies, did any of his ideas alter when he preached on these same themes in the presence of the imperial monarchs themselves?

The sermons on II Thessalonians were preached in Constantinople, in the great church of Hagia Sophia, in 402 (a decade after his homilies on Romans were first preached). The third homily on II Thessalonians begins with the end of the epistle's first chapter and then turns to the beginning of the second chapter:

> They [those who know not God and disobey his commandments] shall suffer the punishment of eternal destruction and exclusion from the presence of the Lord and from the glory of his might, when he comes on that day to be glorified in his saints, and to be marveled at in all who have believed. Let no one deceive you in any way; for that day will not come, unless the rebellion comes first, and the man of lawlessness is revealed, the son of perdition, who opposes and exalts himself against every so-called god or object of worship, so that he takes his seat in the temple of God, proclaiming himself to be God.' (II Thessalonians 1. 9–10, 2. 3–4; 'that day' referring to the Last Day and the end of time when Christ comes again to judge the world, as also in II Peter 3. 10).

John picks up on the theme of doing good, reminding the imperial capital that even though many think hell not so terrible as described by preachers and biblical readings, it is in fact even more terrible than described.[64] Tribulation for the sake of Christ, Chrysostom tells his pampered congregation, is glory: glory for God, who has given strength to his saints and glory for us, who have rendered ourselves worthy

[62] Robert Taft, 'The Pontifical Liturgy of the Great Church According to a Twelfth-century Diataxis in Codex British Museum Add. 34060' in *Orientalia Christiana Periodica* (Rome: Pont. Institutum Orientalium Studiorum, 45, spring 1979), pp. 119–122.

[63] Dvornik writes, 'Christians could not refuse to the state—even a pagan state—the necessary services and contributions which the state needed for the realization of its goal,' in his *Early Christian and Byzantine Political Philosophy*, I, p. 452.

[64] Homily 3 (PG 62, 479–80; NPNCF 13, 384).

by enduring the tribulation.[65] He warns them that the general resurrection of the dead is coming but at a time that no one can predict and that anyone who claims to know—even if they produce a letter they purport is from Paul himself—is lying. It is this tribulation and time of lying that must in fact precede the resurrection and is inspired by the Antichrist.

> Here [St Paul] discourses concerning the Antichrist, and reveals great mysteries. What is the 'falling away?' He calls him Apostasy, as being able to destroy many, and make them fall away. So that if it were possible, [Christ] says, the very elect should be offended [Matthew 24. 24]. And he calls him 'the man of sin.' For he shall do numberless mischiefs, and shall cause others to do them. But he calls him 'the son of perdition' because he is to be destroyed.[66]

The Antichrist, aiming to destroy the faithful, will not be Satan himself, but a man who will set himself up with Satan's aid as an opponent of God. The Antichrist will order men to worship him instead of God and set himself up in the temple of God, 'not that in Jerusalem only, but also in every church'.[67] Performing miracles and winning spontaneous acclaim for himself, the Antichrist will lure humanity to serve him; it is in the temple which is the church of God, gathered and assembled to offer the sacrifice of praise—it is in the corruption of the liturgy—that the Antichrist will be shown for what he is.

Chrysostom turns again to themes that he preached in Antioch: seeds of virtue are planted in each soul, but these seeds need tending; thorns threaten to grow and choke these seeds; wealth is a thorn, and the unmerciful soul is the habitat of thorns. Those who hear his words should heed them, repenting here and now; they should pay attention in response to the the deacon's frequent 'Let us attend!' at the readings and throughout the Eucharist. The should throw themselves into the performance of good works: '[R]epent, and obtain the promised blessings,' John exhorts the wealthy and the powerful.[68] John describes how the wealthy enter the church attended by slaves, decked in their finery, and look around to be sure everybody else notices them. The wealthy can't even be bothered to move another parishioner standing in their way, either; they expect someone else to move others around for them. 'They seem to think that they are doing us, and maybe even God, a favour by coming to church!' he exclaims. John also points out that although the reader announces 'Thus says the Lord' as the introduction to the portion to be read, the congregation seems unaware that it is God himself who speaks to them during these lections in the liturgical assembly. The same folk that would pay rapt attention to a royal messenger ignore the divine prophets. 'The Liturgy is always the same,' the congregation complains;

---

[65] Homily 3 (PG 62, 480; NPNCF 13, 385).

[66] Homily 3 (PG 62, 482; NPNCF 13, 386).

[67] Homily 3 (PG 62, 482; NPNCF 13, 386).

[68] Homily 3 (PG 62, 483–84; NPNCF 13, 386–87).

the world itself is 'always the same' he points out to them and all excuses to avoid taking the Church's liturgy and preaching seriously are just that: excuses. The liturgical experience remains fundamental to John's preaching and his expectations for his congregation.

As he continues his thought in Homily 4, he turns to the apostle's words to the Thessalonians:

> And now you know that which restrains, to the end that he may be revealed in his own season. For the mystery of lawlessness is already at work; only there is one that restrains now, until he be taken out of the way. And then shall be revealed the lawless one, whom the Lord Jesus shall slay with the breath of His mouth, and bring to naught by the manifestation of His coming: even he whose coming is according to the work of Satan.' (II Thessalonians 2. 6–9)

'What restrains?' John asks. Some say the Spirit, he answers, and some say the Roman Empire. John endorses the latter opinion: 'I agree with those who say it is the Empire.'[69] If the apostle Paul had meant the Spirit, he would have said so plainly, John asserts; he had to speak in code because it was dangerous to say out loud that there would come a time when Rome would not be there to restrain the Antichrist.[70] Even though some of those exercising imperial dominion were wicked (or even types of the Antichrist, such as Nero), that does not detract from the central role of the Roman government *per se* (any more than a bad local governor means all 'authority' is ill-founded, as John preached in his series on Romans). Rome, even pagan Rome that persecutes the Christians, staunches the anarchy and chaos that inevitably arise in the absence of a strong civil government; it is in preventing this outbreak of anarchy that Rome restrains the Antichrist who would otherwise seize his opportunity in the confusion following the fall of Rome. Rome is in fact so important in restraining his bid for power that the Antichrist himself will be driven to destroy Rome (the deceiver himself to be destroyed later by Christ, by 'the breath of His mouth' at his second coming).[71]

Chrysostom considered the Antichrist to be the personification of chaos and destruction; there had been many types or anticipations of Antichrist and there would be many more to come, each probably more horrific than the last.[72] It was the power of Rome (even in her pagan days) that kept that complete anarchy and destruction at bay. It was Rome that made the experience of beauty in all its senses[73] and the

---

[69] Homily 4 (PG 62, 485–86; NPNCF 13, 388).

[70] Homily 4 (PG 62, 485–86; NPNCF 13, 389).

[71] Homily 4 (PG 62, 486; NPNCF 13, 389).

[72] Homily 4(PG 62, 486–87; NPNCF 13, 389); compare Homily 3 on II Thessalonians(PG 62, 482; NPNCF 13, 386).

[73] See above, Homily 20 on Romans.

preaching of the Gospel possible by making universal peace a reality.[74] Good citizen that he was, he thought of himself as a 'Roman' living in the 'New Rome' of the ongoing 'Roman Empire' which continued to restrain the Antichrist. In fact, it must be pointed out that Chrysostom never lived to see the fall of the Old Rome in the West and therefore would all the more consider himself a citizen of the 'one empire' which had simply moved its political bureaucracy from Italy to the Bosphorus. This trust in the royal figure fending off supernatural evil is a primeval religious idea with deep roots; Chrysostom is here tapping into ideas which had shaped ancient Jewish practice and would continue to be felt for centuries following John's preaching.[75]

But why, asks Chrysostom, 'did God permit this? What dispensation is this? What is the advantage of his coming, if it take place for the ruin of our race?' The advantage, he says, is that the wicked will be exterminated and there will be no doubt of their perversity: they will have had every opportunity to repent and their refusal to have done so will be apparent to all. Furthermore, the righteous will be vindicated and their glory be made as obvious as the perversity of the wicked (picking up on his opening remarks in Homily 3, that in enduring tribulation the righteous demonstrate their deserving of the acclaim they have won).[76]

John urges the faithful to battle the Antichrist and his minions not with armour 'but with prayers and supplication.'

> For if thus the ancients made war with men in arms, much more ought we to make war with men without arms. So Hezekiah triumphed over the Assyrian king, so Moses over Amalek, so Samuel over the thirty-two kings. If where there was need of arms, and of battle array, and of fighting, they, leaving their arms, had recourse to prayer; here

---

[74] Dostoyevsky articulated a very basic eastern patristic notion when he said—through the mouth of Prince Myshkin in *The Idiot*—that 'Beauty will save the world'. Beauty is one of the primary divine attributes and it is in becoming beautiful that mankind reaches and expresses salvation' or communion with the Divine. The eighth century kontakion (a liturgical hymn) for the first Sunday of Lent states: 'No one could describe the Word of the Father; but when He took flesh from you, O Theotokos, He accepted to be described, and restored the fallen image to its former state by uniting it to divine beauty.' (*The Divine Liturgy*, p. 163) The woman clothed with the sun (Apocalypse 12) is beautiful; the heavenly city, the New Jerusalem (Apocalypse 21) is beautiful; the Scarlet Woman (Apocalypse 17) is alluring and seductive but she is not beautiful.

[75] For an examination of the ancient Israelite belief in the kings of Israel as the 'first line of defense' against the evil angels, see Margaret Barker, *The Lost Prophet* (London: SPCK, 1988), p. 46. The Fathers would say that 'that which restrains the Antichrist' only completely gave way in 1917–1918 with the fall of Austro-Hungary in the West and of imperial Russia in the East—the two last governments representing themselves as the continuation of the Roman Empire.

[76] Homily 4 (PG 62, 487; NPNCF 13, 390).

> where the matter has to be accomplished by prayers alone, does it not much more behoove us to pray?[77]

False or misplaced modesty may prompt some to protest that in the cases John cites it was the rulers who interceded for the people, who were 'wretched and mean persons'. John agrees that in those cases it was the rulers who surpassed the ruled in personal sanctity, but now we 'find among those who are ruled many or rather the greater part excelling their ruler in a great degree; do not deprive us of this succour, raise up our hands that we may not be faint, open our mouth for us, that it may not be closed.' John is here alluding to both Moses's holding his arms aloft in prayer during the battle with Amalek, during which the Israelites triumphed so long as his hands were aloft. When he tired, Aaron and Hur held his arms up so that the Israelites would continue to conquer through the *orans* position in which Christians would stand to pray with hands aloft.[78]

Pointing out that Christians in general and clergy in particular are in the midst of this battle with the forces of chaos and evil, Chrysostom implores his spiritual children to pray for him in his need.

> I am greatly in need of your prayers. Let no one, as I have said, from an excessive humility deprive me of this alliance and succor. If our part be well approved, your own also will be more honorable. If our teaching flow abundantly, the riches will redound to you. Hear the prophet saying, 'Do the shepherds feed themselves?'[Ezekiel 34. 2, LXX].[79]

Anything accomplished by the one prayed for is 'credited to the account', as it were, of the one who does the praying. It is the prayer of a man for others, not himself, that expresses love and is most likely to be heard by God on high. It is this intercession for others that is most becoming for a cleric and makes a layman of equal honour to the cleric. It is in their mutual, public intercessions that love is expressed and power revealed: 'For that which a man praying by himself is not able to receive, that he shall receive praying with a multitude. Why? Because although his own virtue has not, yet the common consent has much power.'[80]

Mutual pardon and reconciliation is the foundation of this mutual common prayer, pardon between layfolk who offend each other and pardon between clergy and laity who offend each other. John admits that clergy make mistakes, and are even more likely to make mistakes than the laity (given that the clergy are responsible for greater numbers than even the most prosperous laity who bear responsibility for their extended households).

---

[77] Homily 4 (PG 62, 489–90; NPNCF 13, 391).

[78] For the battle with Amalek, see Exodus 17; on the *orans* position for prayer, see Tertullian's *Apology* 30.

[79] Homily 4 (PG 62, 490; NPNCF 13, 391).

[80] Homily 4 (PG 62, 491; NPNCF 13, 392).

Taking the analogy of a family household further, John paints a word picture of a father who cares for his multitude of children, and is harassed by the number of his worries. Nevertheless, he does not wish to lose a single child, and shares the same foods of the table with his children. In the case of the household which is the Church, however, the table which the father and children share is the altar, the table of the Lord, and the food is the Lamb of God, the Body and Blood of Christ. They all share the one Lamb and share the same life and honour as a result. The familial sharing of the lamb harks back to the Old Testament injunction that each family should share one lamb at the Exodus and its annual commemoration at Passover as well as the Greek-Christian practice of calling the portion of *prosphora* which becomes the Body of Christ at the Eucharist 'the Lamb.'[81] The eucharistic/liturgical allusion is clearly what Chrysostom had in mind as the reference comes in the midst of the discussion of sharing the sacramental life of the Church as a family.[82] John concludes his sermon by describing his cares and worries for his spiritual children. His pangs and griefs on their behalf are like a mother's birthpangs, but at least a mother's pangs are finished when the child has been born—he claims—whereas his continue until each of his spiritual children see the day of the Lord with confidence and pass through the judgement unscathed. Later Byzantine and Slavic churchmen pick up this thread of Chrysostom's and identify the imperial authority—as well as the clergy—as the father, the *batushka*, of his subjects. The ruler feeds and clothes his children, his subjects, as well as defends them against disorder, oppression, and wickedness.[83]

What can we glean from our examination of John's preaching on Romans 12–13 and II Thessalonians 2? First, in terms of the liturgy itself, we can establish that:

---

[81] For the fully developed practice of reciting verses from Isaiah 53 while cutting and preparing the *prosphora* for use, see *The Divine Liturgy*, pp. 14–16.

[82] Homily 4 (PG 62, 492; NPNCF 13, 392). John is here also tapping into the same set of images and thinking that were employed by Gregory Nanzianzus, one of his predecessors in the episcopal throne of Constantinople, in Gregory's *Oration* XLV (*On Holy Pascha II*, Sections XIV and XXVI; PG 36, 641–4, 657–60). Whether John is directly relying on Gregory's homily or not, the ideas and vocabulary are certainly reminiscent of each other and underscore the interdependence of sheep and shepherd, laity and clergy, congregation and bishop which John is at pains to point out here. John is also pointing out what was probably obvious to his congregation: that the clergy received Communion themselves before giving the mysteries to the laity.

[83] See the mid-eleventh century 'Sermon on Law and Grace' (chs 42–66) by Metropolitan Ilarion of Kiev; English translation available in *Sermons and Rhetoric of Kievan Rus* (Simon Franklin, introduction and translation) of the *Harvard Library of Early Ukrainian Literature* (vol. V, 1991.

*the terms *thusia* (sacrifice) and *prosphora* (offering, as an act and as the bread used in the Eucharist) already evoked liturgical associations and practices for the faithful;

*there were at least three readings at the Divine Liturgy: an Old Testament reading, probably from the prophets, as well as readings from the Epistles and Gospels;

*the reader included 'Thus says the Lord,' as part of the Old Testament reading, either as part of the stylized introduction to the selection or as part of the text itself;

*the congregation was noisy during the readings, making it difficult even for those who wanted to pay attention to hear what the lector was proclaiming;[84] related to this, it is clear that outside the liturgy silence was imposed on the people when an imperial decree was read in public and that the silence was not even so much imposed as a spontaneous reaction of the crowd which was nervously waiting for the reading of the emperor's words;

*the fourth-century congregation was already familiar with the deacon's exclamations still used among eastern Christians, such as 'Let us love one another!' at the kiss of peace and 'Let us stand aright!' at the opening dialogue (which the western Christians would come to call the *sursum corda*) of the *anaphora*;

*the kiss of peace was a prominent liturgical act and considered inseparable from the reception of Holy Communion and it was expected that those able to share the kiss and receive Communion would do so;

*the intercessions (prayer on behalf of others) was a vital liturgical act as well, and the 'Great Litany' following the sermon[85] and the intercessory portions of the *anaphora*(eucharistic or consecration prayer) were emphasized[86] and

*the clergy received Communion amongst themselves before turning and bringing the mysteries to the laity.

---

[84] It is worth noting that Gabriel Bertoniere in his *Historical Development of the Easter Vigil and Related Services in the Greek Church*, Orientalia Christiana Analecta, 193 (Rome: Pont. Institutum Studiorum Orientalium, 1972) cites a rubric directing two simultaneous readings of the Gospel at the Paschal Eucharist in the cathedral of Constantinople: one by the bishop at his throne in the apse, the other by a deacon at the bema in the midst of the church. While his theory is that the deacon is acting as a 'human loudspeaker,' enabling the whole congregation in the vast building to hear the Gospel reading, certainly has merit the practice may also reflect older practice (cf. Anton Baumstark's *Comparative Liturgy* (London: Mowbray, 1958), ch. 2 for the persistence of older customs at Holy Week and Easter) which developed to combat the very problem John was complaining about in his sermons in the Constantinople cathedral: chatting and noise among the congregation, making it impossible to hear the reading being chanted.

[85] On the development of the form of 'litany,' see Dix, *The Shape of the Liturgy*, p. 46, and Mateos, *La Celebration*, pp. 29–31, 162–63, 168–73.

[86] For the historical development of the intercessory portions of the *anaphora*, see Robert Taft, *The Diptychs* (Rome: Pont.Institutum Studiorum Orientalium, 1991).

Secondly, reconciliation and love were the hinges between daily behaviour and liturgical life—what was liturgically enacted on Sunday mornings was to be lived out during the rest of the week or (from an other perspective) one's daily behaviour was to be summarized and fulfilled in the liturgy on Sundays. The love was to be revealed in marital fidelity, sobriety and moderation in consumption of all kinds, alms giving, patience and refraining from judgement of others, intercession for others, and obedience to the government authorities.

Thirdly, in being obedient to the authorities, the faithful would be honouring God and aiding in the struggle to fend off the Antichrist. The coming of the Antichrist, whether considered one man, a series of men or the personification of chaos, might be inevitable, but could be postponed as long as possible by the Roman Empire securing the borders and maintaining the *pax Romana*. The political theory we can tease out of John's preaching had both practical and mystical aspects: in practical terms, obedience was due to the authorities as they were responsible for maintaining order and in mystical terms this obedience was part of a great cosmic struggle between the forces of good and evil, light and darkness, destruction and beauty.

But what about the authorities themselves listening to John's preaching, either in Antioch or in Constantinople? John—although not yet embroiled in the worst of his conflicts with the imperial family, clearly saw on the horizon the trouble coming and refrained from castigating the powerful simply for being powerful.[87] Even wealth, in and of itself, was not an absolute barrier to salvation but did make salvation a less likely prospect for the wealthy; power, on the other hand, could be wielded by the unworthy, but was never itself a threat to their salvation. As the public authorities heard these injunctions to love and these descriptions of the obedience due them as they carried out their duties, what would they conclude about their behaviour during the week following the Sunday liturgy?

One conclusion they might draw would be the need to maintain order by enforcing certain standards of behaviour on the public, taking Chrysostom's castigations and exhortations and compelling the population's adherence to the behaviour he expects: prohibiting prostitution, murder, abortion, and trafficking in magic or charms, setting up government relief agencies or soup kitchens, enforcing public sobriety, punishing treason or other acts of civil disobedience, and rendering obedience themselves to those who bore authority over them as well.[88] In all these acts, they could see themselves as holding chaos and the Antichrist at bay and furthering (or at least maintaining) the life of the Kingdom of God on earth.

When the emperor himself heard these sermons in Constantinople, how might he have received these ideas differently from the authorities in Antioch or his subordinates? It is certainly possible that he would see it as his personal duty to

---

[87] J. N. D. Kelly, *Golden Mouth*, chs 12–15.

[88] Constantine's outlawing of love charms (Dvornik, *Early Christian and Byzantine Political Philosophy*, 2, p. 755) had clearly not had the desired effect.

maintain the imperial unity as a prerequisite to his participating in the Eucharist.[89] He could feel the weight on his shoulders personally to stall the advent of the Antichrist, which would give a further urgency to his imperial responsibility. He might consider it his responsibility to 'assist' his subjects in living ethical, Christian lives as necessary to his participating in the Eucharist in good conscience. We must also bear in mind that Arcadius, the emperor who would have heard John's preaching in Constantinople, was only the second emperor to actually rule as a baptized Christian. When Constantine legalized Christianity in 313 he was enrolled as a catechumen—a candidate preparing for baptism—and was baptized only on his death bed. This tradition of imperial deathbed baptisms continued as the violent responsibilities of ruling—such as war and executions—were considered inappropriate and even impossible for baptized Christians to carry out.[90] It was Theodosius I's recovery after being baptized at death's door [380 AD] that the 'birth pangs' of what it meant to be a baptized Christian emperor began. The conflicts of Theodosius with Ambrose of Milan can be seen at least in part as one aspect of this painful process of transition; furthermore, Theodosius's dismantling of classical pagan culture and the legal establishment of Christianity (which was finalized under Justinian) can also be seen as the results of Theodosius's wrestling with his conscience in his efforts to determine what was appropriate conduct for an emperor who was actually baptized and not merely a catechumen. Chrysostom's preaching, heard by Arcadius and even heeded on occasion, certainly played a role in the emperor's assessment of his dual responsibilities, both as a Christian personally and as ruler of the Roman world politically, and how these roles were to be reconciled.[91] It is not inconceivable that Arcadius and subsequent emperors saw their divinely sanctioned function in world politics as complementary to the ministry of Chrysostom himself: the bishop and the emperor were each charged with facilitating and safeguarding the Christian lives of those committed to their charge. It was the two faces of one ministry committed to two different orders in the Church.[92]

---

[89] See John Meyendorff, *Imperial Unity and Christian Divisions* (Crestwood: St. Vladimir's Seminary Press, 1989), ch. 1, passim, for a discussion of the Byzantine Empire providing a sense of unity in the face of ecclesiastical schisms and cultural pluralism.

[90] Tertullian, *On Idolatry* 17–19.

[91] Chrysostom's sermon on the occasion of Eudoxia using imperial power to seize a widow's vineyard certainly had ramifications for the imperial couple both as private citizens and political personages; see *Vita Porphyrii* (32–54) and Zosimas's *New History* (5.24.1–2). For the conflict between personal responsibility as a Christian and political responsibility as imperial ruler among the newly-converted Rus', see the experience of Vladimir of Kiev in *The Russian Primary Chronicle* (6502–6504).

[92] While complementary, these two ministries of imperial dignity and priesthood were by no means equal in Chrysostom's thinking: 'The office that prevails in the Church excels the civil office as heaven excels the earth.' (Homily 15 on II Corinthians, PG 61, 507; cited by Meyendorff in *Imperial Unity and Christian Divisions*, p. 36).

Chrysostom's preaching certainly laid the groundwork for the emperors to work out God's mandate for their political and personal lives. John created the climate in which it was possible for later Byzantine political theory to flourish and in which it was possible for Justinian, as both a lay member of the Church and as emperor, to proclaim on 6 March 535:

> The greatest gifts that God's heavenly *philanthropia* bestowed upon men are the sacerdotium and the *basileia*, of which the former serves divine matters, the latter presides and watches over human affairs, and both proceed from one and the same principle and regulate human life. Hence, nothing should claim the emperors' care so much as the saintliness of the priests, since these constantly pray to God for them [the emperors]. For, if the priesthood is in every way blameless and acceptable to God, and the *basileia* rules justly and properly over the state entrusted to it, good harmony (*symphonia*) will result, which will bestow whatever is beneficial upon the human race.[93]

Two months later, Justinian is even more explicit: 'The priesthood and the imperium do not differ so very much, nor are sacred things so very different from those of public and common interest.'[94] While not quoting Chrysostom's sermons of more than a century earlier, John's ideas are clearly in the background of Justinian's edicts: the imperial authority is given to the world to act as the primary barrier against chaos, disorder, and ruin. By establishing peace and maintaining order, the imperial authorities acted out of love and charity for those poor and powerless who would otherwise be destroyed by the greed and might of the powerful. A stable society was more conducive to charity and almsgiving than an insecure society in which each citizen would be too preoccupied with the struggle for his own survival to bother caring for his neighbour. While the immediate historical circumstances prompting Justinian's thoughts were very different in their details from the circumstances in which Chrysostom preached, the notion that the imperium is given to the world for mankind's (and the Church's) protection against disarray and confusion—the powers of the Antichrist—echo in Justinian's assertion that good harmony will result when the emperor and his government rule justly and properly. We can see the continuing importance of intercession in Justinian's formulation of the relations between the emperor and the clergy, a reliance that the fourth-century bishop would have approved of in Arcadius's sixth-century successor. Justinian's military policy can also be seen as another aspect of the royal function to restrain the

---

[93] Francis Dvornik, *Early Christian and Byzantine Political Philosophy: Origins and Background.* (Washington DC: Dumbarton Oaks Center for Byzantine Studies, 1966) II, p. 816. It is interesting to note that in this outstanding, monumental study Dvornik thoroughly reviews Chrysostom's political ideas without ever citing the sermons on Romans or II Thessalonians and drops all discussion of patristic ideas about the Antichrist after the late second/early third century authors.

[94] Dvornik, *Early Christian and Byzantine Political Philosophy.* II, p. 816.

Antichrist: by re-establishing Byzantine (i.e. Roman) dominion in the western territories, he was not simply extending his own power or the glory of the state, but was liberating the western territories from barbarian rule reintegrating them into the one Empire as opposed to a multitude of smaller kingdoms and warring municipalities, and freeing them from the confusion and disorder which was inherently a mark of the Antichrist's rule.[95]

John Chrysostom's sermons examined here serve as a cultural link in the tradition of royal figures called to subvert evil and destruction. By referring to the eucharistic liturgy and alluding to various liturgical actions and phrases, John was able to share his vision of the Sunday Eucharist as a stylized enactment of a well-ordered society in which everyone had their proper place and shared their mutual love and self-giving in the varying forms of alms, intercession, *prosphora*, kiss of peace, and Communion.[96] Behaviour in the street should be the free-form, spontaneous version of the stylized behaviour in the church. Why should the one behaviour reflect the other? Because the *polis*, the city or community-at-large, comes to the church to kiss one another and receive Holy Communion together. Each was to serve the other in the streets and in their homes, just as they were each to serve the other in the church.

It was this stylized liturgical action which Chrysostom expected would be the basis for, and the goal of, the weekday behaviour of his congregations in Antioch and Constantinople. These expectations shaped not only the behaviour of fourth-century Antiochenes and Constantinopolitans, but all those who have lived in eastern Christian territories since.

---

[95] Dvornik, *Early Christian and Byzantine Political Philosophy*. II, p. 839.

[96] For a description of who should stand where in church during the liturgy from Antiochene territory in the fourth century, see the *Apostolic Constitutions*, 2.8 and 8.11.

Preaching the Dead from Their Graves: Bernard of Clairvaux's Lament on His Brother Gerard

WIM VERBAAL

Bernard of Clairvaux is known as one of the most formidable preachers in Western Christianity. His fame is based, in the first place, on the corpus of sermons that he published during his life. Among them, his commentary on the Canticle is universally acknowledged a masterpiece. Yet an important pecularity of this corpus has always been forgotten: Bernard's sermons on the Canticle as they are known today meet all the requirements of the highest literary standards. They do not testify so much to Bernard's oratorical skills as to his talents as an author. They are not meant to be heard but to be read, to be studied with attention.[1]

Considering Bernard's sermons to be a literary product instead of the expression of oral preaching has far-reaching consequences for the interpretation of the so-called autobiographical passages they contain. When the sermons must be considered as written literature, the presence of the author in the text ought to be interpreted from the viewpoint of a literary functionality: why does the author think it necessary to confront the reader with his own person? What does his appearance in the text contribute to the message he wants to transfer? If Bernard is as consequential in these passages as he shows himself to be everywhere else, they might need a more careful reading in order to avoid interpreting them in a purely positivistic way as testifying to Bernard's personal opinions and sentiments.[2]

---

[1] In other places I have entered more deeply into this question. See my article 'Réalités quotidiennes et fiction littéraire dans les *Sermons sur le Cantique* de Bernard de Clairvaux', *Cîteaux*, 51 (2000) 201–18, which contains a reaction to Prof. Christopher Holdsworth's article, 'Were the Sermons of St. Bernard on the Song of Songs ever Preached?' in *Medieval Monastic Preaching*, ed. by Carolyn Muessig (Leiden: Brill, 1998), pp. 295–318. Our discussion still continues, as it ought to be, between friends.

[2] For the analysis of his appearance in another sort of text, the *Vita Malachiae*, see my article 'Le saint et moi. Le "narrateur": une donnée structurelle dans l'hagiographie

Bernard, in fact, never wrote anything documentary to give testimony of himself. He did not compose any historical or autobiographical text which provides insight into his mind or heart. In all his writings Bernard addresses the actual reader. With his texts he always pursues concrete and practical aims. For this reason, he never published anything that can be described as *Confessions* or *Soliloquia,*[3] but rather *Sermons* and *Treatises*: texts meant for exhortation and instruction, never personal meditations or prayers. Among Bernard's works that were already published by himself there is not one that does not explicitly refer in some way or another to the presence of a reader. The reader never remains outside. Never an onlooker, he is essential to the textual event.

Very often, therefore, Bernard's use of the first person singular (*ego*) does not refer to his own historical reality. In most cases the *ego* aims at an identification of the reader with the message of the text. The writer offers a sort of *figura* for the reader, who ought to recognize his own reality in the words of the text, which normally elucidate a biblical passage. The *ego* in the text constitutes a bridge between the concrete, historical reality of each reader and the eternal truth of the Bible. Conformation to the *ego* in the text is the first essential step in the transformation of the reader and of his material reality into the spiritual and textual reality of the living Word as expressed in the Bible.[4]

Yet a few passages within the corpus of Bernard's sermons seem to evade a similar interpretation of the *ego*. They are so closely connected to his own personal and unique life-story that it seems impossible to give them any functional interpretation for a reader. Besides, they often constitute rather large and independent texts, whereas the appearance of the *ego* as a *figura* for the reader is normally well prepared in the preceding paragraphs, remains rather limited in proportion and is closely integrated into the context. For this reason, the

---

bernardine', in *Hagiographica*, IX (2002), 19–44 and '*Revocare vitam*. Bernard of Clairvaux writing a friend's life'. *Revue Mabillon*, 75 (2003), 153–78.

[3] In all only one *Soliloquium* is known under Bernard's name but he himself has never published it. It can be found in the third collection of his *Sententiae* as number 125: Jean Leclercq and Henri-Marie Rochais, *Sancti Bernardi Opera* (= SBO) VI–2 (Rome: Editiones cistercienses, 1972), pp. 239–40. This collection was created by the modern editors to put together 127 texts that could be ascribed to Bernard but that had to be collected from the most disparate manuscripts. The *Soliloquium* itself is only found in four manuscripts. Compare Jean Leclercq, *Études sur saint Bernard et ses écrits*. *Analecta Sacri Ordinis Cisterciensis*, 9 (1953), 147–48.

[4] This has been largely elaborated in my 'Een goddelijke tragedie. Triomf en nederlaag in het Woord bij Bernardus van Clairvaux' (unpublished doctoral dissertation, University of Ghent, 2000). Parts of it have found their expression in the article in *Cîteaux*, 51 (2000) and in the article 'Annoncer le Verbe. Les homélies sur le *Missus est* de saint Bernard' in *Collectanea cisterciensia*, 65 (2003), pp. 111–36 and 193–221. Still other publications are in preparation.

'autobiographical' passages have been all too often studied separately without taking their setting into account. Only very recently have the dangers of this approach been indicated and attempts made to interpret Bernard's 'confessions' as an integral part of the textual framework.[5]

1. Bernard's Mourning?[6]

One of the most problematic 'autobiographical' passages in the work of Bernard has always been the lament for the death of his brother Gerard. It takes up most of the twenty-sixth sermon of his commentary on the Canticle. Already Bernard's own contemporaries criticized his fusion of different literary styles that changed the nuptial banquet into a funeral meal, the wedding song into a wake.[7] Indeed, this outburst of personal grief in the middle of an exegetical commentary of the highest literary and spiritual density makes one pause. Is there really no link at all to the structure of the whole commentary?

The lament interrupts Bernard's exegesis on verse 1, 4[b] of the Canticle: 'Sicut tabernacula Cedar sicut pelles Salomonis'.[8] In the beginning of the sermon he first indicates how he will proceed, and he then interprets the first part of the verse. But to go into the more subtle secrets of the second part is too much for him now. He needs the support of his audience.[9] Bernard often ends his sermons with a similar request for aid in his inspiration from the prayers of his audience. Yet this time the phrase is

---

[5] The first attempts were made by literary scientists who were the first to question the personal and spontaneous way a writer expresses his own emotions in his work. Important for Bernard have been Peter Von Moos, *Consolatio. Studien zur mittellateinischen Trostliteratur über den Tod und zum Problem der christlichen Trauer*. 4 vols (Munich: Fink, 1971), Brian Stock, *The Implications of Literacy. Written Language and Models of Interpretation in the Eleventh and Twelfth Centuries*. (Princeton: Princeton University Press, 1983), Marinus Burcht Pranger, *Bernard of Clairvaux and the Shape of Monastic Thought* (Leiden: Brill, 1994).

[6] Bernard's writings were originally intended for Cistercian monks. Therefore, I characterize the reader as male in my analysis. In so doing, I do not intend to minimize the reading experiences of later female readers, but instead to emphasize the revolutionary mental step Bernard was requiring of his clerical and knightly monks. These male readers were asked to identify with the female protagonist of the Canticle.

[7] Compare Berengar of Poitiers in his *Apologia contra sanctum Bernardum*, edited by R. M. Thomson, 'The Satirical Works of Berengar of Poitiers. An Edition with Introduction', *Mediaeval Studies*, 42 (1980), 89–138, esp. p. 121.

[8] Verse 1. 5 in the King James Version: 'As the tents of Kedar, as the curtains of Solomon'.

[9] Sermon on the Canticle (= SC) 26.2, SBO I (1957), pp. 170–71.

immediately followed by a short remark that proves to be the opening of the true sermon: 'Though the end is also imposed by the grief for the calamity that I suffer'.[10]

The distant exegete who has been speaking in the preceding paragraphs seems to utter this short sentence only to explain his premature breaking off. If the phrase had been mirroring a real historic situation, the sermon would have remained one of the shortest in Bernard's corpus. Knowing the reasons for Bernard's grief, the monks surely would have contented themselves with his remark. The chapter would have been dissolved earlier than usual and everyone would have returned to his daily duties.

This reconstruction of an acceptable historical truth does not however meet the exigencies of textual reality. No reader can know the grief that overwhelms Bernard at a certain moment when he wants to explain to his monks a verse of the Canticle. The unexpected breaking-off of the written sermon would leave him perplexed. It asks for a marginal gloss, for a footnote. The sermon could not stand alone. It would give an unfinished impression. Therefore the sermon cannot finish even when, in the text, Bernard is overwhelmed by pain and grief. The strength of his mourning does not allow him to finish, but rather pushes him on to continue. The end he announces is only an ending before the end.[11]

The continuation of the sermon, however, has the effect of a surprise attack on the reader. Nothing in the detached and neutral exposition of the preceding paragraphs prepared the reader for the complete inversion of style which follows. Suddenly the reader hears the cry of despair of a man. An entirely different world enters the text. Just as grief had overwhelmed the speaker and made him abort his exposition of the Bible, now the expression of this grief overwhelms the reader. Not only the exegesis but also the reading itself is interrupted. The distance which the exegete keeps towards the subject of his discourse is swept away and annihilates the reflective attitude of the reader. From now on the reader is less reader than witness. He looks right into the inner self of a suffering fellow man.

This brusque change in the text and the surprise of the reader are the principal reasons for the unshaken belief in Bernard's sincerity when he wrote these words. 'Cette oraison funèbre, ouverte par une explosion involontaire de la douleur et fermée brusquement par des sanglots, est le monument le plus complet et le témoignage le plus irrécusable de la sensibilité de Bernard.'[12] 'Non qu'on doive, généralement, mettre en doute leur sincérité; mais il n'est pas toujours facile de

---

[10] SC 26.2, SBO I (1957) p. 171.

[11] Compare a similar technique at the end of the whole commentary SC 83.6: *Et si probatis, facio finem etiam ante finem [...]*, SBO II (1958), p. 302.

[12] Elphège Vacandard, *Vie de saint Bernard*, 2 volumes (Paris: Victor Lecoffre, 1895) II, p. 55: 'This funeral oration, which opens by an involuntary explosion of pain and stops abruptly in tears, is the most complete monument and the most irrefutable testimony of Bernard's sensitivity.'

distinguer, dans leurs déclarations, ce qui est spontané de ce qui est plus ou moins contraint, imposé par les lois du style ou d'un genre littéraire. [...] l'abbé de Clairvaux y a mis tout son art, parce qu'il y mettait toute son affection.'[13] Even in the most recent edition we can read: 'Ce sermon a toujours beaucoup retenu l'attention. Il interrompt le cours normal de l'exposé. De plus, Bernard devient ici tellement personnel qu'on ressent directement les vibrations de sa vie affective.'[14]

Such expressions are contradicted by Bernard's attitude to writing.[15] He did not write for himself. He did not just want to erect a monument for himself or for the people who were dear to him. He never forgets the reasons for his writing. He seeks the transformation of his readers. His texts are therefore treasures of refinement, literary and spiritual, and especially the passages in which he seems to utter his most intimate affections appear to be masterpieces of a polished literary style.[16]

2. *A Sermon Among Sermons*

First the position of the sermon in the whole of the commentary has to be studied more carefully. It does not seem consonant with Bernard's strength as a composer, by which he manages to master even the hugest compositions, to exclude his most elaborated passages from the deeper structure that underlies each of his works.

---

[13] Jean Leclercq, *Initiation aux auteurs monastiques du Moyen Age. L'amour des lettres et le désir de Dieu* (Paris: Editions du cerf, 1957), p. 125: 'Not that one has to doubt in general as to their sincerity, but it is not always easy to distinguish in their statements what may be spontaneous and what may be artificial, being imposed by the prescriptions of style or literary genre. [...] to this sermon the abbot of Clairvaux has given all of his art, because he has given it all of his affection.'

[14] Paul Verdeyen and Raffaele Fassetta, *Bernard de Clairvaux. Sermons sur le Cantique II*. Sources Chrétiennes 431 (Paris: Editions du cerf, 1998), p. 24: 'This sermon always has retained a lot of attention. It interrupts the normal development of the exposition. Bernard even becomes so very personal that one can perceive immediately the vibrations of his affective life.' Compare also, be it in a more nuanced way, Brian Patrick McGuire, *The Difficult Saint* (Kalamazoo: Cistercian Publications, 1991), p. 141: 'I do not think it likely that Bernard actually burst out in the midst of his sermon in an abrupt way, as suggested by the written text of the twenty-sixth sermon, *but this is possible*.' (my italics)

[15] They have been attacked by Von Moos, *Consolatio*, pp. 279–331 who has pointed out the rhetorical structure of SC 26 (pp. 324–27) and by Pranger, *Bernard of Clairvaux*, pp. 167–80.

[16] As Jean Leclercq acknowledges himself (compare *Initiation aux auteurs monastiques*, p. 125). Of the same author, 'Aspects littéraires de l'oeuvre de s.Bernard', *Recueil des études sur saint Bernard et ses écrits* III (Rome: Edizioni di storia e letteratura, 1969), pp. 13–104, esp. p. 94, n.3.

Concerning the lament on Gerard, an answer ought to be found to the question as to what its function might be inside the commentary on the Canticle.[17]

The sermon on the Canticle (SC) 26 belongs to a group of sermons in which the approach of the Word to the reader is realized. Before SC 20 the divine Word remains some elusive reality that only becomes a little bit more concrete in the name of the divinity, its *nomen.*[18] In SC 20 to 22 the distance between the reader and the Word is slowly reduced. First the love for the Word is evoked (SC 19–20) in its spiritual reality.[19] This spiritual love finds its expression in the next half line of the Canticle: *Trahe me post te, curremus*, which is explained in SC 21–22.[20] The desire to be raised by the Groom who is the Word shows that He is not completely inaccessible. Thanks to the incarnation, the Word has become tangible and visible to mankind. He can be reached and seen, though for the moment the desire is only wakened by his savours.

This vision of the Word, however, will not be opened till SC 45 in which the Bride and the Groom sing their wedding song. The first immediate contact of the reader with the Word takes place in SC 28, in which the Word addresses himself in direct speech to Magdalena. It is too early to rely on the senses of touch and sight. 'Only the hearing has the truth when it perceives the word. [...] Trust the word, acquaint yourself with faith.'[21] Thus, the Word has become accessible. A first contact is made with its spiritual reality. The lament on Gerard in SC 26 might then play a part in reducing this distance between the reader and the Word as it is conveyed by Bernard's text.[22]

2.1 Inside and Outside

In SC 23 a new theme is introduced with the commentary on verse 1. $3^{c\text{–}e}$ of the Canticle: *Introduxit me rex in cellaria sua ; exultabimus et laetabimur in te,*

[17] The first to question the independency of SC 26 is Von Moos, *Consolatio*, pp. 208–82, who studies the links with the end of SC 25 and the beginning of SC 27.

[18] A first climax is reached in SC 15 on Canticle 1. 2^{b}: 'Oleum effusum nomen tuum' (1. 3^{b} in the King James version: 'Thy name is as ointment poured forth').

[19] They treat Canticle 1. 2^{c}: 'Ideo adulescentulae dilexerunt te' (1. 3^{c} in the King James Version: 'Therefore do the virgins love thee').

[20] Verse 1. 4^{a} in the King James Version: 'Draw me, we will run after thee'.

[21] SC 28.8–9, SBO I (1957) pp. 197–98.

[22] The relation of the reader with the Word and the part played by the author was the principal theme of my PhD thesis. The part concerning the sermons on the Canticle is in preparation.

memores uberum tuorum super vinum ; recti diligunt te.[23] Whereas Bernard has so far dedicated several sermons to one half line of the biblical text, in SC 23 he comments on several lines together, although he attributes them to different persons. According to his scenario, the Bride speaks the first half line; the girls speak the next three. By commenting on them in one sermon, Bernard illustrates what is happening here. In the first paragraph of the sermon Bride and girls are separated from each other. The desire of the Bride makes her run on ahead while the girls remain behind. The Bride is admitted into the presence of the Groom, whereas the girls find the door shut. From the inside they hear the voice of the Bride who reassures them that her love will not diminish and that she will share her joy with them. At the end of the second paragraph Bernard confronts the superiors with this image of a loving bride and mother as a model for the care they must take for their own monks.[24]

For the first time in the commentary, a separation is created between those that may enter into the presence of the Groom and those that have to remain outside. The separation comes about because of the differences in love with which each follows the 'savour' of the truth. The Word that began to feel accessible in the preceding sermons suddenly seems to retire once again. A distinction is made between those who seek to reach it. The Bride may enter. She is presented by Bernard as an image for the superiors in their responsibility for those they *have begotten in the gospel.*[25] Bernard himself again and again declares this to be his own task as an author. He strives to be Bride and mother for his readers because of his intimate bond with the Word as a spiritual author and guide. When the Bride, therefore, is admitted to the Groom, this can also be said of Bernard himself.

But where is the Groom to be found? In SC 22 the Word was said 'to be made for us'.[26] It has adopted a more concrete form, thanks to the efforts of the author and of the reader. It still remains outside the immediate grasp of the reader, but by catching the savour of truth and assimilating himself to the narrator, the reader comes close.

---

[23] Verse 1. 4[b-e] in the King James Version: 'The king hath brought me into his chambers: we will be glad and rejoice in thee, we will remember thy love more than wine: the upright love thee'. Bernard replaces the original *cellaria sua* with the alternative reading *cubiculum suum* originating from the Vetus Latina. Yet he opens his exegesis on the official reading but already in the second paragraph is the substitution made. Compare Jean Prosper Deroy, *Bernardus en Origenes. Enkele opmerkingen over de invloed van Origenes op Bernardus' Sermones super Cantica canticorum.* (Haarlem: De Toorts, 1963) pp. 53–56 and pp. 93–95. SC 23 has been treated several times. Deroy takes this sermon as the starting point for his whole textual analysis and comparison of Bernard with Origen. Pranger, *Bernard of Clairvaux*, pp. 51–84, focusses more on the internal dynamics of the text.

[24] SC 23.1–2, SBO I (1957), pp. 138–140.

[25] I Corinthians 4. 15, compare SC 23.1, SBO I (1957), p. 139.

[26] SC 22.5: [...] *ergo in principio erat Verbum, sed Verbum erat apud Deum, factum est autem quatenus esse inciperet apud homines* [...] *quod erat angelis factus est et nobis.* SBO I (1957), p. 132.

The reader's own love for God and Bernard cannot bring them both onto the same level, though. Bernard disappears inside the text like the Bride in the bridal chamber. The reader still remains outside. He is not yet able to grasp the living heart of the text. He is still dependent on the experience of the Bride, on Bernard and on the words the author uses to express the living truth of the text. The text itself has become a wall which separates the author speaking from inside the text from the reader looking for the entrance in order that he may experience this same truth himself. The reading event itself acquires an inside and an outside.

This separation of the author and the reader risks negating all further progress in reading. The author disappears inside the text to sustain a monologue, to which the reader would have to listen from the outside. He would remain a spectator, regarding what happens inside the text, listening to the description of the author, but not experiencing it himself. Bernard seeks at all price to avoid this exclusion of the reader. The reader too has to experience the truth as it is enclosed in the text. The reader must therefore have an absolute confidence in the author that he will not leave him outside, that he is willing to share the joy of his own entry with the reader who cannot follow him yet. Only when the reader trusts the author as much as the girls trust the Bride will Bernard be able to break through the text and let the reader in to experience its truth. The unity of reader and author is essential to their separation, as it is caused by the text.

2.2 Straight and Crooked

The separation of inside and outside in the reading of the sermons will be slowly dissolved in the following sermons. In the end, the harmony between both has to be restored as part of the imitation of the incarnated Word.[27]

As a first step, however, the inside has to conform to the outside. SC 24 is as a whole constructed around the tension between differing insides and outsides, which find their culmination in the opposition that characterizes humankind. Humans have received an upright figure. Their inner core, or soul, must adopt this uprightness and put off its crooked aspect.[28] The tension between a soul, curved downward to earthly occupations, and an upright figure will disappear as soon as a 'crooked' faith straightens itself by its 'right' works and a 'crooked' love for the world will change into the 'right' love for Christ, for the Groom, for the living Word. Humans were created in God's image and God is the absolute 'straightness'. The nucleus of SC 24 is formed by the citation of Psalm 91. 16: *Rectus Dominus Deus noster et non est*

[27] This process will be accomplished in SC 27 and 28 where the Word will reappear and speak in the first person.

[28] SC 24.6, SBO I (1957). p. 157.

iniquitas in eo,[29] indicating that even when talking about external straightness (*Rectus est*) internal uprightness (*et non est iniquitas in eo*) is meant.

The sermon opens with Bernard's returning from Rome after the schism has ended. The external 'uprightness' of the Church has been restored, but, as Bernard explains, this restoration is owed to the inner 'uprightness' of Clairvaux, to which he wants to dedicate himself again: 'I want to live for the efforts and for the welfare of those who make me live by their merits.'[30] Just as God in the centre of the sermon has to be the model for every human 'uprightness', so Bernard himself is the centre of the community in Clairvaux. Likewise, Clairvaux is the 'upright' centre of the Church, which is one of the images of the Bride with whom every human being has to identify.

Inside and outside begin to fuse in what constitutes the core of the sermon: the unequivocal 'uprightness' of God. The reader is confronted with this heart of the sermon. He, too, has to adopt an upright attitude. Reading these words in a 'right' way means to incorporate them, adopt them, conform one's inner attitude to them. Like God in Bernard's sermon, like Bernard in Clairvaux, like Clairvaux in the Church and like the Church in the Bride, the reader must feel himself 'righted' by the inner truth of the text. Only when he experiences this truth of the text will the unity of the reader inside and outside the text be accomplished and the reading be 'right'.

2.3 Black and Beautiful

While in SC 24 Bernard seeks to accommodate the inside to the outside, in the next sermon the movement is turned round. Now it appears that the outside derives its dignity from the inside.[31] But whereas the movement in SC 24 meant a true *conformation* of the inside to its external appearance, the one evoked in SC 25 could better be described as a *transformation*. The external aspect of the Bride does not change: she remains black. The girls, however, learn to see how this external aspect veils her divine nature. It is not the Bride who changes, but the eyes of the spectator. They find their way from the outside into the inside. The Bride herself appears to experience a separation between her outside and her inside, but this does not affect her essential unity. The separation is not cancelled by her, but in the way she is seen by the girls, by the reader. They no longer look at her as do those of her detractors

---

[29] Psalm 92. 16 in the King James Version: 'The Lord is upright and there is no unrighteousness in him'. SC 24.5, SBO I (1957), pp. 156–57.

[30] SC 24.1, SBO I (1957), p. 151.

[31] The commented verse is Canticle 1. 4[a]: *Nigra sum sed formosa, filiae Hierusalem*. Half line 1. 5[a] in the King James Version: 'I am black, but comely, O ye daughters of Jerusalem'.

who incorporate a reverse opposition to hers. She may be black outside and beautiful inside; they seem 'upright' but are black inside.

Again Bernard applies the words of the Bride to the superiors, who have to remain indulgent towards all those for whom they are responsible. Every person deserves to be addressed as a 'daughter of Jerusalem', even when he does not yet meet its spiritual meaning. But then the name will remind him of the division in his own nature between an earthly 'outside' and a heavenly 'inside'.[32] Indicating to others the division in their own being by showing herself divided in hers, the Bride acts in accordance with herself as well as with the saints, with Paul and with Christ himself.[33] They all were black from the outside with the tribulations and the afflictions of life, but inside they were able *to behold with open face as in a glass the glory of the Lord, and to be changed into the same image from glory to glory, even as by the Spirit of the Lord.*[34] The most extreme example is the crucified Christ:

> Black he was, surely, who *hath no form nor comeliness.*[35] Black he was, *a worm, and no man, a reproach of men, and despised of the people.*[36] In the end *he hath made him to be sin* and then should I be afraid to call him black?[37] Look how dirty he is in his rags, beaten black and blue, smeared with spittle, deathly pale. And you will admit he is black. Even the apostles doubted that this was the same man they had seen on the mountain, and the angels that this was the man *into whom they desire to look.*[38] And yet you will admire his beauty. Beautiful he is in himself, black he is for you.[39]

The eyes of the reader and of the spectator are transformed. They have to admit how the internal beauty of the Bride originates in her acceptance of tribulations in which she imitates the divine Groom, though they make her appear black. The harmony between the two aspects of her being is founded on a double conformation to the living Word. In her internal life, she seeks the union with her divine core, being created in the image of God.[40] In her external life, she strives to imitate the example of the living Word on earth.[41] This, however, also means a conformation to humanity, to the other, to the reader.

---

[32] SC 25.2, SBO I (1957), p. 164.

[33] SC 25.5–9, SBO I (1957), pp. 165–69.

[34] II Corinthians 3. 18.

[35] Isaiah 53. 2.

[36] Psalm 21. 7 corresponds to King James Version 22. 6.

[37] II Corinthians 5. 21.

[38] Compare I Peter 1. 12.

[39] SC 25.9, SBO I (1957), p. 168.

[40] Compare SC 25.7, SBO I (1957), p. 167.

[41] Compare SC 25.9, SBO I (1957), p. 168.

To accomplish the transformation of the outsider, whether he is to be found in the girls or in the reader, a double conformation of the Bride and of the author is required. First there is the conformation to the radiant 'inside', a spiritual image strongly desired. Then there is the conformation to the need of the other, to the desire of the girls and of the reader. The Bride disappears into the bridal chamber, but she feels plentiful love and care for those who have to remain outside, even for those who are jealous. The author, too, has disappeared inside the text, while the reader has to remain outside. But from the inside he is able to do more for the reader. By transforming himself into the Word that is speaking in the text, he can address the reader from the inside and evoke the transformation that is necessary to bring over the reader into the textual truth. Similarly, the Bride who was allowed to enter in the bridal chamber addresses herself to the girls outside in order to share her joy with them and to prepare them for their own entrance.

Inside the text, both the living Word and the writer are clothed by the text that, being the active outside, acts on the reader. The reader is still on the outside of it, but as soon as he conforms to the wording of the text, he will have access to the spiritual content. Once he conforms to the textual exterior, to the words he reads, he will at the same time conform to its inner truth, to the sense of the words, i.e. to the living Word that is hiding in the text. His conformation has become a transformation from the outside into the inside. The bridal chamber will be opened where the reader will find the Word.

2.4 Body and Text

SC 25 ends on this positive tone.[42] The conformation of the *ego* to the Word has become possible since the Word did conform to man. 'How beautiful I recognize You to be, Jesus my Lord, even in my shape.'[43] The attention has been focussed again on the appearance, on the human clothing of God. The next sermon starts by developing this theme. The black appearance of the Bride is compared to 'the tents of Kedar'. They serve as a model for the struggle of people on earth, offering but a temporal shelter for the soul. In them the human body can be recognized, being feeble and heavy, *for the corruptible body presseth down the soul, and the earthly tabernacle weigheth down the mind that museth upon many things.*[44] The soul longs for its release, 'to fly away, liberated from the body, in the embrace of Christ'.[45]

---

[42] SC 25.9: *Si non dissimulatis, aderit qui revelat mysteria; nec cunctabitur aperire, qui ad pulsandum invitat. Ipse est enim qui aperit, et nemo claudit, sponsus Ecclesiae, Iesus Christus Dominus noster, qui est benedictus in saecula.* SBO I (1957), p. 169.

[43] SC 25.9, SBO I (1957), p. 168.

[44] Wisdom 9. 15.

[45] SC 26.2, SBO I (1957), p. 170.

A new wall appears which keeps the reader from his union with the Word. At first it was the text into which the author and the Bride disappeared, while the reader was left outside. Then the text turned out to be exactly the way by which the reader could enter the bridal chamber to meet the Word. The reader can open the door by conforming to the words of the text and taking the opportunity to transform himself into the inner spiritual truth as it is concealed inside the text. As soon as the reader accepts this step, his inner transformation is accomplished: his desire will be directed towards the realization of the textual truth in his own life. The reader wants to realize for himself what Bernard's words are telling him. These words (the outer appearance of the text) have become the model for his own inner intentions. Yet a new obstacle is raised in the reader's own external being: his own body offers resistance to such a conformation to the requirements of the text. Reader and author were separated by the text as had been the girls and the Bride by the closed door of the bridal chamber, but both hindrances seemed to be overcome. Now a last division remains and this one resides in the reader himself. His inner intentions turn to the text, while his 'outside', his body, is presented as a burden.

At this point, the exegete breaks off. He does not dare to proceed and to enter the mysteries that are veiled by the second part of the similitude, in which the Bride compares her beauty with 'the curtains of Solomon'. They seem to enclose something 'sublime and holy' which he dares not touch, be it even 'with the permission of Him who laid it down here and sealed it'.[46] The reader suddenly realizes indeed that much has been said on the tension between inside and outside and on their mutual conformation and transformation but that nowhere has the internal beauty of the Bride yet been described. Even now he has to wait. Only in the next sermon will Bernard enter into this subject and show how heaven and earth meet in the living Word, when the earthly bride conforms to the heavenly one so that the Word can descend and live in the soul of the reader. SC 27 is dominated by the ascent of the soul in the heavenly spirit and by the descent of the Word in the soul. This mutual approach will finally open the ears to the speaking of the Word in SC 28.

[46] SC 26.2, SBO I (1957), p. 170.

3. Two Brothers

3.1 Tranquillity and action

Before he treats this double movement of the soul and the Word, Bernard introduces his lament on Gerard. As will appear soon, it does not at all interrupt the line of thought, but rather continues the theme of the preceding sermons. The tension between outside and inside, between internal and external becomes even more pronounced since Bernard himself is involved. For the eye of the reader he paints his own inside and outside and the transformations they underwent because of Gerard's death. During his life Gerard was Bernard's 'outside'. Gerard guaranteed his brother's peace which Bernard needed for his 'studies in the Lord'.[47] 'I owe it to you if I have made any progress, if I have been of any use. You engaged yourself in all and liberated me so I might sit on my own and occupy myself with the saintlier matters of divine service, or apply myself to the more useful matters in the instruction of my sons. And why should I not be safely inside when I knew you acting outside, my right hand, the light of my eyes, my heart and my tongue?'[48]

The existence of both brothers appears to be divided in a similar way to that described by Bernard in the preceding sermons. Gerard had been the action, Bernard the spirit. One was burdened by the cares and duties for the community in its relation with the world outside. The other took care of the spiritual nourishment and of the inner 'uprightness'. Inside the monastery Bernard enjoyed the imperturbable tranquillity of contemplation, while Gerard intercepted the blows. 'In the wisdom of his answers and in the grace he received from above, Gerard knew how to satisfy all, both those familiar to him and those from outside. Nobody could look for me without first happening to bump into Gerard. Whoever arrived, they found Gerard in their way. He opposed himself to them so they might not suddenly disturb my peace. Only those he could not satisfy himself, did he bring to me. The others he sent forth.'[49]

In all he did, Gerard showed himself to be the active or 'black' outside of the saints. He helped everyone in work and deed, preferring rather to wrong himself than others. Finally, this caused him to sacrifice even his own inner peace out of love and affection for his brother and abbot.

'He never asked what was his right to ask. He burdened himself with all the cares so that I might be free. His humility was so great that he expected our tranquillity to be of more fruitfulness than if he had been free himself. [...] As he felt his death

---

[47] SC 26.3, SBO I (1957), p. 171.

[48] SC 26.6, SBO I (1957), p. 174.

[49] SC 26.6, SBO I (1957), p. 174.

approaching, he said: "God, You know that, whatsoever I might have been, I always longed to be in quiet for myself and to be free for You. Yet I remained entangled in all I did because of my awe of You, the will of my brethren, my wish to be found obedient and above all because of a genuine love for my abbot and brother."'[50]

Gerard went even further than the Bride and the saints in the preceding sermons. They managed to preserve the bright and divine core under the 'black' coat of their worldly implications. Gerard, however, sacrificed his desire for the peaceful union with the Word to the activities that made it possible for his brother to enjoy this same peace. In the unity of the brothers Gerard constitutes the 'black' appearance of the Crucified, while Bernard in his peace and tranquillity portrays the divine heart.

This division between the outside and the inside becomes an acutely painful reality at Gerard's death. Both sides are now separated irrevocably. However, this does not cause the greatest problem. Bernard clearly indicates that inside and outside still exist. They have only changed places.[51] Gerard has 'entered the luminous abyss'. He has been 'absorbed into the sea of eternal bliss'. His brother on the contrary is left behind, to be a victim to all sort of cares and torments.[52] 'Together with you all my delights and joys have disappeared. Cares rush in. Troubles beat on all doors. Oppressions from all sides have found me alone. They alone are left for me, now you have gone. Lonely I sigh under the charge.'[53] Death has brought about a complete inversion. Bernard has lost the peace which Gerard's presence ensured. Bernard can no longer be compared to the image of God in His impassibility.[54] It has finally become Gerard's share, his who could not enjoy it during life. Bernard is compelled by the death of his brother to a life of action, to conform to the 'black' outside, while dead Gerard has entered the inside and become one with the Word.

One way or another, this inversion had already been prepared during their common life. Even if Gerard had been a man of action, he did not miss the spirit. 'Why do I say that he acted on the outside as if he knew not the inside and as if he were deprived of spiritual gifts? Those who are spiritual themselves know that his words had a spiritual air. Those who have lived with him know that his manners and his zeal had no carnal taint but were *fervent in spirit*'.[55] This spirituality, however, appears to have been essentially practical. He was consulted on 'building matters, fields, gardens, waters, in short on all agrarian techniques and works. [...] He could easily have been a master to masons, smiths, farmers, gardeners, cobblers and weavers.'[56]

---

[50] SC 26.6, SBO I (1957), p. 174.

[51] Pranger, *Bernard of Clairvaux*, pp. 201–03.

[52] SC 26.5, SBO I (1957), p. 173.

[53] SC 26.8, SBO I (1957), p. 176.

[54] Compare SC 26.5: *[...] impassibilis est Deus*, SBO I (1957), p. 173.

[55] SC 26.7, SBO I (1957), p. 175, ending on a citation from Romans 12. 11.

[56] SC 26.7, SBO I (1957), p. 175.

More important, however, was the significance Gerard had for his brother. He was useful to me in everything and for everything. He was useful in small and in great matters, in private and in public, outside and inside. [...] Deservedly my spirit rested in him, thanks to whom I could *delight in the Lord,*[57] preach in all freedom, pray in security. Thanks to you, I say, my brother, I enjoyed a sober mind and a welcome rest. My speaking was more powerful, my praying more fruitful, my reading more frequent and my affection more fervent.'[58]

The contemplative peace which Bernard enjoyed inside the community found its origins in Gerard. It even caused him to be more active in his preaching and his prayers. Gerard's practical activity had a counterpart in the spiritual activity of his brother, and likewise Bernard's 'spiritual' spirituality was complementary to Gerard's practical spirituality.

3.2 The pains of separation

Death disrupted this harmonious unity of the brothers. Gerard went over into a truly spiritual reality, while Bernard was left behind for active life. Twice in his lament Bernard complains to the reader of his pain, and these two passages frame the central picture of their unity in action and spirit. First the separation of the living and the dead is lamented. In life the brothers were inseparable. Death causes a rupture, giving life in death to him who passed away and leaving a life that is death for the one who remained. 'We loved each other in life: how can we be separated in death? Most cruel separation which nothing but death could create between us! Would you ever desert me, your living brother, here, if you were alive? This really is the work of death, a horrible rupture. Who else did not spare this so sweet bond of our mutual love? Everyone but death, the enemy of all that is sweet! He has done well, death, who furiously has killed both of us by tearing one away. For has not death touched me too? Yes, me even more, since I was left for a life that is worse than any death. I live to die living, and this I ought to call life? How kind you are, severe death, to save me for the use of life but not for its fruits. Then life without fruits is a more heavy death.'[59]

In the second lament the pain is not felt as something outside, but as the result of an inner rupture. Bernard realizes that death has made impossible the unity of his own life. 'While we were one in heart and soul, a sword pierced this soul of mine and his, and cleft it in two. One half was put in heaven, the other was left behind in the dirt. This is me. I am this miserable portion lying in the mud, bereft of its other,

---

[57] Compare Psalm 36. 4 (King James Version, Psalm 37. 4).

[58] SC 26.7, SBO I (1957), pp. 175–76.

[59] SC 26.4, SBO I (1957), p. 172.

its better half. And then they tell me: "You do not weep?" My own intestines are torn out from me and then they tell me: "You do not feel anything?"'[60]

Death proves to have caused a terrible rupture inside Bernard. 'have confessed my affection. I did not deny it. Who could call it carnal? I do not deny it is human any more than I deny being a man. If this does not suffice, neither will I deny it being carnal. Yes, me too, *I am carnal, sold under sin,*[61] sentenced to death, exposed to punishment and labours. I admit, I am not insensible to punishment. I tremble for my own death and for that of those who are mine.'

3.3 Brother and Sons

3.3.1 Brother

Twice Bernard bemoans the pain caused by Gerard's death. Twice he looks for comfort. First, he addresses his dead brother, for whom the division must be as radical as for himself. Only Gerard has received a greater delight for the one he left behind. Just as he had been inseparable from Bernard during life, he now has become inseparable from God. Entering into God, however, means the end of all division, since inside the absolute unity of God no ruptures exist. This might reassure Bernard who can be certain that his brother will not forget him. God may be impassible, but he is certainly compassionate. 'So it must be that you are compassionate too, since you abide in the Compassionate, however little you are now to be pitied: you no longer feel pain, but you feel pity. Your affection has not decreased, it has only changed. Now you have put on God, you have not however put off the care of us. God himself takes care of us. You have thrown away what is weak, not what is pious. Indeed, *charity never faileth:*[62] nor *wilt thou forget me for ever*'.[63]

The union of the brothers will endure, since it is guaranteed by their mutual love. At this same moment Bernard hears Gerard's voice, citing a biblical text. Bernard uses this same technique elsewhere. In the funeral sermon for the Irish bishop Malachy, the voice of the dead friend inspires Bernard to a last exposition on the *refrigerium* which the blessed enjoy. Malachy becomes the voice of the Spirit that inspires in Bernard the last part of the sermon.[64] In our case, however, the effect is quite different. Gerard assures his brother of his lasting love and concern, but

---

[60] SC 26.9, SBO I (1957), p. 177.

[61] Romans 7. 14.

[62] I Corinthians 13. 8.

[63] Psalm 12. 1. SC 26.5, SBO I (1957), p. 173.

[64] *Sermo in Transitu Sancti Malachiae* 8, SBO V (Rome, 1968), p. 422. See my article '*Revocare vitam*. Bernard of Clairvaux writing a friend's life', in *Revue Mabillon*, 75 (2003), 153–78.

Bernard breaks off these comforting words in his own despair. 'I almost seem to hear my brother saying: "Can a woman forget the son of her womb? yea, she may forget, yet will I not forget thee."[65] It is not at all expedient.[66] You know where I wallow, where I lie, where you have left me. There is no one holding out his hand to me.'[67] The comforting consideration of the unity in love with the dead brother fails. The sense of individual impotence is only experienced more poignantly. Though Bernard knows their love will not die, this assurance cannot restore the former unity in the mutual comfort they have known during life.

3.3.2 Brother and Son

The second explosion of pain follows immediately after the portrait of the unity Bernard and Gerard knew in their different activities. Just as the union has been described more intimately, the rupture is now experienced much more as internal suffering. In the first lament Bernard delightedly remembered the pleasure of Gerard's company because of their shared habits, their mutual delight in the presence of the other, the joy of sharing the brother's destination, the sweet conversations. Now he mourns the unity of spirit, the spiritual company, their unanimity, the conformity of their habits.[68] The unity is felt more intimately, so the pain is experienced more deeply. Not the other but the self is at stake. 'My Gerard he was.

---

[65] Isaiah 49. 15.

[66] II Corinthians 12. 1.

[67] SC 26.6: 'Videor mihi fratrem meum quasi audire dicentem: *Numquid mater poterit oblivisci filii uteri sui? Et si illa oblita fuerit, ego tamen non obliviscar tui. Non expedit prorsus.* Scis ubi verser, ubi iaceam, ubi reliqueris me: non est qui porrigat manum.' SBO I (1957), p. 173. That the text from Paul's second letter to the Corinthians breaks off the citation of Isaiah in despair has also been the opinion of Von Moos, *Consolatio*, p. 292: 'Die tröstliche Einsicht vermag den Ton des Planctus zu mildern, nicht zu wandeln. Wie nach einem kurzen Traumanblick (*Videor mihi fratrem meum quasi audire..*) fällt Bernhard in die Trauer zurück. Die unvermittelte Entgegnung zeigt Ernüchterung: *Non expedit prorsus*. Die der Eidolopoiie zugrunde liegende Fiktion "hilft nicht weiter".' In the most recent French edition this cry of despair is clearly misunderstood. The result is a plain translation that does not take into account the biblical text: 'Il me semble presque entendre mon frère me dire: "Une mère pourra-t-elle oublier l'enfant de ses entrailles? Même si elle l'oubliât, moi, je ne t'oublierai pas". *Ce serait bien dommageable en effet*.' [our italics] (Paris: Verdeyen & Fassetta, 1998), p. 291.

[68] Compare SC 26.4: '*Placita fuit pariter utrique* ***societas corporum*** *pro* ***morum concordia****; sed solum me divisio vulneravit. Commune, quod libuit; quod triste et lugubre, meum: in me transierunt irae, in me confirmatus est furor. Erat ambobus alterutrum grata praesentia, dulce consortium, suave colloquium.*' SBO I (1957) p. 172 with SC 26.9: '*Adhaesit anima mea animae illius; et unam fecit de duabus, non consanguinitas, sed unanimitas. Carnis quidem necessitudo non defuit; sed plus iunxit* ***societas spiritus****, consensus animorum,* ***morum conformitas***.' SBO I (1957), p. 177.

He was mine. How could he not be mine, who was my brother in blood, my son in profession, my father in solicitude, my fellow in the spirit, my intimate friend in affection?'[69]

Again Bernard looks for consolation in the pain of this inner rupture. He cannot turn to Gerard, whose assurance of his lasting love has already failed. So now Bernard turns towards his 'sons'. 'Forgive me, my sons. Or rather, if you really are my sons, mourn the fate of your father. *Have pity upon me, O ye my friends,*[70] you who surely will consider how heavy the hand of the Lord rests on me for my sins.'[71] The core of the whole lament has a similar ending and beginning. It also opens with the immediate apostrophe of Bernard's sons. 'You know, my sons, my pain, how I suffer inside, how deplorable my wounds. You surely notice how faithful a companion has left me in the way wherein I walked,[72] how vigilant in his care, how diligent in his acts, how sweet in his habits.'[73]

But who are these 'sons' of Bernard? Nowhere in the preceding sermons has he addressed them. He has only spoken of his brothers, *fratres*. That he changes the appellation of his addressees might be caused by the more intimate tone of the sermon. Yet there exists a link to the subject itself. Gerard is called Bernard's son and father, a son in his monastic profession, a father in his solicitude. Furthermore, on his deathbed, Gerard turns in almost one and the same breath from God to Bernard, appealing to them with the same fatherly name. In the second part of his sermon Bernard evokes what happened: 'As I arrived and heard his clear voice finishing the Psalm, he lifted his eyes to heaven and said: "Father, into thy hands I commend my spirit."[74] Repeating the phrase and sighing again and again: 'Father, Father', he turned to me and then he said: 'Such an honour on the part of God, to be the father of man! Such a glory on the part of man, to be the sons of God, to be the heirs of God! since being sons they must be his heirs.'[75]

As after the first explosion of pain, Gerard's words are once again heard. Yet first it had been the dead and glorified brother who wanted to comfort Bernard in the spirit. Now it is the dying but nonetheless still living Gerard who expresses himself significantly on his relationship to God and his brother. In one single movement and in one single word, God and the abbot are put on one level, both being father. The author arrives exactly at the moment where Gerard speaks the words of the dying Christ. He looks up to heaven and turns almost simultaneously to his brother, each

[69] SC 26.9, SBO I (1957), p. 177.

[70] Job 19. 21.

[71] SC 26.10, SBO I (1957), p. 177.

[72] Psalm 141. 4.

[73] SC 26.4, SBO I (1957), p. 172.

[74] Luke 23. 46.

[75] SC 26.11, SBO I (1957), p. 179.

time repeating twice: Father, Father. Abbot and God are both father to Gerard. In essence their natures coincide. Bernard is like God on earth, as he has been described in the sermon previously, enjoying the imperturbable tranquillity which Gerard ensured him.[76]

3.3.3 Father and Sons

Bernard, then, is justly called father. He may make an appeal to the pity of his 'sons', and it seems almost natural to consider them to be his monks, to whom he is supposed to preach. After all they are his sons by profession. Yet this historical and all too realistic interpretation causes some problems with the textual event. It has been noticed already that the monks did not need this long digression to know why Bernard broke off his exegesis. They would simply have returned to their daily occupations. Such an interpretation, however, expects the commentary to be a truly sermonic and oral instruction on the Canticle delivered inside the monastery. This is in absolute contradiction to the complexity of its deeper structure. It would surely be impossible for the listening monks to understand the function of the lament on Gerard in relation to the rest of the commentary. The audience could never have instantly grasped the continuity of the theme, the tension between inside and outside.

And there is more. The monks themselves participate in the textual event. The whole lament opens with the description of Gerard's interment. This passage is entirely based on Augustine's description of Monica's funeral in the *Confessions*.[77] Like Augustine, Bernard tells his readers how he took part in the funerary ceremony without tears and how all were wondering about his apparent impassibility.

'While the others wept, I followed the bier, as you could have noticed, with dry eyes, I stood at the tomb with dry eyes, until all funerary rites had been accomplished. In my sacerdotal vestments I pronounced the appropriate prayers to him myself. With my own hands I threw the customary earth on this beloved body, soon to be earth itself. Those who saw me wept and wondered that I did not weep, while all did not so much pity him but rather me who had lost him.'[78]

Just as in the *Confessions*, those around the author wonder about his seeming indifference. Those surrounding our author, however, must be his monks. Here they appear in the text as a third participant, who has to be presented to those addressed by the sermon. For a moment, Bernard seems to forget he is addressing exactly those monks he is describing in his text. For a moment, he seems to conform completely to his literary model, the *Confessions*.

---

[76] Compare Pranger, *Bernard of Clairvaux*, p. 204.

[77] *Confessions* XI.32. Von Moos, *Consolatio*, was the first to notice this interdependence of Bernard's text and the *Confessions*. It has been elaborated by Marinus Burcht Pranger, 'Tranen in het antieke christendom. Augustinus en de dood', *Emoties in de middeleeuwen*, ed. by René Stuip and Kees Vellekoop (Hilversum: Verloren Kost, 1998), pp. 29–47.

[78] SC 26.3, SBO I (1957), p. 171.

This forgetfulness, however, is only apparent. In fact Bernard undermines in several ways his own apparently historical account. In a certain sense the group at the tomb is split. There are some who weep and they are indicated as 'the others' (*plorantibus aliis*). There are some who notice that Bernard is not weeping and they are addressed by the author (*ut advertere potuistis*). These groups do not coincide. They form different groups inside the community. One part is formed by those who mourn with Bernard, mourn even instead of him. The other part is regarding Bernard in wonder. They seem hardly to participate in the scene. They do not belong with those standing around the tomb, since they do not feel the grief.

3.4 An author breaking out of the text

An invisible division is made around the tomb between those who are 'inside', who feel for themselves the inner pains of Bernard and weep with him, and those who remain 'outside', just looking in wonder at Bernard's apparent impassibility. And again, an inversion must take place. He who is left 'outside' must be brought in to participate in Bernard's grief and to collect its fruits. For this reason, Bernard has to give up the impassibility that he showed at the tomb and which is nothing other than the distant attitude of the exegete with which the sermon opened. 'But the suppressed grief began to take root deeper inside me and—I feel it—became the sharper as it was not allowed to come out. I admit: I am defeated. Let it come out—it has to—let it come out, what I suffer inside. Let it come out before the eyes of my sons who will judge my weeping more humanly, will comfort me more sweetly, when they know my distress.'[79]

Bernard commits himself. He forces his tears out. His 'inside' is exposed before the eyes of his sons that are outside. He turns himself inside out and thus undermines the carefully constructed attitude of the reader. Bernard abruptly appears to be an outsider himself. He is like the girls who may not enter the bridal chamber. He is like the reader who could not follow the author inside the text. Bernard finds the door closed too, whereas he knows Gerard to be inside with the Groom. His lamentation expresses the pain of each outsider in a spiritual event. In the reading process the text came to be like a wall between the reader and the author. It could only be broken through when the words ceased to be inanimate letters, when the reader conformed to the text and sought to realize it in her own life. Now Bernard finds himself in front of the dead corpse of his brother as before a visible and apparently insuperable obstacle. The spiritual union and the desire to conform can no longer help. The body has become the implacable wall between the *ego* and its unification with the living Word.

[79] SC 26.3: SBO I (1957), p. 171.

Bernard has brought himself to much the same position as he had brought the reader when opening his lament on Gerard. For both, the body appears to be the last obstacle that prevents their being absorbed in the Word. An impasse has been created, that seems to leave no way through. But *with God no word shall be impossible*,[80] nor shall it with the author who seeks to communicate the living Word. The crisis can be solved by the literary action of Bernard. Its solution is to be found in the text. Bernard's lamentation begins as a clear reference to Augustine, then takes a completely different turn. In the *Confessions* the earthly chronology is on the whole respected. Successively, Augustine narrates the conversation in Ostia, Monica's sudden illness, her death and burial. While he appears unaffected to those around him, he feels the pain creeping deeper and deeper till it comes out in tears in the privacy of his bedroom. Only God and the reader are allowed to witness Augustine's pain and tears.

Bernard deliberately departs from his narrative model. He opens on the funeral and on his own unaffected appearance. This impassibility, however, is abandoned almost immediately. The true text consists of Bernard's tears. The ending of Augustine's narration constitutes the beginning for Bernard and his reader.[81] After all, Bernard refuses the intimacy and seclusion. His grief is open and meant to be seen. His tears must flow for his 'sons', for the monks but even more for the reader. Together with the pain that is allowed to come out of him, Bernard himself breaks out of the text. The distant and spiritual reality of the text is broken through. It is filled in by Bernard's own reality, not by his concrete, external reality, but by his internal, affective reality. In tears the author joins the reader. Has the reader sought to conform to the words of the text and still found himself excluded from the inner core? He finds Bernard at his side: 'It's the same with me', he seems to say. 'Me too, I've found the door closed.' The Canticle seems to be lost from view: 'What does this canticle concern me, who am in bitterness?'[82] Yet it does indeed concern him very closely: excluded he is from the Bride in a similar helplessness to the reader's in front of both the dead text and body. The unification with the Word can be accomplished only by way of the death, passing through death, by annihilating death and bringing the dead body to life.

---

[80] Compare Luke 1. 37.

[81] Bernard's and Augustine's attitudes are thus shown to be wholly different. Pranger, 'Tranen in het antieke christendom', pp. 45–46, expresses the alienation of the reader when he realizes that he may be witness to the grief that Augustine has concealed from his closest friends. Bernard's choice to give his lament the form of a sermon prevents this alienated feeling in the reader but likewise sharpens the sense of separation between the author and the reader created by the text.

[82] SC 26.3, SBO I (1957), p. 171.

3.5 The Power of the Word

3.5.1 Limits to Death

With God no word shall be impossible.[83] In keeping with the rhetorical rules Bernard closes his lamentation on some traditional biblical examples. They have been called *topoi* to justify his proper grief.[84] Mentioned in due order are David, lamenting the death of his son Absalom as well as those of Saul and Jonathan, Samuel lamenting Saul, Christ lamenting Jerusalem and Lazarus. They are indeed completely consistent with Christian rhetorical tradition, but for this reason it is the more significant what use Bernard makes of them. They are introduced in the lament when Bernard concludes that it would be impious to weep over Gerard. 'Let me weep then, but let me weep over myself, since reason forbids that I weep over him'.[85] Then Bernard appeals to David who justly wept over Absalom, Saul and Jonathan, justly since he knew that Absalom by his crime was for ever denied escape from the jaws of death. For neither Saul nor Jonathan could there be hope of release from death. 'They will rise but not to live. Or rather to live, indeed, but just to die a more unlucky death, being alive in death. Though, one could righteously think that the sentence on Jonathan is still pending'.[86] A climax can be detected: Absalom died for ever, Saul will rise to die forever, Jonathan might rise to live. And the final barrier of death can thus be broken.

This first gleam of hope, however, cannot still Bernard's pain. The examples seem to have given him a justification only to let his tears flow more freely. His tears find their origin in his love. 'This weighs me down the most, that I love you so ardently.'[87] Love makes him weep for the blow he has received, but also for his house, of which he must now fear the collapse, as Christ foresaw the ruin of Jerusalem. He weeps for the poor who have lost a father in Gerard. He weeps for all the monks because of the strength they have lost in Gerard. 'Yes, I weep, and if I weep not over you, I weep because of you.'[88] The same love which could assure Bernard that Gerard would not forget him, now appears to be the true reason for his pain. It is one and the same love that preserved the union of the brothers, that made the Bride care for her girls left outside, that made possible the conformation of the reader to the text and that now evokes tears on the division. Love also made Christ weep for Jerusalem and for Lazarus. Yet the earthly Jerusalem knows its counterpart in heaven, as will be shown in SC 27: and one word from Christ made Lazarus rise from the grave.

---

[83] Compare Luke 1. 37.

[84] Von Moos, *Consolatio*, pp. 314–17.

[85] SC 26.12. SBO I (1957), p. 179.

[86] SC 26.12, SBO I (1957), p. 179.

[87] SC 26.12, SBO I (1957), p. 179.

[88] SC 26.12, SBO I (1957), p. 179.

For the moment, Lazarus closes the enumeration of the lamented dead who may or may not rise to live. The tears that Christ shed at Lazarus's tomb do justice to Bernard's own tears and make it finally possible for him to accept the loss. 'You have given Gerard, You have taken him away. Even as we grieve that he was taken away, we will not forget that he has been given and we are grateful that we deserved to have him with us. We do not want to miss him for so much as *it is not expedient*.'[89] Just as Gerard, because of his love, could promise that he would never forget his brother, Bernard can now declare the same: his love will prevent him from forgetting Gerard. And while he interrupted his brother in despair, crying out the words of Paul in II Corinthians 12. 1, those same words now give expression to his acceptance, indicating the limits to his own grief.

3.5.2 Inversion of Death

The circle is closed. Bernard has arrived where he had to part from his brother. In the text they have become one again, though separated by death. Bernard's earthly love answers to Gerard's spiritual love and neither will forget the other. But the factual rupture continues. Bernard accepts but remains outside. He now resembles the girls who no longer reproach the Bride with her joy, but who nonetheless remain outside the closed door. He also resembles the reader who wants to conform to the text but whose transformation is hindered by his own body. By joining the reader and breaking through the text with his own affective reality, Bernard manages to give a new impulse to the reading process and to stimulate the unification of the reader with the author, but in the end author and reader both remain outside. They find themselves still in front of the dead bodies of text and brother.

Gerard, however, also appeared to be the outside of Bernard. He realized in the active life of the monastery what Bernard lived in its spiritual inner core. A similarity then exists between Gerard in the monastery and the reader in his reading, since the reader must exteriorize the inner life of the text. He must conform his own life to the words the author speaks from within the text, as Gerard transformed into an active attitude towards the world outside the monastery the words that Bernard spoke from within it. Bernard forces the reader into a double role: he is outside with the author in front of the lifeless corpses of text and brother, but likewise the reader is this same brother alive, and for this reason must also be the living text. The union of Gerard and Bernard is evoked within the reader, just as their separation is a rupture within himself. The active part that ought to be situated on the outside (the living Gerard) is transposed into the 'inside' as the desire for the spiritual truth inside the text (the dead Gerard in his union with the living Word). The spiritual part that normally is to be found inside the text (Bernard the author) has come out to join the reader before the closed door (the living Bernard who is separated from his dead brother). The spiritual core of the text has become its realization in life by the reader.

---

[89] II Corinthians 12. 1. SC 26.13: SBO I (1957), p. 180.

The reader's own intimate desire to become one with the spiritual heart of the text finds itself left outside and weeping, restrained by body and text which both remain dead. If Bernard were to stop his lament by accepting the reality of the separation, he would cause an incurable inner rupture in the reader.

Bernard, therefore, must still proceed. He obliges the reader to recognize both the textual reality and the force of his word. Being an author, he does not need to conform to historical, earthly time. He deviates deliberately from the chronological sequence of the events as his monks and he lived Gerard's death and funeral.[90] For his monks, this deviation of reality would be of no importance. They just had to consult their memories to reconstruct how everything happened. For the reader, however, Bernard's intervention is of the highest importance. The reader cannot be prepared for Bernard's line of thought as it is elaborated in the text. Surely, the reader too will be capable of reconstructing the original chronology as soon as he has heard the whole story, but not before. He will be obliged to depart from the succession of events as they are presented to him by the author. For this reason the textual chronology is basic.[91] This means that for the reader Gerard first is buried. Much later, after the union of the brothers and the inversion of their mutual roles has been described, the reader sees Gerard on his deathbed. The last image of Gerard which Bernard presents will thus be the image that closes the story of the dead brother and that will give it its real significance.

3.5.3 Death of Death

Bernard closes the sermon on a distant memory. During the schism, he travelled through Italy in company of Gerard. Then his brother fell ill.

'As we were last year in Viterbo for the benefit of the Church, he fell ill. The disease worstened and he seemed to be called away. I could not bear at all to leave the companion—and what kind of companion—of my pilgrimage—behind in a strange country and not to return him to those who had entrusted him to me. After all, he was loved by all as he was more than lovable. So I resorted to praying and asked in tears and sighs: "Please, my Lord, wait till we return. Let me render him to our friends and then, if You still desire, You may take him and I will not protest." You heard me, my God. He recovered. We finished the task that You set us. We returned in joy and brought with us our banner of peace.'[92]

[90] Pranger, *Bernard of Clairvaux*, pp. 165–67, shows how the 'earthly' chronology has been restored in the *Exordium Magnum* of Conrad of Eberbach (around 1200).

[91] Pranger, *Bernard of Clairvaux*, pp. 166–67.

[92] SC 26.14, SBO I (1957), pp. 180–81.

The last image of Gerard that the reader will retain is that of the resuscitated dead brother.[93] Gerard is the equal of Lazarus. He, however, is called back to life by his brother. He closes and crowns the sequence of examples that opened with the eternal death of Absalom. In Gerard their figurative meaning finds its fulfilment. Bernard has become a new Christ, whose word has a similar power since in the text he himself has become one with the living Word. He shows himself capable of calling to life those who have become his sons by the love that unites them (*quoniam amabatur ab omnibus, sicut erat amabilis valde*). Bernard is Gerard's father. He is his companion on the way, and finally he is the one who gives him life out of death. The reader, who still is the 'outside' of the text, and who is withheld from the unification with its spiritual core by the death of the text and of his own body, can be called to new life by Bernard's word. He rises again together with (but even more in) Gerard as the 'inside' that comes to life in the 'outside', thanks to the living Word of Bernard inside the text. The last wall is torn down.

Nowhere in all his works does Bernard come towards the reader with such immediacy. Nowhere does he expose himself so much. Yet even now one may not conclude all too rashly. Bernard does not forget what he wants to achieve with the reader. He exposes himself, but only as much as is necessary to accomplish the transformation of the reader. In the end, he himself remains inaccessible. He is the author who knows by his words how to unlock life and death, who even knows how to annihilate them. In the text, he equals the power of the living Word since as an author he has become one with it. Gerard's death and the pain suffered from it help him to break through the wall of the text. Nowhere in the preceding part of the commentary on the Canticle has the text become so lively. Nowhere has the reality of Bernard's words come across with such persuasive force and plenitude. Yet, in the meantime, imperceptibly, the reader himself has become the subject of the text: he is Bernard and Gerard, the author and the text, the living and the dead. As such he will live, only thanks to Bernard's life-giving word that will raise him in the living Word itself.[94]

4. Conclusion

Although Bernard's funerary sermon for his brother Gerard may be considered a masterpiece on its own, it surely is not a digression and an interruption of the

---

[93] In his sermon Bernard does just the thing Berengar of Poitiers wants to deny him: *Sed non talibus instrumentis mortuus suscitatur, nec eloquentiae praestigiis vita mortuo comparatur.* (Thomson, 'The Satirical Works of Berengar of Poitiers', p. 124).

[94] SC 26 is the best and most immediate illustration of what Bernard elsewhere describes as a *renovatio vitae* (Sermon for the Resurrection I.14, SBO V (1968), p. 91) or a *revocatio vitae* (Life of Malachy, Prologue: SBO III (1963) p. 307–09. Compare my article in the *Revue Mabillon*, 75 (2003), 153–78.

commentary on the Canticle, but, on the contrary, it continues and develops the theme under discussion and it even gives it its true and deeper significance. As the sermons which precede it, its real subject constitutes the tension between outside and inside, between action and quiet, between the outward 'black' appearance of the saints and their inner spiritual 'uprightness'. As such, it obeys the underlying structure of this part of the commentary, illustrating in a striking way what these tensions mean in human existence.

SC 26 truly appears to be embedded in the commentary as a whole and to receive its real sense only for those who are able to understand the strong ties which link it to its immediate context. Of course, this raises once again the ongoing debate on the character of these sermons, and of medieval sermons in general. Must they be considered as belonging to some sort of oral literature, meeting the requirements of oratory skills and reported after their deliverance with only slight modifications? Or do they rather comply with all the rules and expectations which are associated with literature in a narrower sense, with a 'prototypical' understanding of literature?[95]

From the reading of SC 26 it will have become clear that for an audience to grasp the underlying meaning of Bernard's lament is too much to ask. It is a text which has to be read and studied, which ought to be 'ruminated' in the proper monastic sense.[96] Undoubtedly, the lament can stand on its own without problems, meeting all the laws and rules of consolatory or funerary panegyrics. Yet, the fact that it does not fill in a whole sermon but is introduced by a prolongation of the commentary itself already shows that it ought not to be separated from the context and that it belongs to the commentary as much as each of the other eighty-five sermons.

This conclusion could be taken as an admonition for every scholar of medieval sermons. They may be less independent and loosely connected as one might suppose when emphasizing too much their function as a part of liturgy. As soon as a sermon collection forms an organized unity, it may very well be that the individual texts have not only to be taken separately, but that they must as well be considered in their sequential continuity. For Bernard's *Sermons on the Canticle* this seems to be rather

---

[95] The 'prototypical' approach to literature as different from a critical one has been discussed by Jim Meyer, 'What is Literature? A Definition Based on Prototypes'. *Work Papers of the Summer Institute of Linguistics, University of North dakota Session*, 41 (1997),which can be found on line:

http://www.und.nodak.edu/dept/linguistics/wp/1997Meyer.htm. The criteria discussed in this paper, which ought to apply to 'a prototypical literary work', are convincing, be it already for their minimalist features, and, though the author clearly restricts himself to the field of modern literary theories, being the nineteenth and twentieth centuries, they prove to be applicable to older texts as well.

[96] The question regarding what kind of audience Bernard had in mind, has been treated in my book, *Een middeleeuws drama. Het conlict tussen scholing en vorming bij Abaelardus en Bernardus*. (Kapellen/Kampen: Pelckmans/Klement, 2002), pp. 233–49.

obvious. Nonetheless, SC 26 with the lament on Gerard has not yet been considered as an integral part of the entire commentary.

It can be shown, however, that even his liturgical sermons, though bearing clearly the marks of their originally oral deliverance, have been elaborated and organized in such a way to fit into the structure which underlies the collection as a whole.[97] The same might be true of other Cistercian sermon collections which have been composed and edited by their proper authors, such as those by Guerric of Igny, Gilbert of Hoyland or John of Ford, but, of course, also of sermon collections in general. Modern readers tend to forget the incredible force of the classical and medieval mind, capable of handling huge compositions so as to give each word its proper place.[98]

Bernard himself provides ample illustrations for his own compositional capacity.[99] The lament on Gerard, its place and role within the entire commentary on the Canticle prove that one can never be prudent enough in reading authors of this stature. Bernard's words on the Canticle could be applied to his proper writings and those of so many antique and medieval authors: 'It incites and entices one easily into reading so as to investigate gladly even under pains what is hiding in it. Neither does the difficulty of the enquiry frighten, wheresoever the sweetness of eloquence charms.'[100]

---

[97] I have worked this out in my paper, 'Bernard of Clairvaux's Sermons for the Liturgical Year: A Literary Liturgy', which was presented at the first International Conference of the Research Institute for the Cultural Heritage of Medieval Rituals, *Genre and Ritual: Traditions and Modifications*, University of Copenhagen 14–16 December 2002. It will be published shortly.

[98] To give two examples from poetry: exactly midway in the first book of the Aeneid, the hero presents himself: *sum pius Aeneas* (I.378[a]); in Dante's *Divine Comedy*, at exactly the centre of the whole poem, there is an allusion to the Trinity: *questo triforme amore* (Purg. xvii.124[a]. At this point, Vergil and Dante are halfway through Purgatory. Dante's three cantos each contain almost the same amount of verses and even of words: 4720, 4755 and 4758 verses, and 33,444, 33,379 and 32,719 words. See the count made in the commentary to Purgatory xxx.139 in the edition by G. A. Scartazzini, *La divina commedia*. (Milan: Hoepli, 1907).

[99] Efforts to show this have been made by Deroy, *Bernardus en Origenes*, who discovered several cryptograms in SC 74 (pp. 150–51). He also found an acrostic in the prayer of Bernard to the Virgin in Dante's Paradiso xxxiii.19–33. See 'Un acrostico nella preghiera di San Bernardo', in *Miscellanea Dantesca* (Utrecht: Spectrum, 1965), pp. 103–13.

[100] SC 1.5, SBO I (1957), p. 5.

‘Spare the Rod and Spoil the Child’: Proverbial Speech Acts, Boy Bishop Sermons, and Pedagogical Violence

EVE SALISBURY

In an officially approved medieval celebration beginning with St Nicholas’s Day (6 December) and extending at least until Holy Innocents’ Day or Childermas (28 December) the traditional hierarchy between schoolboys and their masters was overturned when one schoolboy was elected by his peers to serve as boy bishop.[1] The boy bishop’s duties, much as those of adult bishops, included participating in public processions and preaching homilies that provided a public venue for the boy to admonish his adult audience and to ridicule his master in the sharpest terms possible.[2] What is particularly striking about these sermons, however, is that they disclose a mode of corporal discipline harsh even by medieval standards.

---

[1] E. K. Chambers, *The Mediaeval Stage*, 2 vols (Oxford: Clarendon Press, 1903), pp. 336–71; H. N. Hillebrand, *The Child Actors* (Urbana, IL: University of Illinois Press, 1926), 22–28; V. A. Kolve, *The Play Called Corpus Christi* (London: Edward Arnold, 1966), pp. 135–38; Karl Young, *The Drama of the Medieval Church*, 2 vols (Oxford: Clarendon Press, 1933), I, pp. 104–11; Shulamith Shahar, ‘The Boy Bishop’s Feast: A Case-Study in Church Attitudes Towards Children in the High and Late Middle Ages’, *Studies In Church History*, 31 (1994), 243–60; see also her *Childhood in the Middle Ages* (London: Routledge, 1992), esp. ch. 9; Neil MacKenzie, ‘Boy into Bishop: A Festive Role Reversal’, *History Today*, 37 (1978), 10–16; Eamon Duffy, *The Stripping of the Altars: Traditional Religion in England 1400–1580* (New Haven, CT: Yale University Press, 1992); Arthur F. Leach, ‘The Schoolboy’s Feast’, *Fortnightly Review*, 59 (1896), 241–50; see also *The Medieval European Stage 500–1550*, ed. by William Tydeman (Cambridge: Cambridge University Press, 2001), 107–109; Richard L. DeMolen, ‘*Puer Christi Imitatio*: The Festival of the Boy-Bishop in Tudor England’, *Moreana*, 12 (1975), 17–28. Warren W. Wooden, ‘Childermass Ceremonies in Late Medieval England: The Literary Legacy’, Fifteenth-Century Studies, 4 (1981), 195–205.

[2] The only act he could not participate in was administering the sacraments.

I say 'medieval standards' because the schoolmaster, acting *in loco parentis*, was sanctioned by medieval society to administer discipline in any way he deemed fit. And because many churchmen and scholastics believed that knowledge could be acquired only through adequate suffering, humility, and obedience, the authority of the schoolmaster could be construed both as a legal right and a moral obligation. The proverbial expression often attributed to the wisdom of Solomon—spare the rod and spoil the child—lent additional authority to this rigorous and very physical form of discipline.[3]

The three extant boy bishop sermons examined here—the 1495 sermon delivered at St Paul, the Gloucester sermon in 1558, and Erasmus's *Homily to the Child Jesus* (*Concio de puero Iesu*) in 1512 demonstrate how violence construed both as literal force and as a symbolic acculturation process resides at the very centre of the institutions responsible for the education of boys.[4] Taken together these three sermons reveal the intensity of the premodern debate on how best to raise and educate children, and much in the way of the *ad status* sermons of the thirteenth century,[5] they contribute to our understanding of the pedagogical and childrearing practices of the past. Perhaps even more importantly these sermons enable us to see how literal forms of discipline are gradually institutionalized and accepted as conventional wisdom over time.

As a number of scholars have suggested, the boy bishop ceremonies were not simply carnivalesque ceremonies orchestrated for the purpose of allowing schoolboys to vent typical schoolboy frustrations.[6] Rather, these occasions had serious overtones as public commemoration of scriptural events and acknowledgment of the place of children in sacred history. Ritual re-enactments and liturgical processions both inside and outside sacred space celebrated that sacred history and facilitated its retention in the memories of individuals in the audience: the upside-down carnivalesque world simply rendered the celebratory features of these events more vividly and thus more memorable. But as several episodes surrounding the boy bishop feasts and his sermons suggest, recapitulating sacred history could provoke harsh critique and censure from ecclesiastics both in support

---

[3] The expression as it comes down to us—spare the rod and spoil the child—was coined by Samuel Butler in the nineteenth century. This 'modern' version embodies a number of proverbial statements that advocate corporal punishment as a viable form of discipline.

[4] 'Two Sermons Preached by the Boy Bishop', ed. by J. Nichols, *Camden Miscellany*, n.s., 14 (London, 1875: repr. 1965), pp. i–xxxvi, 1–29. Erasmus, 'Homily on the Child Jesus', in *Collected Works of Erasmus*, ed. by Elaine Fantham, Erika Rummel, and Jozef Ijsewijn, IIIX (Toronto: University of Toronto Press, 1989), pp. 56–70.

[5] Jenny Swanson, 'Childhood and Childrearing in *ad status* Sermons by Later Thirteenth-Century Friars," *Journal of Medieval History*, 16 (1990), 309–31.

[6] Chambers, *The Mediaeval Stage*, I, pp. 336–71; Kolve, *The Play Called Corpus Christi*, pp. 135–38; Karl Young, *The Drama of the Medieval Church*, col. 1, pp. 104–11.

of the festivities and in opposition. While many recognized the spiritual rewards and the financial benefits of the feast, others saw the events and even the boy bishop himself as a challenge to social order. Indeed, mob violence was known to have occurred in Salisbury, at St Peterburg, at Regensburg in Germany, and in Paris where there was a riot during which the boy believed to have been the bishop that year—Bartholomew Divitas—was allegedly murdered.[7] That a similar event occurred across the channel with the apparent homicide of England's most famous boy bishop, Hugh of Lincoln (1255), is an event echoed in Chaucer's Prioress's Tale.[8] To apply the rod then was to tame an individual boy, to keep him in his place, to make him into a pious man, and to subdue the perpetually unruly and rebellious 'next generation'. To apply the rod was to guarantee conformity and respect for authority; to spare the rod was to risk rebellion at all levels of society.[9]

Little is known of the early origins of the boy bishop feast though some scholars surmise that over time it merged with the Feast of Fools and the celebration of St Nicholas, Bishop of Myra, whose cult swept across Europe in the eleventh century. The cult of St Nicholas honoured the patron saint and protector of schoolboys who was also the patron saint of unmarried girls, sailors, thieves, and various others. As incumbent upon all those who attain canonization, Nicholas performed a number of miracles, one of which was to restore the bodies of three boys who had been murdered and pickled in large barrels by an innkeeper. By the logic of miracle St Nicholas reversed the effects of violent crime, literally undoing the injury done to the bodies of these boys. In doing so, he initiated a legend that associates him with the performance of miracles, the prerequisite of which is injury or death.[10]

---

[7] E. K. Chambers, p. 364.

[8] Marie Padgett Hamilton suggests that the original source for Chaucer's tale was a sermon preached by the boy bishop. See 'Echoes of Childermas in the Tale of the Prioress', *Modern Language Review*, 34, no. 1 (1939), 1–8. For a more recent discussion see Lee Patterson, 'The Living Witnesses of Our Redemption: Martyrdom and Imitation in Chaucer's Prioress's Tale', *The Journal of Medieval and Early Modern Studies*, 31, no. 3 (2001), 507–60.

[9] The Feast of Fools which originally consisted of four separate celebrations: St Stephen's Day (26 December), John the Evangelist's Day (27 December), Holy Innocents' Day (28 December), and the Feast of the Circumcision (1 January), traditionally allowed the inversion of ecclesiastical hierarchies—the lower clergy members were permitted to mock church services, to sing, to dance, to celebrate the special holy status of the meek, the humble, and the generally disenfranchised. An extensive discussion is found in Chambers, *The Medieval Stage*, I, pp. 353–71. See also Shulamith Shahar, *Childhood*, pp. 179–82.

[10] The *vita* of St Nicholas is recounted in Jacobus de Voragine, *The Golden Legend: Readings on Saints*, trans. by William Granger Ryan, 2 vols (Princeton: Princeton University Press, 1993), pp. 21–27. This particular episode is missing, though the rescue of the three unmarried girls is present. The entire legend appears in *The Oxford Dictionary of Saints*, ed. by David Hugh Farmer (London: Oxford University Press, 1978), pp. 292–93. The saint is also known to have spurned the nourishment of his mother's breast on Wednesdays and

The boy bishop, who was occasionally called 'Bishop Nicholas', was a metaphor for a saint whose powers transcended the natural world. As representative of Nicholas his words had the power to transform adults into children again, to heal the effects of violence on the bodies and minds of his auditors, if only momentarily. His words promised that innocence could be regained and safety could be assured if only people would follow a certain set of regulations and submit to a higher authority. But St Nicholas was not all the boy bishop could represent to a pre-modern audience; to some he could symbolize the Holy Innocents, to others he represented the twelve-year-old Jesus in the temple, while still others saw in him a symbol of episcopal authority. Whatever he could or did represent to various individuals or groups of people at various times or places, the fact remained that when the boy bishop delivered his sermon, his sanctified authority lent additional meaning to his every word.

That corporal punishment in the schools had become standard practice for keeping rambunctious schoolboys in line 'by the coercion of the birch rod', is attested to by many scholars.[11] But the connection between corporal discipline and proverbial wisdom is made most apparent by Arthur F. Leach. In his oft-cited essay on the boy bishop, he says:

> [T]he medieval schoolboy's life was not a happy one. It was dominated by the stupid, not to say wicked, utterance of the Wise man as to sparing the rod and spoiling the child. The very insignia of a schoolmaster were the instruments of torture. While a canon on installation was given a book for spirituals, and a fish-shaped loaf of bread for the temporalities, the schoolmaster was inducted 'with birch and rod' the latter for constant use on head and hand, and the former for the more ordered application of

---

Fridays when he was an infant. That the St Nicholas plays in the Fleury Playbook were violent is suggested by Clifford Davidson in 'Violence and the Saint Play', *Studies in Philology*, 108 (2001), 292–314. 'In the *Tres clerici*, one of the four St Nicholas plays in the Fleury Playbook (Orléans, Bibliothèque Municipale, MS. 201), the three boys are taken away and butchered by the wicked innkeeper and his wife, who offer their flesh as food to St Nicholas. Refusing the meat placed before him the saint through his prayer brings the boys back to life. In the *Herod* and the *Interfectionem puerorum* (*Slaying of the Innocents*) in the same manuscript, children playing the Innocents who follow the Lamb are as if slain by the king's death-squad in view of the audience, and Rachel weeps and sings movingly for the children of Israel, who in this case will be taken up by an angel into bliss at the end of the play' (293).

[11] Anthony Fletcher, *Gender, Sex and Subordination in England 1500–1800* (New Haven, CT: Yale University Press, 1995), p. 300. See also Marjorie Curry Woods, 'Among Men—Not Boys: Histories of Rhetoric and the Exclusion of Pedagogy', *Rhetoric Society Quarterly*, 22 (1989), 18–26; also her 'Rape and the Pedagogical Rhetoric of Sexual Violence', in *Criticism and Dissent in the Middle Ages*, ed. by Rita Copeland (Cambridge: Cambridge University Press, 1996), pp. 56–86.

> argument *a posteriori*. It was less trouble to beat a boy than to teach him. So the medieval schoolmaster's motto was "Quot verba, tot verbera, a word and a blow".[12]

Leach's remarks are particularly germane to a discussion of proverbial speech acts in relation to corporal discipline of boys since he so explicitly associates the proverb attributed to Solomon with speech: *quot verba, tot verbero*, a word and a blow. The schoolmaster's commands, admonishments, and directives accompanied by a blow with a rod encourages the student to associate the master's word with the blow until eventually the word and the blow become one. In hierarchically arranged social contexts (king/subject, parent/child, abbot or abbess/novitiate, master/student) speech acts, particularly those that fall into the category of command, directive, or legal pronouncement are not static and innocuous. Delivered from those in positions of authority to their subordinates these speech acts produce an effect; they are one-way, forceful, binding, consequential, and often injurious.[13]

The proverb that Leach relates to schoolmasters discloses the inherent violence of Solomon's brand of wisdom: *Qui parcit virgae odit filium suum; qui autem diligit illum instanter erudit.*[14] It also demonstrates how this species of violence is bound up in expressions of parental love, disguised as concern for the child, rendered for his or her moral development; sparing the rod does not translate to an act of compassion, but rather neglect and hatred; applying the rod is understood to be an act of love and concern. The proverb expresses a standard of corporal punishment rendered authoritative by its association with Solomon.

The inherent violence of Solomon's proverb is likely related to another example of his wisdom, relevant here because it narrates how speech functions as an implement of discipline. I am referring to the dispute between two women over an infant, each claiming to be its 'true' mother. When Solomon offers a solution, i.e., to cut the infant boy in half, the biological mother relinquishes her claim because she knows that Solomon represents the law of the land—his statements are legal pronouncements; his words are the law and therefore binding. Spoken in conjunction with a raised sword Solomon's words accrue all the force of the legal system as they threaten to cut the infant body in half to settle the dispute. Solomon's mode of justice demonstrates how words and violent actions are difficult to separate particularly in

---

[12] Arthur F. Leach, p. 128.

[13] Though Michel Foucault does not specifically address medieval education and child-rearing practices, his study of the birth of the prison has some relevance here, especially his chapter on 'Docile Bodies', in *Discipline and Punish: The Birth of the Prison*, trans. by Alan Sheridan (New York: Vintage, 1979), 135–69. Also relevant is Judith Butler's discussion of the power of speech in *Excitable Speech: A Politics of the Performative* (New York: Routledge, 1997).

[14] 'He who spares the rod hates the child; he who loves [the child] vehemently teaches him.' *Biblia Sacra iuxta vulgatam versionem*, ed. by Bonifatio Fischer and others (Stuttgart: Deutsche Bibelgesellschaft, 1983), p. 692.

contexts in which authority is deployed and lessons are to be learned. No less than the proverb attributed to Solomon the narrative of the contesting mothers assures the virtue of weapons used as implements of justice done in the name of love. And because Solomon's wisdom is reiterated in discourses from the Bible to homily to literature to advice manuals and lyric poetry, it was accepted and passed on as conventional wisdom.[15]

Solomon's wisdom emerges in the St Paul's sermon when the speaker addresses the second stage of life which he describes as 'adolescencia' or the 'growynge age.' At this stage of growth and development a young man is subject to constant vacillation between virtue and vice, a point rendered more authoritative by a quote from the author:

> Thre thynges (sayth Salomon) bene harde to me to knowe, and the fourth utterly I knowe not. The flyghte of the egle in the ayer; the waye of the serpent on the erthe; the sayllyng of a shyppe in the see; but the fourth and moost hardest is to understande the waye of a man in his growynge age.[16]

Natural phenomena such as the flight of an eagle, the slithering of a snake, and the wind propelling a ship at sea are easily understood while the adolescent male is unfathomable by comparison. The unpredictability of young men as acknowledged by Solomon contributes to the construction of a stereotype.[17] If *all* young men are subject to moral vacillation and bad behaviour, then it stands to reason that stern disciplinary measures would be justified in order to prevent disruptive behavior. The unfathomability of the adolescent psyche as portrayed here contributes to an already present anxiety about the potential disruption boys could cause, a fear that any adult

---

[15] From Aelfric's *Homilies* and Wyclif's translation of the Bible, to the writings of Dante, Boccaccio, Chaucer, Langland, and Gower; found in hagiography, lyric poetry, iconography, and reiterated in advice literature such as the Middle English version of *Solomon's Book of Wisdom*, 'The Birched School Boy', 'How the Good Wife Taught her Daughter', 'How the Wise Man Taught his Son', and many others. For a discussion of some of these materials see Anna Dronzek, 'Gendered Theories of Education in Fifteenth-Century Conduct Books', in *Medieval Conduct*, ed. by Kathleen Ashley and Robert L. A. Clark (Minneapolis, MN: University of Minnesota Press, 2001), pp. 135–59. There are also depictions of Old Testament events such as the Judgment of Solomon. In Walsoken, for instance is 'a carved Solomon seated on throne with painted canopy behind and flanking [him a] woman standing, woman kneeling.[while on the right] is a soldier with raised sword with child'. See Ann E. Nichols, *The Early Art of Norfolk : A Subject List of Extant and Lost Art Including Items Relevant to Early Drama* (Kalamazoo: Medieval Institute Publications, 2002), p. 44.

[16] 'Two Sermons Preached by the Boy Bishop', pp. 2–3.

[17] There is, of course, some truth present in stereotypes and young men were known to have broken some laws in the Middle Ages. For the widespread nature of this see Natalie Zemon Davis, 'The Reasons of Misrule: Youth Groups and Charivaris in 16th Century France', *Past and Present*, 50 (1971), 41–75.

male writer would know from his own experience. Indeed, the link between boys and men made manifest by the presence of a boy posing as an adult encourages the notion that identities between the two could be mutual. If boys could be men, then men could be boys subject to the same kinds of vacillation and unpredictability.

In perhaps one of the most stunning passages of the St Paul's sermon, the close identification between the boy and his master is disclosed when the boy bishop asks that he might be spared the vision of Jeremiah's 'waking rod' with which he has been beaten so many times in the past. The speaker is reminded of this vision of Jeremiah's rod, he says, when he sees his old master in the audience, at which point his lips tremble in fear. He fantasizes aloud a wish to move his beloved master to action as Seneca was moved to act by Nero. In other words, he wishes he were Nero so that he could compel his master to commit suicide. That this passage expresses an adolescent student's fantasy of killing his teacher might be considered a satirical moment of the boy bishop's sermon, marking what a late medieval or early modern audience might expect him to say but not to act out. Given the carnivalesque practices enlisted in the boy bishop festivities to allow boys to vent their frustrations, this seems quite plausible.[18] On the other hand, we need to remember that this script was written by an adult male. Is it more likely then that the fantasy expresses the master's anxieties? Or is it the expression of the master's own guilty desire? Like the boy, he must remain in a subordinate position in relation to his own superiors. Like the boy, he must suffer the humiliations those superiors could inflict. And while it is tempting to suggest that the schoolmaster may have experienced some pleasure in the act of beating boys, there is only some evidence from the time to support such an assertion.[19] What is possible to claim, however, is that there is an implicit struggle for control of the mind and body of the boy.

The desire to control the mind and body of the boy is the next topic of the sermon, addressed in the emphasis on the necessity for guidance especially between the ages

---

[18] Nicholas Orme, in *Education and Society in Medieval and Renaissance England* (London: The Hambledon Press, 1989), recounts the testimony of Robert Buck who 'claimed to have left school at Clitheroe in 1283 because he was so badly beaten. Robert Eliot of Harnhill (Kent) sued his master in 1390 for beating him' (p. 61). Also, there was a practice called 'barring out' time when schoolboys prevented their masters from entering the school. As Anthony Fletcher suggests, 'Its essence was a reminder to the master of the limits of his authority: the ritual kept alive the possibility of the boy retaliating, yet it never directly challenged the social order' (*Gender, Sex and Subordination*, p. 301).

[19] There are depictions of birching in visual art, including misericordia, but what is extant does not suggest the possibility of pleasure on the part of schoolmasters. If, however, we understand that this mode of violence is perpetuated over time it is possible to look at depictions of later centuries from which we might infer, albeit carefully, that some traditions remain constant. One such study of the nineteenth century looks to the entrenched nature of beating in England. See Ian Gibson, *The English Vice: Beating, Sex and Shame in Victorian England and After* (London: Duckworth, 1978).

of seven and fourteen, and in the designation of who should be responsible for a child's education. The speaker addresses the time at which a father would be expected to requisition a stern schoolmaster to take over his child's education:

> Whan that infant age is ended, the fader provydeth for hys childe for a mayster, the whyche gyveth intstruccyon in small doctrynes, as in hys Donate, Partes of reason, and suche other, the which mayster comunely is called Pedagogus in Latyne. This mayster gevyth commaundementes to the childe in his growynge age. And he breke them he is sharpely correctyd.[20]

After a child reaches age seven, he is considered ready for formal training in the trivium, hence the mention here of Donatus. The master or 'pedagogus' as he is called in Latin leads the child through his adolescence by giving 'commandments' and sharply correcting him should those commandments be broken. It is probably not surprising that this time of life is equated in the sermon with the Law of Moses, which the speaker calls the 'Lawe of Wryten' since the metonymic relation between written law and corporal punishment is underwritten by scriptural authority. As the rod, or 'ferell' corrects so too the commandments and pronouncements made by the schoolmaster correct disobedient or indolent boys. The parallels with the Old Testament are striking since, of course, the schoolmaster has assumed the role of lawgiver and like Moses his authority for correction is validated by God.

In *Spare the Child: The Religious Roots of Punishment and the Psychological Impact of Physical Abuse*, Philip Greven argues that Old Testament texts 'lend additional support to the punishment and violence against children advocated in the name of King Solomon'.[21] He cites a number of scriptural texts among which is Moses's admonition to the Israelites:

> If a man have a stubborn and rebellious son, which will not obey the voice of his father, or the voice of his mothers, and that, when they have chastened him, will not hearken unto them: Then shall his father and his mother lay hold on him, and bring him out unto the elders of the city, and unto the gate of his place; And they shall say unto the elders of his city, This our son is stubborn and rebellious, he will not obey our voice[...] And all the men of his city shall stone him with stones, that he die; so shalt though put evil away from among you; and all Israel shall hear, and fear (Deuteronomy 21. 18–21).

As Greven suggests, Old Testament texts such as these set a precedent for chastisement that marks a 'progression of discipline from pain to death'.[22] Since this is a text from the Pentateuch, the Law of Moses, its meaning is far more significant

---

[20] 'Two Sermons Preached by the Boy Bishop', p. 7.

[21] Philip Greven, *Spare the Child: The Religious Roots of Punishment and the Psychological Impact of Physical Abuse* (New York: Vintage Books, 1992), p. 49.

[22] Greven, *Spare the Child*, p. 49.

even than Greven suggests since obedience is one of its primary themes, and a trajectory from the first implications of rebellion to a son's stoning to death can be construed not merely as an isolated event but as the law. And because Christianity appropriated Old Testament texts, what is said in the Old Testament has a typological relationship to the meaning of the New. Moreover, when Christianity changed the nature of God from Jehovah to Father, the violent acts committed by the Father against his children in the Old Testament function as models for social behaviour. This helps us to see how Old Testament justice can be converted into a Christian mode of justice ostensibly modelled on benevolence and peaceful coexistence but undergirded by admonitory speech acts that promise severe consequences for disobedience. As all three sermons suggest the militant Christ could be a formidable figure, every bit as jealous and demanding as Jehovah.

The Gloucester sermon, delivered by the boy bishop in 1558, is more intensely apocalyptic and noticeably focused on punitive forms of discipline than the St Paul's sermon.[23] These are important features since in this sermon the boy bishop also represents the Holy Innocents as depicted in the Book of Revelation. Typologically related to the first martyrs who shed their blood for Christ, these Holy Innocents are among those chosen to join the elect in heaven. That the sermon invokes a biblical text that advocates a fearsome God is significant since its purpose seems to be to instill apocalyptic fear in its audience.

Perhaps that is why the speaker begins with the passage in Matthew in order to make clear to his audience how adults could ever hope to become as little children and to shock them with the violence of Revelation:

> Lord, how earnest I wold be with the elders of this audience to convert them selves and ther maners to the lykness of litill childer, that thei myght be suer of thy gloriose kyngdom.[24]

He exhorts his audience to understand the spirit of the law rather than its letter and reminds them how Nicodemus was taught to understand spiritual birth at the time of his baptism. The transformation affected by baptism in the example of Nicodemus constitutes a conversion that renders eligible for initiation into the kingdom of heaven those who are not literally babes in arms. Adults are encouraged to appropriate the likeness of children and to submit themselves to religious authority in order to attain the 'gloriose kyngdom'.

The speaker then quotes a passage from the Book of Revelation that describes the kinds of violence associated with spiritual transformation, the prerequisite for entry into heaven. What kind of violence could be directed at the innocent ones? How could Holy Innocents possibly retain their position in heaven? The rhetorical

---

[23] The 1558 date places this in the reign of Mary Tudor, though it was delivered in December after her death the previous month.

[24] 'Two Sermons Preached by the Boy Bishop, p. 19.

questions are answered: virtue resides in the ability to suffer and at the same time retain humility since 'violent suffering' allows only a certain few to attain the kingdom of God. Indeed, in a commemoration of the ultimate judicial event of sacred history, the boy bishop reiterates the description of this select group:

> Centum quadraginta quattuor millia qui empti sunt de terra: hii sunt ui cum mulieribus non sunt coinquinati, virgines enim permanserunt. Ideo regnant cum Deo et Agno, et Angus Dei cum illis.[25]

Apocalyptic passages such as this, according to Lee Patterson, are encoded with sacrifice and death: the Holy Innocents bear 'witness to God not by speaking but by dying—non loquendo, sed moriendo confessi sunt'.[26] In his symbolic representation of the Holy Innocents, the boy bishop signifies the meaning of that event: to take on the likeness of children is to die metaphorically, to submit wholly to God, to be obedient and silent. This seems to be something of a contradiction at first glance since the boy bishop literally speaks these words. However, when we consider that the boy bishop homilies were scripted for him by adult male authors, it is possible to see how the boy himself is silenced despite the fact that he speaks. The 'loss' of the boy's *own* voice, in this sense, casts him into the role of pre-linguistic infant, a child still attached to his mother and dependent upon maternal nurture. As the Latin word from which this stage of life suggests—*infans*—the boy bishop is literally infantilized, rendered 'speechless', in the sense that he is unable to utter his own words, to speak in his own voice.

The boy bishop is an actor playing a role, self-consciously imitating the voice of someone else, re-articulating biblical texts, relinquishing his own voice in the process. At the same time, he is a boy written into a social script that demands the eradication of unruly and rebellious members of society, the group to which he literally belongs; in other words, the boy's performance becomes a scene of ambiguous signification, destabilization, and volatility; neither infant nor adult, innocent nor experienced, he is the manchild caught between attraction to the material/maternal world and resistance to transcendental signification. At the end of the day when the boy takes off his symbolic garb, puts aside his very adult homily, and goes home, he is just another boy.

---

[25] 'The one hundred and forty-four thousand who were redeemed from earth, they are those who were not defiled with women, they remained virgins. Therefore they reign with God, and the Lamb with them.' The 'stage' direction designates the speaker as, not the group of boys, but the boy bishop alone: 'Solus Episcopus Innocencium, si assit, Christum Puerum, verum et eternum Pontificem designans incipiat.' See C. Wordsworth, *Ceremonies and Processions of the Cathedral Church of Salisbury* (Cambridge: Cambridge University Press, 1901), p. 52.

[26] Lee Patterson, 'The Living Witnesses of Our Redemption: Martyrdom and Imitation in Chaucer's Prioress's Tale', *The Journal of Medieval and Early Modern Studies*, 31, no. 3 (2001), 507–60.

That there was a debate about the efficacy of harsh pedagogical practices at the time these sermons were delivered is important to note.[27] What is particularly significant, however, is how that debate is articulated in this sermon. When the speaker turns his attention to the parents in the audience he implores them to understand the efficacy of a 'proper' education and the need for corporal discipline in the education of children. Why are there only bad children nowadays, he asks? The rhetorical question prompts a critical indictment of parents who are inclined toward 'folysh affection', or who 'fondly seke the love of ther child'.[28] Solomon's proverb surfaces immediately hereafter when the speaker turns to the mothers in the audience: 'Dyd you never here, yow fond mothers, what the wise Salomon saith, "Thei that spare the rodd do hate the child?"' He claims that these are the mothers who would rather beat a cushion than their children. What, he asks, has the cushion done to deserve such a beating? The rod cannot hurt the child, he proclaims. Have you not heard the saying: 'The rod breaks no bones?'[29]

There are many points to be made here about this indictment of mothers who refuse to beat their children: first, there is an assumption about the level of chastisement necessary to be considered harmful, no broken bones, no injury. Anything less than the suffering of Christ which functioned as an indicator of tolerable violence, could be acceptable. After all, even he suffered no broken bones. Second, the suggestion that children deserve to be beaten for whatever reason a parent might deem fit opens up a range of possibilities for correction. Virtually any ordinary childhood behavior could be grounds for punishment—prolonged crying; temper tantrums; random, unexplained, or unusual actions. Moreover, such behaviours could suggest demonic possession since original sin and the pervasive presence of the devil were fundamental expectations of everyday life.[30] Certainly a scriptwriter indoctrinated into these religious presuppositions would see temptation of any sort—even the temptation to be kind to one's children—as a real threat to orthodox disciplinary procedures.

But the speaker's attention does not dwell on mothers for very long, and in an address to fathers he deploys another rhetorical strategy. Rather than offering an admonition that implies moral weakness, he suggests to fathers that they simply should not worry about beating their sons. Hard beatings, he says, keep children away from temptation and foster respect. The implication seems to be that men are duty-bound to protect their children from 'evil'. The suggestions that harsh

---

[27] Among those who delineate this argument are Shulamith Shahar in *Childhood in the Middle Ages* and Nicholas Orme in *English Schools in the Middle Ages*.

[28] 'Two Sermons Preached by the Boy Bishop', p. 26.

[29] 'Two Sermons Preached by the Boy Bishop', p. 26.

[30] Though not directly related to medieval practices Murray A. Straus gets to the entrenched nature of this notion in *Beating the Devil Out of Them: Corporal Punishment in American Families* (New York: Lexington, 1994).

discipline encourages respect implies that compassionate benevolence does not, and subtly marks this hands-off approach as soft as the beaten cushion and therefore feminine. Paternal discipline for the purpose of gaining respect—juxtaposed as it is with the admonition of mothers—is masculine by contrast. If fathers do not administer harsh disciplines, their sons are likely to hold them in contempt as lesser men, more closely aligned with reluctant mothers. The implication is that beatings, particularly those rendered by a father, encourage the masculinization of the son's body.

Erasmus's *Homily to the Child Jesus* was written specifically to be spoken by a student of St Paul's whose dean, John Colet, advocated a continuance of the boy bishop tradition despite an increasingly hostile political climate.[31] What distinguishes Erasmus's homily from the other two is the absence of any reference to bodily harm other than that encouraged in the form of self discipline and *imitatio Christi*. Erasmus's philosophy of education did not endorse the kind of pedagogy evident in either the St Paul's or Gloucester sermons because he understood that such treatment did not inspire the acquisition of knowledge.[32] Rather, he replaces corporal discipline with words that convey the meaning of the blow.

Divided into five parts Erasmus's sermon is an example of how artful rhetoric could be in the hands of a skillful rhetorician. In fact the sermon is so eloquent that an explanation needs to be provided early on. The boy describes himself as 'a child among children' whose authority to speak is divinely sanctioned. The child Jesus, the sermon's subject, is then cast in terms of 'teacher', 'champion', and 'general', epithets that confer authority and awe-inspiring heroic status. The military character of the discourse is notable as 'pupils' are soon referred to as 'soldiers' who are subsequently encouraged to follow the example of their glorious leader.[33] There is a subtle hierarchy established here though ostensibly the speaker, his audience, and his subject are characterized as children.

The military metaphors fall away momentarily as the focus shifts to love and the similitude necessary for any audience to identify with the speaker and his subject. The speaker begins to praise his subject in a series of direct addresses: 'you correct

[31] That the themes embodied by the boy bishop would be attractive to John Colet, the dean of St Paul's in the early sixteenth century, appears in his published endorsement of the event: 'Alle these Chyldren shall every Chyldremasse day come to Paulis church, and here the Chylde Bisshoppis sermon, and after be at the hye masse, and eche of them offer a 1d. To the Childe Bisshopps; and with theme the Maisters and surveyours of the schole.' As quoted in J. H. Lupton, *A Life of John Colet, D. D., Dean of St Paul's and Founder of St Paul's School* (Hamden: The Shoe String Press, 1961), p. 175.

[32] Erasmus's philosophy of education is discussed in William Harrison Woodward, *Desiderius Erasmus Concerning the Aim and Method of Education* (London: Clay and Sons, 1904).

[33] 'Homily on the Child Jesus', pp. 56–57.

us by adversity and encourage us by prosperity'.[34] By listing a number of ways in which the child Jesus proved that he would protect and defend 'us' the speaker sets up an obligation particularly binding for children who 'have a special debt towards him'.[35] Then, in a surprising rhetorical move, he refers to the slaughter of the Innocents as a pre-ordained event of sacred history, which he then folds neatly into Christ's concern for children, a rhetorical maneuver that reconciles the violence of the New Testament event with the gospel emphasis on the sanctity of childhood. As in the other two sermons, the speaker mentions Nicodemus as the exemplum of the old man who may become a child again through spiritual rebirth. But unlike the other sermons in which the exemplum remains just an exemplum, Erasmus transforms the notion of rebirth into an ideological abstraction: 'Christianity is nothing other than rebirth, a sort of renewed infancy'.[36]

The renewed infancy reiterates the notion of silence discussed earlier in relation to the Gloucester sermon, but here it takes on an additional implication of prelapsarian sexuality. The speaker reminds the audience that they should desist from 'fleshly passions', for which he uses a description of Jesus's circumcision to drive the point home: just as the foreskin is 'cut off' from its source so too should young men sever themselves from sex. He then begins an explication of the ideal childhood of the twelve-year-old Jesus who refrained from the activities of ordinary children: 'idleness, food, sleep, silly games, foolish tales' and instead spent time 'fulfilling his parents' wishes, or in holy meditation, or in devout and serious conversations with children of his age'.[37] This child was full of wisdom, accrued largely from his association with 'learned men in the temple', the place he was found after having disappeared for three days according to the gospel account in Luke. What does this exemplum teach us, he asks, a rhetorical question that he soon answers. It teaches us 'how docile and obedient we should be toward our parents and teachers (who are the more important kind of parents to us)'.[38] The message is to emulate the child Jesus who leads, teaches, and commands, and like him to be 'chaste, pure, unspotted, meek, simple, docile, free from deceit, ignorant of guile, unknowing of envy, obedient to parents, responsive to teachers, taking no thought for the world, intent on the divine and occupied in the Scriptures'.[39] To do these things is to become a member of this elite company.

The degree of difficulty in following such an exemplary role model is acknowledged in the next part of the sermon in which the focus is on the rewards for living such an austere life and preparing for the same kinds of persecution that Christ

[34] 'Homily on the Child Jesus', p. 61.

[35] 'Homily on the Child Jesus', p. 61.

[36] 'Homily on the Child Jesus', p. 62.

[37] 'Homily on the Child Jesus', p. 64.

[38] 'Homily on the Child Jesus', p. 66.

[39] 'Homily on the Child Jesus', p. 66.

experienced. In this section the speaker's telling paraphrase of Solomon—'the hope of the prize mitigates the whip's force'[40]—suggests that winning such a prize requires a voluntary acceptance of suffering and sacrifice. To suffer for Christ is an honor and even death should 'be the most desirable of events, since we know that we shall pass through it to eternal life'.[41] The speaker concludes by exhorting his audience to fill their minds with thoughts of the child Jesus so that everything they do, think, and feel will 'bear his imprint'. One imagines that the audience would be left in a heightened state of excitement for the challenge that has been placed before them, of becoming one of the 'brave comrades' to achieve membership in this elite new military machine.

Erasmus's reformulation of disciplinary practices brings to fruition what was left inchoate and less eloquently articulated in the earlier sermons. Speech takes the place of the rod, and the discourse that 'pierces deeper than any two-edged sword' displaces the weapon that signifies the militant Christ and the fearsome authority of Revelation. The exhortation to attain wisdom, to learn from teachers, to accept adversity, and to suffer violence in the hope of attaining the final reward is part of an abstract discourse whose meanings can only be grasped through alterations in behavior for everyone in the audience—for parents to relinquish control over their sons, for the boys of St Paul's school to submit silently to the moral teachings of their masters and emulate that ideal Teacher however difficult that might be.

All three homilies presented here rehearse the Gospel of Matthew in which Christ's admonition to the apostles to 'become like little children' is found. The St Paul's and Gloucester sermons address the retention of innocence and humility as a boy grows to adulthood; these two sermons allude to the commemorative function of the festivities, and reiterate the slaughter of the Holy Innocents as the act that produced the first Christian martyrs; both sermons quote Latin Scripture which is then translated into English. And while there are differences in tone, emphasis, and rhetorical flourish, the St Paul's and Gloucester sermons deliver a similar message on the need for harsher discipline of young males, a view the speakers endorse by quoting from Solomon.

Erasmus's *Homily on the Child Jesus*, on the other hand, advocates *imitatio Christi* rather than corporal discipline rendered by schoolmasters or parents. The wisdom associated with Solomon in the other two sermons along with his symbolic signifying power is transformed in the hands of Erasmus to the wisdom of Christ. Solomon's proverb and the discourses attributed to the child Jesus transform a literal understanding of corporal discipline in Erasmus's homily to a symbolic acculturation process in which words replace corporal acts and become the prompts by which discipline is internalized.[42] All three sermons are concerned with the behaviour of

---

[40] 'Homily on the Child Jesus', p. 67.

[41] 'Homily on the Child Jesus', p. 69.

[42] In *De Pueris Instituendis*, under the section entitled 'The Permissible Instruments of

boys to such an extent that the urgency of the matter is noticeable. Given the turbulence of the times perhaps this stands to reason.

Yet Henry VIII's royal decree in 1541 attempted to suppress the feast of the boy bishop; the king declared the unacceptability of counterfeiting practices that allowed children to dress as bishops, priests, and women.[43] Although there is no question that the boy bishop feast provided a venue for antipapist condemnation, Henry's response seems less a result of Reformation politics than it does an articulation of the kinds of collective anxieties that had existed since the thirteenth century. Moreover, since unruly public behaviour had a way of turning into mob violence in England, there existed a ready-made pretext for ending such volatile public occasions. Despite Henry's royal decree, however, the public rituals that surrounded the boy bishop did not succumb to official suppression until the reign of Elizabeth I, and it gave way then, some scholars surmise, only because public theatre with its own stable of child actors supplanted it.[44]

Public repression aside, however, the wisdom of Solomon retains its proverbial appeal as debates on educational reform and the raising of children continue. As even a cursory perusal of the internet demonstrates proverbs such as 'spare the rod and spoil the child' reach into the twenty-first century, suggesting that pedagogical violence and other forms of child abuse are not to be found exclusively in the institutions of the past.[45] Rather, the debate on how best to educate the young has yet to be resolved.

Discipline', Erasmus states: 'Teaching by beating, therefore, is not a liberal education. Nor should the schoolmaster indulge in too strong and too frequent language of blame. Medicine constantly repeated loses its force. You may quote against me the old proverb: "He that spareth the rod hateth his own son.[...]. But I do not accept it as true for Christians today. If we are to "bow the neck" and "chastise," as we are bidden to do, let us see to it that the rod we use is the word of guidance or of rebuke, such as a free man may obey, that our discipline be of kindness and not of vindictiveness.' As quoted in William Harrison Woodward, *Desiderius Erasmus Concerning the Aim and Method of Education* (Cambridge: Cambridge University Press, 1904), p. 208.

[43] Duffy, pp. 430–31.

[44] Michael Shapiro, *Children of the Revels* (New York: Colombia University Press, 1977). The relation between the demise of the boy bishop revelries and children's revels is a slowly developing phenomenon. 'True theatrical performances arise not from the ceremony of the Boy Bishop but from tropes introduced into the Mass after the ninth century' (p. 9).

[45] That Solomon's wisdom is practiced in contemporary life is cited by many. A website of the American Academy of Pediatrics notes that there are still many states in the US in which corporal punishment is legal and currently practiced (http://www.aap.org/policy/re9754.html). Not surprisingly, the aphorism—spare the rod and spoil the child—is cited as a means by which supporters of the corporal punishment of children validate their views.

Bernardino of Siena Visualizes the Name of God

EMILY MICHELSON

In the mid-fifteenth century, the Observant preacher Bernardino of Siena (1380–1444) promoted the Holy Name of Jesus using a tablet with a distinct iconography: a blue background (often with an inscription); a gold sun with twelve large rays and many smaller ones; and inside the sun, the letters IHS, which stood for the name of Jesus. Neither the monogram nor the idea of worshipping the Holy Name was new, but through Bernardino their combination became immensely popular, both in Italy and in much of Europe. Yet the monogram of Jesus had been, and remained, intrinsically hard to understand and lent itself well to radical interpretations. The changes which Bernardino made to the idea of the Holy Name and to its best-known symbol unleashed dangerous potential for both heresy and magic. To avert these risks, Bernardino had to preach a specific iconographical context for the monogram, and to give his various listeners a strict program for interpreting it. Without his sermons, the monogram remained a precariously vague symbol.

In his critical edition of Bernardino's 1427 sermon cycle, Carlo Delcorno describes the monogram as the physical embodiment of Bernardino's preaching and his entire theology.[1] Indeed, Bernardino did advocate the use of the tablet as a representation of his religious thought and of the kind of worship he was trying to foster. And as a result of Bernardino's preaching, the symbol came into widespread independent use in Italy and even in other places in Europe. In the wake of Bernardino's travels, the emblem appeared on doorways, civic buildings, houses, woodcuts, objects, and paintings. The transition from preaching prop to devotional insignia, however, deserves a closer look. In order to be able to understand the fabulous popularity of the monogram in late medieval Italy, it is first important to establish Bernardino's actual goals and intentions for it. These are most accurately

---

[1] Bernardino da Siena, *Prediche Volgari sul Campo di Siena, 1427*, ed. by Carlo Delcorno (Milan: Rusconi, 1989), 'Introduction', pp. 7–8.

gauged by his actual words, that is, by the sermons in which he promoted Christian reform in general, and in particular the worship of the Divine Name of Jesus and the contemplation of that name in tablet form. I will also comment briefly on the use of the monogram in paintings by Italian artists within a generation of Bernardino, in order to suggest ways in which Bernardino's ideas were received and understood.

Bernardino gave his first sermon in 1405, at the age of 25. He was to continue in the role of itinerant preacher of the Observant Franciscan order, travelling throughout Italy almost continuously until his death in 1444.[2] Part of the reason for the popularity of Bernardino's sermons was his commitment to clear speaking. Although he continued to structure his ideas around the traditional rules of the *ars predicandi* and although he addressed nobles and university students as well as peasants, both in Latin and in the vulgar, Bernardino insisted above all on being understood. He used simple language, analogies, parables, and melodrama to convey his theology.[3] He rooted his sermons firmly in the secular world and used them to give his listeners immediate practical advice for improving their behaviour and their morality.[4] He became not only the best-known travelling preacher but also, according to one chronicler, the most famous person in Italy. His audiences numbered in the thousands.[5] After his death, many of the greatest and most popular preachers of the next generation were those who explicitly imitated him and claimed to follow in the 'stile di san Bernardino'.[6]

Bernardino's success, however, was mitigated. He locked horns repeatedly with the theologian Andrea Biglia, and he frequently faced resistance from his own Observant Franciscan order as well as from those he attacked in his sermons.[7] In 1441 an arithmetic teacher from Lodi successfully sued Bernardino for libel after the latter ruined his livelihood by calling him a heretic (the decision was later overturned).[8] Most important for our (and presumably his) purposes, in 1426 Pope Martin V summoned Bernardino to Rome, where Bernardino stood trial for heresy. The main accusation in this trial was the charge that Bernardino was encouraging idolatry with his IHS monogram. Bernardino won his trial so successfully that he

---

[2] Iris Origo, *The World of San Bernardino* (New York: Harcourt, Brace, and World, 1962), pp. 1–2.

[3] Origo, *The World*, pp. 35–37; Franco Mormando, *The Preacher's Demons: Bernardino of Siena and the Social Underworld of Early Renaissance Italy* (Chicago: University of Chicago Press, 1999), p. 9.

[4] Zelina Zarafana, 'Bernardino nella storia della predicazione popolare', in *Bernardino predicatore nella società del suo tempo.* Centro di studi sulla spiritualita medievale, XVI, 9–12 Ottobre, 1975 (Todi: L'Accademia tudertina, 1976), pp. 67–68.

[5] Mormando, *The Preacher's Demons*, p. 1.

[6] Zarafana, 'Bernardino nella storia', 41.

[7] Mormando, *The Preacher's Demons*, pp. 6, 83.

[8] Mormando, *The Preacher's Demons*, p. 82.

was invited to preach in St Peter's to the same crowd that had come to watch his trial and he remained in Rome to give one hundred and fourteen sermons. He was later fully exonerated by Eugene IV.[9] His popularity outstripped the opposition. Most of his listeners were soon convinced that they were in the presence of a saint. As soon as his death was known, rumours of miracles spread, and even his donkey was raided for its value as a relic.[10] Bernardino was canonized soon afterwards in 1450.

Bernardino's tablet portraying the monogram of the name of Jesus seems to have appeared first in Ferrara in 1417, after he preached in that city.[11] For the rest of his life, Bernardino would display it at his sermons and advocate it as an aid to faith. The manner in which he did this is directly recorded by the scribe at the end of one of the sermons of his 1424 Florentine cycle:[12]

> Detto questo frate Bernardino, ardente d'amore di Spirito Santo e dell'amore di Gèsu, con fervore grande, con doppieri accesi, cavò fuori una tavoletta di circa a uno braccio per ogni verso e in essa figurato el nome di Gèsu nel campo azzurro, con uno razzo d'oro con lettere intorno.[13]

At that point, says the scribe, everybody knelt weeping to worship the name.

Bernardino did not invent the IHS formula; it dates from the late-second century. The letters 'IHS' are not Latin at all, in fact, but transliterations of Greek.[14] Copyists of the Greek New Testament, who needed a quick and familiar sign for the oft-repeated name of Jesus (ΙΗΣΟΥΣ), used I H̄ C, I H̄, or I C̄. By the beginning of the third century, the Byzantine Church adopted the two-letter abbreviation I C̄.

---

[9] Mormando, *The Preacher's Demons*, pp. 55, 235.

[10] Origo, *The World*, pp. 241, 244.

[11] Delcorno, *Prediche Volgari*, 7n; T. Lombardi, *Presenza e culto disan Bernardino da Siena nel ducato estense* (Ferrara: Centro culturale città di Ferrara, 1981), p. 16n.

[12] Bernardino's sermons were often recorded by self-appointed scribes, whom Bernardino often tried to accommodate in his speech. (Origo, *The World*, p. 12; Mormando, *The Preacher's Demons*, pp. 40–41).

[13] 'Having said this, brother Bernardino, burning with love of the Holy Spirit and the love of Jesus, with great fervour, and with the candlesticks lit, pulled forth a tablet of about an arm's length on each side, and in it was drawn the name of Jesus on a blue field, with rays of gold and letters around it.' Bernardino da Siena, *Le Prediche Volgare*, ed. by C. Cannarozzi, 2 vols (Pistoia: Pacinotti, 1934) II, p. 213. In writing the name as Iesu o Gesu I have followed the practice of whichever edition I am quoting.

[14] For this information see Peter R. Biasiotto, *History of the Development of the Devotion to the Holy Name* (St. Bonaventure, NY: St. Bonaventure College and Seminary, 1943) pp. 1–4; Theodor Dombart, 'Der Name Jesus', *Die Christliche Kunst*, 11 July 1915, 257–69; and Vicenzo Pacelli, 'Il "Monogramma" bernardiniano: origine, diffusione, e sviluppo', in *San Bernardino da Siena predicatore e pellegrino* (Galatina: Congedo, 1985), pp. 253–60.

The western Church continued to use the three-letter abbreviation, which was carried over into Latin manuscripts with the translation of the Scriptures.[15]

Each individual letter in the monogram underwent transformation over time. 'I' and 'Y' were used interchangeably for the iota, especially in later periods when the monogram was shown in lowercase letters. In place of the sigma, both I $\overline{\text{H}}$ S and I $\overline{\text{H}}$ C were common and even interchangeable in early Christianity for several centuries, but eventually the Latin Church came to prefer the more elegant Ionic 'S' shape to the Doric 'S', which is written 'C'. By far the most enigmatic letter in the monogram is the eta, which is pronounced like and is parallel to a Latin 'E', even though it looks identical to a Latin 'H'.

'IHS' is thus an ambiguous combination, in which the first letter is both Greek and Latin, the last letter is a Latin translation of the Greek, and the middle letter is wholly Greek.[16] The confusion caused by this mixture persisted for centuries, especially as people tried to grapple with the 'H' form, and to superimpose on it a Latin meaning which the letter lacked. Throughout the Middle Ages, as fewer people knew Greek, the 'H' of IHS was commonly considered to be an aspirated letter in the name of Jesus. Many considered the correct spelling of the full name to be 'ihesus,' and the three-letter monogram a straightforward, fully Latin abbreviation of it.[17] As a result, the abbreviated forms 'I $\overline{\text{H}}$ M' and 'I $\overline{\text{H}}$ U' were often given as accusative and otherwise inflected versions of the Latin.[18] Some awareness of Greek, however, persisted throughout the middles ages. Innocent III, for example, decreed that in Latin the name of Jesus is written I $\overline{\text{H}}$ S but pronounced 'Iesus'.[19] The debates about how the name was understood and how it should be written continued until the late nineteenth and early twentieth centuries.[20]

---

[15] Pacelli, 'Il "Monogramma" ', p. 253.

[16] Pacelli, 'Il "Monogramma" ', p. 253.

17 Rosario Jurlaro, 'Il culto del S. Nome nella lettura di S. Bernardino: interpretazione mistica del monogramma grego HIS', in *San Bernardino da Siena predicatore e pellegrino,* pp. 261–62.

[18] Biasiotto, *History*, pp. 4–5.

[19] Jurlaro, 'Il culto del S. Nome', pp. 262.

[20] A diplomatica article from about 1909 asks how the abbreviation ought to be written out in the transcription of medieval documents: Ihesum, Ihesus, Ihesu or Iesum, Iesus, Iesu? The author, G. Bonelli, takes issue with the earlier scholar Monticolo, who had argued for dropping the H lest it be mistaken for an aspirant. Monticolo believed that the true origins of the monogram never disappeared completely in the Middle Ages, even in the age of Carolingian miniscule, and that more educated scribes taught them to their students. It would be absurd to transcribe 'ihs' as 'ihesus', because, given the true Greek function of the 'h', technically it would be equivalent to writing 'ieesus'. Bonelli, in turn, argues that it is impossible that everyone would have known the Greek overtones of the name, even humble, barely-educated scribes. He admits that while 'iesu' is correct historically, the spelling 'ihesu' is more true to the intentions of medieval scribes. Such a spelling would have been universally

With the development of the Carolingian miniscule, the form 'I H̄ S' was rendered into 'i h̄ s' or 'y h̄ s'. These letters, in turn, were transferred into the Gothic script used in the fifteenth and sixteenth centuries.[21] The lowercase rendering 'i h̄ s' proves that by that time, the 'h' was commonly seen as a Latin, not a Greek, letter. At least one scholar argues that the proper lowercase transcription of the monogram would otherwise have contained a lowercase sigma: η.[22] With the humanist reintroduction of both Roman script and capital letters, 'i h s' turned back into 'I H̄ S', by now understood as three fully Latin majuscule letters. Bernardino, however, was aware of the monogram's Greek origins. He never refers to the combination as an acronym nor to 'h' as a full-fledged Latin letter within the monogram.

The abbreviation mark, or cross, above the monogram deserves its own explanation. It has often been argued that when Bernardino was tried for heresy because of his monogram tablet, Pope Martin V insisted that he add a cross above the letters as a sign that the tablet was Christian and orthodox.[23] This argument has been refuted as a 'slanderous assertion', and indeed, the cross appears on Bernardino's tablet as early as 1425, before his heresy trial.[24] Moreover, the cross predates Bernardino entirely. It appears in the manuscript of Henry Suso's *Exemplar* and in sixth-century examples with Roman letters, where the cross is placed on the horizontal bar of the H.[25] With the introduction of lowercase letters, the cross became fully integrated in the monogram. At that point, the abbreviation bar that had been placed over the 'H' now intersected it at one end, forming *ihs*. Over time, the bar was sometimes centred over the monogram, forming a symmetrical cross, for aesthetic as well as religious reasons. With the return to capital letters in the Renaissance, the cross lost its obvious placement, but by then it had become such an entrenched part of the symbol that it was generally maintained, and was again

---

comprehensible and does not require the scholar to ascertain whether that particular scribe knew Greek. Moreover, he dismisses the idea that the presence of an 'h' in the name is a stylistic mark peculiar to the scribes who used it; rather, he argues, it signifies that the 'h' was commonly known, understood, and used. He concludes that the correct form, 'iesu', should only be written out as such when the text provides other indications of the author's erudition. Guiseppe Bonelli, 'Ihesu e Iesu', *Studi Medievali*, 3 (1908–1911), 135–44.

[21] Biasiotto, *History*, p. 5.

[22] Bonelli, 'Ihesu e Iesu', 141.

[23] The *New Catholic Encyclopedia* provides this explanation; Biasiotti gives other examples of scholars who perpetuate the story.

[24] Biasiotto, *History*, p. 7.

[25] Reproduced in Jeffrey Hamburger, *The Visual and the Visionary: Art and Spirituality in Late Medieval Germany* (New York: Zone Books, 1998), p. 262; J. B. Knipping, *Iconography of the Counter-Reformation in the Netherlands: Heaven on Earth* (Nieuwkoop: de Graaf, 1974), p. 110.

centred on the horizontal bar of the H.[26] This chronology suggests an alternative hypothesis about what might have happened at Bernardino's heresy trial; namely, that Martin V, concerned about the potential heresy of the monogram, suggested incorporating the cross precisely because of its familiar and frequent association with the monogram; a cross would satisfy sceptics while making only a subtle change. The actual proceedings of this trial, however, are unknown.

Neither did Bernardino invent the idea of worshipping the name of Jesus. The concept of worshipping the name of God is found in the Hebrew Scriptures. In the Gospels, the apostles preach the power of Jesus's name and act in it. In the long Christian tradition which followed of revering a name as a symbol and token of the person, the name of Jesus always merited extra veneration for being the name of the divine Word made flesh.[27] Devotion to the Holy Name grew considerably during the century before Bernardino's birth, starting with the Council of Lyon in 1274, when Pope Gregory X emphasized the importance of revering the name and of bowing the head when hearing it intoned; he also charged the Dominicans with educating people about these practices.[28] Worship of the Holy Name also found its way into votive masses from the middle of the fourteenth century. Indulgences, both real and fictitious, attached to the Holy Name and its masses, and the foundation of Holy Name confraternities, also encouraged its popularity.[29] The Holy Name also found particular favour among mystics. Richard Rolle in England described the rewards of a life devoted to 'meditation on that lovely Name', and thanked Jesus for preserving the purity of his heart by implanting it with the remembrance of the Name.[30] In Siena, where the monogram would come to mean so much a century later, the blessed John Columbini preached that the name of Jesus was dying and told his disciples to keep it close to their hearts and lips at all times.[31] In Germany, Henry Suso actively promoted devotion to the name among the nuns he mentored. Suso's sense of personal identification with the Holy Name was so strong that he carved the monogram into his chest and thereafter was often depicted with it. Suso also filled his manuscripts with the letters I $\bar{\text{H}}$ S, and encouraged his readers and nuns to imitate him by reproducing the letters and by fostering devotion to the Holy Name in their hearts.[32] In his attachment to the monogram as an emblem which is

[26] Biasiotto, *History*, pp. 8, 10.

[27] Pacelli, 'Il "Monogramma" ', p. 254.

[28] A. Cabassut, 'La Dévotion au Nom de Jésus dans l'Église d'Occident', *La Vie Spirituelle*, 369 (1952), 46–70 (56–57).

[29] R. W. Pfaff, *New Liturgical Feasts in Later Medieval England* (Oxford, Clarendon Press, 1970), pp. 62–63.

[30] Richard Rolle, *The Fire of Love,* ed. by Clifton Wolters (Penguin, London, 1972), pp. 96, 157.

[31] Cabassut, 'La Dévotion', p. 60.

[32] Hamburger, *The Visual and the Visionary*, pp. 233–78.

simultaneously text and image, Suso prefigures Bernardino. Yet Bernardino's love of the Holy Name led to an entirely new form of devotion. It was not, like the Holy Name masses, limited to ritual piety, nor was it the kind of solitary ecstasy experienced by the hermit Richard Rolle. Bernardino combined a specific visual image with a specific devotional program. The combination of the lettered name, the round sun with rays and colors, and the blue background in various shapes allowed Bernardino to teach his listeners how to contemplate the many religious, mystical, and visual associations of Jesus. Its discrete, standardized form also condensed those associations and allowed them to spread in a more codified way.[33] Bernardino made the letters of Jesus's name central to its worship, and most important, taught his ideas to vast numbers of people. With Bernardino, the monogram had celebrity cachet as well as religious appeal.

Bernardino wanted his particular combination of the visual and the verbal to lead his listeners into a more Christian life. But what, exactly, was his plan of action? How did he intend the monogram to help his listeners? Before exploring these questions, it is worth noting that many of his views on the power and potential of the name of Jesus and the use of the monogram seem to become moderated and more sedate after his 1426–27 heresy trial, which had brought the worship of the monogram as evidence against him. Specific examples of this transition will be given as necessary. Nonetheless his overall goals remain constant.

When Bernardino directly mentions the monogram specifically, or the name of Jesus more generally, in his sermons, he has four goals in mind: 1) that the sight of the name of Jesus should be a constant reminder of the faith that Jesus inspired and should bolster the personal faith of all who see or pronounce it; 2) that it should lead them to perform physical acts of faith; 3) that it should become a focus of contemplation for those who can comprehend its mystical meaning; and 4) that it should serve as a healthy substitute for satanic amulets, charms, vanities, and sinful activities. The context and manner in which he refers to the monogram also help us to deduce some of his unstated assumptions and attitudes towards it.

Bernardino's first goal, that the monogram should be a visual reminder of faith, is both his most fervent and his most widely applied; at this level the monogram can affect anyone. In his most famous series of sermons, given in Siena in 1427, he teaches that the gift of the name of Jesus is both universal and uniquely human; anyone who believes in it can learn to go on the right path: 'I, Jesus, am the truest truth, and whoever has faith in me is certain to have eternal life through me [...] everyone has the greatest need of this name, Jesus.' Having been given the capacity to contemplate the name of Jesus, we have a duty to use it to 'direct our minds entirely' towards Jesus himself.[34] Looking at the monogram concentrates the mind

---

[33] See Pacelli, 'Il "Monogramma" ', p. 255.

[34] 'Io, Iesù, so' la verace verità, e chi arà fede in me, sarà certificato di me in vita etterna.di questo nome Iesù ognuno n'ha grandissimo bisogno.' Delcorno, *Prediche Volgari*, pp. 847–48, 852. Bernardino's sermons are cited here according to the editor.

and thereby becomes a form of faith. 'Look at the letters, where it is written "Jesus" or where the cross is [...] just as the words are, direct your mind to them! [...] What does this name Jesus show you? It shows you the divinity in humanity'.[35] It is impossible to reach the same level of faith without contemplation of the name of Jesus: 'And even if you wanted to display [faith] without him, you can in no way display it without this name, Jesus'.[36]

Bernardino understands that strong faith is precarious and might not last without such fortifications as constant visual reminders. He encourages those listeners who cannot read to internalize the painted and sculpted figures of Jesus and to use them to elevate their senses: 'raise yourself to him with mind and with words, which is very useful for the rough and simple people who don't know how to read except in painted stories.'[37] The painted figure, he goes on to say, is on a lower plane than the written word. Bernardino, therefore, also advocates installing the monogram in as many places as possible. When he describes to the Sienese the piety of Perugia and how marvellously well-attended the churches are, he adds that of the thirty most visited, he had the monogram inscribed at least twice on each. He even considers it worthwhile to add the price of each inscription.[38] He anticipates and forestalls any complaints that he is being excessive, insisting that each incidence of the monogram will be a separate reminder and goad to faith. The link between the eyes and the spirit is very direct:

> Ti dissi di questo nome di Iesu, che tu il tenesse in ogni luogo de la tua casa, che tu gli facesse riverenzia, che tu il ricordassi ispesso con buona fede in ogni tua operazione. O lengua serpentina, che dici: 'Che tanti Iesu! Che bisogna in ogni luogo questo Iesu!' E dici: 'Io ho la buona volontà senza tanti nomi.' Dici che hai la buona voluntà ed hai la fede buona! [...] Hai tu a mente ch'io te l'ho detto, e io e degli altri, che 'a buona fede si mangia il lupo la pecora'?[39]

---

[35] 'Guarda le lettare, dove v'è scritto Iesu, o dove è la croce [...] Oh, come so' le parole, così dirizza la mente a quelle! [...] Che ti dimostra questo nome Iesu? Dimostrati la deità in umanità.' 'E però volendo tu dimostrare nulla di lui, tu non poi [puoi] per niuno modo dimostrarlo senza questo nome, Iesu.' 'levati in lui colla mente a colle parole, e molto utile fa alla gente grossa e semplici che non sanno leggere se non nelle storie dipinte.' Delcorno, *Prediche Volgari*, p. 921.

[36] Delcorno, *Prediche Volgari*, p. 922.

[37] Cannarozzi, *Le Prediche Volgare*, II, p. 208.

[38] Delcorno, *Prediche Volgari*, p. 183 and n. 81.

[39] 'I have spoken to you of this name of Jesus, that you should keep it everywhere in your house, that you should give it reverence, that you should remember it often with good faith in everything you undertake. O serpent-like tongue, if you say, "so many Jesuses? Who needs them everywhere", and if you say "I have good faith even without so many names". You say that you have good will and good faith! Do you remember what I have told you, I and others: "good faith is devoured like a wolf eats a sheep".' Siena, Delcorno, *Prediche Volgari*, pp.

Thus the monogram is to serve as a visual stimulus to faith. Even at the times, however, when Bernardino is not discussing his monogram explicitly, he plays with the idea of the visual or written name and of the name internalized in the heart. He claims that the best use of the former is its inscription in the latter, and that the goal of all bodily sight is to encourage mental, internal sight, which is faith. Bernardino's constant treatment of the name of Jesus as something visual and as something which signifies faith ultimately reinforces the use of the monogram. In the Palm Sunday sermon of 1424 in Florence, he tells the story of a bishop (identified in the Golden Legend as Ignatius of Antioch, although Bernardino does not name him) who, as he was martyred, called out the name of Jesus so fervently that after his death the name was found inside every portion of his heart in letters of gold. Immediately after this story, Bernardino tells his listeners to wear the name of Jesus, written or drawn, on their persons, even though at this point in the sermon he has not yet shown them the monogram.[40] At the end of the sermon, when he describes the death of St Paul, calling 'Jesus, my love, Jesus, my love' and lifts his tablet up on display, he has already provided a context and understanding for the monogram and bestowed it with a specific function. The relationship between the visual, oral, and internalized name of Jesus cannot be more closely knit.

The early Renaissance world emphasized the potency of visual images, placing emblems and crests on seemingly every available surface as a sign of power.[41] Richard Trexler adeptly describes how religious objects were seen as the embodiment of divine power in this world; as such, they were perfectly capable of working visible miracles and responding to prayers, curses, or devotion. Symbols this mighty were thus considered dangerous and needed to be 'owned' or controlled by somebody. By the later Middle Ages, ownership of symbols was so important that the owners themselves came into consideration; the efficacy (virtù) of the image was seen as a direct reflection of its owner's 'spiritual athleticism'.[42] In this tournament, Trexler points out, Bernardino was an agile player whose spirituality was never questioned. Creating, and therefore owning, a symbol such as the monogram and advocating its faith-inducing powers was an idea that made perfect sense to Bernardino's listeners.

In the same way, inner faith was meant to show. A second, and secondary, goal in Bernardino's sermons is to teach his listeners to honour the name of Jesus with physical as well as spiritual reverence. He tells them to kneel, bow, or bend their

---

724–25.

[40] Cannarozzi, *Le Prediche Volgare*, II, p. 209. 'Questo nome di Gesu [...] portatelo adosso, o scritto o figurato, e non portrai capitar male.' This sermon culminates with a display of the monogram.

[41] Origo, *The World*, p. 118.

[42] Richard Trexler, *Church and Community, 1200–1600: Studies in the History of Florence and New Spain* (Rome: Edizioni di storia e letteratura, 1987), pp. 40–43, 63–64.

heads, when they either see or hear the name of Jesus. In doing so, he is reinforcing established Church practice, as seen in the decrees of the council of Lyon and again in 1318, when Pope John XXII granted forty days' indulgence to whoever bowed the head in reverence upon saying or hearing the name of Jesus.[43] To the modern reader this insistence may seem petty and the movements themselves perfunctory or token, but for Bernardino's contemporaries, they had great importance. For them, religion was as much a public, communal, and thereby visual practice as it was an internal faith. Then, as now, religious actions were not necessarily any less pious than religious contemplation.[44] When Bernardino tells his readers that 'you must bow to this holy name of Jesus', he means more than just respectful gestures. [45] Physical movements accomplish both internal and external good. They will cement a Christian's inner faith, linking it with his corporeal self, incorporating it into his muscle memory, and jolting him into thinking appropriate thoughts. This is why Bernardino says 'do reverence with your knees, your head, or *your heart*' [Italics added].[46] Those same actions will also display his faith to his companions, creating in them an expectation of his Christian behaviour which will be strengthened whenever any of them enters a church, house, or doorway where the monogram is displayed. Moreover, Bernardino insists on making his religious message is accessible to his listeners no matter what their level. He is explicit in his conviction that everybody has a different level of understanding, and insists over and over in his sermons that different listeners will hear things differently according to their level: 'Hannomi inteso questi parole? Ma meglio m'ha inteso questa donna, e meglio tu, uomo ingegnoso, e meglio intende un dottore. Ma anco lo intese meglio santo Agustino.'[47] As we have seen, he bears in mind the illiterate and tells them to use visual images, instead of words, as an entry into faith. By emphasizing physical gestures, Bernardino provides an intermediate step for people who, for whatever reason, might be daunted by the purely intellectual process of seeing the name of Jesus and translating it directly into personal spiritual improvement. For all these reasons, Bernardino insists on physical reverence at the sight or sound of the name of Jesus and even asserts that in their own way, angels and demons do the same.[48]

---

[43] Jurlaro, 'Il culto del S. Nome', p. 262.

[44] Trexler, *Church and Community*, p. 66.

[45] Delcorno, *Prediche Volgari*, p. 696.

[46] Delcorno, *Prediche Volgari*, p. 695.

[47] 'Have they understood my words? But this woman has understood me well, and this clever man better, and better still a learned one. But St Augustine would understand even better.' Delcorno, *Prediche Volgari*, p. 690.

[48] Delcorno, *Prediche Volgari*, p. 695. For reasons explained in the previous paragraph, I believe that Bernardino's understanding of appropriate behaviour upon hearing the name of Jesus is identical to that upon seeing it, since both are opportunities for internal contemplation.

If, however, Bernardino truly wants to appeal to all his listeners, he has to allow for the most learned as well as the least, and make sure not to preach a message that is oversimplified or boring. As stated earlier, part of the reason for the success of Bernardino's tablet is that its first, immediate impact, while powerful enough for some viewers, could nonetheless lead to further meditation yielding deeper meanings. Bernardino is so insistent and eloquent on this point that it is worth quoting him in full:

> Tolle questo nome, Iesu, il quale è nome sopra ogni nome: fallo dire a uno fanciullo di culla, che ha la boccuccia piena di latte; e aranne dolcezza sì, ma poca poca, però che poco lo intende. Dillo tu, donna, 'Iesù,': altra dolcezza n'arai tu, che'l fanciullo, però che tu senti che questo nome Iesu ti riferische nel cuore che elli è Salvatore, cioè Idio e uomo. Se'l dirà uno uomo devoto con devozione, anco n'arà piu dolcezza, che tu donna. Se 'l dicesse santo Agostino o santo Bernardo, ancho più dolcezza: ellino ne cavavano tanto sugo, tanto mele, tanto zuccaro, che era cosa incredibile.[49]

For the devout listeners and the future Augustines and Bernards in his audiences, then, Bernardino could delve into the various levels of mystical significance represented by the elements of his tablet. Mystical contemplation is Bernardino's third goal in promoting the monogram. The three letters of the abbreviation had been recognized for their mystical significance ever since their former lives as members of the Greek alphabet. The practice in late antiquity of building churches with widths of eighteen Byzantine feet is believed to stem from the numerical values in Greek of the *iota* and *eta* of Jesus's name.[50] The sun, too, was considered a special symbol of Jesus and of spiritual illumination. It is clear that Bernardino knew of these associations, since he incorporates them into his own interpretation of the tablet.

Bernardino's fullest intellectual explanation of the symbol he reputedly designed and certainly promoted took place on Monday, 17 April, 1424, in Florence, the morning after his first dramatic display of the tablet to that audience.[51] In it he makes use of the four senses of scriptural interpretation—literal, anagogic (*divinale*),

---

[49] 'Take this name, Jesus, which is a name above every other name. Make a child in its cradle say it, his mouth full of milk, and he will find sweetness in it, yes, but just a little, because he understands it little. You say it, woman, and you will find a different sweetness in it from the child, because you feel that this name, Jesus, recalls in your heart that he is the Saviour, that is God and man. If a devout man says it with devotion, he will have even more sweetness from it than you, woman. If St Augustine or St Bernard were to say it, they would have even more sweetness: they would reap from it such juice, such honey, such sugar, that it would be indescribable.' Delcorno, *Prediche Volgari*, p. 691.

[50] Jurlaro, 'Il culto del S. Nome', p. 261. The number 18 derives significance in Judaism as well because of the letter associated with it. Exploring the parallels that surely exist between ancient Jewish and Christian numerology must be left to a scholar of the period.

[51] Cannarozzi, *Le Prediche Volgare*, II. pp. 214 et seq.

allegorical, and tropological—which are traditionally applied to text, but which Bernardino instead uses on the tablet. This technique proves not only his facility with traditional preaching methods, but also his ability to stretch their functions and thereby increase their value and relevance. Bernardino then divides each of those four intellects into three sub-intellects: those of the letter, the place, and the form. Despite having created an elaborate structure for his sermon with these divisions, Bernardino does not explain each subdivision equally. He seems to use the form as a means to expound on those interpretations he likes best, particularly with regard to the letters of the divine name. His preferences makes sense—he is a man of words—but in creating and addressing the other subdivisions, he allows for further contemplation of the monogram beyond what he explicitly explains.

At the literal level, Bernardino gives the basic elements of the tablet which he will develop later in his exposition. He says that the *letters* of Jesus's name can be written in three ways: abbreviated, expanded in full (in his spelling, *Iesus*), or in Greek (it becomes clear that he means the Byzantine practice of writing I C̄). The *location* of the letters is a sun on a blue background, symbolizing the most glorious location in the heavens, and the most fitting place for Jesus to be located. The *form* is either square, round, or shield-shaped, with letters around it (the inscription from Philippians).

The anagogical level is the most elaborate, and gives Bernardino the best opportunity to defend his tablet. Bernardino explains the three letters of the Jesus-monogram as follows. Taken together, the three letters represent the Trinity: the Son, the Holy Spirit, and the Father. The letter 'i', being the smallest letter of the alphabet, represents Jesus as a baby, the little son of God. It is the middle of the five vowels just as it is the middle aspect of the Trinity as recited in baptism. It can be either a vowel or a syllable; similarly, Jesus's message could be either simple or obscure, and it is sometimes depicted alone, representing the absoluteness of Christ's divine commands ('sometimes it is just for commanding, "*Ipse disit et fatta sunt*". He commands everything in heaven and on earth and it is done'.). The letter "h" signifies the Holy Spirit, and its shape recalls the presence of the Holy Spirit in the pregnant Mary. 'H' is the eighth letter of the alphabet, signifying Jesus's resurrection on the eighth day. It is not a real letter, but an abstraction (*distrazione di lettera*) and as such it symbolizes the simultaneous pregnancy and virginity of Mary. The 'S' distraction corresponds to the Father in all its written forms: round, to show the roundness of eternity, narrow, to show its unity with human flesh, or 'raised toward the air' to show the harshness of judgment in the Hebrew Scriptures. 'S' kneels down and bends its head to show humility and mercy. Finally, the bar across the top shows redemption in Jesus crucified. Bernardino goes on to add meaning to the other ways of writing the name of Jesus. The five letters 'IESUS' stand for the five wounds and the five woods of the cross. 'I' is again the son, who cries out for our sins; it stands to the side like the lance of the passion. 'S' (by which he might mean 'E', given that he does not otherwise interpret it) has its head bent, 'first to make the world and then to save it'. The round 'S' equals salvation and satisfaction. The 'U' cries out with a great pain and sadness. Because it is closed below and open above, it catches our sins and distributes grace. The 'y' of the Greek abbreviation shows the charity of the incarnation[52] The 'C', of which Bernardino says 'our "C" is the Greek "S" ', is a sign of redemption (perhaps because it may also have a cross, or at least an abbreviation bar, on it). The *location* of these letters is in a sun, for divinity or the incomprehensible glory of God. The twelve rays here stand for the ten commandments plus two 'for the abundance of advice'[sic][53]. There are either eight, ten, or twelve thin rays between each big ray, and as such they signify either the eight days of resurrection, the ten commandments, or the 144,000 redeemed souls (Revelation 14). The form, as before, is either round, square, or shield-shaped, on a blue field to signify faith.

At the allegorical level, Bernardino speaks less directly about the letters, but refers to the faith of the holy Church, of the Trinity, and of the wisdom of the holy Church or of Virgin, who was 'the first blessing, the wisdom of Christians, the wisdom of God and of the Church'. The twelve rays of the sun stand for the twelve apostles or for the twelve articles of faith, and the eight, ten, or twelve little rays show truth, the doctors of the Church, and the perfection of apostolic life, all within the shield of the holy Church.

At this point Bernardino digresses, and in doing so, shows us clearly how central the Holy Name is to his faith: 'The Antichrist, when he comes to the world, will pluck all the names of God and adopt them for himself, but he won't be able to pluck or adopt the name of Jesus in any way at all.' When he goes on to speak of the form of the tablet at this level, a blue field for faith, hope, and charity, he reminds his listeners that St Paul said to take the name of Jesus for a shield and a weapon against the troops of the Antichrist.

At the moral or tropological level, Bernardino recalls the Trinity, teaching his audience that the three letters of the monogram signify different things to three kinds of people: 'For whoever wants to wear it, it is a sign of the Trinity impressed in him; for whoever loves it, it is a sign of his state of grace; whoever is against it will never be saved without changing himself'.[54] The monogram's location in the sun shows the illuminated soul, and the major rays, 'three sweetnesses of solid hope', while the little rays signify God's gift of extra, undeserved grace. Finally, the square shape shows the four cardinal virtues.

This level of detail and explanation serves Bernardino well. On one hand, his belief in graduated levels of human understanding could encourage a trained mind to embark on ever higher journeys of contemplation and illumination. At the same time, it also allows other minds to stay put and be satisfied with the level of

---

[52] 'umanità di mente incarnata per carità'.

[53] 'per l'abbondanza de' consigli; tutta la grolia'. *Grolia* is the Tuscan spelling of *gloria.*

[54] 'Chi lo vuole portare è segno della Trinità dentro per impressione, che n'è innamorate è segno com'è in grazia; chi è el contrario non sarà mai salvato se non si ammenda.'

understanding they already have, or to stretch themselves just enough to grasp the mystical ideas that Bernardino has so clearly told them to think about.

Bernardino offered this very thorough explanation as the last part of a sermon on Revelation 14. 1, 'And I looked, and lo, a Lamb stood on the mount Sion, and with him an hundred forty and four thousand, having his Father's name written in their foreheads'.[55] That name, he says, is a glorious sign, 'the sun of justice' Bernardino then presents the iconography of his tablet, with its cryptic letters and its glorious sun, as a straightforward textual exegesis of this verse, not as a focus of mystical contemplation. The monogram is a tool for teaching basic Christian doctrine to an often unlettered audience.[56] He does not instruct his audience to meditate on the meaning of each letter or promise them new heights of ecstatic union. Instead, he concludes his sermon with an injunction to keep the name in their hearts so that they will be more pleasing to God, and adds examples of instances where the letters of the Holy Name were carved or written in gold. Loving the name leads to grace and glory in eternal life.[57] In other words, he insists that the name is not secret, occult, magical, or mysterious. Its power lies in its dogmatic truth.

This distinction is crucial for Bernardino, an indefatigable warrior against heresy, who had come under suspicion himself. Incantation, charms, amulets, superstitions, and any form of magic were seen as the Devil's chief modus operandi.[58] Earthly pursuits such as games and women's vanities were closely linked to these; they were all satanic distractions from Christian living. Bernardino's fourth objective with his monogram was to replace those things with a similarly tangible, but orthodox, object as a focus of worship. At his own trial, he argued in self-defence that the monogram was specifically intended to be a healthy, orthodox substitute to such superstitious devices as talismans, charms, and magic formulae.[59] In his sermons, he justified his devotion to the Holy Name with scores of biblical quotations. The scriptural passage which often appeared on the tablet was Philippians 2. 10, 'in nomine iesu omne genuflectatur caelestium terrestrium et infernorum'. The legend of the creation of the monogram clearly establishes its function as divine substitute: the story goes that Bernardino had preached such a successful sermon against gambling that it induced the gamblers who heard it to throw their cards into the fire. After the sermon, a man came up to Bernardino in tears, blaming the preacher for ruining his livelihood; he had been a painter of playing cards. In response and compassion, Bernardino quickly sketched the prototype of the monogram in the sun and handed it to the painter, promising that he would survive on that design instead—and, the story concludes, the painter became wealthy producing tablets for Bernardino's listeners.

[55] King James Version.

[56] Pacelli, 'Il "Monogramma" ', 256.

[57] Canarozzi, *Le Prediche Volgare*, II, p. 228.

[58] Mormando, *The Preacher's Demons*, pp. 94–95.

[59] Pacelli, 'Il "Monogramma" ', p. 255.

Such bonfires of vanities, in fact, commonly accompanied his sermons. Bernardino encouraged the public burning of cards, dice, cosmetics, ornaments, and paraphernalia of magic and sorcery. At his canonization, these bonfires would serve as an official example of his saintly accomplishments.[60] Bernardino insisted on the necessity of burning, not just prohibiting, gambling devices, correctly understanding that the human will alone is often insufficient against such a temptation.[61] The role of the monogram in this fiery spectacle, and proof that it replaced vanities in fact as well as in legend, is clear from a miraculously detailed account of Bernardino's visit to Modena in 1423:

> [...]venne a Modena fra Bernardino dell'Osservanza di S. Francesco e predicò suso il pontiglio di piazza...le quali prediche duravano tre et quattro ore; et fece che si abbrugiò in circa a 116 tavoglieri et un sacco di carte, dadi e paltri di giuocare che furono similmente abbrugiati su la piaza di Modena il dì 5 Dicembre; et questo perchè fu tenuto per santo questo frate. Il dì 10 del detto mese fece abbruggiare da 2000 brevi d'ogni ragione e più d'un sacco di capelli da donna e belletti; et poi fecero fare un IHS et fece una predica del nome di Gesu delle più solenni che mai si facesse; et ognuno fecero fare di questi Giesu per le case et per le stanza e da portare adosso, Addì 13 detto, detto frate Bernardino donò il Giesu grande messo a oro in campo azzurro in un quadretto di legno ad uso di madonna a la compagia dell'Annunciata.[62]

In a mysterious and capricious world, subject to unforeseeable natural and unnatural disasters and often under the control of the Devil, the only possible armour and defence was the pursuit of a rigidly moral life.[63] Thus, when Bernardino says 'Look at the letters [...] be careful not to show them any irreverence, which can easily happen through your own fault', he says it not for rhetorical emphasis, but because he believes the monogram to be an immediate and effective remedy against the inscrutable Devil and his snares.

---

[60] Mormando, *The Preacher's Demons*, pp. 106–07.

[61] Delcorno, *Prediche Volgari*, p. 724.

[62] '[...]Fra Bernardino of the Observants of St Francis came to Modena and preached in the piazza[...] his sermons lasted for three or four hours, and he had people burn about 116 game boards, and a bag of cards, dice, and gambling tools which were also burned in the piazza of Modena on December fifth, because the saint had wanted it. On the tenth of that month he had people burn about 2000 pamphlets of every kind and more than a sack of women's hair and trinkets, and then he had them make an IHS and gave a sermon on the name of Jesus more solemn than any he had ever given, and everyone had these names of Jesus made for their houses and rooms and to carry with them. On the thirteenth, brother Bernardino donated the big name of Jesus made of gold on a blue field in a wooden frame to the company of the Annunciation for [devotion to] the Madonna.' Quoted in Lombardi, *Presenza e culto*, p. 36.

[63] Mormando, *The Preacher's Demons*, p. 2.

At times, even Bernardino seems to run the risk of turning the name of Jesus into too much of a talisman by treating it as a cure-all: 'take up the sword and the power, the remedy of the name of Jesus, and you will chase away every evil.'[64] By 1427, however, he has tempered this approach, and modified his views on the human capacity for divine contemplation. Ultimately, he claims, no human can ever reach a true understanding of the name of Jesus in its full complexity and glory:

> E se fussero tutti li valenti uomini del mondo, cercando ciò che se può cercare di perfezione in questo mondo, in tutto ciò che intendono non sarà nulla a rispetto che è inteso in gloria. È questo è solo perché noi non siamo capaci…e così dello intendare di questo benedetto nome di Iesù.[65]

This insistence, however divinely inspired, also serves the very worldly purpose of protecting Bernardino's name-worshipping from higher authorities who might condemn it. If human worship of the divine name will never fully capture all the elements of that name, then the name itself is not cheapened or reduced if that worship turns out to be folly. This is not a negligible concern for Bernardino, who in 1427 had just returned from his heresy trial in Rome, which he had not expected to win.[66] His sermons from this period become a platform both for defending himself publicly and for instructing his congregations in the monogram's true intricacy and sophistication. When Bernardino insists on his own ignorance of heavenly things, 'if you were to say to me, "how should this name Jesus be understood" I would tell you that I don't know, and since I don't know, I could never tell you how to understand it', he is not only making a religious statement but protecting himself against higher authorities.[67] He warns his listeners not to turn the name into a magic formula, and excoriates a preacher who reputedly distorted Bernardino's words to mean that a baptism not made in the name of Jesus is invalid, as if no baptism at all.[68] Ultimately, he believes that the best use of the monogram is as a stepping stone to Christian modes and habits of thought, an indispensable advantage in a dangerous world. When in 1428 Bernardino travelled again through Reggio and Modena, it is recorded that his listeners were so impressed with him and with his discussions of the name of Jesus that they were persuaded to change their lives around. They began to live so

---

[64] Cannarozzi, *Le Prediche Volgare*, II, p. 202.

[65] 'And if all the valorous men of the world were to search for whatever part of perfection can be found in this world, everything they understood would be nothing compared to what is understood in heaven. And this is only because we are not capable of it […] and that is what we can understand of this blessed name of Jesus.' Delcorno, *Prediche Volgari*, p. 692.

[66] Mormando, *The Preacher's Demons*, p. 88.

[67] 'se tu mi decesse:—O come sarà questo nome Iesu inteso?—Rispondoti ch'io nol so, e non sapendolo, mai non tel potrei dare a intendare.'

[68] Delcorno, *Prediche Volgari*, p. 256.

purely that 'having abandoned their internal civil discord, Christian peace was established forever among them'.[69]

Bernardino told his listeners in no uncertain terms that the monogram was not a magical formula, and that divine names did not have magical powers. His rigorous four-part interpretation of the monogram and the specific behaviours that were to accompany it aimed to defend the monogram against misinterpretation, even while they encouraged devotional creativity. Bernardino's explanation of the tablet tried to ensure its orthodoxy by illustrating the Christian nature of each of its elements. Ultimately, Bernardino had no intention of relinquishing control of the monogram to the popular imagination. He told his listeners explicitly what they were and were not to think. This is not to say, however, that he left them no options. Bernardino's sermons were long enough, exciting enough, and well enough attended that he could successfully teach complicated, even contradictory lessons. He was able to convey many ways of believing in and using the monogram while also showing where, in its veneration, the lines fell that must not be crossed. Only after giving his listeners this kind of clear framework to follow could he allow them to fill in the rest mentally.

Bernardino was especially careful to differentiate his name-worship from the Hebrew name of God, the Tetragrammaton, knowledge of which had crept into Christian culture. Because it was an ancient, foreign, and unpronounceable word, it was frequently used in the Christian (or at least non-Jewish) world as a magical code.[70] Invoking the names of God gave a magician the power to invoke demons. Necromancers in their spells drew spells made up of circles surrounding triangular bands; inside the resulting geometric shapes they would depict various powerful objects. Of these, square tablets containing the Tetragrammaton were common.[71] Magic formulae often recited multiple names of God, as in 'I conjure you by the Father and the Son and the Holy Spirit, by Mary the mother of the Lord, by Mary Magdalene, and Mary [the mother] of James, and Salome'. Demons were most commonly conjured up by mention of the Trinity, but also by God as creator, by Christ as the Word by whom God created, or by Christ in his function as judge on the last day. Among these names, the word 'Tetragrammaton' figured prominently.[72] In 1427, Bernardino warns his listeners not to believe that there is another, more secret name for Jesus, possessed of terrible powers 'that if you named it, would make everything that is created tremble'. Bernardino refers to previous cases where such a belief had spread, and calls the believers beasts (*bestione).* Anybody who believes in such a name will not only be dismayed when heaven and earth fail to

---

[69] Quoted in Lombardi, *Presenza e culto*, p. 51.

[70] In the Jewish tradition the accurate pronunciation of the four-letter name of God has been lost, and no substitute pronunciations are ever uttered.

[71] Richard Kieckhefer, *Magic in the Middle Ages* (Cambridge: Cambridge University Press, 1989), p. 159.

[72] Kieckhefer, *Magic*, p. 167.

move upon its pronunciation, but will be considered a full-fledged heretic, worse than a Jew. Bernardino disparages a specific legend which claimed that Jesus worked his miracles by stealing the Tetragrammaton from its guarded spot in the Temple. That kind of name worship, which effectively reduces the divine name to an incantation, he considers a 'cursed madness'.[73]

In Bernardino's sermons, the monogram is a bringer of peace, both internal and communal. The 'Christian peace' and internal reform to which the citizens of Reggio and Modena attest so piously (albeit in a document that is in fact a *vita* of san Bernardino) is the final step in a long progression towards faith as advocated by Bernardino. It is measured gradually by the cumulative effects of the constant visual reminder of the monogram, the physical and spiritual devotion it stimulates, the mystical contemplation of its various components, and its eventual acculturation into the soul at the expense of more sinful and diabolical emblems.

The monogram affected Bernardino as well as his listeners. Throughout his life Bernardino was particularly susceptible to the power of paintings, even though he would devote himself primarily to preaching. His first biographer mentions that the preacher took delight in designing and drawing letters in his moments of leisure.[74] Bernardino describes how as a child he bore a deep affection for a fresco of the annunciation of the Madonna on a public gateway in the Siena walls and considered it the most beautiful Madonna in Siena; indeed, the way he later describes the annunciation in some of his sermons seems to correspond directly to the elements of that painting.[75] The effect of this painting, and presumably others, on Bernardino could easily have helped him to understand how a visual symbol might help his listeners to cement his words in their hearts.

It is no coincidence that the painting which captured so much of Bernardino's attention concerned the Madonna. Bernardino was born on 8 September, the traditional birthday of the Madonna, and always felt a special affiliation with her. He chose that date to be received as a novice in the Franciscan order, to make his final profession of vows, and to perform his first Mass and sermon.[76] In his 8 September sermon of 1427, he tells his audience that because of those vows, it is the day not only of his birth but of his rebirth and the day on which he wishes to die. He mentions that his name derives from St Bernardo, 'so devoted to the Virgin Mary'. As a result, he continues, he wishes to devote his sermon to her, 'in her honor I want to speak of her twelve splendors, with which she illuminates the entire world'.[77] He cites the story of the annunciation, in which the angel who appears to Mary not only

[73] Delcorno, *Prediche Volgari*, pp. 693–94 and n.74.

[74] Enzo Carli, 'Luoghi ed opere d'arte senesi nelle prediche di Bernardino del 1427', in *Bernardino predicatore nella società del suo tempo*, pp. 153–82 (p. 155).

[75] Carli, 'Luoghi', p. 157.

[76] Origo, *The World*, pp. 20–21.

[77] Delcorno, *Prediche Volgari*, p. 684.

announces the news of her pregnancy but also tells her that she should name her child Jesus (Luke 1.28-31). This creates an association between Mary and the name of Jesus.[78] Bernardino continues this connection by choosing the birthday of the Madonna to teach his listeners his own innovations with regard to the worship of the name of Jesus and on the meaning of the monogram.

This choice implies that to Bernardino, the monogram was more than a pedagogical tool; it was central to his theology. In addition, whatever personal identification Bernardino might have had with the monogram would have been strengthened given the nature of Bernardino's heresy trial and the antagonism that preceded it. Because of his monogram, Bernardino was called an idolater and perpetrator of idolatry, a magician, a Hussite, a destroyer of the reverence due the cross, and a beast of the Apocalypse.[79] Bernardino, however, had never believed that he was inventing a new or heretical form of worship with his monogram, merely that he was helping to promote an orthodox one.[80] The summons to Rome must have seemed to him to be based on a misunderstanding of the purposes of his monogram, and thereby of his entire agenda. It must have shocked him deeply, notwithstanding his eventual exoneration.

In Rome, Bernardino was charged with heresy for promoting the worship of the blue and gold colours of the monogram.[81] This perceived distortion of its meaning still begs the question of what Bernardino really intended for it, what he thought its nature was and what kind of worship it merited. Bernardino's sermons tell us explicitly what he thought the monogram could do. The context of his references tell us how important it was to him; namely, that he associated the monogram and the name of Jesus with the Virgin Mary, and also identified it strongly with himself. Perhaps, therefore, it is worth asking what Bernardino himself really was, in order to complete our vision of what the monogram really was. In fine, Bernardino was a man of words, an interpreter who took the text of the scriptural texts and translated them into moral and spiritual lessons to be recounted to his listeners, a speaker who accommodated his transcribers and therefore must have been pleased that his words were being written down.[82] We know that he considered words to be more important than images: 'La migliore iscrittura del nome di Gesu si è quella del cuore, poi quella delle parole, poi è l'esemplare, dipinto e rilevato.'[83] We know that he applied the four techniques of scriptural interpretation to his monogram in a way that he could hardly have done to a fresco of the annunciation. We also know that he liked

[78] Some people consider Mary the first devotee of the name of Jesus.

[79] Mormando, *The Preacher's Demons*, p. 89.

[80] Origo, *The World*, p. 117.

[81] Trexler, *Church and Community*, p. 53.

[82] See note 12.

[83] 'The best inscription of the name of Jesus is the one in the heart, and then the one in words, and then copied, painted, and engraved.' Cannarozzi, *Le Prediche Volgare*, II, p. 208.

to draw, loved paintings, and was so aware of the potential of the visual image that he designed one to house the holiest word he knew. Bernardino considered his monogram to be a hybrid of the visual and the verbal, an image with all the instant appeal of a painting, but ultimately a text with its accompanying status and interpretive elasticity. His creation of the tablet harnesses the power of the visual image in the service of the word in its centre. This conception allows us to understand why Bernardino could honestly advocate contemplation of the monogram's visual aspects, such as its blue colour signifying faith and thereby glory, as a means to deepen faith, and at the same time believe, and convince his prosecutors in Rome, that his fundamental purpose for the monogram was the worship of its letters and the holy name they represented.

Bernardino's detractors succeeded in tarnishing the reputation of the monogram. The controversy it sparked ultimately made it a taboo subject, as the matter of Bernardino's canonization confirms. Of thirty-three articles confirming the case for Bernardino's canonization, none mentions the monogram or even Bernardino's devotion to the name of Jesus.[84] But Bernardino's fans and followers tell a different story. Early paintings of Bernardino—and those who painted him can be assumed to be admirers—show how much his ideas resonated with his listeners.

Paintings here are to be distinguished from instances of the monogram alone being placed as an emblem on doorways, churches, and public buildings. Examples of these abound in the fifteenth century and can be taken as a direct response to Bernardino's injunctions. Paintings, on the other hand, often convey multiple and more complex messages, even if only because the nature and subject of the painting reflect the personal choices of the artist or his patron.

The most famous depiction of Bernardino's charisma and the monogram's appeal is Sano di Pietro's rendering of the saint preaching the 1427 cycle in Siena's Piazza del Campo. Sano shows Bernardino standing very close to but elevated above his audience, and holding up before a rapt, kneeling crowd of men and women the tablet with the monogram clearly represented. Bernardino had preached in Siena previously, in 1424, which justifies Sano's depiction of the identical monogram displayed prominently and publicly on the Palazzo Pubblico behind Bernardino's head. This painting, unlike most from the fifteenth century, can be considered for its historical as well as its aesthetic and religious value, because Sano di Pietro (1408—61, Siena) was both a contemporary and a compatriot of Bernardino, and had memories of their actual interaction.[85] Sano must have prized those memories highly; he would eventually depict Bernardino more than eighty-five times.[86] There are also

[84] Origo, *The World*, p. 129. The articles can be found in *Archivum Franciscanum Historicam*, 44 (1951).

[85] Mormando, *The Preacher's Demons*, p. 255, n. 136.

[86] *Enciclopedia Bernardiniana* (L'Aquila: Centro promotore generale delle celebrazione del VI cnetenario della nascita di s. Bernardino da Siena, 1980-1985); II: *Iconografia*, pp. 27–34, list Sano's paintings of Bernardino.

six or seven other paintings by Florentine or Sienese contemporaries (or almost) of Bernardino depicting very similar scenes, in which Bernardino stands in a lectern and holds his monogram out to the crowd during a sermon.[87]

These paintings cannot all be considered historical evidence, since the painters may not have heard Bernardino speak, and the particulars of the scene may be reconstructed or imagined, but their very existence, recording Bernardino as they remembered or heard about him and not as an abstracted figure in a polyptych, does attest to the power of Bernardino's ceremony of the monogram and the way it captured popular imagination. This was certainly one intent and hope of Bernardino's, and these paintings show that it was fulfilled.

Other paintings of Bernardino in action from the period soon after his death, and often by the same painters as the preaching scenes, depict scenes from his life or scenes representing the miracles he is supposed to have effected.[88] In none of these does Bernardino hold the monogram or use it in his miraculous healing. Neither does anybody gaze at it and find himself transformed. In fact, the monogram does not appear at all. The complete absence of the monogram in these earlier paintings demonstrates an understanding of Bernardino's intentions for it; it may have been powerful, but not as a talisman or amulet or universal remedy. Instead, through their choice of subject, painters maintained the link between monogram and sermon. In so doing, they preserved the monogram in its original context, the context in which it was first explained and promulgated. By associating Bernardino's monogram with his sermons, they also demonstrated its capacity and need for multiple approaches and complex explanations—for a monogram that in some ways was incomplete without the framework of the sermon to elucidate it.

Indeed, the survival of the monogram in any painting of Bernardino at all makes a statement. Painters chose to use the monogram as Bernardino's icon even though Rome, hoping to sever Bernardino's sanctity from his fool-hardy ideas about tablets, gave it no official sanction. They largely rejected more ordinary options such as the three mitres representing the bishoprics he refused, and more obscure ones such as his eyeglass case.[89] Rusconi situates this decision within a general trend in fifteenth-

---

[87] The other painters are Neri di Bicci (Florence, 1418–1492); Benvenuto di Giovanni (Siena, 1436); Giovanni Figuera (1440s, with his colleague R. Thomas); Gian Giacomo da Lodi, who painted a series on Bernardino's life in the 1470s; and Neroccio di Bartolomeo (Siena, 1447–1500) (one generation removed from Bernardino). The paintings are reproduced in *Iconografia*.

[88] This includes, apart from the previously mentioned Sano di Pietro, Gian Giacomo da Lodi, and Figuera/Thomas, Giovanni da Modena (first half of the fifteenth century), Mariano d'Antonio (Perugia, d. 1468), Perugino (b. 1450), and the 'Maestro dell'Annunziazione Gardner', a follower of Perugino's.

[89] Pacelli, 'Il "Monogramma" ', p. 256; O. Scavalcanti, 'Iconografia storica. San Bernardino da Siena (con una incisione)', *Rassegna d'arte antica e* moderna, 7 (1901), 105–106.

century Italian art towards emphasizing the subject's role of preacher and in particular the content of his sermons, using them as a means of both identification and honour: *sermones faciunt sanctitatem*.[90] By choosing the monogram over other symbols the painters aimed, consciously or not, to commemorate Bernardino the way he appeared to them and in the actions they remembered most. They chose a hybrid word and image to label the preacher devoted to both.

Just as Bernardino had considered the monogram central to his calling, over time, the monogram came to identify Bernardino completely. In the paintings made during his life, or from his death mask, or by people removed from him by only a few degrees of separation, Bernardino's likeness in portraiture is strikingly accurate. In the earliest paintings he is so characteristic that his features alone are sometimes his only identification. It has even been argued that Bernardino, whose life coincided with the development of Renaissance painting in general and portraiture in particular, was the first saint to have an authentic portrait.[91] In later paintings, however, he becomes robust, healthy looking, and possessed of more teeth than he ever had in his lifetime—in other words, completely unidentifiable and thereby dependent on external factors, in particular his monogram, to identify him. As memories of Bernardino's character and build faded, however, so did the details of his program for the monogram. An undated but clearly much later painting in the Chiesa di San Bernardino at Carpi shows Bernardino holding the monogram out towards an ill child to cure him.[92]

We have been asking how the tablet was intended, in order to facilitate further investigation of how it was used. We have suggested that the monogram's use as personal icon echoes Bernardino's association of the symbol with him, and perhaps even its function as visual text. We have posited that painters from Bernardino's region and era understood that it was an object of display and veneration, but not an amulet or charm imbued with magical powers. Their paintings of Bernardino preaching show an enthralled crowd on their knees, while their paintings of Bernardino's miracles omit the monogram. The preliminary evidence in early paintings, then, suggests that Bernardino succeeded in making his goals for the monogram clear, and that they were received by the public in the same tone in which he intended them. As for the monogram's subsequent survival, the question is not only whether it survived but whether it did so in ways that would have met with Bernardino's approval. Bernardino's fundamental intention, the one which overshadows all the others, is that the monogram should transform or bolster the faith of the person who beholds and contemplates it. For the monogram to work

[90] Roberto Rusconi, 'Giovanni da Capestrano: Iconografia di un predicatore', in *Predicazione francescana e societa veneta nel Quattrocento* (Padova: Centro studi antoniani, 1995), pp. 25–54 (p. 27).

[91] Mormando, *The Preacher's Demons*, p. 255, n. 136.

[92] Reproduced in Lombardi, *Presenza e culto*, facing page 78.

fully, it must effect an internal transformation, a moral reformation and spiritual deepening that is only imperfectly captured, if at all, by the eye or the paintbrush. Yet, by itself, the monogram could never realize such a transformation. Its powers were limited to the powers of the imagination of each of its viewers. Bernardino's sermons, however, insisted upon the monogram's orthodoxy and gave it form and spiritual direction. Packaged together, the powerful combination of word and image was able to bring doctrinal education, mystical contemplation, and a personal, internalized love of God to a broader audience than ever before.

Sermons Reflecting Upon Their World(s): A Response to Stephen Morris, Wim Verbaal, Eve Salisbury, and Emily Michelson

PETER HOWARD

The chapters reviewed here proffer glimpses into worlds far different, not only from our own, but from each other. Stephen Morris introduces John Chrysostom and the turbulent world of the late antique Byzantine polis where the liturgy acts as the calm centre of the storm. Wim Verbaal explores what the eruption of Bernard of Clairvaux's brother's death into the seemingly tranquil, isolated world of the twelfth-century Cistercian monastery might mean in the context of Bernard's sermons on the Song of Songs. The use made of a blue and gold tablet inscribed with 'IHS' by San Bernardino of Siena to sum up his theology for his hearers in the *piazze* of the Italian Renaissance city-state is the subject of Emily Michelson's contribution. The theatre of the boy bishop—a 'world-turned upside down'—and the implications of the sermons placed on a boy bishop's lips for our understanding of education and corporal punishment in fifteenth and sixteenth-century England is the lively task of Eve Salisbury. It is by adopting particular reading and interpretive strategies for the sermon genre that each author attempts to enter into worlds and reactivate what otherwise might remain dead.[1] The four studies in this section are examples of some of the varied paths such research into sermons is taking. In each, experience is interpreted through texts, but in each one there is a different stance and a different set of assumptions. All the contributions attempt to relate sermons to their particular moment of historical time.

To investigate the way in which sermons relate to their worlds is particularly challenging. If texts produced in past societies confront the historian with an ever-

[1] Erwin Panofsky, 'The History of Art as a Humanistic Discipline', *Meaning in the Visual Arts* (Garden City, NY: Doubleday, 1955), p. 24.

present challenge, then sermons do this in a particular way.[2] They constitute a special form of discourse, shaped as they were by both traditional and classical oratorical techniques, seasoned over time by local usage and particular contextual exigencies. Analytical and methodological skills are sorely tested in the attempt to read traces of society and the circumstances of delivery in the text. How did they relate to writer/speaker? To what degree did rhetorical norms and audience expectation shape the text: its form, its language, its content? How does the original, ephemeral act of speech relate to the text-artifact which is preserved for us? And how were such texts heard and with what impact, emotionally, spiritually, morally? Augustine's ideals, eloquently articulated in his *De doctrina Christiana*, were continually reiterated down the centuries, as we find in one influential fifteenth-century formulation:

> The preacher, when preaching, ought to aim to move people to doing the thing he preaches. So to preach efficaciously he must speak clearly in order to instruct and teach [*doceat*] the intellect of his hearers. Secondly, he must speak in such a way as to delight [*delectet*] his hearer, so as to move [*moveat*] his disposition to hear the word freely. Thirdly he ought to speak thus in order to persuade [*flectat*] him [i.e. the hearer] to fulfill all that is being spoken about, preferably out of love. And, since he does this by the technical skill which Rhetoric teaches (so declares Augustine in Book 4 of the *De doctrina Christiana*), for the honour of God, and the salvation of souls, it is a good and human process or language.[3]

---

[2] For perceptive comments on the problems of interpreting the sermon, see Beverly Mayne Kienzle's 'Conclusion' to *The Sermon*, ed. by Beverly Mayne Kienzle (Turnhout: Brepols, 2000), pp. 965–83. For methodological developments see Augustine Thomson, OP, 'Retrieving the Medieval Sermon as Event', in *Preacher, Sermon and Audience in the Middle Ages* ed. by Carolyn Muessig (Leiden: Brill, 2002), pp. 13–37. Both volumes can be recommended in their entirety for their insights into the current state of the field of medieval sermon studies.

[3] S*ancti Antonini Archiepiscopi Florentini Ordinis Praedicatorum Summa Theologica* (Verona: Augustinus Caratonius, 1740; repr. Graz, 1959). III.XVIII.III, no. III, col.1018a: 'Praedicator, quia ex sua praedicatione debet quaerere homines inducere ad faciendum, quod praedicat; ideo, ut efficaciter praedicet, debet clare loqui, ut instruat, intellectum auditoris, et doceat. Secundo, sic debet loqui, ut delectet auditorem, ut sic moveat affectum, ut libenter audiat verbum. Tertio debet sic loqui, ut flectat, scilicet amando, quae dicta sunt, velit ea implere. Et, quum quis hoc facit industria artis, quam docet Rethorica, ut declarat Augustinus in 4 libro de doctrina Christiana, ad honorem Dei, et salutem animarum, bonum est et humana operatio seu lingua'. See Peter F. Howard, *Beyond the Written Word: Preaching and Theology in the Florence of Archbishpo Antoninus, 1427–1459* (Florence: Olschki, 1995), p. 114. For Augustine, *De doctrina Christiana*, 12.27. 'Dixit ergo quidam eloquens, et verum dixit, ita dicere debere eloquentem ut doceat, ut delectet, ut flectat. Deinde addidit: *Docere necessitatis est, delectare suavitatis, flectere victoriae* [Cicero, *De oratore.* 1, 69]. Horum trium quod primo loco positum est, hoc est docendi necessitas, in rebus est constituta quas dicimus,

The researcher, seeking to link sermon and society and in the putative absence of other evidence, has to assume that Augustine's dicta were observed and that sermons were heard and acted upon and therefore left traces within societies with which they interacted so immediately and intimately. This is an assumption which can be reasonably held for the case-studies that concern us here. All the preachers represented in this section have come down to us as formidable. Three of the preachers were renowned for their eloquence: John Chrysostom as 'the golden tongued' (a reputation carrying over into the Renaissance rehabilitation of the Fathers of the Church); Bernard of Clairvaux as the powerful opponent of Abelard and the champion of such papal causes as the crusades; Bernardino was heralded in the fifteenth century as the 'trumpet of heaven'. The boy bishop can be included, too, since the rhetorically brilliant text, crafted to be spoken before the assembly at St Paul's School—the school founded by Erasmus's friend John Colet—is Erasmus's *Concio de puero Iesu*.

What is implied in the aphorism: 'sermons reflecting upon their world(s)'? Considering the textual artifacts themselves, words and phrases such as reproduce, imitate, replicate, echo, mirror, give back an image, represent, all seem appropriate, but suggest different degrees of interaction. In what way and to what extent can a sermon be said to relate to a particular world? David D'Avray is fond of quoting the dictum articulated by Mark Pattison in the mid-nineteenth century: 'The pulpit does not mould the forms into which religious thought in any age runs, it simply accommodates itself to those that exist. For this reason, because they must follow and cannot lead, sermons are the surest index of prevailing religious feeling of their age'.[4] The notion of 'accommodation' is more mitigated in a recent, exemplary book on Bernardino of Siena as a preacher of peace, which concludes with a concise articulation of the problem of how sermons relate to the worlds which produce them: '[Bernardino's] preaching did not mirror social reality, but did identify pervasive cultural patterns and the hopes and fears which surrounded them.'[5] Surely, Augustine's affirmation of the arts which rhetoric teaches, as quoted above, implies that the speaker of such texts hoped to influence society, not simply mirror it. Cultural tendencies and their attendant hopes and fears were their metier. Preachers can be seen as reflecting and responding to influences which were making themselves felt or noticed within the particular society. But because preachers

---

reliqua duo in modo quo dicimus. Qui ergo dicit cum docere vult, quamdiu non intellegitur, nondum se existimet dixisse quod vult ei quem vult docere; quia etsi dixit quod ipse intellegit, nondum illi dixisse putandus est a quo intellectus non est; si vero intellectus est, quocumque modo dixerit, dixit. Quod si etiam delectare vult eum cui dicit, aut flectere, non quocumque modo dixerit faciet, sed interest quomodo dicat, ut faciat. Sicut est autem ut teneatur ad audiendum, delectandus auditor; ita flectendus, ut moveatur ad agendum'.

[4] David D'Avray, *The Death of the Prince* (Oxford: Oxford University Press, 1993), p. 203.

[5] Cynthia Polecritti, *Preaching Peace in Renaissance Italy: Bernardino of Siena & His Audience*, (Washington, DC: Catholic University of America Press, 2000), p. 243.

thought and articulated their discourse self-consciously on or around fragments of scriptural texts, what they spoke was often articulated through codes which were commonly understood within the culture in question, and so meaning could often turn on the counterpoint of biblical types and biblical phraseology. The medium itself was often a part of the message. This could often mean that there was a gap between what the preacher intended to convey and what he was taken to mean by his audience, especially since, in a Wittgensteinian way, the preacher could not control chains of associations set off in the minds of hearers.

How sermon texts are read, therefore, by modern scholars is largely dependent on the questions which are being asked. Of the authors here under review, Wim Verbaal is the most self-consciously articulate in terms of method. How do we approach texts called sermons? Rightly, Verbaal posits this as a fundamental question. The answer affects how we relate such texts to their contexts–the real and the imagined (assuming that for the historian the real is also imagined). In his crisp, complex, but illuminating opening skirmish, Verbaal outlines the issues facing anyone confronted by texts bequeathed by famous preachers. He questions the way in which medieval sermons are often viewed as 'some sort of oral literature [...] reported after their deliverance with only slight modifications'.[6] His analysis proceeds on the basis of a different assumption, that those of Bernard of Clairvaux, at least, are best considered within the rules and expectations of literature, considered more narrowly as 'prototypical', which can be taken to mean, on the basis of Jim Meyer's approach (to which Verbaal acknowledges a debt towards the end of his piece), as being characterized, among other things, by 'the careful use of language, being written in a literary genre [...], being read aesthetically, and containing many weak implicatures' —that is, being open to interpretation.[7] Because a prototypical reading emphasizes 'a complicated network of similarities overlapping and criss-crossing'[8] the core text of Verbaal's analysis, the twenty-sixth sermon on the Canticles, is open to such a reading since, in his view it was intended by Bernard to be ruminated upon—read and studied—as part of the sermons which precede and ensue. It was, in the end, a product of the *studium*, not the pulpit.

---

[6] This accords with Brian Stock, *The Implications of Literacy: Written Language and the Models of Interpretation in the Eleventh and Twelfth Centuries* (Princeton: Princeton University Press, 1983), p. 410: '[Bernard] did not circulate precisely what he said. His sermons were both oral and rhetorical performances, but on different occasions .[...] But his sermons never completely lost touch with the spoken milieu in which they were conceived and delivered'.

[7] Jim Meyer, 'What is Literature? A Definition Based on Prototypes', *Work Papers of the Summer Institute of Linguistics, University of North Dakota Session*, 41 (1997), p. 4, at http://www.und.nodak.edu/dept/linguistics/wp/1997Meyer.htm.

[8] Ludwig Wittgenstein, *Philosophical Investigations*, trans. by G. E. M. Anscombe (New York: Macmillan, 1953), pp. 31–32, quoted by Meyer, 'What is Literature?', p. 2.

Sermon 26 has not before been considered as an integral part of Bernard's commentary on the Song of Songs, since its focus has been taken to be the eloquent outpouring of the grief that was held in check at Gerard's funeral. Bernard's real grief at the death of the second oldest of his brothers, Gerard, is revealed most in his panegyric which has been called the 'wake' in the midst of the 'wedding banquet' of the commentary of the Song of Songs. Rather than approaching Sermon 26 as an insertion into the commentary of the actual sermon originating in the liturgical event and so an interruption to the commentary's unfolding, Verbaal instead works against the grain of the approaches of medieval sermon scholars and interprets the text from the point of view of literary functionality. Effectively, he is moving the text away from the pulpit, and re-situating the preacher at his desk to engage, not an audience of monks, but his imagined audience with whom he dialogues in his head. This means that the ego of the author merges with that of the reader. Bernard, the author in this instance, in acting as exegete, seeks to use the text to transform the reader into the reality of the Living Word, as expressed in the Bible.

This approach has important consequences. The context within which this text is to be read is not, therefore, the original liturgical setting of Bernard's preaching to his fellow monks; rather it takes its place logically within Bernard's unfolding commentary on the meaning of the Song of Songs. As Verbaal states in his conclusion: 'SC 26 appears to be embedded in the commentary as a whole and to receive its real sense only for those who are able to understand the strong ties which link it to its immediate context.' By context, Verbal does not mean necessarily the historical setting, but rather the textual framework of the passages in question. His strategy of positioning the sermon within the entire commentary means that he interrogates the sermon's functioning within the overall commentary on the Canticle, especially the sermons with which it is grouped which induct the reader into a first contact with spiritual reality, the unfolding theme of the sermons in this part of the commentary. Verbaal carefully links the dynamic of preceding and ensuing sermons to that of the twenty-sixth. In short, it is not an autobiographical insertion which interrupts the flow of the commentary and therefore to be excised separately as part of projects to construct accounts of Bernard's life.

Verbaal's self-conscious, articulate account of a strategy for relating the text of Sermon 26 to the originating event and its new context in the commentary raises questions which are of general importance for sermon studies. Surely, he is right to distinguish the spoken event from the textual event, and the hearer from the reader. It challenges assumptions about the nature of the text as an oral or literary artifact and follows through relentlessly the implications of this. It takes seriously the ongoing importance of the text, now not to be thought of in isolation as a part of an historical event (the funeral of Bernard's brother Gerard) but as an artifice, a constructed text in which the author himself interprets his own experience as an exemplum within his larger account of spiritual transformation, and invites the imagined reader to accompany him in that process. So while it is true to assert that this is the work of the *studium*, not the pulpit, Verbaal clearly understands that Bernard re-worked his initial sermon for a new purpose: to be part of the spiritual work of the monastery, to be pondered in meditation. He is able to envisage how Bernard imagined his words to function. The implications of this realization Verbaal has followed through in a clear, and challenging way.

How the sermons of a late third and early fourth century preacher reflect upon their worlds is approached rather differently in Morris's essay on John Chrysostom. Morris sets up an interesting tension between liturgy and law, with the homilies of John Chrysostom mediating. Through sermons, he claims, we can see the interaction between liturgy books and law books, between prayer and the limits of public behaviour: 'In [Chrysostom's] vision, the Christian community expressing their mutual love through the ritual kiss at the Divine liturgy was the embodiment of Christian virtue which, by its expression and maintenance of both love and order in both the personal and civic or political spheres, would forestall the coming of the Antichrist.' The issues of ritual and civic behaviour, as well as the popularity of Chrysostom's preaching, are linked through appeal to inter-textual resonance and a version of reception theory, articulated as an appeal to 'deep memory' and the compelling metaphors which John Chrysostom could offer his hearers (or readers) to organize reality. In short, through the preaching of Chrysostom, public behaviour was learnt in church. In this view, the preacher is one who is aware of tensions within a society, and is aware of how far it falls short of an ideal. Morris touches on, but does not develop, the extemporaneous origins of the thirty-two homilies on Romans. Like Verbaal, Morris is aware of the difference between the original oral performance of a sermon and the textual artifact which is all that remains of it. Yet he does not explore the implications of the transition from John Chrysostom's thirty-two extemporaneous homilies on the Letter to the Romans recorded by stenographers and the finely finished productions that resulted from John's revisions and what such a process might mean for his claims which relate the sermons to the specific context of their original performance. He is content to give discursive summaries of the sermons in question, first Homilies 20–22 on Romans, then 24, before a return to 23; similar comments apply to the last phase of the discussion when he turns to Chrysostom's Homily 18 on I Corinthians and Homilies 3 and 4 on Thessalonians. Morris proceeds as though the texts before him are the remnant of specific oral performance with slight modifications, rather than thoroughly re-worked as a commentary. This makes less convincing his claims to link sermons, liturgy and law by appeal to 'intertextual resonances' and 'deep memory'—or indeed, his claims to link Chrysostom's sermons to 'their world'. Chysostom's preaching was shaped, Morris argues, by his perception of the issues pertaining to his audience. Yet there is a, perhaps unavoidable, lack of precision in the discussion overall in this respect. For instance, a similar lack of clarity about how to think about the interrelationship of circumstance, scriptural trope, author and audience is evident in Morris's treatment of Homily 22. His explanation of Chrysostom's discourse on the charity of the righteous is linked to the fame of charity organization in Rome, temptations to pride, and speculations on what such pride would mean for Roman

Christians when the logic of his piece would be to work out what it meant for Chrysostom's particular audience in Antioch. There is an assumption that Chrysostom's hearers will recognize their own reality in his discourse, that it will be a transformative recognition, that the hearers will turn themselves into living sacrifices of praise offered to God worthily. So Chrysostom's sermons reflected back on his congregation what was expected from them. The theology of his preaching had political implications and supported the structure of empire. How they might have been heard is speculative, as is reflected by Morris's recourse to such phrases as 'must have heard', 'must have associated', 'resonances', 'both of these allusions would have been familiar to the faithful in Antioch'. The historian's challenge to link text and context is not easily resolved.

For Eve Salisbury, sermons reflect upon their world by disclosing the purported violence within late medieval culture. The sermon here is viewed as the repository of social issues, and in this instance relates to 'the efficacy of harsh pedagogical practices'. Salisbury uses three sermons: two of them are (according to the edition utilized)[9] the only ones extant, written by adults to be delivered by a boy bishop on the Feast of the Holy Innocents, 28 December (dated 1497 and 1558). The third, a 'Homily on the Child Jesus', was written by Erasmus in 1512 'to be spoken by a boy in the School recently founded by Colet in London'.[10] For Salisbury, these sermons 'contribute to our understanding of the pedagogical and childrearing practices of the past' and 'enable us to see how literal forms of discipline are gradually institutionalized and accepted as conventional wisdom over time'.

Salisbury sets her fascinating study of social inversion within a firm setting and is very careful to construct her argument convincingly. The explanation of the way in which institutionalized social inversion could challenge the social order sets up a powerful social context. Skillfully, and rightly, the persona of the boy bishop is established in order to show how his authority, sanctified as 'bishop', 'innocent', 'martyr', and, like all preachers, *in persona Christi*, lent 'additional meaning to every word' of the sermon placed on his lips. The argument then follows several swift shifts. The accepted scholarly opinion that corporal punishment and proverbial wisdom were linked—a word and a blow—in order to keep schoolboys in line leads to the Foucaultian conclusion that hierarchically uttered speech acts produce effects, perhaps even injurious ones. The authority of Leach[11] serves to introduce Proverbs 13. 24—'He who spares the rod hates the child; he who loves [the child] vehemently

---

[9] 'Two Sermons Preached by the Boy Bishop', ed. by J. Nichols, *Camden Miscellany*, n.s. 14 (London, 1875: repr. 1965), 1-29, prefaced 'With an introduction giving an account of the Festival of the Boy Bishop in England' by Edward F. Rimbault, pp. i–xxxvi.

[10] Desiderius Erasmus, 'Homily on the Child Jesus', in *Collected Works of Erasmus*, ed. by Elaine Fantham, Erika Rummel, and Jozef Ijsewijn, XXIX (Toronto: University of Toronto Press, 1989), pp. 56–70 (p. 58).

[11] Arthur F. Leach, 'The Schoolboy's Feast', *Fortnightly Review*, 59 (1896), 241–50.

teaches him'—and the violence inherent in this wisdom of Solomon in relation to schoolmasters vis-à-vis their students. She links this to the traditional *exemplum* of the Wisdom of Solomon: his ploy to distinguish the real mother of a disputed infant child by threatening to have it physically divided between them by the stroke of a sword. In Salisbury's reading this is incontestably a narration of 'how speech functions as an implement of discipline'. Several pages have thus prepared Salisbury's readers to interpret Solomon's wisdom, and the sermons she addresses, as revelatory of violence inherent in the culture. She turns to the first of the sermons.

In her treatment and guided by her own theme, Salisbury ignores the structure of the proem of the text and focuses immediately on adolescence and the quotation from Proverbs to construe that a stereotype about the unpredictability of young men is being constructed, and therefore 'if all young men are subject to moral vacillation and bad behaviour then it stands to reason that stern disciplinary measures would be justified in order to prevent disruptive behaviour'. A further gloss focuses on the anxiety caused to adults by the potential disruption which boys can cause, an anxiety linked to their own remembered experience in childhood. This argument Salisbury pushes further by adverting to the adult words on the lips of a child in an adult ('bishop') role: 'If boys could be men, then men could be boys subject to the same kind of vacillation and predictability'. This may well be so, but it is not a line which the text is following at this point. The text of the sermon declares that 'Y' is like the life of man—according to Isadore of Seville—it is formed of one line which is straight and the other which is crooked. The child is disposed neither to vice nor virtue and is like a tablet on which nothing has yet been drawn (says the philosopher —Aristotole). The problem here is how one respects the integrity of discourse and evidence when pursuing questions of social history.[12] It helps an argument if one assists the reader to contextualize the evidence that is being drawn upon. Salisbury does this for Erasmus's sermon, but not for the two of the boy bishop.

On the other hand, contextual knowledge can sometimes blind the researcher to the possibilities of the text (just as inadequate background knowledge can obscure the possibilities of the text). This leads Salisbury to an apparent overstatement of claims about her second boy bishop sermon, the Gloucester sermon of 1557. A close reading of the text does not reveal it to be more intensely apocalyptic (though like all articulations of Christian theology it has eschatological elements), nor noticeably more focused on punitive forms of discipline than the St Paul's sermon, as she claims. Salisbury has recourse to a secondary source[13] to push the point that the Old

[12] One is reminded here of the late Leonard Boyle's dicta when reading sources, especially for social history: respecting the source itself (one of the key points in his *via inventionis*) and taking care with the evidence (as a way of summing up a number of points he makes in the *via compositionis*). See Leonard Boyle, OP, 'Montaillou Revisited: "Mentalité" and Methodology', in *Pathways to Medieval Peasants*, ed. by J. A. Raftis (Toronto: Pontifical Institute of Mediaeval Studies, 1981), pp. 119–40.

[13] Philip Greven, *Spare the Child: The Religious Roots of Punishment and the*

Testament provides the justification of punishment and violence against children to introduce her discussion of this sermon. Attention to cues within the text itself, though, would have contributed more to her argument than appeal to secondary authority.

In addressing the issue of how fathers might kill the courage of their children (clearly part of the educational debates of the time, indicated by the text, but not addressed by Salisbury), the boy chorister bishop in the Gloucester sermon says that unless a father be willing to beat his child, the child will be stubborn, unbiddable, and in the end contemptuous:

> He will 'hold you nought above all other persons. [...] This is the retorne of such fond tendreness; as experience teacheth by the example of thowsands which have ben brought up so choysely, tendrely, and dangerously. Well, to be breffe, if yow will know the resolucion of this opinion for stowtness, and for [the end] of such corrupt educacion, rede yow the book of the son of Syrac, cap. 30. Ther you shall find the matter playn ynowgh agaynst yow, and I wold now recyte it unto yow if it were not to long for hits short tyme'.[14]

If one were to follow up the boy bishop's suggestion and take the time to read Chapter 30 of Syrac, one would discover a text in praise of the benefits of punitive forms of discipline. The opening verses (30. 1–3) of the chapter from Syrac (Ecclesiasticus or Ben Sira in modern editions) read: 'Whoever loves his son will beat him frequently so that in after years the son may be his comfort. Whoever is strict with his son will reap the benefit, and be able to boast of him to his acquaintances. Whoever educates his son will be the envy of his enemy, and will be proud of him among his friends [...]'.[15] The way in which the boy bishop refers to Syrac 30 implies that it was well known to the audience: parents in the first instance, but also boys and their schoolmasters. Such a passing reference, conjuring up the entire text, was a commonplace in the medieval imagination, and integral to the preaching medium.[16]

Structuring evidence always requires care. As Salisbury approaches her concluding paragraphs the time-frame covered by the three sermons becomes less clear. One begins to have the impression that Erasmus's sermon (1512) is the last written,[17] rather than fourteen years after the St Paul's sermon (1498) and forty-six

---

Psychological Impact of Physical Abuse (New York: Vintage Books, 1992).

[14] Nichols, 'Two Sermons Preached by the Boy Bishop', p. 27.

[15] *New Jerusalem Bible* translation.

[16] In general see D'Avray, *Death of the Prince*, ch. 5. I develop the role of the implications of 'the frozen moment' of a biblical story in my 'The Womb of Mercy: Carmelite Liturgy and the Frescoes of the Branacci Chapel', a contribution to a book to be published by 'Villa I Tatti': The Harvard University Center for Italian Renaissance Studies.

[17] Salisbury writes: 'Erasmus's re-formulation of disciplinary practices brings to fruition

or so years before the Gloucester Sermon (1558). Richard Ramsey, the author of the Gloucester sermon, was of the old religion—that is Catholic. It may well be that the later sermon needs to be further contextualized within the changing religious culture of England, and that questions of how the sort of humanist educational practices evident in Erasmus's text were affected by the broader religious changes initiated by Henry VIII. That Ramsey was removed from his parish in 1559 gives some indication of the turbulence of the time. It could also mean that, in educational terms, the disciplinary practices he was articulating in his Gloucester sermon were reactionary.[18]

Ideas and institutions, and even sermons (which, as 'performative utterances' derive their efficacy, in J. L. Austin's terms, from the institution)[19] often perform functions independently of the intentions of their creators. As Salisbury points out, all three of the sermons she examines rehearse a common text appropriate to a festive season celebrating children in sacred history: 'become as little children' (Matthew 18. 3). As with the rhetorical aim of all sermons, such admonitions as this sought to impel the listeners to imitation and transformation—conversion.[20] Whether intentionally or unintentionally, the language of the sermons of the boy bishop bears traces of the educational practices of the day. In translating these traces into a reconstruction of social practices Salisbury could have extended her analysis by attending more closely to the character and integrity of the discourses, especially the St Paul's and Gloucester sermons, and by pursuing further the implications of some of the cues about context hinted at within the texts themselves.

Emily Michelson's promising piece could be described as a study of the way in which sermons could be used to circumscribe meaning to ensure orthodoxy of interpretations of a visual symbol. In fifteenth-century Tuscany, as with most of Europe, the 'holy' was located in the material world: relics, images, the host.[21] It was a world where sign and signified were well understood, in their ambiguity as well as their specificity. Religious symbols, as Carolyn Walker Bynum has affirmed, were 'polysemic [...] reflecting not just a multiplicity of meanings but a multiplicity of

---

what was left inchoate and less eloquently articulated in the earlier sermons [...]'.

[18] Rimbault in Nichols, 'Two Sermons Preached by the Boy Bishop', p. xxxvi.

[19] J. L. Austin *How to do Things with Words* (Oxford and New York: Oxford University Press, 1976), and Pierre Bourdieu, *Language and Symbolic Power* (Cambridge, MA: Harvard University Press, 1991), ch. 3.

[20] Richard Kieckhefer, 'Convention and Conversion: Patterns in Late Medieval Piety,' in *Church History: Studies in Christianity and Culture* (American Society of Church History), 67 (1998) 32–51.

[21] Though the host was given a separate status, often by civic statute. See Richard Trexler, *Public Life in Renaissance Florence* (New York: Academic Press, 1980; repr. Ithaca: Cornell University Press, 1991), p. 55.

relationships between meanings'.[22] One such polysemic symbol was the *tavoletta*, made famous by one of the most popular preachers of the fifteenth century, San Bernardino of Siena, with its golden sun and twelve rays surrounding the inscription IHS against a blue background. Here the challenge to the historian is to avail herself or himself of the rich contextual, as well as primary materials, to set the image in the complex religious, social and cultural world of Renaissance Italy.

Michelson's aim is to explore the evolution of the *tavoletta* 'from preaching prop to devotional insignia'. Here she shows herself to be acutely aware of an issue which plagues all who work with sermon texts: the distance between intentionality and reception. Her approach, then, is to establish Bernardino's intentions for the monogram through an examination of his sermons on reform, especially those related to the Holy Name of Jesus. Her approach focuses on sermons as a means of verbal communication which establish the iconography. Her way into the preaching of San Bernardino is largely by way of Carlo Delcorno (the editor of the 1427 series of Bernadino's sermons in Siena), Iris Origo and her classic biography, Zelina Zafarana, and Franco Mormando. Absent from her bibliography are some important, recent anglophone studies: those of Cynthia Policretti and Nirit Ben-Aryeh Debby.[23]

The IHS symbol, in the recent study by Cynthia Policretti of Bernardino of Siena as peacemaking preacher, is part of the preacher's well-staged spectacle, aimed at eliciting dramatic group responses at the end of his sermons on the Holy Name. For Policretti, sermons are more than words; they are drama and gesture, and both preacher and audience are complicit. In her evocative, yet incisive chapter on 'The Preacher and the Crowd', the *tavoletta* is evidence of Bernardino's sound grasp of 'the uses of imagery in a culture so oriented towards the visual', the focus for the outpouring of pent-up emotion', and the occasion of spontaneous exorcisms. [24] It is

---

[22] Carolyn Walker Bynum, 'Introduction: the Complexity of Symbols,' in *Gender and Religion: On the Complexity of Symbols*, ed. by Caroline Walker Bynum, Stevan Harrell and Paula Richman (Boston: Beacon Press, 1986), pp. 1–21 (p. 4). Bynum's approach is much influenced by Paul Ricoeur, Victor Turner and Clifford Geertz.

[23] Cynthia L. Polecritti, *Preaching Peace in Renaissance Italy: Bernardino of Siena and his Audience* (Washington, DC: Catholic University of America Press, 2000); Nirit Ben-Aryeh Debby, *Renaissance Florence in the Rhetoric of Two Popular Preachers: Giovanni Dominici (1356–-1419*) and Bernardino da Siena (1380–1444) (Turnhout: Brepols, 2001). Also useful is B. Paton, *Preaching Friars and the Civic Ethos: Siena, 1380–1480* (London: Centre for Medieval Studies, Queen Mary and Westfield College, University of London, 1992). The older biography by Ferrers-Howell is full of useful material and insights. A. G. F. Ferrers-Howell, *San Bernardino of Siena* (London: Methuen, 1913). For the section on Bernardino and painting, recourse should be had also to Nirit Ben-Aryeh Debby, 'The Preacher as Goldsmith: The Italian Preachers' Use of the Visual Arts', in *Preacher, Sermon and Audience in the Middle Ages*, ed. by Carolyn Muessig (Leiden: Brill, 2002), pp. 127–53, esp. pp. 135–45.

[24] Polecritti, *Preaching*, p. 74.

the theatricality of the tactic and the fervent response of the crowd with the risk of enthusiasm degenerating into pure idolatry, rather than the orthodoxy of Bernardino's doctrine, that prompts criticism from such a sober, orthodox theologian like the Augustinian Andrea Biglia. It is the same issue which prompts cautions from Bernardino's friends, the observant Dominican friar Antonino Pierozzi (better known today as Saint Antoninus) and the Servite friar and humanist scholar Ambrogio Traversari.[25] None of their fears were assuaged by Bernardino's sound, orthodox response.[26] They were aware of the problem of 'reception' in all but name and the way in which the *tavoletta* readily evolved into a 'a kind of religious talisman', aided to no little extent by the emotional participation of the crowd.[27]

Michelson claims that after the 1426–27 heresy trial Bernadino's use of the monogram became more moderate, but, nevertheless, the goals with which he framed it, as expressed in his preaching, remained constant, viz. a reminder of faith, a spur to acts of faith, a focus for contemplation, and a substitute for charms, amulets and sinful vanities. To these four which she singles out, Michelson could have added a fifth, which, indeed, she discusses *en passant*: the one *stemma* of unity amidst many *stemme* of factionalism—the IHS monogram uniting the factions of the city, be they familial or political.

Michelson draws on a range of Bernardino's texts to establish her points. Through her exploration of Bernardino's theology of the holy name in relation to the *tavoletta*, Michelson shows the way in which the world of Bernardino was drawn into his pulpit and rearticulated in a way that gave new meaning to his listeners daily concerns, and forged the sort of ethos which resulted in his being numbered amongst the most sought after preachers of his day, by civic authorities as much as religious.[28] As Michelson observes, in a way that is consonant with Polecritti's extended study, '[in] Bernardino's sermons, the monogram is a bringer of peace, both internal and communal.'

More than being a preaching prop, Michelson shows that the monogram and the preaching connected to it were central to Bernardino's personal theology. She shows that Bernardino is susceptible to the visual as much as the verbal. Her argument would have been further enhanced if she had also noted the way in which Bernardino shared with his contemporaries a sophisticated understanding of the role of the

[25] Iris Origo, *The World of San Bernardino*, (London: Cape, 1963), p. 122.

[26] Polecritti, p. 72. The strength of official opposition is a little more prolonged than Michelson allows: three attempts were made to induce the censure of ecclesiastical authority against Bernardino: in 1426 (Martin V), 1431 (quashed 5 January 1432, Bull *Sedis Apostolicae* Eugenius IV, Origo p. 128), 1438 (the Council of Basel).

[27] See most recently Polecritti, *Preaching*, pp. 72–6; Debby, p. 53; also Origo pp. 121–22.

[28] See Howard, *Beyond the Written Word*, pp. 87–89.

image as sign, pointing to further realities.[29] For as he preached to the people of Padua in 1423:

> Yield honour to Holy Church, who would not have you wear amulets round your neck, nor trust in superstitious charms, but would have you trust in the Name of Jesus, from which Name any great miracle may proceed; for Jesus Christ himself hath revealed It to us by His own mouth; and likewise the saints have displayed it to all the world by mighty miracles [...] Believe therefore that every power of doing good is comprised in the mighty Name of Jesus, so that, like as thou worshippest Jesus in the flesh, so thou shouldest worship the Name of Jesus. I mean not the carving or the colouring, but the sweetness; not the sign, but the thing signified: for the Name of Jesus signifies to thee the Saviour, the redeemer, the Son of God. And therefore I suggest that when you stand sponsor to any infant, in lieu of other gifts, you give him one of these silver gilt tablets of the Name of Jesus [...] that the child may wear it for devotion's sake: not because of silver gilt tablets of the Name of Jesus [...] that the child may wear it for devotion's sake: not because it is of silver or gold, but because of the virtue residing in that most holy Name; and that when he comes to years of discretion he may understand the devotion of the Name of Jesus, and bear it continually in mind: just like the pictures which represent to you the Blessed Virgin, or the other Saints; for the purpose of such pictures is, to keep the Saints in mind.[30]

Michelson has allowed a careful reading of her evidence to control her discussion, and has been alert to the interpretive devices available within the culture to build up a complex picture of the contexts to which Bernardino preached. A stronger historiographical background, though, would have strengthened and deepened the argument. Compared with the recent work of Polecritti, intellectually rigorous with a thoughtful use of anthropological insights, Michelson's approach to her sermon studies focuses very much on the intellectual, as is appropriate in view of the inspiration she took from the idea of Carlo Delcorno that the monogram was 'the physical embodiment of Bernardino's preaching and his entire theology'. This admitted, there is the possibility, in view of the sources and the current state of knowledge of this period of Italian history, of a more full-blooded account of the way in which the sermons of fifteenth century reflected upon their worlds.

All the pieces collected here demonstrate that insight, and the courage to undertake the painstaking work of re-constructing historical cultures, can yield an understanding of worlds far removed in time. The sermon and homiletic genres, in the hands of Morris, Verbaal, Salisbury and Michelson, are shown to disclose the contexts in which sermons and homilies were created. The authors also demonstrate that no one technique can force these sometimes unlikely sources to yield their full

[29] For instance, Antonino Pierozzi—Saint Antoninus—the future archbishop of Florence. See Howard, *Beyond the Written Word*, pp. 83–85.

[30] Quoted in Ferrers-Howell, *San Bernardino*, p. 156.

revelatory potential. One lesson to be taken away from these studies is the rich vein of possibility offered by discourse analysis in particular.

A perplexing problem for the modern scholar remains: the spontaneity of the public event has been further distanced, in many instances, by the desire of the preacher to turn his original performance into a more durable, formal, literary genre. The transition from homily to commentary poses particular challenges, as in the case of the texts of both John Chrysostom and Bernard of Clairvaux. The sermons to be spoken by the boy bishop, too, carry the imprint of the *studium* rather than the pulpit and a live performance. The linguistic vividness of San Bernardino, caught in the *reportationes*, is a rarity. But even Bernardino's theatrical performances, ultimately, are lost to the reader. There is no possibility of evoking, only of imagining, the originating events, though admittedly, some anthropological approaches have begun to flesh out the performative element of oral discourse. The power of the preacher, in the end, seems to have rested not in the words alone, but in their delivery. As the fifteenth-century archbishop of Florence, Fra Antonino Pierozzi OP, wrote, and perhaps even preached: 'più muove la voce viva, che la morta—the live voice moves more than the dead one.'[31] Acknowledging this, reading and pondering the studies in this section has enticed us, the readers, into intriguing worlds beyond the texts, worlds which might otherwise have remained, if not dead, at least hidden.

[31] *Lettere di Sant' Antonino, Arcivescovo di Firenze*, ed. by T. Corsetti and D. Marchese (Florence, 1859), p. 81. See Peter Howard, 'The Aural Space of the Sacred in Renaissance Florence', in *Renaissance Florence: A Social History*, ed. by Roger J. Crum and John T. Paoletti (New York: Cambridge University Press, forthcoming 2004).

III

How Sermons are Reflected in other Literatures

Illumination of the Intellect: Franciscan Sermons and *Piers Plowman*

DAVID STRONG

> That the dialectic of hierophanies, of the manifestation of the sacred in material things, should be an object for even such complex theology as that of the Middle Ages serves to prove that it remains *the* cardinal problem of any religion. One might even say that all hierophanies are simply prefigurations of the miracle of the Incarnation, that every hierophany is an abortive attempt to reveal the mystery of the coming together of God and man.[1]

The purport of any Christian sermon is to emphasize an existent connection between the divine and the individual so that the believer forms an active awareness of this relationship. While detractors may claim that sermons should stress the contrasts between these two realms, dominant versus subordinate, such claims minimize the intrinsic bond shared between God and humankind. Consequently, these minimizing sermons function merely to identify God's hierarchical position and then compel the audience to respond simply as passive listeners. Without an informed appreciation of God's interaction with his creation, the layperson's faith lies on rocky ground, vulnerable to the unorthodox persuasions of heretical teachings. This, in fact, is the malady infecting the Church in the eleventh and twelfth centuries. At this time the Cathars, more commonly known as the Albigensians, popularize their religious set of beliefs by advocating an extreme asceticism. Yet, these beliefs directly contradict Catholic dogma, for they reject the doctrine of the Incarnation, replace the biblical story of creation with an elaborate mythology, and recognize a neo-Manichean dualism—a religious dualism founded upon the two principles of good and evil, singling out the

[1] Mircea Eliade, *Patterns in Comparative Religion*, trans. by Rosemary Sheed (New York: Sheed and Ward, 1958), p. 29.

material world as evil.[2] These and other heresies plague the medieval Church and culminate with the Latin Averroist teachings in the mid-thirteenth century. No longer does the Augustinian emphasis upon faith, divine illumination, and grace as the primary means in comprehending God's design define Western thought. Increasingly, scholars focus exclusively upon the intellect alone to discern spiritual truth, often expressing an anticlerical or antifraternal sentiment in the process.[3] The doctrinal disputes inciting these insurgent groups precipitate the Fourth Lateran Council in 1215 and the condemnations of 1277. Both events modify the role of the licenced preacher in rebutting the claims of unorthodox teachings. The appropriation and educational training of the Franciscan Order is a direct result of these changes.

This article will examine in detail the university sermons of the illustrious Franciscan Bonaventure and how they promote a healthy, respectful relationship between God and humankind. The dynamic employed by these sermons inherently possesses a poetic affinity with metaphor and analogy in conveying and explicating this metaphysical link. Specifically, William Langland's didactic poem *The Vision of Piers Plowman* (*c.* 1362) shows how allegory describes this dynamic and, in the process, educates its reading audience. Though facially different genres, each work—sermon and allegorical poetry—seeks an affective and pragmatic effect upon its audience through its emphasis upon Christocentric values. Their substantive import awakens their audience to a divine presence within this world. In effect, *Piers* functions as a literary sermon indebted to Franciscan thought, specifically that strain emphasizing the spiritual value of creation and its innate link to the Creator. Bonaventure, the Seraphic Doctor (1217–74), promulgates a metaphysical system that reveals a connection between this world and the next without demystifying the divine or demeaning human dependence upon God.[4] In his *Collationes in Hexaemeron*, he advances an exemplarist philosophy, maintaining that the objective world is the diffusion into multiplicity of what is fundamentally one in God. Humanity is that point at which creation has become capable of reading the mind of God in the book of the universe and coming back into harmony with God. God, then, entrusts humanity with an exalted destiny. However, sin prevents us from ever attaining this destiny alone; Christ's incarnation both redeems us and the book of nature is made legible again by this historical revelation.[5] The theoretical underpinnings of this

---

[2] For accounts of this heretical group, see Peter the Venerable, PL 189, 719, 850; St Bernard of Clairvaux, PL 182, 434.

[3] For a detailed account of how these sentiments arise at the University of Paris, see Penn R. Szittya, *The Antifraternal Tradition in Medieval Literature* (Princeton: Princeton University Press, 1986), pp. 11–150.

[4] For an introduction into Bonaventure's thought and place within Franciscan intellectual tradition, see Zachery Hayes, 'Bonaventure: Mystery of the Triune God' in *The History of Franciscan Theology*, ed. by Kenan B. Osborne (St. Bonaventure, NY: Franciscan Institute, 1994), pp. 39–126.

[5] All references to *Collationes in Hexaemeron* [hereafter *Hex.*] are from *The Works of Bonaventure: Collations on the Six Days*, trans. by Jose de Vinck, vol. 5 (Paterson, NJ: St.

ideology require Bonaventure's academic audience to embark upon their own self-reflective journey. So too Langland's allegory revolves around an individual's quest for 'Truthe', highlighting this knowledge's source within a heightened awareness of our dependence upon God. This ultimately shows one how to conduct this internal examination. Where Bonaventure's sermons exhort one to realize a personal connection to the divine, *Piers* demonstrates how to make this realization through exercising one's own learning abilities. Both authors exhort their audiences to heed specific Christian mores through cognitive acceptance of faith-based beliefs. And, while Bonaventure tells his academic listeners what to preach about and how to explicate its message properly, a question arises how well his erudite Latin discourse translates in the laity's vernacular world. Felicitously, the vital elements of his philosophy keenly lend themselves to other sermonizing mediums, specifically poetic ones.

The *modus operandi* of Bonaventure's sermons achieves literary expression through Langland's reliance upon similitude and metaphor. These poetic devices describe how the itinerant wanderings of the protagonist, Will, exemplify to the literate, lay Christian how to attain an understanding of the true tenets of Christian faith. As Will's wanderings induce dream visions where he encounters the personified figures defining his very person—Imagynatyf, Anima, etc.—these figures instruct him how studying the world's natural wonder unveils God's manifesto. The conveyance of these ideas, in conjunction with an insistent reference and portrayal of mendicant ways, attests to the poem's indebtedness to Franciscan thought, particularly the cogent preaching of Bonaventure. Langland's use of the vernacular, however, provides him with direct access to the laity.[6] His work typifies the defining elements of a good sermon so much so that its didactic purpose functions as commentary upon the sermonizing ability of mendicants. As he is not constrained by vows to a bishop, Langland can expose the ills undermining preachers at that time. Often, he attributes poor homiletics to personal failings, straying from religious duty. Ultimately, *Piers*, as it reflects Bonaventurean principles, exemplifies the artistic design of sermons in that the preparation and delivery of a sermon is in itself a creative craft. Its artistry does not dwell upon emotionally charged topics, laden with sensational narration, but thoughtfully interprets the import of intangible ideas in this concrete world. And, most importantly, it does so in an engaging and relevant manner. Under this claim, *Piers* then functions as a sermon itself. Consequently, the lessons learned from both Bonaventure's academic sermons and Langland's alliterative poem show that the elements of an effective sermon are its orthodox promotion of the beneficial connection between God and humankind, attentiveness to its particular audience, and presentation of stimulating ideas that enlighten and apply to each individual.

Anthony Guild Press, 1970) *Hex.* 2.20, p. 32; 13.12–13, p. 190–91.

[6] For a complete discussion of the dialect found in the extant copies of *Piers* and relevant critical theories, see M. L. Samuels, 'Dialect and Grammar', in *A Companion to Piers Plowman*, ed. by John Alford (Berkeley: University of California Press, 1988), pp. 223–50.

In order to appreciate the sources giving rise to Bonaventure's theological focus upon the temporal disclosing the eternal, a brief survey of the controversies and factions destabilizing the medieval Church is necessary. This survey, therefore, will include a detailed discussion of Francis's role in determining his followers' pastoral mission to strengthen the laity's belief in the Church and faith in God. This will make clear the spiritual tradition defining Bonaventure as a Franciscan thinker, providing a rationale for his patient and simple methodology towards opposing homiletic instructions. His thought centre's upon Christ's love for humanity and not upon an extensive array of philosophical concepts, distinctions, and proofs. Notably, Bonaventure opens the *Hexaemeron* with a scriptural allusion to acknowledge the theologian's responsibility to the Church and its community: 'In the midst of the Church the Lord shall open his mouth, and shall fill him with the spirit of wisdom and understanding'.[7] Their profession, he points out, ensures confidence in the Church's teachings and fosters harmony within the congregation. Thus, his sermons encourage a critical, practical, and creative approach towards mediation and reconciliation with opposing schools of thought.

In 1215, the Fourth Lateran Council ratifies specific constitutions to defeat the power of heretical movements. One, they mandate that preachers must have the authorization of their bishop.[8] Two, they extend preaching responsibilities beyond that of the bishop to religious preachers who espouse Christian doctrine. They approve and license the mendicant orders to assist the secular clergy in educating lay people to acknowledge and discern the doctrinal veracity of the Church's canon. These mandates substantiate the purpose of the Dominican Order, as an educated order skilled in preaching, and redesign the vocational priorities of the Friars Minor. When Pope Innocent III sanctions the Franciscans, he perceives their mission as a tool for the reclamation of heretic groups.[9] In 1216, at the height of antiheretical activity, Francis of Assisi, the Order's founder, persuades Honorarius II to grant the Portiuncula Indulgence, which also benefits former heretics wishing to escape reprisal.[10] Despite his compassion for heretics, Francis must determine the best means necessary to educate his friars to combat heresy without endangering their commitment to the apostolic life.

The Council's decision accelerates the development and direction of the Order. While preaching plays an integral role from the onset of his religious conversion, Francis's

---

[7] *Hex*. 1.1.

[8] One of the longest of the Lateran constitutions, *Excommunicamus et anathemizamus omnem haeresim*, required that the preacher have the authorization either of the pope or the local bishop before delivering any sermon. The Lateran constitutions are published in the *Conciliorum Oecumenicorum Decreta*, ed. by J. Alberigo and others, 3rd edn (Bologna, 1973).

[9] See Herbert Grundmann, *Religiose Bewegungen im Mittelalter* (Berlin: Emil Ebering, 1935), pp. 70–100.

[10] Raphael M. Huber, 'The Portiuncula Indulgence', *Franciscan Studies*, 19 (New York: Wagner, 1938).

words stress the kingdom of heaven, peace, and penance for the remission of sins.[11] He does not strive to educate through erudite lessons. Rather, his example instructs those around him how to emulate those virtues defining the apostolic ideal. His whole body serves as a tongue to preach the goodness of God.[12] Upon giving his papal blessing for the Rule of 1221, Innocent III ordains the friars' right to preach, provided they heed two conditions. One, their sermons must focus upon penitence, not doctrinal moralizing. Two, no friar may preach unless Francis himself approves. Once they accept these provisions, Innocent III blesses Francis and his followers and gives them the tonsure as a sign of their authority.[13] Although Francis willingly accepts the former condition, his writings show that he is not adamant about enforcing the latter papal instruction:

> Whenever they see fit my friars may exhort the people to praise God with words like these: Fear him and honor him, praise him and bless him, thank and adore him, the Lord almighty, in Trinity and Unity Father, Son, and Holy Spirit, Creator of all. Repent, for the kingdom of heaven is at hand (Matthew 3. 2); remember we soon die.[14]

Francis does not want to inhibit the friars' charisma inspired by the spirit of God. A friar can preach 'whenever' he deems the time and place is proper. Francis's vision, however, proves impractical. Shortly after the first Rule, it becomes clear that he cannot support a liberal interpretation of Innocent III's directive. In the subsequent Rule of 1223, Francis restricts any friar from preaching 'to the people' unless given license by the Minister General.[15] This emphasis upon the people, as opposed to clerics or students, underscores Francis's focus upon a vernacular audience. Wanting to bridge the gap between the educated and uneducated, Francis actively seeks ways to preach that elucidate God's love for humankind without relying upon abstract reasoning. He then concentrates upon earthly objects to instruct his listeners:

> Although the evangelist Francis preached to the unlearned people through visible and simple things, in as much as he knew that virtue is more necessary than words, nevertheless among spiritual men and men of greater capacity he spoke enlivening and profound words. He would suggest in a few words what was beyond expression, and using fervent gestures and nods, he would transport his hearers wholly to heavenly things.

---

[11] All references to the First and Second Life of St Francis by Thomas of Celano [hereafter referred to as I and II Celano] are from 'Lives of Saint Francis by Thomas of Celano', in *Saint Francis of Assisi: Omnibus of Sources*, ed. by Marion A. Habig; I Celano 36, pp. 258–59.

[12] I Celano 97, pp. 311–12.

[13] I Celano 33, p. 255.

[14] Rule of 1221, ch. 21in *Saint Francis of Assisi Omnibus of Sources*, I (Quincy, IL: Franciscan Press, 1991), p. 46.

[15] The Rule of 1223, ch. 9 in *Saint Francis of Assisi Omnibus of Sources*, I (Quincy, IL: Franciscan Press, 1991), p. 63.

> He did not make use of the keys of philosophical distinctions; he did not put order to his sermons, for he did not compose them ahead of time.[16]

With the Fourth Lateran Council allowing friars to preach and with Francis trying to adhere to the conditions imposed upon this religious privilege, the friars implement a number of different preaching techniques which both appeal to the common layperson and preserve their vocation of simplicity.[17] Even though Francis's catechizing skills preclude academic study, the other friars cannot be expected to imitate such a practice. Consequently, the Order chooses to school their novitiates.

Sending incoming vocations to universities marks a significant change not only from Francis's aim but also in the hierarchical structure of the university. To be clear, Francis is not against learning. Rather, he worries about the temptation of pride arising from academic study. He explicitly states that 'those who want to be praised rather as rhetoricians than as preachers, speaking as they do with elegance rather than with sincerity' undo the glory of their holy office.[18] Francis's primary concern is the sanctity of the friars' spirituality; this, more than any academic study, ensures respect amongst the people. To assist the friars in a healthy pursuit of religious studies, the Order establishes both a regular system of training within each convent as well as schools at the main universities in Europe, such as Oxford and Paris.[19] By the middle of the thirteenth century, 'the Order of Friars Minor. . .become one of the most learned institutions in the world'.[20] Their entrance into the world of higher academic thought drastically alters their approaches to sermonizing and redefines their vocation from one of simplistic living to proclaiming the simple beauty found in this Christian life.

When Bonaventure assumes control as the Order's Minister General in 1257, the study of theology becomes a strict obligation upon the priests of the Order. Bonaventure asserts that Francis's stress upon preaching could not have excluded the studies necessary for its preparation.[21] Etienne Gilson explains Bonaventure's line of reasoning:

> If there is a question of the preaching *quam Fratres faciunt*, the reason is that the rule demands of preachers that they shall be able *sermonem facere et sufficienter disponere*. Naturally with such exegetical methods St. Bonaventure had no difficulty in proving that

[16] II Celano 107, p. 450.

[17] For a thorough discussion of the different preaching techniques employed by the Friars Minor, see John V. Fleming, *An Introduction to the Franciscan Literature of the Middle Ages* (Quincy, IL: Franciscan Press, 1977), pp. 110–89.

[18] II Celano 164, p. 494.

[19] For an overview of the Order's commitment to academic learning, see John Moorman, *A History of the Franciscan Order* (Oxford University Press, 1968), pp. 123–39.

[20] Moorman, p. 123.

[21] Bonaventure, *Expositio super regulam fratrum minorum* in *Sancti Bonaventurae Opera Omnia*, XIII (Quaracchi: Collegii S. Bonaventurae, 1898), p. 402.

> the need to give forth only discourses *casta et examinata, ad utilitatem et aedificationem populi* contained in an abridged form a veritable summa of the preacher's art.[22]

This reasoning promotes the scholastic education of friars, if they adhere to the university curriculum. Franciscan studies must prove rigorous enough to realize three aims: an informed understanding of ecclesiology and soteriology, a mastery of argumentative tactics to expose infidels, and a production of good preachers.[23] These guiding principles maintain and fortify the friars' devotion to God and guard them from vain curiosity. Bonaventure's stance on academic learning roots, no doubt, from his education under Alexander of Hales at the University of Paris. But, it is also his university training that both enmeshes him within the anti-mendicant strife of the secular university faculties of the thirteenth century and defines his particular mode of sermonizing. His sermons take the form of collations.

The collations belong to the literary genre of university sermon. Originating from the old monastic tradition, they gain popularity in the University of Paris in 1231.[24] For Bonaventure, the purpose of the collation is to promulgate Franciscan Augustinianism and to champion the orthodoxy of Christian theology. The collations, though ascribed to Bonaventure, are not technically his work; they are recordings of his sermons made by designated university note takers. When the author corrects and proofs these copies, he can then distribute them as the official text. Within the collations, Bonaventure attacks those views espousing the eternity of the world, the oneness of the agent intellect—in other words, Latin Averroism—as well as antifraternal detractors. His greatest achievement, *Collationes in Hexaemeron*, combats the doctrinal crisis at the University of Paris.[25]

In the mid-thirteenth century Latin Averroism, a rationalistic philosophical current that is based on the Aristotelian commentaries of the Islamic commentator Ibn Rushd, or Averroes, as he is known in the Latin West, cuts deep into religious thought. Whereas the previous sojourns of philosophy into theological matters prioritize faith in understanding metaphysical matters, this intellectual movement threatens faith's dominance.[26] The Prologue to Bishop Stephen Tempier's condemnation of 219

---

[22] Etienne Gilson, *The Philosophy of St. Bonaventure*, trans. by Dom Illtyd Trethowan (Paterson, NJ: St. Anthony Guild Press, 1965), p. 47.

[23] *Determinationes quaestionum*, I, 3, t. VIII, p. 339.

[24] M.-M. Davy, *Les sermons universitaires parisiens de 1230–1231. Contribution a l'étude de la predication médiévale* (Études de philosophie médiévale , XV), Paris, Vrin, 1931, 27, note 1.

[25] The twenty-three collations were delivered in Paris between 9 April and 28 May of 1273.

[26] Although Christian thinkers like Augustine and Anselm explore the veracity of certain theological matters via philosophy alone, they never let philosophy subsume the priority of faith-based knowledge. For example, in *On Free Choice of the Will*, Augustine develops an argument for God's existence based both on religious belief and eternal truths that non-Christians could accept. For him, God's existence then becomes true not only by faith, but also by reasoning. See Saint Augustine, *On Free Choice of the Will*, trans. by Anna S. Benjamin and L. H. Hackstaff

Averroistic propositions on 7 March 1277, at Paris, highlights the sensitivity of the faith-reason issue: '[W]hile wishing to avoid Scylla, they fall into Charybdis. For they say that these things are true according to philosophy but not accorded to the Catholic Faith, as if there were two contrary truths'.[27] Though historians today generally agree that no member of the Parisian Arts Faculty propounded a double-truth theory, this passage shows the fear that philosophy is interloping into faith's realm.[28] Traditionally, the arts faculty serves as a preparation for the higher studies of theology, law, and medicine, but by the late 1260s, some of its faculty members choose to remain in the arts faculty instead of teaching the higher disciplines.[29] This causes a significant shift in the direction of university curriculum. Bonaventure in his Lenten sermons of 1267 speaks against an improper use of philosophical inquiry in the arts faculty, and in these sermons as well as those of 1268 he specifically indicates erroneous teachings on the eternity of the world and on monopsychism (the theory that there is only one human intellect). Bonaventure in his fourth sermon *On the Gifts of the Holy Spirit* in 1268 further warns of this educational movement.[30] For Bonaventure, philosophy of whatever sort is only a preparatory stage in the search for a fuller and more complete truth that can be found only in divine revelation.

The Condemnation of 1277 shows how Aristotle's natural philosophy seems to place limits on God's power to effect changes in the natural world and differs from established Christian dogma. Because many theologians hold that God can do anything that

---

(New York: Macmillan, 1964), pp. 35–85.

[27] P. Mandonnet, *Siger de Brabant et l'Averroisme latin au XIIIe siècle*, 2nd edn., 2 vols. (Louvain, 1908, 1911), II, p. 175.

[28] For a thorough overview of this issue, see F. Van Steenberghen, *Thomas Aquinas and Radical Aristotelianism* (Washington, D.C., 1980), pp. 93–109; see also John F. Wippel, *Mediaeval Reactions to the Encounter between Faith and Reason* (Milwaukee: Marquette University Press, 1995).

[29] In the thirteenth century, theology becomes a professional discipline taught in independent faculties of theology at the universities of Paris and Oxford, the most important schools of theology during the thirteenth and fourteenth centuries. See Monika Asztalos, 'The Faculty of Theology', in *A History of the University of Europe: Volume I, Universities in the Middle Ages*, ed. by Hilde de Ridder-Symoens (Cambridge: Cambridge University Press, 1992), p. 414.

[30] In his sermon *Christ, the One Teacher of All*, Bonaventure directly states, 'Aristotle provided a firm foundation for the way of science while neglecting the way of wisdom'. See *What Manner of Man? Sermons on Christ by St. Bonaventure*, trans. by Zachary Hayes (Chicago: Franciscan Herald Press, 1989) p. 37. All citations from this sermon are taken from Hayes's translation, but it should be pointed out that it has more recently been translated in *The Cambridge Translations of Medieval Philosophical Texts*, ed. by Robert Pasnau, III (Cambridge: Cambridge University Press, 2002), pp. 79–92. Hayes's translation will be used because his work exclusively focuses upon Bonaventure's sermons and skill as a preacher.

Aristotle claims are naturally impossible, the following two condemned articles illustrate this dispute.[31]

> 34. That the first cause [that is, God] could not make several worlds.
>
> 48. That God cannot be the cause of a new act [or thing], nor can he produce something anew.

Article thirty-four condemns the claim that God cannot make other worlds if he chose to do so, even though almost no one contends that he had made other worlds.[32] Article forty-eight implies that if God acts to produce a new effect, then the effort itself implies that God is not immutable. Moreover, it also suggests that the world is eternal, because if God cannot produce a new effect, it follows that God could not have produced this world, which would have been a new effect. Two other articles stress the heated intensity of this dispute.

> 37. That nothing should be believed unless it is self-evident or could be asserted from things that are self-evident.
>
> 152. That theological discussions are based on fables.[33]

Etienne Gilson regards these opinions 'as sufficient proof of the fact that pure rationalism was steadily gaining ground around the end of the thirteenth century'.[34] An uneasy compromise arises between these two disciplines. Natural philosophers concern themselves with God's absolute power only by conceding it, moving on, and not seeking to probe it further; theologians are eager to use natural philosophy as long as it is used to seek God by 'faith-guided reason'.[35] Even though philosophy can never completely penetrate divine mysteries, theologians explore those mysteries rationally as is evident from the questions raised and the answers provided.

---

[31] *The Foundations of Modern Science in the Middle Ages: Their Religious, Institutional, and Intellectual Contexts*, trans. by Edward Grant (Cambridge: Cambridge University Press, 1996), p. 78.

[32] For a complete examination of theology's study in late medieval universities, see Edward Grant, *God and Reason in the Middle Ages* (Cambridge: Cambridge University Press, 2002), pp. 115–283.

[33] Edward Grant, *A Source Book in Medieval Science* (Cambridge: Harvard University Press, 1974), pp. 48–50.

[34] Etienne Gilson, *Reason and Revelation in the Middle Ages* (New York: Scribner's, 1938), p. 64.

[35] Gelber uses this phrase in *Exploring the Boundaries of Reason: Three Questions on the Nature of God by Robert Holcot*, ed. by Hester Goodenough Gelber, *Studies and Texts*, 62 (Toronto: Pontifical Institute of Mediaeval Studies, 1983), p. 28.

In the *Hexaemeron*, Bonaventure delimits the bounds of philosophy, ultimately extolling faith in God as the highest level of knowledge attainable to humankind. In the process, he outlines the history of Christian wisdom, asserting that the seeker of truth must acknowledge Christ as the mediator between the human and divine. This outline establishes the primary tenets of Franciscan preaching: 1) central place given to Christ, 2) emphasis on the humanity of Christ, 3) emphasis on God as the Highest Good. Bonaventure's metaphysics revolve around the truths revealed in the embodiment of Christ; for Christ is the key to all reality.[36] The transcendental significance of all created reality lies in the reality of Christ, the symbol of God. This is why the basic metaphysical truth for Bonaventure is not that of origins but the question of exemplarity: the nature of the original after which the many diverse copies are shaped.[37] Therefore, his system of thought is founded upon faith in Christ's revelation. Since the revelation is a historical event, his system acquires meaning through a historical process, but not a history stemming from the chronological events of humankind, but those events comprising the individual Christian's pursuit and embrace of divine love. And, this pursuit can only begin when created reality receives the Exemplar of all creation in the Incarnation.[38] To appreciate the implications of this belief system, consider the following conditional statement: 'If the intelligibility of all things is grounded in their relation to the Word, then in some way all true knowledge must be related to the Word'.[39] Consequently, Franciscan thought objects to Christ being only one *esse*, for such a view would deny Christ's humanity.[40] Creation, then, manifests the revelatory truth of Christ's existence, illustrating the structural law of all reality. It is humankind as a whole, not solely as its spiritual composite—the soul—that reflects divine truth. Despite the complexity of these ideas, Bonaventure's skill as a preacher enables him to discuss them without bewildering his audience. His contemporaries praise this ability. Martin of Fulda avers that he was 'a man of great devotion and integrity, beloved for his life and teaching, but above all for his preaching; Blessed Francis of Fabriano recounts how his preaching to the clergy was so edifying that the listeners fell silent in his presence.'[41]

[36] *Hex.* 1.10; also see, *What Manner of Man? Sermons on Christ by St. Bonaventure*, trans. by Zachary Hayes (Chicago: Franciscan Herald Press, 1974), p. 18.

[37] *Hex.* 1.13.

[38] Bonaventura, *De reductione artium ad theologiam* in *Sancti Bonaventurae Opera Omnia*, V (Quaracchi: Collegii S. Bonaventurae, 1891), p. 324.

[39] *Hex.* 1.10.

[40] Bonaventure, III *Sententiae*, d. 6, a.1, q.1 (III, 148–49); Matthew of Aquasparta, *Quaestiones disputatae de Incarnatione et de Lapsu*, q.9, Bibliotheca Franciscana Scholastica Mediii Aevi, II, 2nd edn (Quaracchi: Collegii S. Bonaventurae, 1957), p. 169–92.

[41] Bonaventura, *Sermones de tempore, de sanctis, de B. Virgine Maria et de diversis*, in *Sancti Bonaventurae Opera Omnia*, IX (Quaracchi: Collegii S. Bonaventurae, 1901), p. 3.

Despite the erudition appropriated to these metaphysical matters, Bonaventure does not preoccupy himself with its recondite nature. Even though his sermons meet the expectations of an academic audience, he touches the listeners' minds with ideas that engage their visceral and emotive responses. His ideas interconnect speculative and scholastic ends with tangible means. For him, God is not an aloof, abstract entity, but a dynamically active creator of both earth and heaven. Pursuing an informed understanding of this fact brings the individual Christian closer to truth, dramatically affecting his or her outlook of spiritual possibilities. In addition, this underlines the affinities shared with *Piers*. Both extol the need for the individual to partake of a spiritual journey to discover truth; the narrative structure of Langland's poem actually utilizes the motif of a pilgrimage in its overriding design. The intrigue aligned with pilgrimage stems from a belief in the practical necessity of knowing God. As Bonaventure states, the 'emanation, exemplarity, and consummation' of Christ directs us towards heaven.[42] Christ is the exemplar both of the created cosmos and incorporeal realm of spiritual truth. This theological position strikes against the Averroistic speculation at the University of Paris in the 1270's, urging the aim of theology as practical and accessible to each individual. By observing nature, the Christian sees vestiges of God. In *The Journey of the Mind to God*, Bonaventure writes:

> For creatures of this visible world signify the invisible things of God: partly, because God is the Origin, Exemplar, and End of every creature . . . every creature is by its very nature a figure and likeness of eternal Wisdom.[43]

Like Augustine, Bonaventure promulgates a view of humans as images of God and the world as a vestige of the Trinity.[44] This view places his ideology onto the mystical plane. This mystical element, which expresses a harmonious integration between the mind and faith, is both central to Franciscan thought and fundamental in seizing the fascination of his audience. His belief that God's goodness is self-diffusive and can be known in a limited capacity establishes an immediacy of God. This immediacy entices Bonaventure's students to learn more in hopes of maximizing the opportunity to penetrate into the unknown. Their natural curiosity acquires a learned direction, requiring a constructive use of their mind in fortifying their religious belief.

Bonaventure's exemplarity impugns the idea of Articles 34 and 48 which considers nature as self-sufficient and an end in itself. In fact, twenty-seven of the two hundred and nineteen condemned articles were directed against some form of the in behalf of the eternity of the world. Such a sublunary perception would endorse human autonomy,

---

[42] *Hex.* 1.17.

[43] Bonaventure, *The Journey of the Mind to God*, trans. by Philotheus Boehner (Indianapolis: Hackett Press, repr. 1990) 2.12.

[44] Augustine, *Contra Faustum*, 20, ed. by Josephus Zycha, CSEL 25, (1891–92) p. 7; *De vera religione*, 7, ed. by J. Martin, CCSL 32 (Turnhout: Brepols, 1982), 13; Augustine, *De Trinitate*, 6.10, 241, ed. by W. J. Mountain, CCSL (Turnhout: Brepols, 1968).

necessarily excluding any reliance upon God's providence. Rather, Bonaventure wants his audience to recognize the affinity between the divine and the mortal: 'it is impossible to understand a creature except through that by which it was made'.[45] While the spiritual and aesthetic valuation of nature in all its forms derives from Plato's cosmic ideology as found in the *Timaeus*,[46] Bonaventure imbues it with a theological significance.[47] While he openly admits a scholarly knowledge of Plato's and Aristotle's epistemologies in his sermons on Christ,[48] he worries that a philosophy isolated from theology tragically neglects what makes creation a system of intelligible signs.[49] In the *Hexaemeron*, he denounces the secularizing philosophical movement of his own time.

> Again, opposing the concelebration of divine praise, we have the spirit of presumption and curiosity, in the sense that the presumptuous does not glorify God but praiseshimself, while the curious is lacking in devotion. There are many men of this kind, empty of praise and devotion although filled with the splendors of knowledge. They build wasps' nests without honeycombs, while the bees make honey.[50]

These mundane thinkers fail to realize how the ultimate value of this world transcends human certitude. By invoking analogy to express this connection between substantially distinct beings, Bonaventure discovers the best means to access and express this value. In his hands, analogy derives from the generating act as it imprints itself upon the being it engenders. He writes: '[Creation] is a trace of God's wisdom wherefore the creature exists only as a kind of imitation of God's wisdom, as a certain plastic representation of it."[51] This analogy refers to how the interior design of one's being necessarily affects the honesty of that person's relation to God. This internal order becomes the very law which directs the actions of an informed Christian intellect.[52] When the individual

---

[45] *Hex.* 1.10.

[46] For a thorough discussion of how Plato's exemplarity affects medieval thought, see M.-D. Chenu, *Nature, Man, and Society in the Twelfth Century* (Toronto: University of Toronto Press: 1997), pp. 1–145. Plato writes in the *Timaeus*, 'Then God, having decided to form the world in the closest possible likeness to the most beautiful of intelligible beings and to a Being perfect in all things, made it into a living being, one, visible, and having within itself all living beings of like nature with itself' (30d. 2–5).

[47] In the Christian West, Plato and the Platonists were given a more positive endorsement than Aristotle. The medieval Latins did have a fragment of Plato's *Timaeus* translated by Cicero, and Chalcidius's translation of and commentary on the first part of the same work was beyond doubt the most influential translation of a Platonic dialogue in the Middle Ages.

[48]. Bonaventure, *Commentarii in II Libri Sententiae* in *Sancti Bonaventurae Opera Omnia*, II (Quaracchi: Collegii S. Bonaventurae, 1885), p. 405

[49] Hayes, p. 37.

[50] *Hex.* 1.8.

[51] *Hex.* 12.14.

[52] *Hex.* 2.23.

recognizes this correlation, the more intimate the relation becomes between these two beings. As a result, the Christian and his community seek to model, or conform, themselves to God. Notably, this claim lies beyond Aristotelian logic. Aristotle considers only a universe of natures to analyze, thus leaving out the means to explore the secrets of a symbolic world such as that of the Augustinian tradition and of Bonaventure in particular. As Gilson writes, 'If the internal law which controls the essences of material or spiritual beings is that of a conformity and, as it were, a configuration to the divine essence, all reasoning that is truly explanatory must demonstrate a certain correspondence between the created and the uncreated'.[53] Seeking the similitude between created reality and God, then, is the spiritual journey that lies before every person—including Christ. As man, he personifies the circle towards a spiritual life; as Son of God, he inspires us to envisage and enter into this circle. This spherical pilgrimage unites individuals to the community, and the community to the Church as it ponders Christ's dynamic.[54] One's spiritual potential is not attained in isolation, but with others to unite in perfect conformity with Christ. This sojourn must seek more than an intellectual or speculative knowledge. It must include a sapient knowledge acquired through an experiential awareness of the world around us.

While Bonaventure's *Hexaemeron* sermons operate on a higher plane of thought—relying upon metaphysical insights to explicate experience—they apply readily to his audience of students and fellow friars, functioning as a model for them.[55] More importantly, he champions the opening of their minds to possibilities other than some of the major secularizing values shaping their society. He declares emphatically that one's spiritual journey begins with accepting Christ's reality.[56] By itself, philosophy knows nothing of Christ, much less appreciates the consequences sin inflicts upon the human condition. Subsequently, Bonaventure accords no faith in classical philosophy to grasp the Church's objective. When he pronounces, 'For you cannot grasp the words of Paul unless you have the spirit of Paul', he makes clear to his learned audience that they must practise what they preach.[57] For preachers, personal meaning in their own spirituality is of chief importance. Spiritual practice must conjoin with professions of religious knowledge. In turn, sermons should not be periphrastic, but deal precisely with the layperson's development of faith. An emphasis upon individual development, interactive

[53] Gilson, p. 209. Bonaventure, *Commentarii in II Libri Sententiae* in *Sancti Bonaventurae Opera Omnia*, II (Quaracchi: Collegii S. Bonaventurae, 1885), p. 405; *Commentarii in I Libri Sententiae* in *Sancti Bonaventurae Opera Omnia*, I (Quaracchi: Collegii S. Bonaventurae, 1882), p. 551

[54] *Hex*. 23.4.

[55] Ferdinand Delorme states in his edition that Bonaventure's audience included up to a hundred and sixty friars. See *Collationes in Hexaemeron*, in *Bibliotheca Franciscana Scholastica Medii Aevi*, 8, ed. by Ferdinand Delorme (Quaracchi: Collegii S. Bonaventurae, 1934) p. 275.

[56] *Hex*. 1.1.

[57] *Hex*. 22.21.

association with the Church, and symbolic sense of nature work together to create a vision for their listeners that rivals the artistry of a poet. As art portrays the most profound elements of the human condition, giving it meaning, the preacher's sermons must capture the audience's imagination, recasting their notion of faith's role in their life. His analogies interpret all dimensions of reality to generate a more complete, fecund expression of humanity. Thus, by urging his students and fellow brothers to deepen their knowledge of creation and their relation to it, Bonaventure preaches not only a way to understand faith but also a means to help the individual realize faith in their everyday life.[58]

Though its historical origins inculcate it with an academic necessity, Bonaventure's rhetoric is not replete with erudite abstractions. His sermons exude a literary quality that inspires the audience's imagination to accept those truths founded upon faith. The etude of his compositions realizes its power through the craft of its creation; this craft, as it praises God's care for humankind, exemplifies the good found in the creative act and substantiates the Christian's belief in the divine. Because poetry is universally admired as a high point of creative achievement, it functions as the perfect vehicle to convey the ideas central to Franciscan sermonizing. Both Bonaventure and Langland use their artist skills to promote, not denigrate, faith-inspired truths.[59] Langland's poetic creation shows how one can explore metaphysical matters without forgoing Christian theology. *Piers Plowman* examines both the natural goodness found in the world and the natural curiosity to know that which lies beyond the bounds of reason, but does not advance epistemological claims exclusive of faith's tenets. This examination attests to a self-reflective awareness of God's imprint upon creation and humankind's dependence upon his grace. Any expression of this truth, whether exhortative or poetic, is creative, for it urges the reader to awaken their senses to the divine's presence and found their belief system upon divine providence. Acknowledging this imprint both enables the poet-creator to imitate the divine model and epitomizes the purport of Franciscan sermonizing. The idea of creation itself is central in comprehending the metaphysical certainty of God, human goodness, and philosophy's need for theology.

The poetic kinship uniting Bonaventure's sermons and Langland's poetic vision lies in their ability to cast images that simultaneously inspire the intellect and the spirit. These conjoint effects cause their audiences to realize how these two disparate modes of knowing complement one another. In addition, by dramatizing an individual's search for

---

[58] For a brief but salient study of the history of creation in philosophical thought, see Zachary Hayes, *The Gift of Being: A Theology of Creation* (Collegeville, MN: Liturgical Press, 2001); Hayes, *Window to the Divine: A Study of Christian Creation Theology* (Quincy, IL: Franciscan Press, 1997); Joseph C. Ratzinger, *Theology of History According to St. Bonaventure* (Quincy, IL: Franciscan Press, 1971).

[59] The most complete study of Langland's tie to Bonaventure's exemplarism is Lawrence M. Clopper, *'Songes of Rechelesnesse' Langland and the Franciscans* (Ann Arbor: University of Michigan Press, 1997), esp. pp. 105–44. This study focuses upon Franciscan poverty practices and their impact upon the poem.

truth 'not in a spirit of humility but in a spirit of speculative curiosity', Langland's narrative simulates the historical causes of Bonaventure's preaching.[60] Contextualizing these origins instructs the reader to appreciate the delicate relationship between analytical faculties and faith when discerning spiritual matters. To convey faith's eminence, Langland situates this search within the literary device of dream vision, thus accentuating the fact that these matters lie in a realm beyond concrete, empirical proof. Rather, this shadowy vestige of reality describes the closest one comes to knowing with certainty faith's veracity. Accepting this truth, then, does not rely upon a learning attainable only through higher study, but through a personal realization of one's own interior search for this truth. In effect, Langland's poetic shaping of these matters addresses the faith-reason debate lying at the heart of Bonaventure's artistic design and purpose.

The polemic thrust of his sermons acquires relevance beyond the academic interests of the university audience when they appear in a vernacular poem designed for the religious edification of the laity. Langland's *Piers Plowman* incorporates vital elements in Bonaventure's exemplarist philosophy as it portrays the search for spiritual truth via human means. This poem puts into relief the internal drive in each human to know all that is intelligible and, ultimately, explicate that which lies beyond cognitive certainty through analogy. Langland, like Bonaventure, relies upon analogies founded upon a community of relations between substantially distinct beings to establish divine wisdom in this world. These analogies stimulate and motivate the reader/listener to grasp a unity between two pairs of different beings.[61] The various degrees of proximity and remoteness of this relation to a higher being appeals to the reader's imagination and provides a schema for literary depictions of metaphysical matters that show the immediacy of God. Appropriately then, Langland expresses these analogies through the personified figure Imagynatyf who lifts Will high onto a mountain called Middle Earth to meet and love 'Kynde my creator' through observing each of his creatures (B.11.325). From this meeting, we learn that any creature, no matter how far removed from the hierarchy of humanity, capably directs the individual's mind to God. Kynde, a figure intelligible through the order of nature, is God in his creative aspect. Imparting to Will that the harmony of creation elucidates the virtue of living righteously, Kynde informs Will to take critical note of the familial care that the animals provide their young. Instinctive behaviour teaches Will about God's goodness and care for all creation (B.11.322–6). Heeding this counsel, Will observes the mating practices of peacocks:

---

[60] David Mills, 'The Role of the Dreamer in *Piers Plowman*' in *Piers Plowman: Critical Approaches*, ed. by S. S. Hussey (London: Methuen, 1969), pp. 180–212.

[61] Explaining created nature as a relation between two beings of which one play the part of a model and the other a copy derives in part from Aristotelian and Augustinian texts. See Aristotle, *Posterior Analytics*, trans. by Jonathan Barnes 2nd edition (Oxford: Clarendon Press, 1994) Book 2.27–28; Augustine, *De Genesi ad litteram inperfectus liber*, 16, ed. by Josephus Zycha, CSEL 28.1, p. 57.

> [. . .] I took kepe how pecokkes bredden.
> Muche merveilled me what maister thei hadde
> And who taughte hem on trees to tymbre so heighe
> That neither burn ne beest may hir briddes rechen. (B.11.358–61)

From his observation, Will learns to appreciate the moral order of nature's creatures. He marvels at their innate ability to shelter and care for themselves. The means by which Imagynatyf instructs Will underline how the human mind can extrapolate from tangible objects. This focus upon the individual objects directly coincides with Franciscan belief. The schema of order illustrated by the birds depicts a higher good. Will's impulse to consider the significance of this order necessarily prompts him to realize the need to do well in this world. Langland lionizes Imagynatyf's role in relation to the other faculties of knowing because Imagynatyf generates the similitudes used by Kynde to link two distinct realms, the intellectual and the spiritual (B.13.14). As Imagynatyf forms likenesses of perceptible objects in the natural world and stores them in memory, Will derives concepts of these images. From them, he can abstract certain truths, spiritual and otherwise. These images awaken him to recognize that both the potentialities of the mind and the presence of divine care vivify his intellectual spirit. Just as the peacock's mating highlights the inborn virtue of animals, Will's exploration of his mind's power points to the channels that he must pursue to attain true wisdom.

By casting the vast majority of action within dream visions, Langland can dramatize Bonaventure's theory of universal analogy. As a realm that intersects the conscious with the imaginative unconscious, the visions extend the bounds of reality. Subsequently, the speeches of the personified allegories attain a level of verisimilitude and function as a primary didactic tool. That these figures, such as Wit, Theology, and Patience, possess an actual existence in relation to Will, their words and actions instruct him of the spiritual capabilities of the human faculties and virtues. These interactions prove that edification does not occur solely by strict academic discourse, for they laud the value of self-knowledge and experiential learning. Langland's visions communicate the essential tools for learning: an interactive instruction that both promotes human thinking abilities and respects the learner's experiences. The resultant knowledge stimulates the imagination to ponder connection to the divine and the divine's prescience to provide us the ability to self-examine and better ourselves. It is, in fact, an intellectualized poem.

Langland's poetic device advances the readers' theological understanding through concrete demonstration of external, present, intelligible, and active realities. His work puts into action the contemplative process of perceiving creation. The consequent vision reveals a design extending Bonaventure's ideas to establish continuity between humankind and the cosmos, the individual and the divine, the intellect and the spirit. In *Sermon II on the Third Sunday of Advent*, Bonaventure elaborates on the educational value of nature. His gloss of the Song of Solomon 6. 11 demonstrates his conviction to this continuity:

> Austerity in the flesh is indicated in the words: 'I went down to the nut garden'; for the nut has a bitter surface, but inside it is sweet. It stands as a symbol of those who have austerity in the flesh externally and devotion within. Humility of mind is indicated by the words: 'To look at the fresh growth of the valley'. As valleys are replete with water, so the water of divine consolation descends upon the humble [...].The sweetness of devotion is mentioned in the words: 'The pomegranates had blossomed'. Pomegranates have many seeds inside, but only one skin, thus symbolizing the soul which must be refreshed with the devotion of manifold sweetness.[62]

Bonaventure's exegesis functions as a key for Christians to comprehend their place in creation: by coming to know creation, they come to know their relation with the divine. They realize that they are a microcosm of nature, infused with the dignity innate within divine goodness. The optimistic intellectuality of this view contrasts starkly with an abstruse or mechanistic interpretation of the universe. The lesson acquired reveals a synthesis of theory and practice that praises the integration of God, humanity, and universe. Both the Franciscan sermons and Langland's poetry assert the omnipresence of this integration.

The allegorical method of instruction in *Piers* centres upon the idea of humankind operating as a microcosm with a divine macrocosm fostering beneficence within cosmic reality. Similarly, Bonaventure draws attention to this correlation. In *Sermon II on the Nativity of the Lord*, he refers directly to this idea:

> It is in this word that we discover the perfection of that greatness of heart which brings all reality to its consummation and completion, since the figure of the circle attests to the perfection of bodies both in the macrocosm and in the microcosm. In the macrocosm, the greater bodies such as the heavens, the sun, and the moon are round in shape. So also in man, who is a microcosm, the more noble members such as the head, the heart, and the eye are round in form.[63]

By personifying the interior 'noble members' of the head, like Imagynatyf, Langland conveys the same lesson of Bonaventure. If Will grasps and exercises the intellectual and sensory potentialities defining his or her person, then he sees an intrinsic connection to those natures lying outside him. This exercise requires no elaborate doctrinal teaching, but an honesty to accept both the abilities and inabilities comprising his person. By looking within, he can see more clearly beyond the rational sphere. Indeed, Bonaventure exhorts that to understand God we must see how living creatures operate as a vestige 'related to God as to the creative principle. An image is related to God, not only as to a principle but as to its motivating object.'[64] As if stressing its fertile philosophical heritage, Langland constructs Will's learning plane upon the premise of

---

[62] Hayes, p. 115.

[63] Hayes, p. 73.

[64] Hayes, p. 35.

imago dei.[65] He cites the famous Pauline passage of 'Hic in enigmate, tunc facie ad faciem'(B.15.162),[66] which aligns with the Genesis declaration 'Faciamus hominem ad imaginem et similitudinem nostram.'[67] Even though Will incorrectly interprets its import, for he pridefully declares that he has never seen Christ in others, 'but [only] as myself in a mirour', his words do convey the seeds of genuine self-discovery, realizing that looking within can redirect him towards the divine image' (B.15.161). Since Will's statement follows an exhortation by his soul—Anima—to embrace Charity with all his being, his presumption seems less impudent. If he heeds this charitable instruction, then Will could see the divine in his soul more clearly. Langland preaches this truth to his literary audience through a sermon spoken by Anima, thus revealing a self-reflective assessment of personal worth.

Because he has been part of 'Cristes court', Anima's sermon holds particular significance (B.15.17). He embodies the most profound elements of the self: sensitive (*sensus*), emotional (*animus*), intellectual (*mens*, *memoria*, *racio*), moral (Conscience), and charitable (*amor*) (B.15.23–39). Anima's words then expound upon the lessons learned so far as well as signify the potential of Will's understanding. Realizing how all these aspects animate Will's being shows how complete self-knowledge reveals the complexity of humankind and its paradisiacal origin: love. Indeed, Anima stresses that he loves 'lelly Oure Lord and alle othere' (B.15.33). Subsequently, Will comes to know charity, or Christ, by looking within and learning about himself. Ultimately then, Anima teaches the reader how to emulate Will in pursuing wisdom and to heed spiritual counsel. First, he warns against academic learning since it will never disclose the essence of divine truth: *Non plus sapere quam oportet sapere* (B.15.69).[68] Next, his decision to castigate the friars' failure to lead a life consistent with their Rule functions self-reflectively, for it both illustrates the purpose of a sermon and points out how sermons fail to edify.

> Freres and fele othere maistres that to the lewed men prechen,
> Ye moven materes unmesurables to tellen of the Trinite,
> That oftetymes the lewed peple of hir bileve doute. . ./
> As wel freres as oother folk, foliliche spenen
> In housynge, in haterynge, in to heigh clergie shewynge
> Moore for pompe than for pure charite. . . . (B.15.70–2, 77–9)

---

[65] See Barbara Raw, 'Piers and the Image of God in Man', in S. S. Hussey *Piers Plowman: Critical Approaches* (London: Methuen, 1969), pp. 143–79; and Daniel Murtaugh, *Piers Plowman and the Image of God* (Gainesville: University Press of Florida, 1978).

[66] I Corinthians 13. 12.

[67] Genesis 1. 26.

[68] [N]ot to think of himself more highly that he ought to think (Romans 12. 3). *The New Oxford Annotated Bible*, ed. by Herbert G. May and Bruce M. Metzger (New York: Oxford University Press, 1973).

He adamantly censures the friars for complicating their sermons with an imbroglio of confusing abstractions. Moreover, he points out how their living fails to typify the religious principles of their avowal. Sermons, therefore, should be expressed clearly and simply so that their message is easily grasped by the listeners and accessible to their level of learning. Anima exemplifies this very principle when, after citing a lengthy Latin text, guilefully states:

> If lewed men wiste what this Latyn meneth,
> And who was myn auctour, much wonder me thinketh
> But if many preest beere, for hir baselardes and hir broches,
> A peire of bedes in hir hand and a book under hir arme. (B.15.119–22)

His words are deceptive because immediately before the macaronic text, Anima had provided a prefatory explanation of its meaning and who the author actually was. Hence, any opposing assertion is false. By employing this rhetorical tactic, Anima illustrates that the most important feature of a sermon is its clarity. While the higher forms of thought and their sources may lie beyond the learning of lay listeners, the information contained within is most applicable to their lives. Subsequently, the preacher must determine the best means to convey this information in a discernible manner. In the above context, the preacher should speak in an indigenous tongue and offer supporting commentary to develop his speculative point. In effect, the preacher must become a vernacular theologian.[69] This does not necessarily mean, however, that the native language must always be spoken, but that the audience understands the words in such a way that they can put the articulated ideas into practice. Determining how to do this is the preacher's paramount concern.

Moreover, Anima points out the errors of the friars in praising position and prestige before the message preached: love. A preacher, like Anima, is not a professional, but a charitable practitioner concerned more about the welfare of others than the position gained by that education. Bonaventure himself writes in the *Hexaemeron*, 'Blessed Francis said that he wanted his brothers to study, but first to practice what they preached. After all, what is the use of knowing a lot, but tasting nothing'?[70] Even if Anima nominally directs his sermon to 'preestes, prechours, and prelates', his intent is Will's instruction. Anima wants every person to acknowledge his insight. As he represents Will's very self, his allegorical import stresses even further that this is what the listener wants: to understand. By framing his discussion of a sermon within a sermon, Anima maintains the constant pedagogical tool of the text—self-reflection.

[69] Archbishop Thoresby of York directed his *Lay Folks' Cathechism* in 1357 against sermons delivered in an arcane manner. See R. N. Swanson, 'The Origins of the *Lay Folks' Catechism*', *Medium Aevum*, 60 (1991), 98; Swanson, 'The "Mendicant Problem" in the Later Middle Ages' in *The Medieval Church: Universities, Heresy, and the Religious Life*, ed. by Peter Biller and Barrie Dobson (New York: Boydell and Brewer, 1999), pp. 217–19.

[70] *Hex*. 22.21.

Will, as a preacher's audience, must be able to look in and discover their ultimate significance as spurred on by the sermon itself.

Notably, Will, when dressed as a mendicant, meets the Doctor of Divinity who is dressed as an academic friar. His actions personify the ills associated with higher learning that Anima subsequently speaks against. Under the guise of proffering certitude, the Doctor manipulates his explication of the Dowel triad—personified figures representing different means to attain virtue—to draw attention away from his own vices of pride and gluttony. He states that Dowel must do as 'clerkes techeth'; Dobet teaches; and Dobest both teaches and acts faithfully to his own instruction (B. 13.116–18). Although Dowel is seen as an action, it is an action that can be identified in a single individual, like Dobet. Hence, the Doctor relies upon a concrete object–a teacher–to enlighten Will, but his use of this object does not have as its purpose the proving of certain truth. Despite the explicit reference to Dobet and Dobest as teachers, the Doctor relies upon this general definition to establish his entire meaning. His interest lies not in identifying the location or ontological primacy of the Dowel triad, but in self-aggrandizing. The Doctor wants Will and the rest of the company to perceive him as a teacher. Sadly though, he knows little of what makes teaching a dignified position. He does not concern himself with whether or not his listener can discriminate the meaning between Dowel, Dobet, or Dobest; he seeks instead only to cloud the waters with a popularized moral claim. He states pompously, 'Qui facit et docuerit magnus vocabitur in regno celorum' (B.13.118b).[71] By hiding behind the veneer of a noble profession, the fallible Doctor shows how selfish desires impair the intellect's exposition of truth. To rely upon one's mind to reveal certain truth is a complex proposition in that no matter how simple and direct certain knowledge may be, impure motives can turn virtue into vice.

As Bonaventure's analogies forgo a strictly rational, linear mode of perceiving the world, his ideology is realized in the denouement of the eighteenth passus in *Piers Plowman*. Here, the poem similarly subverts the inability of human constructs to pierce the veil of spiritual essence without first acknowledging the affinity between the divine and the human as well as with its ultimate ineffability. Langland's transcendent vision gives colour and detail to Bonaventure's mystical philosophy and, likewise, acquires complete clarity only upon accepting Christ's humanity. In *Piers*, Christ's words, dress, and actions defy the audience's expectations of how the Son of God should be portrayed. This unsettling of expectation underlines the pivotal idea that heavenly wisdom can only be known figurally. The intersection between the two realms rewrites itself through a figural understanding of this world as a semblance of divine reality. Though flesh and spirit are different media of human experience, the two are reciprocal and both are necessary for a full realization of Christ's purpose. This idea aligns with the Franciscan Christocentric philosophy that utilizes allegory and angagogy in their sermons.

---

[71] [But] he that shall do and teach, he shall be called great in the kingdom of heaven (Matt. 5. 19).

> Allegory is where one reality signifies another concerning what we have to believe; tropology, or moral teaching, is where from something that is done we learn how to conduct ourselves; anagogy, or the raising of the mind and heart to God, is where we are given to understand what we are to strive after, namely, the eternal joy of the blessed.[72]

Bonaventure's thirteenth collation in the *Hexaemeron* specifically relies upon this method of interpretation to impress upon his audience that only through Christ's appearance does creation's beauty achieve fruition. Like Langland, he focuses explicitly upon Christ's humanity to convey this truth.[73] Through him, all creation manifests a single harmonious theophany of its source. As McGinn asserts, God's presence is expressed as luminously real and immediate in the cosmos as a whole and in each of its elements insofar as they reflect some aspect of the divine fullness.[74] Since created objects communicate the uncreated Word, Will must not fixate upon the outer appearance of creation, but look for its inner meaning in the moral and mystical lessons contained within nature, Christ's incarnation, and the allegorical figures of his soul. By the end of the passus, Will learns that only an acceptance of the figural perspective can provide him with the knowledge he seeks.

From the outset of passus eighteen, Will demonstrates a growing awareness of the temporal world's dependence upon the celestial. He dresses as a penitent who 'weex wery of the world' (B.18.4). Will's disinterest in his waking life relates how his dream world possesses more profundity than his real life. When he drifts off into his sixth dream vision, Will promptly meets the one figure who embodies all the virtues personified in his journey: Christ. Christ's attire reveals how only a figural understanding proffer the kind of knowledge Will seeks, for he appears as a knight. However, He does not wear chain mail on his body; he simply assumes 'humana natura'. Choosing such a common image to depict Christ displays a keen attentiveness to his audience's referential knowledge. By undoing the preconceptions of knightly apparel and exposing Christ's humanity, Langland brings to light an important doctrinal teaching: the Incarnation. Langland can then rely upon Christ's action to supplement the theological explanations disclosed in his jousts, debate with Lucifer, and the explicit responses of the personified allegories Peace, Mercy, Truth, and Righteousness.[75] This redefinition of Christ as a knight stimulates the audience's imagination, thus ensuring that they will heed the poem's didactic message.

---

[72] Bonaventure, *The Works of Bonaventure: Breviloquium*, trans. by Jose de Vinck, II (Quincy, IL: Franciscan Press, 1963), pp. 8–9.

[73] *Hex.* 13.26.

[74] Bernard McGinn, *The Flowering of Mysticism: Men and Women in the New Mysticism (1200–1350)* (New York: Crossroad, 1998), p. 55. Also Roger D. Sorrell, *St. Francis of Assisi and Nature: Tradition and Innovation in Western Christian Attitudes toward the Environment* (New York: Oxford University Press, 1988) chs 5–7.

[75] These allegories are taken from Psalms 85. 10.

Christ's first action is a joust and, just as his dress inverts preconceptions, his battle reinvents the audience's conception of a joust. It depicts the changes inaugurating the new Church. In this portrayal, Pilate's men force the blind Longeus to spear Christ as he hangs upon the cross. When the spear pierces his side, the blood drips into Longeus's eyes and enables him to see. Now seeing what his spear has done, he cries out in sorrow for committing such a heinous act. Christ forgives him. Longeus's sight represents the new means of recognizing sacred virtue: acknowledge Christ's existence. This simple recognition serves as the foundation for the new Church. The individual should not look to ornately stained glass windows or to sophisticated theological learning to defend faith. Rather, he can support the Church against any foes by tilting his open acceptance of Christ's incarnation against them.

Christ's second joust sees him as a much more dynamic force, for he takes up arms against Lucifer. This contest highlights the inability of social standards to judge a person's soul. Clothed in bright light, Christ arrives at the gates of hell as the King of Glory and engages Lucifer in a legal debate to liberate the human souls falsely imprisoned in hell. Watching this drama unfold exposes the powerlessness of reason to safeguard the spirit and the necessity of mercy to counteract the rigidity of human law. When Lucifer declares that he has absolute right to these souls for they have freely chosen to sin, his legal claim seems airtight. Moreover, Truth and Righteousness advocate Lucifer's argument:

> I, Rightwisnesse, recorde thus with Truthe
> That hir peyne be perpetuel and no preiere hem helpe.
> Forthi lat hem chewe as thei chosen, and chide we noght, sustrese,
> For it is botelees bale, the byte that thei eten. (B.18.198–201)

Given their privileged societal rank, their pronouncement sends fear into the reader's heart. The reader momentarily wonders how these pillars of social order are wrong. Yet, as indicative of this passus, both Will and the readers learn to recast their presumptions. They learn about the transposing power of mercy. While mercy may signify a type of kindness given to a person who is under the control of another, this type cannot apply to another dimension of existence. In other words, no person has control over the soul of another. Consequently, the tenets of human law cannot account for the role mercy plays in spiritual justice. Only Christ can do this. Hence, when he refutes Lucifer's claim by citing his evil trickery of humankind, Christ breaks open the gates of hell and mercifully frees the souls. Peace proclaims loudly:

> 'And lete no peple', quod Pees, 'parceyve that we chidde;
> For inpossible is no thyng to Hym that is almyghty'. (B.18.420)

Peace and Mercy acknowledge Christ's power to invert human logic. Upon seeing the redeeming purpose of Christ's actions, Truth and Righteousness embrace their sisters and join them in song to celebrate this event. The debate between the sisters and between Christ and Lucifer emphasizes the principles underlying the Atonement doctrine: Christ's love for humankind. While the reader may not absorb the metaphysical explanations of this doctrine, he must realize the intimate relationship between Christ and humanity. The actions in the text supplement the philosophical elements. Langland's sermonizing, therefore, relies upon the affective state of understanding as well as the intellectual one. And, when the sisters hug one another and break out into song, the reader appreciates how Christ's mercy cannot be expressed by words alone. Will grasps this very fact when he awakes and beckons his family to kiss the cross. He is so moved by Christ's mercy that he does not attempt to discuss its theological ramifications. The profundity of this love transcends linguistic expression. Langland's use of language in this passus is 'a game in which the interplay of love and truth in felt knowledge, intuition, and experience are crucial' and guides the reader to look within to discover wisdom.[76] Learning is not necessarily founded upon great intellectual study, but upon self-reflection of one's innate goodness towards others.

Both Langland and Bonaventure identify the preacher's purpose as establishing a definite link between this world and the next. Each discusses complex theoretical ideas, but does so through sensitivity to their audience's referential knowledge. Even though spiritual truths may ultimately extend beyond rational conclusions, their semblance inheres in nature. Thus, a complementary relationship arises. The incongruity between the two realms is not measured by the otherness of an individual observer, but by the perfection of God's creation. Creation in itself reveals how a divine exemplar imprints itself in this world, and these imprints make the audience constantly aware of the multiple dimensions of insight into the ineffable. Neither Langland nor Bonaventure emphasize stagnant pragmatic methods in instructing their audience. Rather, each employs a commixture of intellectual and artistic techniques to stimulate the listener's interest. In particular, Langland dramatizes Will's revelation that only figural knowledge will aid him in his search, thus validating the aesthetic nature of the text's polemic. This literate audience learns how sensible objects and Christ's person intrinsically conceptualize the divine. Franciscan ideology inspires connections between the erudite and the common, the aesthetic and the natural; Langland embraces this idea, using it to justify his emphasis upon individual capabilities in the search for higher truth. This elevation of human ability empowers the reader to conduct a self-examination that both reveals a harmonious bond to God's providence and distinguishes their individual qualities. By utilizing the literary conventions of allegory, scriptural allusion, and dream vision, Langland ensures that his religious ideas maintain an orthodox quality as they teach the reader how a particular philosophy proffers spiritual perspicacity. Finally, as a work of art, *Piers* illustrates how a sermon must be attentive to the craft of delivering ideas. The preacher must vary his methods of instruction, mixing abstract discussion with natural objects. By doing so, the preacher promotes a correlation between creation and creativity. Bonaventure's *Hexaemeron* employs many natural images which relate an interconnection between the two realms. Without an appreciation of this link, the listener will fail to discern how exemplarity champions the individual's intrinsic bond to

---

[76] Mary Clemente Davlin, *A Game of Heuene: Word Play and the Meaning of Piers Plowman B* (Cambridge: Brewer, 1989), p. 108.

God. Where scholastics embarked on a scientific study of the Christian faith, characterized by three techniques: a methodical commentary on authoritative text, the systematic analysis and solution of dogmatic and moral issues arising from those texts, and the synthetic effort to draw together a coherent and comprehensive presentation of Christian doctrine for instructional purpose, Bonaventure sought to make his theology accessible to his audience so that they could communicate these academic forms to a lay audience. Indeed, where some staid thinkers find transcendence in the lofty and the grand, Bonaventure finds it in the smallest bird or falling leaf. Above all, the experience of the beautiful as it derives from the senses is the primary Franciscan aesthetic experience.[77]

[77] E. Lutz, 'Die Asthetik Bonaventuras nach den Quellen dargestellt', Festgabe Baeumker, *Beitrage zur Geschichte der Philosophie des Mittelalters*, Supplement (Munster in Westphalen: Aschendorff, 1913) 1.202.

Unauthorized Preaching: The Sermon in Jean Bodel's *Jeu de Saint Nicolas*

LYNN T. RAMEY

Jean Bodel is believed to have written the *Jeu de Saint Nicolas* for performance in Arras on 5 December 1200. This remarkable play broke new ground in many areas, including its use of the vernacular to treat a saint's legend. The *Jeu de Saint Nicolas* tells the story of Saint Nicholas's guarding of a vast treasure with the action unrolling in the midst of an epic-like battle between Christians and Muslims. During the battle, a Christian *prudhomme* escapes the massacre and is discovered praying to a statue of Saint Nicholas by the Muslim forces. The Muslim leader mocks the Christian and puts the saint to a test by unlocking the doors to his vast treasury and setting the statue as guardian, with the understanding that if anything is stolen the Christian will pay with his life. Word of the unlocked treasury is spread throughout the kingdom, reaching a tavern where three thieves are playing betting games. The thieves make off with the treasure but are stopped by Saint Nicholas. When the Muslim ruler learns that the saint has saved his treasure, he and his men convert to Christianity and the *prudhomme*'s life is spared.

The *Jeu de Saint Nicolas* has received a good deal of attention not only for being one of the very first vernacular plays, but also for its enigmatic nature. Introductory remarks made by a character called *li preechieres*, or the preacher, summarize the play incorrectly.[1] Hardly what one would expect for a religious play, the tavern

[1] For discussion on the enigmatic prologue, see Jean Claude Aubailly, 'Reflexions sur le *Jeu de Saint Nicolas*: Pour une "dramatologie"', *Le Moyen Age: Revue d'Histoire et de Philologie*, 95 (1989), 419–37; Tony Hunt, 'The Authenticity of the Prologue of Bodel's *Jeu de Saint Nicolas*,' *Romania*, 97 (1976), 252–67; F. W. Marshall, 'The Staging of the *Jeu de Saint Nicolas*: An Analysis of Movement', *Australian Journal of French Studies*, 2 (1965), 9–38; Luciano Rossi, 'L'Oeuvre de Jean Bodel et le renouveau des littératures romanes', *Romania*, 112 (1991), 312–60; Bethany A. Schroeder, 'The Function of the Prologue in *Le Jeu de Saint Nicolas*', *Romance Notes*, 10 (1968), 168–73; Patrick R. Vincent, *The Jeu de*

scene where the thieves learn of the unguarded treasure occupies nearly a third of the play, and the action in the tavern centres around dice games. In looking at the *Jeu de Saint Nicolas* as a play, and therefore a work of literature, critics have failed to point out the way that the play is intimately bound up with the process of preaching. The play begins with the words of a preacher, and within the play there are two instances of mock crusade preaching. Finding a sermon within the 'literary' is probably far more of a surprise for the modern audience than it was for the medieval audience. The early thirteenth century *Jeu de Saint Nicolas* is a mixed-genre piece, including sermons within its overall structure as a play. The sermon found in a literary text is, from the outset, 'unauthorized', since it is located within a genre not its own. In addition, the status of the author may further radicalise the sermon, since he or she, even if a cleric, is unlikely to be considered an appropriate preacher by the Church. Such unusual conditions merit attention, not because they speak of the dominant culture, but precisely because their marginal status may shed light on opaque areas of medieval culture. This article will examine both the importance of the sermons to the reception of the play and the relevance of the play to the history of sermon making. Beginning with a brief history of the medieval crusade sermon and its audience, I will turn to Bodel's work, placing it within the history of theatre and performance. On this background, the play emerges as a hybrid of the two rhetorical forms of sermon and theatre. This mixed nature allows for conclusions about performativity in sermon making and can help explain some of the more puzzling aspects of the play.

The Medieval Crusade Sermon and its Audience

The history of preaching in the Middle Ages can be roughly divided into two periods that were defined by the social systems in place.[2] The first period, which lasted until about 1200, concentrated most religious ceremony and exegesis in the monasteries. Early on, little preaching was done for the common person, though clergy ministered to them through the sacraments. Phyllis B. Roberts notes that, 'The distinguishing mark of most early medieval preaching, however, was that it was essentially preaching by clerics for audiences of clerics, the language being Latin'.[3] Starting

---

Saint Nicolas of Jean Bodel of Arras; a Literary Analysis (Baltimore: Johns Hopkins University Press, 1954).

[2] Paul Scott Wilson, *A Concise History of Preaching* (Nashville: Abingdon Press, 1992), p. 67.

[3] Phyllis B. Roberts, 'Preaching in/and the Medieval City', in *Medieval Sermons and Society: Cloister, City, University*, ed. by Jacqueline Hamesse (Louvain-la-neuve: Fédération Internationale des Instituts d'études médiévales, 1998), p. 152. See Roberts on the importance of the medieval city in effecting a change of audience for the sermon.

with the Carolingian renaissance of the ninth century, religious services gradually became more accessible to the common person. While large parts of the service were still in Latin, by the twelfth century preachers often, but not always, addressed their audiences with a didactic message in the local language. Giles Constable, in exploring the language used in twelfth-century preaching, breaks down the dichotomy between preaching to clerical audiences in Latin and lay audiences in the vernacular. According to Constable, preachers used a variety of languages to get their messages across. Within the same sermon, a preacher might mix his use of language, speaking to different segments of the audience in turn. Ultimately, Constable notes, it was not even necessary that the audience share the language of the preacher, as preaching in the twelfth century was 'a dramatic enterprise'.[4] Other visual and aural elements, such as music and iconography, that made the religious experience poignant for the non-Latin speaker took on increasingly prominent roles in religious services.

In the late eleventh century, the Crusades gave a new impetus to preaching since recruits were vitally needed to accomplish the Church's mission. Travelling priests brought the crusade mission to communities throughout Europe, often setting up impromptu, portable pulpits outdoors where they would preach the crusade. Crusade preaching, while authorized by the Church, often became uncontrollable and was sometimes considered dangerous. Preachers were supposed to be raising armies for the re-conquest of the Holy Land, but many times their audiences included segments of society that were not considered suitable warriors for a crusade. The sermons of very few of these itinerant preachers are extant. Most of what is known about the crusade sermons comes from historians and chroniclers.[5] According to Christoph Maier, the first collection of sermons to have any references to crusade sermon texts was that of James of Vitry in the first half of the thirteenth century.[6] Fulk of Neuilly, a Fourth Crusade preacher authorised by Innocent III, proclaimed the religious crusade to be a concept to which only the poor could truly give themselves.[7] Other crusade preachers encouraged the involvement of women and children, and the armies raised by these preachers were more of a deterrent to the Church's mission than an aid. Yet other preachers encouraged the donation of money or material goods, a call that the Church echoed and amplified over the years.[8]

---

[4] Giles Constable, 'The Language of Preaching in the Twelfth Century', *Viator*, 25 (1994), 131–52, p. 151.

[5] Penny J. Cole, *The Preaching of the Crusades to the Holy Land, 1095–1270* (Cambridge, MA: Medieval Academy of America 1991), p. x.

[6] Christoph T. Maier, *Crusade Propaganda and Ideology: Model Sermons for the Preaching of the Cross* (Cambridge: Cambridge University Press, 2000), p. 4.

[7] Cole, p. 91.

[8] For example, James of Vitry writes, *Nam multi qui ire non possunt pro se mittunt et euntibus tanta de bonis suis largiuntur quod indulgentiam consequntur*, in Maier, p. 122.

Some Crusade preachers left aside the Crusade almost entirely and used their Church-sanctioned portable pulpit as a means of decrying moral decay or perceived societal shortcomings. This tactic became rather common and caused the Church considerable concern, for their messages, preached directly to the common person, were not vetted by local authorities. Co-preachers associated with Fulk of Neuilly garnered negative reputations for keeping monies ostensibly collected for the Crusade and for preaching heretical doctrine.[9] Fulk himself seems to have mixed his moral agenda with recruiting.[10]

D. L. D'Avray, who finds the period around 1200 to be particularly critical in the history of preaching, notes:

> Almost any kind of wandering preacher, it would seem, had a chance of winning a following—one has the impression of a religious atmosphere unusually favourable to preaching of any kind, heretical or orthodox.[11]

This crucial moment in religious history, which marks the beginning of the second phase of medieval preaching, coincides with the time of the *Jeu de Saint Nicolas* (1200). Many factors contributed to the transformation in preaching practices, including a growing, urbanized, mercantile class with the economic power to demand and receive more personalised religious experiences. Crusade and travel to Spain and the East facilitated contact with Islamic and Jewish cultures, reintroducing classical thought to the West through Arabic texts and exposing Christian theologians to Jewish exegesis. Scholasticism in the universities and the work of missionaries and translators such as Ramon Lull opened the door to new ideas and methods. One indication of the importance of this period to the history of preaching is the appearance of various preaching manuals, or *artes praedicandi*. Alan of Lille (1128–1202), author of the first of these manuals, claimed a special status for the preacher and gave 47 example sermons for the use of those who experienced this 'highest calling'.[12]

The twelfth century was also a privileged time for Arras, a community that experienced a tremendous growth in its mercantile class, placing it among the wealthiest and most culturally rich communities in Europe.[13] What were some of the preaching messages that might have been received in bourgeois Arras, where the *Jeu de Saint Nicolas* was written and performed around 1200? Preaching for the Fourth

---

[9] Cole, p. 88.

[10] Cole, p. 90.

[11] D. L. D'Avray, *The Preaching of the Friars: Sermons Diffused from Paris before 1300* (Oxford: Oxford University Press, 1985), p. 25.

[12] Wilson, p. 70.

[13] Carol Lynne Symes, 'The Makings of a Medieval Stage: Theatre and the Culture of Performance in Thirteenth-Century Arras' (unpublished doctoral dissertation, Harvard University, 1999; abstract in *Dissertation Abstracts* 60.6 (1999), 2171–72).

Crusade was in full swing throughout the area of Arras. A contemporary of Fulk of Neuilly, Abbot Martin, was one of the best-known preachers of the Fourth Crusade. Martin had an unusual method of preaching, for he spoke as the mouthpiece of God, as if God had appropriated his voice and body. Penny Cole notes that his message, however, was clearly focused on the success of prior campaigns of the First Crusade, and not the Old Testament stories of martyrdom. Following the rather more upbeat example of Godfrey of Bouillon, Martin emphasizes the rewards that God has in store for those who wage his holy war. According to Cole:

> Martin did not view the crusade principally as an opportunity for martyrdom. He was alive to the fact that all his audience would hope to survive and that many would, in fact, survive; in both cases morale could best be sustained by a package of temporal and spiritual rewards which would serve to cover the eventuality of either life or death.[14]

Martin's questioning of the martyrdom paradigm for Crusade is a theme that will reappear as a central trope in the *Jeu de Saint Nicolas*, defining the play's relationship to preaching.

Jean Bodel's Jeu de Saint Nicolas *and the History of Theatre*

The same factors that led to drastic changes in preaching had their effects on other sectors of social production around the year 1200. A gradual change had been taking place in visual productions—a move from liturgical drama to vernacular drama. Liturgical drama developed from key moments of the Church service that were eventually read or mimed with flair by the clergy in order to increase the attendees' comprehension.[15] Because much of the service was in Latin and therefore incomprehensible to the vast majority of the non-clergy (and some of the clergy, as well), extra-linguistic cues became a vital part of ministry. Music and elaborate artwork, including the magnificent stained-glass windows of the cathedrals, were two of the ways that religion was made more accessible to the masses. Gestures and facial expressions, as foreign language teachers can attest, also greatly increase linguistic comprehension, and these methods became standard practice for the effective preacher. Over time, the preacher used other members of the clergy to act out different parts of his sermon. The audience, too, participated in the drama of the

---

[14] Cole, p. 96.

[15] Liturgical drama is distinct from drama, which owed much to liturgical drama, classical drama and other rhetorical forms, including ritual and debate. See Jody Enders, *Rhetoric and the Origins of Medieval Drama* (Ithaca, NY: Cornell University Press, 1992). For a good summary of the debate on the link between religious ritual and liturgical drama, see William Tydeman, *The Theatre in the Middle Ages: Western European Stage Conditions, c. 800–1576* (Cambridge: Cambridge University Press, 1978), pp. 32–45.

ritual, as Glynne Wickham notes, by dressing in sackcloth and ashes to enact what became known as the Dance of Death.[16] The importance of acting and oratory skills became particularly important qualities in a preacher, as evidenced by the rejection of one scholarly candidate for the position of Archbishop of Canterbury because the king preferred another, lesser-qualified applicant due to his renowned accomplishments as an actor.[17]

Alongside the ritual drama of the Church, plays of longer length were developed to further illustrate important religious messages. The oldest extant play manuscripts written in the vernacular include the Spanish *Auto de los Reyes Magos*, and the two Anglo-Norman plays, the *Jeu d'Adam* and the *Seinte Resurrection*. All three of these plays have been dated to the end of the twelfth century. Not long behind these three plays dealing with biblical themes, Jean Bodel's *Jeu de Saint Nicolas*, dated to around 1200, is the oldest non-biblical (though indeed religious), European vernacular play. Because this play does not deal directly with biblical themes, most scholars have assumed it was performed outside of the Church. Indeed, the length of the play would almost preclude it from being a part of the sacred ritual, but it could have been used to illustrate the instructive daily readings done by the clergy.[18] However, its ties to performative religion are manifest from the outset of the play, which begins with the words of a preacher.

Vernacularity and Performance in the Sermons of the Jeu

There are several moments of preaching in the *Jeu*, the first being the opening words introducing the play, spoken by *li preechieres*, as the rubricator wrote in the manuscript. Two other preaching occasions modelled on Crusade preaching are 1) the call for Arab Crusaders to fight the invading Christian armies by the officially sanctioned crier Connart, and 2) an inverted, mock preaching episode where a tavern worker named Raoulet calls out the news of new wine at the tavern. Each of these instances of preaching is deeply embedded in both the ritual of preaching and in the effect of early thirteenth century preaching. However, the genius and the enigma of the play are produced by the way in which the play uses and at the same time questions both ritual and effect.

The play begins with a 114-line speech to the audience on the part of a preacher. As in any performance, the audience would understand the function of the actor based on prior experience with that type of character. The medieval audience knew

---

[16] Glynne William Gladstone Wickham, *The Medieval Theatre*, 3rd edn (Cambridge: Cambridge University Press, 1987), p. 111.

[17] John Wesley Harris, *Medieval Theatre in Context: An Introduction* (London: Routledge, 1992), p. 46.

[18] Harris, p. 48.

that it was being addressed by a preacher because the audience had seen preachers before who had spoken (and quite possibly dressed) in a similar fashion.[19] Based on this assumption, the following extract from the sermon of *li preechieres* gives important insight into early thirteenth century preaching:

> *Li preechieres*
> Oiiés, oiiés, seigneur et dames
> —Que Dieus vous soit garans as ames—
> De vostre preu ne vous anuit!
> Nous volommes parler anuit
> De saint Nicolai le confés,
> Qui tant biaus miracles a fais. (vv. 1–6)[20]

The preacher addresses his audience in the vernacular, beginning his sermon with a call to listen. This simple action speaks volumes. In her landmark study *Rhetoric and the Origins of Medieval Drama*, Jody Enders discusses the relationship between the drama and forensic debate. Enders rightly points out that legal rhetoric and courtroom performance were intertwined with medieval theatrical performance. Medieval theatre, according to Enders, owes its origins as much to the courtroom as it does to the Church. Her work illustrates the interrelated nature of the different genres of public discourse. Enders quotes Tacitus on the public speaker, who wrote, 'Your public speaker can't get along without "hear, hear", and the clapping of hands. He must have what I may call his stage'.[21] Model sermon books do not show this part of the sermon, the 'hear, hear' or 'oiiés, oiiés' that called the crowd to listen, but this is not surprising since extant sermons can be regarded more as notes for medieval preachers rather than as attempts at recording exactly what was spoken on a particular day.[22] The *Jeu de Saint Nicolas*, however, must convince the audience

---

[19] On the use of costumes in medieval performance, see Tydeman, pp. 36 and 42.

[20] Preacher: 'Oyez, Oyez, lords and ladies, God's blessing be upon you all, to keep you free from every harm! We want to talk to you this evening about Saint Nicholas, the Confessor, who did so many miracles.'

I have used the following edition throughout this article: Jean Bodel, *Le jeu de Saint Nicolas*, ed. by Albert Henry, (Geneva: Droz, 1981).

[21] Enders, p. 69.

[22] This seems to be a commonly agreed upon precept. See Richard H. and Mary A. Rouse, *Preachers, Florilegia and Sermons* (Toronto: Pontifical Institute of Mediaeval Studies, 1979), p. 71, for further details. Michel Zink's work is persuasive in explaining why vernacular sermons were recorded in Latin. See Michel Zink, *La Prédication en langue romane: avant 1300* (Paris: Champion, 1976), pp. 91–101. Louis-Jacques Bataillon goes into greater detail about the mix of vernacular and Latin and how certain sermons may have been recorded and transmitted, Louis-Jacques Bataillon, *La prédication au XIIIe siècle en France et Italie* (Aldershot: Variorum, 1993), pp. 19–35. Christoph Maier concurs that few Crusade sermons were written down. His book includes examples of the few-recorded Crusade sermons, all of

that a preacher is speaking in order to create the proper meaning. We can and must assume then that at least some medieval sermons began with a call to the audience like that of the ritualized courtroom drama. In as much as drama owes some of its origins to legal rhetoric, sermon rhetoric and performance would appear to be as deeply embedded in the same overall format of public speaking. In this case, the play mimics a sermon by beginning with the words of a preacher, and the preacher mimics the lawyer with his call to the audience. Courtroom, stage and pulpit are intertwined in their performative roles.

This moment of performance, when roles are easily confused, has been particularly troubling for readers of the *Jeu de Saint Nicolas*.[23] The preacher's summary of the forthcoming play has a mistake. The preacher claims that the Saracens invade Christian lands, but in the play the Christians take the offensive. The preacher hints of his duplicity by warning members of the audience that they may be surprised by what they see, 'Pour che n'aiés pas grant merveille / Se vous veés aucun affaire' (106–107)[24]. By having the preacher caution the audience to listen closely for differences between his words and the play, Bodel is in essence encouraging his thirteenth-century Arrageois audience to listen critically to preachers and to compare their words with what they see around them.

Crusade preaching, a public phenomenon of the Middle Ages with clear societal repercussions, has left little in the way of written traces. A few famous Crusade speeches, like the accounts of Urban II's preaching of the First Crusade, were recorded from several perspectives. But the vast majority of crusade preaching was recorded only in its effects and not in its performative or literal aspects. Chroniclers give numbers of persons taking up the Cross and sometimes describe the reaction of the audience to a particularly gifted preacher. The *Jeu* gives one example of a call to crusade, as Connart is sent by the pagan king to call troops to fight the Christians. Connart repeats the basic structure of the preacher, again calling to his audience to listen:

Connars
Oiiés! Oiiés! Oiés, signeur!
Oiés vo preu et vo honneur!
Je faç le ban le roy d'Aufrike:
Que tout i viegnent, povre et rique,
Garni de leur armes, par ban;

---

them in Latin. See Christoph T. Maier, *Crusade Propaganda and Ideology: Model Sermons for the Preaching of the Cross* (Cambridge: Cambridge University Press, 2000).

[23] Some of the critics who address the issue of the mistaken preacher include: A. Henry, Tony Hunt, and Bethany A. Schroeder. The debate is divided among those who feel that the prologue, since it does not agree with the play, was added at a later date, and those who account for the difference in some other way.

[24] Thus, don't be very surprised if you should see some mishap.

De le terre Prestre Jehan
Ne remaigne jusques al Coine.
D'Alixandre, de Babiloine,
Li Kenelieu, li Achopart,
Tout vegnent garni ceste part,
Et toute l'autre gent grifaigne.
Seürs soit qui c'onques remaigne
Que li roys le fera tuer. (vv. 225–237)[25]

While Connart's call to Crusade would not provoke the emotional frenzy that the speeches of Fulk of Neuilly and Bernard of Clairvaux did, his words do underscore the basic structure of the rhetoric of public speaking. In a play where the outcome of the Crusade can be read as a deeply ironic call for the audience to re-examine the purpose of the Crusade,[26] Connart's basic argument that troops should come because it is 'par ban' and because those that remain 'li roys le fera tuer' is likely closer to what was felt by the average conscript than a moving religious experience, particularly during the preaching of the Fourth Crusade when the disaster of the Third Crusade was still fresh in the minds of the public.

Connart 'preaches' a second time as the Saracen king asks him to spread the news that the royal treasury has been left guarded only by a statue.

Connars li crieres
Oiiés, oiiés, segneur trestout!
Venés avant, faites me escout!
De par le roi vous fai savoir
C'a son tresor n'a son avoir
N'ara jamais ne clef ne serre;
Tout aussi comme a plaine terre
Le puet on trouver, che me sanle.
Et qui le puet embler, si l'emble,
Car il ne le garde mais nus
Fors seus uns mahomés cornus,
Tous mors, car il ne se remue.
Or soit honnis qui bien ne hue! (574–87).[27]

---

[25] Connart: 'Oyez, oyez, oyez, good men, your honour and your interest! Summons from the King of Africa: that all men come, both poor and rich, furnished with arms, as is required. Let no man dally, from the land of Prester John to Caramania, Alexandrians, Babylonians, the Canaanites, the Achoparts, let all come armed, in this direction and every other savage nation. If anyone remains behind be sure the king will have him killed.'

[26] I have argued elsewhere that the play is, in fact, a call for non-violent crusade. See Lynn Ramey, 'Jean Bodel's *Jeu de Saint Nicolas*: A Call for Non-violent Crusade', *French Forum*, 27:3 (2002): pp. 1–14.

[27] Connart: 'Oyez, oyez, gentlemen all, come along, give me a hearing! On the King's behalf I have to tell you that as from now his treasure hoard will not be under lock and key. Youll find it all laid out, as if on open ground, it seems to me; anyone can help themselves at

The same speaker who before called soldiers to Crusade reuses the same rhetorical framework to dupe the play's tavern crowd, where the future thieves are drinking and gambling. As emissary of the king, Connart knowingly encourages the thieves to commit a crime. While Connart is clearly an official crier and not a member of the clergy, his speech is structured exactly like the prologue and the call to Crusade, both of which were plainly instances of preaching to a medieval audience.[28] In this last case, Connart's speech has the express purpose of causing sin. Since Connart is a Saracen who called for war against the Christians, his words are clearly not to be trusted. By highlighting the duplicitous words of the crier and putting the truth-value of his words into doubt, Jean Bodel has created a suspicion in the minds of his medieval theatrical audience that all public speaking, and by extension all preaching, could be officially sanctioned without being divinely sanctioned.

Connart's mock crusade preaching, though not inspiring, accomplishes the important goal of establishing Connart in the same rhetorical tradition as *li preechieres,* who opened the play with his prologue. Connart's more important task in the play will come as, now established as an officially sanctioned Crusade preacher and mouthpiece for the king, he comes into conflict with Raoulet who is sent by the tavern owner to call the new wine. Connart sees Raoulet about to make a public announcement. The exact movements, properties and physical position taken up by Raoulet are not given in the play's single manuscript, but it can be assumed that the ritual Raoulet started to practice was as recognizable to the audience as it was to Connart. While Raoulet claims that his right to cry the wine comes from the 'homes de la vile' (606) or townsmen, Connart insists upon his exclusive right to make pronouncements based on his long-standing relationship with the 'eskievins de la chité' (601) or city magistrates.

In the conflict between Connart and Raoulet, the *Jeu de Saint Nicolas* enters the contemporary debate over public voice and public space, a debate that remains in the historical record as part of the conflict of power between the commercially successful townsmen and representatives of the crown. Seen in this light, their argument is not a puzzling diversion in a play about the Crusades, as many have suggested.[29] The dispute between the two criers mirrors a contemporary dispute over

---

will. No one's left on guard at all except a single 'horned Mahomet', quite dead, he doesn't move a muscle. Shame on the man who keeps it quiet!'

[28] The preaching of lay people was especially prevalent and equally condemned by the Church at the end of the twelfth century. See Michel Lauwers, 'Praedicatio-Exhortatio: L'Église, la réforme et les laïcs (XIe–XIIIe siècles)', in *La Parole du prédicateur: V^{e}–XVe siècle*, ed. by Rosa Maria Dessì and Michel Lauwers (Nice: Z'éditions, 1997), pp. 187–232.

[29] The tavern interlude has piqued the interest of modern readers, and rightfully so, since it occupies nearly a third of the play. For their analyses of the function or meaning of the long tavern episode, see Andrew Cowell, *At Play in the Tavern: Signs, Coins, and Bodies in the Middle Ages* (Ann Arbor: University of Michigan Press, 1999); Carolyn L. Dinshaw, 'Dice Games and Other Games in *Le Jeu de Saint Nicholas*', *PMLA*, 95 (1980), 802–11; Jane Blythe

who would be allowed to preach to the public. Carolyn Muessig identifies the eleventh and twelfth centuries, the period leading up to the performance of the *Jeu*, as crucial periods in the history of preaching, where monks, clerics and even the laity all claimed the right to preach.[30] For the *Jeu de Saint Nicolas*, the matter is solved by the tavern owner, who strikes a pact between the two criers—Raoulet will call the tavern news and Connart will call all official news. The tavern owner has thus asserted Raoulet's claim to a public voice through the economic power of the town's merchants, while allowing Connart to continue with his work for the king's men. This compromise is really no compromise at all, but rather a successful usurpation of official power by a representative of the city's mercantile class.

Sermon as Theatre and Theatre as Sermon

Jean Bodel's *Jeu de Saint Nicolas* was written and performed at a transformative time for public speaking. Drama was part and parcel of the religious, legal and commercial experience. The sermon had developed to the point where the audience expected a certain level of entertainment. The gestures, the intonation, even the costumes of the priest created a theatre within the Church. Some of the same images known to be used in crusade sermons of the period are repeated in the *Jeu*. The angel that exhorts the Christians in the play finds an echo in sermons *ad crucesignatos* by James of Vitry, Gilbert of Tournai,[31] and Eudes of Châteauroux.[32] James's sermon reads:

> Vidi angelum ascendentem ab ortu solis habentem signum Dei vivi, et clamavit voce magna quatuor angelis quibus datum est nocere terre et mari dicens [...].[33]

James glosses this verse from the Apocalypse, saying:

Dozer, 'The Tavern: Discovery of the Secular Locus in Medieval French Drama' (unpublished doctoral dissertation, 1980; abstract in *Dissertation Abstracts International*, 41 (1980), 1582A–83A; A. Henry; Christine Jacob-Hugon, *L'oeuvre jongleresque de Jean Bodel: l'art de séduire un public* (Bruxelles: De Boeck Université, 1998); Ramey; David Raybin, 'The Court and the Tavern: Bourgeois Discourse in *Li jeus de Saint Nicolai*', *Viator*, 19 (1988), pp. 177–92; Nigel Wilkins, 'Yet More Concerning the Tavern Bills in Jean Bodel's *Jeu de Saint Nicolas*', *Zeitschrift fur Romanische Philologie*, 82 (1966), pp. 339–44.

[30] Carolyn Muessig, *Medieval Monastic Preaching* (Leiden: Brill, 1998), p. 5.

[31] Maier, p. 192–93.

[32] Maier, 168–69.

[33] I saw an angel rising from the sunrise carrying the sign of the living God, and he called in a powerful voice to the four angels whose duty was to devastate land and sea. Maier, pp. 82–83.

> Angelus iste est Christus, paterne voluntatis nuntius [...].dum paulatim per *predicatores mundum illuminavi [...].*[34]

The unusual name of another character from the play, the Emir d'Outre l'Arbre Sec, who resists converting to Christianity, makes more sense in light of James's words:

> Arbores igitur infructuose diabolo exponuntur, que sicce sunt sine humore gratie, non habentes 'fructum bonorum operum' vel folia bonorum verborum.[35]

Finally, the idea of the earthly and heavenly treasures, the central image to the *Jeu de Saint Nicolas*, are themes exploited by Gilbert of Tournai[36] and James of Vitry.[37]

The *Jeu de Saint Nicolas* intentionally capitalized on the horizon of expectations of the sermon genre by putting the prologue in the mouth of a priest. By surrounding the play with the words of a preacher on one end and the *te deum laudamus* (v. 1533) that ended religious ritual on the other, the play itself becomes entwined in religious performance, acting as a sermon itself. The action of the play serves the same function as an exemplum, and it would be difficult to differentiate the play from other exempla that might well have been performed within official Church ritual.[38] The tavern action, where the three thieves play dice games, is not extraneous, but rather functions as an exemplum within the exemplum constituted by the entire play. What the audience learns from the tavern exemplum is that preachers (like Connart) can be dishonest. Those who are foolish enough to follow the words of a false preacher will be undone, as were the three thieves. This *digressio* relates back to the primary theme of the sermon-play as the audience recalls that the words of the original preacher *li preechieres*, the Christian mirror of the Saracen Connart, were also untrue: the Christians invaded the Saracen lands and no one survived the massacre. Finally, the entire play of the *Jeu de Saint Nicolas* provokes the audience to examine the words of itinerant crusade preachers who, in focusing on the success of the First Crusade, are encouraging followers to forget the disastrous consequences of the more recent Third Crusade. Each consequent performance of preaching calls to mind a prior, slightly different performance, with the final result that the *Jeu de Saint Nicolas* undermines any attempt to convince the people of Arras that crusade participation would be either wise or just.

---

[34] This angel is Christ, the messenger of his Father's will [...] as he slowly enlightens the world through his preachers. Maier, pp. 86–87.

[35] The trees that carry no fruit are exposed to the devil; they are dry without the humidity of grace, not carrying the fruits of good works or the leaves of good words. Maier, pp. 90–91.

[36] Maier, pp. 208–09.

[37] Maier, pp. 106–07.

[38] On the subject of the exemplum as mime and eventually as theatrical act, see Carlo Delcorno, 'Medieval Preaching in Italy (1200–1500)', in *The Sermon*, ed. by Beverly Mayne Kienzle (Turnhout: Brepols, 2000), p. 474.

Performance is repetition with a difference, notes Joseph Roach.[39] Religious ritual, including the sermon, was a vital part of performance culture during the Middle Ages. Collections of sermons enabled repetition but show that difference could be inserted through the skill of the performer/preacher and the use of different exempla at different times.[40] Linguistically, as well, sermons could be altered, as preachers no doubt chose different vernacular renderings of the written Latin text. The *Jeu de Saint Nicolas* and other semi-religious medieval theatrical productions mirror and adapt the sermon's performativity. The performance of culture has particular signification at times of cultural confrontation and change, as Roach found in his study of the performance of oral literature in the context of colonialism, and the year 1200 offered myriad opportunities for cultural encounters—Christian and Muslim, clergy and lay, urban and agrarian, and the list goes on.

Acting, while appreciated by the public, was not a mainstream profession and was looked upon with disapproving eye by the Church. Actors' liminal status allowed them to appropriate the action and language of the clergy and repeat it, with a difference. While acting was mostly tolerated, when actors mocked the clergy they could expect harsh condemnation, as decrees against stage representation of the clergy show. While appropriation of the style and manner of the clergy made the actors recognizable as preachers, actors introduced differences that served to question the intentions of the preacher and the role of his audience. The *Jeu de Saint Nicolas* manages to raise considerable doubt about the truth value of the Crusade preacher's message as *li preechieres* proves himself to be unreliable. Jean Bodel's *Jeu de Saint Nicolas* does not simply *contain* preaching: it is *about* preaching, especially unauthorized preaching. The play takes on the contemporary concerns with who has the right to speak God's word and whether those that speak are always telling the truth. Ironically, Bodel undermines his own authority, because his play is as much an unauthorized sermon as the sermons of Connart, *li preechieres*, and the itinerant crusade preacher. *Li preechieres*, by alerting the audience to the play's own duplicity ['Pour che n'aiés pas grant merveille / Se vous veés aucun affaire' (106–7)], casts doubt on the play's own message. Jean Bodel, the courageous and iconoclastic author of the first *fabliaux*, gave his medieval audience a coded warning; that is, one needs to listen to preachers and playwrights with caution, for, as any public voice, their messages can be deceiving.

---

[39] Joseph Roach, "Writing the absent potential: drama, performance, and the canon of African-American literature", in *Performativity and Performance*, ed. by Andrew Parker and Eve Kosofsky Sedgwick (New York: Routledge, 1995), p. 46. Roach is here paraphrasing anthropologist Richard Schechner, who underscores the importance of behaviour that can be rehearsed, repeated and recreated. See Richard Schechner, *Between Theater and Anthropology* (Philadelphia, PA: University of Pennsylvania Press, 1985).

[40] Zink, pp. 204–09.

The Conversion of Mary Magdalene and the Musical Legacy of Franciscan Piety in the Early German Passion Plays

PETER V. LOEWEN

The medieval German Passion plays which flourished between the thirteenth and sixteenth centuries represent some of the most important sources of late medieval Passion exegesis. The nearly one hundred and fifty works in the exant repertory, including the Marian laments (*Marienklagen*), are related to Scripture; however, they are not narrative accounts of the Passion of Christ. Rather, the composers of these dramas elaborate on themes from Scripture using music and poetry to preach to audiences about the virtues of penance. The influence of preaching is palpable in the German Passion plays dating from the late fourteenth and fifteenth centuries, because the characters in the dramas often preach directly to their audience.[1] However, the tradition of preaching in the German Passion plays actually begins with the earliest examples, the *Großes Benediktbeurer Passionsspiel* (*c.* 1250) and the *Wiener Passionsspielfragment* (*c.* 1300). Here, in scenes devoted to

[1] The late repertory of German *Marienklagen* and *Passionen* is filled with overt examples of preaching, a subject too expansive to consider in this study. Some fine examples of preaching in this later body of works may be found in the final song of the Virgin Mary in the *Füssener Marienklage,* 159–70 (*Das Füssener Osterspiel und die Füssener Marienklage, Universitätsbibliothek Augsburg [ehemals: Harburg], Cod. II, 1, 4, 62*, facsimile, ed. by Dietrich Schmidtke, Litterae, Göppinger Beiträge zur Textgeschichte, 69 [Göppingen: Kümmerle, 1983]); the speech performed by the Precursor in the *Bozner Passionsspiel*, 1–74 (*Bozner Passion 1495, Die Spielhandschriften A und B*, ed. by Bruno Klammer, Mittlere deutsche Literatur, 20 [Bern: Lang, 1986]); and the song of Mary Magdalene which occurs at the end of the first day of the *Alsfelder Passionsspiel*, 2847–91 (*The Alsfeld Passion Play*, ed. and trans. by Larry E. West, Studies in German Language and Literature, 17 [Lewiston, NY: Edwin Mellen Press, 1997]).

Mary Magdalene, Latin lyrics and liturgical chants combine with songs in Middle High German to portray her conversion from worldliness to piety. Through music and poetry, composers depict Mary Magdalene's transformation from model sinner to pious Christian by contrasting her secular dance songs, in which she extols the (false) virtues of lechery and vanity, with her songs of penance, in which she laments and entreats her audience to repent.

Because of their overtly homiletical character, it is clear that the *Großes Benediktbeurer Passionsspiel* (*BP*) and the *Wiener Passionsspielfragment* (*WPf*) are connected to the tradition of preaching; but since their authors are unknown, the provenance of these works remains unclear.[2] Several scholars have noted an overall affinity between the compassionate sentiment and moral tone of medieval German Passion plays and the spirituality of the Friars Minor.[3] But a careful comparison of the early German Passion plays to works of Franciscan provenance illustrates that the connection exceeds mere affinity. Indeed, the clear analogy between the songs of Mary Magdalene and principles of German Franciscan theology, sermons, and musical exegesis strongly suggests that the composers of the German Passion plays worked under the influence of Franciscan spirituality and the homiletical programme of its preachers.

---

[2] The *BP* is found in the last *folia* of the famous song collection known as the *Carmina Burana* (107^r–111^r; 112^v). Orthographical and paleographical evidence in its German texts indicate that the play was probably composed in southern Bavaria and that the manuscript was copied in Carinthia, perhaps in Seckau, *c.* 1250. See *Carmina Burana, Facsimile Reproduction of the Manuscript Clm 4660 and Clm 4660a* [Bayerische Staatsbibliothek München], ed. by Bernhard Bischoff, Publications of Mediaeval Musical Manuscripts, 9 (Brooklyn, NY: Institute of Mediaeval Music, 1967), p. 30. Compare Georg Steer, '"Carmina Burana" in Südtirol, Aus Herkunft des clm 4660', *Zeitschrift für Deutsches Altertum und Deutsche Literatur*, 112, no. 1 (1983), p. 1–37. The play was discovered in the library of the Benediktbeuren monastery in 1803, but did not become widely known to scholars until Johannes Andreas Schmeller published his edition of the work in 1847. The *WPf* is the play most closely related to the *BP*. Orthographical evidence in the German texts of the *WPf* indicates that the play is largely composed in a Bavarian dialect, but also compiles material from what was probably a west Central-German model from the Rhenish region of Franconia. The eight *folia* containing the *WPf* were acquired by the Wiener Hofbibliothek in 1849 and now carry the *siglum* Vienna, Österreichische Nationalbibliothek, Ser. Nova 12887 (Suppl. 561). See Rolf Bergmann, *Studien zu Entstehung und Geschichte der deutschen Passionsspiele des 13. und 14. Jahrhunderts,* Münstersche Mittelalter-Schriften, 14 (Munich: Fink, 1972), pp. 41 and 46.

[3] See Bergmann, *Studien*, p. 236; Walther Lipphardt, 'Studien zur den Marienklagen. Marienklage und germanische Totenklage', *Beitrage zur Geschichte der deutschen Sprache und Literatur*, 58 (1934), p. 426; Anthonius Touber, *Das Donaueschinger Passionsspiel* (Stuttgart: Reclam, 1985), p. 9; and Eduard Wechssler, *Die Romanischen Marienklagen: Ein Beitrag zur Geschichte des Dramas im Mittelalter* (Halle: Karras, 1893), p. 4, n.*; pp. 6–7; p. 14; and pp. 30–35.

To lay bare the connection between the music and poetry in the *BP* and *WPf* and programmes of Franciscan homiletics, one must examine how the literal evidence of preaching in the songs of the dramas relates to the music to which it is set. For this reason, the present study will unfold in two phases. I will begin with a philological examination of the dramatic texts through a study of various writings by the Franciscan preachers Berthold of Regensburg, Heinrich of Burgus, and David of Augsburg. The presence of strong literal associations between Franciscan preaching and the German Passion plays leads to further Franciscan reading of the melodies which accompany the secular and penitential texts of Mary Magdalene. In this second phase of my study, I will show that the music Mary Magdalene sings in the *BP* and *WPf* reflects on Franciscan concepts of the *ars musica*. The way composers use music in the settings of the Magdalene texts in these Passion plays coincides with the theories and practices of rhetoric described by Berthold of Regensburg and the Franciscan theologians Bartholomaeus Anglicus and Roger Bacon. Indeed, their views concerning the union of music and preaching are preserved in the German dramas.[4]

This interdisciplinary study of the early German Passion plays contributes to both literary and musical scholarship concerning the role of Mary Magdalene in medieval exegesis. It brings to light a musical aspect of the Franciscan ministry among the German people and offers proof that the German Passion plays reflect an important vestige of Franciscan preaching in the medieval German lands.

Compared to the long tradition of the medieval Easter drama, the Passion play is a small and relatively late development in the history of religious theatre.[5] The presence of laments of the Blessed Virgin Mary in some Passion plays such as the *BP* has led Karl Young and Walther Lipphardt to conclude that the genre evolved within the context of the liturgy for Good Friday, either at vespers or in the ritual of the Adoration of the Cross.[6] However, the liturgical and lyrical materials in scenes that surround and include portrayals of Mary Magdalene make the liturgical orientation of the *BP* and *WPf* seem less certain. The *WPf* includes scenes of Adam and Eve's fall from grace and of Lucifer's temptation and trial of sinners in the court of hell. The *BP* includes liturgical chants from the Palm Sunday processional; scenes

---

[4] All translations of text and editions of music are my own, unless otherwise indicated.

[5] The research of Karl Young and Sandro Sticca shows that the earliest Latin Passion plays appeared at roughly the end of the twelfth and beginning of the thirteenth centuries (Karl Young, *The Drama of the Medieval Church* [Oxford: Oxford University Press, 1933], 2, p. 492; and Sandro Sticca, *The Latin Passion Play: Its Origins and Development* [Albany, NY: State University of New York Press, 1970], pp. 122–25). The liturgical chants that occur in the body of the Passion dramas indicate that they derive from the liturgical observances of holy week and the feasts of those figures who are important to the scriptural narrative of the Passion.

[6] Lipphardt, 'Marienklagen und Liturgie', *Jahrbuch für Liturgiewissenschaft*, 12 (1932), p. 198. Young, *Drama*, 1, pp. 504–06.

that depict the conversation between Jesus and Zacchaeus; portrayals of the raising of Lazarus and the laments of his sisters; and representations of Jesus's preaching. This diverse collection of music shows that the *BP* and *WPf* evolved somewhere between the realms of Church and secular culture, a niche also occupied by the Franciscan preachers.

The Franciscans began their aggressive campaign of spiritual reform among the city-dwellers and nobility in the German lands in 1219.[7] Franciscan preachers quickly became famous for their pastoral charity and energetic ministry. They travelled in pairs from city to city, as Francis recommended, proclaiming to all people, through song and dramatic sermons, the virtues of penance.[8] The Franciscans served the Church by preaching against heresy and served the town by caring for its poor and sick, sometimes at the risk of their own lives.[9] By the mid-thirteenth century, many German Franciscans had joined the ranks of the secular clergy; some had gone on to become bishops.[10] In this new capacity, they were able to extend their influence over the Church. The friars also established a strong reputation for scholarship, especially at their *studia* in Regensburg, Magdeburg, and, later, Cologne. Here, renowned theologians such as David of Augsburg, Bartholomaeus Anglicus, and Duns Scotus advanced the Franciscan programme of education, which helped to transform their order of lay preachers into a movement of poor, educated clerics.[11] Thus, it was not long after their arrival in the German lands that the friars

---

[7] See Loewen 'Francis the Musician and the Mission of the *Joculatores Domini* in the Medieval German Lands', *Franciscan Studies*, 60 (2002), p. 1–46.

[8] 'Tunc beatus Franciscus omnes ad se convocavit, et plura eis de regno Dei, de contemptu mundi de abnegatione propriae voluntatis et proprii corporis subiectione pronuntians, binos illos partes quatuor segregavit, et ait ad eos: "Ite, charissimi, bini et bini per diversas partes orbis, annuntiantes hominibus pacem et poenitentiam in remissionem peccatorum"'. See Thomas of Celano, *Vita prima S. Francisci Assisiensis, et eiusdem Legenda ad Usum Chori* (Quaracchi: Collegii S. Bonaventurae, 1926), p. 29; compare *The Life of Saint Francis*, trans. by Regis J. Armstrong, OFM Cap., and others, Francis of Assisi: Early Documents, 1, *The Saint*, ed. by Regis J. Armstrong, and others (New York: New City Press, 1999), p. 207.

[9] It is believed that the Franciscan friars sustained such heavy losses to their order during the time of the Black Death because they cared for its victims. See P. Konrad Eubel, *Geschichte der oberdeutschen Minoriten-Provinz* (Würzburg: Bucher, 1886), p. 57.

[10] By 1274, thirty-two Franciscan friars had been appointed to the episcopacy; and by 1311, there were fifty-six Franciscan bishops in Europe and North Africa (John Moorman, *A History of the Franciscan Order* [Oxford: Clarendon Press, 1968; repr., Sandpiper, 1998], p. 296).

[11] The friars established schools for their novices at each of their convents and placed their education in the hands of a trained theologian. The most gifted students in the German Franciscan provinces were encouraged to pursue advanced studies at the central *studium*, established in Magdeburg (*c.* 1228) and later moved to Cologne some time before the arrival of Duns Scotus in 1307.

placed themselves in a position to disseminate their spirituality to the widest possible audience.[12]

The collections of sermons, didactic literature, and hagiography extant from the early period of Franciscan expansion in the German lands indicate that the Franciscan programme of spirituality focused mainly on the dichotomy between the sins of vanity and lechery and the virtues of contrition, penance, and atonement. This focus is apparent in the writings of Lamprecht of Regensburg (*c.* 1215–after 1255) and David of Augsburg (*c.* 1200–*c.* 1272).[13] However, the best early examples of Franciscan preaching occur in the German sermons attributed to Berthold of Regensburg (*c.* 1210–*c.* 1272). The sins which most concern him are arrogance (*hôhvart*), which he equates with vanity and wantoness, and lechery (*unkiusche*). In his Sermon 25, Berthold upbraids women for their immodesty, especially for daring to use the offertory in Church as an opportunity to show off their finery. They go nowhere without their fancy wrappers, yellow veils, and ribbons, he says; and they desire to be praised for their beauty.[14] In his Sermon 12, Berthold expresses outrage

---

[12] The history of the Franciscan movement in the medieval German lands is the subject of several important studies, especially the following: *800 Jahre Franz von Assisi: Franziskanische Kunst und Kultur des Mittelalters, Krems-Stein, Minoritenkirche 15. Mai–17. Oktober 1982* (Vienna: Amt der Niederösterreichischen Landesregierung, 1982); Konrad P. Eubel, *Geschichte der oberdeutschen Minoriten-Provinz* (Würzburg: Bucher, 1886); Eubel, *Geschichte der Kölnischen Minoriten-Ordensprovinz*, 1, Veröffentlichungen des historischen Vereins für den Niederrhein (Cologne: J. & W. Boisserée, 1906); Leonhard Lemmens, *Niedersächsische Franziskanerklöster im Mittelalter* (Hildesheim: Lax, 1896); G. E. Friess, *Geschichte der Österreichischen Minoritenprovinz* (Vienna: Gerold, 1882); *500 Jahre Franziskaner der österreichischen Ordens-Provinz* (Vienna: Franziskaner-Provinzialates, 1951); *Franziskanisches Schriftum im deutschen Mittelalter*, 11 and 86, ed. by Kurt Ruh, Münchener Texte und Untersuchungen zur deutschen Literatur des Mittelalters (Munich: Beck, 1965, 1985); Patricius Schlager, *Die deutschen Franziskaner und ihre Verdienste um die Lösung der sozialen Frage, von P. Patricus Schlager Franziskanerordenpriester*, Geschichte Jungend-und Volksbibliothek, 6 (Regensburg: Manz, 1907); and John B. Freed, *The Friars and German Society in the Thirteenth Century* (Cambridge, MA: The Medieval Academy of America, 1977).

[13] Lamprecht of Regensburg is the author of the first German life of Saint Francis (see *Lamprecht von Regensburg: Sanct Francisken Leben und Tochter Syon*, ed. by Karl Weinhold [Paderborn: Schöningh, 1880]). David of Augsburg served as *lector* at the Regensburg *studium* from *c.* 1240 to 1250. His treatise *De exterioris et interioris hominis compositione* (*c.* 1240) is one of the most important theological works to eminate from the German Franciscan provinces (see *Spiritual Life and Progress by David of Augsburg, Being a Translation of His 'De exterioris et interioris hominis compositione'*, ed. and trans. by Dominic Devas, OFM (London: Burns Oats & Washbourne, 1937).

[14] 'Ir fouwen, ir machet ez ouch gar ze noetlîchen mit iuwerm gewande, mit gelwen sleigern, mit gebende, sô mit röckelînen, sô mit dem vorgange ze der kirchen zuo dem opfer etc. [. . .] Ir gêt niwan mit tüechelehe umbe unde mit löbelehe, daz man iuch eht lobe: "jâ

at the *Hôhvertiger*—the arrogant ones. Comparing the value of humility with the transience of worldly pleasure, he writes:

> Phî, hôhvertiger, mit dînem tanzenne! wie tiure dir disiu tugent ist! Wan dû verliusest dîne sêle gar mit einem lîhten dinge, und aller meiste ir frouwen, die niwan mit löbelachen unde mit ir tüechelehen umbe gênt. Wê, ir frouwen! jâ was unser frouwe gar unde gar dêmüetic. Ir habet rehte nihtes niht dar an, dâ mit ir umbe gêt: wan ez ist niwan ein gestüppe und ein gestüppelin und ein gespötte und ein üppiket, unde dir wirt niemer mêr wol dâ mite, daz dû begerst mit aller dîner kraft solicher üppikeite, unde treit dich doch niht für, wan daz dû dâ mite verdampt bist als Lucifer.[15]

In his Sermon 7, Berthold writes that *hôhvart* is a sin to which the young especially fall victim, because of their 'vain arrogance' (*uppige hôhvart*), 'frivolity' (*îtel êre*), and love of pleasure (*freude*).[16]

Heinrich of Burgus, a Franciscan confessor working in Brixen (Bressanone), echoes Berthold's concern for vanity in his mystical allegory *Der Seele Rat* (*c.* 1301–19).[17] Heinrich's text takes the form of a dramatic discourse. Here, characters such as Lady Confession (*Fraw Peichte)*, Lady Atonement (*Fraw Puesse)*, Lady Contrition *(Fraw Rewe)*, angels, and Jesus vie with the Devil for supremacy over the body and soul. Heinrich's portrayal of the conflict between these characters is compelling, especially because it so closely corresponds to the portrayal of Mary Magdalene's struggle with sin in the early German Passion plays. The depiction of the Devil's admiration of the vanity of women, which occurs approximately two-

herre, wie schoene! wart aber ie sô schoenes iht?"' (*Berthold von Regensburg: Vollständige Ausgabe seiner Predigten,* ed. by Franz Pfeiffer and Joseph Strobl [Vienna: 1862, 1882; repr. with forword, bibliography, and history of transmission by Kurt Ruh, Berlin: De Gruyter, 1965], 1, p. 396, 39– p. 397, 12. References to Berthold's text are by page and line).

[15] 'Fie, you vain one with your dancing! How costly this virtue is when you lose your soul completely with fleeting things—especially you ladies who go about not only with wrist frills but with wrappers. Alas, you women! Indeed, Our Lady was perfect and completely humble. You truly have nothing in that which you carry about you, since it is only dust and powder, a mockery, and a vanity. You will never gain happiness when you desire such vanities with all your power. Do not take that path or else you will be as damned as Lucifer.' (Berthold, *Predigten,* 1, p. 173, 1–10).

[16] 'Die jungen liute die vallent dâ von in üppige hôvart durch îtel êre unde durch die freude' (Berthold, *Predigten*, 1, p. 104, 15–6).

[17] *Heinrich von Burgus der Seele Rat aus der Brixener Handschrift*, ed. by Hans-Friedrich Roesenfeld, Deutsche Texte des Mittelalters Herausgegeben von der preussischen Akademie der Wissenschaften, 37 (Berlin: Weidmann, 1932), pp. xxiv–xxv. Hans-Friedrich Rosenfeld proposes that Heinrich of Burgus was a member of the Order of Friars Minor. He probably came originally from Burgeis im Vinstgau and was attached to the convent at Brixen, where he served as a confessor to a community of Poor Clares (ibid., pp. xxiv–xxv).

thirds of the way through Heinrich's text, is especially useful in this comparison. In this passage, the Devil approaches his cronies and produces a sack of finery which he has acquired from a vain woman. He crows over several details of her attire—the seams, knots, and the gaps in the sleeves of her gown, and a lovely garland of flowers—and then remarks on their value.[18] 'Leg die nadelen auch her zu / Und den vaden damit sy sich fru / Freiste an den heren tagen! / Ichwil auch her zu tragen / Dew wе̊hen schapel und den krancz / Den sy trueg an dem tancz'.[19] *Der Seele Rat* of Heinrich of Burgus offers an especially vivid account of the Franciscan view of sin. Heinrich's depiction of the sinner as dancer, singer, and immodest dresser also offers a vivid corollary to Berthold's declarations in Sermon 12.

On the matter of lechery, both Berthold of Regensburg and Heinrich of Burgus write adamantly. Heinrich devotes nearly three hundred lines to a definition of and invective against the sin in *Der Seele Rat.*[20] Berthold of Regensburg teaches that lechery (*unkiusche*) is the 'characteristic sin of the world' (*die werlde süezekeit, unkiusche*) to which especially young people are susceptible.[21] In his Sermon 26, he says that this sin is the chief cause of the devil's fearsome power over people.[22] In Sermon 17, Berthold adds that those who have been trapped by the devil in the sin of lechery delude themselves by believing that their 'false love' (*valsche mine*) is actually the 'true love' (*wâre minne*) which can come only from a love of God and Christ.[23] Those who suffer from *unkiusche* have no choice but to love others who suffer under the same delusions, he says, because to those who have been trapped by the devil, sin has the appearance of virtue.[24] In such cases, he declares, 'Bist dû ein

[18] *Der Seele Rat,* p. 102, 5489–5496. References to Heinrich's text are by page and line.

[19] 'Lay the needle down and also the thread so that they may be praised early on the Lord's day! I also wish to add the lovely crown of flowers and garland that she wore while dancing' (*Der Seele Rat,* p. 102, 5497–5502).

[20] *Der Seele Rat*, lines 278–567.

[21] Stephen L. Wailes, 'The Composition of Vernacular Sermons by Berthold von Regensburg', *Michigan Germanic Studies*, 5.1 (1979), p. 11.

[22] 'Unde von deheiner sünde, die diu werlt ie gewan, hât der tiuvel sô grôzen gewalt über den menschen danne von der unkiusche. Unde dar umbe, ir jungen liute, hüete iuch durch den lebendigen got' (Berthold, *Predigten*, 1, p. 412, 6–9).

[23] 'Sô hât der tiuvel valsche minne geslagen ûf die wâren minne' (Berthold, Predigten, 1, p. 239, 32–33). Berthold does not explicitly define diu wâre minne in this sermon, but elsewhere, particularly in his Sermon 34, he defines wâre minne as a sincere love of Christ. In the same sermon he associates this virtue, emblematically, with the right hand of the crucified Christ. More importantly, he identifies this virtue with Mary Magdalene (Berthold, *Predigten*, 1, pp. 542–43).

[24] 'Unde dû minnest dînen næsten als dich selber, daz ist alsô gestprochen: wan dû selbe unkiusche bist an dem lîbe, sô minnest dû alle die deste gerner die dâ unkiusche sint, unde dû hâst sie dar umbe liep; wan dû trûwest ir geniezen an der unkiusche. Unde dâ mite sô hât der tiuvel valsch geslagen ûf die wâre minne. Wan allez daz dû minne solt an dînem næhsten mit

tanzer oder ein turneisman oder ein luoderer oder ein spiler oder ein frâz, dû bist einem vil holder, der dir des selben hilfet wan der dir dar zuo niht gehelfen kan'.[25] In Sermon 36, Berthold impressively admonishes those who fail to repent their *unkiuscheit* that they will remain in hell for an eternity, and the prayers of all the priests, monks, nuns, angels, saints, and all those who were ever born in the world will not be enough to save them.[26]

The ideal of Christian virtue toward which the Franciscans compelled their audiences was the life of penance. Berthold characterizes penance as an inherently three-fold act of contrition, atonement, and confession.[27] In Heinrich's text, this virtue takes the form of actual characters in his dramatic text. Berthold and David of Augsburg also promote a life of humility *(dêmuot)* as the opposite of vanity and pride. In his treatise *De exterioris et interioris hominis compositione*, David writes that humility has to do with 'repressing self-esteem [. . .] watching for any indications of conceit in words, manner, even sometimes in dress'.[28] Both Berthold and David identify the Virgin Mary as an important model of humility. [29] In fact, Berthold makes a point of saying in Sermon 25 that all the finery of the vain woman is no match for the true beauty of humility represented by the models of the Virgin Mary, Saint Margaret, and others.[30] It is interesting that the *BP* presents that model of beauty in the second half of the drama, which is dominated by a *Marienklage*—a portrayal of the Virgin Mary's sorrow at the scene of the crucifixion. However, the songs of Mary Magdalene in the early German Passion plays illustrate the closest

---

der wâren minne, daz hât der tiuvel allez verkêret in die valschen minne' (Berthold, *Predigten*, 1, p. 239, 33–p. 240, 1).

[25] 'whether you are a dancer, a jouster, a carouser, a gambler, or a mischievous brat, you are far dearer to those who help you in your vice than those who do not' (Berthold, *Predigten*, 1, p. 240, 6–9).

[26] 'Wirdest dû mit der einen sünde funden âne riuwe [. . .] dû muost gein helle varn umbe die selben sünde unde muost êwiclîchen iemer dâ sîn. Unde betten alle pfaffen iemer umbe dich und alle die müniche und alle die nunnen und all die sît anegenge der werlte ie geborn wurden und alle die heiligen und alle engele, sie möhten dich niemer mêr von dannen bringen mit ir gebete' (Berthold, *Predigten*, 1, p. 568, 29–36).

[27] See especially Berthold's exposition on the subject in his Sermon 22 where he writes 'Got der helfe mir, daz ir daz waeger nemet unde hiute also ware riuwe gewinnet unde ze lûterre bîhte komet unde ze rehter buoze (Berthold, *Predigten*, 1, p. 344, 13–15). One should note that Berthold's understanding of penance agrees with his Franciscan contemporary Alexander of Hales, who also sets contrition in a place of priority. See K. F. Lynch, 'The Doctrine of Alexander of Hales on the Nature of Sacramental Grace', *Franciscan Studies*, 19 (1959).

[28] David of Augsburg, *De exterioris et interioris hominis compositione*, 3, p. 24.

[29] See David, *De exterioris*, 3, p. 38 and Berthold, *Predigten,* 1, p. 397, 11–3).

[30] 'Unser frouwe was halt vil schoener danne dû unde was gar herzeclîchen dêmüetic, unde sant Margarêta unde der andern ein michel teil' (Berthold, *Predigten,* 1, p. 397, 11–3).

connections to the themes of sin, penance, and humility described by Franciscan authors.

Lyrical commentary on Mary Magdalene's sins of vanity and lechery dominate the dramaturgy in the *WPf* and the opening passage of the *BP*. Her Latin goliardic song 'Mundi delectatio' (Ex. 1) and the German lyrics that follow it in the *WPf* are the first clear evidence of this focus.[31] In her songs, Mary Magdalene tells her audience that she burns with desire for the pleasures of the world. She lusts for temporal splendour and prizes her own physical beauty above all things. The authors portray Mary Magdalene as a paragon of sin. She behaves shamelessly and champions vanity and lechery as though they were virtues.

In the following scene, the authors of the German dramas elaborate on the worldly life of Mary Magdalene through her dialogue with a merchant from whom she purchases cosmetics. In the *WPf*, stage directions indicate that Mary Magdalene sings her goliardic lyrics while dancing around the merchant.[32] She says, 'Michi confer venditor species emendas / pro multa pecunia tibi iam redendas. / si quid habes insuper odoramtorum / nam volo perungere corpus hoc decorum'.[33] In the German dialogue that follows their Latin songs in the *WPf*, Mary Magdalene identifies the means of her vice—a red felt hat and white flour for her skin, with which she hopes to make herself beautiful and to attract young men.[34] The Merchant encourages her, singing 'Vrowe, nemt der varwe war, wie sie eu gevalle! / sed, mag sie eu wesen gůt, die gib ich eu alle. / wizset, daz sie wol gezimet allen iungen wiben, / die mit mannen wellen ir swere zit vertriben'.[35]

At first glance, the German texts in the *WPf* seem to serve as little more than translations of the Latin verses; however, a careful study of their contents shows that

---

[31] *BP*, p. 151, 19–26 in *Carmina Burana, Die Trink- und Spielerlieder—Die geistlichen Dramen*, 1, ed. by Alfons Hilka and Otto Schumann (Heidelberg: Winter, 1970). See the example below for the original text. The stanzas that make up Mary Magdalene's song 'Mundi delectatio' appear in a sightly different order in the *WPf*; in the later reading, the song follows her dialogue with the merchant 'Michi confer, venditor' and 'Ecce merces optime!' Compare *WPf*, pp. 34–5, 279–306 in *Das Wiener Passionsspiel*, ed. by Ursula Hennig, Litterae, Göppinger Beiträge zur Textgeschichte, 92 (Göppingen: Kümmerle, 1986).

[32] 'Tunc Maria sumat pixides ab eo et circumeat cantando' (Hennig, *WPf*, p. 34, before line 295).

[33] 'Merchant, bring me your finest wares so that I can spend my money on them—especially whatever perfumes you have, for I wish to anoint this beautiful body' (*BP*, p. 151, 27–30).

[34] *WPf*, p. 34, 287–90. The German songs in the *WPf* are not notated with music, though stage directions such as 'resopndeat' and'thetōīc in eadem sunt' suggest that the German texts may have been sung to the same melody as the Latin texts that precede them.

[35] 'Lady, take the cosmetics, as they please you! [. . .] Know that they are well suited to all young women who wish to amuse themselves in the company of men' (*WPf*, p. 34, 291–304).

they are much more. The German lyrics elaborate on specific details of Mary Magdalene's behaviour, which the German audience may have recognized as current examples of vanity. In his Latin text 'Ecce merces optime!', the Merchant encourages Mary Magdalene's immoral behaviour; in the German song 'Vrowe, nemt der varwe war' which follows, he makes clear associations between her vanity and lechery. Thus, the German texts in the *WPf* not only paraphrase the Latin for the benefit of the German-speaking audience, but also clarify the exegetical meaning of the passage in terms that reflect the tirades of German Franciscan preachers.

To complete the representation of Mary Magdalene as a vain lecher, the author of the *BP* concludes the portrayal of Mary Magdalene's worldly life with a courtly *Minnesang* 'Chramer gip die varwe mier' (Ex. 2). An analysis of the German text reveals a verse form that seems to maintain the goliardic meter of the surrounding Latin poetry. The adaptation of this metrical structure becomes awkward at times; it breaks down in the last line of each stanza and in the third strophe of the poem. Nevertheless, in trying to retain the goliardic meter in the German text, the author offers a graceful solution for the problem of linguistic discontinuity in this drama. Here, too, Mary Magdalene extols the virtues of sin, but in the second stanza of the song, her tone changes. She instructs her audience, 'Minnet tugentliche man minnekliche vrǎwen / minne tuo̊t eu hoech gemůt unde lat / euch in hoehen erene schǎven. / Set mich an iungen man [lat mich eu gevallen]'.[36] With these words Mary Magdalene exceeds her role as a model sinner and preaches to her audience of the 'virtues' of vanity and lechery. In this, one can see that the texts of the early German Passion plays develop the character of Mary Magdalene along the same lines as the negative model of female virtue found in the sermons of the German friars. It remains for an angel (and others in the *WPf*) who sings to Mary Magdalene in the scene which follows to convert her to *die wâre minne*—that is to say, a true love of Christ and a desire for penance.

After a scene involving a series of penitential lyrics in the *BP* and *WPf*—sung by an angel in the former play and also by Martha, Simon the Pharisee, and a servant from his household in the *WPf*—Mary Magdalene awakens a changed person. Gone is her desire for carnal pleasure and secular *Minne*; instead, she laments bitterly over her many transgressions. This portrayal of contrition takes the form of a varied strophic *planctus*. German lyrics without musical notation alternate with stanzas of Latin in the *WPf*. In the first stanza of her Latin *planctus* 'Heu, vita preterita' (Ex. 3), Mary Magdalene repents her past life of evil and wickedness. In the German text that follows this stanza in the *WPf*, she repents the sins she committed with cosmetics and with men. She says, 'O we miner missetat / die ich hand begangen / mit verwen an manger stat / vnt mit manigen mannen. / owe ich han gesundet / mit prise vn̄ ouch

[36] 'Virtuous men should love charming women. Love gives you a noble spirit and leads to visions of sublime glory. Look upon me, young men [let me give you pleasure]' (*BP*, p. 152, 35–51). See Ex. 2 below for the complete text.

mit tanzen, / ich trůg geverwet risen / mit mangē ho̊hem cranze'.[37] And as she purges herself of her sins, the lovers, and demons which surround her (stanza 2 'Hinc ornatus seculi'), Mary Magdalene casts off her decorative secular garments in favour of a humble black cloak.[38] She then sets off to find Jesus, so that she may repent her sins before him with tears (stanzas 3–5: 'Ibo nunc ad medicum'; 'O magister optime'; and 'Peccatrici prebeas').

These texts are deeply expressive of Mary Magdalene's new-found piety. She recognizes how disgraceful her behaviour was while she lived only to satisfy her sinful desires. Now, rather than taking pleasure in her worldliness, Mary Magdalene laments over the wretched state into which her vices led her. The confessions of sin she makes in her German lyrics in the *WPf* paraphrase the Latin texts. They also intensify the distinction between sin and virtue by comparing the methods of her worldly life with her new acts of contrition and atonement.

The German text 'Aw̌e, aǔve, daz ich ie wart geborn' (Ex. 4), which concludes the portrayal of Mary Magdalene in the *BP*, summarizes the development of her character and asserts the permanence of her new devotion. The position of this vernacular song at the end of a scene, following a series of Latin lyrics, is especially interesting, because it outlines a parallel between this lyric and her earlier *Minnesang* (Ex. 2), the only other vernacular song Mary Magdalene sings in the *BP*. Mary Magdalene's *Minnesang* was a testimony of her secular spirituality. Now, at a similar climax in the drama, Mary Magdalene returns to the vernacular to proclaim her new pious spirituality and to address her audience on the question of penance. As in her preceding Latin texts, Mary Magdalene laments her misfortunes. She then turns to her audience and tearfully warns them, 'Aw̌e, ich uil vnselaeich wiͤp. / Ow̌e aw̌e, daz ich ie wart geborn, / swenne mich erwechet gotes zorn. / wol uf, ir gůeten man unde wip, / got wil rihten sele vnde leip'.[39]

The transformation which occurs in Mary Magdalene's character reflects the recommendations of David, Berthold, and Heinrich, as though she had been struck by the very message of their writing. She renounces her dancing, decorative habit of dress, and lechery; and she repents through deep contrition, a loud confession, and atonement. Indeed, the dramatic interpretation of Mary Magdalene's penance coincides with the message of a sermon Berthold of Regensburg gave on the occasion of her feast day. In Sermon 34, Berthold extols Mary Magdelene as the greatest saint in heaven and uses her model of penance to admonish his audience:

---

[37] 'Alas I have sinned with praise and with dancing; I have performed decorative steps with many elegant garlands' (*WPf*, p. 38, 407–14).

[38] *BP*, p. 155, 119–22. Compare *WP*, p. 39, 415–8. Stage directions before this text in the *BP* indicate 'Tunc deponat vestimenta secularia et induat nigrum pallium; et amator recedat et diabolus'. The directions in the *WPf* indicate 'et tunc reiciat ornatum'.

[39] 'Take heed good men and women, God will judge your soul and body' (*BP*, p. 158, 158–65).

> Swer noch hiute alse grôzen riuwen hât, dem vergît got alle sîne sünde als gar, als er tet mîner frouwen sant Marîen Magdalênen. Wan si hete sô starke riuwe, daz si unmügelîche vil gewinde unde daz sie unserm herren sîne füeze twuoc mit dem wazzer daz ûz ir ougen flôz. Unde dar umbe vergap er ir unser herre ir sünde lûterlîche unde genzlîche, unde tet daz allen sündern ze einem trôste, daz alle sünder trôst von ir nemen süln swie grôz ir sünde sî.[40]

Berthold elaborates at length on the redemptive light of Mary Magdalene—which he equates cosmologically with the gloomy, tear-stained light of the moon—asserting that it is because she takes it upon herself to lament for many thousands of sinners that they are redeemed from eternal darkness.[41] Like the authors of the German Passion plays, Berthold uses the model of Mary Magdalene and the symbol of the final judgment to preach about the redemptive message of the Passion of Christ. He reminds his audience that those sinners who follow Mary Magdalene will arise from their deadly sins and arrive at holy penance. Just as Jesus revealed himself to Mary Magdalene, he will reveal himself to all sinners who wish to rise up from their sins; and as he arose from the bonds of death, so will they rise up from their sins and stand before him in joy at the final judgment.[42]

Critics have puzzled over the unique organization of events in the portrayal of Mary Magdalene in the early German Passion plays. Richard Froning wondered at the confusion it causes in the Passion narrative, and Karl Young argued that 'there is no reason why Mary, after having been absolved from sin, should depart singing the despairing lament "*Awe, awe daz ich ie wart geborn*"'.[43] On the other hand, Rolf Steinbach has challenged the notion that the *BP* should be interpreted as scriptural narrative. Rather, he asserts that the portrayal of Mary Magdalene in the *BP*—and, by connection, the *WPf*—reflects the author's view of the exegetical meaning of the

---

[40] 'Whoever still today expresses such profound contrition, God forgives their sins entirely as he did with my lady Saint Mary Magdalene. She had such strong contrition and wept so abundantly that she washed our Lord's feet with the water that flowed from her eyes. And for that reason, our Lord forgave her sins fully and completely, and did so to comfort everyone. All sinners should take solace from her no matter how great their sins' (Berthold, *Predigten*, 1, p. 539, 4–12).

[41] 'Ob sie die riuwe an sich nemen wellen, sô wirt noch hiute manic tûsent sünder von der êwigen vinsternisse erlôst' (Berthold, *Predigten*, 1, p. 540, 18–20).

[42] 'Daz er ir erschein, daz bediutet uns daz er allen sündern mit sînen gnâden erschînen wil, ob sie von ir sünden erstên wellen. [. . .] Und als er erstuont von dem tôde sîner menscheit, alsô süln wir in an ruofen, daz wir alsô müezen erstên von unsern sünden, unde danne an dem jungesten tage mit im vor sînem antlitze unde vor sînem zornlîchen gerihte mit freuden müezen erstên' (Berthold, *Predigten*, 1, p. 541, 3–13).

[43] Richard Froning, *Das Drama des Mittelalters: Die lateinischen Osterfeiern und ihre Entwicklung in Deutschland* (Stuttgart, 1891/92; repr. Darmstadt: Wissenschaftliche Buchgesellschaft, 1964), p. 279. Karl Young, *Drama,* 1, p. 536.

Passion.[44] As Steinbach says, Mary Magdalene is a symbol to her audience of the complete decadence of humankind, just as her conversion represents the possibility of redemption.[45] My study of the literal programme of exegesis in the early German Passion plays adds weight to Steinbach's argument. A study of the songs of Mary Magdalene in light of Franciscan preaching reveals an aspect of their exegetical character. Yet, the impact of Franciscan preaching on the early German Passions play exceeds the confirmation of text alone. Using the literal evidence of Franciscan preaching now as a tool of musical criticism, one may discover an even more sublime layer of musical commentary in the dramas which bears witness to the impact of Franciscan notions about the rhetorical art of preaching.

It is clear in the writings of the thirteenth-century Franciscan preachers and theologians that they were eager promoters of the principles of musical homiletics practiced and advocated by Francis of Assisi.[46] Anyone working within their sphere of influence in the German lands and elsewhere must certainly have been aware of their sense of the rhetorical power of music and their notions of how a subtle use of music could evoke the piety of the listener. Among the Franciscan authors who wrote on the subject of music, the works of Bartholomaeus Anglicus, Roger Bacon, and Berthold of Regensburg are most germane to an analysis of the early German Passion plays.

Through his encyclopaedic treatise *De proprietatibus rerum* (*c.* 1247), Bartholomaeus Anglicus taught his novices in Magdeburg and elsewhere in the German lands about the utility of music in scriptural exegesis.[47] He defines music as 'the knowledge of correct performance in sound and singing', a discipline subservient to theology and necessary to one's understanding of the mysteries of sacred Scripture.[48] Quoting from the *Etymologies* of Isidore of Seville,

---

[44] Rolf Steinbach, *Die deutschen Oster- und Passionsspiele des Mittelalters* (Cologne: Böhlau, 1970), p. 110.

[45] 'Wenn in ihm Magdalena klagt "Awve, auwve, daz ich ie wart geborn", dan setzt sie sich selbst damit als Zeichen für die völlige Verlorenheit des Menschen, so wie überhaupt die Darstellung ihrer Bekehrung nicht Wiedergabe eines erregenden Einzelschicksals sein will, sondern beispielhaft die Möglichkeit der Rettung aufzeigt' (Steinbach, *Die deutschen Oster- und Passionsspiele*, p. 110).

[46] For further discussion of this issue, please see Loewen, 'Ars musica and the Rhetoric of Franciscan Piety', forthcoming.

[47] Bartholomaeus Anglicus spent almost his entire career in the German lands (1231–72), first as a lector at the Franciscan *studium* in Magdeburg and later as a bishop and administrator for the order in Bohemia, Austria, and Saxony.

[48] 'Sicut autem subservit theologice discipline ars numerandi et mensurandi, sic eidem famulatur scientia modulandi. Nam musica, que modulationis in sono et in cantu est peritia, sacre scripture mysteriis valde est necessaria' (Bartholomaeus Anglicus, *De proprietatibus rerum: De musica sive Modulatione Cantus*, [Frankfurt: Richter, 1601; repr. Frankfurt: Minerva, 1964], 132, p. 1251).

Bartholomaeus teaches his reader that the effect of music depends on subtle changes in intonation and timbre. When applied to religious purposes, music can evoke the pious emotions of the listener. In his view, the perfect use of music 'delights the ear and attracts and converts the souls of the hearers by caressing them'.[49]

Bartholomaeus's brother theologian Roger Bacon elaborates on the rhetorical value of music in a study of preaching, in the final chapters of his *Opus tertium* (1267). Here, Bacon writes that melody has the power to arouse the devotion of Christians.[50] He also argues that the rhetoric of music informs the art of speech, for the preacher cannot affect the souls of his listeners without using a subtle musical style of declamation. Following the writings of Aristotle, Al-Farabi, Seneca, and Augustine, Bacon teaches that a proper knowledge of music will enable the preacher to persuade his audience with grace and ornamentation. Bacon claims that this happens in the following way:

> [A]ristoteles enim et omnes ejus expositores in libris de his sermonibus testantur, quod hi sermones debent esse in fine decori et sublimes; et hoc non solum prosaïce secundum omne genus coloris et ornatus, sed pro qualitate temporis, et personarum, et locorum, et materiae de qua fit sermo, debent ornari omni genere metri et rythmi, ut animus subito rapiatur in amorem boni et odium mali.[51]

Bacon's statements offer strong testimony about the importance of music in the Franciscan programme of preaching. His interpretation of music in this context shows that its power stemmed from a sensual appeal. Indeed, he asserts that in order to convey to the listener the literal message of a sermon, a preacher must use the tools of music.

---

[49] 'Perfecta autem vox est [. . .] suavis sive dulcis ut auditum non deterreat, sed potius ut aures demulceat et audiencium animos blandiendo ad se alliciat et convertat' (Bartholomaeus Anglicus, *De proprietatibus rerum*, 132, p. 1254). Compare Isidore, *Etymologiarum sive originum*, vol. 3, ed. by W. M. Lindsay (Oxford: Clarendon Press, 1957; repr., 1985), p. 22.

[50] 'Et certe possent tam exquisite excogitari, et cum tanta poetia musicae, quod ad omnem gradum devotionis, quem vellemus, excitaretur populus Christianus' (*Opus tertium*, in *Fr. Rogeri Bacon, Opera Quaedam Hactenus Inedita, I, I.—Opus Tertium, II.—Opus Minus, III.—Compendium Philosophiae*, ed. by J. S. Brewer (London: Longman, 1859; repr., London: Kraus, 1965, LXXIII, p. 298). 'Possent' in this case refers the subject of Bacon's previous discussion about enharmonic music *(enharmonicus)* and its many layers *(multos gradus).*

[51] 'For Aristotle and all of his disciples bear witness in their books about these speeches, that these speeches be graceful and ornamented in the highest degree, and they mean this not in the prosaic sense, according to which every type of color and embellishment should be present, but also to the quality of time, and persons, and places, and subject matter that the sermon deals with. These speeches ought to be adorned with every type of meter and rythym, so that the sould is carried away into a love of goodness and hatred of evil'. (Bacon, *Opus tertium*, LXXV, pp. 306–7).

Bacon's theory of music seems to refer explicitly to the concerns of Franciscan preachers. Certainly the works of Berthold of Regensburg and Heinrich of Burgus are concerned primarily with moral principles and about teaching people how to avoid the evils of sin. In fact, Roger Bacon seems to have recognized this fact, for in the closing statement of his *Opus tertium*, he singles out only one preacher as a perfect practitioner of his concept of musical rhetoric—Berthold of Regensburg.[52] This is resounding testimony to the importance of music in Franciscan preaching. Moveover, Bacon's reference to Berthold of Regensburg has specific implications for one's study of the German Passion plays and, for that matter, any works of music that evolved within the sphere of Berthold's influence. If the texts of the songs of Mary Magdalene in the German dramas show the influence of Berthold's preaching, might they not also preserve his sense of music?

Despite Bacon's statements about Berthold's eager recourse to the rhetoric of music, references to music in his sermons are surprisingly rare. But with Bacon's help, one may be able to piece together Berthold's appreciation of music. In Sermon 42, near the end of his dramatic performance of an allegory on the Passion of Christ, Berthold considers stylistic issues and the importance of musical timbre when singing a German Kyrie. Berthold tells his audience that the song is the best daily remedy for the ravages of demons and is better advice than a pope, angel, bishop, or even a priest could give.[53] They are to sing the Kyrie in the morning and in the evening 'piously and very loudly toward God every time so that the devil may not hinder [their] deep faith at [their] death'. To insure that even the laity sing with feeling, he warns that 'the unlearned people should sing it only in German'.[54] The emphasis that Berthold places on the intelligibility of religous song is interesting. His comments seem to reflect upon the German Passion plays at hand, since they use German songs to convey the meaning of the Latin lyrics that surround them. It is also noteworthy that Berthold's proposal for a vernacular performance of the Ordinary anticipates Luther's reforms by more than two hundred years.[55]

---

[52] 'Sed licet vulgus praedicantium sic utatur, tamen aliqui modum alium habentes, infinitam faciunt utilitatem, ut est Frater Bertholdus Alemannus, qui solus plus facit de utilitate magnifica in praedicatione, quam fere omnes alii fratres ordinis utriusque' (Bacon, *Opus tertium*, LXXV, p. 310).

[53] 'Nû seht, welt ir mir nû volgen, ich gibe iu einen rât, daz der bâbest einen bezzern niht gegeben mac, noch engel, noch bischof, noch priester; niemen in aller der werlte möhte einen bezzern rât niht vinden' (Berthold, *Predigten*, 2, p. 63, 1–5).

[54] 'Ir ungelêrten liute ir sult in niur in tiutsche sprechen' (Berthold, *Predigten*, 2, p. 63, 31). The sense of the passage is that this song is to be sung. Berthold makes this clear when he says 'Nû seht, daz sult ir gar andaehticlichen singen und gar lûte hin ze gote ze allen zîten, daz iuch der tiuvel des rehten gelouben iht geirren müge amtôde' (Berthold, *Predigten*, 2, p. 64, 1–3).

[55] See especially Luther's 'An Order of Mass and Communion for the Church at Wittenberg', trans. by Paul Zeller Strodach, in *Luther's Works*, 53 (Philadelphia, PA: Fortress

Berthold's references to the art of music in Sermon 25 express his appreciation of the power of music in exegesis. Here he asks his audience to help him find a musical solution to the problems of heresy. Heretics are clever, he says, because they spread their heterodox ideas among unsuspecting citizens through the means of simple songs. To stem the erosion of orthodoxy, he devises seven criteria by which the members of his audience might recognize a heretic and then asks:

> Ich wolte halt gerne daz man lieder dâ von sünge. Ist iht guoter meister hie, daz sie niuwen sanc dâ von singen, die merken mir disiu siben wort gar eben unde machen lieder dâ von: dâ tuot ir gar wol an; unde machet sie kurze unde ringe unde daz sie kundegelîch wol gelernen mügen; wan sô gelernent sie die liute alle gemeine diu selben dinc unde vergezzent ir deste minner. Ez was ein verworhter ketzer, der machte lieder von ketzerîe unde lêrte sie diu dint an der strâze, daz der liute deste mêr in ketzerîe vielen. Unde dar umbe saehe ich gerne, daz man diu lieder von in sünge.[56]

The songs in the German dramas are not tirades against heresy, nor are they simple compositions. However, when one interprets the evidence more broadly, the testimony of Berthold does suggest that he inspired composers to produce songs which would serve the spiritual programmes of the Friars Minor, and that he may have instilled in them his concern for musical subtlety. The songs of Frauenlob and other lyrics in German preaching compilations seem to offer evidence for this assertion.[57] Through the lens of Berthold's sermons, the works of Franciscan theologians, and Franciscan writings on music, one may also perceive musical evidence of Franciscan homiletics in the early German Passion plays.

The evidence of musical rhetoric in the early German Passion plays lies in the notation of music in the strophic songs of Mary Magdalene. Rather than supplying only the first stanza of each lyric with music—as was the common practice in other repertories of strophic song such as Troubadour and Trouvère songs, *Minnesang*, and *Laude*—the notators of the *BP* and *WPf* adopted the practice of notation used in Latin hymns and sequences, where every stanza of text is set to music. This approach to musical notation in the songs of Mary Magdalene allows the notator to transmit variations in the repeating melodies for these strophic songs, often through

---

Press, 1965), p. 36.

[56] 'If there is a good composer here who can sing new songs about them, he should mark these seven words well and make songs from them. You would do well by them; and make them short and simple so that it would be child's play to learn them. This way, people learn them better and have less trouble remembering' (Berthold, *Predigten,* 1, p. 405, 38–p. 406, 8).

[57] The impact of Franciscan spirituality on the musical culture of the medieval German lands is the subject of a separate study, though one might consider Frauenlob's invective against sin in his *Langer Ton* and homage to Berthold (see below), and the anonymous songs in Vienna, Österreichische Nationalbibliothek, Cod. 3655 as possible examples. See also my study of 'Ich sezte minen vuoz' in 'Francis the Musician'.

the introduction of ornamental neumes and melodic flourishes. Whether this practice reflects the concerns of the composer, the singer, or the notator is uncertain. Still, if one widens one's focus to include the songs of Mary Magdalene as a whole, one can see that stylistic changes in musical notation are dramaturgical, because they coincide with the pattern of literal exegesis in the two dramas. The point is clearest when one compares examples of music from the two passages of the *BP* and *WPf* whose texts deal with the sinful and penitential behaviour of Mary Magdalene.

Like many of the Latin lyrics found in the *Carmina Burana,* Mary Magdalene's song 'Mundi delectatio' (Example 1, pl. 1) employs a thirteen-syllable trochaic verse pattern, the typical goliardic meter. Since the *BP* transmits its setting of the text using St Gall neumes, notated *in campo aperto*, it is impossible to interpret the pitches of the song; nor can one tell precisely how highly contoured the melody is. However, the later redaction of the song in the *WPf* offers the reader more specific information about its melody.

Example 1 'Mundi delectatio'
Munich, Bayerische Staatsbibliothek, Clm. 4660 (*BP)*, fol. 107r
Vienna, Österreichische Nationalbibliothek, Cod. 12887 (Suppl. 561), (*WPf*), fol. 4v

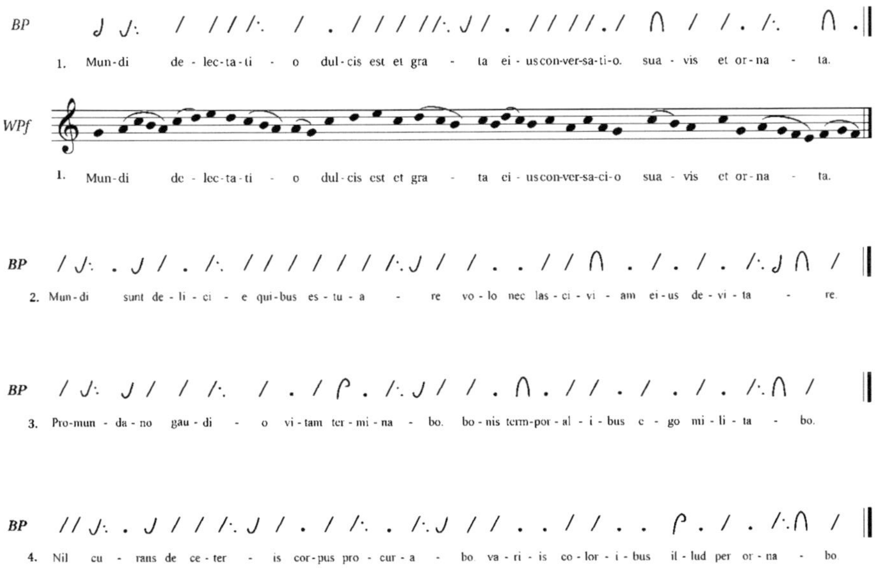

Plate 1 Vienna, Österreichische Nationalbibliothek, Cod. 12887 (Suppl. 561), (*WPf*), fol. 4[v]

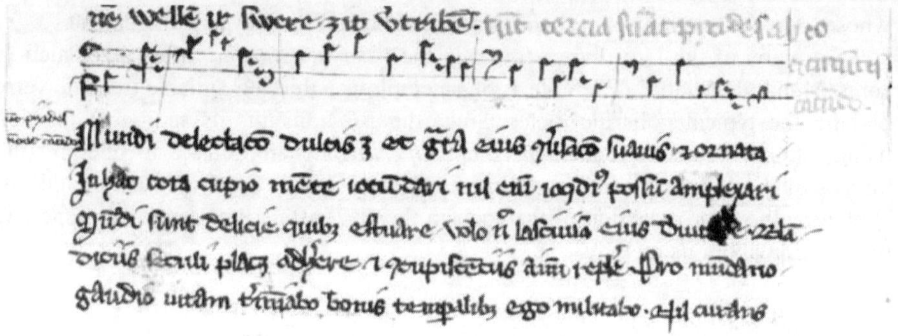

Because it is notated with gothic neumes on staves in the *WPf,* the pitches and the mode of the song are clear.[58] On the whole, the musical notation for 'Mundi delectatio' in the *BP* and *WPf* suggests a syllabic and relatively unornamented setting. The placement of short melodic flourishes, mainly on penultimate syllables, shows that the surface rhythm in each stanza varies slightly. Some variations arise from the introduction of new ornamental neumes such as the liquescent *pes* (√) and *clivis* (∩). The melody for 'Mundi delectatio' appears to be in mode eight, although the cadence on F seems disorienting. It is possible, since the song has a strophic form, that the composer intended it to sound modally unresolved until its conclusion, where the singer might have improvised a cadence on G. In the *WPf,* only the first stanza of the song appears with musical notation.

The song 'Chramer gip die varwe mier' (Ex. 2) is unique to the *BP*. The music that accompanies each stanza of its text indicates that the song has a varied strophic form, like the earlier Latin goliardic lyric, and that it has a simple, syllabic musical setting. Only the refrain appears to be repeated without change. The variations that occur in the notation of the song sometimes advance the ornamental character of the melody, as is particularly clear in the use of the *clivis* in both its regular and liquescent forms (∩ and ρ).[59] However, unornamented pitches—signified by the *virga* (/) and *punctum* (.)—prevail in the setting of this song.

---

[58] The song in the *WPf* is notated on a four-line staff with both C and F clefs (*WPf, fol.* 4[v]).

[59] Timothy McGee writes that the singer would perform a *clivis* by sliding the pitch downwards, which is to say, by deflecting the pitch toward a lower and indistinct note. See McGee, *The Sound of Medieval Song: Ornamentation and Vocal Style According to the Treatises* (Oxford: Clarendon Press, 1998), p. 53.

The musical settings for Mary Magdalene's penitential songs (exx. 3 and 4; and pl. 2) have an altogether different character than the ones that accompany her secular texts. Instead of using syllabic and rather unornamented melodies, Mary Magdalene communicates her literal message of contrition with melodies richly decorated with ornamental neumes and melismatic flourishes. Mary's penitential lyrics consist of several stanzas of varied music, but examples of one Latin stanza and the entire German song will suffice for this study. Once again, the style of musical notation in the *BP* makes it impossible for one to comment on the pitches or melodic contour used in examples derived from that source. Since there are no editions of Mary Magdalene's German lament 'Aw̌e, aǔve, daz ich ie wart geborn' (Ex. 4) which include staff notation, criticism of this lyric will mainly concern the placement of musical symbols. The redaction of the Latin lyric 'Heu vita preterita' (Ex. 3) in the

Example 2 'Chramer gip die varwe mier' *BP*, fol. 107[v]

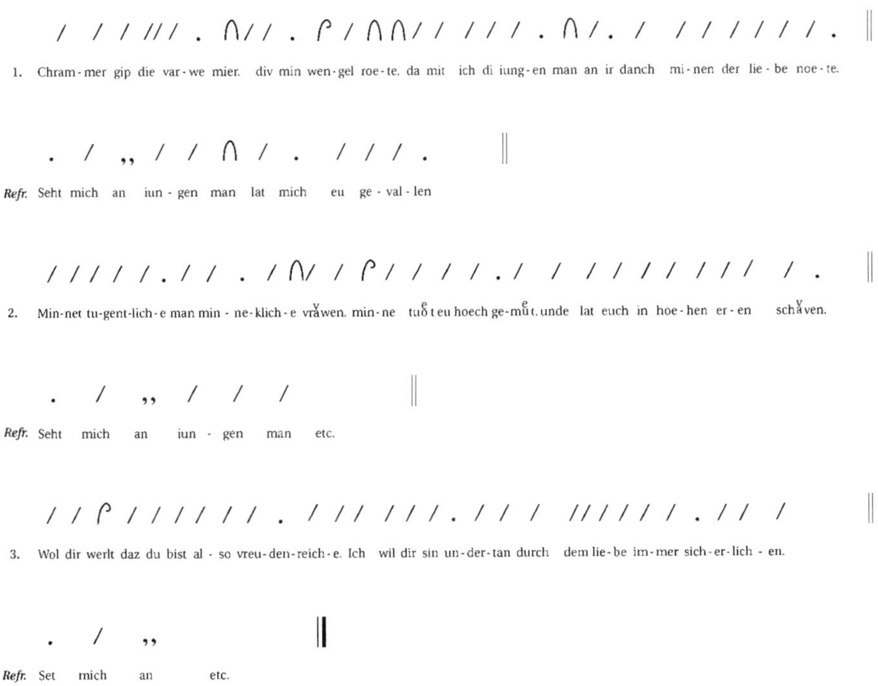

Example 3 'Heu vita preterita' *BP*, fol. 107^{v} *WPf*, fol. 6$^{r–v}$

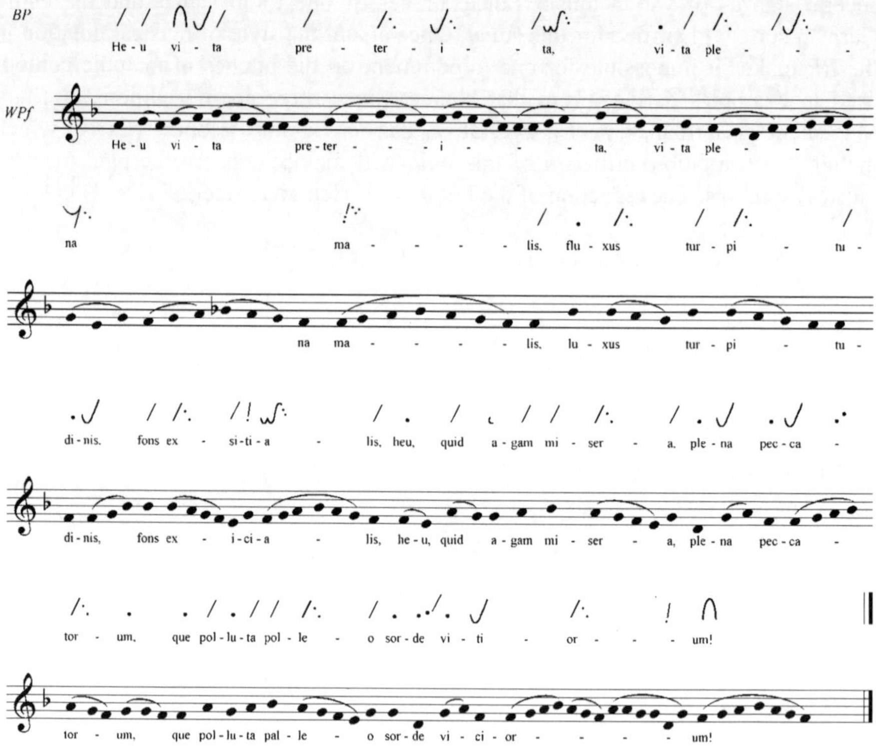

Plate 2 'Heu vita preterita' (FOTO: Bildarchiv, ÖNB Wien), *WPf*, fol. 6$^{r–v}$

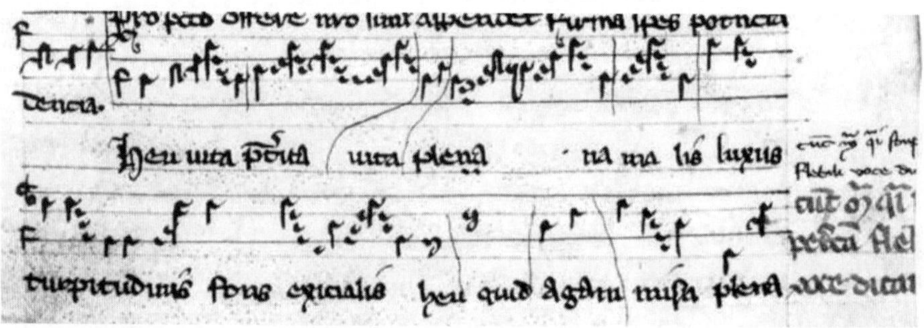

Plate 2 continued

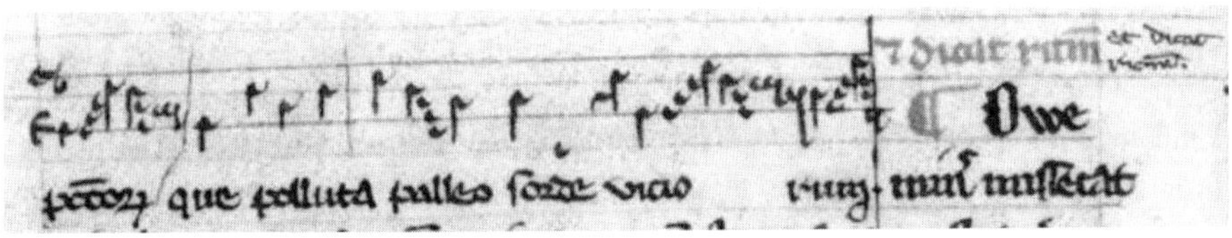

Example 4 ‘Aw̌e, aǔve, daz ich ie wart geborn’ *BP*, fol. 108v

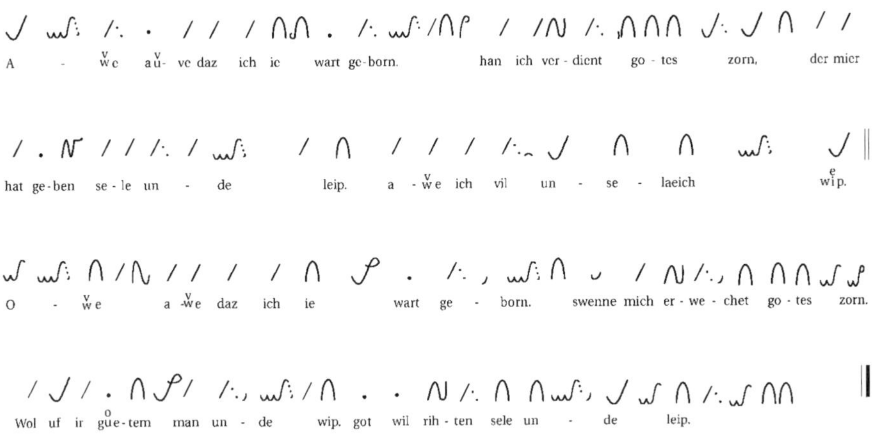

WPf offers clear information about the pitches and contour of the mode-six melody that accompanies that text. One may compare this information to the setting of the text in the *BP*.

At an initial stage of comparison, it is important to note that the formal design of the songs Mary Magdalene sings as a penitent is the same as the ones she sings as a sinner. All of them exhibit goliardic verse structures, except for her German song in example 4. What has changed in these songs is the melody, where it is clear, and the degree of musical embellishment that accompanies the transformation of Mary Magdalene’s character. The impression of change in melodic embellishment is clearest when one focuses on the syllable as the basic unit of measure. The note-to-syllable (syllabic) setting of the worldly songs draws one’s attention to the accentual cadence of the poetry. On the other hand, long vocalizations (melismas) in the penitential songs cause the lyric to flourish with bursts of melody, not only at the beginning and at the final cadence of each stanza, as one would expect, but also within the lines. These melismas might not affect the regular meter of the song if the pace of the syllables were to remain constant; however, they would cause the surface rhythm of the melody to speed and slow frequently and erratically.

The difference in the number of ornaments in the settings of the secular and penitential songs of Mary Magdalene also contributes to one's sense of the contrast between her secular and penitential life. Most of the ornaments in her penitential songs take the form of a *pes* (✓ and ✝), *clivis* (∩ and ∩), *quilisma* (ᴗ∫), or a nuanced variation of these (J, ſ, ϑ, ˥, ᴗ∫). Such neumation indicates that these melodies had a highly varied tone, permeated with sliding and repercussed pitches.[60] In fact, it would appear that a relatively small number of the notes in these penitential songs would have been sung on sustained, centred pitches. Nearly all of the notes in Mary Magdalene's German song (Ex. 4) would have been performed with a slide or a shake. The style of writing in these penitential lyrics is elaborate and meditative in character, like the verses of Graduals and Alleluias. By comparison, the syllabic and unornamented settings of Mary Magdalene's secular songs seem rhythmically regular, perhaps to facilitate her dance steps.

Does this approach to the composition of music in the early German Passion plays constitute a rhetorical programme? Certainly, without the guidance of text, it would be difficult to say what the music might convey, if anything. However, a Franciscan reading of the melodies in the *BP* and *WPf*, by means of Franciscan sermons and theories of music, reveals correlations between textual and musical exegesis in these dramas. Since changes in music seem to correspond to Mary Magdalene's affective statements concerning sin and penitence, it would seem logical to perceive the music she sings as evocative of the feelings she invokes *ad literam*.

When considered from this point of view, it seems ironic that the simple music of Mary Magdalene's secular songs and the decorative settings of her penitential songs contradict the literal meaning of their texts. One can hear that the former songs of Mary Magdalene demonstrate little ornamentation despite what she says about worldly delight, cosmetic decoration, and the sublime glory of secular *Minne*. However, the music which she sings as a humble penitent is resplendent. Even as she pulls off the colourful gown and baubles with which she displayed her physical beauty, she dons a musical garment of flourishing melody, which conveys the spiritual beauty of humility and contrition. This programme of musical commentary seems a surprising corollary to the literal message of piety in the writings of Berthold of Regensburg and David of Augsburg. They, too, recognized distinctions between the false beauty of vanity and the true beauty of humility, and between the

[60] See Timothy McGee, *Medieval Song*, pp. 53 and 55. In singing the *pes*, the performer would begin on a true lower pitch, inflect the voice, and then move away from the upper note. A performance of the *quilisma* involved a smooth sliding between two pitches; strong pulses alternated with weak ones through a slight upward and downward movement in pitch.

false love of lechery and the true love of Christ. The treatment of music in the songs of Mary Magdalene also reflects the views of Franciscan theologians. Her moral, penitential speech is affected with ornaments, subtle inflections of rhythm, and with 'devoted tears in a succession of persuasion', as Roger Bacon suggests. Indeed, one might agree with Bartholomaeus Anglicus that Mary Magdalene uses music to attract and convert the souls of her listeners.

In light of this evidence of literature and music, one might conclude that the early German Passion plays emanated from the ranks of the Franciscan order itself. The portrayal of Mary Magdalene's conversion here is so closely related to the programmes of Franciscan homiletics that one finds it difficult not to leap to conclusions about the provenance of these works. However, to come to this conclusion on the basis of the Magdalene lyrics alone would be inappropriate. The *Marienklage* in the *BP* and the Lucifer play in the *WPf* also offer strong evidence of the impact of Franciscan preaching. On the other hand, these plays demonstrate connections to liturgy, theories of music, and methods of exegesis that were not entirely unique to the Franciscans. The strength of this study does not depend on the positive evidence of authorship, nor is it my intention to offer any such opinion. I wish, instead, to propose two modest conclusions about the German Passion plays which concern the influence of Franciscan spirituality, and a method of musicological study which uses the literal evidence of preaching to analyse the rhetorical voice of music.

By examining the German Passion plays as homiletical works connected to medieval traditions of preaching, one brings to light rhetorical aspects of text which can reflect on the exegetical properties of music. In the evidence of songs such as one finds here, one can see that music was not only a measured art, as medieval music theorists often attest, but was also a form of rhetoric which composers used to express emotion. Works of Franciscan theology and music theory are not the only sources of this evidence. One also finds descriptions of the evocative properties of music in the works of Augustine and Isidore, and among the works of non-Christian philosophers. However, Franciscan descriptions of the *ars musica* offer special sources of evidence because they correlate the rhetoric of music and the art of preaching. It is for this reason that these sources are important for the study of German sacred drama and other repertories of later medieval sacred lyric.

The author or authors responsible for the *Großes Benediktbeurer Passionsspiel* and the *Wiener Passionsspielfragment* seem to have been affected by the spiritual movement of the Franciscans. It may be that they, like other renowned composers such as Frauenlob, took to heart Berthold's call for the assistance of German song writers and put their skills to use in the Franciscan campaign against immorality.[61]

---

[61] See especially Frauenlob's homage to Berthold of Regensburg in *Heinrichs von Meisen, des Frauenlobes Leiche, Sprüche, Streitgedichte und Lieder*, ed. by Ludwig Ettmüller, Bibliothek der gesammten deutschen National-Literatur von der ältesten bis auf die neuere Zeit, 1 (Quedlinburg: Basse, 1843; repr., Amsterdam: Rodopi, 1966), pp. 42–43.

Through poetry the composers of the early German Passion plays portray Mary Magdalene as a 'modern sinner', a perfect mirror of the vain and lecherous people whom Franciscan preachers admonished in their sermons. And following the wisdom of Franciscan theology and preaching, they used the rhetorical voice of music to evoke the spiritual meaning inherent in the Latin and German words of Mary Magdalene's songs. Music and words function together in the German Passion plays as scriptural exegesis. Regardless of their provenance, they are important legacies of the Franciscan movement in the medieval German lands.

Interdisciplinary Craft: A Response to Peter V. Loewen, Lynn T. Ramey, and David Strong[1]

ELIZABETH SCHIRMER

This section, entitled 'How Sermons are Reflected in Other Literatures', attests first and most strikingly to the fluidity of sermon discourse itself. In all three articles, the gestures and goals of preaching blend with chameleon-like ease into compositions never intended for the pulpit, especially *vernacular* compositions. Peter Loewen's analysis of the influence of Franciscan homiletics on early German Passion plays, Lynn T. Ramey's of polemical appropriations of Crusade preaching in the *Jeu de Saint Nicolas*, and David Strong's of *Piers Plowman* as neo-Bonaventuran sermon in poetic form, together establish a close affinity between preaching and those innovative and multi-generic vernacular traditions that would come to be identified as 'literary'. In seeking to explain that relationship, each article locates preaching at the centre of large-scale cultural upheavals, such as the rise of an influential class of urban merchants, contact with Islam and the call for Crusade, or the spiritual and theological revolutions given institutional form in the mendicant orders. And in each, sermon-like gestures reflect and refract through literary texts that record the most profound effects of these cultural shifts.

In this response paper, I consider the specific connections each article draws between preaching and emergent vernacular literatures. I am interested primarily in the methodological issues raised: in the permutations of interdisciplinary approaches represented and in the kinds of historicizing moves they make. I will close by offering a complementary approach to one of the literary texts discussed in this

[1] Some of the material which this response concludes with was presented in a slightly different form at the International Congress on Medieval Studies, Kalamazoo, in 2003. I am grateful to the joint panel of the Lollard Society and the Society of the White Hart, and to its audience, for many helpful responses.

section, William Langland's *Piers Plowman*, in an effort to illustrate briefly the need for a rigorous historicizing of the category of the 'literary' itself.

Preaching, especially when it has lay audiences in mind, emerges from this section as inherently interdisciplinary. Native to the expanding realm between the traditional categories of literate clergy and uneducated lay people, *pro populo* preaching is related on one side to speculative theological movements associated with the universities, and on the other to courtroom rhetoric and popular theatrical performances. Liminal and polysemous, at home in discursive borderlands, preaching becomes ideal material for vernacular literary negotiations as well.[2] For David Strong, the theological value of lay-directed preaching, as well as its literary affinities, reside precisely in its traversal of boundaries between lay and cleric, theology and instruction, knowledge and experience. The best preaching, exemplified for Strong by Bonaventure, is by nature 'poetic' (a characterization to which I shall return at the end of this response), and vernacular poetry is uniquely suited to developing homiletic agendas. Peter V. Loewen and Lynn T. Ramey, in turn, both emphasize the performative nature of preaching and its rhetorical affinities with vernacular drama—which, Loewen notes, 'evolved somewhere between the realms of Church and secular culture, a niche also occupied by Franciscan preachers'. As interdisciplinary 'reflections', all three articles both mimic and illustrate the discursive slipperiness of the texts they study, demonstrating the value (and some of the pitfalls) of interdisciplinary work in medieval studies generally.

Ramey and Loewen both focus their analyses on moments in vernacular plays when discursive boundaries (such as they are) are breached: the songs of Mary Magdalene in the German Passion plays, and the preaching-like moments in the *Jeu de Saint Nicolas*. Such reflections on the intersections, within individual medieval texts, of materials generally the purview of discrete modern disciplines can reveal the limitations imposed by our own disciplinary assumptions—and, and their best, help to transcend them. Vernacular plays themselves, as is evident from both articles,

[2] Recent work on late-medieval vernacularity emphasizes the dual and/or liminal status of the vernacular itself, especially in preacherly contexts. See *The Vernacular Spirit: Essays on Medieval Religious Literature*, ed. by Renate Blumenfeld-Kozinski, Duncan Robertson, and Nancy Bradley Warren (New York: Palgrave, 2002); and *The Vulgar Tongue: Medieval and Postmedieval Vernacularity*, ed. by Fiona Somerset and Nicholas Watson (University Park, PA: University of Pennsylvania Press, 2003). Especially notable are Somerset and Watson's insight, in the Preface to the latter volume, that the 'vernacular' itself connotes both a *local* language and a *universal* one, both a 'common' and a 'mother' tongue; and Claire Waters's parallel emphasis (in her 'Talking the Talk: Access to the Vernacular in Medieval Preaching', Somerset and Watson, pp. 31–42) on the late-medieval preacher's dual 'need both to distinguish himself from and to resemble his flock, and hence the importance of the vernacular in establishing a clerical identity often seen in opposition to it' (p. 32). Through a vernacularity conceived not purely linguistically but more broadly in terms of access, preachers, Waters argues, 'did not so much traverse the imagined space between laity and clergy as embody it' (p. 39).

were themselves frequently 'mixed-genre' affairs. Popular drama allowed for the interplay of a range of performative modes, from preaching to liturgical chants, from courtroom rhetoric to the calling of the new wine. Franciscans preaching repentance (as in Loewen's piece) and Dominicans preaching Crusade (as in Ramey's) were both apt to find their rhetoric appropriated, for better or for worse, in such 'hybrid' theatrical productions.[3] In Loewen's reading of the Passion plays, German songs gloss Latin lyrics in terms that reflect the penitential agendas of contemporary Franciscan preachers. Music, preaching, and theatre become in these moments virtually indistinguishable, as disparate textual and performative modes are harmonized in accordance with Franciscan homiletics broadly conceived. This analysis not only makes excellent sense of the plays themselves, in large part by tracing their indebtedness to the preaching of contemporary German Franciscans, but sheds light as well on previously-obscured medieval understandings of the music *as* rhetoric and of its close kinship to preaching.

Where Loewen finds the early German Passion plays enacting Franciscan homiletic programs, even at those moments when they sound the least like sermons, Ramey offers a much more subversive reading of the preaching-like moments in the *Jeu de Saint Nicolas*, arguing that the play appropriates the form of Crusade preaching precisely in order to undermine its project. Like Loewen, Ramey is interested in those moments when various discursive modes collapse into one another, in this case, that 'moment of performance' when 'courtroom, stage, and pulpit [are] intertwined', and 'roles are easily confused'. In her reading, the inaccuracies and reversals that attend moments of preaching (and preaching-like moments) in the *Jeu* encourage audiences to question officially-sanctioned public speech generally, and the message of Crusade preachers in particular.

The greatest interest of this piece for me lies in the way the play serves Ramey as a window onto the complex and contested discursive cultures of Arras *c.* 1200. In the lively picture she paints, the shift from liturgical to vernacular drama (marked by the production of the *Jeu* itself) interacted with conflicts between urban merchants and the crown over access to public speech, as well as with debates over the right of monastics and even of lay people to preach. Ramey's critical claims about the play itself, and her theoretical claims about 'performativity in sermon-making', are finally narrower than her descriptions of this rich culture invite them to be. By relying, for example, on the simple fact of inaccuracies and reversals—the factual error in *li preechiere*'s opening sermon-like speech, or the fact that the call to Crusade is spoken by a Saracen—Ramey leaves much of their content unaccounted for. Does it matter, for example, that *li preechiere*'s 'mistake' consists of naming the Saracens, rather than the Christians, as the aggressors? Or that the Saracens appropriate not

[3] I borrow both terms in quotation marks from Ramey, who describes the *Jeu de Saint Nicolas*, as 'a mixed-genre piece, including sermons within its overall structure as a play', a 'hybrid of the two rhetorical forms of sermon and theatre'.and passim.

only crusade preaching, but polemic on idolatry?[4] While it may indeed be part of this play's agenda to invite critical reception of public speech, this final totalizing claim elides the different modes of performativity appropriated by the play and the complex interactions between them, rather than offering, as promised, 'conclusions about performativity in sermon-making' per se. This is at least in part a theoretical issue: the 'performative' is a tricky category, getting more so by the day, and I would have liked to have seen it theorized more explicitly here.[5]

This is all by way of saying that Ramey's piece—and, to a lesser extent, Loewen's—remind us that interdisciplinary work tends to raise at least as many questions as it answers. Nor is this necessarily a bad thing. Central to Loewen's thesis, for example, is his claim that Mary Magdalene's songs function as scriptural exegesis, not simply as 'narrative accounts' of the Passion. Moreover, it is their exegetical function that aligns the plays with German Franciscan preaching, for it consists in 'elaborat[ing] on the themes of Scripture using music and poetry to preach to audiences about the virtues of penance' (ibid). Loewen's argument thus would seem to align preaching, music, and poetry with exegesis, as over against narrative. Like Ramey's invocation of the 'performative', Loewen's conflation of exegesis with a model of preaching that is (in Strong's term) 'non-periphrastic' invites further development—especially in relation to contemporary debates generated in large part by the Franciscans themselves, as to what constitutes legitimate exegesis and what relationship should pertain between exegetics and homiletics.[6] I am personally most familiar with later, Insular permutations of these debate: where the Lollards, for example, reject *both* narrative (especially in the form of sermon exempla) *and* the academic exegetical practices of the friars (attacked as overly 'curious' and 'subtle'), characterizing both as pernicious distractions from the

---

[4] Ramey does suggest, along the way, that the *Jeu* sides with the townsmen against the crown. And she claims, finally, that this play in some sense about unauthorized preaching (though it is hard to say what kind of preaching it might advocate).

[5] To begin to grasp the evolving complexity of the concept of 'performative speech', one need only read Judith Butler's extended theoretical reflection on its deployments in contemporary political debates; see her *Excitable Speech: A Politics of the Performative* (New York and London: Routledge, 1997). Fiona Somerset sees connections between Butler's theorizing of performative speech and late-medieval theories of 'emotionally provocative language'; see her 'Excitative Speech: Theories of Emotive Response from Richard FitzRalph to Margery Kempe', in *The Vernacular Spirit: Essays on Medieval Religious Literature*, ed. by Blumenfield-Kosinski and others (pp. 59–79). For a useful study of the specific modes and functions of performativity in late-medieval drama, see Sarah Beckwith, *Signifying God: Social Relations and Symbolic Acts in the York Corpus Christi Plays* (Chicago and London: University of Chicago Press, 2001).

[6] For one version of these controversies, centering on the key concept of 'glossing', see Wendy Scase, *Piers Plowman and the New Anticlericalism* (Cambridge: Cambridge University Press, 1989), pp. 77–83.

Word unsuitable for the pulpit.[7] Such questions may quite legitimately be said to fall outside the scope of Loewen's paper. But it is, I think, part of the virtue of his work that it raises them, encouraging a broadening of discipline-bound perspectives.

I turn now to David Strong's article. Like Loewen and Ramey, David Strong draws connections between preaching and vernacular literature, emphasizing the inter-discursive qualities of both. But where the former two articles emphasize the shared performative qualities of preaching and drama, Strong connects pulpit discourse and poetic making, describing Bonaventuran preaching as 'poetic' and Langland's vernacular poem *Piers Plowman* as a 'literary sermon'. In Strong's analysis, the discursive boundaries between preaching and poetry dissolve under the pressures of Bonaventure's exemplarist theology: the homilest and the poet share a vision of the created world as possessing the imprint of and therefore legibly analogous to its Creator, as well as a valuing of individual faith over scholastic metaphysics. The rhetorical demands of preaching as a pastoral mode complement this theological perspective: to preach sermons focused on the cure of lay souls is perforce to move outside the schools, emphasizing faith over rationalism and finding concrete language and imagery in which to express abstract ideas.[8] In keeping with these demands, Bonaventure's own sermons 'emphasi[ze] individual development, interactive association with the church, and a symbolic sense of nature' thereby 'creat[ing] a vision for their listeners that rivals the artistry of the poet'. Langland's poetic artistry, in turn, furthers Bonaventure's homiletic program: *Piers*'s dream-vision form, for example, dramatizes Bonaventure's theory of analogy and conveys

---

[7] For a thorough discussion of Lollard attitudes towards preaching see Anne Hudson's Introduction to her *English Wyclffite Sermons*, vol. 1 (Oxford: Clarendon Press, 1983). Penn R. Szittya discusses Wyclif's own complicated relation to the Friars and antifraternalism in *The Antifraternal Tradition in Medieval Literature* (Princeton: Princeton University Press, 1986), ch. 4: 'John Wyclif and the Nominalist Seekers of Signs'. There has recently been a resurgence of interest in late-medieval English preaching in particular, and in its relationship both to the emergence of a dynamic literary tradition and to Lollardy. See, e.g., Alan J. Fletcher, *Preaching, Politics, and Poetry in Late-Medieval England* (Dublin and Portland, OR: Four Courts Press, 1998); and H. Leith Spencer, *English Preaching the Late Middle Ages* (Oxford: Clarendon Press, 1993).

[8] While the Bonaventure sermons Strong discusses were given to academic audiences, they ultimately have lay people in mind; for Strong (and, he suggests, for Bonaventure) this is a large part of their theological value. The notion that lay people were more 'flesh-bound' readers than their clerical counterparts, and so not capable of engaging directly with theological abstractions, was commonplace in medieval discussions of preaching and pastoral education. The Franciscans (in this as in so much else) made a theological virtue of lay simplicity: image-, narrative-, and body-based devotional practices were central to Franciscan spirituality; for a good, brief discussion, see Michael Sargent, 'The *Meditationes Vitae Christi* and Franciscan spirituality', from the Introduction to his edition of Nicholas Love's *Mirror of the Blessed Life of Jesus Christ* (New York: Garland, 1992), pp. ix–xxi.

the 'eminence of faith', while Will's journey of self-reflection teaches him the importance of figural understanding.[9]

Strong is at his best when he is explicating Bonaventure's complex exemplarist theology. His reading of *Piers Plowman* also demonstrates nicely how integral Langland's formal decisions are to his theological commitments. Here preaching, poetry, and theology blend seamlessly together in what Strong identifies as exemplary orthodox discourse on a Franciscan model. Eloquent and compelling in many places, this reading of Langland neglects however to treat *Piers* as in any way a product of fourteenth-century England; nor does Strong engage with the poem's complex circumstances of production. In the process he misses much pertinent work that has been done on Langland of late. Why, for example, focus on the B-text, especially when Clopper's detailed account of Langland's Exemplarism relies so productively on the figure of Rechelesness, present only in C?[10] For all its discussion of 'controversies and factions destabilizing the medieval church', this is an oddly ahistorical reading—an impression enhanced by Strong's general claims about orthodox Christian preaching generally, and his equally transcendent construction of the 'poetic.'

Strong's article raises a crucial question: we moderns tend to think of literature as an art form, crafted, aesthetic, self-reflexive, often figural; but in what pre-modern meaning-making systems do these qualities participate, and how did they function in particular medieval texts and cultures? For Strong, aesthetics, the 'experience of the beautiful as it derives from the senses', is central to Franciscan theological and homiletic programs, and Langland's poetics participate in those systems of meaning. This connection seems sound to me; however, Strong uses it not to historicize the literary—for example by engaging the heated debates about poetry and preaching in late-medieval England[11]—but rather to draw transhistorical conclusions about

---

[9] There is some tricky logic here. If Bonaventure's Exemplarism is what makes his sermons 'poetic', then is all poetry in some sense Exemplarist, simply by the nature of literary language? For that matter would Langland or Bonaventure have identified the same conventions as 'literary'? I reflect further on these questions below.

[10] Clopper, Lawrence M., '*Songes of Rechelesnesse': Langland and the Franciscans* (Ann Arbor: University of Michigan Press, 1997). Strong does reference Clopper briefly, but does not engage his detailed analysis of Langland's Bonaventuran investments, an odd omission for this paper. Equally striking in its absence is Scase's study of *Piers Plowman and the New Anticlericalism* (see note 4 above), which argues, for example, that the C-text tends towards a broader and more fully developed anticlericalism, especially in Rechelesnesse's discussion of poverty.

[11] Much good work is being done along these lines. For example, Fletcher reads Reason's sermon in *Piers* (which Strong does not address) against the genre of estates preaching generally, taking Hereford's 1382 Ascension Day sermon and Thomas Wimbledon's St Paul's sermon of 1387 as points of comparison, and finds Langland reflecting on three topics central to contemporary debates about *pro populo* preaching: the correlation between the preacher's

effective preaching: '*Piers*, as a work of art, illustrates how a sermon must be attentive to the craft of delivering ideas'. Langland, I propose, has a very different understanding of 'craft' than does Strong. What I would like offer in response to Strong's article, and in order to render more concrete the methodological points I have made here, is a brief account of how we might begin to historicize the concept of *craft* in late-medieval England. I will do so by considering its deployment in two sermon-like Middle English poems: *Piers* itself, and the roughly-contemporary alliterative poem *Cleanness*.

In *Piers*, craft is nearly always (potentially, contestedly) *work*. And it is as labour, rather than in the modern sense of artistic craftsmanship evoked by Strong's usage, that 'crafte' is most consistently aligned with Langland's self-conscious reflections on his own poetic project.[12] It is also as work that craft functions structurally and theologically in the poem, linking *Visio*/estates/society and *Vita*/individual. The labourers who produce things necessary to the community (whether plowmen, or bakers, brewers, tailors, tinkers, masons, and miners) are allied with the knowledge-seekers (clerks, Church authorities, schoolmen). The work of both is overseen by charity: 'What craft be best to lere? / Lerne to loue, quod Kynde' (C.XII.206–07).[13] 'Craftes' are what the Holy Spirit bequeathed us for our sustenance and our service of God—and the one is not so easy to distinguish from the other in *Piers*. Appropriately, the only time Crafte appears as an allegorical figure is to structure the polity of Holy Church: Grace instructs Piers to 'crouneth counseil kyng and maketh

---

life and his word, preaching for profit, and proper and improper sermon content (see *Preaching, Politics, and Poetry*, ch. 7, 'Langland and Preaching'). Fiona Somerset, in turn, locates *Piers* amongst a growing body of '"extraclergial" texts in late-medieval England, "lewed" or lay in status or alliance, but possessed of "clergie", or learning' (*Clerical Audience and Lay Discourse in Late Medieval England* (Cambridge: Cambridge University Press, 1998) p. 13. She uses this discursive historicizing to illuminate Langland's signature anxieties about his own poetic vocation, as well has his ambivalent treatment of the overlapping categories of 'clergy' (ordained clerics) and 'clergie' (knowledge or learning), see pp. 55–60.

[12] For several excellent accounts of Langland's self-representation in relation to contemporary debates over work and labour (as encoded, for example, in the Statute of Labourers and related legislation), see *Written Work: Langland, Labor, and Authorship*, ed. by Steven Justice and Kathryn Kerby-Fulton (Philadelphia, PA: University of Pennsylvania Press, 1997). It is worth noting that all the articles in this volume focus on the 'Apologia' new in C.V., and so not present in the version of the poem Strong chose to work with. For a slightly different perspective on Langland and work, emphasizing his commitment to Thomist notions of justice in a world where 'constitutions of "lele", "trewe" labor were in serious dispute', see David Aers, *Faith, Ethics and Church: Writing in England, 1360–1409* (Cambridge: Brewer, 2000), ch. 3, 'Justice and Wage–Labor after the Black Death: Some Perplexities for William Langland'.

[13] I cite, here and throughout, from Derek Pearsall's *Piers Plowman by William Langland: An edition of the C-Text* (Berkeley and Los Angeles: University of California Press, 1978).

Craft Šoure styward, / And aftur Craftes consail clotheth Šow and fede' (C.XXI.256–57) (Piers himself is made reeve).

Craft is indeed central, then, to the form of *Piers* and, inseparably, to its theology—but not quite in the way the Strong implies. Indeed *Piers* suggests that 'crafte' (like 'clergie')[14] was a site of the renegotiation in late-fourteenth century England of the proper roles of clergy and laity, and of the relationship between them. This theory gains support from a brief reading of 'crafte' in *Cleanness*, a long, sermon-shaped poem in alliterative long lines that (Lynn Staley has recently suggested) may have been in 'textual dialogue' with *Piers* on questions of sin and Church authority.[15]

Cleanness is an anonymous poem that survives (unlike the ubiquitous *Piers*) in only one manuscript: the justly-famous British Library Cotton Nero A.x, which also preserves the unique surviving copies of *Pearl* and *Sir Gawain and the Green Knight* along with another, shorter sermon-shaped poem dubbed *Patience*.[16] The bulk of *Cleanness* consists of a series of Old Testament narratives: Noah and the Flood, Sodom and Gomorrah, and Balthazar's feast with Daniel's decipherment of the writing on the wall. The poet arranges these stories in chronological order, even when he has to 'rearrange' biblical material to do so, constructing the Old Testament as one long story of humankind's fall away from God.[17] This narrative progression is periodically interrupted by moralizing episodes that reassert a preacherly tone, thereby inserting the individual, as it were, into salvation history. These episodes describe God as a Lord presiding over an ultra-clean court (an image derived from the sixth Beatitude, the poet-preacher's theme text) and the individual seeking salvation as an aspiring courtier, who must become clean enough to serve in God's sight.

---

[14] See Somerset (1998), and note 11 above.

[15] Lynn Staley, 'The Man in Foul Clothes and a Late Fourteenth-Century Conversation about Sin', *Studies in the Age of Chaucer*, 24 (2002), 1–47 (p. 47). Staley finds both texts participating—along with Fitzralph, Chaucer, *St Erkenwald*, and Julian of Norwich—in a larger cultural discussion in which the man in foul clothes was used 'to interrogate the institutional church,' 'explor[ing] the necessarily interlocked issues of sin and judgment as they define the very identity of the church' (1, 2). My reading of the two poems suggests a parallel and related conversation about 'crafte' in the period.

[16] For recent studies of *Cleanness*'s relation to sermon structure and preaching conventions, see Michael H. Means, 'The Homiletic Structure of *Cleanness*', *Studies in Medieval Culture*, 5 (1995), 165–72; Jane K. Lecklider, *Cleanness: Structure and Meaning* (Cambridge: Brewer, 1997); and Richard Newhauser, 'Sources II: Scriptural and Devotional Sources', in *A Companion to the Gawain-Poet*, ed. by Derek Brewer and Jonathan Gibson (Cambridge: Brewer, 1997), pp. 258–75.

[17] The story of the siege of Jerusalem and Balthazar's, for example, is cobbled together from Exodus 25. 31–7, Chronicles 36. 11–21, Jeremiah 52. 1–26, and Daniel 4. 27–5. 31.

For salvation to be possible in *Cleanness*, history must be interrupted or evaded; chronos must be overridden by kairos. God accomplishes this salvific interruption through acts of divine 'cortaysye' (the word is used to describe both the Incarnation and the covenant made with Noah after the Flood). The closest human analogue to divine 'cortaysye' is 'crafte'. 'Crafte', in *Cleanness*, refers to a wide range of creative efforts through which human beings may attempt to restore their natural God-given cleanness: from the priest's sacramental art, to the craft of the vessel-maker, to the lay art of married sexuality. Through craft, the material (the unconsecrated host, the unformed clay, the sexual body) enters the realm of discourse, that is, it is made to function relationally in systems of signification, value, and exchange. And it is by engaging these discursive realms that fallen humans can, as it were, extricate the material from at least some of the constraints of the temporal, and so begin to transcend chronology. Moreover, the specific crafts discussed in *Cleanness* combine to suggest that *all* human creative efforts, clerical and lay alike, are equally necessary to the project of salvation, and equally subject to corruption and abuse.

To take the most striking example: in the second narrative piece of the poem, telling the story of Sodom and Gomorrah, 'crafte' refers exclusively to straight sex within marriage. God's striking paean to married sexuality, shot through with the language of courtly love and devoid of any reference to reproduction, raises sexual pleasure virtually to the level of a sacrament: 'Bytwene a male and hys make such merþe schoulde come,/ [w]elnyše pure paradys mošt preue no better' (703–4).[18] The narrator's reverent citation shortly thereafter of the *Roman de la Rose*, which he calls (significantly) the 'clene *Rose*', (1057), transforms a courtly-love manual into a model for *imitatio Christi*, casting a vernacular literary work in the role of a preacher's authoritative text. In the last half of the poem 'crafte' is used, similarly, to assert the spiritual powers of a primarily lay art form. Here 'crafte' refers to the vessel-making art of King Solomon, and to the Temple vessels themselves. On the one hand these are, of course, ecclesiastical objects, and so instruments of the priest's art. But the vessels also function as instruments of conversion outside of any

[18] I cite, here and throughout, from *The Poems of the Pearl-Manuscript*, ed. by Malcolm Andrew and Ronald Waldron (Berkeley and Los Angeles: University of California Press, 1978). For recent readings of sexuality in *Cleanness* see Elizabeth B. Keiser, *Courtly Desire and Medieval Homophobia:The Legitimization of Sexual Pleasure in Cleanness and its Contexts* (New Haven: Yale University Press, 1997); Allen J. Frantzen, 'The Disclosure of Sodomy in *Cleanness*', *PMLA* 111.3 (1996), 451–64; Michael Calabrese and Eric Eliason, 'The Rhetorics of Sexual Pleasure and Intolerance in the Middle English *Cleanness*', *Modern Language Quarterly*, 56.3 (1995), 247–75); and A. V. C. Schmidt, '*Kynde Crafte* and the *Play of Paramourez*: Natural and Unnatural Love in *Purity*', in *Genres, Themes, and Images in English Literature:From the Fourteenth to the Fifteenth Century: The J. A. W. Bennett Memorial Lectures, Perugia, 1986*, ed. by P. Boitani and A. Torti (Tübingen: Narr, 1988), pp. 105–24.

formal ecclesiastical context, purely by virtue of their artistry: it is the beauty and craftsmanship of the vessels that inspire Nebuchadnezzar to praise the God of the Jews, in a passage that has no equivalent in the Vulgate.

In the key concept of craft—as in *Cleanness*'s hybrid form, mixing sermon and alliterative poem—lay and clerical mediating skills are all but collapsed into each other. This is a linguistic as well as a theological innovation. According to the Middle English Dictionary, 'crafte' in the period had a vast and shifting semantic field. Its meanings comprised learnedness (with specific reference to the seven liberal arts; an academic meaning); knowledge (practical as well as academic); skill (specialized artisans' skills, such as those practised in the urban craft guilds, or simply human ones); and, finally and increasingly, craftiness or deceit. The semantic field of ME 'crafte' thus skirts both the literary and the priestly arts, referring specifically to neither but evoking their shared qualities as well as the charges of hypocrisy and deceitfulness commonly leveled against both. The *Cleanness*-poet finds in this term, I propose, the perfect concept upon which to graft them both. His use of 'crafte' throughout the poem reflects his rethinking of his own poetic and the priest's clerical arts as analogous, imperfect acts of human creation and mediation. This is not unlike Langland's use of the concept; though *Piers*, less sacramentally-minded and more ambivalent about the clerical arts, deploys 'crafte' to set its poetics in relation to sustenance labour, thereby embroiling this vernacular literary project in contemporary controversies over the nature of work and of poverty, and in particular over appropriate clerical manifestations of each.

I return in closing to questions of methodology. In a recent study of Lollard pedagogy, Rita Copeland contends that an over-reliance on 'dense materialist syncretism' can misread cultural phenomena deeply engaged with diachronic developments. Copeland argues instead for 'the force of long-established orders of discourse, especially those that have been naturalized in local cultural relations'.[19] In these terms, my own preliminary reading of 'crafte' in *Piers* and *Cleanness* might be dubbed synchronic, and Strong's discovery of Bonaventuran Exemplarism in *Piers* diachronic. My juxtaposition of what Copeland identifies as two distinct historicist approaches aims to suggest their complementarity while letting each serve as a foil for the other. Strong's discussion of Langland's Exemplarism reminds us that boundaries between poetry, homiletics, and theology in the late Middle Ages were not only different from their modern counterparts but were themselves fluid and open to contest; his article invites us to examine such contests in ever more historically precise ways. I have suggested that late ME 'crafte' was central to the poetics of Langland and the Cleanness-poet precisely because its semantic range encompassed the realms of cleric and lay, homiletics and poetics, labour and artisanship and sacrament—refusing to be contained by traditional disciplinary or

[19] Rita Copeland, 'Childhood, Pedagogy, and the Literal Sense: From Late Antiquity to the Lollard Heretical Classroom', in *New Medieval Literatures I*, ed. by Wendy Scase, Rita Copeland, and David Lawton (Oxford: Clarendon Press, 1997), pp. 125–56 (p. 125).

socio-political boundaries. As such it speaks to the need for interdisciplinary historicist thinking in medieval studies. Ramey and Loewen model this kind of thinking: both are at once carefully particular, drawing on specific cultural contexts to produce insightful readings of literary texts, and methodologically fruitful, using medieval cultures to reflect on modern scholarly practices—and vice versa.

IV

Reflections *Upon* Sermons

Speech-Reporting Strategies in 'Dramatic Preaching': With Examples from East Slavic Festal Sermons

INGUNN LUNDE

The Dramatic Sermon

A branch of Byzantine homiletics which has attracted growing attention during the last few decades is the 'dramatic sermon'. Among the earlier Greek and Syriac representatives of this tradition are Amphilochius of Iconium (d. after 394), Severian of Gabala (d. after 408), Proclus of Constantinople (d. 446 or 447), the presbyter Leontius of Constantinople (fifth–sixth century), Basil of Seleucia (d. after 468), and Severus of Antioch (*c*. 465–*c*. 538), while later homilists include Gregory of Antioch (patriarch 570–593), Andrew of Crete (*c*. 660–725 or 740), Patriarch Germanus I of Constantinople (d. 730 or 742), and George of Nicomedia (metropolitan from *c*. 860). Common to this group of preachers is an ornate homiletic style, characterized by a number of rhetorical devices, such as repetition, anaphora, parallelism, rhythmical and rhyming organization, and, most important, the inclusion of monologues and dialogues. To be sure, several of the listed features are the joint property of the homiletic tradition from its very beginnings; however, their frequency and predominance in these preachers set the latter apart from the earlier tradition.[1]

[1] This homiletic tradition is sometimes labelled *pseudo*- and *post*-Chrysostomian, terms which are not optimal: the first, motivated by the great number of pseudepigraphic *chrysostomica* among the 'dramatic sermons', is vague, the second imprecise. (Severian of Gabala, for instance, was a contemporary of John Chrysostom.)

In the 'dramatic sermons', the protagonists appear as speaking persons, and considerable parts of the text consist of their represented words. The homilist may address them directly and 'quote' their response, but most frequently they enter into conversation with each other. Byzantine sermonists show great creativity in staging such dialogic encounters, occasionally challenging the laws of logic and chronology. We find not only speeches which amplify dialogic sequences of the Gospel narratives, but also imaginary dialogues between, for example, personifications of Hades and Death, or the Devil and Death; Hades laments the raising of Lazarus, the Apostle Thomas enters into a conversation with the heretic Arius (*c.* 250–336), where Thomas, in turn, quotes from his own dialogue with the resurrected Christ (elaborating on John 20. 27–29); or, God and the Son hold a discussion in heaven before the creation of Adam.

Speech-reporting Strategies—A Pragmatic Approach

The study of dialogue in sermons has been approached from several angles. Investigating the literary-historical background, scholars have traced the influence of Syriac and Greek religious poetry and of themes and characters deriving from the repertoire of apocrypha.[2] Moreover, the 'dramatic homilies' have been related to the development of a liturgical drama in Byzantium, a thesis proposed by George La Piana in 1912, but never entirely accepted by other scholars.[3] Another line of inquiry has looked at exegetic, didactic, and rhetorical implications of the sermons' dialogic structure.[4] In this essay, I would like to expand on this latter approach to the tradition

---

[2] See, among others, Sebastian Brock, 'Dialogue Hymns of the Syriac Churches', *Sobornost*, 5 (1983), 35–45; Averil Cameron, 'Disputations, Polemical Literature and the Formation of Opinion in the Early Byzantine Period', in *Dispute Poems and Dialogues in the Ancient and Medieval Near East*, ed. by Gerrit J. Reinink and Hans L. J. Vanstiphout Orientalia Lovaniensia Analecta, 42 (Leuven: Peeters, 1991), 91–108.

[3] George La Piana, *Le rappresentazioni sacre nella letteratura bizantina dalle origini al sec. IX, con rapporti al teatro sacro d'Occidente*, (Grottaferrata: Tip. italo-orientale 'S. Nilo', 1912).

[4] See the following by Judit Kecskeméti, 'Exégèse chrysostomienne et exégèse engagé', *Studia Patristica*, 22 (1989), 136–147;'Doctrine et drame dans la prédication grecque', *Euphrosyne*, 21 (1993), 29–68; 'Deux caractéristiques de la prédication chez les prédicateurs pseudo-chrysostomiens: la répétition et le discours fictif', *Rhetorica*, 14.1 (1996), 15–36; and papers by Mary B. Cunningham, 'Polemic and Exegesis: Anti-Judaic Invective in Byzantine Homiletics', *Sobornost*, 21.2 (1999), 46–68; 'Dramatic Device or Didactic Tool? The Function of Dialogue in Byzantine Preaching', in *Rhetoric and Byzantine Culture: Papers from the Thirty-Fifth Spring Symposium of Byzantine Studies, Exeter College, Oxford, March 2001*, ed. by Elisabeth Jeffreys (Aldershot: Variorum, 2004), pp. 101–113. See also Ingunn Lunde, *Verbal Celebrations: Kirill of Turov's Homiletic Rhetoric and its Byzantine Sources* Slavistische Veröffentlichungen, 86, (Wiesbaden: Harrassowitz, 2001), pp. 161–218 (chapter

of 'dramatic sermons' by adding a further perspective to the analysis of represented speech: linguistic pragmatics.

The analysis of represented, or reported speech is a major field of study within linguistic pragmatics.[5] Pragmatics, which focuses on contextualized uses of language, has developed refined tools and categories for the study of speech-reporting strategies and their possible effects. It should be kept in mind that represented speech as found in the 'dramatic sermons' shares the features of both 'reported speech' and 'projected speech'. The latter usually denotes speech projected onto fictional characters. Naturally, the term 'fictional' is ill-chosen when applied to medieval sermons; however, within the tradition of 'dramatic sermons', homilists expand and elaborate on the protagonists' speeches very freely, even where no or only a few words were uttered in the 'original scene' (as depicted, for example, in the Gospel story), if there is one. It is clear that although the words of the represented persons are definitely perceived to be 'real', the sermonist's intention is rarely to reproduce verbatim some previously spoken utterances. In the following discussion, we shall therefore look for other possible functions and effects which may explain the extended use of represented speech in the 'dramatic sermons'.

Preaching is an interpretive genre. When conveyed in dramatic form, the preacher's voice does not disappear, but the form of theological interpretation and of exhortational aim is different. More specifically, in the 'dramatic sermons', the preacher's ways of engaging the audience, his guidance of their emotions and understanding, are closely connected, I believe, to his manner of organizing the speech of his protagonists. The focus of pragmatics is on the variety of interrelationships between an utterance and its context, involving speaker, audience, framing, perspective, voice, orientation, points of reference (*deixis*), interpretative horizon, communicative goal, etc. By letting the pragmatic approach guide the focus of our attention, we will be able to detect and analyse significant factors of the sermonist's way of rendering the speech of his characters, factors which are relevant for the study of functional nuances and rhetorical effects of speech-reporting strategies within a homiletic context.

Kirill, Bishop of Turov

I shall illustrate my point by a few examples taken from an East Slavic representative of the tradition of 'dramatic sermons', Kirill of Turov (late twelfth century?). We know near to nothing about the historical Kirill, bishop of Turov. No contemporary historical source mentions his name, which is odd in the view of his

---

titled 'Speech and Dialogue').

[5] The term 'reported speech' is used in its broad sense, denoting any form of quoted speech: direct, indirect and anything in between.

literary legacy. If indeed he is the author of what modern scholarship considers to be the *Corpus Cyrillianum*, Kirill of Turov must be regarded as a major figure in the history of early East Slavic literature and spirituality. Alternatively, the label 'Kirill, bishop of Turov' might have been invented at a later point, in order to designate an appropriate authority as the author of a set of texts that were fairly popular and obviously held in high esteem. Kirill of Turov, conventionally dated *c.* 1130–1181,[6] is traditionally considered to be the author of a number of homiletic, hymnographic, and exegetic writings. His homiletic works include (at least) eight festal sermons, from Palm Sunday to the Sunday before Pentecost. These are high-style rhetorical sermons clearly belonging to the tradition of 'dramatic homilies'.[7]

Deixis

The liturgical context of festal sermons constitutes a particular framework for references to time, space, and person. The central theme of the sermons is, more often than not, an event from the history of Christ's life on earth, and thus, has a double reference. It refers both to the historical event, the purpose of the feast-day, and to the present of the service, which takes the form of a celebration through re-enactment of the sacred event.

References to time, space, and person have to do with what pragmatics calls *deixis* (indexality). Any passage of reported speech contains deictic markers which ground information within the dimensions of time, space, and person. In other words, deictic markers tell us something about the network of interrelationships between the quoted words and their surroundings: addressee, quotee, textual and contextual framing, or other particular points of reference. Markers may be of a concrete, easily recognizable nature, such as grammatical form (for example, time

---

[6] For an introduction to Kirill of Turov's life and work, see Simon Franklin, *Sermons and Rhetoric of Kievan Rus*, Harvard Library of Early Ukrainian Literature, English Translations, 5 (Cambridge, MA: Harvard University Press, 1991), pp. lxxvii-cix. The three most recent monographs on Kirill are Wacław Hryniewicz, *Staroruska teologia paschalna w świetle pism św. Cyryla Turowskiego*, (Warszawa: Verbinum, 1993); Aliaksei Mel'nikaŭ, *Kiryl, episkap Turauski: zhytstsio, spadchyna, svetapohliad*, (Minsk: Belaruskaia navuka, 1997, repr. 2000); Lunde, *Verbal Celebrations*.

[7] While it is clear that Kirill has been influenced by the rhetorical tradition of dramatic homilies, the question of his concrete literary sources (that is, the availability of (translated) texts representing this tradition in Kievan Rus') still awaits more thorough analysis. The question of sources has been a cardinal theme in the scholarship on Kirill since the *editio princeps* of his works in 1821. For an overview and critical examination of the earlier scholarship, see Lunde, *Verbal Celebrations*, pp. 85–121.

adverbials, demonstratives and location phrases), or pertain to registers of speech, such as stylistic features, choice of words, interpretive horizon, etc.[8]

If we look at deictic markers within the protagonists' represented speech in Kirill of Turov's sermons, we will soon discover that they are not always 'consistent' within one reported unit. Markers may point in several directions, creating multiple perspectives or even ambiguities with regard to speaker and addressee or other categories and interrelationships within the realm of time, space, and person.

Ambiguities should, I believe, not be dismissed too hastily as reflecting only flaws in the author's literary skills or deficiencies in the grammatical norms of the literary language of his time. Instead, variance in deictic orientation may often be shown to form part of the author's rhetorical strategy, in serving to create a 'perspectival montage' of voices, viewpoints, and references, crucial for the author's homiletic goals.[9]

Perspectival Montage

Let us look at an example, a 'classic' dialogic encounter based on a New Testament episode, the narrative of Thomas the Unbeliever (John 20. 19–31).[10] The dialogue is found in Kirill's *Sermon for Low Sunday*, where Christ responds in a long speech to Thomas's statement of his unbelief (Аще не вложю руки моея в ребра его и в язву гвоздиньную перста моего, не иму вѣры, 417, 41–43)[11]; compare John 20. 25).

[8] To include these last categories within the notion of deixis presupposes a wide understanding of the term, encompassing phenomena such as speaker imprint, subjectivity, and evidentiality. For a recent discussion of these terms from a pragmatic viewpoint, see Ilana Mushin, *Evidentiality and Epistemological Stance: Narrative Retelling*, Pragmatics & Beyond, New series, 87 (Amsterdam: Benjamins, 2001).

[9] For the concept of 'perspectival montage', see the papers of Meir Sternberg, 'Proteus in Quotation-land: Mimesis and the Forms of Reported Discourse', *Poetics Today*, 3.2 (1982), 107–56; 'How Indirect Discourse Means: Syntax, Semantics, Poetics, Pragmatics', in *Literary Pragmatics*, ed. by Roger D. Sell (London: Routledge, 1991), pp. 62–93.

[10] Dialogic elaboration on this episode is not unknown in homiletic tradition; see Pseudo-Chrysostom (Proclus of Constantinople), *Sermon on Thomas* (CPG 5832), Pseudo-Chrysostom, *Sermon for Antipascha* (CPG 5058), and, to a lesser degree, Basil of Seleucia, *Sermon on Thomas* (CPG 6658).

[11] 'Except I shall put my hand into His side and my finger into the print of the nails, I will not believe,' (113). Kirill's sermons were edited in the 1950s by Igor P. Eremin in *Trudy Otdela drevnerusskoi literatury* 11, 12, 13, 15 (1955–1958), reprinted 1989 as *Literaturnoe nasledie Kirilla Turovskogo: arkheologicheskii obzor i izdanie tekstov*, Monuments of Early Russian Literature, 2 (Berkeley: Berkeley Slavic Specialties, 1989). References (page and line numbers) are to the original pagination in Eremin's 1955–1958 edition. English translations (occasionally adjusted) are quoted from Franklin, *Sermons and Rhetoric*, and referred to by page numbers in brackets.

His line of argument is based on references to prophets and other Old Testament figures who acted as 'witnesses' to himself, prefigure his death and resurrection, or in other ways confirm his identity. With the first reference, a 'quotation' is given initially and subsequently confirmed by repetition and interpretation:

> Испытай первое Исаино о мнѣ писание: Копьемь бо—рече—в ребра прободен бысть, и изиде кровь и вода; в ребра прободен бых, да ребром падъша Адама въскресих. (418, 2–4)[12]

The third-person reference of the 'quotation'[13] 'His ribs were pierced[…]' is repeated in the first person by Christ with reference to himself, 'I was pierced through the ribs[…]', while the following 'explanation,' 'in order to[…]' clearly represents the voice of the homilist and follows a very common homiletic and hymnographic manner of interpreting the separate elements of Christ's crucifixion in explanatory parallels.

The interpreting perspective of the homilist is quite strong throughout Christ's address to Thomas, as in many of Kirill's represented speeches. Indeed, Kirill's editor argued that Christ, in this dialogue, 'does only what the homilist could have done for him, with similar success.'[14] If we look more closely, however, there is also a strongly pronounced focus on Christ's personal voice throughout the speech. The third-person reference of the 'Isaiah quotation' just given is found only in this instance. In the subsequent string of references, every quotation where the syntax allows has been changed from the third to the first person when referring to Christ. With Christ's six-time repetition of 'I am (the one who […])' and the frequent first person possessive and personal pronouns pointing to central elements in his life, the homilist highlights the significance of Thomas's personal, dialogic encounter with Christ resurrected:

> Мнѣ бо и преже тебе патриарси и пророци разумѣвше вѣроваша моему въчеловѣчьнию; не буди невѣрен, яко же Ирод, яже слыша мое рожество […] а в сердци о убийствѣ моемь мысляше; Вѣруй ми, Фомо, и познай мя, яко же и Аврам […] познав мя, господа мя нарече; А не буди невѣрен, яко же Валам, иже духомь святымь прорек мое за мир умерьтвие и въскресение […]; И не буди

[12] 'Consider that which was first written about me by Isaiah, as it is said: "His ribs were pierced with a spear, and there came forth blood and water." I was pierced through the ribs, in order to raise Adam, who fell into sin because of his rib.' (113, adjusted).

[13] In actual fact, this is not a quotation from Isaiah, but from John's narrative of the crucifixion (John 19. 34). The naming of the prophet may possibly be explained by Isaiah 53. 2–5, 7 and similar places traditionally understood as prefiguring specific details of Christ's crucifixion.

[14] Igor P. Eremin, 'Oratorskoe iskusstvo Kirilla Turovskogo', *Trudy Otdela drevnerusskoi literatury*, 18 (1962), 56.

невѣрен, яко Навходъносор, иже [...], истиною сына божия нарече мя, etc 417, 44–418, 20)[15]

The dialogic situation is reinforced by Thomas's reply, in his response to Christ's 'I am' with 'you are (the one who[...])'. Correspondingly, the imperative of Christ's repeated demand 'believe!' or 'do not be faithless!' (eight times) is answered in the affirmative by Thomas, who opens and closes his speech with 'I believe'. Meanwhile, in Thomas's response, we see a similar combination of perspectives as in the speech of Christ: statements like 'I see Your ribs, from which You shed blood and water' are supplemented with an interpretation or explanation representing the voice of the homilist addressing the congregation: Вижю ребра, от них же источи кровь и воду; воду же, да очистиши оскверньшюся землю, и кровь же, да освятиши человѣчьское естьство (418, 39–41).[16]

In this way, two distinct perspectives are combined throughout the speech: on the one hand, the focus on the personal, dialogic encounter between Christ and Thomas, the individual unbeliever who comes to believe; and on the other, the wider context of Christ's resurrection for mankind and salvation for every human believer. Crucial for the effect is Kirill's employment of the biblical layer of text and its authority, in particular in the speech of Christ. Scriptural quotations, well-known to the congregation, are reinforced and re-actualized by Christ's own voice within the sermon's here and now.

Temporal Orientation

The example just discussed displays a standard model of double perspective in Kirill's sermons: a speaking person (Christ, an angel, Mary, Joseph of Arimathea, the paralytic (compare John 5. 1–15), the man born blind (compare John 9. 1–38), and others) addresses another person within the narrative of the sermon. Simultaneously, one may perceive in their represented words the preacher's voice and perspective, addressing the audience. A common method of achieving this double effect is, as we have seen, the use of biblical quotations. Here, temporal points of reference play a decisive role. An interesting example is Joseph of

---

[15] 'Before you the patriarchs and the prophets knew me and believed in my incarnation'; 'Be not faithless like Herod, who heard of my birth [...] while in his heart he was scheming to kill me'; Believe in me, Thomas, and know me, as Abraham knew me and called me Lord'; 'Be not faithless like Balaam, who, though he foretold through the Holy Spirit my death for the world and my resurrection [...]'; Be not faithless like Nebuchadnezzar, who, though [...] he called me truly the Son of God' etc. 113–114).

[16] I see Your ribs, from which You shed blood and water: water that You might cleanse the earth of its corruption, blood that You might sanctify mankind.' (115, adjusted).

Arimathea's long plea to Pilate for the dead body of Christ in Kirill's *Sermon for the Third Sunday after Easter* (on the Deposition). Joseph's speech contains a whole string of scriptural quotations, including Old Testament prophecies about Christ, supplied with references to New Testament events, where, in a sequence of scenes, certain 'highlights' from Christ's life on earth are brought in. Instead of a humble plea, Joseph's speech is turned into a chorus-like multiplicity of utterances and voices accentuating Christ's victorious divinity, whilst his dead body still hangs on the cross.

One passage is particularly revealing with regard to temporal constellations; Joseph says: Дажь ми тѣло съняти с креста; хощю бо его в своемь положити гробѣ. Уже бо вся о немь испълнишася пророчества: [...] (422, 14–16).[17] Joseph's viewpoint is that of seeing his own approaching act—the taking down of the body of Christ from the cross—in the context of God's design. All the prophecies concerning the crucifixion of Christ, just quoted by Joseph in his speech, have now been fulfilled; therefore, Pilate must deliver up the body for Joseph to bury. This is, of course, the preacher's viewpoint, yet effectively pronounced rhetorically by Joseph himself. Joseph treats the biblical text in the traditional manner of typological exegesis. The prophecies are re-actualized in his speech, yet at the same time employed as arguments and interpreted from a viewpoint which is possible only in retrospect. Joseph establishes a mutual correspondence between the prophecies and his own act at the moment when he is about to fulfil his mission. This interplay with 'impossible' temporal perspectives is quite characteristic of Kirill's rhetoric. We shall see further consequences of Kirill's treatment of the temporal framework below, in the section on 'immediacy', but let us look at this stage at one additional example, which illustrates the sermons' typical temporal structure as governed by a pattern which is not predominantly linear, but rather hierarchically defined.

References to the raising of Lazarus are remarkably frequent in Paschal sermons, not surprisingly, since the motif is central to the interpretation of the Easter events. In Kirill, one reference to the raising of Lazarus appears in Christ's extended speech to the paralytic in the *Sermon for the Fourth Sunday after Easter*.[18] Now, within the representation of Christ's historical life on earth, such a reference is, of course, 'impossible', since the healing of the paralytic took place before the raising of Lazarus. However, in Kirill's representation of Christ's speech, a parallel is established between the performing of the miracle (the healing of the paralytic, representing humanity) and Christ's death and resurrection, prefigured by his raising of Lazarus. To the audience, who have celebrated both the raising of Lazarus and

---

[17] 'Give me the body to take down from the cross, for I wish to lay it in my own tomb. For already all the prophecies concerning Him have been fulfilled: [...]' (121).

[18] This speech is analysed in more detail below, in the section The Authority of the Spoken Word.

Christ's resurrection a few weeks earlier, the paralytic's 'rising' is easily recognizable as a parallel to the two other events. The rhetorical effect of the reference to the raising of Lazarus is thus dependent on the double structure of Christ's speech to the paralytic, where the performing of the miracle is interpreted as a parallel to Christ's becoming man for man's sake, and is addressed, in this way, to both the paralytic and to Kirill's audience.

Framing and Multiple Addressees

The accumulation of many speakers giving voice to authoritative utterances, as in the speech of Joseph of Arimathea, is regularly found in Kirill's sermons and serves the purpose of amplifying both the message of the speech itself and the scope of addressees, most frequently to the effect of including the congregation among the listeners to the speech. The central theme and scene of any Easter sermon, the announcement of the glad tidings by the angel to the women at Christ's empty grave, is a case in point.

When looking at speech-reporting strategies, it is essential to consider not only the speech itself, but also its immediate textual surroundings, that is, the *framing* of the speech. In Kirill's introduction to the scene at Christ's empty grave in his *Sermon for the Third Sunday after Easter*, we find an original transformation of a traditional motif: the juxtaposition of the four evangelists' slightly diverging accounts of the event.[19] While earlier homilists typically attempt to eliminate the seeming incompatibility of the four evangelists' disparate stories (the problem concerns above all the exact time of the women's visit to the grave, as well as their number), Kirill quotes the four accounts without questioning their discrepancy, introducing the passage with: И минувъши суботѣ и солнцю уже въсиявъшю, вся въкупѣ жены с мюромь, се уже чьтвьртое, придоша. (423, 10–11).[20] Then follow the relevant passages from Matthew, Luke, and John, before the homilist arrives at Mark, who о всѣх повѣдаеть мюроносицах, яже с вонями въ суботу придоша. (423, 23–24).[21] Kirill simply combines the four accounts without reconciling them (chrono)logically, and creates, in the process, not only a choir of voices describing

[19] Earlier homilists juxtaposing the evangelists' accounts include Severus of Antioch, *On the Resurrection* (CPG 7035), Eusebius of Caesaria in his lost *On Discrepancies in the Gospels* (CPG 3470), Hesychius of Jerusalem, *A Collection of Aporias and Solutions* (CPG 6561), and John Barytes, *Sermon on the Resurrection* (CPG 6720); similar passages are also found in one of Romanos the Melode's hymns on the Resurrection and in Theophylact of Ochrid's Gospel commentaries.

[20] 'And when the sabbath was past and the sun was risen, all the women together came with myrrh. This was already the fourth visit' (122).

[21] 'tells of all the spice bearers who came on the sabbath with spices' (123).

the scene, but also the illusion of a multitude of witnesses to the event. This strategy is followed up in the design of the angel's speech.

Immediacy

The angel's announcement of the glad tidings is brought in by his quoting what the women will say to the apostles: Вы же видете тъщь гроб и рьцѣте апостолом: Христос въскресе! (423, 26–27, compare Matthew 28. 7).[22] In this way, the addressees become the speakers, or, put differently, join the angel in proclaiming the sermon's central message. He continues: будѣте благовѣстьцѣ человѣчьскому спасению, рьцѣте апостолом: Днесь спасение миру! (423, 28–30).[23] Here Kirill has the angel quote a passage from the liturgical resurrection troparion (read during the service): 'Today salvation has come to the world' (Днесь спасение миру бысть), significantly, in the present tense.

The ensuing speech of the angel is a retelling and interpretation of salvation history from the Fall of Adam to the Second Coming of Christ. Individual elements of Christ's suffering and death are interpreted within the context of God's plan of salvation; that is, they are lifted out of ordinary historical time and given meaning according to their significance *sub specie aeternitatis*. A few examples:

> за Адама въ тлю падша пострада, того бо ради с небесе сниде и въплътивъся бысть человѣк; да истьлѣвъшаго обновить и на небеса възведет. […] Неповиньн сы продан бысть, да проданыя грѣхомь от дьяволя работы да избавить. На тръсти губою оцьта съ золчию въкуси, да загладить рукописание человѣчьскых съгрѣшений. (423, 32–41)[24]

Here the angel, naturally, merges his voice with that of the explaining homilist (or vice versa) in the manner we observed earlier. In other words, the homilist's retrospective viewpoint is clearly perceived. At the same time, however, the present tense of 'Today salvation comes to the world' is essential; the immediacy of the events portrayed is furthermore reinforced by the speech's dramatic focus on Christ's *descensus ad inferos* (the traditional iconographic, homiletic, and

---

[22] 'Behold, then, the empty sepulcher, and say to the apostles: "Christ is risen!"' (123).

[23] 'Be ye bringers of the glad tidings of man's salvation! Say to the apostles: "Today salvation comes to the world!"' (123, adjusted).

[24] 'For the sake of Adam He descended from heaven and was made flesh and became man, that He might restore him that was corrupt and raise him to heaven. […] He was innocent, and He was sold that He might redeem those that were sold by sin from their servitude to the devil. From the sponge on the reed He tasted vinegar mingled with gall, that He might expunge the book of man's sins' (123–24).

hymnographic manner of depicting his resurrection), which culminates in a rendering of a dialogue between angels and demons at the gates of Hades:

> Съвязан бысть и тьрниемь вѣнчан, да раздрѣшить от уз дьяволь человѣкы и тьрние прельсти вражия искоренить. Солнце помрачи и землею потрясе, и твари всей плакатися створи, да адьская раздрушить скрьвища, и тамо сущих душа свѣт видѣша, и Евжин плачь на радость прѣложи. Въ гробѣ яко мьртв положен бысть, и от вѣка умьршим гробьным живот дарова. Каменьемь с печатьми утвьржен бысть, да адова врата и вѣрѣя от основания скрушить. Стражьми стрѣгомь бѣ всѣми видимо, нъ невидимо съшьд в ад съвязя сотону. Ангельская бо воиньства съ нимь текуще зъваху: Възмѣте, врата, князи ваши, да вънидеть цесарь славы! И ови съвязаныя душа рѣшаче от тьмниць пущаху; друзии же противныя силы вяжюще глаголаху: Где ти, смерти, жало? Где ти, аде, побѣда? Къ ним же оцѣпѣвьше бѣси въпияху: Кто се есть цесарь славы, с толикою на ны пришел властию? Погубил есть князя тьмы и вся его въсхытил скровища, разби смертьный град, адово чрѣво, извоева плѣньникы, иже съ Адамомъ съде, сущая грѣшных душа. (423, 44–424, 16)[25]

Noteworthy is the last instance of direct speech within the angel's speech ('Who is this king of glory[...]'). It is, in fact, difficult to determine exactly where the angel—in the role of interpreting homilist—switches from quoting the demons to speaking 'from himself'. Had it not been for the last deictic 'here' ('that abided here with Adam!'), one would have taken the phrases following the exclamation 'Who is this king of glory that has come against us in such might?' to belong to the homilist's/angel's triumphant depiction of the scene (compare in particular the inserted clarification of the 'captives' of Hades as 'the souls of the sinners'). Or, alternatively, this is indeed the 'here' of the homilist, and the angel, but also of all (other) witnesses to the dramatic scene. The instance shows how Kirill deliberately

---

[25] 'He was bound and crowned with thorns, that He might unbind men from the bonds of the devil and uproot the thorns of the devil's deceit. He darkened the sun and shook the earth, and He caused all creation to lament, that He might smash the vaults of Hades; and the souls of them that abided therein saw the light, and the lament of Eve was turned to delight. He was laid in the tomb as a dead man, and He bestowed life upon the entombed dead of the ages. He was secured with a stone and with seals, that He might smite to their foundations the gates of Hades and the gateposts. He was guarded by watchmen for all to see, but unseen He descended into Hades and bound Satan. For the angelic hosts went with Him and proclaimed: "Lift up your gates, O ye princes, that the king of glory may come in!" And some of the angels untied the bound souls and let them loose from their dungeons, while others bound the hosts of the enemy, saying: "O death, where is thy sting? O grave, where is thy victory?" And the demons were numb with fear and cried out to them: "Who is this king of glory that has come against us in such might? He has destroyed the prince of darkness and has plundered all his treasure vaults. He has smashed the citadel of mortality, the belly of Hades; and He has captured its captives—the souls of the sinners—that abided here with Adam!"' (124–25).

fuses voices, styles and perspectives within one reported unit. Thus the angel's speech combines the 'today' of today's service with both the dramatic 'now' of the events portrayed and the overwhelming temporal perspective of God's plan of salvation, from the Fall to the Second Coming. As a result, the congregation is included among the witnesses or spectators of the (speech) event, which in addition conveys the explaining perspective of the homilist. The including and generalizing stance is reinforced a last time in the concluding section of the speech, where the 'you' address is expanded to 'you all', with a view to the Second Coming:

> Уже бо вся съвьршив Исус, въскрьсе боголѣпьнѣ, и показася прѣже вас приходивъшим женам, възывъя красно: Радуйтася! И апостолом своим в Галилѣю ити повелѣ, да вся тамо с вами освятив с плътию на небеса възидеть, с нею же и пакы придеть судит мирови. (424, 18–22)[26]

Conflicting Voices

The kind of perspectival montage we have seen in both the framing of the angel's speech and in his represented words is characterized by a mutual approval and overall consensus between the different voices: the explaining voice and perspective of the homilist give meaning to the words of the speaker, whilst the 'biblical' voice (Christ, the angel, etc.) adds authority and credibility to the speech, and by implication, to the sermon as a whole. The constellation of voices may be quite different, however.

Let us look at an example of conflicting perspectives within a speech and its framing. Kirill's *Sermons for the Fourth and Sixth Sundays after Easter* deal with two of the 'classic' miracles of Christ: the healing of the paralytic and of the man born blind. In both sermons, Kirill, just as many sermonists before him, portrays the central scene in the form of a dialogue between Christ and the man who was healed (much in the style of the dialogue between Christ and Thomas). Moreover, in both sermons, the dialogue is followed by a dispute with the Jews, who protest against Christ's working miracles on the Sabbath. Anti-judaic polemics of this type form a traditional ingredient in many Byzantine and Slavic Easter sermons.[27] This is the first

---

[26] 'For now Christ has fulfilled all His works, and is risen in splendor. And He appeared to the two women that came before you, with His glorious greeting, "Rejoice!" And He told His apostles to depart into Galilee, that there, with you all, He might bless all and ascend up into heaven in the flesh in which He will come again to pass judgment on the world' (124, adjusted).

[27] See Cunningham, 'Polemic and Exegesis'; for the East Slavic tradition: Alexander Pereswetoff-Morath, *A Grin Without a Cat: 'Adversus Iudaeos' Texts in the Literature of Medieval Russia 988–1504*, I, Lund Slavonic Monographs, 4 (Lund: Lund University Press,

pronouncement of the Jews' protest in Kirill's sermon on the paralytic, with the homilist's introduction:

> Бѣ же в тъ день субота, и видѣвъше его жидове, не порадовашася о съдравии немощьнаго, ни въздаша хвалы богови, въздвигнувъшоому раслабленаго от одра немощи, ни рѣша: Како ти ся, брате, жилы укрѣпиша и телесныя уди утвьрдиша? Нъ акы звѣрие на оружьника нападъше отбѣгоша и богохульная словеса акы стрѣлы к камени пущающе съламахуся: изволиша бо неправду паче, нежели глаголати правьду. И начаша прѣтити носящему одр: Субота есть, и недостоить ти взяти одра. Почто въстал еси от немощи? Почто ицѣлѣл еси от недуга? Почто прѣмѣнилъся еси от болѣзни? Не лѣпо ти бѣ нынѣ одра своего носити. (334, 13–22)[28]

The framing of the speech of the Jews emphasizes their failure to understand and their inability to rejoice before the miracle. Even if the homilist at one point declares his unequivocal denunciation of their words before the antagonists are allowed to pronounce them ('their blasphemous words broke like arrows loosed against a stone'), his discrediting of their speech is performed in a rhetorically dynamic and rather subtle way. Before quoting the speech of the Jews, the homilist quotes what they 'did not say'. This non-uttered, or 'negative' speech contains positively loaded words, words which express genuine amazement before the miracle and stand in sharp contrast to their verbal surroundings. If we look at what the Jews *did* say, we see that their speech contains repeated questions which turn their words into a rhythmical and semantic amplification of the miracle performed by Christ. In fact, the questions echo the words not uttered by the Jews, yet quoted by the homilist, but here small details of address and context determine the approving intonation of the non-uttered words in the former case (the address 'brother'), and their 'real' hostile attitude in the latter ('it is not lawful for thee'; 'It is not meet for you').

The conflicting perspectives and the contrast between the actual words and acts and the unuttered words (and unperformed acts) thus create a twofold effect: they

---

2002).

[28] 'Now it was the sabbath on that day. And when the Jews saw him, they did not rejoice in the health of the sick man, nor did they offer praises to God who had raised up the sick man from the bed of his infirmity, nor did they say, "How, brother, were your sinews thus strengthened? How were the organs of your body made firm?" But instead they ran off like beasts attacking an armed man, and their blasphemous words broke like arrows loosed against a stone. For they desired to speak falsehood more than the truth. And they began to reprimand the man for carrying his bed: "It is the sabbath day, and it is not lawful for thee to take up thy bed. Why have you risen from your sickness? Why are you cured of your infirmity? Why have you ceased to be ill? It is not meet for you now to carry your bed"' (132).

reveal the malevolent attitude of the Jews (their inability to understand and rejoice, their unwillingness to utter the 'positively loaded' words), reinforced by the portended condemnation of the speech to be pronounced, but at the same time, verbalizes through their words, uttered and unuttered, an amplification of the miracle.

It is as if the Jews are sensitively reproached and admonished within the representation of their own speech. It is characteristic of Kirill's style that the juxtaposition generating this effect is not commented on. Instead, the various levels are combined within the represented speech and its immediate surroundings, or framing. In other homilists we can find a similar device spelled out in much more explicit terms, as 'negative' figures openly admit their own misjudgment, or even condemn themselves. The seventh-century Palestinian preacher Theoteknos of Livias, for example, in his *Sermon on the Dormition of the Mother of God*, quotes the Jews saying: 'Truly, we have made a mistake "in our foolishness and have considered her life madness" (Wisdom 5. 4); we have not plucked the fruit of righteousness, for we had a veil of smoke [before our eyes]. [...] Now we know what the prophets meant to reveal to us.'[29]

The Authority of Spoken Word

The rhetorical effect of Kirill's speech-reporting strategies is, as we have seen in several examples, largely linked to the question of authority. A hierarchy of speakers, speeches, and voices manifests itself at several levels and the spoken word in general carries great weight. [30]

We shall return for a moment to the motif of words spoken and deeds performed in Kirill's sermon on the healing of the paralytic, since this sermon demonstrates particularly well the significance given to represented speech in Kirill's sermons. The dramatic centre of the sermon is the dialogic encounter between the paralytic and Christ. Christ asks, in accordance with the Gospel reading (John 5. 6), Хощеши ли сдрав быти? (332, 16–17).[31] The paralytic answers that he would be made whole, but that he has nobody (literally не имам человѣка 'I have no man')[32] to put him in

[29] Brian E. Daley, *On the Dormition of Mary: Early Patristic Homilies* (Crestwood, NY: St. Vladimir's Seminary Press, 1998), p. 78. I owe this example to Mary B. Cunningham's article on anti-Judaic invective in Byzantine homiletics (Cunningham, 'Polemic and Exegesis').

[30] See Lunde, *Verbal Celebrations*, pp. 200–09 for a detailed examination of the 'hierarchy of speakers' in Kirill's sermons.

[31] 'Wouldst thou be made whole?' (129).

[32] Compare modern translations, which render the desemanticized meaning of 'man' in 'I have no man' (Greek ἀνθροπον οὔκ ἔχω) as 'I have nobody'. Kirill's interpretation is not unique in patristic tradition.

the pool when the water is disturbed by the angel (John 5. 7). Then follows a long speech, in which the paralytic laments his illness and complains that he has no one to help him. Christ's response to the sick man takes up the phrase, 'I have no man' and confronts him with the forceful assurance, 'I became man', symmetrically structured anaphorically with the words, 'for your sake' (тебе ради/тобѣ) repeated ten times. At the centre of his speech stands the well-known patristic dictum Аз бых человѣк, да богомь человѣка сътворю (333, 34–35).[33] In this way, the sick man's speech and Christ's response develop Kirill's interpretation of today's theme: the healing of the sick man represents the healing, or salvation, of humanity.

Both speeches are characterized by the double structure we have observed before: the dialogic, personal stance and the homilist's generalizing and explaining perspective. An additional dimension, however, is added to this double perspective if we look again at the dispute with the Jews which follows the healing. The Jews ask the man who was cured: Кто есть он, иже тя створи цѣла? (334, 35),[34] and he answers:

> Нѣсть вълхв, ни чародѣй, ни есть ходатай, ни ангел, нъ сам господь бог Израилев, понеже не осяза мене руками, ни приложи былия к врѣдом удов моих. *Нъ слово его дѣломь бысть; рече бо ми: Въстани и ходи! И въслѣдова слову дѣло, и сдравие телеси.* Тѣм же не судите на лица, ни хулите божия благодати. Нъ праведный суд судите, рцѣте богу: Яко възвеличишася дѣла твоя въ Израили! И господнемь чюдесьмь суботу почьстите, и бога прославите, праздьник украсите! (334, 36–335, 6)[35]

Note that the essence of the man's advice to the Jews amounts to *uttering the right word*: 'say unto God: "How have Thy works been magnified in Israel"'—a Psalm quotation. Throughout, the speech of the Jews is contrasted with Christ's mighty word. Here the formulations of the formerly sick man echo a phrase from the homilist's introduction to the sermon:

---

[33] 'I became man, that I might make man God' (131).

[34] 'Who is the man that made thee whole?' (133).

[35] 'Not a sorcerer, nor a magician, not an ambassador, nor an angel, but the Lord God of Israel Himself; for He touched me not with His hands nor did He apply herbs to my afflicted organs. *But His word became deed. For He said to me, "Rise up and walk." And after the word came the deed, and health to my body.* Therefore judge not according to the appearance, nor slander the grace of God, but judge righteous judgment and say unto God: "How have Thy works been magnified in Israel!" And honor the sabbath in wonder of the Lord, and praise God, and adorn the feast!' (133).

> Ныня же о раслабленѣмь побесѣдуим, […] его же ныня Христос, благый человѣколюбець, *словом ицѣли*: врачь бо есть душам нашим и тѣлом, и *слово его дѣломь бысть*. (331, 8–13)[36]

In the course of the sermon, the homilist establishes a parallel between the *word* uttered by Christ performing the miracle, the healing of one individual, and Christ as the *Word*, the incarnated *Logos* (John 1.1), who was sacrificed for the salvation of all individuals. The lament of the paralytic invokes both these levels. Christ responds to the first by his act *through his words*, and to the second *in his words*, explaining his becoming man for man's sake. Simultaneously, the power of Christ's word is contrasted with the futile speech of the Jews. Whereas the words of the latter are ineffective [акы стрѣлы к камени пущающе съламахуся (334, 17–18)],[37] the word of Christ/Christ the Word performed a miracle, the healing of the paralytic and—in the wider perspective—the salvation of all human beings. Whereas the Jews speak falsely (изволиша бо неправду паче, нежели глаголати правьду [334, 18–19]),[38] the man who was healed turns to Christ at their very last meeting, proclaiming 'Thy word is the truth!' Again it is characteristic of Kirill's rhetorical style that he establishes meaningful parallels without much explicit commentary. The very organization of the speeches, including the hierarchy of speakers and shifting perspectives, becomes part of the overall meaning or message of the sermon.

The Drama of The Word

Represented speech in the 'dramatic sermons' adds, as we have seen, to the immediacy of the depicted events. In my opinion, this is one essential aspect of what is implied by the 'dramatization' of the 'dramatic sermons'. By quoting the voices of the persons portrayed, the author brings them near and into the presence of the audience, in order to have the latter act as witnesses to the represented events. In addition to the voice, the visual element is decisive in achieving this effect. The combination of visual and auditory 'dramatization' is exactly what we can observe in many of the dialogic scenes in Kirill's and other 'dramatic' preachers' sermons.

In Kirill's *Sermon for Ascension Day*, this alliance is illustrated by the combined effect of the central dialogic scene—the exchange of words between the gatekeepers in heaven and the angels with Christ—and its framing, the homilist's representation of Christ's ascension into heaven. Kirill initially invites the congregation to join 'in

---

[36] 'So let us now discourse upon the sick man […] whom Christ in His goodness and loving kindness *made whole* on this day *with His word*. For Christ is the healer of our souls and of our bodies, and *His word became deed*' (128).

[37] 'broke like arrows loosed against a stone' (132).

[38] 'desired to speak falsehood more than the truth' (132).

their minds' the witnesses to the event: Поидѣм же и мы нынѣ, братие, на гору Елеоньскую умомь и узрим мысльно вся преславьная створивъшаяся на ней! (341, 20–21).[39] In the following depiction, dramatic in its imagery and verbal design, the focus is on the visual manifestation of the event, for example, in the way Kirill contrasts the Ascension on the Mount of Olives with God's appearance to Moses on Mount Sinai (Exodus 19): На ону [i.e. on Mount Sinai] бо невидимо съниде, а на сей явьствьно ся показа. (341, 43–44).[40] A few examples:

> Небеса веселяться своя украшающе свѣтила, да благословяться от своего творца, съ плътию сквозѣ тѣх врата на облацѣх възносима. Земля радуеться видящи на себе бога явьствьно ходяща, и вся тварь красуеться от Елеоньскыя горы просвѣщаема, яко на той ангели съ святыми апостолы, по повелѣнию бога отца, съвъкупишася, ожидающе сыновьня пришествия. (341, 37–42)[41]

When Kirill arrives at the crux of the event, the visual stance is replaced by an auditory one:

> И за оны громы и мълния[42] пророчьстии слышатся гласи, яже радостьно ликъствують, глаголюще: Възнесися силою твоею, боже! Поем и въспоем силы твоя! Ангели вся поущают, глаголюще: Въскликнѣте богу вся земля! Пойте же имени его! Патриарси начинають пѣснь: Се бог нашь възноситься, смирив обоя въ едино и съвъкупив земныя с небесными! Преподобнии възглашають: Възнесися на небеса, боже! По всей земли слава твоя! Праведници велегласують: Възнесися, судяй земли, да и мы в свѣтѣ лица твоего, господи, поидем! Давыд же, акы старейшина ликов, уяшняя пѣсеныя гласы, глаголеть: Вси языци, въсплещѣте руками, въскликнѣте богу гласомь радости, да възидеть бог в въскликновении, господь в гласѣ трубьнѣ! (342, 2–12)[43]

---

[39] 'And so, my brethren, let us also now travel in our minds to the Mount of Olives, and let us survey in our thoughts all the glories accomplished thereon!' (144).

[40] 'On Mount Sinai He descended unseen, while on this mountain He made Himself manifest' (145).

[41] 'The heavens rejoice as they adorn their luminaries, that they might be blessed by their Creator as He is borne bodily upwards on the clouds through the gates. The earth rejoices at the sight of God walking manifestly upon it. And all creation radiates beauty, as it is illumined from the Mount of Olives where the angels and the holy apostles are gathered at the behest of God the Father to await the coming of the Son' (145).

[42] Kirill alludes to the event on Mount Sinai, see Exodus 19. 16.

[43] 'And instead of the former thundering and lightening [see previous note], the voices of the prophets are heard in joyful exultation, saying, "Be Thou exalted, O God, in Thy strength: we will sing and praise Thy mighty acts!" And all the angels say in exhortation, "Shout unto God, all the earth. O sing praises to His name!" And the patriarchs begin their song, "Behold our God is exalted, who has joined the heavenly with the earthly and has reconciled the two into one!" And the holy men lift their voices in exclamation: "Be Thou exalted, O God, above

Worthy of notice are the many words semantically related to singing, shouting, and crying in exaltation, not only in the text of the quotations, which are for the most part drawn from the Psalms, but also in the homilist's speech that connects them. By building up this chorus-like effect, Kirill again creates the illusion of a multitude of witnesses to the event. The conflation of biblical quotations continues as Kirill arrives at the central scene at the gates of heaven. Here the angelic hosts are confronted by the gatekeepers, preventing the glorious procession to the entrance into heaven:

> Прѣди же течаху ангельскыя силы страхомь и радостию, отвѣрсти хотяще врата небесныя. Нъ вышьнии вратьници възбраняху, въпиюще: Си врата господня, да никто же земных суду проходить; нам бо положи бог, яже не мимо идуть. Ныня же дивимъся, зряще человѣка на хѣровимьстѣмь престолѣ сѣдяща и прѣже серафим тъщащася врата си проити. Ангели же повѣдаху сына божия силу и сан человѣчьскымь обложена телесемь, и не прѣрѣковати божии воли, вся мудростию творящому: Съниде бо рѣша—на землю, никому же не чювъшю, и се рабий нося образ въсходить. Они же рѣша: Не будем покори [sic], аще не услышим слова божия. Тъгда възгласи Христос: Отвьрзѣте мнѣ врата правьды, и въшьд в ня възвѣщю отцю моему, яже на земли сътдѣях и пострадах. (342, 33–44)[44]

Thus, the culmination of Kirill's portrayal of Christ's ascension, amplified and intensified in every possible way first through dramatic visual imagery, then through the gathering of ever more voices, is Christ's own voice, demanding access to his heavenly kingdom, that is, a manifestation of the central event, as it were, through his own words.

---

the heavens; and Thy glory above all the earth!" And the righteous cry in acclamation: "Be Thou exalted, and judge the earth, that we also may walk, O Lord, in the light of Thy countenance!" And David, the leader of the choirs, who elucidated the voices of song, says, "Clap your hands, all ye nations; shout to God in a voice of exultation, that the Lord may go up with shout, with a sound of a trumpet!"' (146).

[44] 'And the hosts of the angels ran before Him in fear and joy, to open the gates of heaven. But the gatekeepers of heaven prevented them, saying, "These are the Lord's gates; no man from earth may pass hither. Such are God's instructions to us; there can be no circumvention. So we are indeed astonished to see, now, a man sitting upon a throne of cherubs, and in front of Him seraphim trying to open the gates." So the angels told of the power and rank of the Son of God clothed in the body of a man, so they would not be contradicting the will of God, who created all in wisdom: "For", they said, "He descended to earth unnoticed; and behold, now He ascends to heaven in the likeness of a slave." But the gatekeepers said: "We cannot obey unless we hear the word of God." So Christ cried out: "Open to me the gates of righteousness. I will go into them and tell my Father all that I did and endured upon earth"' (147–48).

Concluding Remarks

The 'dramatic sermon' is characterized by a great amount of represented speech, where, more often than not, both a transfer and a transformation of the homiletic task takes place: the sermonist empowers his speaking persons to assist him in conveying and explaining the sermon's central theme. We can speak of a decentralization of the authoritative stance in a genre where authority is of principal concern. In the above, we have looked at several pragmatic categories which are relevant to the study of this process: *deixis* (temporal, spatial, personal), framing, voice, and perspective. Particularly interesting for the dynamic effect of the sermonist's speech-reporting strategies are shifts and combinations within these categories.

Markers affiliated with the relevant categories may be of a grammatical or stylistic nature, creating combinations of different registers of speech which become part of the sermon's overall rhetorical design. We have seen, for instance, how Kirill of Turov's speech-reporting strategies strive to unite different temporal orientations within one reported unit, to the effect that the temporal orientation of the 'original' speech event coincides with the temporal orientation of the new speech event, with consequences for all reference points of both speech and speakers, in particular the scope and number of addressees.

Any segment of reported speech implies a combination of at least two perspectives, that of the quoter, in our case the homilist, and that of the quoted. We have observed significant variance concerning the level of integration of the quoted speech and its perspective into the speech and attitude of the homilist. Here, Kirill deliberately blurs the borderlines in order to achieve some distinct rhetorical effects. Characteristically, he does not strive to separate the different perspectives and stances in order to affirm one or dispute another, but seeks, rather, to combine them within the represented speech and make clear his position by way of juxtaposition, confrontation, and the establishment of meaningful parallels.

In this way, the 'dramatic sermonist' is able to proclaim his homiletic 'truth' in an engaging fashion. The individual speaker's commitment to the truth of what is asserted is constantly subject to evaluation and variation. In other words, the homilist's speech-reporting strategies create a dynamism of evaluative stances and attitudes which maximize the participation of the audience by stimulating their perceptual, emotional, and cognitive involvement.

Relic or Strategy: The Middle Dutch Sermon as a Literary Phenomenon

THOM MERTENS

Medieval sermons are delivered to us through manuscripts and printed editions. They are recognizable as sermons because they distinguish themselves from other text-genres by certain specific characteristics which they have in common with spoken sermons. In this manner, the sermon as a text-genre is defined by the correspondences and analogies with the sermon as a (para)liturgical act, i.e. by its predicatory features.

The written sermon is considered one of the most important means to study the spoken sermon, because *vox audita cito perit, littera autem scripta diu manet.*[1] Often, written and spoken sermons are identified under the silent assumption that statements on the former apply equally to the latter, and vice versa. As a consequence, the written sermon can be perceived only as an incomplete representation of spoken sermon, as described in the *artes praedicandi*. The written sermon is not often understood as a literary genre with its own characteristics and conventions, including the content, structure of the headings, and the organization of sermon collections. The study of the written sermon should focus on the actual transmitted texts, not viewing them primarily from the perspective of the *artes praedicandi*, that privilege the spoken word. By recognizing the difference between

I wish to thank my colleagues Prof. Dr Christoph Burger (Vrije Universiteit Amsterdam), Dr Wybren Scheepsma (Universiteit Leiden), Patricia Stoop (Ruusbroecgenootschap, Universiteit Antwerpen) and Prof. Dr Paul Wackers (Universiteit Utrecht) for their comments on an earlier version of this paper.

[1] Thomas Hemerken a Kempis, *Opera omnia*, ed. by M. J. Pohl (Freiburg i.Br.: Herder, 1902–22), IV, p. 185, l. 7–8: 'The voice one hears, quickly dies away, but written text stays for a long time.'

the spoken and written sermon, we can acknowledge the contributions of women. Women were not allowed to deliver sermons in a liturgical setting, but writing and editing sermons seem to have offered more opportunities to them, as we will see.

The silent identification of the spoken and written sermon blurs on the one side the question of what we actually know about preaching itself, and on the other side the question of the proper characteristics, conventions, and functions of the written sermon. Literary analysis is especially appropriate for evaluation of the written sermon and assessment of the relationships between the written word and oral delivery. The aim of this article is to show that distinguishing between spoken and written sermons can clarify matters considerably. Here, Middle Dutch sermons serve as the materials for illustration, thus giving these texts a wider renown. Before beginning, let us define some important terms.

In the first place, for our convenience and for the sake of clarity, I will use the word *preaching* to designate the spoken sermon, and the word *sermon* for the written text.[2] For the sake of stylistic variation, I will also use the phrases *spoken*, *delivered* or *given*, and *written sermon*.

Furthermore, the concept 'Middle Dutch sermon' has to be delineated. By *sermon* we mean a text which is designated as a sermon by its heading, colophon or in any other way, unless it is clear from its other features that it is not a sermon. This restriction is made because all designations have more than one meaning (e.g. Middle Dutch *sermoen* also can be used for 'speech, utterance'). On the other hand, texts without such a designation, but clearly showing characteristics of liturgical or paraliturgical preaching, also are considered to be sermons. Here, features of style, structure, and content are involved, like an authoritative 'I' addressing a multiple audience, reference to a liturgical 'here and now', a *thema* and *divisio* at the beginning of the text, the appearance of *rationes*, *auctoritates*, and *exempla* in its body, and the typical petition at the end, usually indirectly addressing the Father, the Son, and the Holy Ghost.

By *Middle Dutch* we mean a group of dialects, spoken and written, during three centuries (*c.* 1250–*c.* 1550) in several parts of the Low Countries, i.e. Flanders, Brabant, Limburg, Zeeland, Holland, and perhaps also the Sticht (roughly equivalent to the modernday province of Utrecht). The boundaries between Middle Dutch and German, and chronologically between Middle Dutch and New Dutch are vague.[3] The history of the Middle Dutch sermon starts only a few decades before 1300, from which the earliest preserved specimens date.

---

[2] This distinction and its terminology are inspired by Gerrit Cornelis Zieleman, *Midderlnederlandse epistel- en evangeliepreken*, (Leiden: Brill, 1978), pp. 18–22, pp. 9–10, and G. C. Zieleman, 'Prediking, predikatie, preek: een begripsbepaling', *Kerk en Theologie*, 30 (1979), 115–22.

[3] F. A. Stoett, *Middelnederlandsche spraakkunst: Syntaxis*, 3rd edn (Den Haag: Nijhoff, 1923; repr. 1974), p. 1; A. van Loey, *Middelnederlandse spraakkunst*, I: *Vormleer* (Groningen: Wolters-Noordhoff, 1969), p. 1–3.

Texts as a Basis for the Spoken Sermon

It is likely that preachers, at least sometimes, used their own notes in preaching.[4] As far as we know, there is only one such scheme preserved, and it is even questionable whether this is a scheme serving preaching, because there is no heading mentioning this, of course.[5] It is a list of items in Latin, with some points in Middle Dutch, on paper (14.5 × 21 cm), folded in four. As appears from the writing, this leaf has to be dated in the second half of the fifteenth century. It was found lying loosely in the rent-roll (lease book) of Leeuwenhorst, a convent of Cistercian nuns near Noordwijkerhout in Holland. It remains to be seen whether we can classify preaching schemes like this as sermons.[6] The term *preachable text* represents its function more precisely and is also a broader term because it is not limited to schemes but comprises all texts serving as a basis for preaching.[7] Preachable texts had a practical function, and because of this, they had little chance to survive to the present day. This already slight chance was further reduced by the material form (fly leaves, roll and loose quires) of these draughts, outlines, schemes, and lists.

Preachers did not only use their own notes, but they also employed the texts of others. This brings us to the phenomenon of the model sermons. There are examples of German model sermons reaching back to the ninth century, written in the context of Charlemagne's efforts at Christianization. These sermons were destined for poorly educated clerics. In the course of the thirteenth century, there were also sermons written as reading material for those who were not clerics. The history of the Middle

---

[4] Janne Colijns (see below, quotation at footnote 34) for instance mentions 'rolls, letters and old quires written by the hand of the preacher himself' (*rollen, brieven ende ouden quaternen ghescreven metter hant des selven predicaers*, Brussels, Koninklijke Bibliotheek, MS II 298, fol. 5r).

[5] Picture, edition and discussion by G. de Moor, 'Een Leeuwenhorster preek- of conferentieschema', *Cîteaux: Commentarii Cistercienses*, 35 (1984), 248–57. The texts from the Bethlehem convent near Doetinchem have to be studied, but they do not seem to be concepts, as said by E. Verwijs and J. Verdam, *Middelnederlandsch Woordenboek* (The Hague: Nijhoff, 1885–1952), X: *Bouwstoffen*, p. 354 (art. 776). Five of these sermons were edited by Willem Laurens Bouwmeester, *Het klooster Bethlehem bij Doetinchem (Met tekstuitgave van vijf sermoenen uit het convent afkomstig)* (Doetinchem: Misset 1903), pp. 179–81, 234–82 (edition).

[6] At the end of this paper, in the section, 'The Sermon as a Literary Genre', we will return to this problem.

[7] I borrow the term *preachable text* from G. C. Zieleman, 'Overleveringsvormen van middeleeuwse preken in de landstaal', *Nederlands Archief voor Kerkgeschiedenis*, n.s. 59 (1978–1979), 11–20 (p. 14, n. 15: *predikatietekst*).

Dutch sermon begins here and as a result, there are no collections in Middle Dutch serving primarily as model sermons for preaching. Every written sermon could of course again be delivered orally and could be taken thus as a model sermon. Indeed this was done. It is known that Geert Grote (1340–1384), one of the founding fathers of the Modern Devotion, delivered by heart a sermon of Bernard of Clairvaux:

> Optimam habuit [sc. Gerardus Magnus] memoriam, ut sanctorum patrum sermones, quos semel tantum legisset, cum id placuisset, memoriter retineret. Denique in synodo Traiectensi sermonem beati Bernaerdi de conversione sancti Pauli: 'Saule, Saule, quid me persequeris', de verbo ad verbum coram clero unviserso publice predicavit.[8]

This case proves that existing sermons, which were not meant as model sermons, were taken as a basis for preaching, and one can assume that this could also be done with vernacular sermons.

Even texts that were not at all written as sermons were used in preaching. On the fly leaf of a copy of an incunable *Tboeck vanden leven ons heeren Jhesu Christi* ('The book of the life of Our Lord Jesus Christ')[9], a Middle Dutch 'testament of

---

[8] Johannes Busch, *Liber de origine devotionis modernae*, ch. I, cf. *Des Augustinerpropstes Iohannes Busch Chronicon Windeshemense und Liber de reformatione monasteriorum*, ed. by Karl Grube (Halle: Hendel, 1886; repr. 1968), p. 252: 'He (sc. Geert Grote) had a very good memory, and so he could retain in his memory the sermons of holy fathers, which he had read only once, if he wanted. In this way he delivered in a synod at Utrecht the sermon of Saint Bernard on the conversion of Saint Paul "Saule, Saule, quid me persequeris" (Acts 9. 4), verbatim publicly for the whole clergy.' Middle Dutch translation: *Hy [nl. Geert Grote] hadde ene seer guede memorie, soe dat hy die sermonen der hilligher vaders die hy alleen eens ghelesen hadde, alst hem genoeghede in der memorien onthielt. Hier om in den synodus ende vergaderinghe der clerckscap toe Utrecht predikede hy opelike dat sermoen Sunt Bernts van der bekieringhe Sunte Pauwels: Saule, Saule, waerom vervolgheste my (Acts 9. 4), van woerde toe woerde voer die ghemeyne clerckscap.* Utrecht, Universiteitsbibliotheek, MS 8 L 16, fol. 5, cf. *Het Frensweger handschrift met viten van moderne devoten*, ed. by W. J. Alberts and A. L. Hulshoff (Groningen: Wolters, 1958), p. 7) Probably the sermon *In conversione Sancti Pauli* is meant, from the *Sermones per annum*, cf. *Sancti Bernardi Opera*, ed. by J. Leclerq and H. Rochais (Rome: Editiones Cisterciences, 1957–98) IV, pp. 327–34. There is also a much shorter *Sermo in conversione Sancti Pauli* between the *Sermones varii* (ibid., VI–1, pp. 28–29), but the theme of Acts 4. 6 plays only a marginal role in it. On Geert Grote: P. van Zijl, *Gerard Groote, Ascetic and Reformer (1340–1384)* (Washington: Catholic University of America Press, 1963), esp. pp. 156–69 on Grote's preaching; R. R. Post, *The Modern Devotion: Confrontation with Reformation and Humanism* (Leiden: Brill, 1968), pp. 51–196; Georgette Epiney Burgard, *Gérard Grote (1340–1384) et les débuts de la Dévotion moderne* (Wiesbaden: Steiner, 1970), esp. pp. 182–94 on Grote's preaching.

[9] Printed in Antwerp by Gheraert Leeu on 3 November 1487. Copy: Huntington Library, San Marino, CA, mentioned by Herman Pleij, *De sneeuwpoppen van 1511: Literatuur en stadscultuur tussen middeleeuwen en moderne tijd* (Amsterdam: Meulenhoff; Leuven: Kritak, 1988), p. 400, n. 24. Herman Pleij was so kind to provide me with a photocopy and a

Christ', is written with a note that the famous Dirc Coelde of Münster (d. 1515) preached this text on Good Friday of the year 1488:

> Dit was aldus bescreven te Bruesselle uuytten monde van brueder Dierick van Munstere, minderbruer vander observancien van Bootendale int jair ons heeren dusent CCCC LXXXVII opten goeden vrydach voir den paesschen LXXXVIII des nachts int predecken vander passien in sentthe Goedellen kercke.[10]

This case is somewhat complicated. We have a text, not written to be preached, which was nevertheless used in preaching. This text we know through a transcription of the spoken sermon, i.e. through a written sermon. The text constitution of this testament of Christ is very good, and one can doubt whether this transcription perhaps just pretends to be a transcription of the spoken sermon, but in fact is based on a written text of the testament.[11]

To summarize, preaching schemes and other preachable texts seem to be preserved rarely, and if so, they are difficult to recognize as such. In German there were collections of model sermons composed for clerics who were less educated, but in Middle Dutch no collections seem to have been composed to serve this purpose primarily. Yet there is evidence that existing sermons were used as model texts for preaching. Sometimes even texts were preached which were not at all written for this purpose.

---

transcription of this unedited sermon.

[10] 'Thus this was written at Brussels from the mouth of brother Dirc of Münster, Friar Minor Observant from Botendael, in the year of Our Lord 1487 on Good Friday before Easter of 1488 at night during the preaching of the passion in the church of Saint Goedele.'—Pleij, *Sneeuwpoppen*, p. 400 n. 24 designates the text mistakenly as the well-known 'Letter of Christ', also known as the 'Letter fallen down from heaven' (which was, besides, also preached, cf. R. Jansen-Sieben, 'Ooggetuigen en flagellanten anno 1349', in *De pest in de Nederlanden: Medisch historische beschouwingen 650 jaar na de Zwarte Dood* (Brussels: Koninklijke Academie voor Geneeskunde van België, 1999), pp. 85–108 (p. 100) [also published in *Koninklijke Academie voor Geneeskunde van België: Verhandelingen*, 61 (1999), 175–98 (p. 190)]). On Dirc Coelde: P. J. Goyens, *Un héros du Vieux-Bruxelles, le bienheureux Thiérri Coelde († 1515). Notes et documents* (Malines: S. François, 1929) (pp. 54–92: edition of four sermons); Benjamin de Troeyer, *Bio-bibliographia Franciscana Neerlandica ante saeculum XVI* (Nieuwkoop: De Graaf, 1974), pp. 196–248; Dietrich Schmidtke, 'Dietrich von Münster', in *Die deutsche Literatur des Mittelalters. Verfasserlexikon*, ed. by Kurt Ruh and others, 2nd edn. (Berlin: De Gruyter, 1978-), II, cols. 139–40; Benjamin de Troeyer, 'Kolde (Colde; Coelde), Dietrich, von Osnabrück; von Münster', in *Verfasserlexikon*, V, cols. 19–26.

[11] The text of Dirc Coelde's sermon is not yet edited and the relation to other versions of Christ's testament are not yet studied.

Texts Based on Spoken Sermons

Preachable texts were composed in Middle Dutch both by preachers and listeners. We start here with an illuminating example of a preacher who wrote out his preaching himself. The treatise *Eene oufeninghe vander gracien gods* ('An exercise on the grace of God') is preserved in five manuscripts, and in one of them we find this colophon:

> Dit leste sermoen van gods gracie heeft ghepredict meyster Gosen, doctor in theologi, broder vanden kermeliten t'Utrecht *(added in the margin:* ende na bisscop etc.*)* ende heeftet om beden wil enighe personen ghescreven anno seven ende tsestich *(afterwards completed between the lines with:* M CCCC *and next with* anno Domini M°CCCC° LXVII°), dair dit uut is ghescreven.[12]

This colophon reveals the author of the text: the Carmelite Goswinus Hex, Doctor of Divinity, who became suffragan bishop of Utrecht in 1469.[13] More important to us is, nevertheless, that the finding of this reference to preaching leads to a revision of the view on this treatise.[14] The editor characterized this text in his edition as 'a little treatise from the age of scholasticism and chivalry', but as Robrecht Lievens observed, the text appears to be about one and a half centuries later, and what is more, it appears not to be a treatise but the written reproduction of a spoken sermon.[15] This written sermon clearly shows a lack of predicatory features, although written by the preacher himself according to the colophon.

---

[12] The Hague, Koninklijke Bibliotheek, MS 128 D 9, fol. 293^{r} (dated 1469), cited in Robrecht Lievens, 'Een sermoen van de latere Utrechtse wijbisschop Goswinus Hex', *Spiegel der Letteren*, 7 (1963–64), 44–50 (p. 47): 'The latter sermon on the grace of God was delivered by master Gosen, doctor in theology, brother of the Carmelites in Utrecht *(added in margin:* and afterwards bishop, etc.*)* and he has written it down on the request of some persons in the year sixty-seven *(afterwards completed between the lines with* M CCCC *and next with* anno Domini M°CCCC°LXVII°), and this is copied from that.'

[13] Goswinus Hex was born in Loenhout. He became a Carmelite in Vlissingen, studied theology in Paris and obtained there his doctor's degree. In 1460 he was lector and prior in Vlissingen. In 1469 he became the suffragan bishop of Utrecht. He died in Utrecht on 31 March 1475. Cf. Irenaeus Rosier, *Biographisch & bibliographisch overzicht van de vroomheid in de Nederlandse carmel van 1235 tot het midden der achttiende eeuw* (Tielt: Lannoo, 1950), p. 61 (no. XCII); and Lievens, 'Hex', p. 47–48.

[14] I borrow the term *preachable reference* from G. C. Zieleman, 'Preken als literaire documenten', in Thom Mertens and others, *Boeken voor de eeuwigheid: Middelnederlands geestelijk proza* (Amsterdam: Prometheus, 1993), pp. 70–86, 388–95 (notes, bibliography) (p. 72: *predikatiereferentie*).

[15] L. Reypens, 'Nog een merkwaardig Diets tractaatje uit de scholastische en ridderlijke periode. Eene oufeninghe vander gracien Gods', *Ons Geestelijk Erf*, 34 (1960), 241–70;

There are many texts which are characterized as sermons by their heading or colophon, but in spite of this, have few or no predicatory features. The study of medieval German sermons has raised this problem repeatedly (*Mängel der Predigtform*). For many years, it was supposed that this lack of predicatory features was due to the fact that listeners wrote out the spoken sermon. Preaching could not be noted down verbatim because in the Late Middle Ages, there was no kind of shorthand, and no one would be able to copy out an entire spoken sermon from memory verbatim. Therefore, Paul-Gerhard Völker suggested another explanation in 1963. The preachers themselves, and not the listeners, would have written out their preachable texts, and they would have done this correctly. During transmission, however, the sermons would have been damaged, a circumstance common to almost all spiritual prose in the vernacular.[16]

Hex's sermon clearly shows a lack of predicatory features, although, according to the colophon, the preacher himself wrote it. The absence of predicatory features can hardly be ascribed to a deficient transmission of the text, because the same colophon says that the sermon in the codex is a direct copy of the apograph made by the preacher on request. The manuscript with the colophon dates from 1469, i.e. two years after the sermon was delivered. This case proves that a lack of preaching features does not at all have to be explained by listeners noting down preaching, or from a deficient text transmission. Even when preachers themselves afterwards wrote out their preachable texts, they could omit preaching features. Actually this can be expected. Others (listeners?) had asked for a copy because of the content of the preaching. To convey this content, predicatory features are unnecessary. Preaching as an oral, (para)liturgical medium makes its own demands which can be neglected when the content is conveyed in writing. As far as such written sermons still contain preaching features, these features have to be regarded as relics from the original form.

Hex's sermon does not seem a special case, and it is representative of the few other sermons which have been written down and preserved separate from a sermon collection. Other examples are the sermon on the heap of gold by the Dominican

---

Lievens, 'Hex'.

[16] Paul-Gerhard Völker, 'Die Überlieferungsformen mittelalterlicher deutscher Predigten', *Zeitschrift für deutsches Altertum*, 92 (1963), 212–27 (p. 214). The older vision was worded by Wolfgang Stammler, 'Mittelalterliche Prosa in deutscher Sprache', in *Deutsche Philologie im Aufriss*, ed. by Wolfgang Stammler, 2nd edn. (Berlin: Schmidt, 1960–69), II, col. 981–82. Völker also thinks that the importance of the *artes praedicandi* for the vernacular sermon is overestimated. The fact that written sermons do not meet the prescriptions of the *artes praedicandi*, would not be caused by a difference between spoken and written sermon, but by the fact that the *artes* represent a very theoretical tradition which had no importance for preaching practice. Cf. Paul-Gerhard Völker, *Die deutschen Schriften des Franziskaners Konrad Bömlin*. Vol. I *Überlieferung und Untersuchung* (München: Beck, 1964), pp. 179–81.

Friar Nikolaus of Strasbourg, based on a sermon delivered at Leuven somewhere in the years 1324–31, and the sermon of Henry of Cleve, which we find in a manuscript from 1348.[17] These sermons confirm what is explicit in Hex's sermon. In these sermons, predicatory features also are irrelevant to written transmission of the content.

The number of separately preserved Middle Dutch sermons is comparatively very small. Undoubtedly, far more prose treatises will have been derived from preaching, but this cannot be concluded from their form. When there is no preaching reference, these texts present themselves as short treatises. It is quite normal that spoken sermons, when they are noted down, lose their specific characteristics, thus fading to the less specific prose form which we call treatises. The absence of preaching features, therefore, is not a lack, but a normal procedure which does not need explanation.

As we have seen now, it is quite normal to find no preaching features when preachers themselves write out their spoken sermons. What do we see when listeners copy out what they have heard preached?

In the *Devotio moderna*, it was common for father confessors on the afternoon of holidays to deliver a collation, i.e. a non-liturgical exhortation.[18] In sisterbooks of the *Devotio moderna* we read about sisters taking notes on their wax tablets during these exhortations of their father confessor.[19] Thus Sister Liesbeth of Delft (d. 1423) is

[17] Stephanus Axters, 'De preek op den gulden berg door den leesmeester van Straatsburg', *Tijdschrift voor Taal en Letteren*, 28 (1940), 5–58. Christoph Burger, 'Verassende genadeleer: Nikolaus van Straatsburg, OP: De preek over de gulden berg' (in print). The (unedited) sermon of Henry of Kleve is preserved in Amsterdam, Universiteitsbibliotheek, UvA, MS I G 41, fols 267vb–270va: *Dit es broeder heinrijcs van cleven sermoen*. Cf. J. Deschamps, *Middelnederlandse handschriften uit Europese en Amerikaanse bibliotheken*, 2nd edn (Leiden: Brill, 1972), pp. 149–51 (no. 48).

[18] Post, *Modern Devotion*, pp. 236–37, 244–45, 593. On the collations in the *Devotio moderna*: Thom Mertens, 'Collatio und Codex im Bereich der Devotio moderna', in *Der Codex im Gebrauch (Akten des Internationalen Kolloquiums 11.–13. Juni 1992)*, ed. by Christel Meier, Dagmar Hüpper and Hagen Keller (München: Fink, 1996), pp. 163–82; T. Mertens, 'The Modern Devotion and Innovation in Middle Dutch Literature', in *Medieval Dutch Literature in its European Context*, ed. by Erik Kooper (Cambridge: Cambridge University Press, 1994), pp. 226–41 (pp. 233).

[19] Sisterbooks (German: *Schwesternbücher*) are collections of short biographies portraying sisters of a particular convent. Their function is to create a common history, and by this a shared identity, by keeping alive the memory of the predecessors. The sisterbooks propagated virtues like humility and mutual obedience, also in this manner building the community. On German sisterbooks: Gertrud Jaron Lewis, *By Women, for Women, about Women: The Sister-Books of Fourteenth-Century Germany*, Studies and Texts, 125 (Toronto: Pontifical Institute of Mediaeval Studies, 1996). On the sisterbook of the *Devotio moderna*: Wybren Scheepsma, '"Verzamelt de overgebleven brokken, opdat niets verloren ga." Over Latijnse en Middelnederlandse levensbeschrijvingen uit de sfeer van de Moderne Devotie', in Paul

said to take notes during the collations of the father confessor, Johannes Brinckerinck (d. 1419):

> In groter reverencien ende weerdicheit hadde sij hoer oversten ende wat sij hoer segeden, dat nam sij als uut den monde godes. Ende alse onse vader collacie dede, soe sat sij ende schrief hem dat uutten monde in hoer tafel. Ende dat meeste dat wy van alsulken schriften hebben, dat heeft sie vergadert.[20]

Something comparable is also witnessed in other sisters, e.g. Alijt Bruuns (*c.* 1450?):

Wackers and others, *Verraders en bruggenbouwers: Verkenningen naar de relatie tussen Latinitas en Middelnederlandse letterkunde* (Amsterdam: Prometheus, 1996), pp. 211–38 and 334–46; Wybren Scheepsma, *Deemoed en devotie: De koorvrouwen van Windesheim en hun geschriften* (Amsterdam: Prometheus, 1997), pp. 121–52, 240–45, 306–14; English translation in preparation: Wybren Scheepsma, *Modern Devotion: The Canonnesses of Windesheim and their Writings* (Woodbridge, Suffolk: Boydell & Brewer), ch. 6; Kurt Ruh, *Geschichte der abendländischen Mystik. Vierter Band: Die niederländische Mystik des 14. bis 16. Jahrhunderts*. München, 1999, pp. 313–22; Thom Mertens, 'Het Diepenveense zusterboek als exponent van gemeenschapstichtende kloosterliteratuur', in *Het ootmoedig fundament van Diepenveen: Zeshonderd jaar Maria en Sint-Agnesklooster, 1400–2000*, ed. by Wybren Scheepsma (Kampen: IJsselacademie, 2002), pp. 77–94, 141–43 (notes), 165–66 (bibliography). An English translation of the prologue and some biographies from the beginning and from the end of the Deventer sisterbook: *Devotio Moderna: Basic Writings*, trans. and introd. by John Van Engen (New York / Mahwah: Paulist Press), pp. 121–36.

[20] Sisterbook of Diepenveen, copy of the Meester-Geertshouse at Deventer (MS D), cf. *Van den doechden der vuriger ende stichtiger susteren van Diepen veen ("Handschrift D")*, ed. by D. A. Brinkerink (Leiden: Sijthoff, [1904]), pp. 253–54: 'She held her superiors in great reverence and took what they said to her as if from the mouth of God. And when our father gave his exhortation, she sat and wrote it from his mouth on her tablet. And most of what we have of such writings she collected.' Cf. Sisterbook of Diepenveen, copy of the convent at Diepenveen (MS DV: Deventer, Stads- en Athenaeumbibliotheek, Suppl. 198 (101 E 26)), fols. 58^{v}–59^{r}: *Als onse eerwerdighe pater heer Johan Brinckerinck clacie plach toe done, soe sat suster Elizabet ende scref dat uut synen monde in hoer tafele. Ende dat selve dat wy daer van hebben, heeft sie meestlick vergadert* ('When our reverend father Johannes Brinckerinck used to deliver his collation, sister Elizabet sat down and wrote that from his mouth on her tablet. And most of what we have of it she collected'). On the collations of Brinckerinck: T. F. C. Mertens, 'Postuum auteurschap. De collaties van Johannes Brinckerinck', in *Windesheim 1395–1995: Kloosters, teksten, invloeden: Voordrachten gehouden tijdens het internationale congres '600 jaar Kapittel van Windesheim', 27 mei 1995 te Zwolle*, ed. by A. J. Hendrikman and others (Nijmegen: Katholieke Universiteit Nijmegen, Centrum voor Middeleeuwse Studies, 1996), pp. 85–97. An English translation of some of Brinckerinck's collations: *Devotio Moderna*, trans. by Van Engen, pp. 223–34.

> Seer begherlick was sie dat waert gades toe horen inder clacien ende die marclicste[21] punten scrief sie in hoer tafele om die toe ontholden ende na op pappier toe scriven.[22]

Sister Liesbeth of Delft, like Alijt Bruuns, supposedly noted down separate points. The texts of Brinckerinck, which in the manuscripts are presented to us as being his collations, show no preaching features and even hardly any structure. It is a string of paratactically ordered passages. In the manuscripts, these passages of Brinckerinck are grouped thematically. The nine thematic groups are called 'collations'.[23] Afterwards they have been re-edited slightly by Rudolf Dier of Muiden (d. 1459), an indirect successor of Brinckerinck. In Dier's version they consist of a prologue and eight 'collations'.[24] Text material derived from preaching is involved here, but in both versions preaching characteristics are completely absent. Noting down these loose passages, the sisters tried to record the content of the collations in order to interiorize them. Doing this, they did not try to preserve the whole text structure, but they limited themselves to the citations which were meaningful to them personally and could serve as a basis for the *ruminatio* of short texts to discover and internalize their deeper meaning. This personal, selective approach of all one heard and read was taught systematically as the pre-eminent way to acquire the content of texts.[25] To listeners, the same applies as to preachers: the content was the issue, not the preaching form. When listeners noted down spoken sermons, they left aside the predicatory features, just as the preachers themselves did.

Nevertheless we also find sermons, written out by listeners, which present the complete stock of preaching characteristics. Claus of Euskirchen (d. 1520) was the

---

[21] The manuscript reads *maclicste* ('most easy') here. This is emendated by the present author (T. M.) to *marclicste* ('most notable') according to the designation *puncta notabilia*, which was common use in the *Devotio moderna*.

[22] Sisterbook Diepenveen (MS DV), fol. 81v: 'She had a strong desire to hear the word of God in the exhortation, and she wrote the most notable points on her tablet in order to remember them and afterwards write them on paper.'

[23] Edition: 'Acht collatiën van Johannes Brinckerinck, een bijdrage tot de kennis van den kanselarbeid der Broeders van het Gemeene Leven, uit handschriften der vijftiende en zestiende eeuw medegedeeld', ed. by W. Moll, *Kerkhistorisch Archief*, 4 (1866), 97–167; to be complemented with '"Van swighen", eene collatie van Jan Brinckerinck', ed. by Willem de Vreese, *Het Belfort*, 13 (1898), 231–35.

[24] Edition: 'De collaties van Johannes Brinckerinck', ed. by Ingrid Nagels (unpublished licentiate thesis, University of Antwerp, 1999).

[25] On the function of single points in the spirituality of the *Devotio moderna*: Thom Mertens, 'Lezen met de pen: Ontwikkelingen in het laatmiddeleeuws geestelijk proza', in *De studie van de Middelnederlandse letterkunde: Stand en toekomst: Symposium Antwerpen 22–24 September 1988*, ed. by F. P. van Oostrom and F. Willaert (Hilversum: Verloren, 1989), pp. 187–200; Mertens, 'Modern Devotion', pp. 229–30.

father confessor of two sister houses in Deventer. From one convent, the Master-Geertshouse, originated 312 separate points from his collations.[26] From the other convent, the Buiskens-house, we possess nineteen fairly complete sermons. The texts in the manuscripts of the two sisterhouses are not related to each other. Apparently each collection is derived separately from the sermons given by Euskirchen in the convent concerned.[27] The manuscript containing the nineteen complete sermons displays autographical characteristics, like stylistic corrections and marginal additions of *auctoritates* written with the hand of the copyist. At first sight, one is inclined to conclude that the preacher himself, Claus of Euskirchen, has written out these sermons, and this manuscript is his autograph. This, however, cannot be the case, because the same hand which wrote the corrections and additions, also wrote the rubrics: *Hier beghynnen suverlike punten uut sommighe collacien onses eerweerdigen vaders here Clawes van Euskerke* ('Here begin fine points from some collations of our respectable father Reverend Claus of Euskirchen').[28] Euskirchen would never call himself 'our respectable father', and this means the autograph is not written by him, but by someone who calls him 'our respectable father', therefore by one of the sisters of the convent. In this way, this manuscript proves sisters not only noted down loose points, but apparently also were able to write out complete sermons.

Another manuscript explicitly says that a sister wrote out the collations of the father confessor of her convent:

> *(in red:)* Item dit boeck waert ghescreven int jaer ons heren doe men screef dusent vyfhondert en XVIII en waert gheeynt des donredaechs nae beloken paesschen.
>
> *(in black:)* Item dese collacien heeft suster Agnees van Enghelen alleen onthouden van onsen lieven eerwerdighen vader heer Bernaert en den convent ghelaten den ghenen horen orber in te doen die daer minne toe hebben. En si heeft begheert dattet sal blyven in die leberye en dattet anders nyemont voer syn eyghen houden en sal, want syt alleen becosticht en bearbeyt heeft.

---

[26] 'Goede punten uit de collatiën van Claus van Euskerken (naar hs. no. 686 der Provinciale Bibliotheek van Friesland', ed. by D. A. Brinkerink, *Nederlandsch Archief voor Kerkgeschiedenis*, n.s. 3 (1905), 225–395.

[27] Thom Mertens, 'Ein Prediger in zweifacher Ausführung: Die Kollationen des Claus von Euskirchen', in *Predigt im Kontext: Internationale Fachtagung am Fachbereich Germanistik der Freien Universität Berlin vom 5.–8. Dezember 1996*, ed. by Volker Mertens and Hans-Jochen Schiewer (Tübingen: Niemeyer, forthcoming).

[28] Den Haag, Museum Meermanno-Westreenianum, MS 10 E 48, fol. IV^{v}; cf. fol. 245^{v}: *Hier eynden sommige punten uut onses eerwerdigen vaders here Clawes van Euskerken collacien* ('Here end some points from collations of our respectable father Reverend Claus of Euskirchen').

> En om die minne gods een ave maria voer die scryftster want si cleyn van doechden is M Gro.[29]

For this remarkable fact that sisters wrote out complete sermons of their father confessor, we find more evidence in the sermon collections of the Jericho-convent at Brussels, a convent of Canonnesses.[30] Around 1460 the father confessor, Jan Storm (d. 1488), reformed the spiritual life in this convent. The sermons of this first, inspiring rector of the reformed convent are preserved, provided with a remarkable and interesting prologue:

> Inden name ons heren Jhesu Christi, wien alle knyen gheboecht werden in hemele ende inder eerden ende oec inder hellen, soe hebic dit navolgende boec ghepijnt te vergaderen uut veel collacien die in onsen godshuyse gepredict sijn binnen vijf jaren van eenen weerdigen priester die ons commissarijs was ende biechtvader bi ons stont; niet alsoe te verstaen hi en heefter binnen desen tide ende voer dese jaren voerseit al veel meer ghepredict dan icker uut oft af ghescreven hebben, dwelc mi dicke berouwen heeft geweest dat icker niet meer af onthouden en hebbe om te scriven, aenghemerct die menichfuldege sorghe, uutwendighen last ende arbeit daer hi doen ter tijd met becommert was als hi hem nochtan te deser inwendeger occupatien gaf tot welken hem dwanc die minne van sinen scaepkens, welken hi niet ontrecken en wilde dat voetsel der zielen want hi mindese inden inaderen Christi.
>
> Maer dat ic uuten gronde mins herten beclage, es dat ic soe plomp van begripe ben dat ic alle die scone redenen ende auctorijteyten der heilegen welke hi in sinen sermoenen alligeerde, niet en heb connen van woerde te woerde onthouden om te scriven soe hise

---

[29] The Hague, Koninklijke Bibliotheek, MS 133 M 128, fol. 210^v, cited in G. I. Lieftinck, *Manuscrits datés conservés dans les Pays-Bas*, vol. II, ed. by J. P. Gumbert (Leiden: Brill, 1988), p. 134 (no. 508), planche 895 (picture of fols. 1^r and 8^v): *(in red:)* 'Item, this book was written in the year of our Lord when one wrote one-thousand five-hundred and XVIII, and was finished on the Thursday following the Sunday after Easter.' *(in black:)* 'Item, sister Agnees of Engelen, all by herself, retained these collations of our dear reverend father Bernard and left them to the convent for those who like to profit from it. And she desired that it would remain in the library and also that no-one should keep it as her own, because she herself payed for it and did the work. And, for the Love of God, an Ave Maria for the scribe, since she is scant in virtue. M Gro'. *M. Gro* probably indicates the name of the copyist, possibly Mary Groters, who in the year 1531 wrote Leiden, Universiteitsbibliotheek, MS Ltk. 604 (*ibid*., p. 160 nr 576).

[30] More elaborate on this subject in Middle Dutch literature: Thom Mertens, 'Ghostwriting Sisters: The Preservation of Dutch Sermons of Father Confessors in the Fifteenth and the Early Sixteenth Century', in *Seeing and Knowing: Women and Learning in Medieval Europe 1250–1550*, ed. by Anneke Mulder-Bakker (Turnhout: Brepols, 2004). Völker, 'Überlieferungsformen', p. 217–20, already mentioned sermon collections written out by sisters out of reverence for their father confessors. Völker regarded it as a rather unusual form of sermon writing. Patricia Stoop (University of Antwerp) is studying the Jericho sermon collections.

> schone uutleide. Maer alleen soe hebic den bloeten sin daer af ghepijnt te onthouden soe ic naest conste. [...][31]

In this prologue a nun, Maria van Pee, renders an account of writing out the spoken sermons of the father confessor. She apologizes for any shortcomings in her work. The sermons are not all as deficient as one would expect from reading this prologue. On the contrary, we find very complete sermons, with many predicatory features, including an authoritative 'I' of the preacher addressing an audience. These predicatory features are not just relics, but were deliberately preserved or even heightened. As she writes down and edits the sermons, the nun takes over the role of the father confessor completely.

More sermon collections of father confessors and preachers from outside the convent who preached in the convent church are preserved from the same nunnery.[32] Usually the heading of the sermons mentions the name of the preacher, on which occasion he delivered his sermon and the year he did so. Two of these collections are also preceded by a prologue in which sisters account for their writing down sermons.[33] They claim to have done so for themselves in the first place, in order to

---

[31] Brussels, Koninklijke Bibliotheek, MS 4367–68, fol. 3^{r-v}: 'In the name of our Lord Jesus Christ, to whom every knee shall bow in heaven and in earth and also in hell *(cf. Philippians 2. 10)*, I have tried to compile the following book from many collations which were preached in our house of God within five years by a worthy priest who was our commissary and stood confessor to us; one should not understand this to mean that he did not preach much more during this time and before the years in question than I have written out or copied, and indeed I have often regretted that I have not retained more of them to write down, considering the manifold cares, external (i.e. material) burdens and toil with which he was encumbered, and yet nevertheless gave himself to this inner (i.e. spiritual) occupation. The love of his little sheep compelled him to it; he did not wish to withhold from them that food for the soul, since he loved them in the innermost heart (literally: innards) of Christ. But what I do lament from the bottom of my heart is that I am so dull in my wits that all the beautiful reasonings, and the authorities of the saints which he adduced in his sermons, I have not been able to retain word for word so as to write them down as he explained them so beautifully. But I only tried to retain the bare sense of them as best I could. [...]'. The sermons were delivered in the years 1459–64. The collection was completed on or before 10 August 1466.

[32] The Middle Dutch manuscripts of the Jericho convent are very well preserved in comparison to other convents. Sermon collections are a large part of them and the sisters seem to have had a special interest in them. Cf. Karl Stooker and Theo Verbeij, *Collecties op orde: Middelnederlandse handschriften uit kloosters en semi-religieuze gemeenschappen in de Nederlanden* (Leuven: Peeters, 1997), I, pp. 230–31, II, pp. 79–90.

[33] Gent, Universiteitsbibliotheek, MS 902 (convent of Jericho, 1479): prologue by sister Margriet of Steenbergen CanA; Brussels, Koninklijke Bibliotheek, MS II 298, (convent of Jericho, 1507): prologue by sister Janne Colijns CanA. The third sermon collection with a prologue (of Maria van Pee) is already mentioned above.

internalize the preaching better. Their justification centres primarily on the 'publication' of the sermons for internal use within the convent.

In two of the three cases, the sermon collection was completed during the lifetime of the preacher. The publication of the sermons in the convent must have happened with the knowledge of the father confessor. However, the prologues do not mention any active interference of the preacher in the editing of the sermons or even his approval, which must have been tacit. The marginal role of the preacher in the editing of sermons is confirmed by another collection from the Jericho-convent. A nun, Janne Colijns, gathered this collection nearly twenty years after the death of the father confessor. In doing this, she used the preachable texts of the preacher, and she copied the sermons written out by another sister:

> Ic begheere oec dat nyement en meyne maer zeekerlijc weete dat ic, scriverse dees boecks, dese weerdighe sermoenen som selve hoerende niet en hebben uutghecopiert, want dat en is inder waerheit mijnre plomper verstennisse niet verleent myts dat ic leyder mijn yonghe domheit tot selker gracien niet en hebbe bereyt. Maer ic hebse alleene vergadert eens deel ende oec des meesten deel uuyt rollen, brieven ende ouden quaternen ghescreven metter hant des selven predicaers. Ende die andere sijn uut ghecopieert van sijnre gheestelijker dochter ende religiouse suster ons cloesters van Jericho, met namen suster Barbara Cuyermans, die, inden heere ghestorven, voertijt mijn meerstersse van scrijven gheweest is, waer bij ic met dobbelder scout my hebbe verbonden in ghetrouwigher danckbaerheit bekint dit werck te aengaene ende te willichlijker aenghenomen.[34]

The text must have been noted schematically in those rolls, letters and old quires, because in the heading of one of the sermons, Janne Colijns remarks especially that this sermon was all written out by the father confessor himself.[35] As humble as Janne

[34] Brussels, Koninklijke Bibliotheek, MS II 298, fols 4^{v}–5^{r}: 'I also desire that no one should assume, but should know for certain that I, the woman who writes this book (scriverse *indicates a female writer or scribe, ThM)*, did not copy out any of these worthy sermons from listening to them myself, because in truth that is not granted to my dull understanding, considering that unfortunately I did not prepare my young stupidity for such grace. But I merely (alleene *can mean here either 'merely' or '[gathered] together', ThM)* gathered them together, in part—and in the main part—from rolls, letters and old quires written by the hand of the preacher himself. And the others were copied out by his spiritual daughter, a religious sister of our convent of Jericho, sister Barbara Cuyermans by name, who, now dead in the Lord, in former days was my writing-mistress, for which reason it is with a double debt that, bound in faithful gratitude, I have pledged to undertake this work and have taken it upon me all the more willingly.'

[35] Brussels, Koninklijke Bibliotheek, MS II 298, fol. 227^{r}: *Een schoen sermoen van sinte Marien Magdalenen dat welke ons ghelaten heeft onse eerwerdighe pater Storm, met sijns selfs hant van woerde te woerde ghescreven* ('A fine sermon about saint Mary Magdalene which our reverend father Storm left to us, word for word written with his own hand').

Colijns may be–her humility undoubtedly will have religious motives–she does not express regret for the fact that she cannot submit her texts to the preacher for correction or approval. Nor does she say that there is a problem of authenticity with these texts, due to the fact that the preacher could not authorize these sermons.

Summing up, when listeners write out sermons they have heard delivered, they sometimes compose a loosely structured series of points, largely without the formal sermon's characteristics. In some other cases, this results in complete sermons in which predicatory features are expressly preserved. In these cases, the sisters do not choose the form of *reportatio* with *inquit*-formulas like 'he said', but they completely assume the role of the father confessor. We would think that the preachers themselves wrote these sermons if we had no proof to the contrary, as the codicological indications in the case of the Claus of Euskirchen's collations, and we find very elaborate testimonies of *reportatio* in several sermon collections from the Jericho-convent in Brussels.

One could ask why the predicatory features in these cases have been so explicitly preserved. The nuns themselves say nothing about this. The purpose of this might be in the first place to write 'real' sermons and to harmonize these sermons with other sermon collections, in order that they could serve the same function, i.e. primarily as reading material in the refectory.[36] One also can assume that the preservation of predicatory features is a strategy to minimize their part in writing out the sermons. Sisters, and women in general could not receive holy orders, and as a consequence, they had no ecclesiastical authority to preach. When they wrote out the sermons delivered by a preacher, and at least were responsible for the concrete wording, obviously they only could do this safely by hiding their contribution behind the preaching of the father confessor. Preservation of predicatory elements might also be a literary strategy to bridge this gap of authority. If this is true, sisters would be able to write out and to edit sermons if they could hide their work behind the preaching fiction. In this manner, the sermon as a literary genre lay within the reach of women, as distinct from the liturgical act of preaching which demanded ordination, only accessible to men.

One step further on this way is made by Alijt Bake (d. 1455), the controversial prioress of the Windesheim convent of canonesses of Galilea near Gent, who eventually was banned from her own convent.[37] Bake tried to give the spiritual life of

---

[36] On Middle Dutch sermons as preferred lectures in the refectory of women's convents: Carine Lingier, '"Hongerich na den worden Godes": Reading to the Community in Women's Convents of the Modern Devotion', in *Lesen, Schreiben, Sticken und Erinnern: Beiträge zur Kultur- und Sozialgeschichte mittelalterlicher Frauenklöster*, ed. by Gabriela Signori (Bielefeld: Verlag für Regionalgeschichte, 2000), pp. 123–47.

[37] Alijt Bake, *Tot in de peilloze diepte van God*, introduction and commentary by R. T. M. van Dijk, translated into Modern Dutch by M. K. A. van den Berg (Kampen: Kok / Nijmegen: Titus Brandsma Instituut, 1997); Wybren Scheepsma, *Deemoed en devotie*, pp. 175–201, 251–64 (English translation in preparation: ch. 8); Kurt Ruh, *Geschichte der abendländischen*

her convent a stronger mystical tendency, and she tried to foster it with sermons. To this end she introduced, among others, the sermons of Tauler in Middle Dutch. She also adopted the sermons of Jordanus of Quedlinburg. She considered these incomplete in some respects, and therefore she completed them with her own sermons. Palm Sunday had a special place in her spiritual life. After four sermons from Jordanus on Palm Sunday follow five sermons written by Alijt. The first has this heading:

> Hier beghint dat derde stuc vanden[38] palmzondaghe dat doen overbleef ende dat den eerbaren wizen leerare ontviel. Dat heeft deze hier opgheraept. Ende dat hem hier in ontbleef dat heeft die heylege geest door deze arme creature vervult, gode lof. Deerste sermoen.[39]

These five texts by Alijt Bake are called *sermoenen* because of their affinity with the sermons of Jordanus of Quedlinburg. However, they show few predicatory features. Bake does not mention her name, but on the other hand, she clearly marks the fact that Jordanus is no longer speaking here. She does not hide her authorship behind the authority of a preacher. How far these sermons reflect Bake's addresses to her convent is not known.[40]

To summarize this section, besides loosely structured compilations of notes, there are also collections of complete sermons, also preserved, written by listeners. The expressed preservation of predicatory features aims at writing genuine sermons, but might also serve as a strategy to bridge the gap of authority between the preacher as *auctor intellectualis* and the editor. The writing out of sermons delivered by father confessors seems to have been more usual in Middle Dutch than was thought before. The sermon as a literary genre offered women more possibilities than preaching as a (para)liturgical performance would, even so much so that Alijt Bake, as an author of sermons in some degree, dares to come forward from the shadow of an authorized preacher.

Mystik, IV (München: Beck, 1999), pp. 252–67.

[38] *vanden vanden* MS.

[39] Brussels, Koninklijke Bibliotheek, MS 643–44, fol. 159r: 'Here begins the third part of Palm Sunday that was left over and fell from the wise teacher. This *(sc. Bake)* has picked it up here. And what escaped from him *(sc. Jordanus)*, this the Holy Spirit has fulfilled through this poor creature *(sc. Bake)*, praise God. The first sermon.' The five sermons were edited by B. Spaapen, 'Middeleeuwse passiemystiek, V: De kloosteronderrichtingen van Alijt Bake', *Ons Geestelijk Erf*, 42 (1968), 5–32, 225–61, 374–421; 43 (1969), 270–304.

[40] Scheepsma takes the position that in these complements to Jordanus's sermons lies the germ from which Bake's authorship developed. Cf. Wybren Scheepsma, 'Alijt Bake (1415–1455) und die deutschen Prediger des 14. Jahrhunderts', in *Predigt im Kontext. Internationale Fachtagung am Fachbereich Germanistik der Freien Universität Berlin vom 5.–8. Dezember 1996*, ed. by Volker Mertens and Hans-Jochen Schiewer (Tübingen: Niemeyer, forthcoming).

Written Sermons With No Relation to Spoken Sermons

The sermon was not a favoured literary form for Middle Dutch authors, not even for authors who belonged to the preaching orders. It is striking how few Franciscan and Dominican friars used the Middle Dutch sermon as a literary medium. The Franciscan, Hendrik Herp (d. 1477), used the sermon form for all his Latin writing, but the only text he wrote in Middle Dutch, the *Spieghel der volcomenheit* ('The Mirror of Perfection'), has the form of a treatise.[41] From the most famous Dutch preacher, the Franciscan Jan Brugman (d. 1473) relatively few sermons have been preserved.[42] His preaching to the laity in the towns made him famous, but virtually nothing from the sermons is preserved in writing. The question remains as to what extent Brugman had a share in the disparate methods used in preserving his spoken sermons. The Franciscan Dirc Coelde of Münster also reached for the treatise form for his catechetical writing, the *Kerstenspiegel* ('The Mirror for Christians').[43] The role of the Dominicans in Middle Dutch spiritual literature is comparatively small. Moreover, they rarely used the sermon as a literary medium, in contrast to their German colleagues.[44] The Dominican Dirc of Delft (d. 1404) is the father confessor and preacher at the court of the count of Holland, but when he takes up his pen to expound Christian doctrine, he uses the treatise form of the encyclopaedic *summa*.[45]

---

[41] Hendrik Herp, *Spieghel der volcomenheit*, ed. by Lucidius Verschueren (Antwerpen: Neerlandia, 1931). Ruh, *Geschichte*, IV, pp. 219–28. *Eden* and *Collatio I* were translated in Middle Dutch, but they have only few predicatory features. The *Eden*-translation was edited by Franz Jostes, 'Beiträge zur Kenntniss der niederdeutschen Mystik', *Germania*, 31 [= N.R. 19] (1886), 1–41, 164–204. The translation of the *Collatio I* is not yet edited; it was mentioned by J. Alaerts, 'Een Middelnederlands handschrift met werken van Herp en Ruusbroec (Brussel, K.B., IV 37)', *Ons Geestelijk Erf*, 49 (1975), 18–28. The collations of Herp are translated in modern French: Henri Herp, *Trois conférences spirituelles*, introd. and trans. by Georgette Epiney-Burgard (Genève: Steiner, 1983).

[42] On Brugman: F. A. H. van den Hombergh, *Leven en werk van Jan Brugman ofm. (± 1400-1473)* (Groningen: Wolters, 1967); Ruh, *Geschichte*, IV, pp. 212–18. On Brugman's writings and their transmission: De Troeyer, *Bio-bibliographia Franciscana*, pp. 65–102. Editions of Brugman's sermons: Jan Brugman, *Verspreide sermoenen*, ed. by A. van Dijk (Antwerp: De Nederlandsche Boekhandel, 1948); *Onuitgegeven sermoenen van Jan Brugman ofm*, ed. by P. Grootens (Tielt: Lannoo, 1948).

[43] *Der Christenspiegel des Dietrich Kolde von Münster*, ed. by Clemens Drees (Werl in Westfalen: Dietrich-Coelde, 1954) On Dirc Coelde of Münster, see n. 10.

[44] A survey of the writings by Dominican authors in Middle Dutch manuscripts: Stephanus G. Axters, *Bibliotheca Dominicana Neerlandica Manuscripta 1224–1500* (Leuven: Publications Universitaires de Louvain, 1970); Stephanus G. Axters, 'Bibliotheca Dominicana Neerlandica Manuscripta 1224–1500. II', *Ons Geestelijk Erf*, 50 (1976), 309–36.

[45] This text was completed in 1404. Dirc van Delf, *Tafel van den Kersten Ghelove*, ed. by L. M. F. Daniëls (Antwerpen: Neerlandia / Nijmegen / Utrecht: Dekker & Van de Vegt, 1937–38), 3 vols. Cf. F. P. van Oostrom, *Court and Culture: Dutch Literature 1350–1450*

At the same time as the German Dominicans chose the sermon as the preferred form of mystical literature, Dutch mystic writing was dominated by Jan of Ruusbroec, who wrote predominantly treatises. Though Ruusbroec does not use the sermon form, he uses, nevertheless, preaching methods in his treatises. The principal work of his, *Die geestelike brulocht* ('The Spiritual Espousals') departs from the theme *Siet de brudegom coemt, gaet ute hem te ontmoetene* ('See, the bridegroom cometh; go out to meet Him').[46] By a four-part, textual division, this theme determines the structure of the whole text: each of the three books of the *Brulocht* consists of four parts corresponding to the parts of the theme: *Siet, / de brudegom coemt, / gaet ute / hem te ontmoetene* ('See, / the bridegroom cometh; / go out / to meet Him', Matthew 25. 6). His *Rike der gelieven* ('The Realm of Lovers') is also structured according to a five-part, textual division of a biblical theme.[47] Furthermore, it is likely that Ruusbroec used the traditional preacher's manuals and borrowed etymologies and the like from them, but this is not studied yet. Even so, Dirc of Delft probably consulted such manuals for his *Tafel*.[48] Therefore, Middle Dutch authors borrowed occasionally, the literary means of style and structure from the sermon form, and they consulted predicatory manuals, but they do not take the sermon as a literary form for the transmission of their matter.

(Berkeley: University of California Press, 1992), ch. 5. In his doctoral thesis, Daniëls points out the sermonlike character of the first three chapters of the summer part, which discuss the three names of the fourth Sunday in Lent (Mid Lent). Cf. F. A. M. Daniëls, *Meester Dirc van Delf: zijn persoon en zijn werk* (Nijmegen: Dekker & Van de Vegt; Utrecht: Van Leeuwen, 1932), pp. 54–56. Stephanus G. Axters, 'Frères Precheurs, VI: Pays-Bas', in *Dictionnaire de Spiritualité*, ed. by Marcel Viller and others (Paris: Beauchesne, 1933–95), V (1964), cols. 1502–1509 (col. 1505): two sermons which we owe to a master in theology who, according to various indications, could be Dirc of Delft. Those sermons are extant only in a single manuscript (Library of Bruges, MS 408, fols 265^r–279^r), where the author deals especially with devotion to the angels and the gifts of the Holy Spirit.

[46] Matthew 25. 6; Jan van Ruusbroec, *Die geestelike brulocht*, ed. by J. Alaerts, English trans. by H. Rolfson (Tielt: Lannoo/Turnhout: Brepols, 1998), pp. 150–51, l. 1.

[47] Wis. 10. 10. Jan van Ruusbroec, *Dat rijcke der ghelieven*, ed. by J. Alaerts, English trans. by H. Rolfson (Tielt: Lannoo/Turnhout: Brepols, 2002), p. 151, l. 1–2: *Die here / hevet weder leidet / den gherechten / die gherechte weeghe, / ende hevet hem ghetoent dat rike gods* ('The Lord / led back / the just / along the right ways / and showed him the realm of God'). Cf. also Paul Wackers, 'Een wereldbeeld in één zin', in *Hoort wonder! Opstellen voor W. P. Gerritsen bij zijn emeritaat*, ed. by Bart Besamusca, Frank Brandsma and Dieuwke van der Poel (Hilversum: Verloren, 2000), pp. 177–81; Hilde M. P. Noë, *In een verwonderen van al deser rijcheyt: Het beeldgebruik in Jan van Ruusbroecs Dat rijcke der ghelieven* (Leuven: Peeters, 2001), pp. 15–19.

[48] Daniëls, however, does not mention these manuals as sources. Cf. Daniëls, *Meester Dirc van Delf*, pp. 34–91: ch. 2 'De bronnen van de "Tafel van der kestenre ghelove"'.

One particular friar did however value the sermon form as a vehicle for Christian doctrine, and that was Dirc of Delft's predecessor, the Carmelite Willem de Biechtvader ('William the Confessor'). To him, *Een nuttelijc boec den kerstenen menschen* ('A usefull book for the Christian People') is ascribed. Willem moulds his catechetic matter in the form of a cycle of sixty-three sermons on the Sunday pericope, in which the Epistle or (more often) the Gospel is translated or paraphrased and then provided an elucidatory gloss. This cycle seems to be the product of the desk, not of the pulpit. The sermon form is nevertheless explicitly used, including the fiction of orality and references to a liturgical 'here and now'. The use of this literary form to convey the Sunday Gospel with the glosses in vernacular, reflects the Sunday preaching in the mass. Attending mass on Sundays was one of the few obligations of each Christian and, by this, an important opportunity for catechesis to the laity. Attending mass was a very passive affair in the Middle Ages and for a long time after. The sermon was the only time in mass the priest addressed the lay people directly in the vernacular. Therefore, Sunday preaching was very important for contact between the Church and laity. It can be expected that further catechization embroiders on this kind of preaching. Using the preaching form, the Sunday Gospel with the gloss stresses the analogy with the Sunday's preaching. The preaching form clearly is a literary strategy here, expressing the functional congeniality with Sunday preaching by a formal analogy.

The combination with the Gospel pericopes made these sermons attractive. Sermon collections as *Een nuttelijc boec* could be used as pericope collections. The pericope collection was a very dominant text form. This is clear from the fact that every text lending itself even slightly to this purpose was prepared for use as a pericope collection: to translations of the New Testament, the Old Testament pericopes and a reading scheme were added, and also to translations of the Gospels, diatessarons, or paraphrases of the life of Jesus. Pericope collections containing the Epistles and especially the Gospels in the order of the ecclesiastical year were part of the established book collection of advanced pupils.[49] Spiritual authors stimulated lay people to employ themselves in reading spiritual literature on Sunday afternoons. Even when this was done as a pastime, it was better than dancing or visiting taverns.[50] It is known that devout lay people indeed engaged in community reading of spiritual literature on Sunday afternoons. In some towns after the vespers, collations where held, during which a text was read and discussed or an exhortation

---

[49] Cf. Thom Mertens, 'The Last Judgement in Middle Dutch Sermons on the Sunday Gospel', in *The Last Judgement in Medieval Preaching*, ed. by Thom Mertens, Hans-Jochen Schiewer and Maria Sherwood-Smith (Turnhout: Brepols, forthcoming); Geert Warnar, '"Die donkerheit vercleren": Over de literairhistorische achtergronden van de Middelnederlandse evangeliënharmonie', *Queeste*, 6 (1999), 112–26 (pp. 121–24).

[50] See also the prologue on the Middle Dutch translation of the Pentateuch by the 'Bible-translator of 1360', cited and translated in Mertens, 'Last Judgement'.

was delivered in the form of a sermon.[51] The success of the pericope collections was based on their use as school texts and as instructions for educated lay people.[52] Pericopes with glosses could not only be used as a pericope collection, but they also offered an explanation of those pericopes. In the case of *Een nuttelijc boec* the glosses offered an all-round catechesis which was presented to the reader in small, temporized pieces. The preaching form here is staged. It is a literary strategy in order to express a functional congeniality with the Sunday preaching by an analogy of form.

Een nuttelijc boec belongs to the genre of Middle Dutch glossed Epistles and Gospels. There are more examples of this genre. On the whole, we know six collections, which are not all completely preserved—if they ever were complete. Four collections have had a wider diffusion, if we may depend on the preserved manuscripts and printed editions. None of these collections has been edited, with the exception of a few sermons. There is, however, a survey, made by G. C. Zieleman, who also studied the most complex collection more thoroughly.[53] The oldest manuscripts date from the first quarter of the fourteenth century. All collections have been delivered anonymously and only two on the basis of circumstantial evidence have been assigned an author's. *Een nuttelijc boec* is one of the two.

The glossed Epistles and Gospels seem therefore the only sermon collections from preachers showing predicatory features. There is no (proven) connection with actually delivered sermons, and if there were, it would be of marginal importance.

It may be concluded from what we have discussed so far that in Middle Dutch, the sermon as a form was not a popular medium to convey religious matter, except in the case of the glossed Epistle and Gospel collections. In these texts the preaching fiction is staged to express the kinship and analogy in content and function with the preaching during Sunday mass.

---

[51] Cf. Mertens, 'Collatio', pp. 166–68.

[52] A study of the provenance of the manuscripts could inform us better or force us to refine or revise these explanations. There seems to be a tendency that most of the vernacular spiritual literature originally written for lay people got its most wide reception in semi-religious communities. Cf. for example the secondary and tertiary reception of Dirc of Delft's *Tafel van den kersten ghelove*, as analyzed by Frits van Oostrom, *Aanvaard dit werk: Over Middelnederlandse auteurs en hun publiek* (Amsterdam: Prometheus, 1992), pp. 152–70, 298–99 (first published: F. P. van Oostrom and others, 'Over Dirc van Delft en zijn lezers', in *Het woord aan de lezer: Zeven literatuurhistorische verkenningen*, ed. by W. van den Berg and J. Stouten (Groningen: Wolters-Noordhoff, 1987), pp. 49–71).

[53] Zieleman, *Epistel- en evangeliepreken*, pp. 49–159. A seventh cycle (*ibid.*, pp. 78–81) is incomplete and is (partly) collected from texts from other cycles

The Sermon as a Literary Genre

It should be clear by now that the relationship between the written and spoken sermon is not straightforward. An answer to the question of who wrote out spoken sermons—the preacher himself or his listeners—says nothing about the literary form or the quality of the text. There are sermons written out by listeners, which nevertheless have many predicatory features and there are sermons written out by the preacher himself which do not show such features. We find that contrary to expectation, the preservation of predicatory features requires explanation, not their absence. Are preaching features unintended relics of the previous history of the text, or are they intentionally preserved as a literary strategy serving a certain purpose?

On the basis of all this, it would be possible, though in my opinion not advisable, to conceive of the sermon as a purely literary phenomenon and its relation to preaching as an interesting fact which is actually irrelevant for the text. This position could be defended with a reference to the existence of sermons which are not based on actual preaching, such as the glossed Epistle or Gospel. This would mean, however, that the sermon as a literary phenomenon would be detached from preaching, even in the cases in which the texts preserve predicatory features or use them as a strategy to link up with preaching. Complete disconnection of preaching and the written sermon would lead to disregarding the question of why a particular text is linked with preaching and what this literary strategy is aiming at.

All texts related to sermons should be checked for the generic features of preaching. In this manner the difference between oral preaching and the written discourse of sermons will be noticed and, even more importantly, in this way the study of sermons is not disconnected from its soil. If we consider all these texts as sermons, we will have to divide the genre into subgenres and to discriminate on the one hand texts presenting themselves explicitly as sermons, and on the other hand texts in which the present predicatory features are only relics. Also the very rarely preserved preachable texts, written by the preachers themselves as a basis for preaching, should be considered as a category within the genre. They live on the same soil as the sermons, and they are functionally akin to model sermons.

The issue of written and oral literacy, of text and performance is not confined to the sermon. There are more genres which in the first place take shape in performances, such as theatrical plays and *sproken* (spoken moralistic poems).[54] Likewise, the written texts are secondary here, sometimes considered separately, though not completely divorced from their origins. In this context we have to dwell on parodic sermons for a moment.[55] The designation of this (sub)genre suggests that

[54] Cf. Reinder P. Meijer, *Literature of the Low Countries* (The Hague—Boston: Nijhoff, 1978), pp. 38–40. Van Oostrom, *Court and Culture*, ch. 2. Dini Hogenelst, *Sproken en sprekers: Inleiding op en repertorium van de Middelnederlandse sproke* (Amsterdam: Prometheus, 1997). 2 vols.

[55] On the parodic sermon in Middle Dutch: Dick Kaijser, 'Het laatmiddeleeuwse

these texts satirize written sermons. They actually satirize preaching as a liturgical act, and it would be better to call them mock preaching. The same question as with sermons arises with these mock spoken sermons. Are we dealing with texts which are the basis of the performance, like a score for a musical performance, or are we dealing with an imitative representation of such a performance? Are the texts analogous to preachable texts or to written sermons? And there are more questions to ask. Do these mock spoken sermons present us with predicatory features which we otherwise do not see in sermons? Precisely which parts or aspects of the preaching were satirized? Is the image of the preaching they give (apart from their ridicule) another than the image reflected in 'ordinary' sermons? If so, parodic sermons might give us another perspective on preaching than sermons do. And thus comparative study of parodic and non-parodic, ordinary sermons might give us also indications of literary conventions of the sermon unrelated to the preaching. Anyhow, in more than one respect, parodic sermons are a distinct category in sermon literature.

Therefore, we suggest using a wide conception of the literary genre of the sermon and to distinguish several categories or subgenres according to their relation to preaching. Surely, there will be marginal and dubious cases, like the example of Goswinus Hex's sermon, which in most manuscripts is preserved as a treatise and is only recognizable as a derivitive of preaching by the explicit testimony in one manuscript. There will always be such doubtful cases, no matter which delineation of the genre one chooses.

This brings us to the issue of genres in general. Because it is impossible to make a sound demarcation between the genres, the problem as a whole sometimes is considered as a hopeless venture. Often, nevertheless, it is clear which features are characteristic for the genre, though it is impossible to design a kind of taxonomic system of clearly delineated genres. It is even more difficult to identify the generic category of individual texts.[56] All this is no reason to consider it useless to speak about genres. A discussion of generic features in a particular text makes it possible to analyze this text thoroughly, clearly and exactly. In this context this plea for a wide, but subdivided, concept of the genre 'sermon' has to be understood. It is a useful tool that raises fruitful questions, not a filing cabinet with labels.

---

spotsermoen', *Spektator*, 13 (1983–84), 105–27; Hogenelst, *Sproken*, I, p. 76, 194–95, II, nos R3, R260, R265

[56] Cf. Nico H. J. Bogaard, 'La définition du fabliau', in *Epopée animale, fable, fabliau: Actes du IVe Colloque de la Société Internationale Renardienne, 7–11 septembre 1981* (Paris: PUF, 1984), pp. 657–68 (p. 667) proposes a 'familial' concept of genre.

Fashioning Devotion: The Art of Good Friday Preaching in Chaucerian England

HOLLY JOHNSON

Christ's Passion holds the central place in late-medieval Christianity. Thomas Bestul calls the Passion 'the master narrative' of the late Middle Ages, which 'describes the central act of human history, the redemption of mankind, in relation to which every other event in history is referred and acquires meaning.'[1] According to Richard Kieckhefer, devotion to the Passion had reached 'a feverish intensity' by this period.[2] Passion plays, religious lyrics, meditative treatises, the writings of the mystics, and the pictorial arts of this period manifest this intensity. However, it was on Good Friday, the day set aside by the Church to commemorate Christ's suffering and death, that devotion to the Passion found its most dramatic public expression. A group of macaronic (mixed Latin-vernacular) Good Friday sermons, composed and preached in late medieval England, *c.* 1350–1450, attest to the centrality of Good Friday in dramatizing and communicating the Passion narrative. The sermons were used to create a world in which their audiences enter experientially into the events of Good Friday. This paper will explore three macaronic Good Friday sermons that exemplify the striking ways preachers construct these dramas. Each sermon has the same primary aim—to draw the audience into the liturgical present, making Christ's suffering and death a felt reality and simultaneously fashioning a devotional response to this reality, one which calls for sorrow, compassion, contrition, even at times outrage, and, above all, gratitude.

---

[1] Thomas Bestul, *Texts of the Passion: Latin Devotional Literature and Medieval Society* (Philadelphia, PA: University of Pennsylvania Press, 1996), p. 24.

[2] Richard Kieckhefer, 'Major Currents in Late Medieval Devotion', in *Christian Spirituality: High Middle Ages and Reformation*, ed. by Jill Raitt, World Spirituality: An Encyclopedic History of the Religious Quest, 17 (New York: Crossroad, 1996), 75–108 (p. 89).

Mircea Eliade has argued that 'every ritual has the character of happening *now*, at this very moment. The time of the event that the ritual commemorates or re-enacts is made present, "re-presented" so to speak, however far back it may have been in ordinary reckoning.'[3] For the late-medieval Church in England, this statement applies especially to the Good Friday liturgy which included, among a number of rituals unique to Good Friday, three that support Eliade's point particularly well. Of these rituals, one was the reading—or chanting—of the entire Passion according to St John's Gospel. Another was the veneration of the cross, which the English called the creeping to the cross, when both priests and laity 'crept' barefoot and on their knees up to a cross and kissed it. The third was the office of burial when the Church ceremonially 'buried' Christ by carrying the cross that had been venerated to a special sepulchre within the church, where it remained with one candle burning and with a 'watch' kept continually until it was 'raised' again at Easter.[4] The creeping to the cross was rendered more affecting by the concurrent chanting of the *Improperia*, or Reproaches, a set of rebukes drawn from the Old Testament and placed in Christ's mouth that contrast what he has done for the Jews with the way they are treating him now, on Good Friday. Such rituals were intended to re-enact the events of the first Good Friday, making them present again and drawing the participants into these events as if they were there. In the medieval view, this was not a mere act of the imagination, a sort of suspension of disbelief; the events *were* happening again because they happened both in time and outside of time, both historically and eternally. The liturgy was the place where eternity and temporality met. What happened during the liturgy could be said to happen in the liturgical present.

We cannot be sure exactly when, amidst the Good Friday rituals, the congregation heard a sermon, but the number of extant Good Friday sermons suggests that they did hear one, and often a rather long one.[5] Sermons may have been preached at the Good Friday liturgy and/or possibly later in the afternoon. According to John Stow's *A Survey of London* (1603), preaching on the afternoon of Good Friday was apparently a venerable tradition by the early sixteenth century. 'Time out of mind', Stow remarks, 'it hath beene a laudable custome that on Good Friday in the afternoone some especial learned man by appointment of the Prelates, hath preached

---

[3] Mircea Eliade, *Patterns in Comparative Religion*, trans. by Rosemary Sheed (Lincoln, NE: University of Nebraska Press, 1996). pp. 392–93. First published New York: Sheed and Ward, 1958.

[4] Eamon Duffy, *The Stripping of the Altars: Traditional Religion in England 1400–1580* (New Haven, CT: Yale University Press, 1992), pp. 29–30.

[5] J. W. Tyrer, *Historical Survey of Holy Week: Its Service and Ceremonial* (London: Oxford University Press, 1932), p. 117, notes that the Anglo–Saxons called Good Friday 'Langa Frigedæg' as do the Danes, which he suggests is a comment upon the length of time one spends in church. One of the macaronic sermons, if preached in its entirety, would probably have taken at least two hours.

a sermon at Paules Crosse treating of Christ's passion.'[6] In her study of English sermons *c.* 1370–*c.*1500, Helen Spencer gives evidence that sermons were preached outside—and often at crosses—on Sunday afternoons.[7] Thus, it is quite possible that Stow's 'time out of mind' reaches back into the late Middle Ages and that Good Friday sermons were also preached outside in the afternoon. The sermons themselves reveal little about when during the liturgy they were preached although one might assume they were preached following the reading of the Passion according to St John and before the veneration of the cross. A smidgen of evidence for this placement can be found in one of the model sermons by Jacobus de Voragine, the thirteenth-century Dominican friar and author of the *Legenda aurea*. In a sermon explaining the significance of each of the Good Friday rituals, Jacobus, when discussing the veneration of the cross, describes four people—Mary, Simon, Mary Magdalene, and Judas—who kissed Christ on Good Friday and explains what these kisses signify.[8] Jacobus then turns to the congregation and uses the only future tense in the sermon, saying, 'Quicumque igitur crucem hodie osculabitur, videat qualiter osculetur.'[9] In his sermon for Good Friday, the fourteenth-century English preacher John Mirk also uses future tense only when explaining the reason for venerating the cross: 'Then, aftyr þe oryson, þe cros is broȝt forþe, þe whech ych cristen man and woman schall worschip þys day, in worschip of hym þat as þys day dyed on þe cros.'[10] If the sermons were preached prior to the veneration of the cross , preachers may have seen the need to prepare a congregation to respond appropriately to this ritual, making the sufferings of Christ on the cross as vivid as possible so that congregants felt the full weight of them while they crept to the cross on their knees and heard the *Improperia*. The macaronic Good Friday sermons this paper examines and others like them use rhetorical and stylistic devices that seem designed specifically for preparing audiences to respond to this event.

---

[6] John Stow, *A Survey of London* (Stroud: Alan Sutton, 1994. Facsimile of edition published London: Routledge, 1912). Originally published as *A Survey of London* (London: Windet, 1603), 1, p. 167.

[7] Spencer, *English Preaching in the Late Middle Ages* (Oxford: Clarendon Press, 1993), pp. 71–72.

[8] *Sermo cviii* in *Sermones de tempore et de sanctis* (Basel: Johann von Amerbach, 1488), unpaginated: 'Notandum quod quattuor persone christum erant osculate, scilicet, Maria in signum amoris, Symeon in signum deuotionis, Magdalena in signum reconsiliationis, Judas in signum perditionis.'

[9] *Sermo cviii* in *Sermones de tempore et de sanctis*: 'Therefore whoever will kiss the cross today, let him take care how he kisses.'

[10] John Mirk, *Mirk's Festial:A Collection of Homilies, by Johannes Mirkus (John Mirk)*, ed. by Theodore Erbe, EETS, e.s., 96 (London: K. Paul, Trench, Trübner, 1905), p. 123, ll. 18–23: 'Then, after the prayer, the cross is brought forward, which each Christian man and woman shall worship this day, in honor of him who on this day died on the cross.'

The Macaronic Sermons

These sermons share several elements that unify them, perhaps the most striking of which is their mixed Latin-vernacular, or macaronic, texture. They are recorded with Latin as their base language but with Middle English words, phrases, and verses blended into the Latin text. The sermons always use Middle English verses or words for their sermon divisions, which act as mnemonic devices for both preacher and audience and give shape to the sermon material. Such English verses suggest that, while the sermons were recorded macaronically, they were, or were intended to be, preached in English.[11] One preacher, however, states explicitly that he will preach in both Latin and English: he will use Latin first to summarize for the clerics what he will then preach in English for the rest of the audience.[12] But while the first part apparently spoken in Latin is recorded in the manuscript entirely in Latin, by contrast the rest of the sermon is dotted with words and phrases in English. So although the preacher may have in fact preached the rest of the sermon in English, the sermon was recorded in both English and Latin. Whatever one might make of the admixture of Latin and English, Siegfried Wenzel, in his recent study of macaronic sermons, maintains that this phenomenon did not result from the preacher's carelessness or inadequate mastery of the Latin language. Such sermons, he argues, 'in the form they have come down to us, are first of all products of literary composition.'[13] The Middle English in these sermons is not used because the preacher lacked Latin vocabulary or because he was using some technical word for which there was no Latin equivalent, nor was it used because the preacher did not have a firm grasp of his material. Wenzel suggests that the macaronic texture may have been used for rhetorical purposes; sermons are more likely to be recorded in mixed language when the preachers are dealing with highly emotional material or 'favorite topics', one of which was Christ's Passion.[14] Furthermore, Wenzel argues that the macaronic form of these sermons, whether or not it was 'deliberately

[11] Siegfried Wenzel, *Macaronic Sermons: Bilingualism and Preaching in Late-Medieval England* (Ann Arbor: University of Michigan Press, 1994), p. 107, articulates the commonly held scholarly view regarding the language used to preach sermons in the late Middle Ages: 'Modern students of medieval preaching have fairly unanimously asserted that sermons given to the common people were delivered in the vernacular, whereas sermons to the clergy were preached in Latin, but both were written out or down in Latin, the official language of the clergy.'

[12] London, Lambeth Palace, MS 352, fol. 217v:'Nunc pro processu sermonis, notabitis primo breuiter in Latinis pro istis clericis et postea in Anglicis pro vobis omnibus.'

[13] Wenzel, *Macaronic Sermons*, p. 79. Wenzel includes an edition and translation of a macaronic Good Friday sermon as one of the appendices to this study.

[14] Wenzel, *Macaronic Sermons*, p. 67.

intended', was 'certainly tolerated, and it was tolerated by writers who otherwise show a high level of intelligence and clerical training.'[15]

Of the macaronic sermons written in England, the Good Friday sermons in particular reveal their creators' rhetorical sophistication. Each sermon uses a *thema*, protheme and introduction, divisions and subdivisions, and each includes exempla, *distinctiones*, and prooftexts from a variety of authorities—in short, all the trappings of fully developed scholastic sermons.[16] Within this seemingly rigid structure, the preachers construct richly imaginative, highly rhetorical, and unified literary works intended to elicit a multilayered response to Christ's suffering and death. They use a great variety of material to this end, as seemingly disparate as a proof-text from Avicenna to the immensely popular devotional text, the *Quis dabit*, known to the English as the Lament or Complaint of the Virgin Mary.[17] They also undertook with earnestness their role as pedagogues, teaching to their audiences the theology of the redemption and the Passion's place within salvation history. Thus, these sermons are both devotional and doctrinal, the two carefully balanced; they seek to elicit a highly affective response to the Passion within a solid theological setting.

Bishop Thomas Brinton

Before examining the art employed by these macaronic sermons, I would like briefly to discuss, by way of contrast, a Good Friday sermon preserved in Latin and preached around the same time by Thomas Brinton, Benedictine monk and Bishop of Rochester from the years 1373–1389. W. A. Pantin calls him 'an outstanding monk-bishop', well known 'above all as a preacher [...] thanks especially to the collection of one hundred and three sermons, preached between 1373 and 1383, that has survived'.[18] Like the preachers of the macaronic sermons, but unlike some of his more familiar contemporaries such as John Mirk and John Wyclif, Brinton uses the scholastic form; however, he does so with very little conscious artistry. While this

---

[15] Wenzel, *Macaronic Sermons*, p. 112.

[16] There is no scholarly consensus on what term to use for this sermon form. It has been called the 'thematic' sermon, the 'modern' sermon, and the 'university' sermon. For discussions of these terms, see Spencer, *English Preaching,* pp. 231–32, and Wenzel, *Preachers, Poets and the Early English Lyric* (Princeton: Princeton University Press, 1986), pp. 61–62. I follow Wenzel in choosing 'scholastic'.

[17] For the Latin text of the *Quis dabit*, see C. William Marx, 'The *Quis dabit* of Oglerius de Tridino, Monk and Abbot of Locedio', *Journal of Medieval Latin*, 4 (1994), pp. 118–29. For a Middle English version, see *The Middle English Prose Complaint of Our Lady and Gospel of Nicodemus*, ed. by Marx and Jeanne F. Drennan, Middle English Texts, 19 (Heidelberg: Winter, 1987).

[18] W. A. Pantin, *The English Church in the Fourteenth Century* (Cambridge: Cambridge University Press, 1955), pp. 182–83.

particular sermon was ostensibly preached to a monastic audience, it does not differ in style or purpose from his sermons, Good Friday or otherwise, which were apparently preached to lay or mixed audiences. Brinton's primary role is that of the teacher, not that of the rhetorician; he seems to make little attempt to elicit an emotional response to the Good Friday events. Examining Brinton's prosaic use of the form will highlight the rhetorical and literary art of these three macaronic sermons.

This particular Brinton sermon was probably preached (in some form) on Good Friday in 1376 to the monks of Rochester priory;[19] it uses the *thema*, *Requiescite sub arbore* (Genesis 18. 4: 'Rest under the tree'), a line taken from the words Abraham says to the three angels who visit him. The central metaphor developed from this *thema* is that the tree under which we should rest is the tree of the cross and that resting under this tree is comparable to meditating on the Passion, a point set forth in both the protheme and the *introductio thematis*. To make this point Brinton introduces and allegorizes a number of biblical references to trees as well as several exempla, mostly taken from civil law and natural history. The metaphor of the tree shifts several times during the sermon, depending on context. For instance, Brinton begins the protheme with an example from civil law of those who seek refuge by fleeing to the statues of a ruler, statues made from trees or rocks. He then immediately turns to a more elaborate example from nature, taken from Pliny, of a precious tree in India whose flowers and sweet odour were hated so much by the serpent that it poisoned the tree's root until the tree dried up. The people who saw this took treacle and poured it into a branch, which dissolved the poison, and the tree bore fruit. People then held the treacle in great honour.[20] Brinton compares the Indian tree to the human race before original sin, the serpent to the 'old serpent' (Satan), and the treacle to Christ who was sent into the Virgin Mary, the branch of the tree of Jesse. Brinton then points out that Christ also redeemed the human race *on* a tree, the tree of the cross, and thus we should honour this tree (not just the treacle) on which is 'our salvation, resurrection, and life', more than we do a statue of a ruler, who only offers bodily safety.[21] Brinton has now returned to his earlier example from civil law, which he had not developed when he first introduced it.

---

[19] Thomas Brinton, Bishop of Rochester. *The Sermons of Thomas Brinton, Bishop of Rochester (1373–1389)*, ed. by Mary Aquinas Devlin, 2 vols, Camden Third Series, 85 (London: Offices of the Royal Historical Society, 1954), p. 307.

[20] Brinton, *Sermons*, p. 307: 'Narrat *Plinius* in India fuisse arborem preciosam, cuius flores et fructus dulcem habebant odorem, quam multum odiens serpens nomine iaculus intoxicauit radicem et statim exaruit. De quo dolentes illi de patria tiriacam acceperint et in quamdam virgam arboris infunderunt.'

[21] Brinton, *Sermons*, p. 308: 'Igitur si imperatoris statua iuxta premissa in tanta fuit reuerencia quia saluauit corporaliter a confusione et morte, certe maiori honore est arbor crucis adoranda in qua est salus nostra, resurrectio atque vita.'

He proceeds in this way throughout both protheme and *introductio thematis*, the latter of which is more lengthy and involved than the actual 'process' (body) of the sermon. By the end of the *introductio thematis*, Brinton has primarily made clear why monks especially should meditate on the Passion and the effect this meditation should have. Finally, after the introduction, Brinton divides his *thema* into four principal parts, using as his dividing motif the four trees from which the cross was traditionally believed to have been made—cedar, cypress, palm, and olive—and likening each tree to a disposition we receive from some aspect of the cross. The actual plan of the sermon is far simpler (and much shorter) than the preceding introduction. Brinton subdivides the first principal part only into two parts and uses one exemplum for each of the other parts, each of which he allegorizes in some detail.

What he does not do, although one might expect him to do so given the protheme and introduction, is show what meditating on the Passion entails or offer narrative content to guide such a meditation. Nor does he attempt to create what William Hodapp, in an article concerning Richard Rolle's Passion Meditation B, has called the 'meditative pause, during which Jesus's Passion becomes immediate and present for those who enter and participate in the present dramatic world.'[22] Brinton's introductory material could be used for a very different sermon on the Passion, suggesting, in Jean Greatrex's words, the 'pick' and 'mix' approach to composing sermons.[23] While the ideas in individual sections are organically linked, there is no compelling underlying logic to the entire sermon, and the protheme and *introductio thematis* are so thematically similar that one wonders whether Brinton may not have included both when composing the sermon but only used one when preaching it. This would then depend on the audience, the protheme being more suited to a mixed audience and the introduction to a monastic audience. Brinton also does not make much reference to the fact that it is Good Friday, that Christ is presently suffering, nor does he allude to the Good Friday liturgy in any significant way. At one point, he does note the refrain of Fortunatus's hymn *Pange lingua*, sung during the veneration

[22] William Hodapp, 'Ritual and Performance', p. 242. Hodapp is here discussing one of John of Grimestone's Passion lyrics which is found in Grimestone's handbook for preachers and was probably intended to be used in sermons. See Wenzel, *Preachers, Poets*, ch. 4.

[23] Jean Greatrex, 'Benedictine Sermons: Preparation and Practice in the English Monastic Cathedral Cloisters', in *Medieval Monastic Preaching*, ed. by Carolyn Muessig (Leiden: Brill, 1998), pp. 271–79 (p. 277). Greatrex is referring to the use of sermon collections in Benedictine monasteries and suggests that there is evidence that monks picked and mixed different parts from different sermons, 'facilitated by reference to the subject indexes and also to the *exemplum* collections for a few illustrative and edifying stories selected with the particular audience in view'. Wenzel has pointed out to me that the unusual thing about Brinton is that he seems to pick and mix from his own sermon material, sometimes transplanting whole sections verbatim from one sermon to another.

of the cross,[24] but this is because the line—'Crux fidelis inter omnes arbor una nobilis'[25]—refers to the cross as a tree and thus fits his *thema* well.[26] For Brinton is nothing if not dogged in the way he exploits every reference or exemplum connecting trees with the cross. While there are occasional moments of rhetorical ardor, the predominant mode of the sermon is pedagogical, although Brinton trots out so many scriptural references and exempla, and these exempla are so varied, that it might be a wonder if any of them stuck in the audience's memory.

The Scholastic Framework

The macaronic Good Friday sermons are also pedagogical, but this is not their predominant mode, which should be called meditative. Unlike Brinton's sermon, several of them do offer narrative content, recreating scenes from the Passion with graphic images, descriptive narration, and imaginary dialogues. They periodically stop the narrative to offer moral and exegetical commentary on these scenes very like *Vita Christi* texts, the meditative treatises popular in the late Middle Ages that take their readers through Christ's life, instructing them to make themselves present at each event and exhorting them to have compassion and to imitate in their own lives what they see in Christ's.[27] Using the Good Friday sermon to narrate the Passion in this way goes back at least to the 13th century; Nicole Bériou discusses a 13th-century macaronic sermon from France whose Dominican preacher 'recites a complete and colourful story of the Passion, in a succession of dramatic events, interrupted by doctrinal or moral comments.'[28] Some of the macaronic sermons find clever ways to use their principal parts to narrate the events chronologically, while others place the events wherever they fit the larger organizational scheme the sermon has set up, even if the events are then out of order. But the intention in both cases is the same: to paint vivid scenes of Christ's Passion as if it were happening in the

---

[24] Tyrer, *Historical Survey*, p. 131.

[25] 'The faithful cross is the noblest tree among all'.

[26] Brinton, *Sermons*, p. 308.

[27] The two texts central to this tradition are the *Meditationes vite Christi*, traditionally attributed to Bonaventure but now believed to have been written by John of Caulibus, and Ludolph of Saxony's *Vita Jesu Christi*. For a discussion of the latter's relationship to preaching, see Lawrence F. Hundersmarck, 'Preaching the Passion: Late Medieval "Lives of Christ" as Sermon Vehicles', in *De Ore Domini: Preaching and Word in the Middle Ages*, ed. by Thomas L. Amos, Eugene A. Green, and Beverly Mayne Kienzle (Kalamazoo: University of Western Michigan Press, 1989), pp. 147–67.

[28] Nicole Bériou, 'Latin and Vernacular. Some Remarks about Sermons Delivered on Good Friday during the Thirteenth Century', in *Die deutsche Predigt im Mittelalter*, ed. by Volker Mertens and Hans-Jochen Schiewer (Tübingen: Niemeyer, 1992), pp. 268–84 (p. 277).

timeless now and to fashion devotion by eliciting the affective response sought in private meditation. Thus, when one macaronic sermon says in its introductory material that it is important on Good Friday to listen again to the events of Christ's suffering and death, to be filled with deep sorrow, and to weep three kinds of tears, it then becomes the vehicle by which the audience will hear these events and through which it will—if the preacher is successful—feel such sorrow. It creates the meditative pause lacking in Brinton's sermon and strengthens the liturgical present.

One predominant way that the macaronic sermons create this pause is by using the scholastic structure itself to place the Passion narrative into a larger drama, often one that intimately involves the audience. By inviting the audience to participate—at least implicitly—in this larger drama, the sermons make of the Passion a more immediate reality that demands a more immediate response. The first of the three examples, perhaps the most meditative, is a very long sermon that seems largely indebted to the *Vita Christi* tradition. The preacher uses the *thema*, *Dilexit nos et lavit nos a peccatis nostris in sanguine suo* (Revelation 1. 5:'He loved us and washed us from our sins in his own blood') to create a great love-story between Christ and the audience.[29] Christ becomes the lover-knight, and his Passion becomes the battle he fights and wins, but dies winning, in order to gain back his beloved's inheritance. Such a narrative would have been familiar to an English audience; lover-knight exempla, common in Good Friday sermons and other genres, are well known from the *Ancrene Wisse*, wherein a king willingly battles the enemies of a disdainful lady, and from *Piers Plowman*, in which Christ himself battles in Piers's armor.[30] In this sermon the exemplum becomes the main event, a narrative the preacher maintains throughout the sermon so that it appears to be the primary story. This overarching narrative brings the Passion into the liturgical present by making its implications more immediate for the contemporary audience. The preacher, however, specifies from the beginning of the sermon that what is made present on Good Friday is a *memoria* of the Passion. He begins with the words, 'Reuerendi mei, sponsa grata, pro cuius amore sponsus eius in bello fuerit occisus, solet diem obitus sui anniuersariam diligenter obseruare eiusque dileccionem et beneficia ac eciam mortis ystoriam ad memoriam non sine dolore lacrimabiliter reuocare.'[31] This initial

---

[29] This sermon is known to be extant in one manuscript: London, Lambeth Palace, MS 352, fols 216^{r}–224^{v}.

[30] See Rosemary Woolf, 'The Theme of Christ the Lover-Knight in Medieval English Literature', *Review of English Studies*, 13.49 (1962), 1–16; *The English Religious Lyric in the Middle Ages* (Oxford: Clarendon Press, 1968), pp. 44–55; J. A. W. Bennett, *Poetry of the Passion: Studies in Twelve Centuries of English Verse* (Oxford: Clarendon Press, 1982), pp. 63–84; Douglas Gray, *Themes and Images in the Medieval English Religious Lyric* (London: Routledge, 1972), p. 131; Wenzel, *Preachers, Poets*, pp. 233–38.

[31] Lambeth 352, fol. 216^{r}: 'My dear sirs, a wife, grateful to her husband who was killed in battle for love of her, is accustomed to observe attentively the anniversary day of his death and to recall to memory his love and blessings and also the history of his death not without

statement establishes what will become the controlling metaphor for the rest of the sermon. The audience is the grateful wife, Christ the husband for whose death she grieves yearly; the rest of the sermon becomes the means by which she will recall the memory of his battle and death. The audience is thus asked to bring these events into the present through memory in order to respond with gratitude and sorrow, to undertake, in other words, a public meditation.

The preacher controls this *memoria* by using the scholastic sermon form to set up a series of frames in which he places the events. Before dividing the sermon material, he names three degrees of faithful love. The first degree transforms a lover and changes him into the thing that he loves; the second deforms him through the pains he suffers; and the third unforms him, when he loses his life for his beloved. These three degrees of love give the sermon its organizational scheme with each principal part representing one degree. The preacher then likens each degree to a 'truelove', a clover-like plant with four leaves, an image which then becomes a visual grid in which to place the narrative. The four leaves of the truelove are used to subdivide each of the three principal parts into four subsections, which become four actions by which Christ demonstrates that particular degree of love. Each leaf is then assigned a Middle English verse that will be used as the overarching motif for that section of the narrative. For instance, the third degree of love, when the lover loses his life for the beloved, comprises the following verses:

Love did hym ys armes spredin,
Love did him wel lovd to gredin,
Love did ys hert bledin,
An wit ys bloud vr saules fedin.[32]

Each verse represents one action by which Christ proves his love and each action comprises a number of events from the Passion narrative. For example, the second leaf of the third degree of love—'Love did him wel lovd to gredin'[33]—comprises Christ's seven last words from the cross, which he 'cried out'. The leaves of the truelove thus become a means of organizing and managing the events of the Passion and of connecting them to the overarching story of the lover-knight. The image itself helps shape the narrative and fix it more firmly in the audience's memory.[34] Because a truelove is easy to visualize, it sticks in the mind and, when one next sees an actual 'truelove', it may recall the Middle English verses and the narrative to which they

lamentable sorrow.'

[32] Lambeth 352, fol. 217^{v}.

[33] 'Love made him cry out very loudly.'

[34] Mary Carruthers, *The Book of Memory: A Study of Memory in Medieval Culture* (Cambridge: Cambridge University Press, 1990), p. 17, notes that, according to early writers, 'retention and retrieval are stimulated best by visual means, and the visual form of sense perception is what gives stability and permanence to memory storage'.

refer, as well as all that is implied by the concept of 'true love'. And it may evoke the emotions one felt when hearing this narrative. Emotions become part of the memory.

The truelove motif also had rich associations for an English audience and appears in several English poems and exempla. In an article investigating the Middle English poem, *The Quatrefoil of Love*, Helen Phillips notes that the word 'truelove' is itself common in Middle English devotional literature, sometimes as a synonym for the 'divine Lover, like "lemman" and "derelyng", and occasionally used of Mary too'.[35] Phillips finds three main aspects of what she calls the Truelove tradition:

> Firstly, the truelove flower may be associated with the search for the divine lover in Canticles 3. 2, *per vicos et plateas*; secondly, *true love* may be used to define an ideal of a love which is reciprocal and entirely without thought of profit: 'love for love' alone; thirdly, the truelove may be visualized as an emblem, sign or love-token of some kind, sometimes with an inscription with different significations assigned to each leaf.[36]

Each of these aspects is suggested in this sermon. The Truelove is the true lover, Christ, willing to perform the three degrees of 'true love' to demonstrate his love for his beloved. The truelove flower then becomes a visualizable emblem that represents each sign of Christ's love and thus also a love-token, for these signs are intended as proof of his love. By using the image of the truelove, the preacher, when he begins his narrative, can therefore rely on these cultural associations already established. By setting up a husband-wife relationship between Christ and audience and linking it to the truelove plant and thus to 'true love', the preacher constructs for the audience a personal *memoria*, just as a meditative text does. The audience is thus invited to enter into the events as participants, as it will during the creeping to the cross. Like a meditative text, the sermon guides the audience's responses to these events; it fashions the appropriate devotion.

Other sermons are not so explicitly meditative but still reinforce the liturgical present and establish an intimacy between the audience and the suffering Christ. The second example is a comparatively short sermon preached in the early fifteenth century, possibly by a Franciscan, William Melton.[37] He crafts this intimacy by heightening the role of the Virgin Mary and her grief over the death of her Son, using the *thema*, *Ve michi mater mea* (Jeremiah 15. 10: 'Woe unto me, my mother') to foster this role and create a mood of lament, a mood the sermon sets up from its

---

[35] Helen Phillips, '*The Quatrefoil of Love*', in *Langland, the Mystics and the Medieval English Religious Tradition: Essays in Honour of S. S. Hussey*, ed. by Helen Phillips (Rochester: Boydell & Brewer, 1990), 243–58 (p. 257).

[36] Phillips, '*The Quatrefoil of Love*', p. 257.

[37] A. Little, 'A Fifteenth-Century Sermon', in *Franciscan Papers, Lists, and Documents* (Manchester: Manchester University Press, 1943), 244–56 (p. 245).

beginning. In the short protheme the preacher first refers briefly to the biblical story of Joseph's bloody tunic, focusing on the point in the story when Jacob's sons ask him whether this tunic is indeed Joseph's and he responds that it is, believing that a wild animal tore Joseph to pieces (Genesis 37. 32–33). The preacher then allegorizes the tunic as Christ's body, which was given 'into the hands of the Virgin' just as it was given to Jacob, but then it is she who asks the question, not Jacob's sons. The sermon says that Mary 'clamauit dicens: "O pater misericordie, vide si hec est tunica filii tui annon? Vide, summe deus, si caro Christi est quod celo obumbrante spiritu sancto nunciante Gabrieli concepi".'[38] The Virgin Mary thus becomes the father who is given the tunic, Christ's dead body, and the interrogator who demands to know if this is the Father's son. The preacher then verbally creates an arresting image of the pietà. 'The Virgin', he says, 'wrapped this tunic around herself from her head to her feet. She saw the head pricked, etc., the body bloodied.'[39] This prompts her to ask Christ the question, 'My Son, why is your apparel red?'—a question from Isaiah traditionally related to Christ's Passion. In her anguish, the Virgin essentially poses two theological questions: can God's Son die and why must he? These questions are then answered in the sermon's first principal part, but the preacher makes of her interrogation a seemingly eternal lament, a lament that knowledge of Christian doctrine will not silence. He ends the protheme with the words: 'Vox igitur eius in rama sonabat plorans filium suum, interrogans patrem; si tunica filii sit annon?'[40] Hers then becomes the 'voice heard in Ramah, Rachel, weeping for her son who refused to be consoled.'[41]

In a short space, the protheme accomplishes a number of rhetorical tasks: it creates a striking image of the pietà, establishes a mood of lament, places the Passion in a larger theological framework, and sets up a dialogue that will pervade the rest of the sermon, a dialogue in which the Virgin Mary is the primary participant. She becomes, in J. A. W. Bennett's words, the 'mouthpiece of human protest and human compassion,'[42] and her words are, for the most part, the words of a lamenting mother, the 'vox plorans', imploring God for answers. Throughout the sermon she speaks sometimes to God the Father, sometimes to her son who in turn speaks to her, and at the end of the sermon, when Christ has presumably died, she speaks to John

[38] Ibid., p. 247: 'cried out to heaven, saying, "O Father of mercy, see whether or not this is the tunic of your Son? See, highest God, if Christ's flesh is that which I conceived after the Holy Spirit's overshadowing and Gabriel's annunciation."'

[39] Ibid., pp. 247–48: 'Voluebat intra se virgo hanc tunicam a capite usque ad pedes, videbat capud spinatum etc., corpus cruentatum.'

[40] Ibid., p. 248: 'Her voice therefore sounded in the branches, lamenting her son, asking the Father whether this was his son or not.'

[41] Jeremiah 31. 15; Matthew 2. 18.

[42] Bennett, *Poetry of the Passion*, p. 53.

the Evangelist, to whom Christ had just entrusted her. Many of her speeches are excerpted from the *Quis dabit*. Because this is a devotional text most likely familiar to an English audience, by weaving the text throughout the sermon, the preacher draws on a remembered response to this text. Mary thus lives out the Passion in the immediate moment, becoming the meditative or even liturgical link for the audience. The audience is encouraged to take part in this drama, to enter fully into the event, even if it is only as helpless witness.

A preacher may also evoke the liturgical present and fashion devotion by giving the audience a primary role in the dialogue. This strategy is used in the third example, a Good Friday sermon preached in the late 14th century by a Franciscan named Henry Chambron. This sermon uses as its *thema* the question from Isaiah—*Quare rubrum est indumentum tuum* [43]—to present a multifaceted exposition of medieval theories of the Atonement.[44] Chambron keeps this exposition from being dry and abstract by turning his sermon into an imaginary theological debate or *disputatio* of which the audience becomes part. He begins the sermon by naming three occasions on which Christ is asked the question—'Why is your apparel red?'—at the Ascension by the angels who did not accompany Christ when he came to earth, on Judgment Day by the souls awaiting judgment, and on Good Friday by every faithful Christian. Chambron then uses his protheme to develop two dialogues, the first between the angels and Christ on Ascension Day, the second between the elect and damned and Christ on Judgment Day. These dialogues serve as models for the exchange between Christ and the audience that takes place on Good Friday during the main part of the sermon, and they place the events of Good Friday into a larger theological context. They also evoke an image of Christ as triumphant knight (in the first dialogue) and angry judge (in the second), in both cases exploiting the topos of Christ in the winepress, both treader and trodden on, developed from the passage in Isaiah from which the *thema* is taken.[45]

Once Chambron has established by means of these two dialogues a set of participants and a larger context for the Passion, he turns to the audience and

---

[43] Isaiah 63. 2: 'Why is your apparel red?'

[44] This sermon exists in two versions, a longer one which is known to be extant in four manuscripts and a shorter version known to be extant in two manuscripts. Incomplete copies of the longer version are extant in Cambridge, University Library, MS Ii.3.8, fols 106^{r}–1104bis, verso (i.e., canceled 114^{v}); Cambridge, University Library, MS Ee.6.27, fols 73^{r}–84^{v}; and Oxford, Balliol College, MS 149, fols 77^{v}–83^{v}. The only complete copy of the longer version is in Arras, Bibliothèque Municipale, MS 184 (254), fols 61va–68va. The shorter version of this sermon is in Oxford, Balliol College, MS 149, fols 84^{r}–86^{v}, directly following the longer version, and in Padua, Biblioteca Antoniana, MS 515, fols 82^{v}–87^{r}.

[45] See James H. Marrow, *Passion Iconography in Northern European Art of the Late Middle Ages and Early Renaissance: A Study of the Transformation of Sacred Metaphor into Descriptive Narrative*, Ars Neerlandica I (Kortrijk: Van Ghemmert, 1979), pp. 83–94, for the development of and variations on this topos.

reminds them that the question, 'Why is your apparel red?' can be asked by each faithful Christian on Good Friday. He then says, 'Ad hanc tamen questionem oportet me respondere hac vice, sicut possum, quia Christus a quo queritur hec questio est ita afflictus quod ei non vacat respondere ad presens; necesse ergo est michi quod faciam sicut facit responsalis in scolis theologorum.'[46] Through this curious manoeuvre Chambron creates a fiction he then maintains throughout the sermon, a fiction in which the audience, the implicit 'faithful Christian', is confronted with the suffering Christ bloodied by the instruments of the Passion and wants to know how this has happened, just as the Virgin does who asks the same question in the sermon discussed above. But Christ's present suffering makes it impossible for him to explain the cause of this suffering. The preacher thus places before the audience the *imago pietatis* (or the Man of Sorrows), the crucified Christ who looks directly out at the spectator in pain and anguish and often points to his wounds, the *ostentatio vulnerum*, which are usually bleeding.[47] There is no sense of time in these images. Christ has all the wounds, including the wound in his side, which he received after his death, yet he is alive. The audience has thus been given a key role in this imaginary *disputatio*, that of *disputans*, the one who poses the question. But this is a *disputans* who does not ask a theological question as an academic exercise but rather asks in response to the painful reality confronting him, just as in the sermon *Ve michi mater mea* where the Virgin is similarly confronted by the body of her dead son. This situation makes the answer to the question of immediate—even urgent—concern to the ones who are asking it. The preacher, instead of preaching to them, has now transformed himself into Christ's respondent; Christ is, then, the *magister*, the master who stands behind the respondent, his student. In this way all have been placed in the context of a theological school, but an odd theological school it is in which the Master and the subject are one and the same. Chambron thus combines an overarching drama, the scene of a theological debate, with an hieratic image, the *imago pietatis*, and this combination of drama and image acts as a unifying and emotionally evocative backdrop against which the events of Good Friday are re-enacted and re-experienced. While the imaginary scene may be that of a dry theological debate, the mood Chambron creates is one of mourning; the suffering Christ is ever-present throughout the sermon. The audience, as *disputans*, is asked to

[46] Oxford, Balliol College, MS 149, fols 84^r–84^v: 'Yet it is necessary for me to respond to this question at this time because Christ, to whom this is addressed, is so afflicted and tormented, that he cannot respond. Therefore it is necessary for me that I do as does a respondent in the schools of theology.'

[47] For recent studies of this image, see Bernhard Ridderbos, 'The Man of Sorrows: Pictorial Images and Metaphorical Statements', in *The Broken Body: Passion Devotion in Late-Medieval Culture*, ed. by A. A. MacDonald, H. N. B. Ridderbos and R. M. Schlusemann (Groningen: Forsten, 1998), pp. 145–81; and Michael Camille, 'Mimetic Identification and Passion Devotion in the Later Middle Ages: A Double-sided Panel by Meister Francke', in *The Broken Body*, pp. 183–210.

respond to the event before it not just with curiosity, but with concern, outrage, and compassion.

Other Devices

The scholastic structure in each of these Good Friday sermons, and others like them, sets up a backdrop against which Christ's suffering and death are brought dramatically to life. These sermons thus both reinforce the liturgical present of the Good Friday rituals and bring the act of private meditation into the public realm. To intensify and sustain this meditation and 'fix' it in their audience's memory, preachers use a number of rhetorical and stylistic devices. For instance, they sometimes drop their preaching persona and slip into pious address, becoming living models of devotion and penitence. They also excerpt well-known devotional texts, such as the *Quis dabit* or St Bernard's homilies on the Song of Songs, that draw their audiences into an intimate moment with Christ while simultaneously transforming such moments into public expressions of piety. As we have seen with the use of the truelove image, the *imago pietatis*, and the lover-knight exemplum, the sermons also share with other genres images, topoi, and metaphors that may have elicited a remembered emotional response. The scholastic structure provides a framework within which the preacher can shift from preacher to teacher to pious meditator, from exhortation to explanation to mystical reverie, without losing control of the larger devotional mood.

Of these devices visual images operate perhaps in the subtlest and most effective way in fashioning devotion. Such visual images are not only used to structure individual sections of these sermons, pictorially framing the verbal material, as was seen with the image of the truelove, but they also help create for the audience a memory, both of the content contained by the image and of the response sought from that content. In his study of Chaucer's imagery, V. A. Kolve argues that 'the images most central to the late Middle Ages carried with them a weight of accumulated cultural meaning—historical, religious, moral and psychological. They are images with a human past.'[48] Kolve also states that the 'memory receives not only the image but its consequence for the perceptor. [...] Because an image contains both a likeness and an intention, it has the capacity both to remind and to move the soul.'[49]

---

[48] V. A. Kolve, *Chaucer and the Imagery of Narrative: The First Five Canterbury Tales* (Stanford: Stanford University Press, 1984), p. 61.

[49] Kolve, *Chaucer and the Imagery of Narrative*, p. 45. Carruthers, *The Craft of Thought: Meditation, Rhetoric, and the Making of Images, 400–1200* (Cambridge: Cambridge University Press, 1998), pp. 14–15, makes a similar point about the way memory works. Memories 'are all images, and they are all and always emotionally "colored"'. But, she continues, 'more is involved than simply an emotional *state* associated with a memory. [...] Memories are not tossed into storage at random, they "are put in" their "places" there, "colored" in ways that are partly personal, partly emotional, partly rational, and mostly

Although Kolve's focus is *The Canterbury Tales*, his assertion also applies to images used by Good Friday preachers, which, like the image of the truelove, are not original to these sermons; rather they have 'accumulated cultural meaning' and invite the audience 'to recognize as being *like*—as being in "approximate register" with—symbolic images known from other medieval contexts, both literary and visual.'[50] Literary and pictorial images of the suffering Christ had a multiplicity of expressions by the late Middle Ages, which had seen, according to James Marrow, an 'extraordinarily inventive expansion of Passion imagery in which the simple formulas of earlier centuries were replaced by elaborately detailed and moving descriptions of Christ's tormentors, torments, and sufferings.'[51] The preachers employ many such images, including the Charter of Christ, Christ in the Mystical Wine Press, the Instruments of the Passion (or the *Arma Christi*), Christ as a man 'wrapped in woe'—all variations on the *Imago pietatis*. They also exploit a number of metaphors related to these images, metaphors likewise invested with cultural meaning, such as Christ as the harp or Christ's Passion as a book. The preachers can assume the audience will readily recognize such metaphors and images, and they can also invoke them in often suggestive ways, assured that their basic outlines are already formed in the audience's memory.

The interplay between images and narrative in these sermons creates a tension between stasis and action, a tension connected to that which is created by the interplay between doctrine and drama, or theology and pathos. The sermon *Ve michi mater mea* discussed above, which uses as its controlling image the pietà and its controlling drama the Lament of the Virgin Mary, exemplifies this tension particularly well in its first principal part, a narrative very like an exemplum but perhaps better thought of as a dramatic vignette. Instead of involving knights or kings as allegorical representations of Christ, this vignette involves Christ directly; he himself plays the leading role. In this vignette Christ is tried under three laws—the law of nature, the law of Moses, and the law of grace—each of which condemn him to die. This vignette allows the preacher to place Christ's Passion before the audience as an event taking place in the timeless now at the same time as it allows him to dramatize a theological point: to explain theologically why Christ must die and thus answer the question posed by the Virgin in the sermon's protheme. It also places the significance of Christ's Passion within salvation history, the largest possible context, thereby preparing the audience for the full impact of the narrative it will hear in the next two parts of the sermon which narrate the events of the Passion in roughly chronological order.[52]

---

cultural'.

[50] Kolve, *Chaucer and the Imagery of Narrative*, p. 61.

[51] Marrow, *Passion Iconography*, p. 1.

[52] The second principal part uses the alphabet as its organizational device to narrate the Passion up until the crucifixion; each letter represents one or two of the ways Christ suffered.

The Christ-on-trial vignette functions as both allegory and drama. Each trial has its own jury and four judges derived from Scriptures as well as two advocates, one of which argues against Christ's death, the other for it. While it is 'true' that an innocent man should not have to die for a guilty man, it is necessary that an innocent man die for a guilty man since a guilty man cannot save himself nor can God in his divinity die. This is the Anselmian logic of *Cur Deus Homo*, placed in the mouths of two allegorical figures. The jury for this trial is made up of the twelve patriarchs, whose speaker, Joseph, uses his own typology—'I was solde to egipte pro 30 d. and saued all my kynde'—to prove that Christ must also be sold to save the 'genus humanum.'[53] The four judges—Abel, Abraham, Noah, and Lot—do likewise. Thus the first trial gives both doctrinal and exegetical reasons for Christ's death. The trial ends with Christ's reaction—he 'pleynynge hymself to his speciall frende dixit verba thematis *Ve michi* etc'[54]—and Mary's response, which is a lengthy complaint the preacher attributes to Bernard, but is in fact excerpted from the *Quis dabit*, the devotional text that appears throughout this sermon.[55] 'My son, my son', she bewails, 'Woe unto me, woe unto me, who will make it so that I die for you? O, I am wretched; what would I do? My son dies. Why does not his mother die? O wretched death, do not spare me, slaughter the mother with the son because woe unto me among all women.'[56] She then adds a Middle English verse which acts as a transition to the next trial: 'To the law of Moses my appeal I make. The law of nature I will forsake.' This pattern is repeated at the end of the second trial, but at the end of the third Christ speaks out himself, complaining to his mother in his own Middle English rhyme: 'Der moder myn, to me is gret dole and pyne.'[57] Christ and Mary's responses give this trial an affective dimension not found in the real trials on which Christ was placed on Good Friday, during which he was falsely accused and thus unjustly condemned to die. All three trials act almost as tableau; they place before the audience a series of characters who each soberly deliver a reason for Christ's death, in response to which Christ and Mary deliver heart-rending complaints. The allegorical and biblical figures speak from a timeless perspective; they speak the doctrinal voice. Christ and his mother speak in the immediate moment. Their

---

The third principal part uses the metaphor of Christ as a harp to narrate five out of Christ's seven last words from the cross.

[53] Little, 'A Fifteenth-Century Sermon', p. 248.

[54] He 'lamenting to his special friend, said the words of the *thema*, "Woe unto me", etc.'

[55] For a discussion of its attribution to Bernard, see Bestul, *Texts of the Passion*, pp. 52–53.

[56] Little, 'A Fifteenth-Century Sermon', p. 249: 'Fili mi, fili mi, ve michi, ve michi, quis dabit ut ego morior pro te? O misera quid faciam? Moritur filius, cur non moritur mater? O mors misera, noli michi parcere, trucida matrem cum filio quia inter omnes mulieres ve michi'.

[57] 'Dear mother mine, for me is great suffering and pain'. Little, 'A Fifteenth-Century Sermon', p. 251.

complaints are in contrast to Christ's relative impassivity in the Gospel accounts, making these narratives more affective and therefore memorable; without losing the larger theological perspective, they invite the audience to experience the Passion from the human perspective of mother and son.

While the sermon relies heavily on the *Quis dabit* to lend pathos to these trials (and trigger a familiar response in the audience), there are marked differences between the devotional text and its use in this sermon. The trials in the sermon are rendered affective by Christ and his mother's plaintive reaction, but they are set up primarily to answer in narrative form the larger question of why Christ must suffer and die. The *Quis dabit* presents the story of the Passion from the point of view of the Virgin Mary, so hers are the eyes through which the reader sees the events; it is a maternal view of a beloved child suffering with little outside narrative voice and no preacher to mute the Virgin's pathos. The *Quis dabit* is thus intended to draw its readers into an intimate experience of the Passion based almost entirely on an affective response. The sermon *Ve michi mater mea* offers something else. The preacher's voice frames that of the Virgin, exerting control over the material and offering a larger dimension to the view; it never allows sentiment to get out of control. The form of the scholastic sermon itself tempers the emotionalism, as does the theological meaning of the Passion. This keeps *Ve michi mater mea* from falling into the near histrionics sometimes displayed by the *Quis dabit* and by fifteenth-century Middle English lyrics of the Compassion of the Virgin Mary, which Rosemary Woolf criticizes for lacking a 'substantial theological frame of reference, which could control invention and feeling.'[58] The Christ-on-trial vignette sets up this frame of reference but does so dramatically, by letting the participants in salvation history speak for themselves. The preacher thus maintains his role as pedagogue without diminishing the pathos of the Passion; in fact, it is in his role as pedagogue that he constructs the appropriate response to this pathos.

Conclusion

In their attempt to underscore the liturgical present, the macaronic Good Friday sermons share many rhetorical and stylistic devices with other late-medieval genres, especially religious lyrics, meditative treatises, and Passion plays. They thus illuminate the rich cross-fertilization among genres. They also reveal more fully the imaginative milieu out of which works like *Piers Plowman* were born. In discussing Langland's indebtedness to sermons, Wenzel suggests that we 'think of the poem's sermon background as a diffuse and widely dispersed influence, furnishing commonplaces and perhaps even structural patterns that floated from pulpit to pulpit

[58] Woolf, *Religious Lyric*, p. 272.

and settled in many written texts.'[59] But sermons also help us better understand Langland's liturgical imagination, his evocation of the timeless now. For example, the Christ-on-trial vignette discussed above works very much the way sections of *Piers Plowman* work and with a similar effect. In Passus 16 of *Piers Plowman*, the dreamer meets Abraham, Moses, and the Samaritan from Christ's parable and sets out with them to witness Christ's 'joust' in Jerusalem. In discussing this scene, Joseph Wittig notes that this 'sort of imaginative simultaneity, this 'omnitemporalness,' creates exactly the kind of overlaid experiences for which the liturgy strives as it re-enacts biblical events (both Old Testament 'figures' and their New Testament fulfillments) and applies them to current time.'[60] The Christ-on-trial vignette, with its large cast of characters from the Old and New Testaments joined by pairs of allegorical figures which are all placed together in a fictional trial scene set in the timeless now of the Good Friday liturgy, creates just this sort of 'overlaid experience'. These sermons thus offer us a wider view of the imaginative mode in which medieval artists worked and of the expectations they may have had for their audiences, who were trained to experience the 'omnitemporalness' created not only by *Piers Plowman* and sermons, but by Passion plays, religious lyrics and devotional images like the *imago pietatis*.

The macaronic sermons also offer us a more balanced understanding of late-medieval piety. The feverishness of the piety assumed by scholars who study devotional texts may somewhat obscure the more everyday, tempered piety experienced by a majority of medieval people, whose devotion was fashioned by sermons where this feverishness is controlled and given substance by talented preachers trained not only in the rhetorical and literary arts but also in doctrine and exegesis. While the primary aims of these sermons were to make the events of the Passion immediately present and to elicit from the audience an affective response to those events, it was not enough to encourage the audience to enter experientially into these events; the audience must be taught how to respond—and this response must be carried over into daily life. None of the sermons engages in the overwrought emotionalism of a devotional text like the *Quis dabit*. The sermons control feeling partly by way of the scholastic form, with its divisions and subdivisions which place all the material into an ordered structure, and partly by way of the theology that underpins the narratives and devotional images. Never far beneath the surface, even while the preachers use graphic descriptions to narrate the most highly affective scenes, lie the larger doctrinal explanations of the Passion. Thus a balance is struck between the feelings of tenderness and compassion that should result from a meditation on Christ's suffering on the one hand and a theological understanding of

[59] Wenzel, 'Medieval Sermons', in *A Companion to* Piers Plowman, ed. by John A. Alford (Berkeley: University of California Press, 1988), pp. 155–72 (p. 168).

[60] Joseph Wittig, *William Langland Revisited*, Twayne's English Authors Series, 537 (New York: Twayne Publishers, 1997), p. 128.

what that suffering means on the other. An affective response is never sought for its own sake; these preachers are not the counterparts of the preachers of the modern tent revival. For a contemporary audience this doctrinal dimension might undermine the affective response that preachers claim to seek; but more imaginative effort—or greater imaginative sophistication—may have been expected from the medieval audiences to whom these preachers preached.

Finally, these sermons exemplify well the highly developed art of late-medieval preaching. For while they employ many topoi found in other genres, they cannot rightly be designated as devotional texts intended for private meditation or literary texts intended for private enjoyment. They are sermons: public, oratorical, and occasional. Each of them is a literary and rhetorical construct intended for the specific occasion of Good Friday. None has the 'pick' and 'mix' quality that the Brinton sermon has. Although the sermons rely on cultural associations and popular devotions, the way they transform these devotions into the sermon form may have served as a jolt for a potentially indifferent audience that had heard the Passion narrative itself time and again. By placing this narrative into a new context, each sermon also creates for its audience memorable content, a way of 'fixing' the narrative in the audience's memory for future reflection. By placing highly emotionally content within the fairly rigid scholastic sermon structure, these sermons create a tension between two seemingly disparate modes. But this may be the same tension found in the liturgy itself, which is, after all, a formalized set of rituals re-enacting a violent historical event.

A Statistical Treatment of Sin and Holiness in Sermons from the Early Middle Ages (500–1100)

MARTINE DE REU

1. The Use of Computers and Statistics for Medieval Mentality Studies

As yet, few articles on medieval mentality studies involve (even elementary) statistical data, although in other fields of medieval research, such as demographic studies, taxation, and so forth, statistics are readily used. Two reasons for this phenomenon are apparent. Firstly, the method is deeply mistrusted by researchers working in the field of the history of ideas. They fear, as R. Busa puts it, that texts will be consulted and not read.[1] The unity of the text seems to be lost,

[1] R. Busa, 'Nouvelles perspectives d'herméneutique thomiste', in *Méthodologies informatiques et nouveaux horizons dans les recherches médiévales*, ed. by J. Hamesse (Turnhout: Brepols, 1992), pp. 66–67: 'Il y a, en effet, des livres à consulter et des livres à lire. Une chose est lire, une autre est consulter: je lis une histoire, je consulte un répertoire. Je pense que, entre lire pour lire et lire pour consulter, il y a au fond deux différences. La première est qu'en consultant je cherche une information particulière que je veux insérer dans un autre ensemble: tandis que, quand je lis, je cherche l'"idée" d'ensemble de ce que je lis. La seconde est qu'en consultant, je sais déjà ce que je cherche, mais pas nécessairement quand je lis: en lisant, je ne cherche pas, mais je chemine, je regarde, je'observe et je relève'. In their article D. I. Holmes, L. J. Gordon, C. Wilson, 'A Widow and her Soldier: Stylometry and the American Civil War', *Literary and Linguistic Computing*, 16 (2001), 403–20 (p. 404), the authors forestall criticism from historians: 'Historians have not always welcomed new techniques into their craft, and no doubt, there will be those sceptical of the conclusions presented below. We simply ask historians to consider stylometry as an additional tool to understanding the past, one that complements more traditional scholarship and allows historians to think anew some old questions.'

and consequently the researcher can no longer grasp the deepest sense of the text. Secondly, the primary sources for medieval mentality studies are texts, i.e. documents consisting of words, grouped together in sentences, paragraphs, chapters and forming a unity in which the order of the different elements is important. Studies in the field of economics, demography, and suchlike use mostly data from historical sources with a repetitive structure—with a recurring series of similar entries.[2] Data from the latter sources are 'more suitable' for entering into databases and for treating automatically and/or statistically.

The automatic analysis of texts gained important impetus during the last decades of the twentieth century, when growing numbers of machine-readable texts became available for historians and philologists. In this context, the gigantic databases of the Louvain-la-Neuve-based CETEDOC, and its successor institution in Turnhout, CTLO, immediately come to mind,[3] although also a multitude of other initiatives led to similarly successful results.[4]

---

[2] O. Boonstra, 'De computer in een historisch onderzoek', in *Historische Informatiekunde. Inleiding tot het gebruik van de computer bij historische studies*, ed. by O. Boonstra, L. Breure, P. Doorn (Hilversum: Verloren, 1990) pp. 49–50; H. Voorbij, 'Analyse en ontsluiting van teksten met behulp van de computer', in *Historische Informatiekunde. Inleiding tot het gebruik van de computer bij historische studies*, ed. by O. Boonstra, L. Breure, P. Doorn (Hilversum: Verloren, 1990), pp. 131–39.

[3] See for the CETEDOC the publications of L. Genicot and P. Tombeur. L. Genicot, 'Les concordances et listes de fréquence des textes narratifs latin composés en Belgique avant 1200', in *Actes du Colloque: L'utilisation des ordinateurs et la recherche en sciences humaines*: extra issue of *Archives et Bibliothèques de Belgique* (Brussels: Association des archivistes et bibliothécaires, 1971), pp. 241–48 ; idem, 'Le traitement électronique des textes diplomatiques belges antérieurs à 1200', in *Informatique et histoire médiévale*, Communications et débats de la Table Ronde CNRS, organisée par l'École française de Rome et l'Institut d'Histoire Médiévale de l'Université de Pise (Rome, 20–22 mai 1975), ed. by L. Fossier, A. Vauchez, C. Violante, Collection de l'École française de Rome 31 (Rome: École française de Rome, 1977), pp. 97–104; id., 'Some elementary remarks on the utility of computers in medieval History', in *Computer applications to medieval studies*, ed. by A. Gilmour-Bryson (Kalamazoo: Medieval Institute Publications, Western Michigan University, 1984), pp. 45–50 ; P. Tombeur, 'Informatique et étude de textes. Pour une meilleure connaissance du vocabulaire medio-latin', *Archivum Latinitatis medii aevi*, 40 (1977), 124–38; id., 'Vox Latina. Belgian initiatives in data-processing: the intellectual language of Europe, AD 197–1965', *Computers and the Humanities*, 12, 1–2 (1978), 13–18; id., 'Informatique et étude de textes médiévaux', in *L'homme et son univers au moyen âge*, ed. by C. Wenin, Philosophes médiévaux 27 (Louvain-la-Neuve Institut supérieur de philosophie, 1986), pp. 174-86; id., 'Latinité et informatique: travaux réalisés par le CETEDOC. Perspectives et implications méthologiques', in *The Editing of Theological and Philosophical Texts from the Middle Ages*, Acts of the conference arranged by the Department of Classical Languages, University of Stockholm, 29–31 August 1984, ed. by M. Asztalos, Studia Latina Stockholmiensia 30 (Stockholm: Almqvist & Wiksell, 1986), pp. 35–57; id., 'Banques de données textuelles et lexicales pour l'étude de la tradition occidentale', in *Méthodologies*

Gradually, medievalists interested in the history of ideas came to accept the use of the computer—and even to praise it—for very specific purposes. At first, they only used the printed or microfilmed listings of computers, such as concordances and lists of lemmata.[5] Later, some medievalists were convinced to work directly with the computer, instead. One was encouraged to explore machine readable texts when looking for the first appearance of a certain word,[6] the occurrence of a term with a chosen author and, last but not least, the identification of citations. Enthusiasm for this application was so overwhelming that *L'ordinateur et le médiéviste* devoted a complete issue to the topic.[7]

Computer studies has invited us to go further, though: as soon as a text is in machine-readable format, it can be explored in many different ways. Some scholars use the computer (and statistics) for the style analysis of texts. While, in general, researchers gained a deeper insight in the style of a particular author, the method also provided several anonymous texts with an author. Stylometry is a set of quantitative methods used to decipher texts, making abstraction of the contents of the texts and concentrating on stylistic characteristics. Some stylistic characteristics include the analysis of function words such as articles, prepositions, adverbs; the ratio of different lemmata on the total of *formae*; average word length; average sentence length, and cluster analysis of the most frequently used words in complete or partial texts.[8] In recent stylometric research one tries also to include syntactically based

informatiques et nouveaux horizons dans les recherches médiévales, ed. by J. Hamesse, Rencontres de philosophie médiévale, 2 (Turnhout: Brepols, 1992) pp. 225–47.

[4] See for 'medieval' examples: J. Deploige, M. De Reu, L. Milis, 'Informatique et études médiévales', in R. Van Caenegem, *Introduction aux sources de l'histoire médiévale* (Turnhout: Brepols, 1997), pp. 533–50 and note 12 for sites or portals to other examples.

[5] See for example the works of R. Busa, L. Génicot and P. Tombeur mentioned earlier.

[6] See for a concrete example: P. Tombeur, 'Informatique et étude de textes médiévaux', in *L'homme et son univers au moyen âge*, ed. by C. Wenin, Philosophes médiévaux, 27 (Louvain-la-Neuve, 1986), pp. 185–86.

[7] *Le médiéviste et l'ordinateur*, no. 22, fall 1990. Some examples of studies (partially) based on the counting of citations: M. De Reu, *La Parole du Seigneur. Moines et chanoines médiévaux prêchant l'Ascension et le Royaume des Cieux*, IHBR Bibliothèque, 43 (Brussels, Rome: IHBR, 1996); J. Deploige, *In nomine femineo indocta. Kennisprofiel en ideologie van Hildegard van Bingen (1098–1179)* (Hilversum: Verloren, 1998).

[8] General introductions: H. H. Somers, Statistical methods in literary analysis, in *The Computer and Literary Style: Introductory Essays and Studies*, ed. by J. Leed (Kent, OH: Kent State University Press, 1966), pp. 128–40; A. Kenny, *The Computation of Style. An Introduction to Statistics for Students of Literature and Humanities* (Oxford: Pergamon Press, 1982); H. Voorbij, 'Analyse en ontsluiting van teksten met behulp van de computer', in *Historische Informatiekunde. Inleiding tot het gebruik van de computer bij historische studies*, ed. by O. Boonstra, L. Breure, P. Doorn (Hilversum: Verloren, 1990), pp. 130–83; D. I. Holmes, 'Authorship Attribution', *Computers and the Humanities*, 28.2 (1994), 87–106;

techniques. This type of research necessitates amply tagged texts, which are time consuming to produce.[9]

In a similar manner, methodologies for content analysis of groups of texts have been developed. These methods, equally quantitative, are mostly applied for the analysis of responses to open questions in questionnaires used by sociologists, psychologists, market researchers, and so forth. Recently, the methods for content analysis have also been used for the attribution of an author to an anonymous text.[10] Content analysis aims to evaluate the frequency of types of words in a text and by doing so to get at the deepest meaning of the text. Content analysis can be effectuated by different methods. Basically, one can choose a set of words and check the frequency of their presence in the text. For instance, a list of aggressive words can be compiled for analyzing the hostile tone of a speech. Additionally, all the words in a given text or set of texts can also be analyzed. In practice this means that only the most frequently used words are analyzed and grouped in function words indicating time, function words indicating space, adverbs indicating intensity, nouns referring to the family circle, and so on. Putting these data in a matrix with the different types of the words in the rows and the different texts in the columns, allows the regrouping of the texts according to their content. The sociologist can even assign a particular set of answers to a specific segment of the population if the questionnaire included some closed questions enquiring about age, sex, education and so on. Separating the different groups needs advanced statistical methods such as univariate or multivariate analyses of variance, cluster analysis, neural-network

---

Holmes, 'The Evolution of Stylometry in Humanities Scholarship', *Literary and Linguistic Computing*, 13 (1998), 11117; E. Stamatatos, N. Fakotakis, G. Kokkinakis, 'Computer-Based Authorship Attribution without Lexical Measures', *Computers and the Humanities*, 35.2 (2001), 193–214. See for a critical approach of cluster analysis used in some studies of stylometry: D. L. Hoover, 'Statistical Stylistics and Authorship Attribution: an Empirical Investigation', *Literary and Linguistic Computing*, 16.4 (2001), 421–44. Studies based on "stylometrics": A. Ellegård, *A Statistical Method for Determining Authorship: the Junius Letters, 1762–1772*, Gothenburg Studies in English 13 (Göteborg, 1962); F. Mosteller, D. L. Wallace, *Inference and Disputed Authorship: 'The Federalist'* (Reading, MA: Addison-Wesley, 1964); F. Mosteller, D. L. Wallace, *Applied Bayesian and Classical Inference, the Case of the Federalist Papers* (New York: Springer-Verlag, 1984); R. Thisted, B. Efron, 'Did Shakespeare Write a Newly Discovered Poem?', *Biometrika*, 74 (1987), 445–55, D. I. Holmes, 'A Stylometric Analysis of Mormon Scripture and Related Texts', *Journal of the Royal Statistical Society, Series A—Statistics in Society*, 155,1 (1992), 91–120.

[9] D. I. Holmes, 'The Evolution of Stylometry in Humanities Scholarship', *Literary and Linguistic Computing*, 13 (1998), 116–17.

[10] C. Martindale, D. McKenzie, 'On the Utility of Content Analysis in Author Attribution: The Federalist', *Computers and the Humanities*, 29 (1995), 259–70.

algorithms, etc. By now, an impressive number of specific computer programs is at the disposal of the researcher.[11]

As stated before, medievalists working outside the field of socio-economic studies are hesitant to consider the computer as a possible ally in their research. There have been, for some decades, a great many initiatives regarding the electronic publication of texts in order to facilitate the reading, or maybe more accurately, the consultation of these texts. Fortunately, many of these were encoded. Investigating the encoding process is not the scope of this article.[12] Except for charters, the full potential of electronically available texts is seldom exploited.[13] The purpose of this article is to count selected words in electronically available texts and interpret the results with simple statistical techniques.[14] One must not replace an attentive reading of texts

---

[11] See footnote 10 and G. Salton, *Automatic Text Processing: The Transformation, Analysis and Retrieval of Information by Computer* (Reading, MA: Addison-Wesley, 1989); L. Lebart, 'Sur les analyses statistiques de textes', *Journal de la Société de statistique de Paris*, 135.1 (1994), 17–36; L. Lebart, A. Salem, *Statistique textuelle* (Paris: Dunod, 1994); E. Mergenthaler, 'Computer-Assisted Content Analysis', in *Zuma-Nachrichten. Spezial: Text Analysis and Computers* (Mannheim: ZUMA, 1996), pp. 3–32; U. Kelle, 'Computer-Aided Qualitative Data Analysis: An Overview', in ibid., pp. 33–63; F. Guérin-Pace, 'La statistique textuelle. Un outil exploratoire en sciences sociales', *Population*, 52.4 (1997), 865–87.

[12] We refer to more recent issues of *Le médiéviste et l'ordinateur* treating *Le texte médiéval sur Internet I. Chercher et trouver* (nr 37–hiver 1998), *Le texte médiéval sur Internet 2. Mettre des textes sur Internet* (nr 38–hiver 1999), *La numérisation des manuscrits médiévaux* (nr 40—automne 2001) and the following sites / portals for examples of electronic publishing: Ménestrel (www.ccr.jussieu.fr/urfist/mediev.htm), Labyrinth (www.georgetown.edu/labyrinth/), Reti Medievali (www.retimedievali.it/), Internet Medieval Sourcebook (www.fordham.edu/halsall/sbook.html), TEI (www.tei-c.org).

[13] See for the use of electronically available charters the results of the DEEDS-project in Toronto (M. Gervers) and of the 'Atelier des textes diplomatiques' of the ARTEM in Nancy (B.-M. Tock). See further the proceedings of the conference on charters held at the Collegium Budapest/Institute for Advanced Study in March 1999: *Dating Undated Medieval Charters*, ed. by M. Gervers (Woodbridge, Suffolk: Boydell & Brewer, 2000) and for Dutch charters: M. Leroy, 'The Thirteenth-Century Middle Dutch Charters (1272–1300) of Saint John's Hospital in Bruges: A Diplomatic and Paleographic Approach', in *Secretum Scriptorum. Liber Alumnorum Walter Prevenier*, ed. by W. P. Blockmans, M. Boone, T. de Hemptinne (Leuven, Apeldoorn: Garant, 1999) pp. 93–128.

[14] See for some examples of content analysis of medieval texts based on statistics: L. Breure, 'The Modern Devotion: The Structure of a Concept', in *Computer Applications to Medieval Studies*, ed. by A. Gilmour-Bryson (Kalamazoo: Medieval Institute Publications, 1984), pp.135–46; J.-P. Genet, 'Automatic Text Processing and Factorial Analysis: A Method for the Determining the Lexicographical Horizon of Expectation', in *Computer Applications to Medieval Studies*, ed. by A. Gilmour-Bryson (Kalamazoo: Medieval Institute Publications, 1984), pp. 147–76; M. De Reu, *La Parole du Seigneur. Moines et chanoines médiévaux prêchant l'Ascension et le Royaume des Cieux*, IHBR Bibliothèque, 43 (Brussels, Rome: IHBR, 1996); T. De Meester, 'Kronieken in grafieken. Methodologische perspectieven voor

with 'counting words'. It is a complementary way to look at texts. 'Counting' offers a more objective basis to 'intuitive' feelings occurring while reading texts. In those cases where statistical methods yield unexpected results, they exhort us to return to the texts and start reading them over again from a new point of view.

The type of research presented in this article has many problems in common with the content analysis as it is done by linguists, sociologists, psychologists and others: word forms have to be grouped under their lemmata, some words have homonyms or have several meanings. Unlike the researchers of modern texts, we do not deal with a (more or less) uniform spelling, and we cannot use dictionaries to analyze words automatically (i.e. to separate homonyms or words with more than one meaning into several groups). Furthermore, our collection of texts is much bigger than the corpus treated by our colleagues dealing with modern writings—*in toto* I studied 10,666,325 words in the CLCLT and 23,610 columns in the PL and some manually counted sermons. Furthermore, the corpus was not written at one moment in history, but over six centuries. The latter fact means that one has to check also for new words developing, old words disappearing, and changes in meaning. Of course it is impossible, even with the aid of a computer, to examine the complete content of all those texts. So, I have chosen a set of concepts to analyze, and I will concentrate here on vices and virtues. During my research, I have asked the following questions: which vices are more often mentioned than others? which virtues are more popular than others? are vices more often stressed than virtues? and are there evolutions over time? The results obtained by analyzing sermons are always compared with the occurrences of vices and virtues found in other sources from the same period.

2. Defining a Corpus for Analysis

Statistical analysis necessitates several basic data requirements.[15] Firstly, one has to analyze sufficient numbers; ideally, one should analyze 'everything'. While this

---

de kwantitatieve analyse van middeleeuwse monastieke historiografie', *Bulletin de l'institut historique belge de Rome*, 70 (2000), 299–336; S. Vanderputten, 'Clusterpatronen in de middeleeuwse monastieke historiografie', *Revue belge de philologie et d'histoire*, 78 (2000), 773–95; S. Vanderputten, *Sociale perceptie en maatschappelijke positionering in de Middeleeuwse monastieke historiografie (8e–15e eeuw)*, Algemeen Rijksarchief en Rijksarchief in de provinciën. Studia, 87 (Brussels: Algemeen Rijksarchief, 2001); J. Deploige, *Hagiografische strategieën en tactieken tegen de achtergrond van kerkelijke en maatschappelijke vernieuwingstendensen. De Zuidelijke Nederlanden, ca 920–ca 1320* (unpublished doctoral thesis, Ghent University, 2002).

[15] See, for example, J. T. Lindblad, *Statistiek voor historici* (Muiderberg: Coutinho, 1984); S. Heyes, M. Hardy, P. Humphreys, P. Rookes, *Starting Statistics in Psychology and Education. A Student Handbook* (Oxford: Oxford University Press, 1986); R. J. Shavelson, *Statistical Reasoning for the Behavioral Sciences* (Boston: Allyn and Bacon, 1988); O.

ideal is seldom possible, it can a priori never be attained for medieval studies. For one thing, not every source has been preserved. As M. Garrison puts it: 'The survival of a poem or manuscript from the ninth century to the twentieth [...] reflects the complex interaction of chance and intention'.[16] It is indeed superfluous to posit that this is a valid statement for all medieval sources. Secondly, counting sufficient numbers in an efficient way supposes that these sources are edited and electronically available. These necessities diminish even further the corpus of texts at one's disposal.

Since the analysis of early medieval sermons is the primary goal, I first discuss the constitution of a body of sermons. One of the first problems in establishing a corpus is the wide variety in context of the early medieval sermon. Sermons were/are often delivered during mass (usually after the gospel), but this was/is not the only occasion of their occurrence. Innumerable sermons were pronounced during the night offices. The practice of praying during the night developed as early as the first century. During the following centuries (night) vigils became more frequent and more elaborate, especially in monastic communities.[17] The *Regula Benedicti* prescribes a vigil (*vigiliae*) with two nocturns during weekdays and three nocturns during Sundays and feast-days. In practice, this meant that on winter weekdays the monks had to listen to three lessons of 'normal' length and to one short lesson. The longer lessons had to be chosen from the Bible and from the writings of the *orthodoxi catholici Patres*. During the summer, one lesson from the Old Testament was substituted for the three lessons. On Sundays and feast-days, the monks had to listen to twelve lessons. Benedict only gives precise indications for the last four lessons (the third nocturn): those have to be taken from the New Testament. The other lessons could be chosen from the same books as designed for the *vigiliae* held during the week.[18] However, sermons were also used outside the church. If it happened that a long lesson could not be completed during the night office, then the remainder of the text was read out in the refectory.[19]

Boonstra, P. Doorn, F. Hendrickx, *Voortgezette statistiek voor historici* (Muiderberg, 1990).

[16] M. Garrison, 'The Emergence of Carolingian Latin Literature and the Court of Charlemagne (780–814)', in *Carolingian Culture: Emulation and Innovation*, ed. by R. McKitterick (Cambridge: Cambridge University Press, 1994), p. 111.

[17] H. Leclercq, in *Dictionnaire d'Archéologie Chrétienne et de Liturgie*, t. 12.2 (Paris: Letouzey et Ané, 1936), col. 1962–2017 (*s.v.* Office divin); A. -G. Martimort, *L'Église en priére. Introduction à la liturgie* (Paris: Desclée, 1961), pp. 791–837.

[18] *Regula Benedicti*, cap. 8–11, ed. and trans. by A. de Vogüé, J. Neufville, Sources chrétiennes, 181–86 (Paris: Les éditions du Cerf, 1971–1972), vol. 2, pp. 508–17. See also A. -G. Martimort, *Les lectures liturgiques et leurs livres*, Typologie des sources du moyen âge occidental, 64 (Turnhout: Brepols, 1992), especially pp. 78–96 and A. Davril, E. Palazzo, *La vie des moines au temps des grandes abbayes, Xe–XIIIe siècles* (Paris, 2000), especially pp. 121–54.

[19] R. Étaix, 'Répertoire des homéliaires conservés en France (hors la Bibliothèque

Most monastic communities gathered daily for chapter. During this *officium capituli*, Benedictine monks had to listen to the appropriate paragraph of a martyrology and a necrology; then they were informed on the several duties to be done during the day, and listened to a chapter of the Rule and a commentary upon it or a sermon. Chapter was concluded by a benediction pronounced by the abbot.[20] Other communities, such as canons, had similar dispositions. Sermons were also used for private meditation. Ample provisions in this regard were made in the *Regula Benedicti.*[21] Finally, some sermons were delivered outside any liturgical context or even religious building. This occurred when missionaries were preaching for pagans or neophytes or, some centuries later, when heretics explained their opinions to potential followers.

It is clear that early medieval sermons were used on many occasions and their audience was, as a consequence, most diversified. The greater part of the sermons was 'consumed' in a monastic context, by religious persons who had received at least a basic education, while some monks belonged to the restricted circle of real erudites. However, sermons were also meant to edify 'simple' parishioners and were the most important means of communication with the pagans.

Since early medieval sermons were used in very different contexts and for audiences with varying levels of education, their form and content are most diverse. Several scholars have tried to distinguish between two types of sermons: the homily and the sermon *stricto sensu*. The homily is defined as a verse by verse (or sometimes a phrase by phrase) explanation of a complete pericope, while the sermon *stricto sensu* focuses on one verse (the theme) or on a particular idea.[22] Furthermore, one assumed that the patristic and monastic homily composed before the twelfth century gradually evolved into the monastic and then mendicant sermon.[23] This is a

---

Nationale)', in idem, *Homéliaires patristiques latins: Recueil d'études de manuscrits médiévaux,* Collection des Études Augustiniennes, Série Moyen Âge et Temps Modernes, 29 (Paris: Institut d'études augustiniennes, 1994), pp. 3–4 mentions that monastic communities owned in some cases a double set of lectionaries: one for the choir and one for the refectory. That way the monks didn't have to carry the big volumes from one place to the other. See for a later period: R. Étaix, 'Le lectionnaire cartusien pour le réfectoire', in *Homéliaires patristiques latins*, pp. 105–36.

[20] A. -G. Martimort, *L'Église en prière. Introduction à la liturgie*, p. 834.

[21] *Regula Benedicti*, cap. 48, vol. 2, pp. 598–605; see also the graphics of A. Barbero, C. Frugoni, *Medioevo. Storia di voci, racconto di immagini* (Rome, Bari: Laterza, 1999), p. 62.

[22] For example J. W. O'Malley, 'Introduction: Medieval Preaching', in *De Ore Domini. Preacher and Word in the Middle Ages*, ed. by T. L. Amos, E. Green, B. M. Kienzle, Studies in Medieval Culture, 27 (Kalamazoo: Medieval Institute Publications, 1989), pp. 1–11.

[23] For example J. W. O'Malley, 'Introduction: Medieval Preaching', p. 3: 'We can, in fact, easily justify dividing the history of medieval preaching into at least two stages, with the line of demarcation somewhere around the twelfth and thirteenth centuries, as might be expected. The earlier stage was characterized by sermon forms and preaching practices that were

very broad generalization, masking a more complex reality, since the two types and many mixed forms existed at the same time and homilies evolved into sermons and sermons imitated homilies.[24] While sermons and sermon collections existed serving only one purpose and remaining (nearly) unchanged for centuries, there are also sermons that were often remodeled and used in different contexts or transformed into other literary types. Gregory the Great composed his *Homiliae in evangelia* for his parishioners, while the Venerable Bede 'used' those homilies in his commentary on the gospels of Mark, *in Marci evangelium expositio*. Smaragdus of Saint-Mihiel, in his turn, took the text of Bede and mixed it with quotations from the *De consensu evangelistarum* of Augustine for his *Collectiones in epistolas et evangelia*. Finally, Rabanus Maurus used the text of Smaragdus for his *Homiliae in evangelia et epistolas*, compiled at the request of the emperor Lothar .[25] Some decades before Rabanus Maurus and Smaragdus of Saint-Mihiel put themselves to work, Paul the Deacon had already inserted the text of Gregory the Great without any changes into his homiliary.[26]

The employment of Gregory's *Homiliae in evangelia* shows how a sermon might be composed for parishioners to be heard in mass, but later adapted for different audiences and functions.

In the preceding paragraphs, I demonstrated the variety in form, content and use of sermons. Because of this variety and the frequent evolutions of one type into another, it is impossible to formulate strict definitions for each type of text.

---

obviously modeled on such Fathers of the Church as Augustine and Gregory the Great. Whether the sermons were delivered in a monastery or in a parish church (or its equivalent), the "sermon" tended to be dependent on the paraphrastic form of the so-called homily popularized in the West by Augustine and his followers'.

[24] T. L. Amos, 'The Italian Homiliary: From Sermon Collection to Monastic Homiliary', *Medieval Sermon Studies Newsletter*, 29 (1992), 47–48 (= paper presented at the 26th International Congress on Medieval Studies, Western Michigan University, May 1991).

[25] Concerning Rabanus Maurus and Smaragdus of Saint-Mihiel, see: H. Barré, *Les homéliaires carolingiens de l'école d'Auxerre: authenticité, inventaire, tableaux comparatifs, initia*, Studi e testi, 225 (Vatican City, 1962), pp. 4–5 and 12–13. On p. 5 we find the following odd sentence: 'Liturgiques par leur ordonnance et leur objet, leurs homéliaires ne le sont plus par leur destination; au lieu de fournir des *lectiones* pour l'Office divin, ils servent à la lecture méditée ou bien à la prédication; "ad legendum vel ad praedicandum", précise Raban'. The formulation of this sentence tends to suggest that the author doesn't consider predication as part of the liturgy (of mass).

[26] On the homiliary of Paul the Deacon see: R. Grégoire, *Homiliaires liturgiques médiévaux. Analyse de manuscrits*, Biblioteca degli Studi medievali, 12 (Spoleto: Centro Italiano di Studi sull'Alto Medioevo, 1980), pp. 423–78 and A.-G. Martimort, *Les lectures liturgiques et leurs livres*, pp. 87–89. See M. De Reu, *La parole du Seigneur. Moines et chanoines médiévaux prêchant l'Ascension et le Royaume des Cieux*, pp. 24–25 and pp. 48–49. The examples are taken from the commentaries on Matthew 16. 14–20.

Consequently, I will consider the words homily and sermon as synonyms in this article, as is common among most historians today.[27]

Sermons are often collected in *homiliaria* or *sermonaria*. These concepts too have been strictly defined by some authors, while others use the words in a much broader sense. According to Barré, Étaix and Grégoire 'une collection prend le nom d'homéliaire, lorsque, en correspondance avec le sacramentaire, elle est ordonnée suivant le cycle de l'année liturgique et l'englobe en son entier'.[28] Consequently, they deny the term homiliary for collections of sermons of one author (e.g. Augustine, Caesarius of Arles, Gregory the Great) or around one theme (an apostle, the Virgin). This narrow definition is difficult and ambiguous. What if the sermon collection of one author covers the whole year? Only fifteen lines below his definition, Barré writes: *L'homéliaire, lui, est consacré aux lectures patristiques. Primitivement, un seul auteur, tel Augustin, a pu suffire à les fournir, mais on fera bien vite appel à l'ensemble des "Pères catholiques et orthodoxes".*[29] In this article I will use the words *homiliare* or *sermonare* in their broad sense, i.e. as a collection of sermons.

The vast number of preserved texts, combined with a limited number of good editions, presents another problem to be tackled by whomever wants to study the early medieval sermon. Earlier studies list as many as about 1450 sermons for the period 500–950,[30] but their present number is larger. About twenty years ago, only one out of four (known) Carolingian sermons was edited. One can assume that this proportion is still valid today.[31]

The study of the early medieval sermon is further complicated by the fact that there is no single list of all the sermons of that period. In order to establish a list of sermons I consulted the works mentioned in Appendix I.

---

[27] J. Longère, *La prédication médiévale* (Paris: Études augustiniennes, 1983), p. 15: 'La distinction sermon-homélie n'est pas toujours nette, ainsi qu'en témoignent le *Liber sermonum* d'Alain de Lille ou les collections de Raoul Ardent. De plus, par commodité littéraire, beaucoup d'études emploient indifféremment les deux termes, il en sera ainsi au cours du présent travail'. See also B. M. Kienzle, Introduction, in *The Sermon*, p. 161: 'The homily, for the authors of this volume, falls within the bounds of the sermon genre'.

[28] H. Barré, in *Dictionnaire de Spiritualité ascétique et mystique*, VII (Paris: Beauchesne, 1969), col. 598 (*s.v. homéliaires*); a less strict definition is given by I. W. Frank, in: *Theologische Realenzyklopädie*, 27 (Berlin; New York: De Gruyter, 1997), p. 254 (*s.v.* Predigt): 'Wie aus der frühmittelalterlichen Homilie die Schulpredigt wurde, so aus den Homiliaren die Sermonesreihen'.

[29] Frank, 'Predigt', p. 254.

[30] T. N. Hall, 'The Early Medieval Sermon', in *The Sermon*, p. 237, borrows the figures of E. Dekkers and A. Gaar for the period 500–750: 475 sermons and from T. Amos for the period 750–950: 970 sermons.

[31] T. N. Hall, 'The Early Medieval Sermon', in *The Sermon*, p. 237: of those 970 Carolingian sermons, 235 have been edited.

In the present article only sermon collections meeting the following requirements are investigated:

1) the authorship, or at least the place and time of compilation of the homiliary, are generally accepted.

2) the collection is edited and, preferably, electronically accessible.

Since, as we have seen, (nearly) identical sermons were used on several occasions, no distinction was made regarding the form of the text (homily or sermon), the intended audience (laity or monks), or the context (use during mass, Offices etc).

The collections upon which this study is based are mentioned in Appendix II. For each collection I indicate the length (in words, columns or occasionally in pages for the texts that I counted manually). *In toto*, I explored a corpus of sermon collections of 1,176,841 words and 1404 columns from the PL and forty small pages. These numbers have to be augmented with the sermons composed during the tenth and eleventh century which are treated in my article published in the proceedings of the twelfth Medieval Sermon Studies Symposium.[32] In order to study the evolution of the occurrences of vices and virtues over a longer period of time, the results obtained for the tenth and eleventh century are included in the present article.

It seemed interesting to compare the results obtained by studying the sermons with other types of sources. Since the results obtained from the sermons were compared to those yielded by the investigation of *paenitentialia* and 'society' in 'Vertus chrétiennes et vices démoniaques aux Xe et XIe siècle', I wanted to study these two additional types of sources between 500 and 900 as well. The category 'society' consists of 'all available' sources from 500 till 900, as I will explain later. For the *paenitentialia*, I could not gather sufficient data. The CLCLT-4 contains for the Merovingian *paenitentialia* only 9953 words and for the Carolingian *paenitentialia* 20,020 words. This means that a number of virtues and vices are not even represented. Roughly, this small analysis showed that in the *paenitentialia, ira* and *luxuria* were the most important vices (*superbia* is not even mentioned in the Merovingian *paenitentialia*, though, as stated, the sample is too small for valid results). The most important virtue is *fides*.

The constitution of the category 'society' was made in a practical way. It is of course impossible to read all the surviving sources from between 500 and 900. Consequently, an analysis of all the texts contained on CLCLT-4[33] for the sixth to ninth centuries was decided upon. This meant 5,504,076 words in two hundred and ninety works for the Merovingian period and 3,170,914 words in one hundred and

[32] M. De Reu, 'Vertus chrétiennes et vices démoniaques aux Xe et XIe siècle', in *Preaching and Society in the Middle Ages: Ethics, Values and Social Behaviour*, Padova, 14-18 July 2000, ed. by L. Gaffuri, R. Quinto, Centro Studi Antoniani, 35 (Padova: Centro Studi Antoniani, 2002), pp. 93–118.

[33] During spring 2002 the CLCLT-5 was released. For the this article I continued to work with the CLCLT-4, since more than half of the statistical research had already been done.

sixty works for the Carolingian period. The Merovingian works were selected with the command 'titulus = s 6, s 7, s 8 .AND. aetas = patres'; the Carolingian works were selected via the command 'titulus = s 8, s 9 .AND. aetas = medii aevi'. Of course, the Patrologia Latina Database could have been analyzed together with the CLCLT as was done for the sermons from the tenth and eleventh centuries. For the present research, this option seemed impossible. While I analyzed twenty-one and a half volumes of the *Patrologia Latina* for the tenth and eleventh centuries, more than sixty volumes of this series should have been examined in order to cover the complete period. Even for computers, this is time consuming and one would have to repeat the searches over again for 'smaller' manageable units. This huge extra cost in computer and research time would furthermore have brought little extra knowledge. Since the experience for the tenth and eleventh centuries has been effectuated, it is clear that the final results make very little difference when taken from the CLCLT or the PLD. In statistical terms, both selections are random samples. If numbers are high enough, contents matter less with random samples. In 'Vertus chrétiennes et vices démoniaques aux Xe et XIe siècle', I show a precise example of how a corpus with a different content shows the same results.[34]

Chart 1: Merovingian period, all sources (CLCLT-4), calculated by total of words

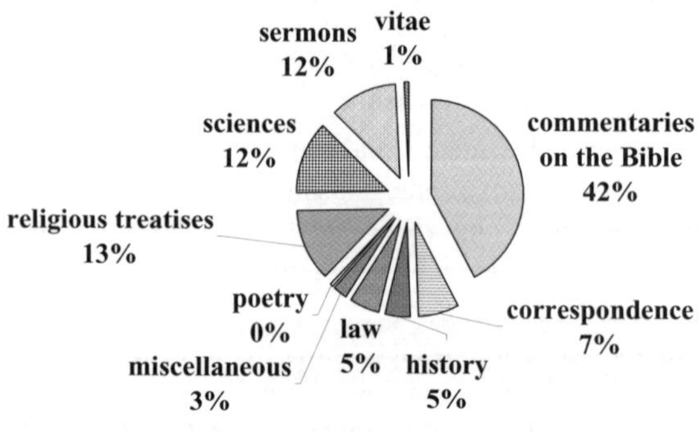

Charts 1 and 2 give an overview of the several types of texts that have been studied in this article. The importance of the several types of sources is determined by the number of words they represent in the corpus—and consequently not by the number of titles that enters in each category. Counting titles means that a work of

[34] Pp. 107–09.

Chart 2: Carolingian period, all sources (CLCLT-4), calculated by total of words

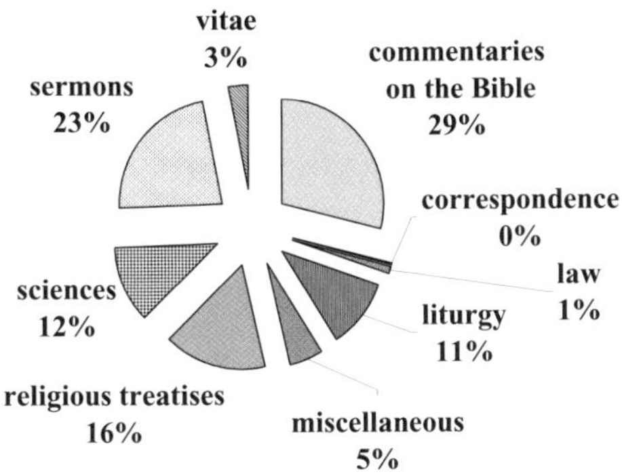

400,000 words would have the same weight as a work of 4000 words. For the rules of entering a work in a particular category, I refer again to 'Vertus chrétiennes et vices démoniaques aux Xe et XIe siècle'.

While charts are altogether lacking in the CLCLT, one sees that some categories are not represented in a particular period on the CD-ROM. Thus there is no category 'liturgy' in the Merovingian period, while the category 'history' does not exist for the Carolingian period. Other categories are 'almost' absent: *vitae* and poetry in the Merovingian epoch, and correspondence and law during the Carolingian times. In both periods the commentaries on the Bible are the most important group, while sermons, sciences and religious treatises are significant groups in both periods (>10%). It has to be noted that during the Carolingian period sermons are the most important group and liturgy exceeds ten percent.[35]

3. Terminology of Vice and Virtue

After having defined the literature to be analyzed, a decision has to be made about the words to work with. For the sake of comparison, I decided to retain the same words as I had done for my research on the vices and virtues in the tenth and

[35] See e.g. R. McKitterick, *The Frankish Church and the Carolingian Reforms, 789–895* (London, 1977), ch. 3: 'The Instruction of the People: Preaching' (pp. 80–114) for the significance of preaching to the Carolingian rulers and ch. 4: 'The Instruction of the People: the Liturgy' (pp. 115–54) for the importance of liturgy in the reform program of the Carolingians.

eleventh centuries.[36] The list of the researched terminology for vices and virtues is as follows:

the seven vices
superbia, vana gloria, inanis gloria
tristitia, tristicia, accedia, accidia, acedia, acidia
gula, ventris ingluvies, gastrimargia
avaritia, avaricia
luxuria, fornicatio, fornicacio, concupiscentia carnis or carnalis
invidia
ira (ira, iram, irae, iras, irarum; ire and *iris* controled separately), *iracundia*

the seven virtues
fides
spes
caritas, charitas
temperantia, temperancia
fortitudo
prudentia, prudencia
iustitia, iusticia, justitia, justicia

Since most collections were compiled in a monastic context, I thought it interesting to include two important 'monastic' values as well in the present research.

the monastic values
humilitas
obedientia, obediencia, oboedientia, oboediencia

As indicated in the first section of this article, several 'problems' were encountered during the analysis of the texts: (a) identical forms can be derived from different lemmata (homonyms), (b) identical lemmata can have several meanings (polysemy), (c) a specific combination of words can have a particular meaning that cannot be derived from the individual words and (d) orthography is not yet standardized.

(a) homonyms: all occurrences of *ire* and *iris* were verified separately
(b) polysemy: I checked manually all forms of *fides* and retained (counted) only the 27,552 occurrences of *fides* in the sense of faith, thus I did not take into account

[36] The motivation of this choice is explained in 'Vertus chrétiennes et vices démoniaques aux Xe et XIe siècle', in *Preaching and Society in the Middle Ages: Ethics, Values and Social Behaviour*, Padova, 14–18 July 2000, ed. by L. Gaffuri, R. Quinto, Centro Studi Antoniani, 35 (Padova: Centro Studi Antoniani, 2002), pp. 93–118.

the sense of loyalty to a liege lord, fidelity between spouses, to believe a story etc. For *iustitia* the occurrences of the word in the sense of privilege or right were not retained, leaving only the 11,121 occurrences of justice.

(c) specific combinations of words with a particular meaning: for *prudentia* and *caritas*, the forms of courtesy *prudentia vestra* or *caritas vestra* were not taken into account, nor for *ira* were the occurrences of the locutions *ira Domini*, *ira Dei* or *dies irae* retained.

(d) orthography: as is clear from the list mentioned above, I checked the different orthographies of the concepts analyzed in this research.

4. *The Results*

a) general view

I begin by comparing the presence (in percentages) of vices, virtues and the monastic values in sermons from three periods: the Merovingian and Carolingian periods and the tenth and eleventh centuries. Because of its importance, *fides* is separated from the other virtues. Chart 3 demonstrates that the data for the Merovingian period and the tenth and eleventh centuries correspond more or less. The Carolingian period is characterized by the emphasis on *fides* (38%), while all the other concepts are de-emphasized.

Chart 3: Vices, virtues, *oboedientia* and *humilitas* in sermons from 500 till 1100

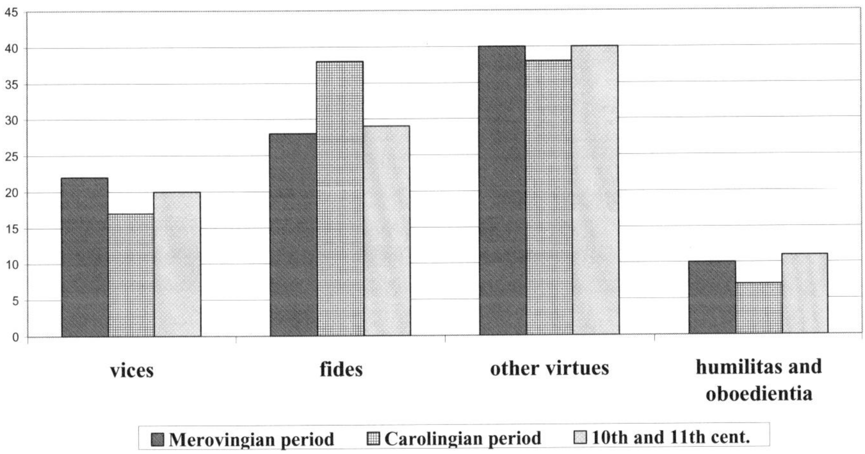

The overall figures of the previous chart mask some particularities of those preachers who made the most serious efforts to adapt their discourse to a lay audience. Chart 4 shows separate data on Caesarius of Arles, Abbo of Saint-Germain and an anonymous author of the ninth century; by way of comparison, I also added the data on the Bible commentary of Paschasius Radbertus. The three collections intended for the laity stress roughly the same points. They pay much attention to the vices, while *fides* is less stressed than in the work of Paschasius Radbertus. As far as monastic values are concerned, one detects an evolution. Caesarius stressed less the virtues of *humilitas* and *oboedientia*, and as a result more time was devoted to the other virtues. From the Carolingian period on these monastic values were also preached frequently to the laity. In the Bible commentary of Paschasius Radbertus—and I reiterate that this commentary is an adaptation of his preaching for monks—50% of all time devoted to vices or virtues, is dedicated to *fides*. Concretely, this means 1312 occurrences of *fides* per 415,244 words, of which 2653 concern vices and virtues (0.64% of total of words). Caesarius of Arles mentions a vice or a virtue from the aforementioned list 2032 times; this is 0.79% of the total (258,369 *formae*).

Chart 4: Vices, virtues, *oboedientia* and *humilitas* in specific collections from 500 till 1100

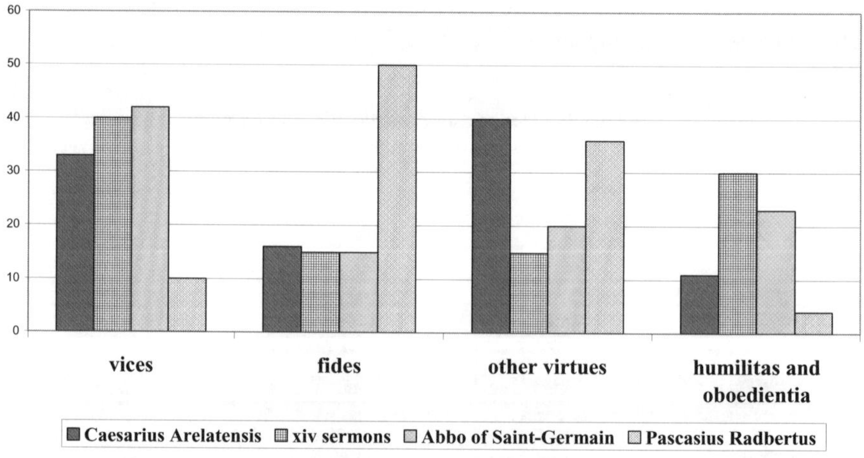

Chart 5 presents the data for the occurrences of vices, virtues, *oboedientia* and *humilitas* for 'all' the sources from the sixth to the eleventh centuries. One detects here, just as for the sermons, the similarities between the data for the Merovingian period and those for the tenth and eleventh centuries. Only for 'other virtues' is there no perfect symmetry. This is most probably due to the small differences in percentages. As far as the Carolingian period is concerned, the increased importance of *fides* is achieved at the expense of all the other vices and virtues.

Chart 5: Vices, virtues, *oboedientia* and *humilitas* in all sources (CLCLT-4) from 500 till 1100

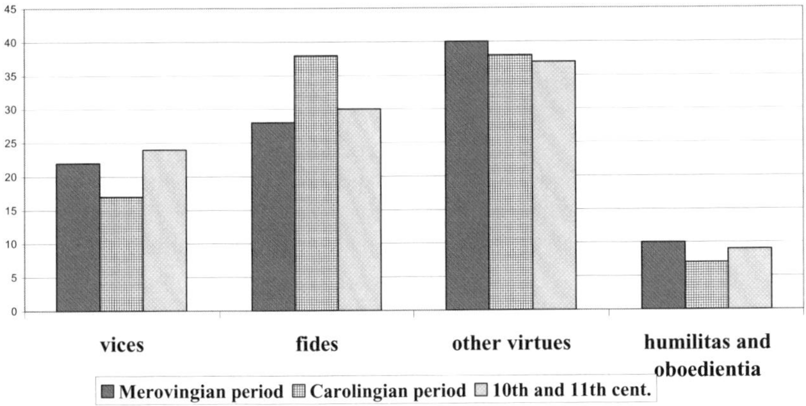

b) the vices

I now turn to the details and examine the presence of the different vices in Chart 6. The order of importance between the several vices is unique for the Carolingian period, where one finds *ira* (25%) in the first place, followed by *superbia* (20%) and *luxuria* (18%). In the Merovingian period and the tenth and eleventh centuries, however, *superbia* (25% and 31% respectively) seems to be the most important vice,

Chart 6: Vices in sermons from 500 till 1100

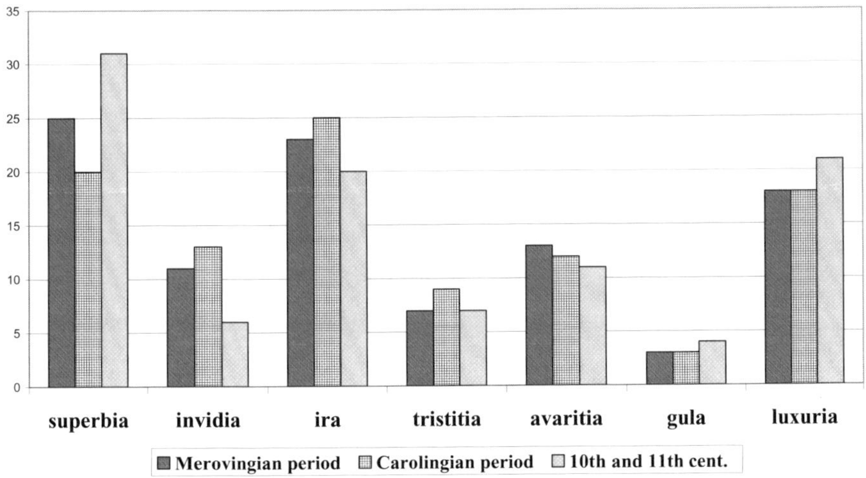

followed by *ira* and *luxuria*. Just as in the previous charts, the Carolingian sermons have characteristics of their own, while the sermons from the tenth and eleventh centuries fit in with the Merovingian ones.

The emphasis on the several vices varies widely from one sermon collection to another, as is shown in Chart 7. As mentioned above, statistical analysis requires large numbers in order to obtain valid results. These results, however, mask individual characteristics of authors. In the *XIV Sermons* of northern Italy, *superbia* accounts for about half of the occurrences (46%) of vices, while other vices such as *gula* and *tristitia* do not appear at all. In this particular collection the preacher seems to exhort his hearers mainly to live together peacefully within the Christian community. The vices that do not necessarily have a bad influence on community life (*gula* and *tristitia*) are omitted. One could argue that *superbia* does not necessarily influence the community, either. Apparently this was not the opinion of the anonymous preacher in the north of Italy. Chart 4 shows that precisely the anonymous Italian preacher stresses more than any other author the need for *humilitas* and *oboedientia*.

Paschasius Radbertus treats the several vices in his Bible commentary more equally. As in most Carolingian collections, *ira* is the most important vice, but it wins only with 2%, an insignificant lead. *Ira* is followed by three vices with almost the same weight. Even *avaritia* and *tristitia* appear frequently in the commentary. Only *gula* is almost dismissed. Paschasius Radbertus holds the opinion that the monks not only must reflect upon their attitude towards their brethren, but also have to behave correctly while alone in their cells as well.

Chart 7: Vices in specific collections from 500 till 1100

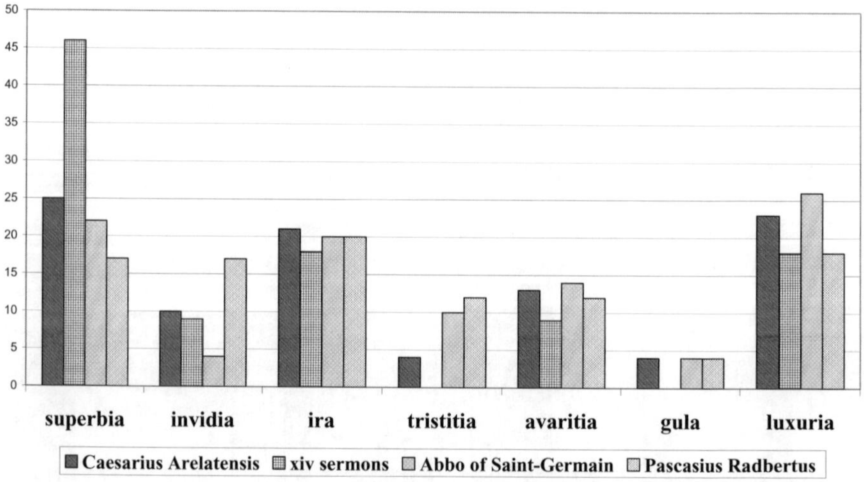

Chart 8 allows the examination of the vices in all the sources from 500 to 1100. The strong similarities between Charts 3 and 5 are repeated in Chart 6 and 8. And once more, the Carolingian period has its own characteristics: a low point for *superbia* and peaks for *ira* and *tristitia*. *Ira* is clearly the most important vice (28%) in all the sources from the Carolingian period, followed by *superbia* (21%) and *luxuria* (15%). The sermons show the same 'top three'.

Chart 8: Vices in all sources (CLCLT-4) from 500 till 1100

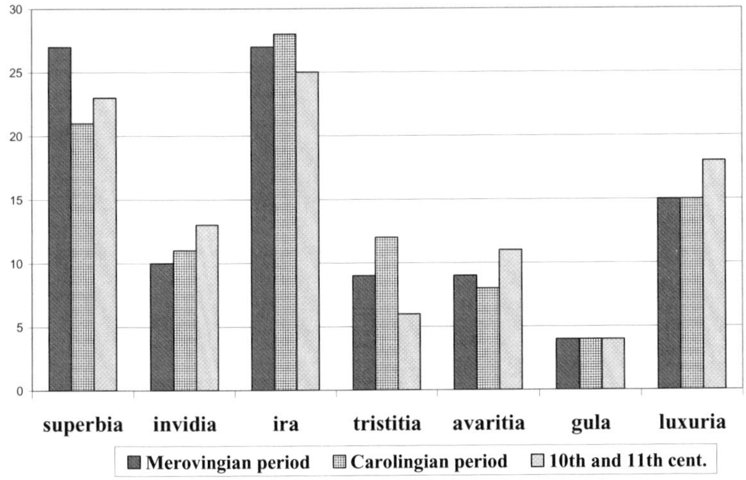

c) the virtues

The comparison of the virtues over the three periods in Chart 9 shows a familiar picture. The weight of the different virtues in the Merovingian sermons and those from the tenth and eleventh centuries corresponds very well, while the Carolingian sermons are set apart. *Fides* is for all periods by far the most important virtue, followed by *caritas* and *iustitia*. Only in the Carolingian period is *iustitia* (19%) slightly more important than *caritas* (17%).

Chart 9: Virtues in sermons from 500 till 1100

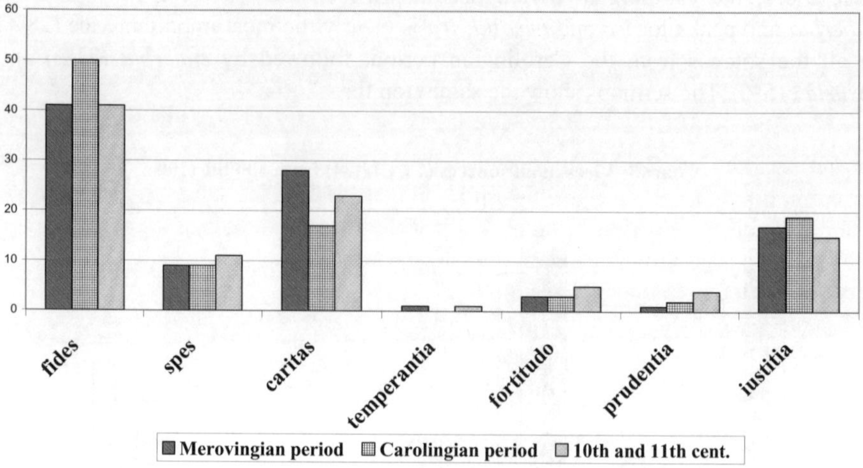

Chart 10: Virtues in specific collections from 500 till 1100

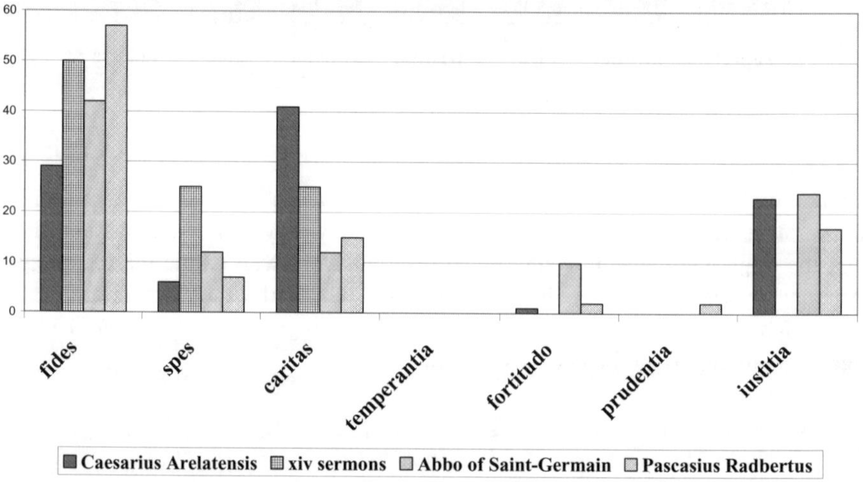

Chart 10 presenting the spread of the virtues in individual collections is more difficult to interpret. The authors do not seem to agree on the importance of the several virtues. While the three other authors think that *fides* is the most important virtue, Caesarius of Arles preaches in the first place *caritas* (41%). The anonymous author of the *XIV Sermons* sticks to the basics: he instructs only on *fides* (50%), *spes* and *caritas* (both 25%). Most of these individual authors consider *iustitia* more important than *spes*, though the anonymous author does not mention this virtue.

Just as on previous occasions, there are remarkable similarities between the data for the sermons and those for 'society' (Chart 9 and Chart 11). However, while the sermons and other sources from the different periods hold the same 'top three' in the same order in the previous charts, this seems not to be the case here. Instead of showing a peak during the Carolingian period, *iustitia* shows here a low point between 750 and 900 (15%, while in the previous and subsequent periods 18%). Consequently, for the general analysis of all the sources between 500 and 1100, one detects the following order for the Merovingian and Carolingian period: 1 *fides*, 2 *caritas*, 3 *iustitia*. For the tenth and eleventh centuries the same virtues remain important, but *iustitia* is now slightly more important than *caritas*.

Chart 11: Virtues in all sources (CLCLT-4) from 500 till 1100

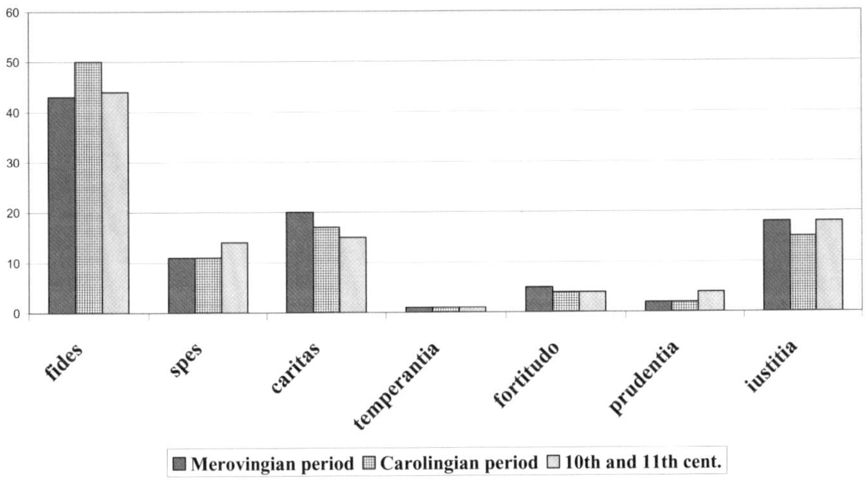

5. Conclusions

The time has come for conclusions. Let me first summarize the results. When analyzing Chart 3, one detects that the Carolingian sermons have a clearly distinct identity. Only in Chart 5 (all sources) do the 'other virtues' not retain the emphasis they had in the Merovingian period. The analysis of the vices in Chart 6 and 8 shows again a clear identity for the Carolingian period, even though for some vices one cannot detect a 'back to normal' movement after the collapse of the Carolingian empire. The sermons indicate a continuing decrease in the weight of *avaritia*, while Chart 8 with all types of sources reveals an increasing importance of *invidia*, mainly at the expense of *superbia*. The Charts 9 and 11 on virtues make clear that this analysis is not really different from the one made before: the Merovingian period and the tenth and eleventh centuries have more in common than they have with the Carolingian epoch. In Chart 11 with all virtues one detects the continuous decrease in importance of *caritas*, while *prudentia* increases gradually in weight. The latter characteristic is even more prominent in Chart 9 with the sermons. While *iustitia* is more important in the Carolingian sermons than in the homilies from the other periods, the inverse picture can be seen in Chart 11 with all types of sources.

It is striking how the Carolingian preachers succeeded in giving their sermon collections an identity, all the while borrowing so extensively from their predecessors. While reading the Carolingian sermons in the traditional way, one has the strong impression of reading once more the 'old stuff' in a slightly different arrangement. This statistical content analysis, however, shows that the Carolingian preachers knew very well how to adapt the older material in order to put a new emphasis in their texts.

The final question now is: are the changes that one discerns in the Carolingian sermon intentional? And if the answer to this question is yes, then whose intentions do they reflect?[37] Who thought that one should pay more attention to *fides*? Who thought that the vice of *ira* was more detestable than *superbia*, and who held the opinion that *iustitia*, instead of *caritas,* should counter *ira*? A possible answer may be found in the legislation issued during the reign of Charlemagne and his immediate successor. In order to communicate his programme to his subjects, Charlemagne relied on preaching. In R. McKitterick's work on the Carolingian reforms one reads:

> What is so distinctive about the sermon and preaching in the Frankish epoch is that they had the sanction of the law, for the spoken, like the written word was seen by the Frankish clergy to be one of the effective means for the implementation of the Carolingian reform programme. Charlemagne and his clergy legislated for the propagation of the Christian faith, and promoted the sermon to be one of the principal vehicles for the instruction of the people.[38]

---

[37] J. L. Nelson, 'Kingship and Empire in the Carolingian World', in *Carolingian Culture*, p. 53: 'The relationship of ideas to reality is a general problem in the history of political thought. Peculiar to the earlier Middle Ages, however, is the difficulty with so much of the material of answering such basic questions as: who wrote it and for what audience? Is it a public work in the sense of expressing the 'offical line' of the regime?'

[38] R. McKitterick, *The Frankish Church and the Carolingian Reforms, 789–895* (London: Royal Historical Society, 1977), p. 81.

The *Admonitio generalis* is the most important source if one wants to know Charlemagne's opinions on preaching.[39] Preaching is mentioned in four *capitula* (32, 61, 66, 82). These *capitula* indicate the desired contents for the sermons: preachers should preach the faith in the Trinity (32) and explain the Creed (32, 61, 82); they have to condemn vices such as hate, avarice, greed (66), lechery, envy, drunkenness (82) and recommend virtues as hope, charity, etc. (82). Later legislation repeated parts of the *Admonitio generalis*.[40] Also other sources indicate that the propagation of the correct faith was considered among the main duties of the ruler of the Franks: *Nostrum est secundum auxilium divinae pietatis sanctam undique Christi ecclesiam ab incursu paganorum et ab infidelium devastatione armis defendere foris, et intus catholicae fidei agnitione munire*.[41] For Charlemagne and his successor the *fideles* of God were also their own loyal subjects: *fideles Dei et regis*.[42] As such, the Carolingian rulers did not make a clear distinction between *fides* = faith, and *fides* = the oath of loyalty to a lord.

Charlemagne considered himself God's lieutenant on earth.[43] Next to faith, order had an important place in his empire, hence the numerous *capitularia* or the appointment of *missi dominici*.[44] 'Peace and public order were a sign of holiness.'[45] *Iustitia* could only exist where order ruled.[46] *Ira* meant a threat to order and hence to *iustitia*. This view was not shared by the authors of 'all sources' in the Carolingian period. They consider *caritas* as slightly more important than *iustitia*. For those authors, *ira* should be combated by *caritas*. It is only during the tenth and eleventh centuries, when disorder reigns in the former Carolingian empire, that the authors of 'all sources' assess the value of *iustitia*. In this period *iustitia* is slightly more important than *caritas*, while *ira* remains the most frequently cited vice.

The assertion that the Carolingian emperors tried to influence preaching is not new: as we have seen in the above quotation from the work of R. McKitterick, some

---

[39] Edited by A. Boretius and V. Krause in *Capitularia Regum Francorum*, in: MGH LL in 4, section II, vol. 1 (Hannover, 1883), n. 22, pp. 52–62.

[40] R. McKitterick, *The Frankish Church and the Carolingian Reforms, 789–895*, pp. 1–44.

[41] *Codex Carolinus*, ed. by W. Gundlach, in MGH Epp. III (Hannover, 1892), no 93, p. 137.

[42] H. Helbig, 'Fideles Dei et regis', *Archiv für Kirchengeschichte*, 33 (1951), 275–306.

[43] See J. L. Nelson, 'Kingship and Empire in the Carolingian World', in *Carolingian Culture*, pp. 58–59; S. Vanderputten, *Een heilig volk is geboren. Opkomst en ondergang van een christelijke staatsideologie uit de vroege Middeleeuwen (c. 750–900)* (Hilversum: Verloren, 2001); P. Riché, *Les carolingiens. Une famille qui fit l'Europe* (Paris: Hachette, 1983), especially Part V, Chapters I and II.

[44] J. H. Lynch, *The Medieval Church. A Brief History* (London, New York: Longman, 1992), p. 67: 'To put it simply, the Carolingian programme of reform was intended to restore proper "order" to society, including the church'.

[45] Vanderputten, *Een heilig volk is geboren*, p. 29: 'Vrede en openbare orde waren een teken van heiligheid'. See also p. 47.

[46] Vanderputten, *Een heilig volk is geboren*, pp. 85–86.

of the homiliaries were even written at their request. A precise example of how preaching was adapted however, was till now lacking. I hope to have provided such an example in this article.

Appendix I: Works consulted to establish our list of relevant collections of sermons composed between 500–900

T. L. Amos, *The Origin and Nature of the Carolingian Sermon*, (unpublished doctoral dissertation, Michigan State University, 1983).

H. Barré, *Les homéliaires carolingiens de l'école d'Auxerre: authenticité, inventaire, tableaux, initia*, Studi e testi, 225(Vatican City, 1962).

F. Brunhölzl, *Histoire de la littérature latine du Moyen Age*, Reference Works for the Study of Mediaeval Civilization (Turnhout, 1990–1996).

E. Dekkers, *Clavis patrum latinorum*, Corpus Christianorum. Series Latina (Turnhout, Steenbrugge, 1995).

R. Étaix, 'Les homéliaires carolingiens de l'école d'Auxerre', in: *L'école carolingienne d'Auxerre de Murethach à Remi 830–908*, ed. by D. Iogna-Prat, C. Jeudy, G. Lobrichon, D. Duby, Entretiens d'Auxerre 1989 (Paris, 1991).

R. Étaix, *Homéliaires patristiques latin: Recueil d'études de manuscrits médiévaux*, Collection des Études Augustiniennes, Série Moyen Âge et Temps Modernes, 29 (Paris, 1994).

R. Grégoire, 'Les homéliaires mérovingiens du VIIe—VIIIe siècle', *Studi Medievali*, 13 (1972), 901–917.

R. Grégoire, *Homéliaires liturgiques médiévaux. Analyse de manuscrits* (Spoleto, 1980).

J. Longère, *La prédication médiévale* (Paris: Études Augustinnienes, 1983).

J. Machielsen, *Clavis Patristica Pseudoepigraphorum Medii Aevi. Opera Homiletica*, 2 vols, CCSL (Turnhout, 1990).

The sermon, ed. by B. M. Kienzle, Typologie des sources du moyen âge occidental, 81–83 (Turnhout, 2000), especially G. Ferzoco, C. Muessig, Bibliography (paragraph V), pp. 30–34 and T. N. Hall, The Early Medieval Sermon, pp. 203–69.

G. M. Verd, 'La predicacion latina en la transicion medieval' (451–751), *Miscelanea Comillas*, 30 (1972), 157–204.

G. M. Verd, 'La predicacion carolingia (751–910)', *Miscelanea Comillas*, 35 (1977), 297–344.

<u>Appendix II</u>: Collections of sermons composed between 500 and 900 and analyzed in this article; this list has to be completed by the sermons composed between 900 and 1100 and enumerated in 'Vertus chrétiennes et vices démoniaques aux Xe et XIe siècle', in *Preaching and Society in the Middle Ages: Ethics, Values and Social Behaviour*, Padova, 14–18 July 2000, ed. by L. Gaffuri, R. Quinto, Centro Studi Antoniani, 35 (Padova, 2002), pp. 93–118.

<u>Caesarius Arelatensis</u>: southern France, 470— d. 542/3
238 sermons; 258,369 words
Sermones, ed. by G. Morin, Turnhout, 1953 (CCSL 103-104).
initially composed for his parishioners

<u>Gregorius Magnus</u>: central Italy, *c.* 540–d. 604
40 + 22 homilies (and some fragments); 81,848 and 106,486 words
Homiliarum xl in evangelia libri duo, ed. by R. Étaix, Turnhout, 1999 (CCSL 141).
initially composed for his parishioners
Homiliae in Hiezechihelem Profetam, ed. by M. Adriaen, Turnhout, 1971 (CCSL 142).
initially composed for his parishioners?

<u>Beda Venerabilis</u>: England, 672/2–d. 735
50 homilies and two Bible commentaries; 107,147 + 137,312 + 70,435 words
Homiliarum evangelii libri II, ed. by D. Hurst, Turnhout, 1955 (CCSL 122).
In Lucae evangelium expositio–In Marci evangelium expositio, ed. by D. Hurst, Turnhout, 1960 (CCSL 120).
initially composed for the private reading of monks and for use in the night offices

<u>Paulus Diaconus</u>: Lombardy (also Montecassino and Carolingian court), *c.* 730–d. 799
202 (de tempore) and 96 (de sanctis) homilies, 408 columns
Homiliare, in PL 95, 1159–1566.
initially composed for use in the night offices

<u>Smaragdus Sancti Michaelis ad Mosam</u>: Carolingian empire, ?–d. 825
80 occasions, appr. 170 homilies, 538 columns
Collectiones in epistolas et evangelia (= *Liber Comitis*), in PL 102, 15–552.
initially composed for preaching in mass (to monks) or for the offices

<u>Hrabanus Maurus</u>: Francia, 780/1–d. 856
70 + 163 homilies; 458 columns
Homiliae de festis praecipuis, item de virtutibus (ad praedicandum populo), in PL 110, 9–134.

initially composed for preaching in mass, dedicated to archbishop Haistulfe of Cologne

Homiliae in evangelia et epistolas, in PL 110, 135–467.

initially composed for emperor Lothair for his own edification (date of composition: 854–855)

Paschasius Radbertus: Francia, 790–d. *c*. 859

Bible commentary; 415,244 words

In Matheo, ed. by B. Paulus, 3 vols, Turnhout, 1984 (CCCM 56–56A).

initially composed for the private reading of monks, though the contents are taken from his preaching to the monks

XIV Sermons: Italy between 801 and 845

14 homilies; 40 small pages

XIV homélies du IXème siècle d'un auteur inconnu de l'Italie du Nord, ed. with a French translation by P. Mercier, Paris, 1970 (SC 161).

initially composed for parishioners.

Multilingualism in Medieval Sermons: A Response to Thom Mertens, Martine De Reu, Ingunn Lunde, and Holly Johnson

SIMON FORDE

In my response to this section entitled 'Reflections *Upon* Sermons', I intend to deal with the issue of language—the language of both medieval sermons and the scholars who study them. Three of the four papers presented in Section IV are composed by scholars whose native tongue is not English; nor is it necessarily their first foreign language. The fourth paper (Johnson) explores macaronic sermons, which testify to the multilingual nature of late-medieval Europe. While I do not intend to analyse her paper in detail, the multilingual environment that she has sketched in this article is in fact the template against which I wish to discuss the modern day challenge of sermons scholars. From diverse linguistic heritages themselves, sermons scholars attempt to convey, in English, research on texts that are written in variety of languages.

The papers by Mertens, De Reu and Lunde are more technical in orientation than Johnson's, which might be fairly described as typical of a contemporary medieval article from North America. The other three papers, in turn, explore a taxonomy for dealing with preaching and sermons texts. By analysing what is probably a typical, but manageable, corpus of material in Middle Dutch, Mertens creates a vocabulary for exploring both the genres of sermons literature and their relationship to either preaching or meditation. In a statistical analysis of a rather large dataset of electronically searchable Latin texts from the early Middle Ages, De Reu examines the terminologies for virtue and vice in sermons. Finally, employing 'linguistic pragmatics' as a tool for studying a collection of 'dramatic sermons' by Kirill of Turov, a (probably) twelfth-century Russian preacher, Lunde explains the sermons' theatrical effects. Regardless, however, of each contributor's own technical aims, all of the essays deal with the issue of working with foreign languages, either in a plurilingual medieval environment, or a contemporary academic world where scholars are operating in a new, effectively global, *koine*.

In the humanities, and more particularly medieval sermon studies, it is only within the last decade that English has become so predominant. When an international network of scholars operating in this field was established via an informal newsletter (now the *Medieval Sermon Studies* journal) by Gloria Cigman in the late 1970s, English and French were equally influential and, if anything, the greater experience of French scholars who had been active for longer in the field than the Anglophone scholars gave French the edge. The earliest symposia of this network were bilingual, and when a constitution was developed in the early 1990s for what had grown into the International Medieval Sermon Studies Society, it too was bilingual.

One remarkable feature of this sermons network from its foundation was the active effort to welcome scholars from throughout the world, and to ensure that the sermons studied were not restricted to the Christian West, but were fully comparative, with input from scholars of Jewish preaching and other Middle-Eastern religious traditions. For inclusiveness, it is valuable that Ingunn Lunde offers this volume an introduction to sermons from medieval Russia, since Russia in particular and the Eastern Church in general has—perhaps with the exception of input from Mary Cunningham—been relatively neglected in the dialogue over Christian preaching of the Middle Ages.[1] Lunde admirably perseveres with this dialogue, so that scholars of the Latin and vernacular West can gain more knowledge not only of the historical and ecclesiastical context and literary heritage in which Kirill of Turov and his fellow preachers operated, but also of Kirill's achievement. We have a presentation here of a dramatic type of preaching ,common in Byzantium, that reached its audience effectively. Although Kirill's linguistic methods have not been explored in Western sermons, his dramatic purpose is similar to the theatrical Good Friday preaching in England, described by Holly Johnson. Beyond linking East and West, Lunde makes a strong case that Kirill should be considered a major figure of medieval European preaching for his powers to engage his audience through reported speech.

While Lunde is concerned with a linguistic terminology for dramatic preaching, De Reu looks closely at the terms for virtue and vice and their contexts in the preaching of the early middle ages. De Reu's thesis is based on searches of the Patrologia Latina Database (PLD) and the CETEDOC Library of Christian Latin Texts (CLCLT-4 databases). She has defined a set corpus of sermon texts in her Appendix 2, and has established some control groups against which to compare her findings. She has set down clearly the search strategy that she has followed. It is worth discussing this further, not because her strategy or findings are likely to be flawed, but because the complexity and dangers can be neglected by observers. It is

[1] Mary Cunningham, *Faith in the Byzantine World* (Oxford: Lion Publishing, 2002).

also worth stressing that De Reu's undertaking differs markedly from conventional scholarship, where the source studied is either brought to light by the scholar herself or available through the critical edition of another. In both of these more conventional cases, the scholar is intensely familiar with the text at hand. In De Reu's case, however, she is entirely dependent for her source data on the editorial, computing and analytical decisions made by a sizeable number of people, many of whom are invisible. Scholars are well aware that the texts brought together into the PL by J.-P. Migne are of a far from uniform quality, but it is a major undertaking for one scholar working on the complete set to know the comparative merits of individual volumes in the series. Even though CLCLT is drawn from self-proclaimed modern critical editions, almost entirely from the post-1945 period, the underlying Corpus Christianorum volumes alone contain a variety of editorial practices and decisions. And the support tools offered to scholars by the Centre Traditio Litterarum Occidentalium research unit (CTLO, formerly CETEDOC) may not always be available in a particular library, whilst other tools are currently in development (e.g. lemmatized word-forms, Latin-vernacular and vernacular-Latin dictionaries for identifying synonyms and variants). I have been fortunate to have been offered access to some such tools which are not yet publicly available, thanks to the assistance of Eddy Gouder of CTLO.

The first selection criterion that De Reu has applied in choosing her control groups concerns her definition of 'Merovingian' texts and those she classes as 'Carolingian'. This she has done by selecting all titles from the sixth to eighth centuries which are classified in CLCLT as being 'patristic' (*aetas* = *patres*), and those from the eighth and ninth centuries which are classified as being 'medieval' (*aetas* = *medii aevi*). To understand the rationale of De Reu's selection, one has to understand the logic of CLCLT, which is in turn derived from Corpus Christianorum. Here, the patristic age is defined as the period up to and including the death of Bede in 735. The medieval period commences with works that can be dated to 736 or later. De Reu has therefore been forced to define 'Merovingian' according to the chronology adopted in patristic studies, such that Merovingian writings are those dated by CLCLT to the period 501–735 and Carolingian writings are those dated to 736–900. This is not, therefore, the periodization commonly accepted by historians, but the database prevents a tighter definition. And, of course, the strategy is dependent on the accuracy of the dating of texts adopted in CLCLT.

The second selection criterion is based on searches for word forms associated with vices and virtues (plus two important monastic virtues). De Reu has listed the nominative forms in her paper, but we can assume that she will have searched under the related word forms (*superbia, -am, -ae, -as, -arum, -is*). She may have consulted the browse lists offering orthographic variants for the same root form (*superbie*, and so forth). She has clearly been imaginative in identifying synonyms: for *gula*, the synonyms *ventris ingluvies* and *gastrimargia*. She may have consulted the CLCLT handbook to identify common orthographic variants within medieval Latin: 'c' for 't' in *fornicatio*, and 'ch' for 'c' in *caritas*. She has shown particular awareness with 'ire' to realise that *ire* and *iris* have more than one lemma and need to be checked separately to ensure that the forms here do indeed refer to 'anger'. Of course, the results of a search depend entirely on the appropriateness of the search strategy and the quality of the data searched. To emphasize how complex the task is, let us examine three aspects further. First, spelling of medieval Latin allows far greater orthographic diversity than we would expect, particularly if we have become influenced by normalized editions and classical forms in dictionaries. The extent to which the richness of medieval spellings remains intact depends on the editorial policy of numerous editors of Corpus Christianorum volumes. Nonetheless, the diversity is partly glimpsed through the *Thesaurus Formarum*, produced by CTLO as a guide to use with CLCLT. For *tristitia* alone, we might readily guess the variant *tristicia*, but *triscicia* and *triscitia* may be less obvious. The variant *–ie* for classical *–iae* is also no surprise. But the 5th declension nominative equivalents in *–es* to the 1st declension forms in *–a*, that is, *tristicies* and *tristities* were, for me, a surprising possibility. Second, De Reu's argument is based on the same semantic form remaining constant over six centuries. If a semantic equivalent replaced an earlier form, the concept could remain important, but under a different guise. But semantic equivalents are very hard to identify. Familiarity with the texts through extensive close reading is one way of identifying such words; but this process rather contradicts the benefit of working with these large database searches. Till now, the major Latin dictionaries have not been searchable. Nonetheless, a quick search of the opening letters in Blaise's *Dictionnaire Latin-Français des auteurs chrétiens*, for French *orgueil*, generated the following putative Latin synonyms for *superbia*: *ambitio*, *authadia*, *barriditas*, *cervicula*, and *elatio*. A further study would be required to discover whether any of these were significant in the period and in the texts covered by De Reu. But this example indicates how important electronically-accessible Latin-vernacular dictionaries could be for future research in this field. A final complexity derives from word-combinations, such as *vana gloria*. Here a full understanding of the computer software becomes required of the scholar. A search for 'vana gloria' alone would, in the CLCLT software, only generate nominative (and ablative) forms where the words appear in this order and without any intervening words. Thus *vanam gloriam* would not be found; nor would *gloria vana* and nor would *vana autem gloria* and the enclytical *gloriaque vana* (which is treated by the software as 'gloria que vana'). The solution is to enter a proximity operator which allows one or more words to come between the forms and for the forms to appear in reverse order. Thus 'vana /1 gloria' would find results for *vana gloria*, *gloria vana*, *vana autem gloria* and *gloriaque vana*, while 'vana /2 gloria' would find, for instance *vanaque siue gloria*.

Let us now examine further the terminology generated by Thom Mertens for Middle Dutch sermons, supplemented by terms drawn from the other authors here, and elsewhere. Mertens'ss work seems important for generating a typology of sermon-texts that can apply across fields normally delineated by linguistic heritage. He has made a powerful case for the appropriateness of considering some Middle

Dutch sermon-texts apart from any possible preaching context. Indeed, he so clearly delineates the oral from the written that he must make a plea not to divorce sermon texts entirely from preaching—this is their ground, after all. This is a *volte-face* from the tradition encapsulated by G. R. Owst and those who sought in sermons evidence for preaching as a medieval mass medium.[2] More recently, collections of sermons that were 'preachable', but not records of preaching acts, tended to be lumped into a single category of 'model sermon'. But 'model sermon' has been used as a description for a sermon written to be a model used directly in preaching.

Mertens writes:

> The glossed Epistles and Gospels seem therefore the only sermon collections from preachers showing predicatory features. There is no (proven) connection with actually delivered sermons.

In other words, Mertens is claiming that no sermon collections exist in Middle Dutch that have what he calls preaching features. His only exception are glossed pericope collections and here there is also no proven link to preaching acts. Indeed, he says that their similarity to sermons is a 'fiction' which is 'staged to express the kinship and analogy in content and function with the preaching during Sunday Mass'.

Mertens's terminology warrants a revisitation, I think, and a framework that encourages broad adoption by other scholars. He is proposing a series of 'categories or subgenres according to their relation to preaching'. These include the following concepts:

Preaching—a spoken act (although the act may be referred to in a text)

- Preaching reference (*predikatiereferentie*)—allusion in a text to a preaching event or occasion
- Preaching (or predicatory) features—use in a sermon-text of first and second persons addressing a congregation (though this can be inserted as a literary device)
- Collation—a non-liturgical exhortation, namely, a particular locale for preaching

Sermon—a text with its 'soil' rooted in preaching, however far removed it may be from any acts of preaching (though note that Middle Dutch *sermoen*, as Latin *sermo*, should not be confused with the sense 'discourse, speech, utterance'). Mertens describes further classifications by formal, compositional and generic criteria, as follows:

---

[2] G. R. Owst, *Preaching in Medieval England: An Introduction to Sermon Manuscripts of the Period c.* 1350–1450 (Cambridge: Cambridge University Press, 1926).

Sermon form(s)—a formal criterion for identifying and classifying sermons:

- 'Modern form' associated with the schools and the mendicants based on the establishment of a theme and a mnemonic but quite elaborate division of it
- 'Homily' or sermon of the 'ancient' type, involving verse by verse commentary of the pericope

Preaching method(s)—compositional criteria identified with sermons, involving a study of the rhetorical or literary techniques associated, particularly, with the modern preaching form, together with the use of characteristic preaching tools or aids (manuals, etymological reference works etc.):

- 'Dramatic' sermons, a particular rhetorical device used to engage the audience
- Mnemonic devices, such as macaronic triads

Preachable text *(predikatietekst)*—notes or material that have the potential for use in preaching:

- Preaching outlines (notes for preaching), or *schema*

Individual sermons—the subgenres describe different formal characteristics, but also different relationships between the text and any possible preaching act:

- Random notes (*losse punten*), probably composed by listeners
- Random extracts—records of parts of sermons or collations for further rumination, in order to internalize parts of the message which the writer found meaningful
- Treatise—in certain cases, this can be a sermon excised of preaching features
- A '*reportatio*'—a record of a preaching event, with characteristics such as *inquit*-formulas

Sermon collections—collections of sermons, normally following a liturgical structure, and probably primarily meant for spiritual or preparatory reading; they may in some cases represent reworked material by preachers or listeners, 'published' for use in a different context:

- Pericope collections—a 'dominant form' of sermon; these sermons were composed as reading matter organised around the readings of the liturgical year.

- Glossed Gospels or Epistles—a subset of the pericope collections.

Aids for preachers—genres of works aimed at assisting preachers:

- *Artes praedicandi*—manuals on how a sermon should be composed
- Preaching manuals—reference works for use in constructing a sermon (e.g. etymologies, biblical commentaries)
- Model sermons—works which were used by other preachers in preaching; note that other material could be preached even though it seems not to have been written for that purpose.

Mock sermons—parodic or satirical texts using stereotypical features associated with preaching.

Thom Mertens's article is an impressive attempt to provide a terminology for studying the distinct forms of sermon text that survive, their composition and relationship to acts of preaching. His corpus is Middle Dutch, and he draws on terms from Dutch scholarship in this field, but he is offering a taxonomy that can be applied, at least, to sermons across the late-medieval West.

Mertens's attempt at developing a terminology based on concepts from one language and forming it in another (English) is not straightforward; in some respects, Dutch offers a richer selection of vocabulary with which to create various nuances or distinctions. Martine De Reu also draws on a number of advantages typical of her educational formation in Belgium. She demonstrates an impressive ability not only to deal with Latin texts and vocabulary, but an understanding of computing and statistics. We can be confident that the conclusions she draws about the qualitative difference of Carolingian preaching on the vices and virtues (in comparison with Merovingian and post-Carolingian sermons) are based on a good understanding of the dataset with which she is working.

Mertens, De Reu, Johnson, and Lunde are operating in a global language for communication, English, at just the point when relationships between different varieties of English are in flux. Until recently the various official forms for instance, Indian, Canadian, British, American could be said to have equal value but distinct geographical areas of preeminence. Very recently, through particular computer software, the spelling and grammar of American English is becoming imposed worldwide. Conversely, dialectal or non-standard forms of English have gained a high value in certain fields of popular culture and speech. At the same time, the native speakers of English have, arguably, not come to terms with 'their' language becoming the property of non-native speakers. In mainland Europe, at least, non-native practitioners are developing particular national or super-national variants of English. These new forms of English are a fusion of different varieties of English reflecting the receptivity of each country to the particular varieties, together with the interpolation of certain grammatical or semantic peculiarities that are influenced by their indigenous language. To medievalists familiar with Latin and its relationship with the European vernaculars, the patterns are familiar. Holly Johnson's article describes an earlier transitional moment within English, when one particular dialect was gaining dominance—at the expense of other indigenous dialects and the language of the political elite which was becoming seen as 'foreign'—, and it is this same dialect that is now the basis for a global language.

The adoption of English as this global medium offers a certain facility of communication. But it has disadvantages which are worth acknowledging. It disadvantages those who are not bilingual in English, even if their knowledge of several other major languages is impressive. Moreover, English at present embeds and privileges inherited cultural and educational values drawn from its native-speaking communities. Two weaknesses of the educational training in many English-speaking countries are often acknowledged: the relatively poor acquisition of foreign-language skills, and the separation between the sciences and the humanities such that students of the one branch may lack basic competencies in the other. The research undertaken by Martine De Reu shows no such failings. Her work is predicated on the development of two large-scale computer databases, one of which is still growing. But its growth is dependent on sufficient scholars with the ability to undertake traditional philological and editing work on Latin texts, and a team of philologists able to integrate these texts and create software and other tools for their analysis. And her work presumes that there are fellow scholars who share an ability to conduct such quantitative and qualitative analyses with Latin, and, and that there is a professional community that supports the creation of such databases and rewards those who work in this way on them. The scholarly communities in the UK and North America, often under pressure from public bodies, have a poor record in developing these skills and fostering such work.

The challenge that I have tried to identify here is one whereby sermonists, in particular, can converse in a shared, single language, yet not lose their ability to bring insights and strengths from their own academic traditions and to construct a place for dialogue that is truly pan-European.

Bibliography

GEORGIANA DONAVIN

STUDIES IN INTERDISCIPLINARITY

Ankersmit, Frank, 'Historicism: An Attempt at Synthesis', *History and Theory,* 34.3 (Middletown, CT: Blackwell Publishers for Wesleyan University Press, 1995), 143–62.

Austin, Ann E., 'Faculty Cultures, Faculty Values', in *Assessing Academic Climates and Cultures*, ed. by W. G. Tierney (San Francisco: Jossey Bass, 1990), pp. 61–74.

—, and Roger G. Baldwin, *Faculty Collaboration: Enhancing the Quality of Scholarship and Teaching* (Washington, DC: George Washington University Press, 1991).

Bal, Mieke, *The Practice of Cultural Analysis: Exposing Interdisciplinary Interpretation, Cultural Memory in the Present* (Stanford: Stanford University Press, 1999).

Bann, Stephen, *Reading 'Rembrandt': Beyond the Word-Image Opposition* (New York: Cambridge University Press, 1991).

—, *Romanticism and the Rise of History* (New York: Cambridge University Press, 1995).

Barthes, Roland, 'The Discourse of History', trans. and intro. by Stephen Bann, in *Comparative Criticism Yearbook*, 3 (Cambridge: Cambridge University Press, 1981), pp. 3–20.

Becher, Tony, 'The Disciplinary Shaping of the Professorate', in *The Academic Profession: National, Disciplinary and Institutional Settings*, ed. by Burton R. Clark (Berkeley: University of California Press, 1987), pp. 271–303.

—, 'Interdisciplinarity and Community', *Academic Community: Discourse of Discord?*, ed. by Ronald Barnett (London: Taylor and Francis, 1994), pp. 55–71.

Boxer, Marilyn J., 'Unruly Knowledge: Women's Studies and the Problem of Disciplinarity', *NWSA Journal*, 12 (Bloomington: Indiana University Press, 2000), 119–30.

Culler, Jonathan, *Framing the Sign: Criticism and Its Institutions* (Norman, OK: University of Oklahoma Press, 1988).

Damrosch, David, *We Scholars: Changing the Culture of the University* (Cambridge, MA: Harvard University Press, 1995).

Foucault, Michel, *The Archaeology of Knowledge*, trans. by A. M. Sheridan Smith (New York: Pantheon Books, 1972).

Friedman, Susan Stanford, *Mappings: Feminism and the Cultural Geographies of Encounter* (Princeton: Princeton University Press, 1998).

Frost, Susan H. and Paul M. Jean, 'Bridging the Disciplines: Interdisciplinary Discourse and Faculty Scholarship', *The Journal of Higher Education*, 74.2 (Columbus: Columbus University Press, 2003), 119–49.

Geertz, Clifford, *The Interpretation of Culture* (New York: Basic Books, 1973).

Graff, Gerald, *Professing Literature: An Institutional History* (Chicago: University of Chicago Press, 1987).

Grewal, Inderpal, and Caren Kaplan, eds, *Scattered Hegemonies: Postmodernity and Transnational Feminist Practices* (Minneapolis: University of Minnesota Press, 1994).

Holly, Michael Ann, 'Past Looking', *Critical Inquiry*, 16.2 (Chicago: University of Chicago Press, 1990), 371–96.

Holsinger, Bruce W., 'Medieval Studies, Postcolonial Studies, and the Genealogies of Critique', *Speculum*, 77 (2002), 1195–1227.

Hunt, Lynn, 'The Virtues of Disciplinarity', *Eighteenth-Century Studies*, 28 (Baltimore: Johns Hopkins University Press for the American Society for Eighteenth Century Studies, 1994), 1–7.

Kant, Immanuel, 'Idea for a Universal History', ed., trans. and intro. by Lewis Beck in *Kant on History* (Saddle River, NJ: Prentice Hall, 1963), pp. 11–26.

Klein, Julie Thompson, *Crossing Boundaries: Knowledge, Disciplinarities, and Interdisciplinarities* (Charlottesville, VA: University Press of Virginia, 1996).

Kockelmans, Joseph J., ed., *Interdisciplinarity and Higher Education* (University Park, PA: Pennsylvania State University, 1979).

Lattuca, Lisa R., *Creating Interdisciplinarity: Interdisciplinary Research and Teaching Among College and University Faculty* (Nashville: Vanderbilt University Press, 2001).

Lyotard, Jean Francois, *The Postmodern Condition: A Report on Knowledge*, trans. by Geoff Bennington and Brian Massumi (Minneapolis: University of Minnesota Press, 1984).

Neubauer, John, 'Music and Literature: The Institutional Dimensions', in *Music and Text: Critical Inquiries*, ed. by Steven Paul Scher (Cambridge: Cambridge University Press, 1992), pp. 3–20.

Newell, William Henry, and Julie Thompson Klein, 'Interdisciplinary Studies into the 21st Century', *The Journal of Education*, 45.1 (1996), 152–69.

Newman, John Henry, Cardinal, *The Idea of a University Defined and Illustrated* (London: Longmans, Green, 1926).

Said, Edward W., *The World, the Text and the Critic* (Cambridge, MA: Harvard University Press, 1983).

Scholes, Robert, *The Rise and Fall of English* (New Haven, CT: Yale University Press, 1998).

Weber, Max., *Methodologische Schriften, Studienausgabe* (Frankfurt a.M.: S. Fisher, 1968).

Wissoker, Ken, 'Negotiating A Passage Between Disciplinary Borders', *Chronicle of Higher Education*, 14 April 2000, p. B4.

PRIMARY SOURCES

Abelard, Peter, *Sermones*, PL 178, 379–610.

Ælfric, Abbot of Eynsham, *Ælfric's Catholic Homilies: The First Series Text*, ed. by Peter Clemoes, Early English Text Society, s.s. 17 (Oxford: Oxford University Press, 1997).

—, *Aelfric's Catholic Homilies. Introduction, Commentary and Glossary*, ed. by Malcolm R. Godden, Early English Text Society, s.s. 18 (Oxford: Oxford University Press, 2000).

—, *Ælfric's Catholic Homilies. The Second Series*, ed. by Malcolm R. Godden, Early English Text Society, s.s. 5 (London: Oxford University Press, 1979).

—, *Ælfric's Lives of Saints, Being a Set of Sermons on Saints' Days Formerly Observed by the English Church*, ed. by Walter William Skeat, Early English Text Society, o.s. 46, 82, 94, 114 (Oxford, 1881, 1885, 1890, 1900), repr. in 2 vols (Oxford: Oxford University Press, 1966), with a Modern English translation.

—, *Homilies of Ælfric: A Supplementary Collection*, ed. by John C. Pope, Early English Text Society, o.s. 259, 260 (Oxford: Oxford University Press, 1967, 1968).

Aelred of Rievaulx, *Sermones I–XLVI. Collectio Claraevallensis prima et secunda*, ed. by Gaetano Raciti, CCCM 2B (Turnhout: Brepols, 1989).

Alan of Lille, *The Art of Preaching*, trans. by Gillian Rosemary Evans, Cistercian Fathers Series, 23 (Kalamazoo: Cistercian Publications, 1981).

—, *Liber Sermonum*, PL 210, 197–226.

Albert the Grand, *Alberts des Grossen Augsburger Predigtzyklus über den hl. Augustinus*, ed. by Johann Baptist Schneyer, in *Recherches de théologie ancienne et médiévale*, 36 (Louvain: Abbaye du Mont César, 1969), pp. 100–47.

Alexander of Ashby, *Aux origines des artes praedicandi. Le De artificioso modo predicandi d'Alexander d'Ashby*, ed. by Franco Morenzoni, *Studi Medievali*, 3rd series, 32.2 (1991), and CCCM 188 (Turnhout: Brepols, 2004).

Amadeus of Lausanne, *Huit homélies mariales*, introduction and notes by G. Bavaud, ed. by Jean Deshusses, trans. by Antoine Dumas, Série des textes monastiques d'Occident, 5 (Paris: Editions du Cerf, 1960).

Ambrosius Autpertus, *Ambrosii Autperti opera*, ed. by Robert Weber, CCCM 27B (Turnhout: Brepols, 1979), pp. 963–1036.

Aquinas, Thomas, *Les Collationes in decem praeceptis de saint Thomas d'Aquin. Édition critique avec introduction et notes*, ed. by Jean-Pierre Torrell, in *Revue des sciences philosophiques et théologiques*, 69 (Paris: Libraire Philosophique Vrin, 1985), pp. 5–40, 227–63.

—, *The Sermon-Conferences on the Apostles' Creed*, ed. by Nicholas Ayo (Notre Dame: University of Notre Dame Press, 1988).

Atto of Vercelli, *Sermones*, PL 134, 833–60.

Augustine, *Ancient Christian Writers: Sermons for Christmas and Epiphany*, trans. by Thomas Comerford Lawler (Westminster, MD: Newton Press, 1952).

—, *Epistola*, PL 33, 1001.

—, *Nine Sermons of Saint Augustine on the Psalms*, intro. and trans. by Edmund Hill (London and New York: Kennedy Press, 1958).

—, *On Christian Doctrine*, trans. by D. H. Robertson, Jr. (New York: Liberal Arts Press, 1958).

—, *Selected Easter Sermons of Saint Augustine*, with introduction, notes and commentary by Philip T. Weller (St Louis, MO: Herder, 1959).

—, *Selected Sermons of St Augustine*, trans. and ed. by Quincy Howe, Jr. (London: Gallancz, 1967).

—, *Sermons on the Liturgical Seasons*, trans. by Mary Sarah Muldowney (New York: Fathers of the Church, 1959).

Auzzas, Ginetta, 'Dalla predica al trattato: Lo Specchio della vera penitenzia di Iacopo Passavanti', *Lettere Italiane*, 54 (2002), 325–42

Babilas, Wolfgang, ed., *Untersuchungen zu den Sermoni Subalpini. Mit einem Exkurs über die Zehn-Engelchor-Lehre*, Münchener romanistische Arbeiten, 24 (Munich: Hueber, 1968).

Baldwin, Abbot of Ford, *Baldwini de Forda Opera: Sermones de commendatione fidei*, ed. by David N. Bell, CCCM 99 (Turnhout: Brepols, 1991).

Barcelona, P. Martí de (O Min Cap), ed., *L'Ars Prædicandi de Francesco Eiximenis*, in *Homenage a Antoni Rubió i Luch,* II (Barcelona: [s.n.], 1935), pp. 301–40.

Bartolomeo of Breganze, *Bartolomeo da Breganze, O.P., I sermones de beata Virgine (1266)*, ed. by L. Gaffuri (Padua: Editrice Antenore, 1993).

Bartolomeo of Vicenza, *Mariale*, ed. by Laura Gaffuri, Fonti per la storia della terraferma veneta, 7 (Padua: Editrice Antenore, 1994).

Bazire, Joyce and James E. Cross, *Eleven Old English Rogationtide Homilies,* Toronto Old English Series, 7 (Toronto: Centre for Mediaeval Studies—University of Toronto Press, 1982).

Bede, *Bedae Venerabilis Opera Pars* III *Opera Homiletica*, CCSL 122 (Turnhout: Brepols, 1955).

—, *Bede the Venerable: Homilies on the Gospels*, trans. by Lawrence T. Martin and David Hurst, 2 vols, Cistercian Studies Series, 110–11 (Kalamazoo: Cistercian Publications, 1991).

Bernard of Clairvaux, *On the Song of Songs I–IV*, 4 vols, trans. by Kilian Walsh, Cistercian Fathers Series, 4, 7, 31, 40 (Kalamazoo: Cistercian Publications, 1979–83).

—, *Sancti Bernardi Opera*, ed. by Jean Leclercq, Charles H. Talbot, and Henri-Marie Rochais, 8 vols (Rome: Editiones Cistercienses 1957–77).

—, *Sermons for the Summer Season: Liturgical Sermons from Rogationtide and Pentecost*, trans. by Beverly Mayne Kienzle and James Jarzembowski, Cistercian Fathers Series, 53 (Kalamazoo: Cistercian Publications, 1990).

—, *Sermons on Conversion*, trans. by Marie-Bernard Said, Cistercian Fathers Series, 25 (Kalamazoo: Cistercian Publications, 1981).

Bernardino of Siena, *Sancti Bernardini Senensis Opera omnia*, 8 vols (Ad Claras Aquas, Florence: Collegii S. Bonaventurae, 1950–65).

—, *Le prediche volgari dette nella Piazza del Campo l'anno MCCCCXXVII ora primamente,* ed. by L. Banchi, I Classici Rizzoli, 3 vols (Siena, 1880–88), repr. ed. by P. Bargellini (Milan: Rizzoli, 1936).

—, *Le prediche volgari. Quaresimale fiorentino del 1424–1425*, vols 1–7, ed. by Ciro Cannarozi (Pistoia and Florence: Pancinotti, 1934–58).

—, *Prediche Volgari sul Campo di Siena, 1427*, ed. by Carlo Delcorno (Milan: Rusconi, 1989).

Bernardino Tomitano da Feltre, *Sermoni nella redazione di fra Bernardino Bulgarino da Brescia*, ed. by Carlo Varischi of Milan, 3 vols (Milan: Renon, 1964).

Berthold von Regensburg, *Berthold von Regensburg: Vier Predigten. Mittelhochdeutsch/Neuhochdeutsch*, trans. and ed. by W. Röcke (Stuttgart: Reclam, 1983).

—, *Welt und weltliches Treiben im Spätmittelalter: aus den Predigten des Volks- und Sittenpredigers Berthold von Regensburg (gest 1272)*, ed. by Gerhard E. Sollbach (Hamburg: Kovac, 1994).

Blake, Norman Francis, ed., *Quattuor sermones, Printed by William Caxton*, Middle English Texts, 2 (Heidelberg: Winter, 1975).

Blumrich, Rüdiger, *Marquard von Lindau, Deutsche Predigten. Untersuchungen und Edition*, Texte und Textgeschichte, 34 (Tübingen: Niemeyer, 1994).

Bonaventure, *Sancti Bonaventurae Sermones de diversis*, ed. by Jacques-Guy Bougerol, 2 vols (Paris: Éditions Franciscaines, 1993).

—, *Sancti Bonaventurae Sermones de tempore. Reportations du ms. Milan Ambrosienne A 11 Sup.*, ed. by Jacques-Guy Bougerol (Paris: Éditions Franciscaines, 1990).

—, *Sancti Bonaventurae Sermones dominicales*, ed. by Jacques-Guy Bougerol, Bibliotheca franciscana scholastica Medii Aevi, 27 (Grottaferrata: Collegio S. Bonaventura Padri, Quarrachi, 1977).

Brinton, Thomas, *The Sermons of Thomas Brinton, Bishop of Rochester (1373–1389)*, ed. by Mary Aquinas Devlin, Camden Third Series, 85–86 (London: Offices of the Royal Historical Society, 1954).

Brixiensis, Albertanus, *Sermones quattuor*, ed. by Marta Ferrari, (London: Fondazione Ugo da Como, 1955).

Bruguera, Jordi and Joan Coromines, *Homilies d'Organyà*, Llibres del Millenari, 1 (Barcelona: Fundació Revista de Catalunya, 1989).

Caesarius of Arles, *Caesarius of Arles: Sermons*, trans. by Mary Magdeleine Mueller (Washington DC: Catholic University of America Press, 1956).

—, *Sermones ad populos*, ed. by Germain Morin, *Sancti Caesarii Arelatensis Sermones*, CCSL 103, 2 vols (Turnhout: Brepols, 1953).

Caplan, Harry, ed., 'A Late Mediaeval Tractate on Preaching', in *Studies in Rhetoric and Public Speaking in Honor of J. A. Winans* (New York: The Century, 1925), pp. 61–90.

—, '"Henry of Hesse" On the art of preaching', in *Publications of the Modern Language Association of America*, 48 (Baltimore: The Association, June 1933), pp. 340–61.

Caracciolo, Roberto, *Quaresimale padovano 1455*, critical edition with introduction and notes, ed. by Oriana Visani, Centro Studi Antoniani, 6 (Padua: Messaggero, 1983).

—, *Opere in volgare*, ed. by Enzo Esposito, introduction by Raul Mordenti, Biblioteca di scrittori salentini, I/4 (Galatina: Congedo, 1993).

Cátedra, Pedro M., *Los sermons atribuidos a Pedro Marín*, Acta Salmanticensia: Textos Recuperados, 1 (Salamanca: University of Salamanaca, 1990).

Caterina de' Vigri, *I sermoni*, introduction and commentary by Gilberto Sgarbi, with a critical edition by Enzo Lodi (Bologna: Barghigiani, 1999).

Cigman, Gloria, *Lollard Sermons*, Early English Text Society, o.s. 294 (Oxford: Oxford University Press, 1989).

Comestor, Peter, *Sermones* in PL 171, 476–81, 583–744; PL 198, 1809–44.

Corominas, Joan, 'Les homilies d'Organyà: edició critica millorada i anotada', in *Entre dos llenguatges* (Barcelona: Curial, 1976), pp. 126–53.

Cross, James E., *Cambridge Pembroke College Manuscript 25: A Carolingian Sermonary used by Anglo-Saxon Preachers*, King's College London Medieval Studies, 1 (London: King's College Publishers, 1987).

—, and J. Morrish Tunberg, eds, *The Copenhagen Wulfstan Collection. Copenhagen Kongelige Bibliothek Gl. Kgl. Sam. 1595,* Early English Manuscripts in Facsimile, 25 (Copenhagen: Rosenkilde and Bagger, 1993).

De Leeuw Van Weenen, A., ed., *The Icelandic Homily Book. Perg. 154 in the Royal Library, Stockholm,* Íslensk handrit: Icelandic Manuscripts, Series in Quarto, 3 (Reykjavík: Stofnun Árna Magnússonar á Islani, 1993).

Dykmans, Marc, ed., *Robert of Anjou, La Vision Bienheureuse. Traité envoyé au Pape Jean XXII* (Rome: Grégorienne University Press, 1970).

Eckhart, Meister, *Die deutschen und lateinischen Werke* (Stuttgart: Kohlhammer, 1936).

—, *Mystische Schriften*, ed. by Gustav Landauer (Berlin: Schnabel, 1995).

—, *Werke*, vol. 1, *Predigten*, ed. by Josef Quint, ed. and commentary by Niklaus Largier, vol. 2, *Predigten, Traktate, Lateinische Werke*, ed. by Ernst Benz and others, with commentary by Niklaus Largier (Frankfurt a.M.: Deutscher Klassiker, 1993).

—, *Werke in zwei Bänden, Bibliothek deutscher Klassiker*, ed. by Niklaus Largier (Frankfurt a.M.: Deutscher Klassiker, 1993).

Einarsson, Sigurbjörn, Guðrún Kvaran, and Gunnlaugur Ingólfsson, *Íslensk Hómiliubók. Fornar Stólræður* (Reykjavík: Híð íslenska bókmenntafélag, 1993).

Eudes of Châteauroux, *Odo da Châteauroux. Politica e Religione nei sermoni inediti,* Deputazione Abruzzese di Storia patria, Studi e Testi, 14 (Padua: Bottega d'Erasmo, 1993).

Ferrer, Vincent, 'Le Sermon en langue vulgaire prononcé à Toulouse par Saint Vincent Ferrier le vendredi saint, 1416', ed. by C. Brunel, *Bibliothèque de l'École des Chartes*, 151 (1953), 5–53.

—, *Quaresma de Sant Vicent Ferrer, predicada a València l'any 1413,* ed. by J. Sanchis Sivera (Barcelona: Atenes, 1927).

—, *Sermons*, ed. by Josep Sanchis Sivera, Els Nostres Clàssics (Barcelona: Editore Barcino, 1932; repr. 1971).

—, *Sermons*, ed. by Xavier Renedo and Lluís Cabré, Tria de Clàssics, 7 (Barcelona, 1993).

—, *Sermons de Quaresma*, ed. by Manuel Sanchis Guarner, 2 vols (Valencia: Albatros Edicions, 1973).

Fishacre, Richard, *The Virgin as Olive-Tree: A Marian Sermon of Richard Fishacre and Science at Oxford*, ed. by R. James Long, *Archivum Fratrum Praedicatorum*, 52 (1982), 77–87.

—, *Two Versions of a Sermon by Richard Fishacre, O.P., for the Fourth Sunday of Lent on theTheme: Non enim heres erit filius ancille cum filio libere*, ed. by Maura O'Carroll, *Archivum Fratrum Praedicatorum*, 54 (1984), 113–41.

Gilbert of Hoyland, *Sermons on the Song of Songs*, 3 vols, trans. by Lawrence C. Braceland, Cistercian Fathers Series, 20, 26, 34 (Kalamazoo: Cistercian Publications, 1978–1979).

—, *Treatises, Epistles and Sermons*, trans. by Lawrence C. Braceland, Cistercian Fathers Series, 34 (Kalamazoo: Cistercian Publications, 1981).

Giles of Rome, *Aegidii Romani Opera omnia*, I, 6, *Repertorio dei Sermoni*, ed. by Concetta Luna (Florence: Olschki, 1990).

Giordano da Pisa, *Quaresimale fiorentino 1305–1306*, ed. by Carlo Delcorno (Florence: Sansoni, 1974).

—, *Del Vangelio della nave*, ed. by Carlo Delcorno (Pisa: Giardini, 1978).

—, *Sul terzo capitolo del Genesi*, ed. by Cristina Marchioni, Biblioteca della Rivista di Storia e letteratura religiosa. Testi e documenti, 13 (Florence: Olschki, 1992).

Grant, Raymond J. S., ed. and trans., *Three Homilies from Cambridge, Corpus Christi College 41: The Assumption, St. Michael and the Passion* (Ottawa: Tecumseh Press, 1982).

Gregory the Great, 'The Book of Pastoral Rule', *The Book of Pastoral Rule and Selected Epistles of Gregory the Great Bishop of Rome*, ed. and trans. by Rev. James Barmby, NPNCF, Second Series, Vol. XII: *Leo the Great, Gregory the Great* (Grand Rapids, MI: Eerdmans, 1989), xxxi–72.

—, *Grégoire le Grand: Homélies sur Ezechiel*, ed. by Charles Morel, Sources Chrétiennes, 327, 360 (Paris: Editions du Cerf, 1986–90).

—, *Gregory the Great: Forty Gospel Homilies*, trans. by Dom David Hurst, Cistercian Studies Series, 123 (Kalamazoo: Cistercian Publications, 1990).

—, *Homiliae in Evangelia*, PL 76, 1075–1312.

—, *Registrum Epistularum Libri I–VII*, ed. by Dag Norberg, CCSL 140 (Turnhout: Brepols, 1982).

—, *Sancti Gregorii Magni Homiliae in Hiezechihelem Prophetam*, ed. by Marc Adriaen, CCSL 142 (Turnhout: Brepols, 1971).

Guerric of Igny, *Liturgical Sermons I*, trans. by Monks of Mount Saint Bernard Abbey, Cistercian Fathers Series, 8 (Paris: Editions du Cerf, 1971).

—, *Sermons*, 2 vols, ed. by John Morson and Hilary Costello, trans. by Placide Deseille, Source Chrétiennes, 166, 202 (Paris: Editions du Cerf, 1970–73).

Guibert of Nogent, 'Guibert de Nogent. A Book about the Way a Sermon Ought to be Given', trans. by Joseph M. Miller, in *Readings in Medieval Rhetoric*, ed. by Joseph M. Miller, Michael H. Prosser, and Thomas W. Benson (Bloomington: Indiana University Press, 1973), pp. 162–81.

—, *Quo ordine sermo fieri debeat; De bucella Iudae data et de veritate Dominici corporis; De sanctis et eorum pigneribus*, ed. by Robert B. C. Huygens, CCCM 127 (Turnhout: Brepols, 1993).

Hauf, Albert G., ed., 'El 'Ars praedicandi' de Fr. Alfonso d'Alprão, O.F.M. Aportación al estudio de la teoría de la predicación en la Península Ibérica', in *Archivum Franciscanum Historicum*, 72 (1979), pp. 233–329.

Haymo of Auxerre, *Homiliae de tempore*, PL 118, 11–746.

—, *Homiliae in aliquot de sanctis*, PL 118, 747–805.

—, *Homiliae in aliquot epistolas Pauli*, PL 118, 803–16.

Heinrich Kalteisen, *'Von der minnenden Seele'. Drei Predigten Heinrich Kalteisens O.P.*, ed. by Bernhard D. Haage, Göppinger Arbeiten zur Germanistik, 373 (Göppingen: Kummerle, 1983).

Heiric of Auxerre, *Heirici Autissiodorensis Homiliae per circulum anni*, ed. by Richard Quadri and Rolando Demeulenaere, CCCM 116 (Turnhout: Brepols, 1994).

Helgason, Jón, ed., *Hauksbók*, Manuscripta Islandica, 5 (Copenhagen: Munksgaard, 1960).

Higden, Ranulph, *The Ars componendi sermones of Ranulph Higden O.S.B. A Critical Edition*, ed. by Margaret Jennings, Davis Medieval Texts and Studies, 6 (New York: Brill, 1988).

Hildegard of Bingen, *Expositiones evangeliorum*, ed. by Jean-Baptiste Pitra, *Sanctae Hildegardis Opera Spicilegio parata*, Analecta Sacra, 8 (Farnborough: Gregg, 1882), pp. 245–327.

Hrabanus Maurus, *Homiliae de festis praecipuis, item de virtutibus*, PL 110, 9–134.

—, *Homiliae in Evangelia et epistolas*, PL 110, 135–467.

Hudson, Anne and Pamela Gradon, eds, *English Wycliffe Sermons*, 5 vols (Oxford: Clarendon Press, 1983–96).

Humbert of Romans, *Treatise On Preaching*, trans. by The Dominican Students Province of St Joseph, ed. by Walter M. Conlon (London: Blackfriars, 1995).

Iacobus de Marchia, *Sermones Dominicales*, ed. by R. Lioi, 4 vols (Falconara and Maritima: Biblioteca Francescana, 1978–84).

Indrebø, Gustav, ed., *Gamal Norsk Homiliebok. Cod. AM 619 4*, repr. 1966, Norsk historisk kjeldeskrift-institutt, Skrifter, 54 (Oslo: Hovudkommisjon hjaa Jacob Dybwad, 1931).

Irvine, Susan, *Old English Homilies from MS. Bodley 343*, Early English Text Society, o.s. 302 (Oxford: Oxford University Press, 1993).

Isaac of Stella, *Sermons I,* ed. by Anselm Hoste and Gaston Salet, Sources Chrétiennes, 130 (Paris: Editions du Cerf, 1967).

—, *Sermons II*, ed. by Anselm Hoste, Gaston Salet and Gaetano Raciti, Sources Chrétiennes, 207 (Paris: Editions du Cerf, 1974).

—, *Sermons III*, ed. by Anselm Hoste, Gaston Salet and Gaetano Raciti, Sources Chrétiennes, 339 (Paris: Editions du Cerf, 1987).

Ivo of Chartres, *Sermones*, PL 162, 505–71.

Jacques de Troyes, *Les Sermons donnés à Laon en 1242 par le chanoine Jacques de Troyes, futur Urbain IV*, ed. by Jacques Foviaux, in *Recherches Augustiniennes*, 20 (Paris: Études Augustiniennes, 1985), pp. 203–56.

Jacques de Vitry, *The Exempla or Illustrative Stories from the Sermones vulgares of Jacques de Vitry*, ed. by Thomas Frederick Crane, Folklore Society Publications, 26 (New York: Franklin, 1890; repr. 1967).

—, *The Faces of Women in the Sermons of Jacques de Vitry. Commentaries, Editions and Translations*, ed. by Carolyn Muessig (Toronto: Peregrina Publishing, 1999).

—, *Jacques de Vitry, deux sermons de mortuis du recueil inédit de sanctis*, in *Moines et moniales face a la mort. Actes du colloque de Lille, 2–4 octobre 1992*, ed. by Jean Longère, Histoire médiévale et archéologie, 6 (Paris: Université de Paris, 1993), pp. 235–82.

—, *Quatre sermons ad canonicos de Jacques de Vitry*, in *Recherches Augustiniennes*, 23, ed. by Jean Longère (Paris: Études Augustiniennes, 1988), pp. 151–212.

—, *Un sermon de Jacques de Vitry (†1240) 'Ad Praelatos et Sacerdotes'*, in *L'Écrit dans la société médiévale. Divers aspects de sa pratique du XIème au XVème siècle. Textes en hommage à Lucie Fossier*, ed. by Jean Longère (Paris: CNRS, 1991), pp. 47–60.

Johannes Geiler Von Kaysersberg, *Sämtliche Werke*, ed. by G. Bauer (Berlin: De Gruyter, 1989, 1991).

Johannes Nas, *The Corpus Christi Sermons*, ed. by Richard Ernest Walker, Göppinger Arbeiten zur Germanistik, 394 (Göppingen: Kummerle, 1988).

Johannes von Staupitz, *Salzburger Predigten 1512. Eine textkritische Edition*, ed. by Wolfram Schneider-Lastin (Tübingen: Niemeyer, 1990).

John Chrysostom, 'Sermons', in PG 60, 595–628.

John of Ford, *Sermons on the Final Verses of the Song of Songs*, 7 vols, intro. by Hilary Costello, trans. by Wendy Mary Beckett, Cistercian Fathers Series, 29, 39, 43–47 (Kalamazoo: Cistercian Publications, 1977–84).

—, *Super extremam partem–Cantici canticorum–Sermones CXX*, ed. by Edmund Mikkers and Hilary Costello, CCCM 18 (Turnhout: Brepols, 1970).

Julian of Vézelay, *Sermons*, ed. by Damien Vorreux, Sources Chrétiennes, 192–193 (Paris: Editions du Cerf, 1972).

Kaeppeli, Thomas and Emilio Panella, *Gammelnorsk Homiliebok etter AM 619 qv.*, Corpus Codicum Norvegicorum Medii Aevi, Quarto Serie, 1 (Oslo: Selskapet til utgivelse av gamle norske handskrifter, 1952).

—, *Scriptores ordinis praedicatorum Medii Aevi*, 4 vols (Rome: Ad S. Sabinae, 1970–93).

Langton, Stephen, *Selected Sermons of Stephen Langton*, ed. by Phyllis B. Roberts (Toronto: Pontifical Institute of Mediaeval Studies, 1980).

Llull, Raymond, *Ars brevis praedicationis*, ed. by Curt Wittlin, *Arts Abreujada de prediccació,* Biblioteca Escriny, Collecció de textos medievals breus, 4 (Barcelona, 1982).

—, *Libre de praedicatione*, ed. by Abraham Soria Flores (Palma de Mallorca: Patronat de Ramón Llull, 1961).

—, *Libre de virtuts e de pecats o Art major de predicació*, ed. by F. Domínguez Reboiras (Palma de Mallorca: Patronat Ramón Llull, 1990).

—, *Selected Works of Ramón Llull (1232–1316)*, ed. and trans. by Anthony Bonner (Princeton: Princeton University Press, 1985).

—, *Summa sermonum in civitate Maioricensi annis 1312–1313 composita*, ed. by F. Dominguez Reboiras and A. Soria Flores, CCCM 76 (Turnhout: Brepols, 1987).

Lombard, Peter, *Sermones*, PL 171, 339–967.

Longère, Jean, *Œuvres oratoires de maîtres parisiens au XIIe siècle: étude historique et doctrinale*, 2 vols (Paris: Études Augustiniennes, 1975).

Martín de Córdoba, '*Ars praedicandi* de Fray Martin de Cordoba', ed. by Fernando Rubio, *La Ciudad de Dios*, 172 (Madrid: Real Monasterio de el Escorial, 1959), 327–48.

Matthieu of Aquasparta, *Matthaei ab Aquasparta sermones de beata Maria Virgine*, ed. by Caelestinus Piana, Bibliotheca franciscana ascetica Medii Aevi, 9 (Quaracchi: Collegi S. Bonaventurae, 1962).

—, *Matthaei ab Aquasparta sermones de sancto Francisco, de sancto Antonio et de sancta Clara. Appendix: Sermo de potestate pape*, ed. by Gedeon Gál, Bibliotheca franciscana ascetica Medii Aevi, 10 (Quaracchi: Collegi S. Bonaventurae, 1962).

Maurice of Sully, *Maurice of Sully and the medieval vernacular homily with the Text of Maurice's French Homilies from a Sens Cathedral Chapter Ms.*, ed. by C. A. Robson (Oxford: Blackwell, 1952).

Menot, Michel, *Sermons choisis de Michel Menot*, ed. by Joseph Nève (Paris: Champion, 1924).

Mertens, Volker, ed., *Das Predigtbuch des Priesters Konrad. Überlieferung, Gestalt, Gehalt und Texte,* Münchener Texte und Untersuchungen zur deutschen Literatur des Mittelalters, 33 (Munich: Beck, 1971).

—, and Hans-Jochen Schiewer, *Die Postille Hartwigs von Erfurt* (Berlin: Akademie Verlag, 2000).

Mirk, John, *Mirk's Festial: A Collection of Homilies*, ed. by Theodore Erbe, Early English Text Society, e.s. 96 (London: Paul, Trench, Trubner, 1905).

Molho, M., ed., *Les homélies d'Organyà*, *Bulletin Hispanique*, 63 (Bordeaux: Editions Biere, 1961), 186–210.

Moran I Ocerinjauregui, J., *Les Homélies de Tortosa*, Textos e Estudis de Cultura Catalana, 20 (Barcelona: Curial, 1990).

Morris, Richard, ed., *The Blickling Homilies of the Tenth Century*, Early English Text Society: o.s. 58, 63, 73 (Oxford: Oxford University Press for the Early English Text Society, 1874–80, repr. with corrections, 1967).

Nevalinna, Saara, ed., *The Northern Homily Cycle: The Expanded Version in MSS Harley 4196 and Cotton Tiberius E. vii.,* Mémoires de la Société Néophilologique de Helsinki, 38, 41, 43 (Helsinki: Société Néophilologique, 1972–1984).

Nicola da Milano, *Collationes de Beata Virgine*, ed. by M. Michèle Mulchahey, Toronto Mediaeval Latin Texts, 24 (Toronto: Pontifical Institute for Mediaeval Studies, 1997).

Nicolas of Cusa, *Opera omnia Nicolai de Cusa*, 19 vols (Leipzig and Hamburg: Meiner, 1932–93).

Nicholson, Lewis E., ed., *The Vercelli Book Homilies: Translations from the Anglo-Saxon* (Lanham, MD: University Press of America, 1991).

O'Carroll, Mary E., *A Thirteenth-Century Preacher's Handbook: Studies in Manuscript Laud Misc., 511*, Pontifical Institute of Medieval Studies, Studies and Text, 128 (Toronto: Pontifical Institute of Mediaeval Studies, 1997).

Odo of Canterbury, *The Latin Sermons of Odo of Canterbury*, ed. by C. De Clercq with the assistance of Raymond Macken, Verhandelingen van de Koninklijke Academie voor wetenschappen, letteren en schone kunsten van België. Klasse der letteren, 105 (Brussels: AWLSK, 1983).

Odo of Cluny, *Sermones*, PL 133, 709–52.

Odo of Morimond, *Sermones*, PL 188, 1645–58.

Önnerfors, Ute, ed., *Abbo von Saint-Germain-des-Prés: 22 Predigten*, Lateinische Sprache und Literatur des Mittelalters, 16 (Frankfurt a.M.: Lang , 1985).

Paasche, Fredrik, ed., *Homilíu-bók (Icelandic Sermons). Perg. 4 to No. 15 in the Royal Library Stockholm,* Corpus Codicum Islandicorum Medii Aevi, 8 (Copenhagen: Levin & Munksgaard, 1935).

Palmer, Nigel F., ed., *Die 'Klosterneuburger Bußpredigten'. Untersuchung und Edition,* in *Überlieferungsgeschichtliche Editionen und Studien zur deutschen Literatur des Mittelalters. K. Ruh zum 75. Geburtstag*, ed. by Konrad Kunze and others, Texte und Textgeschichte, 31 (Tübingen: Niemeyer, 1989), pp. 210–44.

Patavini, S. Antonii, *Sermones dominicales et festivi ad fidem codicum recogniti curantibus*, ed. by Beniamino Costa, Leonardo Frasson, Joanne Luisetto, with the help of Paulo Marangon, Centro Studi Antoniani (Padua: Centro Studi Antoniani: Edizion Messagero, 1979).

Paul the Deacon, *Homiliae*, PL 95, 1159–1666.

Pelagius Parvus, *The Sermons of Brother Paio, Thirteenth Century Dominican Preacher's Sermones in Latin Text*, ed. by John-Gaston Tuthill (Ann Arbor: University Michigan Press 1982).

Perarnau I Espelt, Josep, 'La compilació de sermons de sant Vicent Ferrer de Barcelona, Biblioteca de Catalunya, Ms. 477', Arxiu de Textos Catalans Antics, 4 (1985), 213–402.

—, *Els quatre sermons catalans de sant Vicent Ferrer en el manuscrit 476 de la Biblioteca de Catalunya*, Arxiu de Textos Catalans Antics, 15 (1996), 109–340.

Peter of Celle, *De nativitate Sanctae Mariae*, ed. by Gerard De Martel, 'Recherches sur les manuscrits des sermons de Pierre de Celle', *Scriptorium*, 33 (1979), 3–16.

—, *Selected Works*, ed. and trans. by Hugh Feiss, Cistercian Studies, 100 (Kalamazoo,: Cistercian Publications 1987), 43–62.

—, *Sermones*, PL 202, 637–926.

Peter the Venerable, *Petri Venerabilis Sermones Tres*, ed. by Giles Constable, *Revue Bénédictine*, 64 (Namur: Abbye de Maredsous, 1954), pp. 224–72.

Pfeiffer, Franz, *Berthold von Regensburg*, vol. 1 (Vienna, 1862; repr. Berlin: De Gruyter, 1965).

— and Joseph Strobl eds, *Berthold von Regensburg*, vol. 2 (Vienna, 1880; repr. Berlin: De Gruyter, 1965).

Poggio, Bracciolini, *Facezie. Liber facetarium*, with an essay by Eugenio Garin, intro., trans. and notes by Marcello Ciccuto (Milan: Biblioteca Universale Rizzoli, 1983).

Poliziano, Angelo, *Detti piacevoli*, ed. by Tiziano Zanato, Bibliotheca biographica. Sezione artistico-letteraria (Rome: Istituto dela Enciclopedia Italiana, 1983).

Ranulphe of the Houblonnière, *La prédication de Ranulphe de la Houblonnière. Sermons aux clercs et au simples gens à Paris au XIIIème siècle*, ed. by Nicole Bériou, Études Augustiniennes, 2 vols (Paris: Études Augustiniennes, 1987).

Remigius de Auxerre, *Sermones*, PL 131, 865–932.

Richard of St Victor, *Richard de St-Victor. Liber exceptionum*, ed. by Jean Châtillon, Textes philosophiques du moyen âge, 5 (Paris: Vrin, 1958).

—, *Sermones centum*, PL 177, 901–1210.

—, *Sermones et opuscules spirituels inédits*, ed. by Jean Châtillon and William-Joseph Tulloch, Bibliothèque de Spiritualité médiévale (Paris-Bruges: Desclée, De Brouwer, 1951).

Robert of Basevorn, 'The Form of Preaching (*Forma Praedicandi*)', ed. by James J. Murphy, trans. by Leopold Krul, OSB, in *Three Medieval Rhetorical Arts* (Berkeley: University of California Press, 1971), pp. 109–215.

Rodrigo Lizondo, M., *Les corts generals de Jerusalem. Sermó allegoric del segle XIV sobre la mort de Jesucrist* (Barcelona: Edicions del Mall, 1985).

Rogerius de Platea, O. Min., *Sermones*, I, ed. by Cataldo Roccaro, Officina de studi medievali, Collana Franciscana, 5 (Palermo: Enchiridion, 1993).

Ross, Woodburn O., 'Brief *Forma predicandi*', *Modern Philology*, 34 (1937), 337–44.

—, *Middle English Sermons*, Early English Text Society, 209 (London, Milford: Oxford University Press, 1940).

—, *Middle English Sermons*, Early English Text Society, o.s. 262 (London, Milford: Oxford University Press, 1969).

Salvesen, Astrid, trans., *Gammelnorsk Homiliebok*, introduction and commentary by Erik Gunnes (Oslo-Bergen-Tromsø: Universitetsforlaget, 1971).

Sanchez, M. A., 'El sermón del Formamiento del Hombre (estudio y edición)', *Atalaya*, 3 (1992), 9–24.

Savonarola, Girolamo, *Prediche sopra l'Esodo*, ed. by Pier Giorgio Ricci, Edizione Nazionale delle opere, 2 vols (Rome: Belardetti, 1956–57).

—, *Prediche sopra Ezechiele*, ed. by Roberto Ridolfi, Edizione Nazionale delle opere, 2 vols (Rome: Berlardetti, 1955).

—, *Prediche sopra Giobbe*, ed. by Roberto Ridolfi, Edizione Nazionale delle opere, 2 vols (Rome: Berlardetti, 1957).

—, *Prediche sopra Ruth e Michea*, ed. by Vincenzo Romano, Edizione Nazionale delle opere, 2 vols (Rome: Berlardetti, 1961–62).

—, *Prediche sopra Aggeo e Trattato circa il reggimento della città di Firenze*, ed. by Luigi Firpo, Edizione Nazionale delle opere (Rome: Berlardetti, 1965).

—, *Prediche sopra Amos*, ed. by Paolo Ghiglier, Edizione Nazionale delle opere, 2 vols (Rome: Berlardetti, 1971–72).

—, *Prediche sopra i Salmi*, ed. by Vincenzo Romano, Edizione Nazionale delle opere, 2 vols (Rome: Berlardetti, 1969–74).

—, *Sermones in primam Divi Ioannis epistolam con il volgarizzamento toscano*, ed. by Armando F. Verde, Edizione Nazionale delle opere (Rome: Berlardetti, 1989).

Schönbach, A. E., ed., *Altdeutsche Predigten*, 3 vols (Graz, 1886; repr. Darmstadt: Wissenschaftliche Buchgesellschaft, 1964).

Schiewer, Hans-Jochen, ed., *Entstehungs- und Überlieferungsgeschichte der Sonntags- und Heiligenpredigten. Mit einer Musteredition* (Tübingen: Niemeyer, 1996).

Schmitt, Peter and others, eds, *Fest- und Heiligenpredigten des 'Schwarzwälder Predigers'* (Munich: Fink, 1982).

Schnyder, A., ed., 'Jakob Sprengers Predigt auf Johannes Evangelist (1465). Edition und Beiträge zur Interpretation', *Zeitschrift für deutsches Altertum und deutsche Literatur*, 123 (1994), 55–75.

Scragg, Donald G., ed., *The Vercelli Homilies and Related Texts*, Early English Text Society, o.s. 300 (London: Oxford University Press, 1992).

Sisam, C., ed., *The Vercelli Book,* Early English Manuscripts in Facsimile, 19 (Copenhagen: Rosenkilde and Bagger, 1976).

The South English Legendary, ed. by C. d'Evelyn and A. J. Mills, Early English Text Society, o.s. 235, 236 (London: Oxford University Press, 1956–59).

The South English Nativity of Mary and Christ, ed. by O. S. Pickering, Middle English Texts, 1 (Heidelberg: Winter, 1975).

Stephen of Tournay, *Sermones*, PL 198, 91–429.

Szarmach, Paul E., ed., *Vercelli Homilies IX–XXIII*, Toronto Old English Series, 5 (Toronto: University of Toronto Press, 1981).

Tauler, Johannes, *Sermons*, trans. by Maria Shrady (New York: Paulist Press, 1985).

Terrones del Cano, F., *Instrucción de Predicadores*, ed. by F. G. Olmedo, Clásicos Castellanos, 126 (Madrid, 1946; 1st edn, Madrid, 1617).

Thomas of Chobham, *Summa de arte praedicandi*, ed. by Franco Morenzoni, CCCM 82 (Turnhout: Brepols, 1988).

Thomas of Todi, *The Art of Giving Sermons and of Preparing Conferences*, ed. by Joseph M. Miller, Michael H. Prosser and Thomas W. Benson, trans. by Joseph M. Miller, in *Readings in Medieval Rhetoric* (Bloomington: Indiana Unversity Press, 1973), pp. 273–79.

Tugwell, Simon, ed. and trans., 'Treatise on the Formation of Preachers', in *Early Dominican Selected Writings* (New York: Paulist Press, 1982), pp. 183–385.

Umiltà of Faenza, *Sermones*, ed. by A. Simonetti, in *I sermoni di Umiltà de Faenza. Studio e edizione*, Biblioteca di Medioevo Latino, 14 (Spoleto: Centro Italiano di Studi sull'alto Medioevo, 1995).

—, *The Vercelli Book Homilies*, ed. by Lewis E. Nicholson (Lanham, MD: University Press of America, 1991).

Walker, R. E., ed., *Johannes Nas. The Corpus Christi sermons. An edition with notes and commentary*, Göppinger Arbeiten zur Germanistik, 394 (Göppingen: Kummerle, 1988).

Walther of St Victor, and others, *Sermones ineditos triginta sex*, ed. by J. Châtillon, CCCM 30 (Turnhout: Brepols, 1975).

Warner, Ruby D.-N., *Early English Homilies from the Twelfth-Century Manuscript. Vespasian D. XIV*, Early English Text Society, o.s. 152 (London, 1917, repr. 1971).

Whinnom, Keith, ed., *Diego de San Pedor: Obras completas*, 1 (Madrid: Castalia, 1979).

Willard, R., ed., *The Blickling Homilies*, Early English Manuscripts in Facsimile, 10 (Copenhagen: Rosenkilde and Bagger, 1960).

William of Auvergne, 'Un manuel de prédication médiévale', ed. by A. de Poorter, *Revue néoscholastique de philosophie*, 25, (1923), 192–209.

Wimbledon, T., *Wimbledon's Sermon, Redde rationem villicationis tue*, ed. by I. K. Knight, Duquesne Studies, Philological Series, 9 (Pittsburgh: Duquense University Press, 1967).

Wittlin, Curt, ed., *Art abreujada de predicacio*, Biblioteca Escriny, 4 (Barcelona: Edicions del Mall, 1982).

Wittlin, C., *Un sermón en latín de fray Antonio Canals, hecho en Valencia el 8 de setiembre de 1392: la virgen Maria, un libro*, in *Escritos del Vedat*, 27 (Valencia: Facultad de Teología San Vicente Ferrer de Valencia, 1997), 287–302.

Worstbrock, Franz Josef, 'Herolt, Johannes (Discipulus)', in *Die deutsche Literatur des Mittelalters Verfasserlexikon: Band 3*, ed. by Wolfgang Stammler, Karl Langosch, Kurt Ruh, and Gundolf Keil (Berlin: De Gruyter, 1981), pp. 1123–27.

Wulfstan, *The Homilies of Wulfstan,* ed. by Dorothy Bethurum (Oxford: Clarendon Press, 1957).

—, *Sermo Lupi ad Anglos* ed. by Dorothy Whitelock (London: Methuen, 1939; 2nd edn, 1952; 3rd edn, 1963).

SECONDARY SOURCES

Allen, Pauline, 'John Chrysostom's Homilies on I and II Thessalonians: The Preacher and His Audience', *Studia Patristica*, 31 (1997), 3–21.

—, 'Caesarius of Arles, the Medieval Sermon and Orthodoxy', *Indiana Social Studies Quarterly*, 35 (1982), 11–20.

Amos, Thomas L., and Beverly M. Kienzle, eds, *De Ore Domini: Preacher and Word in the Middles Ages*, Studies in Medieval Culture, 27 (Kalamazoo: Medieval Institute, Western Michigan University, 1989).

Anastasi, Rosario, 'Sulla funzione della retorica nell'omiletica in Michelle Psello', *Koinonia*, 7.1 (1983), 57–59.

Bataillon, Louis-Jacques, 'Approaches to the Study of Medieval Sermons', *Leeds Studies in English*, n.s. 11 (1980), 19–35.

—, 'La prédication au XIIIe siècle en France et Italie: études et documents', (Aldershot: Variorum, 1993).

—,'Les images dans les sermons au XIIIème siècle', *Freiburger Zeitschrift für Philosophie und Theologie*, 37 (1990), 327–95.

—, 'Les problèmes d'édition des sermons et des ouvrages pour prédicateurs au XIIIème siècle', in *The Editing of Theological and Philosphical Texts from the Middle Ages, Acts of the Conference Arranged by the Department of Classical Languages, University of Stockholm, 29–31 August 1984,* ed. by Monica Asztalos (Stockholm: Almqvist & Wiskell, 1986), pp. 105–20.

—, 'De la *lectio* à la *praedicatio*: Commentaires bibliques et sermons au XIIIème siècle', *Revue des sciences philosophiques et théologiques*, 70 (1986), 559–74.

—, 'Sermons rédigés, sermons reportés (XIIIème siècle)', *Medioevo e Rinascimento, Aunnuario del Dipartmiento di Studi sul Medioevo e il Rinascimento dell'Università di Firenze,* 3 (1989), 69–86.

—, '*Similitudines* et *exempla* dans les sermons du XIIIe siècle', in *The Bible in the Medieval World: Essays in Memory of Beryl Smalley*, *Studies in Church History*, ed. by Katherine Walsh and Diana Wood, Subsidia, 4 (Oxford: Blackwell Publishers, 1985), pp. 191–205.

Bauer, Christian, *Geistliche Prosa im Kloster Tegernsee. Untersuchungen zu Gebrauch und Überlieferung deutschsprachiger Literatur im 15. Jahrhundert,* Münchener Texte und Untersuchungen zur deutschen Literatur des Mittelalters, 107 (Tübingen: Niemeyer, 1996).

Bériou, Nicole, *L'art de convaincre dans la prédication de Ranulphe d'Homblières*, in *Faire croire. Modalités de la diffusion et de la réception des messages religieux du XIIème au XVème siècle,* ed. by *L. Duval-Arnould*, Collection de l'École française de Rome, 51 (Rome: Bottega d'Erasmo, 1981), pp. 39–65.

—, *L'avènement des maîtres de la Parole: La prédication à Paris au XIIIe siècle.* Collection des Études Augustinennes, Série Moyen Age et Temps Modernes, 31, 2 vols (Paris: Études Augustiniennes, 1998).

—, 'La Madeleine dans les sermons parisiens du XIIème siècle dans Mélanges de l'École française de Rome', *Moyen Âge*, 104 (1992), 269–340.

—, *La prédication de Ranulphe de la Houblonnière: Sermons aux clercs et aux simples gens à Paris au XIII*[e] *siècle*, 2 vols (Paris: Études Augustiniennes, 1987).

—,'La reportation des sermons parisiens à la fin du XIIIème siècle', in *The Editing of Theological and Philosophical Texts from the Middle Ages, Acts of the Conference Arranged by the Department of Classical Languages, University of Stockholm, 29–31 August 1984*, ed. by Monica Asztalos (Stockholm: Almqvist & Wiskell, 1986), pp. 87–123.

Berlioz, Jacques, 'La mémoire du prédicateur, Recherches sur la mémorisation des récits exemplaires (XIIIe–XVe siècles)', in *Temps, mémoire, tradition au Moyen-Age: actes du XIII*[e] *Congrès de la Société des historiens médiévistes de l'enseignement supérieur public, Aix-en-Provence, 4–5 juin 1982* (Aix-en-Provence: Universite de Provence, 1983), pp. 157–83.

—, 'Le récit efficace: l'example au service de la prédication (XIIIe–XVe siècles)', *Mélanges de l'École française de Rome, Moyen Âge-temps modernes*, 92 (1980), 113–46.

Biggs, Frederick M., 'The Fourfold Division of Souls: The Old English Christ III and the Insular Homiletic Tradition', *Traditio,* 45 (1989–90), 35–51.

Blumrich, R., 'Feuer der Liebe. Franziskanische Theologie in den deutschen Predigten Marquards von Lindau', *Wissenschaft und Weisheit*, 54 (1991), 44–55.

Borgehammer, Stephan, 'De dedicatione ecclesiae, Formell analys av några vadstena predikningar avsedda för kyrkoinvigningsfesten', in *I Heliga Birgittas trakter: Nitton uppsatser om medeltida samhälle ock kultur i Östergötland 'västanstång'*, ed. by Göran Dahlbäck (Stockholm: Humanistisksamhällsvetens-kapliga forskningsrådet, 1990), pp. 151–67.

Bouhot, Jean-Paul, 'L'homéliaire de Saint-Pierre du Vatican au milieu du VIème siècle et sa postérité', *Recherches Augustiniennes*, 20 (1985), 87–115.

Briscoe, Marianne G., '*Artes praedicandi*', *Typologie des sources du moyen âge occidental*, 61 (Turnhout: Brepols, 1992).

—, 'How Was the *Ars praedicandi* Taught in England?' in *The Uses of Manuscripts in Literary Studies: Essays in Memory of Judson Boyce Allen*, ed. by Charlotte Cook Morse and others, Studies in Medieval Culture, 31 (Kalamazoo: Kalamazoo Medieval Institute, Western Michigan University, 1992), pp. 41–58.

Broek, Marinus A. van den, 'Sprichwort und Redensart in den Werken des Leipziger Volkspredigers Marcus von Weida', *Beiträge zur Erforschung der deutschen Sprache*, 7 (1987), 168–81.

Brown, D. Catherine, *Pastor and Laity in the Theology of Jean Gerson* (Cambridge: Cambridge University Press, 1987).

Cabré, L. and Renedo, X., '*Et postea applicetur thema*. Format in the Preaching of St Vicent Ferrer, OP', *Archivum Fratrum Praedicatorum*, 66 (1996), 245–56.

Capitani, O., C. Leonardi, E. Menestò and R. Rusconi, eds, *Da Gregorio VII a Bernardino da Siena. Saggi di storia medievale* (Florence and Perugia, 1987).

Cátedra, Pedro M., *Dos estudios sobre el sermón en la España medieval* (Barcelona: Universidad Autónoma de Barcelona, 1981).

—, 'La modificación del discurso religioso con fines de invectiva. El sermón', in *L'invective au Moyen Âge: France, Espagne, Italie: actes du colloque 'L'invective au Moyen Âge', Paris, 4–6 février 1993*, ed. by Eric Beaumatin and Michael Garcia, Atalaya, 5, 1242–5869 (Paris: Presses de la Sorbonne nouvelle, 1995), pp. 101–22.

—, 'La mujer en el sermón medieval (a través de textos españoles)', in *La condición de la mujer en la Edad Media*, ed. by Y. R. Fonquerne and Alfonso Esteban (Madrid, Ed. de la Univ. Complutense, 1986), pp. 39–50.

Nebrija y la predicación, in *Antonio de Nebrija: Edad Media y Renacimiento*, ed. by C. Codoñer and J. A. González Iglesias, Acta Salmanticensia. Estudos Filologicos, 257 (Salamanca, Universidad de Salamanca, 1994), pp. 129–50.

—, 'La predicación castellana de San Vicente Ferrer', *Boletín de la Real Academia de Buenas Letras de Barcelona*, 39 (1983–84), 235–309.

—, *Sermón, sociedad y literatura en la Edad Media. San Vicente Ferrer en Castilla (1411–1412)* (Salamanca: Junta de Castilla y Leâon, Consejerâia de Cultura y Turismo, 1994).

Chavasse, Antoine, 'Un homéliaire liturgique romain du VIème siècle', *Revue bénédictine*, 90 (1980), 194–233.

Chazan, Robert, *Daggers of Faith: Thirteenth-Century Christian Missionizing and Jewish Response* (Berkeley: University of California Press, 1989).

Cigman, Gloria, 'Luceat Lux Vestra: The Lollard Preacher as Truth and Light', *Review of English Studies*, 40 (1989), 479–96.

Clayton, Mary, 'Delivering the Damned: A Motif in Old English Homiletic Prose', *Medium Ævum*, 55 (1986), 92–102.

—, 'Homilaries and Preaching in Anglo-Saxon England', *Peritia*, 4 (1985), 207–42.

Cole, Penny, *The Preaching of the Crusades in the Holy Land (1095–1270)*, Medieval Academy Books, 98 (Cambridge, MA: Medieval Academy of America, 1991).

Connolly, John M., 'Applicatio and Explicatio in Gadamer and Eckhart,' in *Gadamer's Century: Essays in Honor of Hans-Georg Gadamer*, ed. by Jeff Malpas, (Cambridge, MA: MIT Press, 2002), pp.76–96.

Constable, Giles, 'The Language of Preaching in the Twelfth Century', *Viator*, 25 (1994), 131–52.

Cormeau, C., 'Essen und Trinken in den deutschen Predigten Bertholds von Regensburg', in *Essen und Trinken in Mittelalter und Neuzeit. Vorträge eines interdisziplinären Symposions vom 10–13. Juni 1987 an der Justus-Liebig-Universität Gießen*, ed. by I. Bitsch and others (Sigmaringen, 1988), pp. 77–83.

Costard, M., and Hans-Jochen Schiewer, 'Predigt', in *Marienlexikon*, 5 (1993), pp. 297–310.

—, 'Zwischen Mystik und Moraldidaxe. Deutsche Predigten des Fraterherren Johannes Veghe und des Dominikaners Konrad Schlatter in Frauenklöstern des 15. Jahrhunderts', *Ons Geestelijk Erf*, 69 (1995), 235–59.

Cross, James E., 'A *Sermo de Misericordia* in English Prose', *Anglia*, 108 (1990), 429–40.

—, 'The Use of Patristic Homilies in the Old English Martyrology', in *Anglo-Saxon England*, 14 (1985), 107–28.

—, and Alan Brown, 'Literary Impetus for Wulfstan's Sermo Lupi', *Leeds Studies in English*, n.s. 20 (1989), 271–91.

—, and Alan Brown, 'Wulfstan and Abbot of Saint-Germain-des-Prés', *Mediaevalia*, 15 (1993), 71–91.

—, and Julia Crick, 'The Manuscript: Saint-Omer, Bibliothèque Municipale, 202', in *Two Old English Apocrypha and their Manuscript Source: 'The Gospel of Nichodemus and 'The Avenging of the Saviour'*, Cambridge Studies in Anglo-Saxon England, 19 (Cambridge: Cambridge University Press, 1996), pp. 10–35.

—, and Thomas N. Hall, 'Fragments of Alanus of Farfa's Roman Homiliary and Abridgments of Saints' Lives by Goscelin in London, British Library, Harley 652', in *Bright is the Ring of Words: Festschrift für Horst Weinstock zum 65, Geburtstag*, ed. by Clausdirk Pollner, Helmut Rohlfing and Frank-Rutger Hausmann, Abhandlungen zur Sprache und Literatur, 85 (Bonn: Romanistischer, 1996), pp. 49–61.

Cunningham, Mary B., 'Andrew of Crete's Homilies on Lazarus and Palm Sunday: The Preacher and his Audience', *Studia Patristica*, 31 (1997), 22–41.

—, and Pauline Allen, *Preacher and Audience: Studies in Early Christian and Byzantine Homiletics*, *A New History of the Sermon*, 1 (Leiden and Boston, MA: Brill, 1998).

D'Avray, David L., *Medieval Marriage Sermons: Mass Communication in a Culture Without Print* (Oxford: Oxford University Press, 2001).

—, *The Preaching of the Friars: Sermons Diffused from Paris before 1300*, (Oxford: Clarendon Press, 1985).

Dahmus, John, 'Preaching to the Laity in Fifteenth-Century Germany: Johannes Nider's "Harps"', *Journal of Ecclesiastical History*, 34 (1983), 5–68.

Dank, Ute, *Rhetorische Elemente in den Predigten Bertholds von Regensburg*, Deutsche Hochschuleditionen, 36 (Neuried: Ars Una, 1995).

Dauven-van, Knippenberg, C., 'Predigt und predigthafte Elemente in den deutschsprachigen Spielen des Osterfestkreises', *Jahrbuch der Oswald von Wolkenstein Gesellschaft*, 7 (1992/93), 115–32.

—, 'Über den Zusammenhang zwischen Osterpredigt und dramatischer Darstellung des Ostergeschehens', in *Osterspiele, Texte und Musik. Akten des 2. Symposiums der Sterzinger Osterspiele (12.–16. April 1992)*, ed. by M. Siller, Schlern-Schriften, 293 (Innsbruck: Universitatsverlag Wagner, 1994), pp. 33–50.

—, 'Ein Anfang ohne Ende: Einführendes zur Frage nach dem Verhältnis zwischen Predigt und geistlichem Schauspiel des Mittelalters', *Amsterdamer Beiträge zur Älteren Germanistik*, 38/39 (1994), 143–60.

Delcorno, Carlo, 'Eremo e solitudine nella predicazione dei Francescani', *Lettere Italiane,* 54 (2002), 493–523.

—, 'La diffrazione del testo omiletico. Osservazioni sulle doppie reportationes delle prediche bernardiniane', *Lettere italiane*, 4 (1986), 457–77.

—, 'La predicazione volgare in Italia (sec, xii–xiv), Teoria, produzione, ricezione', *Revue Mabillon,* 65, n.s. 4 (1993) 83–107.

—, 'L'*ars praedicandi* di Bernardino da Siena', *Lettere Italiane*, 32 (1980), 441–75.

—, 'Rassegna di studi sulla predicazione medievale e unamistica (1970–1980)', *Lettere Italiane,* 33 (1981), 235–76.

Deyermond, A., 'The Sermon and its Uses in Medieval Castilian Literature', *La Corónica*, 8 (1979–80), 127–48.

—, 'Problems of Language, Audience, and Arthurian Source in a Fifteenth-Century Castilian Sermon', *Miscelánea Solá Solé*, I (Barcelona, 1984), 43–54.

Domínguez Reboiras, F., ed., 'Moltes novelles raons. La originalidad del *Ars praedicandi* de Ramon Llull en su contexto medieval', *Anuario medieval*, 4 (1992), 93–137.

Donavin, Georgiana, '*De sermone sermonem fecimus*: Alexander of Ashby's *De artificioso modo predicandi*', *Rhetorica*, 15.3 (1997), 279–96.

Douglass, E. Jane Dempsey, *Justification in Late Medieval Preaching. A Study of John Geiler of Keisersberg*, Studies in Medieval and Reformation Thought, 1 (Leiden: Brill, 1989).

Egerding, M., 'Leben in Demut: Zu einer Grundhaltung in den Predigten von Johannes Tauler', *Geist und Leben*, 63 (1990), 99–110.

Eisenmann, S., '*Sed corde Dicemus*'. *Das volkstümliche Element in den deutschen Predigten des Geiler von Kaysersberg*, Europäische Hochschulschriften, Reihe, 1 (Frankfurt a.M.: Lang, 1996).

Elschenbroich, A., '*Purgare, illuminare, perficere*. Johann Geiler von Kaysersberg als Fabelerzähler und Fabelinterpret in seinen Predigtzyklen', *Deutsche Vierteljahrsschrift*, 61 (1987), 639–64.

Englisch, E., 'Deutsche Predigten als Vermittler zwischen Gelehrtenkultur und Volkskultur', in *Volkskultur des europäischen Mittelalters*, ed. by P. Dinzelbacher and H.-D. Mück, Böblinger Forum, 1 (Stuttgart: Kröner, 1987), pp. 147–58.

Étaix, Raymond, L'ancienne collection de sermons attribués à saint Augustin 'De Quattuor Birtutibus Caritatis', *Revue bénédictine*, 95 (1985), 44–59.

—, 'L'homéliaire carolingien d'Angers', *Revue Bénédictine,* 104 (1994), 148–90.

—, 'L'homéliaire composé par Raban Maur pour l'empereur Lothaire', *Recherches Augustiniennes*, 19 (1984), 211–40.

—, 'Les homéliaires carolingiens de l'école d'Auxerre', in *L'école carolingienne d'Auxerre de Murethach à Remi 830–908*, ed. by Dominique Iogna-Prat, Colette Jeudy, Guy Lobrichon, and Georges Duby (Paris, 1991).

—, *Homéliaires patristiques latins: recueil d'études de manuscrits médiévaux*, Collection des études augustiniennes, Série Moyen-Age et temps modernes, 29 (Paris: Études Augustiniennes, 1994).

—, 'Le recueil de sermons composé par Raban Maur pour Haistulfe de Mayence', *Revue des Études Augustiniennes*, 32 (1986), 124–37.

—, *Homéliaires patristiques latins: recueil d'études de manuscrits médiévaux*, Collection des Études Augustiniennes, Serie Moyen-Age et Temps Modernes, 29 (Paris: Études Augustiniennes, 1994).

Evans, Gillian Rosemary, *Alan of Lille: The Frontiers of Theology in the Later Twelfth Century* (Cambridge: Cambridge University Press, 1983).

—, *The Thought of Gregory the Great*, Cambridge Studies in Medieval Life and Thought, Series 4, 2 (Cambridge: Cambridge University Press, 1988).

—, and David L. D'Avray, 'An Unusual *Ars Praedicandi*', *Medium Aevum*, 49 (1980), 26–31.

Evans, Ruth, 'An Anonymous Old English Homily for Holy Saturday', *Leeds Studies in English,* n.s. 12 (1981), 129–53.

Fauser, M. and W. Hilgendorff, eds, 'Predigt und Homiletik in der deutschsprachigen Forschungsliteratur 1975–1985. Eine Bibliographie', *Rhetorik*, 5 (1986), 149–87.

Ferrando Francès, A., 'L'Omelia sobre lo psalm "De profundis" de Jeroni Fuster', in *Miscellània Joan Fuster. Estudis de llengua i literatura*, ed. by A. Ferrando and A. Hauf, Publicacións de l'Abadia de Montserrat, 6 (Barcelona: Publicacións de l'Abadia de Montserrat, 1993), pp. 79–106.

Ferruolo, Stephen C., 'Preaching to the Clergy and Laity in Early Thirteenth-Century France: Jacques de Vitry's *Sermones ad status*', *Proceedings of the Annual Meeting of the Western Society for French History*, 12 (Las Cruces, NM: New Mexico State University Press, 1985), 12–22.

Fletcher, Alan J., '*Benedictus qui venit in nomine Domini*: A Thirteenth-Century Sermon for Advent and the Macaronic Style in England', *Mediaeval Studies*, 56 (1994), 217–45.

—, 'John Mirk and the Lollards', *Medium Ævum*, 56 (1987), 217–24.

—, '"Magnus predicator et deuotus": A Profile of the Life, Work, and Influence of the Fifteenth-Century Oxford Preacher, John Felton', *Mediaeval Studies*, 53 (1991), 125–75.

—, 'The Preaching of the Pardoner', *Studies in the Age of Chaucer*, 11 (1989), 15–35.

—, *Preaching, politics and poetry in late-medieval England* (Dublin and Portland, OR: Four Courts Press, 1998).

—, 'Unnoticed Sermons from John Mirk's Festial', *Speculum*, 55 (1980), 514–22.

Forde, Simon N., 'Nicholas Hereford's Ascension Day Sermon, 1382', *Mediaeval Studies*, 51 (1989), 205–41.

Forni, Arnaldo, 'Kerygma e addattamento: Aspetti della predicazione cattolica nei secoli XII–XIV,' *Bullentino dell'istituto storico italiano per il medio evo e Archivio Muratoriano*, 89 (1980–81), 261–348.

Fournier, G., 'Un sermonnaire allemand du temps de maître Eckhart. Le "Paradisus animae intelligentis". Conditions d'une redécouverte', *Revue des sciences religieuses*, 70 (1996), 102–12.

Francescanesimo e cultura in Sicilia (sec. XIII–XVI). Atti del Convegno internazionale di studio nell'ottavo centenario della nascita di S. Francesco d'Assisi, Palermo, 7–12 marzo 1982, Officina di studi medievali. Schede medievale 12–13 (Palermo, 1987).

Franceschini, D., 'Un ritrovato codice di prediche di Giordano da Pisa', *Lettere italiane*, 43 (1991), 570–86.

Frugoni, C., 'L'immagine del predicatore nell'iconografia medievale', *Medioevo e Rinascimento. Annuario del Dipartimento di Studi sul Medioevo e il Rinascimento dell'Università di Firenze*, 3 (1989), 287–99.

Gallo, D., 'Predicatori grancescani nella cattedrale di Padova durante il Quattrocento', in *Predicazione francescana e società veneta nel Quattrocento: commitenza, ascolto, ricezione. Atti del Il Convegno internazionale di studi francescani, 26–28 marzo 1987.* Le Venezie Francescane, n.s. 6 (Padua, 1989), pp. 175–85.

Gamboso, V., 'I due sermoni in lode di S. Antonio di Albertino da Verona', *Il Santo*, 27 (1987), 77–120.

Garfagnini, G. C., *Ser Lorenzo Violi e le prediche del Savonarola*, in *Medioevo e Rinascimento. Annuario del Dipartimento di Studi sul Medioevo e il Rinascimento dell'Università di Firenze*, 3 (1989), 261–85.

Gatch, Milton McC., 'The Unknowable Audience of the Blickling Homilies', *Anglo-Saxon England*, 18 (1989), 99–115.

Geier, Martin, *'Drumb muss ein newer Daniel auffstehn'. Müntzers Fürstenpredigt: ein theologischer Intertext, Die Schrift und die Tradition. Studien zur Intertextualität,* ed. by Martin Geier, (Munich: Fink, 1985).

Gillespie, Vincent, '*Doctrina* and *Predicacio*: The Design and Function of Some Pastoral Manuals', *Leeds Studies in English,* n.s. 11 (1980), 36–50.

Giombi, S., ed., 'Teorie sulla predicazione nei secoli XVI–XVII e l'Ordine dei Cappuccini', in *Girolamo Mautini da Narni e l'Ordine dei Cappuccini fra '500 e '600* (Rome: Istituto Storico del Cappuccini, 1998), pp. 149–84.

Gnädinger, L., 'Das Altväterzitat im Predigtwerk Johannes Taulers', in *Unterwegs zur Einheit. Festschrift für H. Stirnimann*, ed. by Johannes Brantschen and Pietro Selvatico (Fribourg: Herder, 1980), pp. 253–67.

—, *Johannes Tauler. Lebenswelt und mystische Lehre* (Munich: Beck, 1993).

Godfroy, M.-F., 'Le prédicateur franciscain Thomas Illyricus à Toulouse (novembre 1518 - mai 1519)', *Annales du Midi*, 97 (1985), 101–14.

Gregg, Joan Young, *Devils, Women, and Jews: Reflections of the Other in Medieval Sermon Stories*, SUNY Series in Medieval Culture (Albany, NY: State University of New York Press, 1997).

Grégoire, R., *Homéliaires liturgiques médiévaux: analyse de manuscrits*, Biblioteca degli Studi Medievali, 12 (Spoleto: Centro Italiano de Studi sull'alto Medioevo, 1980).

Hall, Thomas N., 'III, Articles and Notes: A Basic Bibliography of Medieval Sermon Studies', *Medieval Sermon Studies*, 36 (Autumn 1995), 26–42.

Hamesse, J., 'Les problèmes posés par l'édition critique des reportationes', *Franciscan Studies*, 24 (1986), 107–17.

—, and Xavier Herman, eds, *De l'Homélie au Sermon: Histoire de la Prédication Médiévale* (Louvain-la-Neuve, 1993).

—, and Beverly M. Kienzle, Debra L. Stoudt, Anne Thayer, eds, *Medieval Sermons and Society: City, Cloister, University*, Textes et études du Moyen Âge, 8 (Louvain-la-Neuve: Fédération Internationale des Instituts d'Études Médiévales, 1998).

Hasebrink, B., *Formen inzitativer Rede bei Meister Eckhart. Untersuchungen zur literarischen Konzeption der deutschen Predigt*, Texte und Textgeschichte, 32 (Tübingen: Niemeyer, 1992).

—, 'Grenzverschiebung. Zu Kongruenz und Differenz von Latein und Volkssprache bei Meister Eckhart', *Zeitschrift für deutsches Altertum und deutsche Literatur*, 121 (1992), 369–98.

—, 'Der Rebdorfer Eckhartkommentar. Überlieferung und Kommentierung der Armutspredigt Meister Eckharts in der Rebdorger Handschrift Cgm 455', in *Mystik*, ed. by C. Cormeau, *Zeitschrift für deutsche Philologie*. Sonderhefte, 113 (1994), pp. 207–22.

Hasse, Hans-Peter, *Karlstadt und Tauler. Untersuchungen zur Kreuzestheologie*, Quellen und Forschungen zur Reformationsgeschichte, 58 (Gütersloh: Mohn, 1993).

Heffernan, Thomas J., 'The Authorship of the *Northern Homily Cycle*: The Liturgical Affiliations of the Sunday Gospel Pericopes as a Test', *Traditio*, 41 (1985), 289–309.

Herzog, U., 'Die Predigt', in *Prosakunst ohne Erzählen. Die Gattungen der nicht-fiktionalen Kunstprosa*, ed. by K. Weissenberger, Konzepte der Sprach- und Literaturwissenschaft, 34 (Tübingen: Niemeyer, 1985), pp. 145–67.

Hjelde, O., *Norsk preken i det 12. århundre: Studier i Gammel Norsk Homiliebok* (Oslo: Hjelde, 1990).

Holloway, Julia Bolton, ed., *Beata Umiltà: Sguardo su Beata Umiltà: Contemplating on Holy Humility* (in Italian and English), trans. by Fabrizio Vanni (Florence: Editoriale gli Archipressi, 2003).

Horner, Patrick J., 'Benedictines and Preaching in Fifteenth-Century England: The Evidence of Two Bodleian Library Manuscripts', *Revue bénédictine*, 99 (1989), 313–32.

Hudson, A. and H. L. Spencer, 'Old Author, New Work: The Sermons of MS Longleat 4', *Medium Ævum*, 53 (1984), 220–38.

Iohn, F., *Die Predigt Meister Eckharts: Seelsorge und Häresie*, Beiträge zur alteren Literaturgeschichte (Heidelberg: Winter, 1993).

Johnston, Mark D., *The Evangelical Rhetoric of Ramon Llull: Lay Learning & Piety in the Christian West Around 1300* (Oxford: Oxford University Press, 1996).

Jones, Malcolm, 'The Parodic Sermon in Medieval and Early Modern England', *Medium Aevum,* 66 (1997), 94–114.

Kannengiesser, Charles, 'The Homiletic Festal Letters of Athanasius', in *Preaching in the Patristic Age. Studies in Honor of Walter J. Burghardt*, ed. by David G. Hunter and Walter J. Burghardt (New York: Paulist Press, 1989), pp. 73–100.

Karlsson, S., ed., 'Ögn og háls i hómilíu', *Gripla*, 4 (1980), 135–37.

Kienzle, Beverly Mayne, *Cistercians, Heresy and Crusade in Occitania, 1145-1229: Preaching in the Lord's Vineyard* (Rochester, NY: Boydell, 2001).

—, 'Cistercian Preaching Against the Cathars: Hélinand's Unedited Sermon for Rogation, B.N. MS. Lat. 14591', *Cîteaux*, 39 (1988), 297–314.

—, 'Deed and Word: Hélinand's Toulouse Sermons I', in *Erudition at God's Service*, ed. by John R. Sommerfeldt, Cistercian Studies. Studies in Medieval Cistercian History, 11 (Kalamazoo: Cistercian Publications, 1987), pp. 277–90.

—, 'Mary Speaks Against Heresy: Hélinand of Froidmont's Unedited Purification Sermon, Paris Bib. Nat. Ms. Lat 14591', *Sacris Erudiri*, 32 (1991), 291–308.

—, and Edith Wilks Dolnikowski, Rosemary Drage Hale, Darleen Pryds, Anne Thayer, eds, *Models of Holiness in Medieval Sermons: proceedings of the International Symposium (Kalamazoo, MI, 4–7 May 1995)*, *Textes et études du moyen âge*, 5 (Louvain-la-Neuve: Fédération internationale des Instituts d'études médiévales, 1996).

—, *The Sermon*, Typologie des sources du moyen âge, 81–83 (Turnhout: Brepols, 2000).

—, *'Verbum Dei et Verba Bernardi:* The Function of Language in Bernard's Second Sermon for Peter and Paul', in *Bernardus Magister. Papers presented at the Nonacentury Celebration of the Birth of Saint Bernard of Clairvaux, Kalamazoo, MI, (...), 10–13 may 1990*, ed. by John R. Sommerfeldt, Cistercian Studies, 135 (Kalamazoo: Cistercian Publications, 1992), pp. 149–59.

—, and Pamela J. Walker, eds, *Women Preachers and Prophets through Two Millennia of Christianity* (Berkeley: University of California Press, 1998).

Knapp, F. P., *Admonter Predigten und Bibelkommentare. Die Literatur des Früh- und Hochmittelaters* in *den Bistümern Passau, Salzburg, Brixen und Trient von den Anfängen bis zum Jahre 1273* (Graz: Akademische Druk- und Verlagsanstalt, 1994).

Le Goff, Jacques, 'L'exemplum et la rhétorique de la prédication au XIIIe et XIVe siècles', in *Retorica e poetica tra i secoli XIIe XIV: atti del secondo Convegno internazionale di studi dell'Associazione per il Medioevo e l'unmanesimo latini (AMUL) in onore e memoria di Ezio Franceschini, Trento e Rovereto 3–5 ottobre*

1985, ed. by Claudio Leonardi and Enrico Menestò, Quaderni del 'Centro per il collegamento degli studi medievali e unmanistici nell'Università di Perugia', 18 (Perugia: Regione dell'Umbria, 1988), pp. 3–29.

Leclercq, Jean, 'Were the Sermons on the Song of Songs Delivered in Chapter?', in *Sermons on the Song of Songs*, II, trans. by Kilian Walsh, Cistercian Fathers Series, 7 (Kalamazoo: Cistercian Publications, 1976), pp. vii–xxx.

Lemarie, J., 'L'homéliaire carolingien de Mondsee, témoin de sermons d'un Pseudo-Fulgence', in *Philologia Sacra: Biblische und patristische Studien für Hermann J. Frede und Walter Thiele zu ihrem siebzigsten Geburtstag*, vol. 2, ed. by R. Gryson, H. J. Frede and W. Thiele, Vetus Latina, Aus der Geschichte der lateinischen Bibel, 24/1–2, 2 vols (Freiburg im Breisgau, 1993), pp. 568–81.

Lesnick, Daniel R., *Preaching in Medieval Florence. The Social World of Franciscan and Dominican Spirituality* (Athens: University of Georgia Press, 1989).

Lo Cicero, Carla, 'Rufino traduttore di Basilio: Emulazione e citazioni bibliche', in *Tra IV e V secolo: Studi sulla cultura latina tardoantica,* ed. by Isabella Gualandri (Milan: Cisalpino, 2002), pp. 97–117.

Longère, Jean, 'Deux sermons de Jacques de Vitry', in *L'image du pélerin au Moyen Âge et sous l'Ancien Régime. Actes du Colloque International de Rocamadour, 30 septembre – 4 octobre 1993*, ed. by P.-A. Sigal (Gramat: Association des Amis de Rocamadour, 1994), pp. 93–103.

—, *La prédication médiévale* (Paris: Études Augustiniennes, 1983).

—, 'Le prélat selon Alain de Lille (d. 1205)', in *Les Prélats, L'Église et la société, XIe–XVe siècles: Hommage à Bernard Guillemain*, ed. by Françoise Bériac and Anne-Marie Dom (Talence: CROCEMC, Université Michel de Montaigne Bordeau III, 1994), pp. 101–08.

—, 'Le sacrement de pénitence dans les sermons de S. Antoine', in *Le fonti e la teologia dei Sermoni Antoniani. Atti del Congresso Internazionale di studio sui sermones di S. Antonio di Padova, Padova, 5–10 ottobre 1981*, ed. by A. Poppi, Centro Studi Antoniani, 5 (Padua: Messagero, 1982), pp. 559–77.

Macmullen, Ramsay, 'The Preacher's Audience (A.D. 350–400)', *Journal of Theological Studies*, 40 (1989), 503–11.

Mageroy, H., 'In dedicatione ecclesiæ sermo: Om overleveringa av "Stavkyrkjepreika"', in *Opuscula*, VIII, Bibliotheca Arnamagnæana, 38 (Copenhagen: Munksgaard, 1985), pp. 96–122.

Marinangeli, G., 'La settecentesca collezione dell' Opera omnia di S. Giovanni da Capestrano in riproduzione anastatica', *Bullettino della Deputazione Abruzzese di Storia Patria*, 75 (1985), 453–82.

Martin, Hervé, *Le Métier de Prédicateur: En France Septentrionale à la fin du moyen âge (1350–1520)* (Paris: Editions du Cerf, 1988).

—, 'Un prédicateur franciscain du XVème siècle: Pierre-aux-Bœufs, et les réalités de son temps', *Revue de l'histoire de l'Église de France*, 70 (1984), 107–26.

Mastronardi, Maria A., 'La predicazione volgare di R. Caracciolo, Questioni preliminari', *Annali della Facolotà di Lettere e Filosofia,* 25–26 (1982–83), 291–321.

—, 'Persuaione e mimesi, Modelli retorici e prassi omiletica nella predicazione di Roberto Caracciolo', *Lares: Rivista trimestrale di studi dem-etno-antroplogici diretta da*, 56 (1990), 59–81.

—, 'Retorica umanistica e modelli francescani nell'oratoria sacra di Roberto Caracciolo', *Annali della Facolotà di Lettere e Filosofia,* 32 (1989), 305–25.

—, 'Tradizione retorica e 'actio' giullaresca in un sermone semidrammatico del Quattrocento', *Lares: Rivista trimestrale di studi dem-etno-antroplogici diretta da,* 56 (1990), 587–602.

Mattoso, José, 'Estratégias da pregação no sécolo XIII', in *Fragmentos de uma composição medieval* (Lisbon: Editorial Estampa, 1987), pp. 191–202.

Mayer, Wendy, 'The Dynamics of Liturgical Space: Aspects of Interaction between John Chrysostom and his Audiences', *Ephemerides Liturgicae,* 111 (1997), 104–15.

McGuire, Brian Patrick, 'Cistercians and the Rise of the Exemplum in Early Thirteenth Century France: a Reevaluation of Paris B.N. Ms. Lat. 15912', in *Classica et Medievalia*, 34 (1983), 211–67.

McLaughlin, R. Emmet, 'The World Eclipsed? Preaching in the Early Middle Ages', *Traditio*, 46 (1991), 77–122.

Menzel, Michael, 'Predigt und Predigtorganisation im Mittelalter', *Historisches Jahrbuch*, 111 (1991), 337–84.

Merrix, Robert P., 'Sermon Structure in The Pardoner's Tale', *Chaucer Review*, 17 (1983), 235–49.

Mertens, Volker, 'Authentisierungsstrategien in vorreformatorischer Predigt: Erscheinungsform und Edition einer oralen Gattung am Beispiel Johannes Geilers von Kaysersberg', in *Editio: Internationales Jahrbuch für Editionswissenschaft/ International Yearbook of Scholarly Editing/Revue Internationale des Sciences de l'Edition Critique*, 16 (2002), 70–85.

—, 'Der "implizierte Sünder". Prediger, Hörer und Leser in Predigten des 14. Jahrhunderts, *Zur deutschen Literatur und Sprache des 14. Jahrhunderts*'. *Dubliner Colloquium 1981*, ed. by Walter Haug and others, Reihe Siegen, 45 (Heidelberg: Winter, 1983), pp. 76–114.

—, and Hans-Jochen Schiewer, eds, *Die deutsche Predigt im Mittelalter. Internationales Symposium am Fachbereich Germanistik der Freien Universität Berlin vom 3.–6. Oktober 1989* (Tübingen: Niemeyer, 1992).

—, 'Studien zu den "Leipziger Predigten"', *Beiträge zur Geschichte der deutschen Sprache und Literatur*, 107 (1985), 240–66.

Millett, Bella, 'The Songs of Entertainers and the Song of the Angels: Vernacular Lyric Fragments in Odo of Cheriton's *Sermones de Festis*', *Medium Ævum*, 64 (1995), 17–36.

Mischlewski, A., 'Eine deutsche Antoniterpredigt aus dem 15. Jahrhundert', in *Aus Archiven und Bibliotheken. Festschrift für R. Kottje zum 65. Geburstag*, ed. by H. Mordek, Freiburger Beiträge zur mittelalterlichen Geschichte. Studien und Texte, 3 (Frankfurt a.M.: Lang, 1992), pp. 477–88.

Moran I Ocerinjauregui, J., 'Les homilies d'Organyà en relació amb les homilies provençals de Tortosa', in *Miscellània Pere Bohigas, 2*: Estudis de Ilengua i literatura catalanes, 4 (1982), pp. 67–84.

Muessig, Carolyn, *Medieval Monastic Preaching*, Studies in Intellectual History, 90 (Leiden: Brill, 1998).

Müller, O., 'Mündlichkeit und Schriftlichkeit in der deutschen Predigt des Mittelalters', in *Beiträge zur Schriftlinguistik*, ed. by P. Ewald and others, Sprache, System u. Tätigkeit, 15 (Frankfurt a.M.: Lang, 1995), pp. 191–200.

Neuendorff, Dagmar, 'Berthold von Regensburg zugeschriebene Predigten als Herausforderung an die Editionswissenschaft und die Literaturgeschichtsschreibung', *Jahrbuch für Internationale Germanistik*, 34 (2002), 147–66.

—, 'Die typisierte Wirklichkeit: Zu Predigten Bertholds von Regensburg', in *Zur Rolle der Sprache im Wandel der Gesellschaft,* ed. by Matti Luukkainen, and Riitta Pyykkö, Suomalaisen Tiedeakatemian Toimituksia/Annales Academiæ Scientiarum Fennicæ, Humaniora, 317 (Helsinki: Finnish Academy of Science and Letters, with Finnish Society of Sciences and Letters, 2002), 216–27.

—, 'Überlegungen zur Rezeptionsgeschichte Berthold von Regensburg zugeschriebener deutscher Predigten vor dem Hintergrund seiner lateinischen Sermones', in *Bildungsexklusivität und volkssprachliche Literatur. Literatur vor Lessing - nur für Experten? Akten des VII. Internationalen Germanisten-Kongresses Göttingen 1985*, ed. by K. Grubmüller, G. Hess, and A. Schöne, Kontroversen, alte und neue, 7 (Tübingen: Niemeyer, 1986), pp. 69–73.

Nigro, S. and E. Sanguineti, *Le brache di San Griffone. Novellistica e predicazione tra '400 e '500. Prefazione di E. Sanguineti*, Biblioteca di cultura moderna, 879 (Bari: Laterza, 1983).

Nolcken, Christina Von, 'Some Alphabetical Compendia and How Preachers Used Them in Fourteenth Century England', *Viator*, 12 (1981), 271–88.

Odber de Baubeta, Patricia Anne, 'Towards a History of Preaching in Medieval Portugal', *Portuguese Studies*, 7 (1991), 1–18.

O'Mara, Veronica M., 'A Middle English Sermon Preached by a Sixteenth-Century "Athiest" [sic]: A Preliminary Account', *Notes and Queries*, n.s. 34 (1987), 183–85.

Pacini, G. P., 'La predicazione laicale nelle confraternite', *Ricerche di storia sociale e religiosa*, n.s. 17–18 (1980), 13–27.

Papi, M., 'Crociati, pellegrini e cavalieri nei "Sermone" di Gilberto di Tournai', *Studi Francescani*, 73 (1976), 373–409.

Paton, Bernadette, *Preaching Friars and the Civic Ethos: Siena, 1380–1480* (London: Centre for Medieval Studies/University of London Press, 1992).

Paz, Francisco-Javier Tovar, *Tractatus, sermones atque homiliae: el cultivo del género literario del discurso homilético en la Hispania tardoantigua y visigoda*, *Anejos del Anuario de estudios filológicos*, 15 (Cáceres: Universidad de Extremadura, Servicio de Extremadura, 1994).

Pelligrini, L., 'Tabula super sermones. Gli indici dei sermonari domenicani nei codici centro-italiani (sec. XIII–XV)', *Archivum Fratrum Praedicatorum*, 64 (1994), 119–42.

Pensel, F., 'Reimfassung einer Predigt Bertholds von Regensburg über die Messe', *Beiträge zur Geschichte der deutschen Sprache und Literatur*, 117 (1995), 65–91.

Perarnau I Espelt, Josep, 'L'antic ms. 279 de la Catedral de València, amb sermons de san Vicente Ferrer, perdut durant la guerra del 1936–1939. Intent de reconstrucció', *Butlletí de la Biblioteca de Catalunya*, 10 (1982–84 [1986]), 29–44.

Pernler, S.-E., 'Predikan ad populum under svensk medeltid', in *Predikohistoriska perspektiv: Studier tillägnade Åke Andrén*, ed. by A. Härdelin, Skrifter utgivna av Svenska kyrkohistoriska föreningen. II. Ny följd, 35 (Alusjo: Skeab Verbun, 1982), pp. 73–95.

Pini, A. I., 'Bologna e la Romagna nella "Cronica sive Liber exemplorum ad usum praedicantium" di Salimbene de Adam', ed. by G. Petti Balbi in *Salimbeniana, Atti del Convegno per il VII centenario di fra Salimbene* (Bologna: Radio Tau, 1991) pp. 174–97.

Polecriti, Cynthia L., *Preaching Peace in Renaissance Italy. San Bernardino of Siena and his Audience* (Berkeley: University of California Press, 1988).

Powell, Sue, 'A New Dating of John Mirk's Festial', *Notes and Queries*, n.s. 29 (1982), 487–89.

Rapp, Francis, 'Un prédicateur strasbourgeois à l'époque de Tauler', *Revue des sciences religieuses*, 70 (1996), 125–35.

Reinitzer, Heimo, *Beiträge zur Geschichte der Predigt: Vortäge und Abhandlungen*, Vestigia Bibliae, 3 (Hamburg, 1981).

Reiter, P., *Der Seele Grund. Meister Eckhart und die Tradition der Seelenlehre*, Episthemata. Würzburger Wissenschaftliche Schriften. Reihe Philosophie, 139 (Würzburg: Königshausen & Neumann, 1993).

Roberts, Phyllis Barzillay, 'The Pope and the Preachers: Perceptions of the Religious Role of the Papacy in the Preaching Tradition of the Thirteenth-Century English Church', in *Religious Roles of the Papacy: Ideals and Realities, 1150–1300*, ed. by Christopher Ryan, Papers in Mediaeval Studies, 8 (Toronto: Pontifical Institute of Mediaeval Studies, 1989), pp. 277–97.

—, *Thomas Becket in the Medieval Latin Preaching Tradition: An Inventory of Sermons about St. Thomas Becket c. 1170–c. 1400* (Steenbrugge; The Hague: Nijhoff, 1992).

Rouse, Mary A. and H. Richard, '"*Statim invenire*": Schools, Preachers, and New Attitudes to the Page', in *Authentic Witnesses: Approaches to Medieval Texts and Manuscripts* (Notre Dame, IN: University of Notre Dame Press, 1991), pp. 191–220.

Roussel, Henri, and François Suard, eds, *Alain de Lille, Gautier de Châtillon, Jakemart Giélée et leur temps: Actes du Colloque Lille, octobre 1978* (Lille: Presses Universitaire de Lille, 1980).

Ruh, Kurt, 'Deutsche Predigtbücher des Mittelalters', *Vestigia bibliae*, 3 (1981), 11–30.

—, *Meister Eckhart. Theologe, Prediger, Mystiker*, 2nd edn, (Munich: Beck, 1989).

Rusconi, Roberto, 'De la prédication à la confession: transmission et contrôle de modèles de comportement au XIIIème siècle', in *Faire croire. Modalités de la diffusion et de la réception des messages religieux du XIIème au XVème siècle*, ed. by Louis Duval-Arnould, Collection de l'École française de Rome, 51 (Rome: Bottega d'Erasmo, 1981), pp. 67–85.

—, 'Giovanni da Capestrano. Iconografia di un predicatore nell'Europa del '400', in *Predicazione francescana, societa veneta nel Quattrocento: committenza, ascolto, ricezione* (Le Venezie francescane, 6 [1989], pp. 31–60, then Padua, Centro Studi Antoniani, 1995, pp. 25–53).

—, 'Predicatori e predicazione (secoli IX–XVIII)', *Intelletuali e potere*, ed. by C. Vivanti, Soria d'Italia. Annali, 4 (Turin: Einaudi, 1982), pp. 951–1035.

—, *Predicazione e vita religiosa nella società italiana: da Carlo Magno alla Controriforma*, Documenti della storia, 30 (Turin: Loescher, 1981).

—, La Predicazione: parole in chiesa, parole in piazza', in *Lo Spazio Letterario del Medioevo: I, II Medioevo Latino, II: La Circolazione del Testo*, ed. by Guglielmo Cavallo and others, (Rome: Salerne, 1994), pp. 571–603.

—, '"Predicò in piazza": politica e predicazione nell'Umbria del '400', in *Signorie in Umbria tra Medioevo e Rinascimento: l'esperienza dei Trino* (Perugia, 1989), pp. 113–41.

—, 'Vincent Ferrer e Pedro de Luna: sull'iconografia di un predicatore fra due obedienze', in *Conciliarismo, stati nazionali. Inizi dell'Umanesimo. Convegno Storico Internazionale, Todi, 9–12 ottobre 1988*, Atti dei Convegno dell'Accademia Tudertina e del Centro di Studi sulla Spiritualita Medievale. n.s. 2 (Spoleto: Centro italiano di studi sull'alto Medioevo, 1990), pp. 213–33.

Samson, Annie, 'The South English Legendary: Constructing a Context', in *Thirteenth-Century England. Proceedings of the Newcastle upon Thyme Conference*, ed. by P. R. Cross and S. D. Lloyd (Rochester, NY: Boydell, 1986), pp. 185–95.

Schiewer, Hans-Jochen, *'Die Schwarzwälder Predigten': Entstehungs-und Überlieferungsgeschichte der Sonntags-und Heiligenpredigten: mit einer Musteredition*, Münchener Texte und Untersuchungen zur deutschen Literatur des Mittelalters, 105 (Tübingen: Niemeyer, 1996).

—, 'Ein maere ist daz – Narrative Exempla in der frühen deutschen Predigt', in *Erzählungen in Erzählungen. Phänomene der Narration in Mittelalter und Früher Neuzeit*, ed. by Harald Haferland and Michael Mecklenburg, Forschungen zur Geschichte der älteren deutschen Literatur, 19 (Munich: Fink, 1996), pp. 199–219.

—, '"Predigt". B. Volkssprachliche Literaturen des Westens. i. Deutsche Literatur', *Lexikon des Mittelalters*, 7 (Munich-Zurich, 1994), cols. 174–76.

—, 'Spuren von Mündlichkeit in der mittelalterlichen Predigtüberlieferung. Ein Plädoyer für exemplarisches und beschreibend-interpretierendes Edieren', *Editio*, 6 (1992), 64–79.

—, and Volker Mertens, *Repertorium der ungedruckten deutschsprachigen Predigten des Mittelalters*, vol. I, *Die Handschriften aus dem Straßburger Dominikanerinnenkloster St. Nikolaus in undis und benachbarte Provenienzen* (Tübingen: Niemeyer, 2000).

Schiewer, Regina D., 'Die Entdeckung der mittelniederdeutschen Predigt. Überlieferung, Form, Inhalte', *Oxford German Studies*, 26 (1997), 24–72.

—, 'Predigtforschung in Aufwind', *Jahrbuch der Oswald von Wolkenstein-Gesellschaft*, 12 (2000), 291–309.

Schmidtke, Dietrich, 'Eichstätter Fragmente von Eckhartpredigten. [Mit Textpublikation]', *Zeitschrift für deutsches Altertum und deutsche Literatur*, 112 (1983), 73–82.

Schmitt, Jean-Claude, ed., *Prêcher d'exemples: récits de prédicateurs du moyen âge* (Paris: Stock, 1985).

Schneider, K., 'Felix Fabri als Prediger', in *Festschrift W. Haug und B. Wachinger* (Tübingen: Niemeyer, 1992), pp. 437–68.

Schneyer, Johann Baptist, *Repertorium der Lateinischen Sermones des Mittelalters fur die Zeit von 1150–1350*, 9 vols (Münster: Aschendorff, 1969–90).

Schulze, Manfred, 'Der Hiob-Prediger. Johannes von Staupitz auf der Kanzel der Tübinger Augustinerkirche', in *Augustine, the Harvest and Theology (1300–1650). Essays dedicated to Heiko Augustinus Oberman in Honour of his Sixtieth Birthday*, ed. by Kenneth Hagen (Leiden: Brill, 1990), pp. 63–88.

Schumacher, M., '"Eyn meyster und s. Gregor sprechent". Das "Höhlengleichnis" Gregors des Großen bei Heinrich Seuse und in deutschen Predigten des Spätmittelalters', *Literaturwissenschaftliches Jahrbuch*, 33 (1992), 361–66.

Schüppert, H., 'Frauenbild und Frauenalltag in der Predigtliteratur', in *Frau und spätmittelalterlicher Alltag. Internationaler Kongress Krems an der Donau 2.–5. Oktober 1984*, ed. by H. Kühnel, Österreichische Akademie der Wissenschaften. Veröffentlichungen des Instituts fur mittelalterliche Realienkunde Österreichs, 9 (Vienna: Verlag der Österreichischen Akademie der Wissenschaften, 1986), pp. 103–56.

—, 'Geiler von Kaysersberg. Ein Beitrag zur Imagologie der Predigt', in *Albertus Magnus und der Albertinismus*, ed. by J. F. Maarten and others, Studien und Texte zur Geistesgeschichte des Mittelalters, 48 (Leiden: Brill, 1995), pp. 333–52.

Scragg, Donald G., 'An Old English Homilist of Archbishop Dunstan's Day', in *Words, Texts and Manuscripts, Studies in Anglo-Saxon Culture presented to Helmut Gneuss*, ed. by Michael Korhammer (Cambridge: Brewer, 1992), pp. 181–92.

Seidel, Kurt Otto, ed., *Die St. Georgener Predigten. Ausgewählte Abbildungen zur handschriftlichen Überlieferung*, Litterae, 89 (Göppingen: Kummerle, 1982).

—, 'Eine Bielefelder Handschrift der Buchwaldschen "Heiligenpredigten" nach Art des Schwarzwälder Predigers', *Zeitschrift fur deutsches Altertum und deutsche Literatur*, 114 (1985), 141–46.

Sims, S., 'Relative Chronology in the Old Icelandic Homily Book', *Arkiv för nordisk filologi*, 104 (1989), 143–59.

Spencer, H. Leith, *English Preaching in the Late Middle Ages* (Oxford: Clarendon Press, 1993).

—, 'The Fortunes of a Lollard Sermon-Cycle in the Later Fifteenth Century', *Mediaeval Studies*, 48 (1986), 352–96.

Stancliffe, Clare, 'The Thirteen Sermons attributed to Columbanus and the Question of Their Authorship', in *Columbanus: Studies on the Latin Writings*, ed. by Michael Lapidge (Rochester, NY: Boydell, 1997), pp. 93–202.

Steer, Georg, 'Bettelorden-Predigt als "Massenmedium"', in *Literarische Interessenbildung im Mittelalter. DFG-Symposium 1991*, ed. by Joachim Heinzle, Germanistische Symposien. Berichtsbände, 14 (Stuttgart: Metzler, 1993), pp. 314–36.

—, 'David von Augsburg und Berthold von Regensburg. Schöpfer der volkssprachigen franziskanischen Traktat- und Predigtliteratur', in *Handbuch der Literatur in Bayern: vom Frühmittelalter bis zur Gegenwart, Geschichte und Interpretationen*, ed. by Albrecht Weber (Regensburg: F. Pustet, 1987), pp. 99–110.

—, 'Meister Eckhart-Predigten in Handschriften des 14. Jahrhunderts', in *Deutsche Handschriften 1100–1400. Oxforder Colloquium von 24.–28. März 1985*, ed. by Volker Honemann and Nigel F. Palmer (Tübingen: Niemeyer, 1988), pp. 399–407.

—, 'Zur Authentizität der deutschen Predigten Meister Eckharts', in *Eckardus Theutonicus, homo doctus et sanctus. Nachweise und Berichte zum Prozeß gegen Meister Eckhart*, ed. by Heinrich Stirnimann and Ruedi Imbach, Dokimion, 11 (Freiburg, Switzerland: Universitätsverlag, 1992), pp. 127–68.

—, and Loris Sturlese, *Lectura Eckhardi. Predigten Meister Eckharts von Fachgelehrten gelesen und gedeutet* (Stuttgart: Kohlhammer, 1998).

Stiegmann, E., 'The Literary Genre of Bernard of Clairvaux's *Sermones Super Cantica Canticorum*', in *Simplicity and Ordinariness*, ed. by John R. Sommerfeldt, Cistercian Studies, 61 (Kalamazoo: Cistercian Publications, 1980), pp. 69–93.

Stormer, U., '*In dubio pro sermone* oder was ist eine Lesepredigt?', *Jahrbuch für internationale Germanistik*, 24 (1992), 48–52.

Sturlese, Loris, 'Die Kölner Eckhartisten. Das Studium generale der deutschen Dominikaner und die Verurteilung der Thesen Meister Eckharts', in *Die Kölner Universität im Mittelalter: geistige Wurzeln und soziale Wirklichkeit*, ed. by Albert Zimmermann and Gudrun Vuillemin-Diem, Miscellanea Mediaevalia, 20 (Berlin and New York: De Gruyter, 1989), pp. 192–211.

—, 'Tauler im Kontext. Die philosophischen Voraussetzungen des "Seelengrundes" in der Lehre des deutschen Neuplatonikers Berthold von Moosburg', *Beiträge zur deutschen Sprache und Literatur*, 109 (1987), 390–426.

Sypher, G. Wylie, 'Comme un chien mort: Preaching About Kinship in France', *Proceedings of Western Society for French History*, 22 (1995), 157–70.

Szarmach, Paul E., 'The Earlier Homily: "De Parasceve"', in *Studies in Earlier Old English Prose*, ed. by Bernard F. Huppé (Albany, NY: State University of New York Press, 1986), pp. 381–99.

—, 'The Latin Tradition of Alcuin's *Liber de Virtutibus et Vitiis*, cap. xxvii–xxxv, with Special Reference to Vercelli Homily XX', *Mediaevalia,* 12 (1989 for 1986), 13–41.

Taylor, Larissa J., *Soldiers of Christ: Preaching in Late Medieval and Reformation France* (New York: Oxford University Press, 1992).

Thompson, Augustine, *Revival Preachers and Politics in Thirteenth-Century Italy: The Great Revival of 1233* (Oxford: Clarendon Press, 1992).

Tkahashi, Yumiko, 'Das Erzählschema bei Johannes Pauli. Eine textlinguistische Untersuchung frühneuhochdeutscher Predigterzählungen', *Studien des Instituts für Kultur der deutschsprachigen Länder*, 11 (Tokyo, 1993), 19–49.

—, 'Die narrative Struktur der Predigterzählung—eine Studie über die Schimpf-Exempel von Johannes Pauli', *Doitsu Bungaku*, 88 (1992), 66–76.

Troeyer, B. De, 'Dietrich von Münster (um 1435–1515)', *Franziskanische Studien*, 65 (Werl: Deitrich-Coede, 1983), 156–204.

Trout, John M., 'Alain of Lille and the Art of Preaching in the Twelfth Century', *Bulletin de Théologie ancienne et médiévale*, 12 (1980), 642–53.

Varanini, Giorgio and Guido Baldassarri, eds, *Racconti esemplari di predicatori del Due e Trecento*, t. 2: *Esempi di Giordano da Pisa*, I Novellieri Italiani, 4 (Rome: Salerno Editrice, 1993).

Vàrvaro, Alberto, 'Dallo scritto al parlato (II): la predica di fra' Simone del Pozzo (1392)', in *La parola nel tempo: lingua, società e storia*, ed. by Alberto Vàrvaro, Studi linguistici e semiologici, 20 (Bologna: Mulino, 1984), pp. 205–20.

Vasoli, Cesare, 'Arte della memoria e predicazione', *Medioevo e Rinascimento. Annuario del Dipartimento di Studi sul Medioevo e il Rinascimento dell'Università di Firenze*, 3 (1989), 301–21.

Vecchio, Silvana, 'Il decalogo nella predicazione del XIII secolo', *Cristianesimo nella storia*, 10 (1989), 41–56.

—, 'Le prediche e l'istruzione religiosa', in *La predicazione dei frati dalla metà del '200 alla fine del '300. Atti del XXII Convegno internazionale, Assisi, 13–15 ottobre 1994*, Società internazionale di studi francescani, Centro interuniversitario di studi francescani (Spoleto: Centro italiano di studi sull'alto medioevo, 1995), pp. 303–35.

Vicaire, Marie-Humbert, and Etienne Delaruelle, eds, *La prédication en Pays d'Oc (XIIe—début XVe siècle)*, Cahiers de Fanjeaux, 32 (Toulouse: Privat, 1997).

Viera, David J., 'Vicent Ferrer's Catalan Sermon on Margaret of Antioch', in *Actes del Vuitè Colloqui d'Estudis Catalans a Nord-Amèrica (Bloomington, 1995)* (Barcelona: Publicacions de l'Abadia de Montserrat, 1998), pp. 293–304.

—, and Jordi Piqué, 'Vicent Ferrer i el sermó del dia de Sant Jordi', in *Actes del Setè Colloqui d'Estudis Catalans a Nord-Amèrica (Berkeley, 1993)*, ed. by August Bover and others (Barcelona: Publicacions de l'Abadia de Montserrat, 1996), pp. 275–85.

Volk-Birke, Sabine, *Chaucer and Medieval Preaching: Rhetoric for Listeners in Sermons and Poetry*, ScriptOralia, 34 (Tübingen: Narr, 1991).

Waters, Claire M., *Angels and Earthly Creatures: Preaching, Performance, and Gender in the Later Middle Ages*, The Middle Ages Series (Philadelphia: University of Pennsylvania Press, 2003).

Wells, David A., 'The Journeys of the Apostles in the German Premendicant Sermons: On the Feast of the Separation of the Apostles', in *German Narrative Literature of the Twelfth and Thirteenth Centuries. Studies presented to R. Wisbey on his Sixty-fifth Birthday*, ed. by Volker Honemann and others (Tübingen: Niemeyer, 1994), pp. 99–121.

Wenzel, Siegfried, 'Academic Sermons at Oxford in the Early Fifteenth Century', *Speculum* 70, 2 (1995), 305–29.

—, *Macaronic Sermons: Bilingualism and Preaching in Late-medieval England*, (Ann Arbor: University of Michigan Press, 1994).

—, *Preachers, Poets, and the Early English Lyric* (Princeton: Princeton Univerity Press, 1986).

Wetzel, R., 'An Account of the Reception of Augustine in his Tübingen Sermons', in *Via Augustini. Augustine in the Later Middle Ages, Renaissance and Reformation. Essays in Honour of D. Trapp*, ed. by Heiko Augustinus Oberman, Studies in Medieval and Reformation Thought, 48 (Leiden: Brill, 1991), pp. 72–115.

—, 'Johann Geiler von Kaysersberg in Augusburg. Zum Predigtzyklus "Berg des Schauens"', in *Literarisches Leben in Augsburg während des 15. Jahrhunderts*, ed. by Johannes Janota and Werner Williams-Krapp, Studia Augustana, 7 (Tübingen: Niemeyer, 1996), pp. 265–80.

Zafarana, Zelina, 'La predicazione francescana', in *Francescanesimo e vita religiosa dei laici nel '200. Atti dell'VIII Congresso della Societa Internazionale di studi francescani, Assisi, 16–18 ottobre 1980* (Perugia: Maggioli, 1981), pp. 203–50.

Zieleman, Gerrit Cornelius, 'Das Studium der deutschen und niederländischen Predigten des Mittelalters', in *Sô predigent etelîche. Beiträge zur deutschen und niederländischen Predigt im Mittelalter*, ed. by Kurt Otto Seidel, Göppinger Arbeiten zur Germanistik, 378 (Göppingen: Kummerle, 1982), pp. 5–48.

Contributors

Leo Carruthers was educated at University College Dublin before moving to France in 1977 to pursue research at the Sorbonne, where he obtained both the PhD and the *Doctorat d'Etat* for his work on Middle English devotional texts, in particular *Jacob's Well*. His article 'Richard Lavynham and the Seven Deadly Sins in *Jacob's Well*' (*Fifteenth-Century Studies*, 18 [1991], 17–32) is one of several studies on this text. In 1988 he was elected first President of the International Medieval Sermon Studies Society. He has taught at several French universities and has been professor of Medieval English at the Sorbonne (Paris IV) since 1994.

Martine De Reu received her PhD in medieval history at the University of Ghent and studied informatics for her BA at the Hogeschool Gent. Since 1994 she has worked as Keeper of Manuscripts and Rare Books in the Ghent University Library, and in 2004 she was also appointed as head of its repository library. She has published on church history and on book archaeology, and is author of *La parole du Seigneur: moines et chanoines médiévaux prêchant l'ascension et le royaume de cieux* (Turnhout: Brepols, 1996).

Georgiana Donavin, Professor of English at Westminster College in Salt Lake City, is co-editor of the book series Disputatio, this volume, and three additional books. Her scholarship focuses on representations of the family and also the uses of medieval rhetorical techniques in late Middle English literature. Her interest in sermons derives from work on the *artes praedicandi*, and she is author of '*De sermone sermonem fecimus*: Alexander of Ashby's *De artificioso modo predicandi* (*Rhetorica*, 15.3 [Summer 1997], 279–96). She has also written articles and a book on John Gower's *Confessio Amantis* (*Incest Narratives and the Structure of Gower's 'Confessio Amantis*', English Literary Studies, 56 [Victoria, BC: University of Victoria Press, 1993]).

Simon Forde is the Publishing Manager of the English language publications in medieval and renaissance studies for Brepols Publishers. He was formerly the director of the International Medieval Institute at the University of Leeds and creator of the annual International Medieval Congress there. His research interests are in the Latin sermon collection of Philip Repingdon, a follower of Wyclif. Forde is author of 'Lay Preaching and the Lollards of Norwich Diocese, 1428–1431' (*Leeds Studies in English*, 29 [1998], 109–206). He was formerly editor of the journal *Medieval Sermon Studies*.

Peter Howard is Senior Lecturer in the School of Historical Studies at Monash University, Australia. He has published in the area of medieval sermon studies and the Florentine renaissance, including *Beyond the Written: Preaching and Theology in the Florence of Archbishop Antoninus 1427–1459* (Florence: Olschki, 1995). He has held fellowships at the European University Institute, Florence, the Istituto per le Scienze Religiose, Bologna, and 'Villa I Tatti': the Harvard University Center for Italian Renaissance Studies.

Holly Johnson is Assistant Professor of English at Mississippi State University. She is currently completing a critical edition of macaronic Good Friday sermons. Also in progress is a book investigating the rhetorical art of Passion preaching in late medieval England. Her research interests include the medieval art of memory and the exegetical imagination.

John Kitchen received his doctorate in 1995 from the University of Toronto's Centre for Medieval Studies. His previous publications include *Saints Lives and the Rhetoric of Gender: Male and Female in Merovingian Hagiography* (New York: Oxford University Press, 1998), as well as articles treating medieval Christianity. He is currently Assistant Professor in the Department of History and Classics at the University of Alberta.

Peter V. Loewen is Assistant Professor of music history at Eastern Illinois University. He received his PhD in musicology from the University of Southern California in 2000. His research interests concern medieval secular and religious song, chant, drama, and the use of music in preaching and other forms of devotion in the Middle Ages. His book *The Music of the Medieval Franciscans*, and articles entitled 'Ars Musica and the Rhetoric of Franciscan Piety', and 'Mary Magdalene Preaches through Song: Female Language in The Shrewsbury *Officium Resurrectionis* and in German and Czech Easter Dramas', are forthcoming.

Ingunn Lunde, Professor of Russian Literature, University of Bergen, is the author of *Verbal Celebrations: Kirill of Turov's Homiletic Rhetoric and its Byzantine Sources* (Slavistische Veröffentlichungen, 86 [Wiesbaden: Harrassowitz, 2001]. She has published articles on medieval East Slavic literature and culture, nineteenth- and twentieth-century Russian literature (Tolstoy, Pushkin, Dostoevsky; Zoshchenko), rhetorical theory and linguistic pragmatics. Lunde is editor and co-editor of six books, and founder and general editor of the series Slavica Bergensia. Her current research project focuses on the dynamics of linguistic liberation and literary development in Russia in the 1920s and 1990s.

Thom Mertens studied Dutch language and literature at the Catholic University Nijmegen (Netherlands). He is Director of the Ruusbroec Society (Antwerp) and professor of the history of Dutch religious literature at the University of Antwerp. His research is mainly concerned with the literary aspects of late medieval Dutch literature. Mertens is co-editor of the new Dutch-Latin-English edition of Ruusbroec's *opera omnia*.

Emily Michelson is a doctoral candidate in History and Renaissance Studies at Yale University, studying vernacular preaching in Italy and its relationship to the Reformations of the sixteenth century. Her projected thesis title is *Anti-Protestant Preaching and Catholic Reform in Italy*.

Stephen Morris has degrees from Yale, St Vladimir's Seminary, and Hunter College (CUNY). Currently an independent scholar from New York City, he works primarily on patristics and subjects related to Byzantine ecclesiastical life. His published work deals with fourth-century commentaries on the Apocalypse, and he is author of '"Clothed in Scarlet, Clothed with the Sun": Thoughts on the Women of the Apocalypse 12 and 17' (in *Earth's Abominations; Philosophical Studies of Evil*, ed. by Daniel M. Haybron [Amsterdam/New York: Rodopi, 2002]).

Cary J. Nederman is Professor and Graduate Director in the Department of Political Science at Texas A&M University, College Station. He is the author or editor of more than a dozen books, including most recently *English Political Thought in Early Fourteenth-Century England* (Medieval and Renaissance Texts and Studies, 2003); *Talking Democracy: Historical Approaches to Rhetoric and Democratic Theory* (Penn State, 2004); and *John of Salisbury* (Medieval and Renaissance Texts and Studies, 2005). He has also published over eighty articles and book chapters, including contributions to many leading journals in political science, history, philosophy, and medieval studies.

Lynn T. Ramey is Assistant Professor of French at Vanderbilt University. Her interest in crusade preaching stems from work on medieval cultural interactions, including a book, *Christian, Saracen and Genre in Medieval French Literature* (London / New York: Routledge, 2001), and 'Jean Bodel's "Jeu de Saint Nicolas": a Call for Non-violent Crusade' (*French Forum*, 27. 3 [2002], 1–14). She is currently working on a study on concepts of difference in the Middle Ages and their effects on modern constructions of race.

Jeffrey Burton Russell is Professor Emeritus of History at the University of California, Santa Barbara. He is the author of seventeen books and over seventy articles, specializing in the history of Christianity, theology, and the middle ages. He has published one book on heaven (*A History of Heaven* [Princeton: Princeton University Press, 1997]) and is currently working on another on the same subject for Oxford University Press.

Eve Salisbury, Assistant Professor in English at Western Michigan University, is the author of articles on violence, medieval romance, Chaucer, and Gower. She has edited a volume entitled *The Trials and Joys of Marriage* (TEAMS [Kalamazoo: Medieval Institute Publications, 2002]) and has co-edited a collection of essays—*Domestic Violence in Medieval Texts*—with Georgiana Donavin and Merrall L. Price (Gainesville: University Press of Florida, 2002). She is currently working on a book on Chaucer's domestic ethics.

Elizabeth Schirmer is Assistant Professor of English at New Mexico State University, having received her PhD from the University of California, Berkeley in 2001. Her research centers on the vernacular religious writing of late fourteenth- and early fifteenth-century England, with a particular interest in evolving cultures of lay reading. She is the author of 'Reading Lessons at Syon Abbey: The *Myroure of Oure Ladye* and the Mandates of Vernacular Theology' (forthcoming in *Voices in Dialogue: New Problems in Reading Women's Cultural History*, ed. by Katherine Kerby-Fulton and Linda Olson (Chicago: Notre Dame University Press), and of 'Orthodoxy, Textuality, and the "Tretys" of Margery Kempe' (*Journal x* 1.1 [1996] 31–56).

David Strong received his PhD in British Literature from Indiana University and is an Assistant Professor at the University of Texas at Tyler. He has published various essays on Langland and Shakespeare. His most recent article is 'The Questions Asked, the Answers Given: Langland, Scotus and Ockham' (*The Chaucer Review*, 38. 3 [2004], 255–75).

Catherine Brown Tkacz is an independent scholar in Spokane, Washington. Her areas of special study are women in the medieval Roman Catholic Church and church art. She co-edited *'Nova Doctrina Vetusque': Essays on Early Christianity in Honor of Fredric W. Schlatter, S.J. with Douglas Kries*, (American University Studies, Series VII, Theology and Religion, vol. 207 [New York: Lang, 1999]) and is author of *The Key to Brescia Casket: Typology and the Early Christian Imagination* (Collection Des Etudes Augustiniennes, Série Antiquité, 165 [Chicago: University of Notre Dame Press, 2002]).

Richard Utz, one of the co-editors of this volume, is a 'University of Northern Iowa Distinguished Scholar' and Professor of English. He is the author of *Chaucer and the Discourse of German Philology: A History of Critical Reception and an Annotated Bibliography of Studies, 1793–1948* (2002) and *Literarischer Nominalismus im Spätmittelalter: Eine Untersuchung zu Sprache, Charakterzeichnung und Struktur in Geoffrey Chaucers 'Troilus and Criseyde'* (1990), and (co-)editor of twelve essay collections and over forty articles and book chapters in the areas of late medieval English literature, medievalism, literary nominalism, and the history of English (medieval) studies as a discipline.

Wim Verbaal studied biology at the Landbouwhogeschool Wageningen (Netherlands) and afterwards classical philology at the University of Ghent (B), where he took his PhD in 2000 on the writing strategies of Bernard of Clairvaux. He published a book in Dutch on the conflict between Bernard and Abelard, *Een middeleeuws drama: het conflict tussen scholing en vorming bij Abaelardus en Bernardus* (Kapellen: Pelckmans; Kampen: Klement, 2002), and is preparing another in English on Bernard's writing techniques. Besides several articles on Bernard, others focus on Walahfrid Strabo, Gerard Zerbolt of Zutphen, and the poetics of late antiquity.

Index of Names

COMPILED BY NATHAN GALE AND RICHARD UTZ

Abbo of Saint–Germain, 350
Abelard, Peter, 75, 79, 183
Absalom, 134
Aelfric of Eynsham, 14
Aidon, St, 24
Alcuin of York, 13, 75
Alexander IV, Pope, 20
Alexander of Hales, 203
Al–Farabi, 248
Alfred, King, 13
Allan of Lille, 224
Alypius, 33, 48
Amalek, 106
Ambrose, St, 65, 66, 67, 68, 69; *see* also Ambrose of Milan
Ambrose of Milan, 110
Amphilochius of Iconium, 273
Ananias, 9
Andrew of Crete, St, 273
Anima, 199, 214–16
Antonius, the Hermit, 66
Antony, St, 9
Arcadius, Emperor, 90, 110, 112
Arelatensis, Caesarius, 359
Aristotle, 188, 204–05, 208–09, 248
Arius, 274
Asser of St David's, John, 13
Athenagoras of Athens, St, 56
Augustine of Hippo, St, xvi, 8, 30–34, 36–41, 43–51, 56, 59, 66–68, 70–73, 75, 79, 81–85, 131, 133, 166–67, 182–83, 207, 248, 257, 343–44
Austin, J. L., 190
Averroes, 203

Bacon, Roger, 237, 247–49, 257
Bake, Alijt, xxiii, 307–08
Basil of Caesarea, St, 8, 9
Basil of Seleucia, 273
Basil the Great, *see* Basil of Caesarea
Barré, H., 344
Bartholomaeus Anglicus, 237–38, 247–48, 257
Baudovinia of Radegund, 56
Bede, The Venerable, 58, 74, 75, 79, 343, 359, 365
Benedict, 341; *see* also Benedict of Subiaco and Monte Cassino, St
Benedict of Subiaco and Monte Cassino, St, 10
Benedict of Nursia, St, *see* Benedict of Monte Cassino, St
Bennett, J. A. W., 326

Bériou, Nicole, 322
Bernard of Clairvaux, St, xviii–xix, 11, 16, 18, 113–39, 181, 183–86, 193, 229, 329, 331
Bernadine of Siena, St, *see* Bernardino of Siena, St
Bernardino of Siena, St, xv, xix, 157–79, 181, 183, 191–94
Bernardo, St, 174
Berthold of Ratisbon, *see* Berthold of Regensburg
Berthold of Regensburg, xxi, 237, 239–42, 245–47, 249–50, 256–57
Bestul, Thomas, 315
Biglia, Andrea, 158, 191
Bishop of Myra, 143; *see* also Nicholas of Myra, St
Blaise, 366
Bodel, Jean, xx–xxii, 221–22, 225–26, 228, 231, 233–34
Bomgardner, David L., 35, 37, 41
Bonaventure, St, xx, xxv, 198–200, 202–04, 206–13, 215–20, 260, 263–64
Bridget, St, 21, 22, 23, 24, 25
Brig, Celtic Goddess, 22
Brigantia of Rome, 22
Brigid of Kildare, St, 22, 24
Brigitta, St, *see* Bridget, St
Brinton, Thomas, xxv, 319–23, 334
Brugman, Jan, 309
Bruno, St, 10
Busa, R., 335
Bynum, Carolyn Walker, 190

Caesar, 83
Caesarius of Arles, St, 8, 10, 344, 350, 355
Carruthers, Leo, xv–xvii, xxv, 3–27, 81, 82,
Castro, Fidel, 86
Catherine of Siena, St, 21
Chambron, Henry, xxiii, 327–28
Charlegmagne, xxiv, 13, 295, 356–57
Charles of Franks, King, 13; *see* also Charlemagne
Charybdis, 204
Chaucer, Geoffrey, 143, 329
Chavasse, Antoine, 73
Chrysostom, St John, xvii–xviii, xxiv, 56, 59, 89–112, 181, 183, 186–87, 193
Cigman, Gloria, 364
Cistertians, 10, 11, 18
Claus of Euskirchen, xxii, 302–03, 307
Clement of Alexandria, St, 6, 56
Clement of Rome, St, 7, 8
Cleopatra, 83
Clopper, Laurence M., 264
Coelde of Münster, Dirc, 297, 309
Cole, Penny, 225
Colet, John, 152, 183, 187
Colijns, Janne, 306–07
Columbanus, St, 10
Columbini, John, 162
Confession, Lady, 240
Connart, Saracen, 226, 228–34
Constable, Giles, 223
Constantine, Emperor, 13, 110
Copeland, Rita, 268
Cunningham, Mary, 364
Cyprian, 59
Cyril of Alexandria, St, 59

d'Arbrissel, Robert, 23
d'Avray, David, 183, 224
David of Augsburg, 237–39, 242, 245, 256
Debby, Nerit ben, 191
Delcorno, Carlo, 191, 193
De Reu, Martine, xxiii–xxvi, 335–60, 363–65, 369–70
Desert Fathers, The, 9, 12
Diaconus, Paulus, 359
Diego of Osma, 20

Dier of Muiden, Rudolf, 302
Dirc of Delft, 309–11
Divitas, Bartholomew, 143
Dominic, St, 19, 20
Domitian, Emperor, 6
Donatus of Fiesole, 148
Donavin, Georgiana, xiii–xxv 371–404
Dowel, 216

Egeria, 17
Eliade, Mircea, 315
Elizabeth I, Queen, 155
Enders, Joy, 227
Erasmus, Desiderius, xix, 142, 152–54, 183, 187–90
Eudes of Châteauroux, 231
Eudiox, Empress, 90
Eugene IV, 159
Eutychus, 6

Fathers of the Church, 183
Felicitas, St, xviii, 29–32, 34, 39, 41, 44, 46–47, 50
Felicity, St, 83; *see* also Felicitas, St
Forde, Simon, xxvi, 363–70
Fortunatus, 321
Francis of Assisi, St, 19, 20, 200–02, 238, 247
Francis of Fabriano, 206
Friars Minor, 236, 250
Froning, Richard, 246
Fulk of Neuilly, 223–25, 229

Garnerus of Saint Victor, 50
Garrison, M., 341
George of Nicomedia, 273
George La Piana, 274
Gerard, xviii, 115, 118, 125–39, 185
Germanus I, St, 273
Gilbert, Lewis E., xv
Gilbert of Hoyland, 139
Gilbert of Tournai, 231–32
Gilson, Etienne, 202, 205, 209
Godfrey of Bouillon, 225
Gouder, Eddy, 365
Greatrex, Jean, 321
Grégoire, 344
Gregory VII, Pope, 18
Gregory of Antioch, 273
Gregory the Great, 72, 343–44
Greven, Philip, 148
Grote, Geert, 296
Guerric of Igny, 139

Haimo of Auxerre, 75, 79
Handel, G. F., 65
Harding, St Stephen, 10
Heinrich of Burgus, 237, 240–42, 245, 249
Henry V, King, 23
Henry VIII, King, 155, 190
Henry of Cleve, 300
Herp, Hendrik, 309
Hex, Goswinus, 298–300, 314
Hilda, St, 24
Hildegard of Bingen, St, 11, 12, 21
Hippolytus of Rome, 64, 74
Hodapp, William, 321
Holland, Duchess Margaret, 23
Honorarius II, 200
Hosden, Philip, xvii, 77
Howard, Peter, xix, 181–94
Hugh of Lincoln, 143
Hur, 106

Ignatius of Antioch, St, 7, 165,
Innocent III, Pope, 14, 160, 200–201
International Medieval Sermon Studies Society, 26–27
Irenaeus, St, 56
Isaiah, 73, 75, 326–27
Iscariot, Judas, 68, 70, 96, 317
Isidore of Pelusion, 90
Isidore of Seville, St, 7, 188, 247, 257

Jaicus, 56
James of Vitry, 223, 231–32
Jan of Ruusbroec, 310
Jephthah, 56
Jeremiah, 147
Jerome, St, 9, 32, 62
John XXII, Pope, 166
John of Cassian, St, 10
John of Damascus, St, 7
John of Ford, 139
Johnson, Holly, xxiii–xxv, 315–34, 362–64, 369
Jonathan, 134
Jordanus of Quedlinburg, 308
Joseph of Arimathea, 279–81
Justinian, Emperor, 111, 112

Kempe, Margery, 17, 23
Kieckhefer, Richard, 315
Kienzle, Beverly Maine, xiv
Kirill of Turov, xxiv, 275–91, 363–64
Kitchen, John, xvi–xvii, xxiv, 29–54, 83, 84,
Klein, J. T., xiv
Kolve, V. A., 329–30

Lamprecht of Regensburg, 239
Langland, William, xx, 198–99, 207, 210–14, 216–17, 219, 260, 263–65, 268, 332–33
Langton, Stephen, 14
Leach, Arthur F., 144–45, 187
Leo VI of Byzantine, Emperor 13, 15
Leontius of Constantinople, 273
Lewis, C. S., 81
Liesbeth of Delft, Sister, 300, 302
Lievens, Robrecht, 298
Lipphardt, Walther, 237
Loewen, Peter V., xxi, xxiv, xxv, 235–58, 259–63, 269
Longére, Jean, 26
Longeus, 218
Lother, Emperor, 343
Louis IX, King, 15
Lowden, John, 77
Lull, Ramon, 224
Lunde, Ingunn, xxii, xxiv–xxix, 273–91, 363–64, 369

Magdalena, 118
Magdalene, Mary, xv, xxi, 173, 235–37, 240, 242–47, 249–51, 253, 255–58, 260, 262, 317
Magnus, Gregorius, 359
Maier, Christoph, 223
Malachy of Ireland, 128
Mandeville, Sir John, 17
Margaret, St, 242
Marrow, James, 330
Martin V, Pope, 158, 161–62
Martin, Abbot, 225
Martin of Fulda, 206
Maurus, [H]Rabanus, 343, 359
Maximus of Turin, 57, 62–66, 68, 77–79, 85
McGinn, Bernard, 217
Mckitterick, R., 356–57
Mead, Luther, xiv
Mead, Margaret, xiv
Melton, William, xxiii, 325
Mertens, Thom, xxii–xxiii, xxv, 293–314, 363, 366–67, 369
Meyer, Jim, 184
Michelson, Emily, xv, xix, xxiv, 157–79, 181, 190–93
Migne, Jacques–Paul, 9, 365
Mirk, John, 317, 319
Monica, 131, 133
Morris, Stephen, xvii–xix, xxiv, 89–112, 181, 186–87, 193
Morrison, Karl, 32–33
Mormando, Franco, 191
Muessig, Carolyn, 231

Nebuchadnezzar, 268
Niceta(s) of Remesiana, St, 6

Nicholas, St, xviii, xx, 141, 143–44, 221
Nicodemus, 149, 153
Nikolaus of Strasbourg, 299
Nonnus, 59
Novatian, 65, 78, 79

Olaf, King, 22
Olympias of Constantinople, St, 56
Origen, 8, 59
Origo, Iris, 191
Owst, G. R., 367

Pachomius, St, 9
Pantin, W. A., 319
Patrick, St, 22
Patterson, Lee, 150
Pattison, Mark, 183
Pee, Maria van, 305
Perkins, Judith, 36
Perpetua, xviii, 29–37, 39, 41, 44–50, 83–85
Philippa of Sweden, Queen, 23
Phillips, Helen, 325
Pierozzi, Antonio, 191, 194; *see* also Antoninus the hermit
Piers, 265, 323
Pietro, Sano di, xix, 176
Pilate, Pontius, 60, 61, 62, 63, 65, 68, 76, 77, 218, 280
Plato, 208
Pliny, 320
Policretti, Cynthia, 191–93
Proclus of Constantinople, 273

Radbertus, Paschasius, 350, 352, 360
Ramey, Lynn T., xx–xxii, xxiv, 221–34, 259–63, 269
Ramsey, Richard, 189–90
Raoulet, 226, 230–31
Reed, Thomas, 49, 50
Roach, Joseph, 233
Robert of Anjou, King, 15
Robert of Molesme, St, 10
Robert of Sorbon, 14
Roberts, Phyllis B., 222
Rolle, Richard, 321
Rupert of Dentz, 58, 76, 79
Rusconi, Robert, 177
Rushd, Ibn, 203
Russell, Jeffrey Burton, xvii, 81–86

Salisbury, Eve, xviii, xix, xxiv–xxv, 141–55, 181, 187–90, 193
Salome, 173
Samson of St Edmunds, 11
Scylla, 204
Scotus, Duns, 238
Severiah of Gabala, 273
Severus of Antioch, 273
Severus, Septimius, 30
Seneca, 147, 248
Schirmer, Elizabeth, xxiii, 259–69
Sigfrid, St, 22
Simon, 244, 317
Sira, Ben, 189
Smaragdus of Saint-Mihiel, 343, 359
Solomon, King, 142, 145–46, 148, 151, 154–55, 188, 267
Spencer, Helen, 317
Staley, Lynn, 266
Steinbach, Rolf, 246–47
Storm, Jan, xxiv, 304
Stow, John, 316–17
Stradella, Alessandro, 65
Strong, David, xx–xxii, xxv, 197–220, 259–60, 263–66, 268
Susanna, xiv, xvii, 55–79, 84–85
Susanna of Rome, 73
Suso, Henry, 161–63
Syrac, 189

Tacitus, 227
Tempiers, Stephen, 203
Tertullian, 8, 32, 46, 59
Thecla, 66

Theodosius I, 110
Theodosius II, 90
Theology, 212
Theophilus of Antioch, St, 56
Theoteknos of Livias, 286
Thomas of Canterbury, St, 17
Thomas the Apostle, 274, 277–79
Tkacz, Catherine Brown, xiv–xv, xvii, 55–79, 84
Traversari, Ambrogio, 192
Trexler, Richard, 165

Umiltà of Faenza, St, 12
Urban II, Pope, 16, 18, 228

Verbaal, Wim, xviii, xxiv, 113–39, 181, 184–86, 193
Vitry, Jacques de, 19
Völker, Paul–Gerhard, 299
Voragine, Jacobus de, 317

Wenzel, Siegfried, 318, 332
Wickham, Glynne, 226
William de Biechtvader (William the Confessor), 311
Wittig, Joseph, 333
Woolf, Rosemary, 332
Wulfstan of York, 14
Wyclif, John, 15, 319
Wynter, Symon, 23

Young, Karl, 237, 246

Zacchaeus, 237
Zafarana, Zelina, 191
Zarephath, 56, 79
Zieleman, G. C., 312

Disputatio

Titles in series

Speculum Sermonis: Interdisciplinary Reflections on the Medieval Sermon, ed. by Georgiana Donavin, Cary J. Nederman, and Richard Utz, Disputatio 1 (2004).

Rhetoric and Renewal in the Latin West 1100–1540: Essays in Honour of John O. Ward, ed. by Constant J. Mews, Cary J. Nederman, Rodney M. Thomson, Disputatio 2 (2003).

The Appearances of Medieval Rituals: The Play of Construction and Modification, ed. by Nils Holger Petersen, Mette Birkedal Bruun, Jeremy Llewellyn, and Eyolf Østrem, Disputatio 3 (2004).